Fodor's

CHILE

WELCOME TO CHILE

A long sliver of land wedged between the Andes and the Pacific, Chile packs a wealth of diverse landscapes in its narrow borders. In the north, the Atacama Desert enthralls with the world's highest geyser field and alpine salt flats dotted with flamingos. Vibrant beaches, first-rate vineyards, and bustling cities like Santiago and Valparaíso make it easy to tap into the good life in central Chile. In Patagonia, outdoor enthusiasts revel in exciting adventures, from climbing snow-capped volcanoes to trekking through the majestic Torres del Paine National Park.

TOP REASONS TO GO

★ **Stunning Scenery:** Postcard-perfect backdrops from Chiloé to San Pedro de Atacama.

★ **Wine:** Full-bodied reds and crisp whites flourish in wineries on the Andes foothills.

★ **Patagonia:** Immense blue glaciers, dramatic mountain peaks, and crystalline lakes.

★ **Outdoor Activities:** Hiking and spotting unique wildlife are just a few top options.

★ **Easter Island:** Mesmerizing stone moai loom large on this isolated island.

★ **The Central Coast:** Alluring beaches, fresh seafood, and Valparaíso's colorful hills.

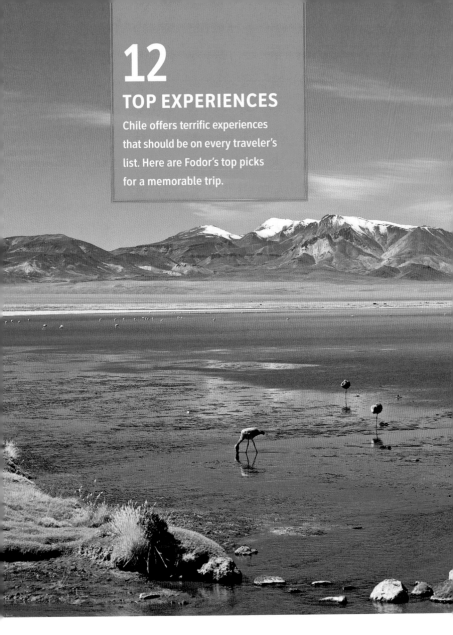

12
TOP EXPERIENCES

Chile offers terrific experiences that should be on every traveler's list. Here are Fodor's top picks for a memorable trip.

1 San Pedro de Atacama

In the heart of the Atacama Desert, San Pedro is renowned for its breathtaking scenery. Explore erupting geyser fields and blue alpine lakes, and watch multihued sunsets across lunar-like landscapes. *(Ch. 5)*

2 Chiloé's Churches

More than 150 wooden chapels dot Chiloé's rugged, misty landscapes. These historic chapels are elegant reminders of the island's missionary past. *(Ch. 8)*

3 Valparaíso

A UNESCO World Heritage Site, the port town of Valparaíso charms with its candy-color metal houses, dramatic hills overlooking the Pacific, and wooden funiculars. *(Ch. 3)*

4 Santiago

Surrounded by the Andes, Chile's vibrant capital is filled with top-notch museums, colorful crafts markets, colonial buildings, and trendy restaurants. *(Ch. 2)*

5 Wineries

Sample flavorful reds and crisp whites at the vineyards that line Chile's Central Valley. The often-stunning settings and generous tasting sessions are added bonuses. *(Ch. 2, 3, 6)*

6 Wildlife Spotting

Chile's ecosystems support a variety of wildlife. Expect to see penguins and guanacos (above) in Patagonia and alpacas and flamingos in the Atacama Desert. *(Ch. 5, 10)*

7 Seafood

You're never far from the ocean in Chile. Local restaurants serve delicious seafood throughout the country, from Patagonian king crab to mouthwatering stews. *(Ch. 1)*

8 Pablo Neruda's Houses

Even those unfamiliar with Neruda's poetry will be captivated by the whimsical objects and unusual architecture at his houses in Santiago, Valparaíso, and Isla Negra (below). *(Ch. 2, 3)*

9 Torres del Paine

This national park is Chile's premier destination for hikers and nature lovers. Its aquamarine lakes, abundant wildlife, and jagged peaks are spectacular. *(Ch. 10)*

10 Lakes and Volcanoes

Whether you prefer fishing, hiking, kayaking, climbing, or horseback riding, Chile's snow-capped volcanoes and glistening lakes offer outdoor activities for everyone. *(Ch. 7)*

11 Easter Island

Wandering among the mysterious moai, the colossal stone statues that keep watch over the most isolated island in the world, is truly awe-inspiring. *(Ch. 11)*

12 Beaches

Take your pick of gorgeous beaches—from the glamorous strands along the Central Coast to windswept beauties in the south—on the long Pacific coastline. *(Ch. 3, 4, 5)*

CONTENTS

CONTENTS

MAPS

ABOUT THIS GUIDE

Fodor's Recommendations
Everything in this guide is worth doing—we don't cover what isn't—but exceptional sights, hotels, and restaurants are recognized with additional accolades. Fodor's Choice★ indicates our top recommendations; and **Best Bets** call attention to notable hotels and restaurants in various categories. Care to nominate a new place? Visit Fodors.com/contact-us.

Trip Costs
We list prices wherever possible to help you budget well. Hotel and restaurant price categories from $ to $$$$ are noted alongside each recommendation. For hotels, we include the lowest cost of a standard double room in high season. For restaurants, we cite the average price of a main course at dinner or, if dinner isn't served, at lunch. For attractions, we always list adult admission fees; discounts are usually available for children, students, and senior citizens.

Hotels
Our local writers vet every hotel to recommend the best overnights in each price category, from budget to expensive. Unless otherwise specified, you can expect private bath, phone, and TV in your room. For expanded hotel reviews, facilities, and deals visit Fodors.com.

Top Picks
★ Fodor's Choice

Listings
⊠ Address
⊠ Branch address
☎ Telephone
🖷 Fax
⊕ Website
✉ E-mail
🎟 Admission fee
⊙ Open/closed times
Ⓜ Subway
⊹ Directions or Map coordinates

Hotels & Restaurants
🏨 Hotel
🛏 Number of rooms
🍽 Meal plans
✗ Restaurant
🍷 Reservations
👔 Dress code
⊟ No credit cards
$ Price

Other
⇨ See also
☞ Take note
🏌 Golf facilities

Restaurants
Unless we state otherwise, restaurants are open for lunch and dinner daily. We mention dress code only when there's a specific requirement and reservations only when they're essential or not accepted. To make restaurant reservations, visit Fodors.com.

Credit Cards
The hotels and restaurants in this guide typically accept credit cards. If not, we'll say so.

EUGENE FODOR

Hungarian-born Eugene Fodor (1905–91) began his travel career as an interpreter on a French cruise ship. The experience inspired him to write *On the Continent* (1936), the first guidebook to receive annual updates and discuss a country's way of life as well as its sights. Fodor later joined the U.S. Army and worked for the OSS in World War II. After the war, he kept up his intelligence work while expanding his guidebook series. During the Cold War, many guides were written by fellow agents who understood the value of insider information. Today's guides continue Fodor's legacy by providing travelers with timely coverage, insider tips, and cultural context.

EXPERIENCE CHILE

WHAT'S WHERE

Numbers correspond to chapter numbers.

2 Santiago. Although it doesn't get the same press as Rio or Buenos Aires, this metropolis is as cosmopolitan as its flashier South American neighbors. Ancient and modern stand side by side, and the Andes are ever present to the east.

3 The Central Coast. Anchoring the coast west of Santiago, port city Valparaíso has stunning views from the promenades atop its more than 40 hills. Next door, Viña del Mar has nonstop nightlife and the country's most popular stretch of shoreline.

4 El Norte Chico. A land of dusty brown hills, the "little north" stretches for some 700 km (435 miles) north of Santiago. The lush Elqui Valley grows the grapes used to make *pisco,* Chile's national drink. Astronomers flock here for the clear night skies.

5 El Norte Grande. Stark epitomizes Chile's great north, a region bordering Peru and Bolivia. This is the driest place on Earth, site of the stunning landscapes of San Pedro de Atacama.

6 The Central Valley. Chile's wine country lies south of Santiago, from the Valle Maipo to the Valle Maule. Some of the world's best wines come from this fertile strip of land trapped between the Pacific and the Andes. A drive through the valley is beautiful any time of year.

7 The Lake District. The austral summer doesn't get more glorious than in this compact stretch of land between Temuco and Puerto Montt. It has fast become vacation central, with resorts such as Pucón, Villarrica, and Puerto Varas.

8 Chiloé. More than 40 islands sprinkled across the Golfo de Ancud make up the archipelago of Chiloé. Dozens of wooden churches, constructed by Jesuit missionaries during the colonial era, dot the landscape.

9 The Southern Coast. This stretch of coastline between the Lake District and Patagonia is one of the Earth's most remote regions. Anchoring its spine is the Carretera Austral, an amazing road trip.

10 Southern Chilean Patagonia. Look up "end of the world" in the dictionary and you might see a picture of Chile's southernmost region. It's home to some of the most stunning landscapes on the planet, including the majestic Torres del Paine.

1

PERU

Arica ✈

Iquique ✈

BOLIVIA

EL NORTE GRANDE 5

Calama

San Pedro de Atacama

Antofagasta ✈

NORTHERN CHILE

PACIFIC OCEAN

Copiapó 4

A N D E S

El Norte Chico

Vallenar

Pan American Hwy

ARGENTINA

La Serena

Ovalle

THE CENTRAL COAST
Zapallar
Viña del Mar
Valparaíso 3

SANTIAGO ✈ 2

Rancagua

Curicó
Talca

THE CENTRAL VALLEY 6

Chillán

Concepción

Curicó
Talca

Chillán

Concepción

Pan-American Hwy

Temuco

Villarrica   Pucón

Valdivia   THE LAKE DISTRICT 7

Osorno

ARGENTINA

Puerto Varas

Puerto Montt ✈

Castro

Isla Grande de Chiloé 8

PACIFIC OCEAN

Puerto Puyuhuapi

A N D E S

THE SOUTHERN COAST 9 Coyhaique   Balmaceda

SOUTHERN CHILE

Cochrane

Parque Nacional Torres del Paine

ARGENTINA

Puerto Natales

Estrecho de Magallanes

SOUTHERN CHILEAN PATAGONIA 10

Punta Arenas ✈

Tierra del Fuego

Puerto Williams

0   100 mi
0   100 km

NEED TO KNOW

Pacific Ocean

Santiago

CHIILE

Atlantic Ocean

AT A GLANCE

Capital: Santiago

Population: 17,619,700

Currency: Peso

Money: ATMs common; cash more common than credit

Language: Spanish

Country Code: 56

Emergencies: 133

Driving: On the right

Electricity: 220v/50 cycles; plugs are U.K. standard three-prong or Chilean standard with three round prongs

Time: Same as New York during daylight savings time; two hours ahead otherwise

Documents: Up to 90 days with valid passport; visa on arrival required

Mobile Phones: GSM (850 and 1900 bands)

Major Mobile Companies: Movistar, Entel, Claro

WEBSITES

Chile: ⊕ www.chile.travel

Pro Chile: ⊕ www.prochile. gob.cl/int/united-states

GETTING AROUND

✈ **Air Travel:** Santiago's Arturo Merino Bentez International Airport is the largest; others include Punta Arenas, Calama, Easter Island, and Puerto Montt.

⛴ **Boat Travel:** Boats and ferries are the best way to reach many places in Chile, such as Chilo and the Southern Coast.

🚌 **Bus Travel:** Long-distance buses are safe and affordable. The biggest drawback is the time to cover the distances involved.

🚗 **Car Travel:** Rent a car outside of Santiago. Some regions, such as parts of the Atacama Desert, are impossible to explore without your own wheels.

PLAN YOUR BUDGET

	HOTEL ROOM	MEAL	ATTRACTIONS
Low Budget	42,000 pesos	4,000 pesos	Museum of Pre-Colombian Art, 3,500 pesos
Mid Budget	83,000 pesos	7,000 pesos	Flight of wine at a vineyard, 20,000 pesos
High Budget	139,000 pesos	11,000 pesos	Half-day trip to see Atacama Saltlake, 45,000 pesos

WAYS TO SAVE

Eat Chilean fast food. Stop at a mom-and-pop place to feast on the ubiquitous empanada or a churrasco sandwich (thin strips of beef) for a low price.

Take a tax holiday. Hotels in Chile do not charge taxes (known as IVA) to foreign tourists. When checking the price, make sure to ask for the *precio extranjero, sin impuestos* (foreign rate, without taxes).

Take the fancy bus. Luxury bus travel between cities costs about one-third that of plane travel and is more comfortable, with reclining seats, movies, and snacks.

Hassle Factor	Medium. Flights to Santiago are frequent, and a wealth of domestic flights and luxury buses connect Santiago to Chile's far reaches.
3 days	Explore the neighborhoods of Santiago. Rent a car one day and head 90-minutes west from Santiago to Valparaíso or Viña del Mar.
1 week	Explore Santiago and overnight it in either Valparaíso or Viña del Mar. Fly north to spend several days in San Pedro de Atacama and the Atacama desert.
2 weeks	Spend your first week in Santiago and the north. Then head south to the Lake District and then farther south to the Patagonian city of Punta Arenas to explore Chilean Patagonia in depth.

WHEN TO GO

High Season: Across Chile, high season runs from December to March, peaking during January and February, except in Santiago, which tends to empty as most Santiaguinos take their summer holiday.

Low Season: May to September is considered the low season. The wettest months are June and July. During this time, places like Chiloé and Easter Island can feel forlorn and El Norte Grande and the desert can be cold and rainy.

Value Season: The high season tapers off in March, and April is an excellent time to visit for more tranquillity. November is also quiet, but colorful. Expect vast north-to-south climatic differences, because Chile's distances span the equivalent of Cancún to Hudson Bay.

BIG EVENTS

February: Chile's equivalent of Eurovision, the annual Festival Internacional de la Cancin in Viña del Mar is Chile's best music festival.

February: The annual Tapati Rapa Nui festival is a two-week celebration of Easter Island's Polynesian heritage.

July: The town of La Tirana in Chile's northern Tarapac Region hosts the country's most important folklore festival, Fiesta de La Tirana.

September: On September 18, Chileans all over the country celebrate their independence day with traditional activities and foods.

READ THIS

■ **Residence on Earth,** Pablo Neruda. Breakthrough work by the Nobel laureate and arguably Chile's most famous literary figure.

■ **The House of Spirits,** Isabel Allende. The spiritual story of four generations of a Chilean family, filled with magic, history, and drama.

■ **Distant Star,** Roberto Bolaño. A searing short novel that takes place in first years of Pinochet's military dictatorship.

WATCH THIS

■ **Il Postino.** Italian film detailing the passionate relationship between Pablo Neruda and his third wife.

■ **No.** A Chilean film about the creative advertising tactics that helped defeat the Pinochet dictatorship.

■ **Machuca.** Socially conscious film about the lives of two youths right before the military coup.

EAT THIS

■ **Empanada de pino**: savory pastry stuffed with meat, onions, olives, egg

■ **Paila marina**: a seafood stew served in an earthenware bowl

■ **Curanto**: a fish stew from Chiloé prepared in a pit with shellfish, meat, and potatoes

■ **Manjar**: milk caramel made from boiled condensed milk

CHILE TODAY

Women and the Family

Over the past decade, women in Chile have become increasingly influential in both the government and the private sector. When the country's first female President, Michelle Bachelet, began her first term in 2006, she launched a campaign to promote gender equality in Chile and named women to a number of influential posts in her cabinet. Since her reelection in December 2013, she has proposed legislation on women's sexual reproductive rights and same-sex marriage, which is considered groundbreaking for this predominantly Catholic nation. Despite many advances, salaries for men and women remain unequal in Chile, and men typically occupy the most influential positions, particularly in the private sector.

Two government policies have had a particularly important impact on women and the family in Chile. In November 2004, divorce became legal for the first time. Then, in 2006, state-run hospitals were given clearance to distribute the morning-after pill free of charge. Before the passage of the law legalizing divorce, Chile was one of the few countries in the world to prohibit this practice, which resulted in many Chileans forming new families without legally divorcing. Those who could afford it had their marriages annulled. These new policies have directly challenged the influence of the Roman Catholic Church in Chile (about 60% of Chileans are Catholic), and were resisted by the powerful conservative sectors of the Chilean population.

Chilean Identity

Due in part to its overall economic success, Chilean identity is in flux. While Chileans are proud of their nationality and celebrate the *fiestas patrias* (independence-day holidays) with fervor, they also increasingly value cultural and material imports from abroad. Many Chileans flock to malls to buy the latest technological toys, and SUVs are common, despite high gas prices. Many members of the expanding middle class are moving to the suburbs and sending their children to private, bilingual schools; incorporating English words into conversations and having coffee at Starbucks have become status symbols.

Other sectors of the Chilean population, however, resist these influences, including members of the political left and indigenous groups. A number of popular Chilean artists have also commented on Chile's increasingly materialistic and outward-looking culture, including writer Alberto Fuguet and musicians Los Chancho en Piedra and Joe Vasconcellos.

An interesting example of these tensions in Chilean identity is the annual pre-Christmas charity event, the Teletón. Modeled on telethons in the United States, the Teletón is billed as "27 hours of love" and presided over by Chilean TV personality Don Francisco. Despite its growing commercialization—companies showing off with big donations to strengthen their branding—the event is remarkable not only because it raises large sums of money for children with disabilities, but also because almost all Chileans watch it and contribute funds, despite class, ethnicity, or geographic differences. The Teletón is truly an expression of modern *chilenidad* (Chileanism).

Export Industries

Chilean export industries continue to be a crucial source of jobs and national income. Foremost among these are the nation's copper mines, which are more

productive than any others in the world. In 2013, Chilean copper exports reached US$40.5 billion; mining products constituted 60% of the Chilean export market and 20% of the country's GDP. Chile's principal nonmineral exports include wine, wood, fruit, vegetables, and fish. The top three markets for Chilean exports are China (23%), the United States (12%), and Japan (11%).

Despite the positive economic impacts of Chile's vibrant export sector, the success of these businesses has also resulted in domestic conflicts. The mining and salmon industries have been criticized for negative environmental effects. The Mapuche, Chile's most significant indigenous group, have challenged the construction of hydroelectric plants in the south of Chile on environmental, territorial, and cultural grounds. And following the infamous mining accident of 2010, when 33 Chilean miners found themselves trapped underground for more than two months before their miraculous rescue, workers have raised concerns about mine safety, as well as pertinent questions about working conditions and higher wages.

Chile on the International Stage

Since its return to democracy, Chile has been active in international politics and trade relations. A strong proponent of free trade, Chile has signed more than 20 Free Trade Agreements (FTAs) with 50 countries worldwide. It participates actively in United Nations agencies and has sent Chilean soldiers on UN peacekeeping missions in countries such as Haiti and Iraq. The reelection of Chilean José Miguel Insulza as secretary general of the Organization of American States (OAS) makes Chile a high-profile force in the hemisphere.

Despite its increasingly important role on the global stage, Chile's relations with its immediate neighbors are somewhat contentious. Chile and Argentina have ongoing disputes over natural gas, and Bolivia and Chile have maintained only consular relations since 1978 due to a long-standing conflict over Bolivia's sea access. After Peru elevated its dispute over the demarcation of the coastline between the two countries to The Hague, the court ruled against Chile in 2014. While Chile lost 8,000 square miles of maritime territory, it was able to keep its rich coastal fishing waters.

Chile had maintained cordial but somewhat distant relationships with Bolivia and Venezuela since Evo Morales (Bolivia) and Hugo Chávez (Venezuela) came to power. Under Nicolas Maduro's leadership in Venezuela, the relations between the countries have become more strained.

Language

It's no coincidence that *How to Survive in the Chilean Jungle,* a dictionary of Chilean slang, remains popular. Chileans use an astonishing amount of slang—known as *chilenismos* (Chileanisms). Some frequently heard examples are *¿Cachai?,* an interrogative that roughly means "Get it?" and supposedly comes from the English expression "to catch," and *al tiro,* which means "right away" (which in Chile could mean a time frame of 30 seconds or several hours).

The word *gringo*—which refers mostly to North Americans but in some cases may refer to other foreigners—is considered relatively neutral and is used freely, but can take on a negative connotation depending on the tone. Used with the diminutive (*gringuito, gringuita*), it can also be affectionate.

FLAVORS OF CHILE

Not to be outdone by neighboring Peru and Argentina, whose culinary traditions are famous throughout South America and beyond, Chilean cooking is currently undergoing a culinary renaissance with several pioneering chefs taking traditional dishes and giving them a modern touch.

Highlights of Chilean cuisine include a bounty of regional seafood, like salmon, sea bass (*corvina*), and conger eel (*congrio*). Mussels and scallops are widely available, and *locos* (abalone) and *jaiba* (crab) are frequently prepared as *chupes* (stews) or *pasteles* (pies). In addition, due to the Central Valley's temperate climate, a wide variety of fresh fruit and vegetables are available.

Fish and Shellfish

Although there isn't much variety in the way it's prepared, Chilean fish is so tasty that you probably won't mind that your options are mostly limited to grilled, baked, or fried. A trip to Punta Arenas would not be complete without trying *centolla* (the local king crab), nor should you leave Easter Island without savoring a yellowfin tuna ceviche (made by marinating the fish in lemon juice and adding a selection of shellfish, as well as onions, bell peppers, chili, and cilantro).

Many coastal towns have a central fish market where you can buy fresh catch or enjoy a *paila marina* (a seafood stew that is a mouthwatering combination of white fish, plus shellfish such as mussels, scallops, and razor clams, and white wine and seafood broth).

Barbecues

Asados (barbecues) are a national pastime, and any excuse—from birthdays to baptisms to national holidays—is used to start up the grill. While the uninformed might liken the country's asados to their North American counterpart, the Chilean version starts with *choripan,* a spicy sausage served in a bun and topped with *pebre,* a mixture of tomatoes, cilantro, onions, and chilies, as well as mayonnaise. Women are generally relegated to making salads (with *ensalada a la chilena* being a firm favorite) and providing drinks, including the obligatory pisco sour, while men gather around the barbecue offering advice to the official *parrillero* (designated grill master).

Merken

Although Chilean cuisine is not renowned for its spice, the indigenous Chilean seasoning, merken (*merquén*), is added to many of the country's dishes, providing a flavorful touch. Hailing from the native Mapuche tribe in southern Chile's IX Region, merken is a powdered mixture of *cacho de cabra* chili, toasted coriander seeds, and salt. It is used to season everything from peanuts (for a tasty snack) to meats, such as venison and duck.

Empanadas

You can order an empanada as a starter or a main course. These come most commonly as *empanadas de pino*—stuffed with meat, onions, olives, egg, and raisins, or with *queso* (cheese); occasionally they'll be stuffed with *mariscos* (shellfish).

Fast Food

Along with the ubiquitous empanada, some of the most popular fast foods in Chile are the *completo* (a large hotdog in a bun), *churrasco* sandwich (thin strips of beef on your choice of white sliced bread or in an oversized bun), and *lomito* (a pork sandwich). Since all of them are available with a mind-boggling array of toppings, you just can't go wrong.

An *italiano* will get you a mountain of avocado, diced tomato, and mayonnaise;

the *dinámico* version adds sauerkraut to the mix; and the *chacarero* has green beans and green chilies. A common accompaniment for all of these is *ají chileno,* a spicy local version of ketchup.

Curanto

Chiloé is famous not only for its churches but also for its unique dish called *curanto.* No trip to the south would be complete without trying it, especially because the ritual of cooking the dish usually becomes an event in itself.

The stew is prepared outdoors buried in a pit in the ground, which is lined with stones that have been heated to red-hot over an open fire. Layers of shellfish, sausage, smoked pork ribs, potatoes, and pulses are added, and then covered with sodden earth and damp sacks to create a kind of pressure cooker. Everything is left to cook for an hour or so. Curanto is usually served with *milcao,* a moist and delicious potato cake steamed above the curanto; don't let its rather unappetizing gray color put you off.

Traditional

Robust and comforting Chilean dishes such as Mapuche *charquicán* (a hearty beef stew with potatoes, squash, and other vegetables) and *cazuela* (a beef or chicken casserole) are popular to ward off the chill of winter. *Humitas* (a lightly seasoned corn paste wrapped in corn leaves, normally eaten plain or sprinkled with sugar as a main course) and *pastel de choclo* (a mixture of minced beef, chicken, olives, hard-boiled egg, and raisins, topped with a layer of creamy mashed corn and served in a heavy clay bowl) are more common in the summer, when their main ingredient, corn, is in season.

Fruit

Walk into one of the *ferias* (street markets) during summer months and you will be overwhelmed by the colors and smells of all the freshly grown fruit. Papayas are particularly plentiful in Easter Island and La Serena, where they are used to make liquor and sweets. A wide range of berries—strawberries, raspberries, and blueberries—are grown in the central and southern regions and used to make fresh juices and tasty *kuchen* (tarts).

Custard apples (*chirimoyas*), with their mottled green skin and creamy texture, are divine on their own or can be made into juices or to flavor ice cream. It is not unusual to see succulent football-size *sandías* (watermelons) being sold at the side of the road on the highways leading to Santiago. And given Chile's reputation as a major wine-producing nation, it goes without saying that succulent table grapes are widely available.

A popular summertime drink sold on vendor carts is the traditional *mote con huesillo,* made from peaches and husked wheat, and served in a tall, chilled glass with a spoon.

Manjar

Manjar (known as dulce de leche in other South American countries) is a national obsession. Made from boiled condensed milk, this caramel-like sweet substance is used as a filling for everything from *alfajores* (two cookies sandwiched together and covered in chocolate) and *cuchuflis* (thin wafers rolled into cylinders), to crepes and *brazo de reina* (the Chilean equivalent of the Swiss roll).

Manjar is also sold in bar form and can be found at almost every street kiosk. It's commonly used as an ice-cream flavor, often combined with nuts or banana.

WINES OF CHILE

History

For the 19th and much of the 20th century, most Chilean wine was cheap and consumed domestically. It had been initially brought to the country by the first European settlers to make sacramental wine. With the rise of cross-Atlantic trade in the 19th century, some Chileans made fortunes in the mining industry. They returned from Europe and many began building their own Chilean-style chateaux, particularly on the outskirts of Santiago. French varietals such as Cabernet Sauvignon, Malbec, and Carmenère thrived in the Central Valley's rich soils and the near-perfect climate.

Chilean wineries stagnated through much of the 20th century. The introduction of modern equipment such as stainless steel tanks and national and international investment in the industry made Chilean wine a tasty and affordable option in the 1980s. Continued advances in growing techniques and wine-making methods throughout the 1990s and into the early 21st century have resulted in the production of excellent wines of premium and ultrapremium quality.

What to Taste

Cabernet Sauvignon. The king of reds grows well almost anywhere it's planted, but Cabernets from the Alto Maipo are particularly well balanced, displaying elegance and structure with a distinctive freshness.

Carmenère. Chile's signature red wine-producing grape arrived in Chile during the mid-19th century from France, where it was usually a blending grape in Bordeaux. At the time, it could be found throughout Europe, but became nearly extinct in the late 19th century due to a continent-wide infestation of aphidlike insects. Over time Chileans forgot about it, mistaking it for a cousin of the Merlot vine.

It wasn't until the Chilean boom times of the 1990s that they realized they had a unique grape hidden among the other vines in their vineyards. It had thrived thanks to the country's unique topography, which provides natural barriers to the aphids. Today, Chile is the largest exporter of Carmenère wine in the world.

Malbec. True, this is Argentina's grape, but Chile produces award-winning bottles of this red wine that have appealing elegance and balance.

Sauvignon Blanc. Due to cooler climates, the region of Valparaíso is most notable for its Sauvignon Blanc, Chile's second-biggest varietal after Cabernet Sauvignon. Vineyards from Elqui to Bío Bío also produce this exciting white wine with fresh green fruit, crisp acidity, and often an enticing mineral edge.

Syrah. Chile produces two distinct styles of this emerging red variety. Be sure to try both: luscious and juicy from Colchagua or enticingly spicy from coastal areas, such as Elqui or San Antonio.

Where to Go

Chile's appellation system names its valleys from north to south, but today's winegrowers stress that the climatic and geological differences between east and west are more significant. The easternmost valleys closest to the Andes tend to have less fog, more hours of sunlight, and greater daily temperature variations, which help red grapes develop deep color and rich tannins while maintaining bright acidity and fresh fruit characteristics.

On the other hand, if you're after crisp whites and bright Pinots, head to the coast, where cool fog creeps inland from the sea each morning and Pacific breezes keep the vines cool all day. Interior areas in the Central Valley are less prone to extremes and favor varieties that require more balanced conditions, such as Merlot and Carmenère. Syrah, a relatively new grape in Chile, does well in both cold and warm climates.

Casablanca Valley. The name of this cool-climate coastal region, located 75 km (47 miles) northwest of Santiago, translates appropriately to "white house." Unsurprisingly, it turns out excellent, crisp white wines, including aromatics such as Riesling and Gewürztraminer. Several wineries in this area can be visited as day-trips from either Santiago or Valparaíso.

Central Maipo and Alto Maipo. This is the cradle of Chile's Cabernets, with more than half of its 30,000 acres of vineyards dedicated to what many believe is the country's best grape. In part due to its proximity to the capital of Santiago, this region is the most productive and the easiest to visit for most visitors.

While Alto Maipo extends into the foothills, boasting a microclimate ideal for viticulture, Central Maipo borders the Maipo River and is much warmer with less rainfall, allowing for the growth of highly praised Carmenère wines as well as Cabernet.

Colchagua Valley. The wines of this well-known Chilean region are regular headliners on the world's top lists, including robust red varietals such as Malbec, Carmenère, Syrah, and Cabernet, but also white Chardonnay and Sauvignon Blanc varietals as well. The Colchagua Valley is roughly 180 km (110 miles) to the south of Santiago, and the vineyards stretch from the western Coastal Range to the eastern foothills of the Andes Mountains.

The best town to stay when exploring this area is the picturesque Santa Cruz.

Curicó Wine Valley. Thanks to its varied climate and fertile, high-yielding soil, more than 30 varieties of grapes—more than anywhere else in the country—can be found in Curicó's vineyards. The dominant grapes are Cabernet Sauvignon and Sauvignon Blanc in this region, which is located approximately 200 km (124 miles) south of Santiago.

Maule Valley. Chile's largest wine-growing region is also one of its oldest and most diverse. Roughly 250 km (155 miles) south of Santiago, the Maule Valley is home to both traditional, family-run vineyards and innovative, modern wineries, with an increasing focus on sustainable, organic wine-making techniques.

Tips for Visiting Chilean Wineries

1. The number one wine travel rule in Chile? Make reservations. Unlike wineries in the United States, certain wineries are not equipped to receive drop-in visitors.

2. Don't expect wineries to be open on Sunday or holidays.

3. The distances between wineries can be longer than they look on the map. Allot plenty of travel time, and plan on no more than three or four wineries per day.

4. Contact the wine route offices in the region you're visiting. They can be helpful in coordinating visits to wineries.

5. Hire a driver, or choose a designated driver.

6. Keep in mind there are not only many different types of wineries available to visit, from family-run small businesses to large, mechanized operations, but also different ways to see them. Some wineries offer everything from thrill-seeking zip line courses to leisurely bike tours.

IF YOU LIKE

Sports and the Outdoors

The Lake District is Chile's outdoor-tourism center, with outfitters and guides ready to fix you up and take you out for any activity your adventurous heart could desire. Fly-fishing, hiking, and rafting top the list, but the entire country has caught the outdoor bug, and activities abound.

■ **Pucón.** Chile's all-around adventure destination is the area around Pucón and Villarrica, where everything from rafting and kayaking to climbing and horseback riding is available.

■ **Sendero de Chile.** Though incomplete, the ambitious Chilean Trail will provide a continuous north-south trail running the entire length of the country (8,500 km/5,282 miles).

■ **Southern Coast.** Fly-fishermen should explore the trip options in southern Chile. There are numerous places to fish, most of which are much less crowded and much more remote than any place you may have been before.

■ **Valle Nevado.** Since Chile's seasons are the opposite of the Northern Hemisphere's, you can ski or snowboard from June to September. Most of Chile's ski resorts are in the Andes close to Santiago. With the top elevations at the majority of ski areas extending to 3,300 meters (10,825 feet), you can expect long runs and deep, dry snow.

■ **Volcán Ojos del Salado.** If you're a mountaineering enthusiast, you likely already know about Ojos de Salado in El Norte Chico. The world's highest active volcano, it soars to 6,893 meters (22,609 feet). There are dozens of other challenging climbs all along the eastern border of the country.

Natural Wonders

Norway has fjords. Bavaria has forests. Nepal has mountains. Arizona has deserts. Chile offers all these—so it's understandable if you feel disoriented each time you step off a domestic flight that's whisked you from one region to another.

■ **The Andes.** A defining feature of Santiago is its proximity to the Andes. They dwarf downtown office buildings, and serve as a convenient way to get oriented. Everywhere else you might go in Chile, the Andes will be there as a defining characteristic, and a reminder of the isolation from which Chile is recently emerging.

■ **Atacama Desert.** The most arid spot on Earth is in El Norte Grande's Atacama Desert; no measurable precipitation has ever been recorded there. The region's Cerros Pintados form the world's largest group of geoglyphs.

■ **Laguna San Rafael.** A cobalt-blue mountain of ice, this 4-km (2½-mile) glacier south of Coyhaique in the Aisén Region is a doubly arresting attraction: it gives off thunderous sounds as chunks of it break off and stir up the water as you pass by (safely on your ship, of course).

■ **Parque Nacional Fray Jorge.** This is Chile's only cloud forest, and a great retreat from the relentless sun of El Norte Chico.

■ **Torres del Paine.** No photo can ever do justice to the ash-gray, glacier-molded spires of Patagonia's most visited attraction.

■ **Volcán Villarrica.** This volcano in the Lake District is one of the world's most active—although you shouldn't let this deter you from hiking to the snow-covered summit.

Beachgoing in Chile

With more than 4,300 kilometers (2,672 miles) of coastline stretching between the northern border with Peru to the Strait of Magellan in Patagonia, there's no shortage of beach activity and watersports to be enjoyed. From sunbathing on white sandy beaches to surfing and diving, there's a *balneario* (beach resort) for everyone in Chile. Here are only a few of the most notable:

■ **Anakena.** Lapis-lazuli water, coconut palms, and white coral sand are yours to be had—if you don't mind taking a plane five hours from Santiago. This paradise-like tropical beach is located on one of the most remote inhabited islands in the world, where you will also find the infamous stone statues, or *moai*, for which Easter Island is most famous.

■ **La Serena.** Less crowded than Viña del Mar, some of the country's longest stretches of beach can be found near La Serena. While it's generally unsafe for swimming due to strong rip currents and rough waters, the beaches of La Serena are popular with surfers and windsurfers.

■ **Viña del Mar.** Easily accessible from Santiago by bus, this is Chile's most famous beach. The upper classes have flocked here to see and be seen since the 1870s. It's referred to as the Chilean Riviera and has numerous thriving resorts and restaurants.

■ **Zapallar.** The hills above this beach are dotted with European-style villas and adobe working-class homes. Scuba-diving and kayaking are popular activities on this Central Coast area.

Chilean Literary History

Chile's rich literary history include such prominent authors as Pablo Neruda, Gabriela Mistral, and Isabel Allende,

to name only a few. Both Neruda and Mistral were awarded the Nobel Prize in Literature, which is no small feat for a relatively small country. Bookworms wishing to pay tribute to Chilean literary history should not miss these key sites:

■ **Casa de Isla Negra.** Of Pablo Neruda's three houses in Chile, this is where he spent most of his time. In the small coastal town of Isla Negra, about 96 km (60 miles) west of Santiago, this house was built to resemble a ship; inside, the objects that Neruda collected throughout his life, many nautically related, overflow in each room. Both Neruda and his third wife, Matilde Urrutia, are buried outside, overlooking the rough Pacific Ocean.

■ **La Chascona.** This Pablo Neruda house in the artsy Bellavista neighborhood of Santiago is one of the city's top attractions. The house features a quirky bar, winding garden paths, and a wide assortment of objects and knickknacks that inspired Neruda's poetry.

■ **La Sebastiana.** At the top of one of Valparaíso's hills, this striking Pablo Neruda house has magnificent views of the city's harbor and Pacific Ocean. The house itself looks like an ocean liner rising from a town filled with beautiful houses.

■ **Museo Gabriela Mistral.** In Vicuña, a small city in the Elqui Valley, roughly 530 km (329 miles) north of Santiago, this museum documents the life of the first Latin American author to win the Nobel Prize in Literature. There are numerous artifacts from Mistral's life along with a pleasant garden.

HIGHLIGHTS OF PATAGONIA

Patagonia is a wild and rugged land filled with breathtaking landscapes and eye-catching wildlife. There are few other places in the world where you can feel such a great isolation and vast emptiness, and yet see waters teeming with wildlife; visit gauchos living on windswept estancias; and get so close to ancient glaciers that you can actually walk inside these ice cathedrals. With an area that spans over a million square kilometers between Chile and Argentina, be prepared to gasp at the majesty of the Patagonian wild.

Glaciers

The Patagonia ice field covers much of the southern end of the Andean mountain range, straddling the Argentina-Chile border. The glaciers that spill off the high altitude ice field are basically rivers of slowly moving ice and snow that grind and push their way across the mountains, crushing soft rock and sculpting granite peaks.

Most of Patagonia's glaciers spill into lakes, rivers, or fjords. Chunks of ice calve off the face of the glacier into the water, a dramatic display of nature's power that you can view at several locations. There are multiple options for viewing these majestic icebergs, whether by strapping on a set of crampons for a trek, horseback riding over the pampas, boating, 4x4 driving, or kayaking through the fjords. Some are accessible only through boat tours or by helicopter, though the stunning rugged scenery makes the travel time more than worthwhile.

Glaciar Grey, Parque Nacional Torres del Paine, Chile. Perhaps the most stunning of the many glaciers in this must-see national park, Glaciar Grey, with its fragmented icebergs, is an easy and rewarding site to hike to here.

Glaciar Martial, Ushuaia, Argentina. In a mountain range just above Ushuaia, this glacier can be reached by a panoramic ski lift. There are lovely hikes all around the glacier with great views.

Glaciar Perito Moreno, El Calafate, Argentina. One of the continent's most awe-inspiring sights, this majestic glacier is renowned for its sparkling blue façade, accessibility, and the blocks of ice that spill dramatically off it into the nearby lake.

Upsala Glacier, El Calafate, Argentina. Part of the Los Glaciares National Park in Argentina, the Upsala Glacier is the largest glacier in South America, and one of the most visually impressive. It is accessible only by boat.

Mountain Trekking

In Patagonia, mountains mean the Andes, a relatively young range that stretches for more than 4,000 miles down South America. Some of the most breathtaking summits are in southern Patagonia. Glacial activity has played an important role in chiseling the most iconic Patagonian peaks. The spires that form the distinctive skylines of Torres del Paine and the Fitzroy range are solid columns that were created when rising glaciers ripped away weaker rock, leaving only hard granite skeletons that stand rigid at the edge of the ice fields. There is no shortage of paths in the region that will get you up close and personal with these impressive peaks, and provide you with unobstructed views of the spectacular scenery.

Mt. Fitzroy and Cerro Torre, El Chalten, Argentina. More than a dozen well-marked routes are available here within the Parque Nacional Los Glaciers. Awe-inspiring views of this massive granite structure, the highest mountain in the park, are well worth getting up early for.

Osorno Volcano, Lake District, Chile. Visible from every point in Osorno, the volcano reaches a height of 2,661 meters (8,730 feet) above sea level and takes six hours to ascend, usually in an organized group with a local guide.

Parque Nacional Torres del Paine, Chile. This national park offers wild rock climbing and no shortage of wildlife-spotting, including condors and guanacos, a smaller cousin of the alpaca and llama.

Penguin Colonies

The best time to see penguins is from November through February, which coincides with the best weather in coastal Patagonia. Most of the penguins you'll see in Patagonia are Magellanic penguins, black-and-white colored birds that gather in large breeding colonies on the beaches here in summer and retreat to warmer climes during winter. They're smaller than the Emperor penguins in Antarctica, standing about 30 inches tall and weighing between 15 and 20 pounds. Due to oil spills and the effects of climate change, Magellanic penguins have been classified as a threatened species.

Some of the most convenient and impressive penguin colonies to visit are:

Isla Magdalena, Chile. Home to 120,000 Magellanic penguins, this one-square-kilometer island is the site of one of the largest such colonies in southern Chile. It's an easy boat ride away from Punta Arenas.

Pingüinera del Seno Otway, Punta Arenas, Chile. This protected colony has more than 11,000 feathered residents in peak season. Just an hour from Punta Arenas, this is one of the best spots on mainland Chile to visit penguins.

Puñihuil, Chiloé, Chile. Southwest of Ancud in Chiloé, the three small islets of Puñihuil are home to an abundant colony of Humboldt and Magellanic penguins.

National Parks

There is no better place to experience the majesty of Patagonia than in a national park. The most spectacular national parks include:

Los Glaciares National Park, Argentina. A UNESCO World Heritage site, Los Glaciares National Park is home to stunning lakes and natural scenery. About 40% of it is covered by ice fields that contain nearly 50 glaciers.

Parque Nacional Tierra del Fuego, Argentina. Accessible by car or train, this is the southernmost national park in the world. There are breathtaking wildlife refuges, mountain-ringed lakes, strikingly green lagoons, peat bogs, and wild cherry forests.

Parque Nacional Torres del Paine, Chile. Chile's most popular national park offers classic hikes with spectacular views of waterfalls and glaciers, and unusual wildlife like the guanaco and the ñandú. Its most spectacular attractions are its lakes of turquoise and emerald waters; and the Cuernos del Paine ("Paine Horns"), the geological showpiece of the immense granite massif.

Wildlife Spotting

Other than Magellanic penguins, animals you might see in Patagonia include whales, Andean condor, rhea, pumas, Albatross, and sea lions. Be sure to pack a good pair of binoculars, sunglasses, and sunblock to protect yourself from the glare of the sun's rays.

GREAT ITINERARIES

THE CITY, THE BEACH, AND THE DESERT IN 10 DAYS

Days 1–3: Santiago

No matter where you fly from, you'll likely arrive in Chile's capital early in the morning after an all-night flight. Unless you can sleep the entire night on a plane and arrive refreshed at your destination, reward yourself with a couple of hours' shut-eye at your hotel before setting out to explore the city.

The neighborhoods, small and large, that make up Santiago warrant at least a day and a half of exploration. A trip up one of the city's hills—like **Cerro San Cristóbal** in Parque Metropolitano or **Cerro Santa Lucía**—lets you survey the capital and its grid of streets. Any tour of a city begins with its historic center; the cathedral and commercial office towers on the **Plaza de Armas** reflect Santiago's old and new architecture, while the nearby bohemian quarter of **Bellavista**, with its bustling markets and colorful shops, was built for walking. But Santiago's zippy, efficient metro can also whisk you to most places in the city, and lets you cover ground more quickly. Avoid taking the metro during the morning and evening rush hour.

Alas, if you're here in the winter, gloomy smog can hang over the city for days at a time. Your first instinct may be to flee, and one of the nearby wineries in the **Valle de Maipo** will welcome you heartily. If it's winter and you brought your skis, **Valle Nevado**, Chile's largest downhill resort area, lies a scant 16 km (10 miles) outside Santiago.

Days 4–6: Valparaíso and the Central Coast

A 90-minute drive west from Santiago takes you to the Central Coast and confronts you with one of Chilean tourism's classic choices: Valparaíso or Viña del Mar. If you fancy yourself one of the glitterati, go for Viña and its chic cafés and restaurants and miles of beach. But "Valpo" offers you the charm and allure of a port city, rolling hills, and cobblestone streets with better views of the sea.

Here's a solution: Why not do them both? Only 10 km (6 miles) separate the two cities, and it's easy to travel between them, whether by taxi or the metro system that connects them. Besides, they offer their own distinct charms.

Spend the first day in **Valparaíso**, where you can ride the funiculars up the city's many hills, wander through streets lined with brightly painted houses, and feast on some of the country's freshest seafood near the port. Don't miss a visit to **La Sebastiana**, one of Pablo Neruda's houses. From the poet's bedroom window is one of the best panoramic views of Valparaíso that you'll encounter.

The following day, make your way to **Viña del Mar** and prepare to soak in the rays. Some of the best and most glamorous beaches in the country can be found here. When you've had enough sun, you can stroll through the numerous shopping galleries in downtown Viña.

Round out your visit the following day with a trip to the charming coastal town of **Isla Negra**, 90 km (56 miles) south of Valparaíso. The unmistakable highlight is another of Pablo Neruda's houses, easily the best of his three residences. It's chock-full of artifacts and curios from his many travels and overlooks a rough part of the

Pacific Ocean. Head back to Santiago at night in preparation for the next leg of the journey.

Days 7–10: San Pedro de Atacama

You certainly *could* drive the nearly 1,500 km (900 miles) to Chile's vast El Norte Grande, but a flight from Santiago to **Calama**, then a quick overland drive to **San Pedro de Atacama** will take you no more than 3½ hours. This is one of the most-visited towns in Chile, and for good reason: it sits right in the middle of the Atacama Desert, with sights all around.

You'll need at least two days here to do justice to the alpine lakes, ancient fortresses, Chile's largest salt flat, and the surreal landscape of the **Valle de la Luna**. Your best bet is to find a reputable tour agency in San Pedro—and there are many—and make at least two day trips: one to the **Geysers del Tatio**, which requires a pick-up around 4 in the morning; and one to the **Reserva Nacional Los Flamencos**, where you can watch flamingos fly over jagged salt flats and cobalt lakes.

Just remember that you'll be in a high-altitude zone, so it's best to take it easy during your first day here, wandering through the charming town and popping into the numerous gift shops. Don't miss the stunning sunsets over the nearby Valle de la Luna.

Transportation

It's quite easy, and even preferable, to explore Santiago, Viña del Mar, and Valparaíso using public transportation, and a car is not needed in San Pedro de Atacama if you use tour agencies. Once in San Pedro de Atacama, you can hook up with various tour agencies to visit sights

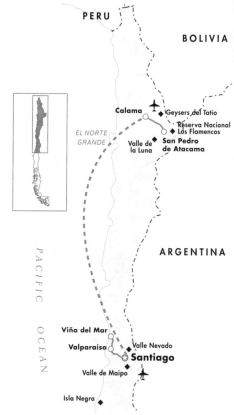

not accessible by bus. There are frequent flights from Santiago to Calama and back.

HIGHLIGHTS OF PATAGONIA IN 14 DAYS

Days 1 and 2: Santiago

Arrive in Santiago early the morning of your first day. After a brief rest, set out to explore the city's museums, shops, and green spaces using the power of your own two feet and the capital's efficient metro.

Days 3–6: The Lake District

Head south 675 km (420 miles) from Santiago on a fast toll highway to **Temuco**, the gateway to Chile's Lake District, or even better, take one of the frequent hour-long flights. Temuco and environs are one of the best places in the region to learn about the indigenous Mapuche culture.

About an hour south, and just 15 minutes apart on the shores of **Lago Villarrica,** lie the twin resort towns of flashy, glitzy **Pucón** and quiet, pleasant **Villarrica.** Base yourself in the latter if you're in peso-saving mode. Drive south through the region from the graceful old city of **Valdivia** to **Puerto Montt,** stopping at the various resort towns. Frutillar, Puerto Octay, and Puerto Varas still bear testament to the Lake District's German-Austrian-Swiss immigrant history. Be sure to make time for one of the region's many hot springs.

Days 7–9: Chiloé

From Puerto Montt, drive or take a bus 65 kilometers (40 miles) southeast toward Pargua and catch the ferry to Chiloé. Base yourself in **Castro,** the capital, which allows for easy side trips through the island. Take a full day to photograph the rows of multicolor homes on stilts, called *palafitos*, in Castro, and then visit as many of the UNESCO World Heritage Site churches in surrounding towns as possible.

For those seeking to get away from it all, set out for a day-hike in **Parque Nacional Chiloé**, with its heavily forested trails and dramatic lookout points. Roughly 29 km (18 miles) southwest of the town of Ancud, you can visit **Puñihuil** and its colony of Humboldt and Magellanic penguins. Don't forgot to dine on the island's famous curanto at night.

Days 10–14: Parque Nacional Torres del Paine

After taking a return ferry and bus ride back to Puerto Montt, take a spectacular morning flight over the Andes to the Patagonian city of **Punta Arenas.** On the next day take a bus north to **Puerto Natales,** gateway to the **Parque Nacional Torres del Paine.** You'll need at least two days to wander through the wonders of the park. On your final day, head back to Punta Arenas, stopping en route at one of the penguin sanctuaries, and catch an afternoon flight to Santiago.

THE ULTIMATE CHILEAN WINE TRIP IN 6 DAYS

Days 1 and 2: Santiago and the Maipo Valley

Start your oenophile adventure in the capital city of **Santiago,** from where some of Chile's best wineries are only a cork's throw away in the **Maipo Valley.** Look for bilingual tour availability and accessibility to public transit.

Our top recommendations include **Viña Undurraga,** started and run by the same family since 1885; **Viña Concha y Toro,** Chile's largest wine producer and perhaps its most entertaining winery tour, with a visit to the Casillero del Diablo, the famed wine cellar where the devil supposedly dwells; and **Viña Santa Rita,** with an impressive on-site museum and Pompeiian-style manor.

Days 3 and 4: Casablanca Valley

From Santiago, it's a mere 45-minute drive to the **Casablanca Valley.** Just three decades ago, the land here was considered inhospitable for vineyards, but now winemakers have discovered that the valley's proximity to the sea is its main asset, because cooler temperatures give the grapes more time to develop flavor as they ripen.

The three can't-miss vineyards in this area are **Casas del Bosque,** which offers a vineyard tour in an old wagon; **Viña Matetic,** which has a stunning bodega that resembles a bunker worthy of a James Bond villain; and **House of Morande,** which is one of the valley's oldest wineries and a superb place to stop for lunch during your tours.

If you grow tired of vineyard-hopping, make your way to **Viña del Mar**, a mere 30 kilometers (18.6 miles) away from the heart of the valley. It's a great place to spend the night while exploring the Casablanca Valley. You can walk along the beach in the morning and then indulge in the vibrant nightlife when you've returned in the evening.

Days 5 and 6: Colchagua Valley

From Santiago, drive 90 minutes south to the **Colchagua Valley**. Stay overnight at an inn or B&B in **Santa Cruz**, the main town of the valley, with an attractive central square and several craft shops. There are numerous vineyards to visit throughout this valley, but one of the better ones to start with is **Viña Montes**. It's known for its deep reds, crisp whites, and Feng Shui design principles. Nearby, **Viña Lapostolle-Clos Apalta** is housed in one of the most handsome pieces of architecture in Chile: the barrel-stave-shape beams rising impressively above the vineyards create a wooden nest for the winery, which is built into a hillside to facilitate the gravity-flow process.

Be sure to make time to visit **Viña Santa Cruz**, which is less a winery and more an entire wine complex. It features a cable car, astronomical center, and indigenous museum. Plan to spend several hours here.

Transportation

There are a variety of options available. If you prefer the independence of a self-guided tour, rent a vehicle in Santiago and pick up a map of the Chilean wine region, which is available at many bookstores and wine shops. From Santiago to Casablanca, you can take a public bus and

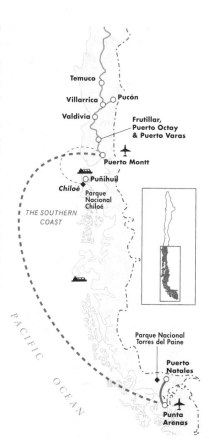

then a taxi from the terminal to your wineries of choice.

Most organized tours are offered as either half- or full-day, and include guides as well as meals. There are alternatives to the tedium of bus tours; options can combine horseback riding, bicycling, and even zip-lining along with your wine tastings.

HISTORY YOU CAN SEE

Precolonial Chile

The indigenous groups living in Chile before the arrival of the Spanish can be categorized as the pre-Incan cultures in the north, the Mapuche in the region between the Choapa River and Chiloé, and the Patagonian cultures in the extreme south. Although the Incan Empire extended into Chile, the Mapuche successfully resisted their incursions; there is a debate about how much of Chile the Incans conquered.

The **geoglyphs** constructed between AD 500 and 1400 in the mountains along ancient northern trade routes are some of the most important in the world. The **Chinchorro mummies,** relics of the Chinchorro people who lived along the northern coast, are the oldest in the world, dating from 6000 BC. They are visible at the Museo Arqueológico de San Miguel de Azapa near Arica.

In Temuco, the **Museo Regional de la Araucanía** provides a fairly good introduction to Mapuche art, culture, and history. Temuco and its environs also offer a sense of modern Mapuche life. Farther south, the **Museo Salesiano de Maggiorino Borgatello** in Punta Arenas has an interesting collection of artifacts from various Patagonian cultures. Finally, in Santiago, the **Museo Chileno de Arte Precolombino** has an excellent collection of indigenous artifacts from Mexico to Patagonia.

Colonial Chile

While Ferdinand Magellan and Diego de Almagro both traveled to Chile earlier, it was Pedro de Valdivia who founded Santiago in 1541. Before being killed in battle by a Mapuche chief, Valdivia established a number of other important towns in Chile. The Mapuche successfully resisted Spanish conquest and colonization, ruling south of the Bío Bío River until the 1880s.

The **Plaza de Armas** is where Pedro de Valdivia founded Santiago in 1541. The **Iglesia San Francisco** is Santiago's oldest structure dating from 1586, although it was partially rebuilt in 1698 and expanded in 1857. The **Casa Colorada** is a well-preserved example of colonial architecture. It was the home of Mateo de Toro y Zambrano, a Creole businessman and Spanish soldier, and now houses the Museo de Santiago. On Chiloé near Ancud, the **San Antonio Fort** constructed in 1786 is all that remains of Spain's last outpost in Chile.

Independence

September 18, 1810—Chilean Independence Day—is when a group of prominent citizens created a junta to replace the Spanish government. However, full independence was achieved several years later in 1818 with the victory of the Battle of Maipú by Bernardo O'Higgins and José de San Martín. Chiloé remained under Spanish control until 1826.

The **Temple of Maipú** on the outskirts of Santiago was constructed in honor of the Virgin of Carmen, patron saint of Santiago, after the Battle of Maipú. While the original temple was destroyed, its foundations still exist near the new structure built in the 1950s.

The **Palacio Cousiño** in Santiago, built by one of Chile's most important families in 1871, provides an excellent sense of how the elite lived in an independent, modernizing Chile. Note that the building suffered significant damage during the February 2010 earthquake and, as of this writing, was closed until further notice.

Military Dictatorship

In 1973, Chile's first socialist president, Salvador Allende, was overthrown by a military coup by the Chilean Air Force.

Some of the bullet holes from their bombardment of the **Palacio de La Moneda,** where Allende committed suicide after refusing to surrender, can still be seen today. Today, this building is the site of the country's presidential offices; construction first began on it in 1784.

A junta led in part by Augusto Pinochet, the commander-in-chief of the Chilean army, seized power and began to detain thousands of people whom they considered potential subversives, including political activists, journalists, professors, and trade unionists. The junta used the **Estadio Nacional** in Santiago as a prison camp and torture site for tens of thousands of detainees. The stadium is considered a national site and has since been renovated and expanded. First-division soccer matches and large concerts are now held in this stadium.

The most important site used by the Chilean secret police to torture and interrogate political prisoners during the Pinochet era is on the outskirts of Santiago. Once a spot where artists and progressives would meet up, **Villa Grimaldi** held more than 4,000 detainees in the mid-1970s.

Today, it is a memorial site and peace park featuring a wall of names of its prisoners and a memory room containing personal items and mementos of the people who "disappeared" at Villa Grimaldi.

Two other prominent sites that the Pinochet regime used for torture and imprisonment are found in the Atacama Desert to the north of Santiago. In **Chacobuco,** a ghost town roughly 70 km (43 miles) north of Antofagasta in El Norte Grande, the regime established a notorious prison camp, and the artwork of its former inhabitants still lines the walls. Farther north, around 168 km (100 miles) north of Iquique, **Pisagua** was where the Pinochet regime established a camp for missing persons and political prisoners. The camp still haunts the small town even now.

One of the largest cemeteries in Latin America, the **Cementerio General de Santiago,** is an important national monument that reveals a lot about traditional Chilean society. Most Chilean presidents are buried here, with the notable exception of Pinochet. Salvador Allende, who was originally buried in a makeshift grave outside of Viña del Mar, was transported here when democracy was restored to the country. His grave, along with the memorials for those disappeared during the Pinochet regime, make this cemetery an important pilgrimage site.

CHILE MADE EASY

How expensive is Chile?

Chile is among the most expensive countries in Latin America. Prices of hotels and transportation go up considerably from mid-December through mid-March and again in July and August.

What should I pack for a trip to Chile?

Many of Chile's attractions are outdoors, so packing sturdy, all-weather gear is a good idea. Sunglasses, a hat, and sunscreen are all musts because the ozone layer over Chile is particularly deteriorated. For your electronic gear, keep in mind that you will need a two-pronged plug adaptor and that voltage in Chile is 220 volts, 50 cycles (220V 50Hz).

Do I need to or should I rent a car? Is driving hectic?

You definitely don't need to rent a car in Santiago because you can take a combination of taxis, buses, and the metro to get around town. For day trips from Santiago to the coast or wine country, renting a car is probably the most convenient option, although buses to these destinations are also frequent and reasonably priced.

If you do rent a car, be aware of one-way streets and signs indicating right of way. You are not allowed to turn on red at a stoplight unless there is a specific sign indicating otherwise. To drive legally in Chile you need an international driver's license as well as your valid national license, although car rental companies and police do not often enforce this.

Can I drive between Chile and Argentina?

Yes, you can drive between Chile and Argentina, but there are a few things to keep in mind. First, because it is an international border, be sure to have your passport, along with your driver's license. Also, special insurance is required.

If you rent a car, the rental company will provide you with a permit to drive into Argentina (for a price, of course), which includes all the necessary paperwork to cross the border (including the insurance). The permit must be requested several days in advance of the day the rental begins. The rental car must be returned in Chile, and the permit is valid for one exit to Argentina and one entrance into Chile. Common border crossings include the route from Santiago to Mendoza and Valdivia to Bariloche.

Do U.S. citizens still have to pay a reciprocity fee upon entering Chile?

No. Until early 2014, all U.S. citizens entering Chile for the first time had to pay a reciprocity fee of US$161 before passing customs. Because the United States recently made Chile a country eligible for its U.S. Visa Waiver Program, Chile has dropped the reciprocity fee for U.S. citizens.

Do I need to speak Spanish?

It is always helpful to speak the language of the country where you are traveling, but it is less crucial in Chile. Particularly in Santiago, there is generally at least one person who can speak basic English in most restaurants, hotels, and shops. However, if you plan on traveling to less tourist-oriented destinations, fewer people will speak English, and you may need to resort to nonverbal means of communication or trying out those basic Spanish phrases you have learned.

SANTIAGO

WELCOME TO SANTIAGO

TOP REASONS TO GO

★ **The Andes:** Towering, jagged peaks over 15,000 feet high keep you oriented in Santiago, where "uptown" is always due east, toward the mountains.

★ **Great crafts markets:** Fine woolen items, lapis lazuli jewelry, carved wooden and terra-cotta bowls, and other handicrafts from the length of the country are bountiful in Santiago.

★ **Vibrant food scene:** Long considered a destination for the non-foodie, change is afoot in Santiago. Restaurants showcase some of Chile's finest agricultural products with innovative and traditional preparations, and many local ingredients are now given reputable "Denomination of Origin" status.

★ **World-class wineries:** Santiago is in the Maipo Valley, the country's oldest wine-growing area, home to some of Chile's largest and most traditional wineries. Concha y Toro and Santa Rita are within an hour's drive of the city, as is the lovely Casablanca Valley.

2

same name, and now has become a focal point for restaurant-seekers. Lastarria abuts Bellas Artes, where there are more stores than sit-down restaurants.

4 **Parque Forestal.** A leafy park along the banks of the Río Mapocho gives this tranquil district its name. The city's two main art museums share space with jugglers and families on weekends, and this is a new locus for luxury and boutique hotels.

5 **Bellavista and Parque Metropolitano.** On the north side of the Río Mapocho, Bellavista is Santiago's "left bank," a bohemian district of cafés, small restaurants, crafts shops, and one of the homes of famed poet Pablo Neruda.

6 **Parque Quinta Normal Area.** Slightly off the beaten track in western Santiago, the Quinta Normal is one of the largest parks in the city and home to four museums, including one with old locomotives.

7 **Las Condes.** This business area, specifically the street Isidora Goyenechea, has a concentration of upscale eateries, design and gift shops, and a few high-end hotels.

8 **Providencia.** This is where most tourists find themselves at night. It's slightly less urban and historical than the center and is subdivided into smaller neighborhoods linked by a metro station.

1 **Santiago Centro.** This area is undergoing a renaissance. The areas around La Moneda presidential palace and the Plaza de Armas are where you find most of the historic monuments and museums.

2 **La Alameda.** Also known as Avenida Libertador Bernardo O'Higgins, La Alameda marks the southern boundary of Santiago Centro and is lined with sights that include the San Francisco church, ochre-color Universidad de Chile, and Gabriela Mistral Cultural Center (GAM).

3 **Bellas Artes/Lastarria.** Lastarria started with the cobblestoned street of the

GETTING ORIENTED

Pedro de Valdivia wasn't very creative when he mapped out Santiago, sticking to the simple grid pattern typical of almost all colonial towns. The city didn't grow much larger before the meandering Río Mapocho impeded these plans. You may be surprised, however, at how orderly the city remains. It's difficult to get lost downtown, using the Andes as your compass. They're always to the east. Much of the city, especially districts such as Bellavista, is best explored on foot. The subway is the quickest, cleanest, and most economical way to shuttle between neighborhoods. To travel to more distant neighborhoods, or get anywhere in the evening after the subway closes, it's probably best to hail a taxi.

KEY

M *Metro stops*

i *Tourist information*

`===` *Cable-car line*

Updated by
Eileen Smith

Plazas, parks, and fountains share space with street performers, urban photographers, and historical buildings in downtown Santiago. Underneath it all, an ultramodern metro system whisks residents to and from work and play. It is this mix of old and new, neo-Baroque architecture and glass towers, haute cuisine and streetside sopaipillas (fried dough) that makes Santiago what it is today. All over, the city's fairly bursting at the seams with restaurants, cafés, and hotels.

Santiago has come a long way from the triangular patch of land hemmed in by the Río Mapocho (which has since been rerouted, and has only one branch), when the city was founded by Pedro de Valdivia in 1541. Today the area of the original municipality is known as Santiago Centro, and is just one of 32 comunas (districts)—each with its own distinct personality—that make up the city.

In the city, the comuna names rule conversation, and can make or break friendships. The most moneyed semi-central districts like Las Condes, Vitacura, and to a lesser extent, Providencia and Ñuñoa are considered part of the *barrio alto* (literally "high neighborhood, referring to both topography and social strata). It's considered more bohemian to live and spend time in Santiago Centro, particularly the neighborhoods of Lastarria, Bellas Artes, near Parque Forestal, or even down in Barrio Brasil, where some of the city's oldest architecture is found.

That is not to say that well-heeled Santiaguinos do not spend time downtown. Santiago Centro is central to many businesses, and all the bank branches and government architecture is here, including the stock market (though trading is mostly done online now). It's also home to several arts and performance spaces including the Universidad de Chile Theater, Municipal Theater, and the Gabriela Mistral Cultural Center.

Parks are a major meeting point for friends and families in the city, including Parque Quinta Normal (at the metro of the same name), Parque O'Higgins, where the military parade is held every year for Fiestas Patrias, Parque Forestal, and Parque Metropolitano, commonly referred to as Cerro San Cristobal, the larger of the two hills that overlooks the city. Farther uptown in Vitacura, the new Parque Bicentenario, with its duck and waterfowl feeding ponds and dog park, attracts families with children. In nearly all of the city parks you can find people playing *fútbol*, riding bikes, or just enjoying the green space as a retreat from what can be a busy city.

And it is busy. Santiago today is home to more than 6 million people—nearly a third of the country's total population. The city continues to spread outward to the barrios altos east of the center, and all over the city there are cranes building both office and apartment buildings. The tallest building in South America (another good orientation landmark) is the nearly 1,000 foot-tall Costanera Center, steps from the Los Leones metro station and home to a flashy, upscale mall, which some consider a shrine to Chilean consumerism.

Yet, residents are just as likely to run into each other at the supermarket, Vega, weekend fruit and vegetable markets called *ferias,* or in the neighborhood plaza. When they do, they stop to greet each other and talk for at least a minute or two, because even though at times it's a hectic city, in many ways Santiago is just a giant small town at heart.

PLANNING

WHEN TO GO

Santiaguinos tend to abandon their city every summer during the school holidays that run from the end of December to early March. February is a particularly popular vacation time, when nearly everybody who's anybody is out of town. If you're not averse to the heat, this can be a good time for walking around the city; otherwise spring and fall are better choices, as the weather is more comfortable. Santiago is at its prettiest in spring when gentle breezes sweep in to clean the city's air of winter smog and the lavender-blooming *jacaranda,* and the yellow-blooming *aromo* (a type of acacia) come into flower.

Spring and fall are also good times to drive up through the Cajón del Maipo, when the scenery is at its peak. In spring, the plum and cherry trees are in bloom, and in fall, you get some foliage change, and maybe an early snow. Also in fall, the vineyards around the city celebrate the *vendimia*—the grape harvest—with colorful festivals that are an opportunity to try traditional Chilean cuisine as well as some of the country's renowned wines. Winters in the city aren't especially cold— temperatures rarely dip below freezing—but days are sometimes gray and gloomy, and air pollution is at its worst, making it a good time to head to the beach or mountains.

PLANNING YOUR TIME

Santiago is a compact city, small enough to visit all the must-see sights in a few days. Consider the weather when planning your itinerary—on the first clear day your destination should be Parque Metropolitano, where you are treated to exquisite views from Cerro San Cristóbal. After a morning gazing at the Andes, head back down the hill and spend the afternoon wandering the bohemian streets of Bellavista, with a visit to Nobel laureate Pablo Neruda's Santiago residence, La Chascona. Check out one of the neighborhood's colorful eateries, or take a side trip down to Patronato for a falafel or some cheap clothes shopping.

The next day, head to Parque Forestal, a leafy park that runs along the Río Mapocho. Be sure to visit the lovely old train station, Estación Mapocho. After lunch at the Mercado Central, or across the river at Vega or Vega Chica, cover the city's colonial past in Santiago Centro. Requisite sights include the Plaza de Armas, where the cathedral and old post office are, and the nearby Museo Chileno de Arte Precolombino. Stop for coffee or tea in Lastarria or Bellas Artes and do some wandering in Plaza Mulato Gil de Castro and the connected Lastarria or Bellas Artes neighborhoods, ending at the culture and arts center GAM. On your third day explore the sights along La Alameda, especially the presidential palace of La Moneda and the landmark church, Iglesia San Francisco. For a last look at the city, climb Cerro Santa Lucía. That night try dinner in trendy Las Condes or more upscale Vitacura.

GETTING HERE AND AROUND

AIR TRAVEL

Santiago's Comodoro Arturo Merino Benítez International Airport is about a 30-minute drive west of the city. An official taxi or private transfer from the airport to Centro is about 18,000 pesos (slightly more to Providencia and Las Condes); get tickets from the counters before entering the arrivals hall. A shared transfer (which departs when there are enough passengers) costs about 6,000 pesos; get this also from the counters. The cheapest option is to take one of two buses that depart from the airport to Pajaritos and Los Héroes metro stations (Los Héroes is more centrally located), for about 1,600 pesos one way, per person. These buses leave from the far end of the international arrivals terminal.

Airport Contact Comodoro Arturo Merino Benítez International Airport ⊠ *Avda., Armando Cortínez Norte, Pudahuel* ☏ *2/2690–1752* ⊕ *www. aeropuertosantiago.cl.*

Airport Transfers CentroPuerto ☏ *2/2601–9883* ⊕ *www.centropuerto.cl.* **Taxi Oficial** ☏ *2/2601–9880* ⊕ *www.taxioficial.cl.* **Transvip** ☏ *2/2677–3000* ⊕ *www. transvip.cl.*

BUS TRAVEL

Buses are relatively efficient and clean, although very crowded at peak times. Fares on the subway and buses are paid using the same prepaid smart card (most easily acquired in subway stations), called a BIP (say: BEEP). The card itself costs 1,400 pesos. You can also buy single-use tickets for the metro, but not the bus. Fares vary from 590 to 700 pesos, depending on the time of day, and transfers taken (one free transfer from bus to bus, one paid transfer from bus to metro within 120 minutes). At night, there is emergency use of the BIP card on buses only, which allows you to travel, even if you do not have enough money on the card, though most tourists stick to the subway for simplicity's sake.

Bus Depots Terminal Alameda ⊠ *Av. Libertador Bernardo O'Higgins (Alameda) 3750, Estación Central* ☏ *2/2270–7500* ⊕ *www.terminaldebusessantiago.cl.* **Terminal Los Héroes** ⊠ *Tucapel Jiménez 21, Santiago Central* ☏ *2/2420–0099* ⊕ *www.terminaldebuseslosheroes.cl/.* **Terminal San Borja** ⊠ *San Borja 184, Estación Central* ☏ *2/2776–0645* ⊕ *www.terminaldebuses.com/terminales-de-buses.* **Terminal Santiago** ⊠ *Av. Libertador Bernardo O'Higgins (Alameda) 3850, Estación Central* ☏ *2/2376–1750.*

Bus Lines Transantiago ⊠ *Moneda 975, 4th fl., Santiago Central* ☏ *800/730–073, 600/730–0073* ⊕ *www.transantiago.cl/.* **Tur-Bus** ⊠ *Alameda 3750, Estación Central* ☏ *600/660–6600, 2/2822–7500* ⊕ *www.turbus.cl.*

CAR TRAVEL

You don't need a car if you're not going to venture outside the city limits, as most of the downtown sights are within walking distance of each other. A car is the best way to see the surrounding countryside, and the highways around Santiago are excellent. There is an iPhone and Android app called Carretera that helps estimate cost of travel in Chile, calculating cost of gasoline and tolls.

SUBWAY TRAVEL

Santiago's subway system is the best way to get around town. The metro costs between 580 and 690 pesos per ride (depending on time of day and bus transfers). You can buy a single-use ticket or a smart (BIP) card. The metro is safe but gets very crowded at peak hours, and you should keep a hand on valuables. The system operates weekdays 5:40 am–11:30 pm, weekends 8 am–11 pm, with some variation depending on the metro line. Metro opening and closing hours are listed at each station above the turnstiles.

TAXI TRAVEL

Taxis are plentiful, especially outside of bus stations and in touristy neighborhoods. The taxi service Uber is just catching on, and some people prefer to use the app SaferTaxi to ensure that there is a record of their journey. Be prepared with small bills in taxis, as some drivers may not have change. It is customary to round to the closest 500 or 1,000 pesos, but tipping is not customary.

Taxi Companies Alborada ⊠ *Badajoz 12, Las Condes* ☏ *2/2246–4900* ⊕ *www. radiotaxilascondes.cl/.* **Andes Pacífico** ⊠ *José Pedro Alessandri 30, Macúl* ☏ *2/2912–6000* ⊕ *www.andespacifico.cl/.* **Apoquindo** ⊠ *Bilbao 7202, Las Condes* ☏ *2/2210–6200* ⊕ *www.transportesapoquindo.cl/.* **Italia** ⊠ *Coquimbo 1469, Santiago Central* ☏ *2/2591–8900* ⊕ *www.ritalia.cl/.* **Neverías** ⊠ *Apoquindo 4830, Office 22/23, Las Condes* ☏ *2/2207–0003* ⊕ *www.neverias.cl/.*

SAFETY

Despite what Chileans claim, Santiago is no more dangerous than most other large cities and considerably less so than many other Latin American capitals. As a rule of thumb, watch out for your property, preferably keeping physical contact with it, but unless you venture into some of the city's outlying neighborhoods, your physical safety is unlikely to be at risk. Beware of pickpockets particularly in the Centro, near Los Leones metro, and on buses. Don't keep valuables in outside pockets, and exercise caution when using smartphones in very busy areas.

Visitors should be wary of parking attendants. During the day, they should only charge what's on their portable meters when you collect the car but, at night, they ask for money—usually 1,000 pesos—in advance. This is a racket but, for your car's safety, it's better to comply.

TOURS

Sernatur, the national tourism service, maintains a listing of experienced individual tour guides, who run half-day tours of Santiago and the surrounding area.

FoodyChile. Colin Bennett's tour company's name FoodyChile is a play on words, meaning both "foodie Chile" and "food and Chile." He's got several years of experience in the field and has been living in Chile for more than 10 years. Tours are always small, personalized, and focus on consumables, including wine, craft beer, and sweets. There are lunches and dinners hosted in private homes, as well as market tours. ⊠ *José Manuel Infante 100, Office 204, Providencia* ☏ *9/9538–4342* ⊕ *www. foodychile.com* ✉ *From 45,000 pesos.*

Fotoruta. Cat Allen, a photographer with lots of experience leading people around Santiago on foot, has a lovely way of encouraging your own pictures, no matter the skill level. There's even an iPhoneography class. Some classes have a photo-sharing session at the end. ⊠ *Bellavista* ☏ *9/8766–6844* ⊕ *www.foto-ruta.com* ✉ *From US$32.*

Santiago Adventures. This adventure tour company prides itself on running tours no one else does, such as heliskiing at Ski Arpa and thematic tours of Santiago, including Jewish culture, bicycling, and food. The company also organizes multiday trips inside and outside of Santiago, extending to the north and south of the country and beyond to Argentina and Uruguay. ⊠ *Doctor Manuel Barros Borgoño 198, 2nd fl., Providencia* ☏ *2/2244–2750* ⊕ *www.santiagoadventures.com* ✉ *From US$74.*

Turismo Cocha. One of the biggest players in the Chilean tourism industry, Cocha books tours inside and outside of Chile, as well as hotels, airfare, cruises, and even English classes. Single-day city tours are available, but the main focus is on multiday tours with lodging at three-, four-, and five-star hotels. The main office is in El Golf (Las Condes), but there are nearly 20 offices around the city, including one at the airport. ⊠ *El Bosque Norte 0430, Las Condes, Santiago* ☏ *2/2464–1000* ⊕ *www. cocha.com* ✉ *From 100,000 pesos.*

VISITOR INFORMATION
Visitor Information Sernatur ⊠ *Av. Providencia 1550, Providencia* ☏ *2/2731–8310* ⊕ *www.sernatur.cl* ⏲ *Weekdays, 9–6, Sat. 9–2.*

EXPLORING

SANTIAGO CENTRO

Shiny new skyscrapers may be sprouting up in neighborhoods to the east, but Santiago Centro has its share of construction going on, too. During the past decade, the population downtown has nearly doubled, but that's for the whole comuna, not just the *casco histórico*, which is close to the Alameda and runs from La Moneda up to about Santa Lucía. Take the metro down here, not a taxi, for easy transportation, as the usual traffic headaches apply to downtown Santiago.

TIMING AND PRECAUTIONS
In this part of the city you can find interesting museums, performance spaces, galleries, imposing government buildings, and bustling commercial streets. Don't worry about getting lost in a sprawling area—it takes only about 15 minutes to walk from one edge of the historic center to the other.

TOP ATTRACTIONS

Gabriela Mistral Cultural Center (GAM). This giant cultural center just steps from the Universidad Católica metro houses some of Santiago's most interesting folk museum exhibits, as well as a nice wine store and theater. There is a large atrium between the two halves of the building with a colorful skylight, restaurant, and café. Outside the building, to the north side is an amphitheater that is occasionally used to host events. An antiques market takes place on the west side of the building Tuesday through Saturday, if it's not raining. ⊠ *Alameda 227* ☎ *2/2566–5500* ⊕ *gam.cl* Ⓜ *Universidad Católica.*

Metropolitan Cathedral. Conquistador Pedro de Valdivia declared in 1541 that a house of worship would be constructed at this site bordering the Plaza de Armas. The first adobe building burned to the ground, and the structures that replaced it were destroyed by the earthquakes of 1647 and 1730. The finishing touches of the neoclassical cathedral standing today were added in 1789 by Italian architect Joaquín Toesca. Be sure to check out the baroque interior stained-glass-topped arched colonnade, and look out for the sparkling silver altar of a side chapel in the south nave. ⊠ *Plaza de Armas 444* ☎ *2/2671–8105* ⊙ *Daily 9–7:30* Ⓜ *Plaza de Armas.*

Museo Chileno de Arte Precolombino. This well-endowed collection of artifacts of the region's indigenous peoples, much of it donated by the collector Sergio Larraín García-Moreno, is displayed in the beautifully restored Royal Customs House that dates from 1807. The permanent collection, on the upper floor, showcases ceramics and textiles from Mexico to Patagonia. Unlike many of the city's museums, the displays here are well labeled in Spanish and English. Guided tours in English are available at no extra cost, but must be booked in advance. There is a shop with a good selection of on-topic books and an airy café as well. ⊠ *Bandera 361, at Av. Compañía* ☎ *2/2928–1500 general, 2/2929–1522 tours* ⊕ *www.museoprecolombino.cl* 💲 *3,500 pesos; free 1st Sun. of every month* ⊙ *Tues.–Sun. 10–6* Ⓜ *Plaza de Armas.*

Museo Histórico Nacional. The colonial-era Palacio de la Real Audiencia served as the meeting place for Chile's first Congress in July 1811. The building then functioned as a telegraph office before the museum moved here in 1911. It's worth the small admission charge to see the interior of the 200-year-old structure, where exhibits tracing Chile's history from the preconquest period to the 20th century are arranged chronologically in rooms centered on a courtyard. Keep an eye out for Allende's eyeglasses. Ask for the English brochure and free audio guide, and if you are not heights-averse, take a tour up the tower for a bird's-eye view of the Plaza de Armas, cathedral, and downtown Santiago. ⊠ *Plaza de Armas 951* ☎ *2/2411–7001* ⊕ *www.museohistoriconacional.cl* 💲 *Tues.–Sat., 600 pesos; Sun., free* ⊙ *Tues.–Sun. 10–5:45* Ⓜ *Plaza de Armas.*

Fodor's Choice **Plaza de Armas.** This square has been the symbolic heart of Chile—★ as well as its political, social, religious, and commercial center—since Pedro de Valdivia established the city on this spot in 1541. The Palacio de los Gobernadores, the Palacio de la Real Audiencia, and the

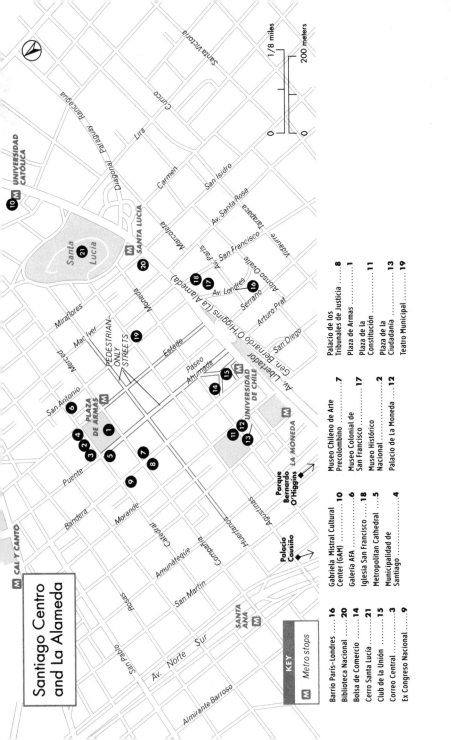

Santiago Centro and La Alameda

KEY

Ⓜ *Metro stops*

Barrio París-Londres **16**
Biblioteca Nacional **20**
Bolsa de Comercio **14**
Cerro Santa Lucía **21**
Club de la Unión **15**
Correo Central **3**
Ex Congreso Nacional **9**

Gabriela Mistral Cultural
Center (GAM) **10**
Galería AFA **6**
Iglesia San Francisco **18**
Metropolitan Cathedral **5**
Municipalidad de
Santiago **4**

Museo Chileno de Arte
Precolombino **7**
Museo Colonial de
San Francisco **17**
Museo Histórico
Nacional **2**
Palacio de La Moneda **12**

Palacio de los
Tribunales de Justicia **8**
Plaza de Armas **1**
Plaza de la
Constitución **11**
Plaza de la
Ciudadanía **13**
Teatro Municipal **19**

Municipalidad de Santiago front the square's northern edge. The dignified cathedral graces the western side of the square. The plaza has historically been very lively, with chess players in a gazebo, street performers, and caricaturists. Recent improvements have increased the number of trees and installed Wi-Fi. ⊠ *Compañía at Estado* Ⓜ *Plaza de Armas.*

WORTH NOTING

Correo Central. Housed in what was once the ornate Palacio de los Gobernadores, this building dating from 1715 is one of the most beautiful post offices you are likely to see. It was reconstructed by Ricardo Brown in 1882 after being ravaged by fire and is a fine example of neoclassical architecture, with a glass-and-iron roof added in the early 20th century. It has occasional exhibits in the main hall, plus an extensive collections of stamps from around the world and other postal and telegraph memorabilia in the adjoining Postal and Telegraph Museum (free admission). ⊠ *Plaza de Armas 989, at Puente* ☎ *2/2956–5145* ⊕ *www.correos.cl* ☉ *Post office: weekdays 8–7, Sat. 9–2; museum: weekdays 9:30–6:30* Ⓜ *Plaza de Armas.*

Ex Congreso Nacional. Once the meeting place for the National Congress (the legislature moved to Valparaíso in 1990), this palatial neoclassical building became the Ministry of Foreign Affairs for a time but was returned to the Senate for meetings after the Ministry moved to the former Hotel Carrera in the Plaza de la Constitución in December 2005. The original structure on the site, the Iglesia de la Compañía de Jesús, was destroyed by a fire in 1863 in which 2,000 people perished. Two bells from that church now grace the elaborate gardens. To coordinate a tour, write an email to protocolostgo@senado.cl with at least two days' notice. More formal attire is appreciated, and neither shorts nor baseball caps are permitted. The tour is free and lasts approximately 30 minutes. ⊠ *Catedral 1158* Ⓜ *Plaza de Armas.*

Galería AFA. If for no other reason, you should go to the AFA gallery because it's tucked away in a fascinating little plaza and alleyway just steps from Santiago's Plaza de Armas. You will be rewarded with free art exhibits across three gallery rooms: contemporary exhibitions of photography, sculpture, painting, and more by emerging and established Chilean artists. It's occasionally closed during installations. ⊠ *Psje. Phillips 16, Apartment 2A* ☎ *2/2664–8450* ⊕ *www.galeriaafa. com* ☉ *Tues.–Fri. 11–5, Sat. 11–3.*

Municipalidad de Santiago. Today's city hall for central Santiago can be found on the site of the colonial city hall and jail. The original structure, built in 1552, survived until a devastating earthquake in 1730.

GOOD TO KNOW

There are few public restrooms in Santiago. Ecobaños operates four public restrooms in El Centro that are clean and brightly lighted. The uniformed attendants even wish you good day. All this for 400 pesos! They are located at Morandé and Huérfanos, Ahumada and Moneda, Ahumada between Compañía and Huérfanos, and Estado between Moneda and Agustinas. Sure-thing (free) bathrooms are also located in the basement at the Biblioteca Nacional.

2

Joaquín Toesca, the architect who also designed the presidential palace and completed the cathedral, reconstructed the building in 1785, but it was destroyed by fire a century later. In 1891, Eugenio Joannon, who favored an Italian Renaissance style, erected the structure standing today. On the facade hangs an elaborate coat of arms presented by Spain. The interior now houses a tourist office as well as a small gallery and souvenir shop. The tourism office runs free tours on Monday, Wednesday, and Friday at 10 am with no previous registration required. ⊠ *Plaza de Armas* ☉ *Weekdays 9–6, weekends 10–4* Ⓜ *Plaza de Armas.*

Palacio de los Tribunales de Justicia. During Augusto Pinochet's rule, countless human-rights demonstrations were held outside the Courts of Justice, which house the country's Supreme Court. The imposing neoclassical interior is worth a look, but the guards reserve the right to admission and prefer more formal attire (no shorts, flip-flops, tank tops). It is open for visits 9–2. ⊠ *Av. Compañia 1140* Ⓜ *Plaza de Armas.*

OFF THE BEATEN PATH

Parque Bernardo O'Higgins. Named for Chile's first president and national hero, whose troops were victorious against the Spanish, this park has plenty of open space for everything from ball games to military parades. Street vendors sell *volantines* (kites) in the park year-round; breezy September and early October comprise prime kite-flying season, especially around September 18, Chile's national holiday. There are pedalcab and rollerblade rentals on weekends, a competitive rollerblade track, and a terrain park with a deep bowl for skateboarders and rollerbladers. The park has a beautiful covered pool, which costs 5,000 pesos for a day visit; goggles and bathing cap are required. Both the Movistar Arena and Teatro La Cupola theater are at this park as well. ⊠ *Autopista Central between Av. Blanco Encalada and Av. Rondizonni* ☐ *Free* ☉ *Daily dawn–dusk* Ⓜ *Parque O'Higgins.*

LA ALAMEDA

Avenida Libertador Bernardo O'Higgins, more frequently called Alameda, is the city's principal thoroughfare. Along with the Pan-American Highway (Avenida Norte Sur) and the Río Mapocho, it forms the wedge that defines the city's historic district. Many of Santiago's most important buildings, including landmarks such as the Iglesia San Francisco, stand along the avenue. Others, like Teatro Municipal, are just steps away.

TIMING AND PRECAUTIONS

You could spend an hour alone at the Palacio de la Moneda—try to time your visit with the changing of the guard, which takes place every other day at 10 am on weekdays, and 11 on weekends. Under the Plaza de la Constitución, which is on the Alameda side of the Moneda, there's the Centro Cultural Palacio la Moneda—a culture, arts, and exhibition space with a few shops and cafés. Across the Alameda, take at least an hour and a half to explore Iglesia San Francisco, the adjacent museum, and the Barrio París-Londres. You could easily spend a bookish half hour perusing the stacks at the Biblioteca Nacional, where you can also get 30 minutes of free Internet if you present identification. Plan for an hour or more at Cerro Santa Lucía with its splendid view of the city and adjacent crafts markets.

TOP ATTRACTIONS

Fodor's Choice ★ **Cerro Santa Lucía.** The mazelike park of Santa Lucía is a hangout for park-bench smoochers and photo-snapping tourists. Walking uphill along the labyrinth of interconnected paths and plazas takes about 30 minutes, or you can take an elevator two blocks north of the park's main entrance (no fee). The uppermost lookout point affords an excellent 360-degree view of the entire city; two stairways lead up from the Plaza Caupolicán esplanade; those on the south side are newer and less slippery. Be careful

near dusk as the park, although patrolled, attracts the occasional mugger. There is a tiny tourism office near the Alameda entrance, open weekdays, but closed for lunch from 2 until 3 pm, and a small indigenous crafts fair called the Centro de Exposición de Arte Indígena (or Gruta Welén) in a natural cavern carved out of the western flank of the hill. ⊠ *Santa Lucía at La Alameda, Santiago Centro* ☎ *2/2664–4206* ⏱ *Nov.–Mar., daily 9–7; Apr.–Oct., daily 9–6* Ⓜ *Santa Lucía.*

Iglesia San Francisco. Santiago's oldest structure, greatest symbol, and principal landmark, the Church of San Francisco is the last trace of 16th-century colonial architecture in the city. Construction began in 1586, and although the church survived successive earthquakes, early tremors took their toll and portions had to be rebuilt several times. Today's neoclassical tower, which forms the city's most recognizable silhouette, was added in 1857 by architect Fermín Vivaceta. Inside are rough stone-and-brick walls and an ornate coffered wood ceiling. Visible on the main altar is the image of the Virgen del Socorro (Virgin of Perpetual Help) that conquistador Pedro de Valdivia carried for protection and guidance. ⊠ *Av. Libertador Bernardo O'Higgins (Alameda) 834, Santiago Centro* ☎ *2/2638–3238* ⏱ *Mon.–Sat. 7:30 am–8:30 pm, Sun. 9–2. Mass, Tues.–Sat. 9, 10, and 7:30; Sun 10, 11, noon, 1, and 7:30* Ⓜ *Santa Lucía, Universidad de Chile.*

Palacio de La Moneda. Originally the royal mint, this sober neoclassical edifice designed by Joaquín Toesca in the 1780s and completed in 1805 became the presidential palace in 1846, serving that purpose for more than a century. It was bombarded by the military in the 1973 coup, when Salvador Allende defended his presidency against the assault of General Augusto Pinochet before (it was determined in 2013) committing suicide there. Free tours can be arranged by email with at least two days' notice. Tell them you want to see the Salón Blanco if you'd like to go upstairs. ⊠ *Plaza de la Constitución, Moneda between Teatinos* *and Morandé, Santiago Centro* ☎ *2/2690–4000* ✆ *visitas@presidencia. cl* ⊕ *www.gob.cl* ☽ *Daily 10:30–6* Ⓜ *La Moneda.*

Fodor's Choice   **Plaza de la Constitución.** Palacio de la Moneda and other government
★   buildings line Constitution Square, the country's most formal plaza.
The changing of the guard takes place every other day at 10 am within
the triangle defined by 12 Chilean flags. Adorning the plaza are four
monuments, each dedicated to a notable national figure: Diego Portales,
founder of the Chilean republic; Jorge Alessandri, the country's leader
from 1958 to 1964; Eduardo Frei Montalva, president from 1964 to
1970; and Salvador Allende (1970–73). ⊠ *Moneda at Morandé, Santiago Centro* Ⓜ *La Moneda.*

WORTH NOTING

Barrio París-Londres. Many architects contributed to what is frequently
referred to as Santiago's Little Europe, among them Alberto Cruz
Montt, Jorge Elton Alamos, and Sergio Larraín. The string of small
mansion houses lining the cobbled streets of Calles París and Londres
sprang up in the mid-1920s on vegetable patches and gardens once
belonging to the convent adjoining Iglesia San Francisco. The three- and
four-story town houses are all unique; some have brick facades, while
others are done in Palladian style. ⊠ *Londres at París, Santiago Centro.*

Biblioteca Nacional (*National Library*). Near the foot of Cerro Santa
Lucía is the block-long classical facade of the National Library. Moved
to its present premises in 1925, this library, founded in 1813, has one
of the oldest and most extensive collections in South America. The
second-floor Sala José Toribio Medina (closed Saturday), which holds
the most important collection of early Latin American print work, is
well worth a look. The three levels of books, reached by curved-wood
balconies, are lighted by massive chandeliers. The café on the ground
floor is a quiet place to linger over a coffee. There is free Internet in a
few locations. ⊠ *Av. Libertador Bernardo O'Higgins (Alameda) 651,
Santiago Centro* ☎ *2/2360–5232* ⊕ *ww.bibliotecanacional.cl* ✆ *Free*
☽ *Weekdays 9–7, Sat. 9–2* Ⓜ *Santa Lucía.*

Bolsa de Comercio. Chile's stock exchange is housed in a 1917 French
neoclassical structure with an elegant clock tower surmounted by an
arched slate cupola. Business is now done electronically but you can
visit the old trading floor with its buying and selling circle called *rueda*.
You must leave your ID at the door. ⊠ *La Bolsa 64, Santiago Centro*
☎ *2/2399–3000* ⊕ *www.bolsadesantiago.com* ✆ *Free* ☽ *Weekdays 9–6*
Ⓜ *Universidad de Chile.*

Club de la Unión. The facade of this neoclassical building, dating to 1925,
is one of the city's finest. The interior of this private club, whose roster
has included numerous Chilean presidents, is open only to members and
their guests, except for the last Sunday in May, when it is sometimes
open for the *Día del Patrimonio.* ⊠ *Av. Libertador Bernardo O'Higgins
(Alameda) 1091, Santiago Centro* Ⓜ *Universidad de Chile.*

Museo Colonial de San Francisco. This monastery adjacent to Iglesia San
Francisco houses the best collection of 17th-century colonial paintings
on the continent. Inside the rooms wrapping around the courtyard
are 54 large-scale canvases portraying the life of St. Francis painted

in Cuzco, Peru, as well as a plethora of religious iconography and an impressive collection of silver artifacts. Most pieces are labeled in Spanish and English. There are peacocks roaming the central courtyard. ⊠ *Av. Libertador Bernardo O'Higgins (Alameda) 834, Santiago Centro* 🕾 *2/2639–8737* ⊕ *www.museosanfrancisco.com* 🎫 *1,000 pesos* ⊙ *Tues.–Fri. 10–1:30 and 2:30–6, Mon. and Sat. 10–1:30 and 2:30–4* Ⓜ *Santa Lucía, Universidad de Chile.*

Plaza de la Ciudadanía. On the south side of the Palacio de la Moneda, this plaza was inaugurated in December 2006 as part of a public works program in preparation for the celebration of the bicentenary of Chile's independence in 2010. Beneath the plaza is the Centro Cultural Palacio de la Moneda, an arts center that puts on interesting exhibitions. The Artesanías de Chile crafts shop there has top-quality work, and the Tienda Centro Cultural is a good place to buy unusual souvenirs and jewelry. Also here are a restaurant, a café, a bookshop, and two movie theaters. ⊠ *Plaza de la Ciudadanía 26, Santiago Centro* 🕾 *2/2355–6500* ⊕ *www.ccplm.cl* 🎫 *Bldg.: free. Exhibition: Chileans and residents 2,000, foreigners 5,000, foreign students 2,500. Half-price entry before noon weekdays* ⊙ *Centro Cultural exhibitions daily 10–6:30* Ⓜ *La Moneda.*

Teatro Municipal. The opulent Municipal Theater is the city's cultural center, with performances of opera, ballet, and classical music. Designed by French architects, the theater opened in 1857, with major renovations in 1870 and 1906 following a fire and an earthquake. The Renaissance-style building is one of the city's most refined monuments with a lavish interior that deserves a visit. The cobblestoned walk around the building completes the picture. ⊠ *Plaza Alcalde Mekis, Av. Agustinas 794, at Av. San Antonio, Santiago Centro* 🕾 *2/2463–8888* ⊕ *www.municipal.cl* Ⓜ *Universidad de Chile, Santa Lucía.*

LASTARRIA AND BELLAS ARTES

This contiguous area is really two neighborhoods, but elements of modern and artsy Bellas Artes and the more traditional and cobblestoned Lastarria flow in and out of each other. Bellas Artes has gone from seedy to universally popular within a decade. It is full of budget-friendly empanada joints, pizza places, ice-cream parlors, and all-natural food shops.

Mostly cobblestoned Lastarria starts at Merced, and extends south to the imposing new Gabriela Mistral Cultural Center. It's a better-heeled crowd in Lastarria, and the area has more upscale dining. Both areas have street-level commerce with clothing boutiques and art supplies, and both are popular among Chileans and foreigners.

TIMING AND PRECAUTIONS

You can't go wrong with a late afternoon in Bellas Artes, as restaurants and street-side cafés fill up with people off work early. In Plaza Mulato Gil de Castro, allot at least 30 minutes for the Museo de Artes Visuales and adjoining Museo Arqueológico. Because both of these areas are busy and attract people who've come to spend money, simple precautions like keeping your purse in your lap, not on the back of your chair, are recommended. Consider coming down into Lastarria after a walk up Cerro Santa Lucía, the smaller of the two hills that overlooks the city.

TOP ATTRACTIONS

Museo Arqueológico de Santiago. This archaeological museum, devoted specifically to the indigenous peoples of Chile, more than makes up for its small size with the quality of the exhibits, labeled in English and Spanish. Artifacts include an outstanding collection of the Andean headwear used to distinguish different ethnic groups, pottery, jewelry, and a collection of the woven bags used by Andean peoples to carry the coca leaves that sustained them during their long treks at high altitudes. It is located inside the Museo de Artes Visuales, and one entry fee pays for both visits. ⊠ *José Victorino Lastarria 307, 2nd fl., Lastarria* ☎ *2/2664–9337* ⊕ *www.mavi.cl* ✉ *Tues.–Sat. 1,000 pesos (includes Museo de Artes Visuales), Sun. free* ☉ *Tues.–Sun. 10:30–6:30* Ⓜ *Universidad Católica.*

Fodor$Choice **Museo de Artes Visuales.** This dazzling museum of contemporary art
★ displays the combined private holdings of Chilean industrial moguls Manuel Santa Cruz and Hugo Yaconi, and has one of Chile's finest collections of contemporary Chilean art. The building itself is a masterpiece: six gallery levels float into each other in surprising ways. The wood floors and Plexiglas-sided stairways create an open and airy space where you might see—depending on what's on display when you visit—paintings and sculptures by Roberto Matta, Arturo Duclos, Gonzalo Cienfuegos, Roser Bru, José Balmes, and Eugenio Dittborn, among others. ⊠ *José Victorino Lastarria 307, at Plaza Mulato Gil de Castro, Lastarria* ☎ *2/2684–9337* ⊕ *www.mavi.cl* ✉ *Tues.–Sat. 1,000 pesos (includes Museo Arqueológico de Santiago), Sun. free* ☉ *Tues.–Sun. 10:30–6:30* Ⓜ *Universidad Católica.*

PARQUE FORESTAL

You wouldn't think building-happy Santiago would let the prime real estate that is Parque Forestal go without construction, but the narrow strip of land was left over after a canal was built in 1891 to tame the unpredictable Río Mapocho. The area quickly filled with the city's refuse. A decade later, under the watchful eye of Enrique Cousiño, it was transformed into the leafy Parque Forestal. It was and still is enormously popular with Santiaguinos, and recent investments have cleaned it further, installed playgrounds for children, and created a bike path along the northern edge.

On weekends, the area near the Contemporary Art Museum fills with jugglers, people doing aerial silks, and acrobatics. The eastern tip of the park, near Plaza Baquedano (also referred to as Plaza Italia, though that plaza is further north) is distinguished by the Wagnerian-scale *Fuente Alemana* (German Fountain), donated by the German community of Santiago. The bronze-and-stone monolith commemorates the centennial of Chilean independence.

TIMING AND PRECAUTIONS

You can have a pleasant, relaxing day strolling through the city's most popular park, losing yourself in the art museums and exploring the Mercado Central. You can easily spend an hour or two in the Museo Nacional de Bellas Artes and the Museo de Arte Contemporáneo. The Vega Chica, Tirso de Molina, and Vega Central are usually crowded, so keep an eye on your personal belongings. When the markets close around sunset, it's best to return to more lively neighborhoods south of the river.

TOP ATTRACTIONS

Mercado Central. At the Central Market you'll find a matchless selection of edible products from the sea. Depending on the season, you might see the delicate beaks of *picorocos,* the world's only edible barnacles; *erizos,* the prickly shelled sea urchins; or heaps of giant mussels. If the fish don't capture your interest, the architecture may: the lofty wrought-iron ceiling of the structure, reminiscent of a Victorian train station, was prefabricated in England and erected in Santiago between 1868 and 1872. Diners are regaled by musicians in the middle of the market, where a few larger restaurants compete for customers. You can also find a cheap meal at the smaller restaurants around the edge of the market. ⊠ *Ismael Valdés Vergara 900* ☎ *2/696–8327* ⊕ *www.mercadocentral.cl* ☉ *Sat.–Thurs. 7–5, Fri. 6 am–7 pm* Ⓜ *Puente Cal y Canto.*

Museo Nacional de Bellas Artes. Unfortunately, Chile's main art museum now has only a small part of its excellent collection of Chilean painting on display, confining it to just six small rooms on the second floor. The rest of the museum is given over to temporary exhibitions of varying interest. The elegant, neoclassical building, which was originally intended to house the city's school of fine arts, has an impressive glass-domed ceiling, which illuminates the main hall. Guided tours in English are available in January and February. ⊠ *Bounded by José M. de la Barra and Ismael Valdés Vergara* ☎ *2/2499–1600* ⊕ *www.mnba.cl* ☜ *Tues.–Sat. 600 pesos, Sun. free* ☉ *Tues.–Sun. 10–6:50 pm* Ⓜ *Bellas Artes.*

WORTH NOTING

Estación Mapocho. This mighty edifice, with its trio of two-story arches framed by intricate terra-cotta detailing, is as elegant as any train station in the world. The station was inaugurated in 1913 as a terminus for trains arriving from Valparaíso and points north, but after trains were diverted to Estación Central, the space was turned into one of the city's principal arts and conference centers. The Centro Cultural Estación Mapocho houses two restaurants, a café, a large exhibition hall, and arts space. The cavernous station that once sheltered steam engines now hosts musical performances and other events, such as the Cumbre Guachaca, a celebration of city-meets-down-home-country culture, usually held in April. ⊠ *Plaza de la Cultura, Independencia at Balmaceda* ☎ *2/2787–0000* ⊕ *www.estacionmapocho.cl* ☜ *Station free, exhibition fees vary* ☉ *Daily 10–6; exhibitions closed Mon.* Ⓜ *Puente Cal y Canto.*

Museo de Arte Contemporáneo. After an ambitious restoration, completed in 2008, followed by the destructive earthquake of 2010 and

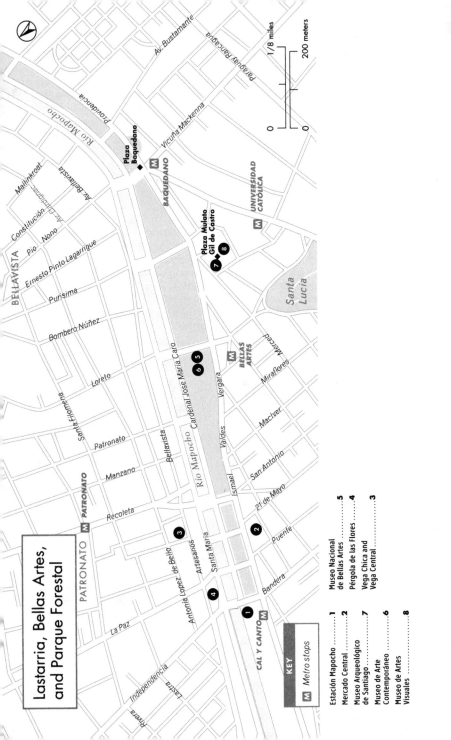

Lastarria, Bellas Artes, and Parque Forestal

200 meters

1/8 miles

then another renovation, the elegant Museum of Contemporary Art has a sparkling new interior in this classic building. The museum showcases modern Latin American paintings, photography, and sculpture. The museum is run by the art school of Universidad de Chile and isn't afraid to take risks. Look for Fernando Botero's pudgy *Caballo (Horse)* sculpture out front, and drop in at its new café serving gourmet pour-over coffee and homemade treats. There is another location of this museum near Quinta Normal, with different exhibits and a bus-turned-café called *Central Placeres* or simply *La Micro* ("the bus," in Chilean slang) parked outside. ⊠ *Bounded by José M. de la Barra and Ismael Valdés Vergara* ☎ *2/2977–1741* ⊕ *www.mac.uchile.cl* 💲 *600 pesos* ☉ *Tues.–Sat. 10–6:30, Sun. 10:30–6* Ⓜ *Bellas Artes.*

OFF THE BEATEN PATH

Parque de las Esculturas. Everyone who lives in Providencia, a commercial and residential community, knows this as one of the city's most captivating—and least publicized—public parks. Its gardens are filled with sculptures by Chile's top artists and because of its pastoral atmosphere, the park is popular with joggers and cuddling couples. In the center is a wood pavilion that hosts art exhibitions. To get here from the Los Leones metro stop, walk up Pedro de Valdivia towards Cerro San Cristóbal, and over the river. The park is on your right. It hosts a jazz festival every January, and a little farther west, is one of the free exercise stations that dot the city. ⊠ *Pedro de Valdivia and Santa María, 750000.*

Pérgola de las Flores. Santiaguinos come to the Pérgola de las Flores (literally: "gazebo of flowers") markets to buy wreaths and flower arrangements for decoration or to bring to the city's two nearby cemeteries. *La Pérgola de las Flores,* a famous Chilean musical, is based on the conflict that arose in the 1930s when the mayor of Santiago wanted to shut down the market, then located near the Iglesia San Francisco on the Alameda. Find a chatty florist at one of the two open-air markets—Pégola San Francisco and Pérgola Santa María, each with about 40 vendors—and you may learn all about it. ⊠ *Av. La Paz at Artesanos, Recoleta* ☉ *Daily sunrise–sunset* Ⓜ *Puente Cal y Canto.*

Vega Chica and Vega Central. From fruit to furniture, meat to machinery, these lively markets stock just about anything you can name. Alongside the ordinary items you can find delicacies like *piñones,* which are giant pine nuts found on monkey puzzle trees. If you're undaunted by crowds, try a typical Chilean meal in a closet-size eatery, or *picada* in the Vega Central, chowing down on brothy cazuela or a plate of fried fish. For a little more selection and a little more space, go to the second floor of the Vega Chica (now called Tirso de Molina) where Chilean, Colombian, Thai, Mexican, and Peruvian food is all dished out in large portions at fair prices. As in any other crowded market, be extra careful with your belongings. ⊠ *Antonia López de Bello between Av. Salas and Nueva Rengifo, Recoleta* Ⓜ *Patronato or Puente Cal Y Canto.*

BELLAVISTA AND PARQUE METROPOLITANO

If you happen to be in Santiago on one of those lovely winter days when the sun comes out after rain has cleared the air, head straight for Parque Metropolitano. In the center is Cerro San Cristóbal, a hill reached via funicular railway, taxi, a 45-minute trail, or an hour-plus uphill walk on the main road. Atop the hill are spectacular views of the city below the snow-covered Andes Mountains.

In the shadow of Cerro San Cristóbal is Bellavista. The neighborhood has but one sight—poet Pablo Neruda's hillside home of La Chascona—but it's perhaps the city's best place to wander. Strike out on your own, or start out in Patio Bellavista (an open-air mall/arcade); either way you're sure to find interesting shops, small art galleries, souvenirs, and food to suit most budgets and tastes.

TIMING AND PRECAUTIONS

Plan on devoting an entire day to visiting Parque Metropolitano's major attractions. During the week the park is almost empty, and you can enjoy the views in relative solitude. If you decide to walk up from the Bellavista side, take the road about 5 km (3 miles), or take a right at a sign about half a mile in that says Zorro Vidal and follow the path for a hike about 40 minutes to the top. This is best done on weekends. Avoid walking down the hill if you decide to watch the sunset from the lofty perch—the area is not well patrolled. Give yourself at least an hour to wander through Bellavista, and another hour for a tour of La Chascona.

TOP ATTRACTIONS

FAMILY
Fodor'sChoice
★

Cerro San Cristóbal. This large, iconic hill within Parque Metropolitano is one of the most popular tourist attractions in Santiago. From the western entrance at Plaza Caupolicán (Pio Nono) you can take a steep but enjoyable one-hour walk to the summit, or take the funicular. (The funicular, which opened in 1925, is a historic monument.) At the top is the gleaming white statue of the Virgen de la Inmaculada Concepción. Until it fell into disrepair in 2009, a *teleférico* (cable car) ascended from the eastern entrance, seven blocks north of the Pedro de Valdivia metro stop. At this writing *teleférico* operations are suspended, with no firm plans for repairs as the process has stalled at the request for proposal stage. Driving up costs to 3,000 pesos per car during the week and 4,000 on weekends. ✉ *Cerro San Cristóbal, Bellavista* ☎ *2/2730–1331* ⊕ *www.parquemet.cl* 🎫 *Round-trip funicular: weekdays 2,000 pesos, weekends and holidays 2,600 pesos* ☉ *Park daily 8:30 am–9 pm. Funicular Mon. 1–6, Tues.–Sun. 10–7* Ⓜ *Baquedano, Pedro de Valdivia.*

Fodor'sChoice
★

La Chascona. This house designed by the Nobel Prize winning poet Pablo Neruda was dubbed the "Woman with the Tousled Hair" after Matilde Urrutia, the poet's third wife. The two met while strolling in nearby Parque Forestal, and for years the house served as a romantic hideaway before they married. The pair's passionate relationship was recounted in the 1995 Italian film *Il Postino*. There are audio guides, available in English, Spanish, French, Portuguese, and German, and the house is visually fascinating, with winding garden paths, stairs, and bridges leading to the house and its library, which is stuffed with books. There's Neruda's old bedroom in a tower, and a secret passageway. Scattered throughout are collections of butterflies, seashells, wineglasses, and other odd objects that inspired Neruda's tumultuous life and romantic poetry. Although not as magical as Neruda's house in Isla Negra, La Chascona can still set your imagination dancing. The house is on a

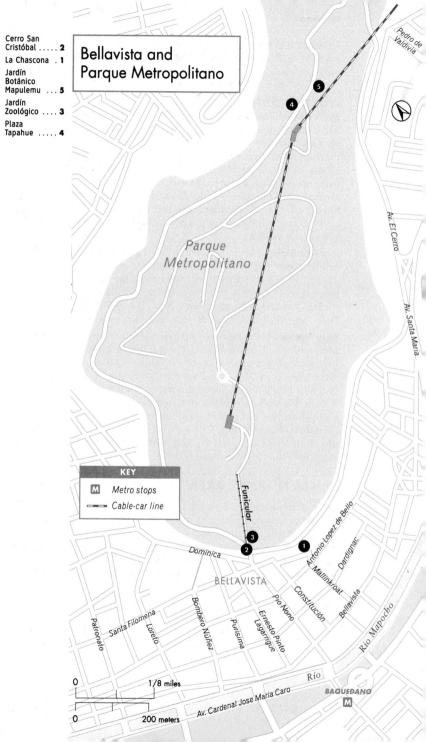

Bellavista and
Parque Metropolitano

Parque
Metropolitano

Pedro de Valdivia

Av. El Cerro

Av. Santa María

Funicular

Dominica

Antonio Lopez de Bello

Mallinkroat

Dardignac

Bellavista

BELLAVISTA

Patronato

Santa Filomena

Loreto

Bombero Núñez

Purísima

Pio Nono

Ernesto Pinto Lagarrigue

Constitución

Río Mapocho

Río

BAQUEDANO

KEY

M Metro stops
⊏⊐ Cable-car line

0   1/8 miles

0   200 meters

Av. Cardenal Jose María Caro

little side street leading off Constitución. ✉ *Fernando Márquez de la Plata 0192, Bellavista* 📞 *2/2777–8741* ⊕ *www.fundacionneruda.org* 🎧 *Audio guide 5,000 pesos* ⊙ *Mar.–Dec., Tues.–Sun. 10–6; Jan. and Feb., Tues.–Sun. 10–7* Ⓜ *Baquedano.*

WORTH NOTING

Jardín Botánico Mapulemu. Gravel paths lead you to restful nooks in the Mapulemu Botanical Garden, dedicated to native Chilean species. Every path and stairway seems to bring you to better views of Santiago and the Andes. On weekends, the Instituto Nacional de Deportes conducts classes starting from 9:30 am. These free municipality-run seminars may include yoga, Zumba, aerobics, aeroboxing, or a spinning-like activity called "bicicleta estatica." There are also paid yoga classes on Sunday 10–noon. The easiest access is from the Pedro de Valdivia side. ✉ *Cerro San Cristóbal, Bellavista* 📞 *2/2730–1331* 🎧 *Free* ⊙ *Daily 10–6* Ⓜ *Pedro de Valdivia.*

FAMILY **Jardín Zoológico.** The Zoological Garden is a good place to see Chilean animals, some nearly extinct, that you might not otherwise encounter. As is often the case with many older zoos, the animals aren't given much room. ✉ *Cerro San Cristóbal, Bellavista* 📞 *2/2730–1368* ⊕ *www.zoologico.cl* 🎧 *3,000 pesos* ⊙ *June–Sept., Tues.–Sun. 10–5; Oct.–May, Tues.–Sun. 10–6 (ticket booth closes at 5 Tues.–Sun.* Ⓜ *Baquedano.*

FAMILY **Plaza Tupahue.** The main attraction in summer of this area inside Parque Metropolitano is the delightful Piscina Tupahue, an 82-meter (269-foot) pool with a rocky crag running along one side. Beside the pool is the 1925 Torreón Victoria, a stone tower surrounded by a trellis of bougainvillea. If Piscina Tupahue is too crowded, try the nearby Piscina Antilén. From Plaza Tupahue you can follow a path below to Plaza de Juegos Infantiles Gabriela Mistral, a popular playground. ✉ *Cerro San Cristóbal, Bellavista* 📞 *2/2730–1300* 🎧 *Piscina Tupahue 6,000 pesos; piscina Antilén 7,500 pesos* ⊙ *Piscina Tupahue and Antilén, Nov.–Mar., Tues–Sun. 10–7* ⊙ *Pool closed Mon.* Ⓜ *Pedro de Valdivia.*

PARQUE QUINTA NORMAL AREA

Just west of downtown is shady Parque Quinta Normal, a 75-acre park with three museums within its borders, another just across the street, and two more down the block. This is an especially good place to take kids. The park was created in 1841 as a place to experiment with new agricultural techniques. On weekdays it's great for quiet strolls; on weekends you have to maneuver around noisy families. Pack a picnic or a soccer ball and fit right in.

Near the park is the Museo de la Memoria, a museum in memory of the dictatorship, and the modern Biblioteca de Santiago. Closer to the Alameda is the arts and performing center Matucana 100 and the Quinta Normal branch of the Museo de Arte Contemporáneo, both of which have cafés outside.

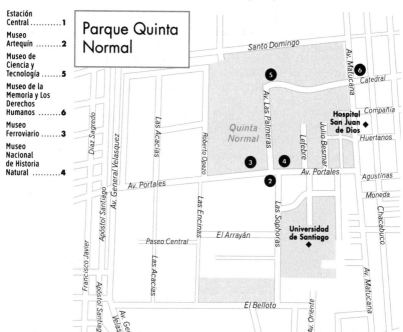

TIMING AND PRECAUTIONS

You can visit the museums in and around the park, stroll along a wooded path, take a pedal boat in the lagoon, rent a pedal car, or take the motorized pretend train around the park all within a couple of hours. Be sure to check out the dilapidated greenhouse mid-park for photo ops, though one day soon, this may be turned into a café.

TOP ATTRACTIONS

Estación Central. Inaugurated in 1897, Central Station is the city's last remaining train station, serving the south as far as Chillán. The greenish iron canopy of the station that once shielded the engines from the weather is flanked by two lovely beaux arts edifices. A lively market keeps this terminal buzzing with activity. The grand entrance has a colorful, illuminated carousel and a couple of cafés. As in any busy place, keep a close watch on valuables. ⊠ *Alameda 3170, Estación Central* ☎ *600/585–5000* 🎟 *Free* 🕙 *Daily 6 am–midnight* Ⓜ *Estación Central.*

OFF THE
BEATEN
PATH

Cementerio General. It may be an unusual tourist attraction, but this cemetery in the northern part of the city reveals a lot about traditional Chilean society. Through the lofty stone arches of the main entrance are well-tended paths lined with marble mausoleums and squat mansions belonging to Chile's wealthy families. The 8- or 10-story "niches"—concrete shelves housing thousands of coffins—resemble middle-class apartment buildings. Their inhabitants lie here until the rent runs out and they are evicted. Look for former President Salvador Allende's final resting spot; a map at the main entrance to the cemetery can help you find it. Ninety-minute Historic Heritage Tours in Spanish run Tuesday, Wednesday, and Thursday at 10 am and 3 pm. General tours are on Monday and Friday (by prior arrangement) and last 90 minutes. Three different 75-minute night tours are available at 8 pm for kids and adults. All tours require reservations and cost 2,500 pesos. ⊠ *Av. Prof. Alberto Zañartu 951, Recoleta* ☎ *2/2637-7800* ⊕ *www.cementeriogeneral.cl* ▢ *Free* ☉ *Daily 8:30–5:30* Ⓜ *Cementerios.*

FAMILY **Museo Artequín.** The resplendent Pabellón París houses this interactive museum that teaches the fundamentals of art to children, but the pavilion itself—with its glass domes, Pompeian-red walls, and blue-steel columns—is the real jewel. It was designed by French architect Pierre-Henri Picq to house Chile's exhibition in the 1889 Paris International Exposition (where Gustave Eiffel's skyline-defining tower was unveiled). After the show the structure was shipped back to Santiago. On weekdays, school groups explore the two floors of reproductions of famous artworks hung at kid-height. There are occasional interactive exhibits and workshops. ⊠ *Av. Portales 3530, Parque Quinta Normal* ☎ *2/2681-8656* ⊕ *www.artequin.cl* ▢ *800 pesos; free Sun.* ☉ *Tues.–Fri. 9–5, weekends 11–6, closed Feb.* Ⓜ *Quinta Normal.*

Fodor'sChoice **Museo de La Memoria y Los Derechos Humanos.** This museum is a pow-
★ erful testimony to the coup that established the Chilean dictatorship of Augusto Pinochet; the resulting detention, torture, and murder of Chilean citizens; and the country's historic vote to return to democracy. There is a heavy audio-visual component as well, with moving letters by children about the events of the times. There are some images and artifacts here that may be harder for children to process, but it's an important part of Chilean history and arguably the country's best museum. Admission is free, and it's just across the street from the Parque Quinta Normal. Audio guides in several languages are available for 2,000 pesos. ⊠ *Matucana 501, Parque Quinta Normal* ☎ *2/2597-9600* ⊕ *www.museodelamemoria.cl* ☉ *Winter, Tues.–Sun. 10–6; summer, Tues.–Sun. 10–8* Ⓜ *Quinta Normal.*

FAMILY **Museo Ferroviario.** Chile's once-mighty railroads have been relegated
Fodor'sChoice to history, but this acre of Parque Quinta Normal keeps a bit of the
★ romance alive. More than a dozen steam locomotives and three passenger coaches are set within quiet gardens with placards in Spanish and English. You can board several of the trains. Among the collection is one of the locomotives used on the old cross-Andes railway to Argentina, which operated between Chile and Argentina from 1910 until 1971. Guided tours are available. ⊠ *Av. Las Palmeras, Parque Quinta Normal* ☎ *2/2681-4627* ⊕ *www.corpdicyt.cl/mferroviario* ▢ *800 pesos* ☉ *Apr.–Nov., Tues.–Fri. 10–6, weekends 11–6; Dec.–Mar., Tues.–Fri. 10–6, weekends 11–7* Ⓜ *Quinta Normal.*

WORTH NOTING

FAMILY **Museo de Ciencia y Tecnología.** Children can spend a happy half-hour at this small science-and-technology museum's interactive exhibits, while adults can peruse its collection of old phonographs, calculators, and computers. A small part of the Museo Infantil's (Children's Museum) collection was also moved to this museum after the 2010 earthquake, and they have exhibits for ages three and up on astronomy and vision. ✉ *Parque Quinta Normal, Parque Quinta Normal* ☎ *2/2689–8026* ⊕ *www.mucytec.cl* ✉ *800 pesos* ⊗ *Mar.–Dec., Tues.–Fri. 10–5:45, weekends 11–5:15; Jan. and Feb., Tues.–Fri. 10–6:15, weekends 11–6:15* Ⓜ *Quinta Normal.*

FAMILY **Museo Nacional de Historia Natural.** The National Museum of Natural History is the centerpiece of Parque Quinta Normal. Paul Lathoud, a French architect, designed the building for Chile's first international exposition in 1875. After suffering damage from successive earthquakes, the neoclassical structure was rebuilt and enlarged. There are large dioramas of stuffed animals against painted backdrops, descriptions of wrongs committed against indigenous people, and occasionally, paleontologists working in glass-walled exhibits that you can watch. The skeleton of an enormous blue whale hangs in the central hall, delighting children of all ages. Exhibits are not labeled in English, but audio guides in English are available. ✉ *Parque Quinta Normal s/n* ☎ *2/2680–4603* ⊕ *www.mnhn.cl* ✉ *Tues.–Sat. 600 pesos, Sun. free* ⊗ *Tues.–Sat. 10–5:30, Sun. and holidays 11–5:30* Ⓜ *Quinta Normal.*

VITACURA

Vitacura is not only Santiago's top shopping spot, it is also—with its tree-shaded streets, gardens, and wide sidewalks—a great place for a stroll, especially on a Saturday morning when residents are out jogging, walking their dogs, or simply picking up a newspaper and some fresh *marraquetas,* Chile's roll-shape answer to French bread. Parque Bicentenario is a great place for a run, or taking kids to feed the fish, geese, and other birds that live in the pond there (animal feed is sold on-site).

TOP ATTRACTIONS

FAMILY **Museo de la Moda.** The Fashion Museum, opened in 2007 by a son of Jorge Yarur Banna, one of Chile's most successful textile barons, hosts small but choice exhibitions around different themes using clothes—mostly women's dresses—that date to the 1600s. Housed in the Yarur family's former home, designed by Chilean architects in the style of Frank Lloyd Wright in the early 1960s and decorated by a brother of Roberto Matta, one of Chile's most famous painters, the museum also offers a fascinating insight into the lifestyle of the Chilean oligarchy in the run-up to the upheaval of Salvador Allende's socialist government and the ensuing military coup. The main rooms are on show with their original furnishings, and the pink 1958 Ford Thunderbird driven by Mr. Yarur's wife is parked in a courtyard. It's best to call before visiting as the museum closes for as much as two months between exhibitions. The museum café, which is always open, serves light meals and snacks at reasonable prices. ✉ *Av. Vitacura 4562, Vitacura* ☎ *2/2219–3623*

⊕ *www.museodelamoda.cl* ✉ *3,000 pesos* ⊗ *Tues.–Sun. 10–6* Ⓜ *No metro.*

WHERE TO EAT

Menus cover the bases of international cuisines, but don't miss the local bounty—seafood delivered directly from the Pacific Ocean. One of the local favorites is *caldillo de congrio,* the hearty fish stew celebrated by poet Pablo Neruda in his "Oda al Caldillo de Congrio." (The lines of the poem are, in fact, the recipe.) A pisco sour—a cocktail of grape brandy and lemon juice—makes a good start to any meal, especially when accompanied by a plate of *machas a la parmesana,* small razor clams served au gratin, baked in lemon juice, or with white wine, butter, and grated cheese.

Tempted to try heartier Chilean fare? Pull up a stool at one of the counters at Vega Central and enjoy a traditional *pastel de choclo* (pie filled with ground beef, chicken, olives, and a boiled egg, topped with mashed corn). Craving seafood? Head to the Mercado Central, where fresh fish is brought in each morning. Want a memorable meal? Trendy new restaurants are opening every day in neighborhoods like Bellavista, where hip Santiaguinos come to check out the latest hot spots.

In the neighborhood of Vitacura, a 20- to 30-minute taxi ride from the city center, a complex of restaurants called Borde Río attracts an upscale crowd, but other reservations-only restaurants worth a look are on Alonso de Córdoba and Nueva Costanera. El Golf, an area including Avenida El Bosque Norte and Avenida Isidora Goyenechea in Las Condes, has numerous restaurants and cafés. The emphasis is on creative cuisine, so familiar favorites are given a Chilean twist. This is one of the few neighborhoods where you can stroll from restaurant to restaurant until you find exactly what you want.

Santiaguinos dine a little later than you might expect. Most fancy restaurants don't open for lunch until 1. (You may startle the cleaning staff if you rattle the doors at noon.) Dinner begins at 7:30 or 8, although most places don't get crowded until after 9. Many eateries close for a few hours before dinner and on Sunday night. People do dress smartly for dinner, but a coat and tie are rarely necessary. Avoid shorts, sneakers, and athletic gear, and you should be fine in most places.

WHAT IT COSTS IN CHILEAN PESOS (IN THOUSANDS)				
	$	$$	$$$	$$$$
AT DINNER	Under 6	6–9	10–13	over 13

Restaurant prices are the average cost of a main course at dinner or, if dinner is not served, at lunch.

SANTIAGO CENTRO

$$ CHILEAN 🍴 **Blue Jar.** This restaurant, a block from the Palacio de la Moneda, is an oasis of quiet on a small pedestrian street. The food—simple but creative dishes using the best and freshest Chilean ingredients—appeals to locals and visitors alike, whether it's a sandwich, a soup-salad combo, or a hearty ham and egg breakfast. The menu changes seasonally, with dishes like chicken cashew curry and venison with caponata sharing menu space with grilled bass and passionfruit mousse. The restaurant has a good wine list and does upper-crust business lunches. Reservations are advisable for lunch, particularly for an outside table. They serve a full dinner the first Thursday of every month but otherwise there's an abbreviated menu in the evenings, with service stopping at 9 pm (kitchen closes at 8:30). So arrive early for evening drinks, sandwiches, and snacks. [$] *Average main: 9900 pesos* ✉ *Almirante L. Gotuzzo 102 at Moneda* ☎ *2/2696–1890* 🌐 *www.bluejar.cl* 🕒 *Closed weekends* [M] *Moneda.*

$$$$ CHILEAN 🍴 **Bristol.** This restaurant inside the Hotel Plaza San Francisco serves inventive dishes like marinated scallops over octopus carpaccio and cold tomato-and-pepper sauce. The restaurant has won several awards and often makes it onto top lists in local media. It's not as bright as it could be and doesn't have much of a view, but what you've got on your plate should make up for it. [$] *Average main: 15000 pesos* ✉ *Hotel Plaza San Francisco, Alameda 816* ☎ *2/2639–3832* 🌐 *www.plazasanfrancisco.cl* [M] *Universidad de Chile.*

$$$ CHILEAN 🍴 **Confitería Torres.** José Domingo Torres, a chef greatly in demand amongst the Chilean aristocracy of his day, decided in 1879 to set up shop in this storefront on the Alameda. It remains one of the city's most traditional dining rooms, with red-leather banquettes, mint-green tile floors, and huge chandeliers with tulip-shape globes. The food, such as *lomo al ajo arriego* (sirloin sautéed with peppers and garlic), now comes from recipes by the mother of owner Claudio Soto Barría. This restaurant also has a branch for snacks and light meals in the Centro Cultural Palacio La Moneda, and another location on upscale Isidora Goyenechea in El Golf (Las Condes). [$] *Average main: 9400 pesos* ✉ *Alameda 1570* ☎ *2/2688–0751* 🌐 *www.confiteriatorres.cl* 🕒 *Closed Sun.* [M] *Moneda.*

$ CHILEAN 🍴 **Dominó.** This 50-year-old fast-food chain is a Chilean institution and now has a score of restaurants around the city. This is the place to try an *Italiano* (a hotdog with tomatoes and avocado) or another Chilean favorite, *chacarero* (hotdog or beef sandwich with green beans, tomato, and chili pepper). *Jugo de melon tuna* (honeydew juice) is a traditional favorite as well. The restaurants have no-frills decoration but are impeccably clean, and the service is fast and friendly. The chain also does delivery, though credit cards aren't accepted for delivery orders. [$] *Average main: 4000 pesos* ✉ *Ahumada 146* ☎ *2/2411–0600* 🌐 *www.domino.cl* 🕒 *Closed Sun.*

$$ FRENCH 🍴 **Les Assassins.** Although at first glance this appears to be a rather somber bistro, nothing could be further from the truth. The service is friendly and the Provence-influenced food first-rate. The steak au poivre and beef Bourguignon would make a Frenchman's mouth

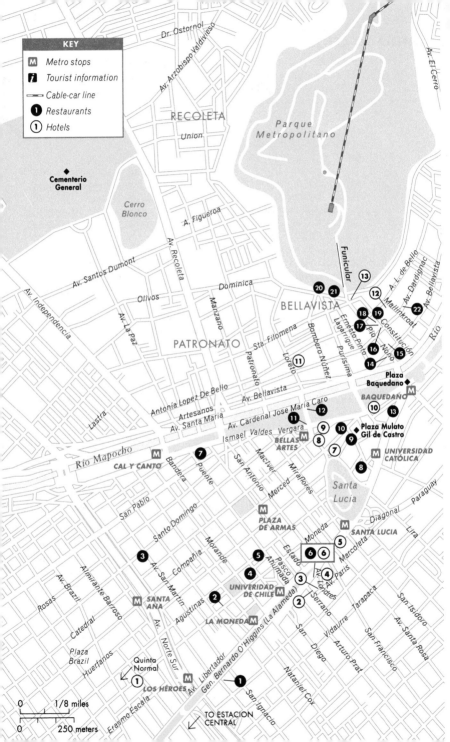

KEY

M	Metro stops
i	Tourist information
▭▭	Cable-car line
1	Restaurants
①	Hotels

Dr. Ostornol

Av. Arzobispo Valdivieso

RECOLETA

Union

Av. El Cerro

Parque Metropolitano

◆ **Cementerio General**

Cerro Blanco

A. Figueroa

Av. Recoleta

Av. Santos Dumont

Av. Independencia

Av. La Paz

Olivos

Dominica

PATRONATO

Manzano

Sta. Filomena

Patronato

Loreto

Bombero Núñez

Purísima

Ernesto Pinto Lagarrigue

Pio Nono

Constitución

Mallinkroat

A. L. de Bello

Av. Dardignac

Av. Bellavista

Rio

Funicular

BELLAVISTA

20 **21** **13**
12
18 **19** **22**
17
16 **15**
14

11

Plaza Baquedano ◆

M

BAQUEDANO

Antonia Lopez De Bello

Artesanos

Av. Santa Maria

Av. Bellavista

Av. Cardenal Jose Maria Caro

12

Ismael Valdes

Vergara

11

9 **10**

8

7

13

Plaza Mulato Gil de Castro ◆

Lastra

Rio Mapocho

M

CAL Y CANTO

Bandera

puente

San Antonio

Maciver

Merced

Miraflores

BELLAS ARTES

M

9

8

7

8

M

UNIVERSIDAD CATÓLICA

7

San Pablo

Santo Domingo

San Martin

Compañia

Morande

Santa Lucia

Paraguay

Diagonal

Lira

San Diego

San Isidoro

San Francisco

Av. Santa Rosa

Arturo Prat

Vidaurre

Tarapaca

Almirante Barroso

Av. Brazil

Rosas

Catedral

Plaza Brazil

Huerfanos

San Pablo

M

SANTA ANA

Agustinas

2

UNIVERIDAD DE CHILE

M

4

Paseo Ahumada

Estado

5

Moneda

3

Av. Paris

6 **6**

5

4

3

2

M

PLAZA DE ARMAS

M

Marcoleta

M

SANTA LUCIA

3

Av. Londres

Serrano

San

LA MONEDA

M

Av. Libertador Gen. Bernardo O'Higgins (La Alameda)

Norte Sur

Nataniel Cox

San Ignacio

Quinta Normal

①

Erasmo Escala

M

LOS HÉROES

1

↓ **TO ESTACIÓN CENTRAL**

0	1/8 miles
0	250 meters

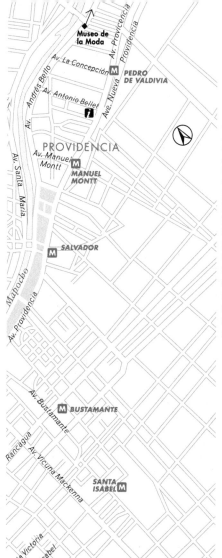

Where to Eat and Stay
in Santiago Centro
and Bellavista

water. $ *Average main: 9000 pesos* ✉ *Merced 279B, Parque Forestal* ☎ *2/2638–4280* ⊕ *www.lesassassins.cl* ⌕ *Reservations essential* ⊗ *Closed Sun. No lunch Sat.* Ⓜ *Universidad Católica.*

$$$ ✕ **Majestic.** Oddly located in the downtown Best Western Hotel, this
INDIAN was Santiago's first Indian restaurant and some consider it the best. Whether you order a simple lentil dal or one of the more sophisticated curries, you're in for a good meal. As with all Indian restaurants in Chile, rice and naan cost extra. The main drawback is that unless you're downtown, it's a bit out of way, but there's a second branch in the Alto Las Condes shopping mall on Avenida Kennedy. The downtown restaurant is heavy on tapestries and shiny adornments. $ *Average main: 12500 pesos* ✉ *Santo Domingo 1526* ☎ *2/2695–8366* ⊕ *www.majestic.cl* ⌕ *Reservations essential* Ⓜ *Santa Ana.*

$$ ✕ **Mercado Central.** There are more than a dozen places to eat here. Try
SEAFOOD La Joya del Pacífico or one of the tiny restaurants with names like Marisol or Francisca around the inner edge of the market. Many are little more than a kitchen with a few tables, but these are where locals and the market workers eat. The tables may be rickety, but the fish couldn't be fresher and cheaper or the service friendlier. Credit cards are accepted at larger restaurants like Donde Augusto and La Joya del Pacífico, but not by smaller establishments like Marisol and Francisca. The mercado and its restaurants close at 5 pm. $ *Average main: 6000 pesos* ✉ *San Pablo 967* ⊕ *www.mercadocentral.cl* ⊗ *No dinner* Ⓜ *Cal y Canto.*

$$ ✕ **Salvador Cocina y Café.** On a tiny pedestrian-only street in the middle
CHILEAN of downtown, this hidden two-story lunch option is one you don't want
Fodor'sChoice to miss. On weekdays, there's a variety of set menus, which include
★ an appetizer, main dish, iced tea, and choice of coffee and dessert. All dishes adopt modern spins on Chilean and international favorites. You might have a grain salad with *mote* (hulled wheat kernels), beef carpaccio, kidneys in cream sauce, or spinach-filled pasta. There are vegetarian choices, too, but the meat dishes are often more adventurous. $ *Average main: 6000 pesos* ✉ *Bombero Ossa 1069* ☎ *2/2673–0619* ⊗ *Closed weekends. No dinner* Ⓜ *Universidad de Chile.*

LASTARRIA AND BELLAS ARTES

$$$ ✕ **Bocanariz.** Getting a prime table at trendy Bocanariz in Lastarria at
CHILEAN the last minute Thursday through Saturday night is not just difficult,
Fodor'sChoice it's impossible. That's how popular this wine bar with accompanying
★ menu is. The waiters are all someliers and have about 300 kinds of wine on hand for any given evening, many of which can be drunk by the glass or small pour. The menu is set up for pairing, separating out food types by notes such as smoky, spiced, citrus, light, creamy, herbed, and sweet. There are also themed flights of wine, including one called *huaso* for the Chilean cowboy. The interior design is tasteful, on the romantic side, and the restaurant attracts mostly young professionals and international tourists. $ *Average main: 12000 pesos* ✉ *José Victorino Lastarria 276, Bellas Artes* ☎ *2/2638–9893* ⊕ *www.bocanariz.cl* ⌕ *Reservations essential* ⊗ *No lunch Sun.*

$$ ✕ **Café Sur Patagonico.** Owned by an Argentine couple, this little res-
CHILEAN taurant, with its black-and-white floor and bottle-lined wood-paneled

walls, serves loads of atmosphere along with its impressive homemade pasta, meats, and seafood. If you're not sure what to order, share a *tabla*, a charcuterie board, which might also have seafood or mushrooms. ■ TIP→ **This is a good place to try lamb or venison.** [$] *Average main: 8000 pesos* ✉ *José Victorino Lastarria 92, Lastarria* ☎ *2/2664–5341.*

$$$$ FRENCH 🍴 **Castillo Forestal.** French food made with Chilean ingredients is what's for dinner (or lunch) at this converted castle with a turret room, a gorgeous outdoor balcony, and antique toy museum in the basement. Castillo Forestal attracts a well-heeled clientele, many of whom are here for special occasions. It has 60 tables, but don't let that make you think you don't need a reservation. There is a set brasserie lunch with onion soup and black angus fillet, or if you want something lighter (or less expensive), try a turkey club or Mediterranean sandwich on focaccia with fresh Chilean mozzarella. [$] *Average main: 18500 pesos* ✉ *Cardenal José María Caro 390, across from Bellas Artes museum, Parque Forestal* ☎ *2/2664–1544* 🌐 *www.castilloforestal.cl* 🕒 *Closed Mon.*

$ SPANISH Fodor's Choice ★ 🍴 **Colmado Coffee & Bakery.** This café is a welcome part of the trend in Santiago toward serving excellent coffee. It's a comfy, rustic two-story nook tucked into a courtyard, with gourmet bites including Spanish sausage and cheeses, regular and gluten-free sweets, and one of the city's best vegan sandwiches. Coffee is made by Chemex and siphon, and several kinds of tea are available. [$] *Average main: 5000 pesos* ✉ *Merced 346, Location E2-Interior Patio, Bellas Artes* [M] *Bellas Artes.*

BELLAVISTA

$$$ SEAFOOD Fodor's Choice ★ 🍴 **Azul Profundo.** When it opened, this was the only restaurant on this street near Cerro San Cristóbal. Today it's one of dozens in trendy Bellavista, but its two-level dining room—with walls painted bright shades of blue and yellow, and racks of wine stretching to the ceiling—ensure that it stands out in the crowd. Choose your fish from the extensive menu—swordfish, sea bass, shark, salmon, and tuna are among the choices—and enjoy it *a la plancha* (grilled) or *a la lata* (served on a sizzling plate with tomatoes and onions). [$] *Average main: 10000 pesos* ✉ *Constitución 111* ☎ *2/2738–0288* ✍ *Reservations essential* [M] *Baquedano.*

$$$ PERUVIAN 🍴 **Bandarián.** In the past several years, Peruvian restaurants have proliferated in Santiago. This restaurant is a bit expensive but does not compromise on quality. Bandarián was originally founded by one of the chefs to the Peruvian embassy and serves traditional favorites, like *ají de gallina*, a mild creamy chicken stew, among other meat, fish, shellfish, and pasta dishes. The restaurant has a cozy layout with bright red walls and wood accents. If only passing by, you still might catch the savory smell of delicious food. [$] *Average main: 10000 pesos* ✉ *Constitución 38, Locale 52* ☎ *2/2737–0725* 🌐 *www.barandiaran.cl.*

$$$ CHILEAN Fodor's Choice ★ 🍴 **Como Agua Para Chocolate.** Inspired by Laura Esquivel's romantic 1989 novel *Like Water for Chocolate*, this Bellavista standout started out focusing on the aphrodisiacal qualities of food but has since shifted to more standard Chilean dishes. It is, however, still one of the most popular eateries in Bellavista, though it's more traditional than experimental. Reserve the "bed table" if you want to be showy (it has a headboard

but is not actually a bed). $ *Average main: 10000 pesos* ✉ *Constitución 88* ☎ *2/2777-8740* ⊕ *www.comoaguaparachocolate.cl* ⚑ *Reservations essential* Ⓜ *Baquedano.*

$$$ ✕ **El Mesón Nerudiano.** To evoke another time and place, El Mesón Neru-
CHILEAN diano relies on traditional recipes, poetry, music, and live theater, all in homage to one of Chile's great poets, Pablo Neruda. The old house where the restaurant is located is decorated inside with bric-a-brac and has an entire wall lined with wine bottles. It is just a stone's throw from La Chascona, Neruda's house-turned-museum, which means it attracts lots of tourists. The menu at the restaurant has some Chilean favorites, like *caldillo de congrio,* a fish soup cooked from the recipe given in one of Neruda's poems, and other Chilean dishes, including a few with *róbalo* (European sea bass). There is also meat, gnocchi, and one vegetarian dish. $ *Average main: 12000 pesos* ✉ *Dominica 35* ☎ *2/2737-1542* ⊕ *www.elmesonnerudiano.cl.*

$$ ✕ **Fuente Alemana.** Close to the Pío Nono bridge into Bellavista, this is
CHILEAN the place to eat one of the vast, overflowing sandwiches (called sand-wiches, as in English) that Chileans consider unique to their country. Try a *lomito completo* with thin tender slices of pork with sauerkraut, mayonnaise, and tomato sauce, or a *chacarero,* with slices of beef with tomatoes, green beans, and chili pepper—get it "*sin ají*" if you don't like spicy food. $ *Average main: 6000 pesos* ✉ *Av. Libertador Bernardo O'Higgins (Alameda) 58, Santiago Centro* ☎ *2/2639-3231* ⊗ *Closed Sun.* Ⓜ *Baquedano.*

$ ✕ **Galindo.** Join artists and the young crowd of Bellavista for traditional
CHILEAN Chilean food in an old adobe house. This restaurant goes back 60 years, when it started life as a canteen for local workmen. Although sometimes crowded, it's a great place to try pastel de choclo or a hearty *cazuela,* a typical meat and vegetable soup that is a meal in itself. The fish is fresh and sandwiches hearty as well. $ *Average main: 5000 pesos* ✉ *Dardig-nac 098* ☎ *2/2777-0116* ⊕ *www.galindo.cl* Ⓜ *Baquedano.*

$$$ ✕ **La Bodeguilla.** This authentic Spanish restaurant is a great place to stop
SPANISH for a glass of sangría after visiting Cerro San Cristóbal. After all, it's right at the foot of the funicular. The dozen or so tables are set among wine barrels and between hanging strings of garlic bulbs. Nibble on tasty tapas like *chorizo riojano* (a piquant sausage), *pulpo a la gallega* (octopus with peppers and potatoes), and *queso manchego* (a mild white cheese) while perusing the long wine list. Then consider order-ing the house specialty—*cabrito al horno* (oven-roasted goat). $ *Av-erage main: 10000 pesos* ✉ *Av. Dominica 5* ☎ *2/2732-5215* ⊕ *www. labodeguilla.cl* ⚑ *Reservations essential* ⊗ *Closed Sun.* Ⓜ *Baquedano.*

$$$ ✕ **Patio Bellavista.** This multilevel complex of bars, eateries, cafés, and
ECLECTIC souvenir shops, which stretches from Pío Nono to Constitución, and between Calle Bellavista and Dardignac, has become a centerpoint of Bellavista, somewhat defying its more bohemian reputation. Still, it fills day and night with Chileans and foreigners alike, by offering a little bit of everything, including tourist offices, the occasional free concert or *cueca* (national dance) performance in the central plaza, a live music space, a theater, galleries, and an Irish pub, French bistro, and Peru-vian and Middle-Eastern restaurants. There's even a Starbucks and a

McDonald's. The patio is open daily from 8 am until the wee hours of the morning, though on Sunday they call it an early night and close by 2 am. Shops are open 10–9. Underground parking is at Bellavista 052. $ *Average main: 12000 pesos* ✉ *Pío Nono 73* ☎ *2/2249–8700* 🌐 *www.patiobellavista.cl* [M] *Baquedano.*

$$ CHILEAN 🍴 **Peumayén.** This restaurant follows a pre-Hispanic theme, with traditional touches from all the regions of Chile. Every meal starts with a colorful and varied "bread basket," a slate plate with examples from the north to the south of Chile. Entrées include llama and horse meat, lamb, fish, and the much celebrated potato. The restaurant interior is part romantic, part rustic, and there's an agreeable plant-filled courtyard for outside dining in warmer months. $ *Average main: 8000 pesos* ✉ *Constitución 136, Providencia* ☎ *2/2247–3060* 🌐 *www.peumayenchile.cl* 🕒 *No lunch Tues.–Sat. No dinner Sun.* [M] *Baquedano.*

$$ AMERICAN FAMILY 🍴 **Uncle Fletch.** All-beef burgers, onion rings, and three kinds of veggie burgers all share space at this American-style restaurant in Bellavista owned by a French expatriate. These are some of the best burgers in the city, with patties made from meat, mushroom, chickpea, quinoa, or shrimp. $ *Average main: 6000 pesos* ✉ *Dardignac 0192* ☎ *2/2777–6477* [M] *Baquedano.*

LAS CONDES

$$$ THAI 🍴 **Anakena.** With tables overlooking the hotel's lovely garden, this elegant eatery emphasizes fresh ingredients. You can order Thai favorites like pad thai (rice noodles, peanuts, egg, sprouts, and shrimp) and one of many different curries. A wide selection of spring rolls with interesting combinations of seafood and vegetables starts the meal. If it's on the menu, don't pass up the grilled swordfish. This is part of the Grand Hyatt hotel but has a separate entrance, so you don't have to go through the hotel lobby. $ *Average main: 11500 pesos* ✉ *Grand Hyatt Santiago, Av. Kennedy 4601* ☎ *2/2950–3179* 🌐 *www.anakenathaimarket.cl* [M] *No metro.*

$$ CAFÉ 🍴 **Café Melba.** Breakfast is served all day at this storefront restaurant—something that's almost unheard of in Chile. If you're particularly hungry, order the Works—baked beans, mushrooms, sausage, and bacon. Drink it down with a caffè latte, served in a large white bowl. For lunch, there's a selection of hot dishes, quiches, salads, and sandwiches. The interior is open and airy, with wooden tables scattered about the wood-floored dining room. In warm weather, grab a seat on the covered patio in front. It closes around 7 pm on weekdays and 3:30 on weekends. $ *Average main: 7000 pesos* ✉ *Don Carlos 2898, off Av. El Bosque Norte* ☎ *2/2232–4546* 🕒 *No dinner* [M] *Tobalaba.*

$$$ CAFÉ 🍴 **Coquinaria.** Whether you want a full English breakfast, lunch on a shady terrace, or a good cup of tea to linger over, this restaurant down the steps to one side of the W Hotel doesn't disappoint. Options include soups and sandwiches, as well as entrées. The bonus is that it's also a gourmet food shop, packed with temptations such as fresh pasta and cheeses not easily found elsewhere in Santiago. The restaurant has another location on Alonso de Córdova. It's also one of the few restaurants in Santiago that does a complete brunch, which costs about

10,000 pesos. [$] *Average main: 12000 pesos* ✉ *Isidora Goyenechea 3000* ☎ *2/2245–1958* 🌐 *www.coquinaria.cl* [M] *El Golf.*

$$$ JAPANESE 🍴 **Matsuri.** With a sleek design that calls to mind Los Angeles as much as Tokyo, this Japanese restaurant in the Grand Hyatt is one of Santiago's most stylish eateries. After passing through a foyer painted vivid red, you enter the calm dining area with a view of a waterfall. Downstairs are a sushi bar and two tatami rooms (no shoes allowed, but slippers are provided) with sliding screens for privacy, and upstairs are two grill tables. Reservations are a must on weekends. [$] *Average main: 12000 pesos* ✉ *Grand Hyatt Santiago, Av. Kennedy 4601* ☎ *2/2950–3051* 🌐 *www.matsuri.cl* ✍ *Reservations essential* [M] *No metro.*

PROVIDENCIA

$$$$ SEAFOOD 🍴 **Aquí Está Coco.** This restaurant—by far the best place in Santiago to eat seafood—is run by the admittedly showy chef "Coco" Pacheco. The restaurant, which burned down in 2008 but was rebuilt soon thereafter, is intimate and kooky at the same time, with a variety of different themed dining rooms, including one which has diners eating at a boat-turned-table. Traditional specialties, like grilled *corvina* (sea bass) and the classic Chilean *machas a la parmesana* (razor clams au gratin) are very popular items. But that doesn't mean you should skip the urchins, octopus, king crab, or swordfish with *charquican* (a Chilean stew), either. You might want to go in a group, so you can try a bit of everything. [$] *Average main: 14000 pesos* ✉ *La Concepción 236* ☎ *2/2410–6200* 🌐 *www.aquiestacoco.cl* ✍ *Reservations essential* ⏲ *Closed Sun. Closed Feb.* [M] *Pedro de Valdivia.*

$$$$ CHILEAN 🍴 **Astrid y Gastón.** The Santiago branch of the restaurants owned by Lima-based chef Gastón Acurio introduced Peru's wonderful food to Chile, but according to many people, it is not as good as it used to be and a bit overpriced. That said, the *causas* (stacks of food on rounds of mashed potatoes) are great, as is anything with giant prawns. Winning combinations of flavors in Astrid's deserts, taken from all over South America, include (at times) sugared citrus rinds, carrot cake, and herb-flavored ice cream. The wine list also impresses. [$] *Average main: 15000 pesos* ✉ *Antonio Bellet 201* ☎ *2/2650–9125* 🌐 *www.astridygaston.cl* ✍ *Reservations essential* ⏲ *Closed Sun. No lunch Sat.* [M] *Pedro de Valdivia.*

$ ECLECTIC 🍴 **Café Clementina.** This tiny café-bakery is handily located between Providencia's Sculpture Garden and the Pedro de Valdivia entrance to Cerro San Cristóbal. They make sweet and salty treats, perfect for a quick coffee stop or a picnic. If you opt for a light lunch, you can dine on the grassy Padre Letelier plaza—you will get a tablecloth with your couscous salad, chicken with mustard vinaigrette, or quiche. Don't miss dessert—the brownies sell quickly. There is a small seating area inside and benches in the plaza as well. [$] *Average main: 4000 pesos* ✉ *Los Conquistadores 2242, cross street Padre Letelier* ☎ *2/2231–6832* 🌐 *www.cafeclementina.cl* ⏲ *Closed Feb. Closed Sun. No dinner Sat.*

$ VEGETARIAN 🍴 **Café del Patio.** This popular, lively vegetarian eatery does most of its business at night, when it turns into a lively rock café with a DJ. Lunches and dinners consist of pizza, pasta, salads, and sandwiches and

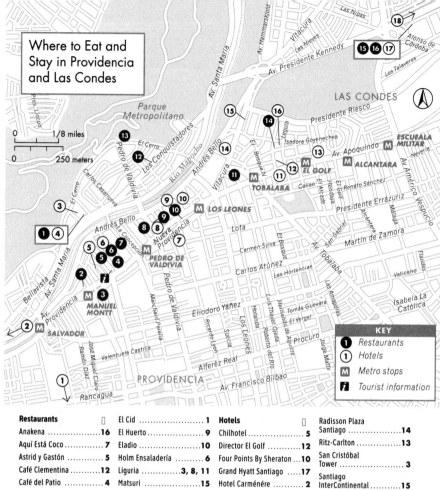

Where to Eat and Stay in Providencia and Las Condes

LAS CONDES

PROVIDENCIA

KEY

🔴 1	*Restaurants*
⚪ 1	*Hotels*
Ⓜ	*Metro stops*
🅸	*Tourist information*

Restaurants 🔴		
Anakena	....	**16**
Aquí Está Coco	....	**7**
Astrid y Gastón	....	**5**
Café Clementina	....	**12**
Café del Patio	....	**4**
Coquinaria	....	**14**
Divertimento Chileno	.....	**13**

El Cid	....	**1**
El Huerto	....	**9**
Eladio	....	**10**
Holm Ensaladería	....	**6**
Liguria	.............**3, 8, 11**
Matsuri	....	**15**
Normandie	....	**2**

Hotels ⚪		
Chilhotel	....	**5**
Director El Golf	....	**12**
Four Points By Sheraton	...**10**
Grand Hyatt Santiago	....**17**
Hotel Carménère	....	**2**
Hotel Orly	....	**8**
Italia Suite Bed & Breakfast	**1**
Le Rêve	....	**9**
Meridiano Sur Petit Hotel	.. **6**
Neruda Express	...........**11**

Radisson Plaza Santiago	...................**14**
Ritz-Carlton	...............**13**
San Cristóbal Tower	....	**3**
Santiago InterContinental	...........**15**
Santiago Marriott Hotel	.............**18**
Santiago Park Plaza	....	**7**
Sheraton Santiago	....	**4**
W Santiago	................**16**

a daily menu that includes a main dish, natural juice, and whole wheat or rye bread for 3,990 pesos. The menu is called call *"naturista,"* which means fish is served but not red meat or chicken. $ *Average main: 3900 pesos* ⊠ *Cirujano Guzmán 39* ☎ *2/2235–2865* ⊕ *www.cafedelpatio.cl* ⊘ *No lunch Sun.* Ⓜ *Manuel Montt.*

$$$
CHILEAN
FAMILY

✕ **Divertimento Chileno.** A favorite with Chilean politicians, journalists from the nearby television stations, and, on Sundays, local families, this restaurant serves both homemade pasta—the spinach and ricotta ravioli served with butter and sage is excellent—and traditional Chilean fare such as *pastel de choclo* (beef and corn casserole). Its main attraction, however, is its tranquil tree-shaded setting at the base of the San Cristóbal hill. This is a good place to go with children; they can play safely outside while the adults linger over their meal. The restaurant offers kids' meals for 6,000 pesos. $ *Average main: 10000 pesos* ⊠ *Av. El Cerro at Av. Pedro de Valdivia Norte* ☎ *2/2975–4600* ⊕ *www. divertimento.cl* ⋗ *Reservations essential* Ⓜ *Pedro de Valdivia.*

$$
CHILEAN

✕ **Eladio.** You can eat a succulent *bife de chorizo* (sirloin), mouthwatering *costillas de cerdo* (pork ribs), or just about any other meat cooked as you like—with a good bottle of Chilean wine—and your pockets wouldn't be much lighter. Finish with a slice of *amapola* (poppy-seed) sponge cake. This restaurant also has a branch in Bellavista at Pío Nono 251. Both get full and don't take bookings, so you may have to wait a little while for a table. $ *Average main: 7000 pesos* ⊠ *Providencia 2250* ☎ *2/2231–4224* ⊕ *www.eladio.cl* ⊘ *Closed Sun.* Ⓜ *Los Leones.*

$$$$
CHILEAN
Fodor's Choice
★

✕ **El Cid.** Considered by critics one of the city's top restaurants, El Cid is the culinary centerpiece of the Sheraton Santiago. The dining room, which overlooks the pool, has crisp linens and simple place settings. All the excitement here is provided by the food, which is served with a flourish. Don't miss the famous grilled seafood—king crab, prawns, squid, and scallops with a sweet, spicy sauce. If you're new to Chilean cuisine, you can't go wrong with the excellent lunch buffet, which includes unlimited wine. $ *Average main: 18000 pesos* ⊠ *Av. Santa María 1742* ☎ *2/2233–5000* ⊕ *www.restaurantelcid.com* Ⓜ *No metro.*

$$
VEGETARIAN

✕ **El Huerto.** One of Santiago's oldest vegetarian restaurants, this wood-paneled eatery in the heart of Providencia is no longer as innovative as it once was, but the hearty soups and fresh-squeezed juices still make it worth a visit. The vegan set lunch is good value, and every day there's a three course "menú" that consists of an appetizer, main course, and dessert for 7,400 pesos. $ *Average main: 6500 pesos* ⊠ *Orrego Luco 054* ☎ *2/2233–2690* ⊕ *www.elhuerto.cl* ⊘ *No dinner Sun.* Ⓜ *Pedro de Valdivia.*

$
EUROPEAN

✕ **Holm Ensaladería.** This salad and brunch place is the brainchild of Victor Holm, a Danish entrepreneur who wakes up before the crack of dawn every day to source the fresh ingredients for his salads. Youngish patrons choose from a selection of predressed salads, such as pasta salad with pesto, bean salad, and chicken or fish (optional)—all of which are served over a plate of mixed fresh greens. There is also a large selection of vegetable juices. For brunch—a steal at 7,500 pesos—there are three different options, with meat and vegetarian plates, including eggs, fresh bread, avocado, soup, dessert, and a broiled caramelized grapefruit half.

The restaurant fills up at lunch and in places it gets so narrow that you have to sidle through to get to the bathroom. The best seating is outside. $ *Average main: 4000 pesos* ⊠ *Padre Mariano 125* ☎ *7/7764–1149* ⊗ *No dinner weekends.*

$$
CHILEAN
Fodor's Choice
★

✕ **Liguria.** This extremely popular restaurant and bar is always packed, so you might have to wait to be seated in the chandelier-lighted dining room or at one of the tables that spill out onto the sidewalk. A large selection of Chilean wine accompanies such favorites as *cazuela* (a stew of beef or chicken and potatoes) and *mechada* sandwiches (tender and thinly sliced beef). The restaurant also serves several signature cocktails, including many that are pisco-based but not pisco sours. There are three branches of Liguria, but this one is the original. No reservations are accepted. $ *Average main: 8000 pesos* ⊠ *Av. Providencia 1373* ☎ *2/235–7914* ⊕ *www.liguria.cl* ⊗ *Closed Sun.* Ⓜ *Manuel Montt* $ *Average main: 8000 pesos* ⊠ *Pedro de Valdivia 047* ☎ *2/2334–4346* ⊗ *Closed Sun.* Ⓜ *Pedro de Valdivia* $ *Average main: 8000 pesos* ⊠ *Luis Thayer Ojeda 019* ☎ *2/2231–1393* ⊕ *www.liguria.cl* ⊗ *Closed Sun.* Ⓜ *Tobalaba.*

$$
FRENCH

✕ **Normandie.** This unassuming French restaurant is easy to miss, but it's a good place to linger when you do find it. Join the regulars for a steaming bowl of onion soup and beef Bourguignon with french fries (made from real potatoes) in winter, or a glass of wine at one of the pavement tables in summer. The service is as friendly as the food is good, and the wooden bar and slightly haphazard decor give it atmosphere. $ *Average main: 7000 pesos* ⊠ *Providencia 1234* ☎ *2/2236–3011* ⊕ *www. normandie1234.cl* ⚑ *Reservations essential* ⊗ *Closed Sun.* Ⓜ *Manuel Montt.*

VITACURA

$$$$
CHILEAN
Fodor's Choice
★

✕ **Boragó.** With food foraged from every corner of Chile and prepared in innovative ways, Rodolfo Guzmán's restaurant Boragó seemed destined to be a hit before it even opened. In its stark space in Vitacura, waiters serve tables one of two tasting menus of 7 or 12 courses with wine pairings. The innovative presentation also impresses, with food served on rocks and in egg-shape bowls. The chef's signature dish is a spin on the *curanto* clambake from Chiloé, which is made with rainwater from Patagonia and served in what looks like a small clearing in a tiny thicket. All the fussy preparation does come at a price, though. The smaller of the two tasting menus costs about 50,000 pesos. $ *Average main: 50000 pesos* ⊠ *Nueva Costanera 3467* ☎ *2/2953–8893* ⊕ *www. borago.cl* ⚑ *Reservations essential* ⊗ *No lunch.*

$$$$
SEAFOOD
Fodor's Choice
★

✕ **Europeo.** You're in for a fine meal at this trendy yet relaxed eatery on Santiago's most prestigious shopping avenue. The menu changes regularly but leans toward fish—try the succulent *mero*, a white fish, or the shellfish risotto topped with a foam of fish stock. This is also one of the few places in town that serves wild game, such as venison ragout. Small and quiet, the restaurant is frequented by the wealthiest Chileans but is not overly pretentious. Set lunch is the steal here, for about 15,000 pesos. Dinner can be à la carte, or a tasting menu with wine pairings, which runs a hefty (but most say worth it) 48,000 pesos.

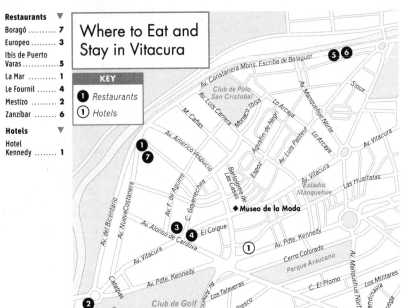

Where to Eat and Stay in Vitacura

KEY

❶ Restaurants
① Hotels

The simple decor and uncluttered tables are designed to give pride of place to the outstanding food, served by unobtrusive waiters. $ *Average main: 13500 pesos* ✉ *Av. Alonso de Córdova 2417* ☎ *2/2208–3603* ⊕ *www.europeo.cl* ⌨ *Reservations essential* ☉ *No lunch Sat. Closed Sun.* Ⓜ *No metro.*

$$$
SEAFOOD
✕ **Ibis de Puerto Varas.** Nattily nautical sails stretch taut across the ceiling, pierced here and there by mastlike wood columns, and the walls are a splashy blue at this stylish but casual seafood restaurant with a slightly innovative take on Patagonian food. Choose from appetizers such as ceviche or a plate of oysters and, for a main course, tuna grilled with dill and coriander or bell peppers stuffed with shrimps, cream, and cheese. This restaurant is in BordeRío, a free-standing restaurant enclave a short taxi ride from El Golf. $ *Average main: 11000 pesos* ✉ *Borde Río, Av. Monseñor Escrivá de Balaguer 6400* ☎ *2/2218–0111* ⊕ *www.ibisdepuertovaras.cl* ⌨ *Reservations essential* Ⓜ *No metro.*

$$$$
SEAFOOD
Fodor'sChoice
★
✕ **La Mar.** Opened by chef Gastón Acuria (also of Astrid y Gastón), this restaurant serves a wide range of Peruvian-style fish dishes, but its specialty is ceviche—it has seven different varieties that you can eat at a special bar as well as at the tables. The restaurant, which also has branches in other Latin American capitals and in San Francisco, California, may be right on a busy street, but you feel as if you were by the sea, an effect skillfully conjured by its airiness, turquoise chairs, and,

above all, the terrace's white canvas roof, mounted on poles and mimicking the sails of a boat. The pisco sours are among the best you'll find in Santiago. [$] *Average main: 20000 pesos* ✉ *Nueva Costanera 4076* ☎ *2/2206–7839* 🌐 *www.lamarcebicheria.cl* ✍ *Reservations essential* ⏲ *No dinner Sun.* [M] *No metro.*

$$ FRENCH FAMILY 🍴 **Le Fournil.** This restaurant serves hot meals, but it's primarily a bakery and a place for a light lunch or supper of quiche and salad or—even better—a unique version of pizza, known as *tartine,* with slices of the bakery's own bread as a base. There are several other branches of Le Fournil around Santiago, including at the Parque Arauco shopping mall and Patio Bellavista, as well as at the international arrivals area in the airport. Unusually for Chile, the restaurant has a children's meal. This branch is in Paseo El Mañío, a short pedestrian street lined with several restaurants, so if you get here and change your mind, you have options. [$] *Average main: 7000 pesos* ✉ *Av. Vitacura 3841* ☎ *2/2228–0219* 🌐 *www.lefournil.cl* [M] *No metro.*

$$$ CHILEAN 🍴 **Mestizo.** This restaurant, with a view over the Parque Bicentenario, is a bit out of the way but well worth the trip for a leisurely lunch or, on a summer evening, a perfect and generous-size pisco sour as the sun sets between the hills. The restaurant's design, with a roof supported on large boulders, makes the best of its setting, and the eclectic menu brings together some of the best of Chilean and Peruvian cuisine. With an emphasis on fish, the menu also offers some great meat dishes such as *plateada,* a slow-cooked cut of beef on a bed of mashed potatoes and basil. Reserve a table with their online reservation service, or call if you specifically want an outdoor table, but be warned that temperatures drop at night even in summer. [$] *Average main: 11000 pesos* ✉ *Av. Bicentenario 4050* ☎ *9/7477–6093* 🌐 *www.mestizorestaurant.cl* [M] *No metro.*

$$$ MIDDLE EASTERN 🍴 **Zanzíbar.** Although you can order hummus or lamb stew, this ostensibly Middle Eastern restaurant is more about conjuring up an exotic atmosphere than recreating the cuisine of the region. (The first clue is that Zanzibar isn't in the Middle East.) The food is tasty, but the real reason to come is to glide across the multicolor mosaic floors and settle into a chair placed beneath dozens of silver lanterns. Tables are just as fanciful, with designs made from pistachio nuts, red peppers, and beans. It's all a bit over the top but fun nonetheless. This restaurant is located in Borde Río, a collection of upscale restaurants a short metro ride from El Golf. [$] *Average main: 11000 pesos* ✉ *Borde Río, Av. Monseñor Escrivá de Balaguer 6400* ☎ *2/2218–0118* 🌐 *www.zanzibar.cl* ✍ *Reservations essential* ⏲ *No dinner Sun.* [M] *No metro.*

WHERE TO STAY

Santiago's accommodations range from luxurious *hoteles* to comfortable *residenciales,* which can be homey bed-and-breakfasts or simple hotel-style accommodations. All the construction in the past decade means competition between hotels is steep, but they still fill in the high summer season and when large trade fair or business conventions occur (March is a peak month). Outside these dates, you can often find a room for up to 20% less than the advertised rack rates, particularly if you stay for more than a couple of days. Call several hotels and ask for the best possible rate. It's a good idea to reserve in advance during the peak seasons (January, February, July, and August).

Some hotels, particularly more expensive ones, quote prices in U.S. dollars rather than pesos. Visitors from abroad are exempt from the 19% sales tax, provided they pay in foreign currency or with an overseas credit card. *Hotel reviews have been shortened. For full information, visit Fodors.com.*

WHAT IT COSTS IN CHILEAN PESOS (IN THOUSANDS)				
	$	$$	$$$	$$$$
FOR TWO PEOPLE	Under 51	51–85	86–115	over 115

Hotel prices are the lowest cost of a standard double room in high season.

SANTIAGO CENTRO

$$$$ HOTEL **The Aubrey.** Two 1920s mansions next to Cerro San Cristóbal were joined together in 2009 to form this hotel, giving it ample outdoor space, including a pool and an indoor-outdoor patio bar. **Pros:** well-lit; knowlegeable and friendly staff; 20% discount on rooms in winter. **Cons:** less expensive rooms lack hillside views and private terraces. [$] *Rooms from: 147000 pesos* ✉ *Constitución 317, Bellavista* ☎ *2/2940–2800* 🌐 *www.theaubrey.com* 🛏 *13 rooms, 2 suites* 🍴 *Breakfast.*

$$$$ HOTEL **El Castillo Rojo.** This boutique hotel in a red castle just off the beaten path in Bellavista is a step back in time, in all the right ways. **Pros:** great location in Bellavista; attention to detail; superior customer service. **Cons:** decoration feels fussy at times; main areas can be dark. [$] *Rooms from: 116000 pesos* ✉ *Constitución 195, Bellavista* ☎ *2/2352–4500* 🌐 *www.castillorojohotel.com* 🛏 *19 rooms* 🍴 *Breakfast.*

$ HOTEL **Foresta.** Staying in this seven-story hotel across the street from Cerro Santa Lucía is like visiting an elegant old home that has seen better days. **Pros:** great location near the quaint cafés and shops of Plaza Mulato Gil de Castro. **Cons:** rooms are small (though matrimonial rooms—with a sitting area and a double bed instead of two twins—are just a few thousand pesos extra). [$] *Rooms from: 41500 pesos* ✉ *Victoria Subercaseaux 353* ☎ *2/2639–6261* 🛏 *35 rooms* 🍴 *Breakfast* [M] *Bellas Artes.*

$ HOTEL **Happy House Hostel.** From the gorgeous Baroque facade with balconies to the original ceiling medallion from which the chandelier in the giant salon and living room hangs, it's clear that Happy House Hostel is something special. **Pros:** historical architecture; a beautiful plaza; close to nightlife and Barrio Yungay. **Cons:** a bit farther afield from some sights. [$] *Rooms from: 40000 pesos* ✉ *Moneda 1829, Barrio Brasil* ☎ *2/2688–4849* 🌐 *www.happyhousehostel.com* 🛏 *25 rooms* 🍴 *Breakfast* [M] *Los Héroes.*

$$$ HOTEL **Hotel Fundador.** On the edge of the quaint Barrio París-Londres, this hotel has rooms that, although small, are bright, airy, and attractive. **Pros:** tucked away from downtown traffic noise; on the doorstep of a

subway station; free Wi-Fi. **Cons:** not an area for a stroll at night; few restaurants or bars in the immediate vicinity. $ *Rooms from: 112700 pesos* ⊠ *Paseo Serrano 34* ☎ *2/2387–1200* ⊕ *www.fundador.cl* ⇆ *119 rooms, 28 suites* ⦿ *Breakfast* Ⓜ *Universidad de Chile.*

$ ⛉ **Hotel París 813.** In the heart of Barrio París-Londres, this mansion-
HOTEL turned-hotel has old-fashioned, clean rooms with the basic furnishings. **Pros:** excellent value for a modest price; friendly service; free Internet. **Cons:** breakfast room too small for hotel size; no elevator; no parking. $ *Rooms from: 22000 pesos* ⊠ *París 813, La Alameda* ☎ *2/664–0921* 🖷 *2/639–4037* ⊕ *www.hotelparis813.com* ⇆ *50 rooms* ⦿ *Breakfast* Ⓜ *Universidad de Chile, Santa Lucía.*

$$$ ⛉ **Hotel Plaza San Francisco.** Across from Iglesia San Francisco, this busi-
HOTEL ness hotel has everything traveling executives need. **Pros:** helpful Eng-
Fodor'sChoice lish-speaking staff; on-site restaurant offers interesting cuisine. **Cons:**
★ nightlife and other good restaurants are a metro or taxi ride away. $ *Rooms from: 104000 pesos* ⊠ *Alameda 816* ☎ *2/2639–3832* ⊕ *www. plazasanfrancisco.cl* ⇆ *137 rooms, 9 suites* ⦿ *Breakfast* Ⓜ *Universidad de Chile.*

$ ⛉ **Hotel Vegas.** This colonial-style building, adorned with a bullet-shape
HOTEL turret, sits in the heart of the charming Barrio París-Londres. **Pros:** good location for downtown sightseeing; free Wi-Fi. **Cons:** some rooms smell musty; cramped lobby, bar, and café; no elevator; no parking. $ *Rooms from: 30000 pesos* ⊠ *Londres 49* ☎ *2/2632–2514* ⊕ *www.hotelvegas. net* ⇆ *20 rooms* ⦿ *Breakfast* Ⓜ *Universidad de Chile.*

$$ ⛉ **Loreto Hotel.** This airy hotel just steps into the Recoleta neighborhood
HOTEL makes it close enough to Bellavista to walk, but not too near to hear any of the noise. **Pros:** great breakfast buffet; very helpful staff. **Cons:** you need to take a taxi at night. $ *Rooms from: 70000 pesos* ⊠ *Loreto 170, Bellavista* ☎ *2/2777–1060* ⊕ *www.loretohotel.cl* ⇆ *20 rooms, 4 suites* ⦿ *Breakfast.*

$$ ⛉ **Mercure Santiago Central.** It's hard to beat the location of this hotel,
HOTEL close to Cerro Santa Lucia. **Pros:** central location; within walking distance from many points of interest downtown. **Cons:** it's a bit impersonal. $ *Rooms from: 60000 pesos* ⊠ *Alameda 632, Santiago Centro* ☎ *2/2595–6622* ⊕ *www.mercure.com* ⇆ *140 rooms, 2 suites* ⦿ *Breakfast.*

LASTARRIA AND BELLAS ARTES

$$$ ⛉ **Hotel Ismael 312.** You couldn't pick a better place to put a design hotel
HOTEL in downtown Santiago, with expansive views over Parque Forestal and a rooftop pool from which to enjoy it. **Pros:** unbeatable location; high design elements. **Cons:** the rooms can feel a bit sterile; rooms overlooking the street (as opposed to the park) do not have much of a view. $ *Rooms from: 109000 pesos* ⊠ *Ismael Valdes Vergara 312, Parque Forestal* ☎ *2/2616–7600* ⊕ *www.hotelismael312.com* ⇆ *44 rooms, 1 suite* ⦿ *Breakfast.*

$$$$ ⛉ **The Singular.** This new luxury lodging in downtown Santiago is sure
HOTEL to be a hit with international travelers and locals alike. **Pros:** courtyard for leisurely breakfasts. **Cons:** exposed concrete of old buildings visible from rooftop deck. $ *Rooms from: 170,000 pesos* ⊠ *Merced 294,*

Bellas Artes ☎ 2/2306–8820 ⊕ *www.thesingular.com/santiago/lastarria* 🛏 *61 rooms, 1 suite* ⏐◉⏐ *Breakfast* Ⓜ *Bellas Artes.*

$$$
HOTEL
🖼 **Su Merced.** This small boutique hotel in a historic building has stunning views over Parque Forestal with sleek design and art inside. **Pros:** design-focused; family owned; attentive staff. **Cons:** less expensive rooms have a view of the street. Ⓢ *Rooms from: 112000 pesos* ✉ *Coronel Santiago Bueras 121, Parque Forestal* ☎ 2/2584–7230 ⊕ *www.sumercedhotel.com* 🛏 *8 rooms, 1 suite* ⏐◉⏐ *No meals.*

LAS CONDES

$$$$
HOTEL
🖼 **Director El Golf.** Aside from its location near the center of the El Golf entertainment district, this hotel has an important plus in that rooms—all spacious suites—have a kitchenette and small dining area. **Pros:** a good choice for longer-stay visitors who don't want to eat out every night. **Cons:** decoration is a bit dated. Ⓢ *Rooms from: 116000 pesos* ✉ *Carmencita 45* ☎ 2/498–3000 ⊕ *www.director.cl* 🛏 *49 suites* ⏐◉⏐ *Breakfast* Ⓜ *El Golf, Tobalaba.*

$$$$
HOTEL
Fodor'sChoice
★
🖼 **Grand Hyatt Santiago.** The soaring spire of the Grand Hyatt resembles a rocket (and you might feel like an astronaut when you're shooting up a glass elevator through a 24-story atrium). **Pros:** garden and swimming pool are particularly lovely; great views of Andes; three excellent restaurants. **Cons:** out of the way and, although one of city's main shopping malls is close, there isn't much else nearby; fee for Internet. Ⓢ *Rooms from: 175000 pesos* ✉ *Av. Kennedy 4601* ☎ 2/2950–1234 ⊕ *www.santiago.hyatt.com* 🛏 *287 rooms, 23 suites* ⏐◉⏐ *Breakfast* Ⓜ *No metro.*

$$$
HOTEL
🖼 **Neruda Express.** This "express" version of the larger Hotel Neruda (on Avenida Pedro de Valdivia) lacks the space and other frills, but rooms are tastefully modern and bright. **Pros:** convenient to fashionable Las Condes but priced lower; close to Costanera Center; free Wi-Fi. **Cons:** although all windows have double glass, rooms on Avenida Apoquindo still get traffic noise (those at the back are quieter). Ⓢ *Rooms from: 90000 pesos* ✉ *Vecinal 40 at Av. Apoquindo* ☎ 2/233–2747 ⊕ *www.hotelneruda.cl* 🛏 *50 rooms, 2 suites* ⏐◉⏐ *Breakfast* Ⓜ *El Golf, Tobalaba.*

$$$
HOTEL
🖼 **Radisson Plaza Santiago.** Santiago's World Trade Center is also home to the Radisson, a combination that makes sense to many corporate travelers. **Pros:** all the comfort and facilities of a top hotel (such as concierge service) at a more modest price; easy walking distance to the metro. **Cons:** the presence of the nearby Costanera Center and an increase in car ownership snarls traffic during peak commuting hours. Ⓢ *Rooms from: 105000 pesos* ✉ *Av. Vitacura 2610* ☎ 2/2433–9000 ⊕ *www.radisson.com/santiagocl* 🛏 *134 rooms, 25 suites* ⏐◉⏐ *Breakfast* Ⓜ *Tobalaba.*

$$$$
HOTEL
🖼 **Ritz-Carlton.** The rather bland brick exterior of this 15-story hotel, the first Ritz-Carlton in South America, belies the luxurious appointments within. **Pros:** prime location on Avenida Apoquindo; close to the main El Golf business and restaurant area. **Cons:** some find the elaborate decoration fussy and oppressive; Wi-Fi is free in the lobby, but there is a charge for in-room use. Ⓢ *Rooms from: 197000 pesos* ✉ *El Alcalde 15* ☎ 2/2470–8500 ⊕ *www.ritzcarlton.com* 🛏 *189 rooms, 16 suites* ⏐◉⏐ *Breakfast* Ⓜ *El Golf.*

2

$$$ HOTEL **Santiago InterContinental.** Attendants wearing top hats usher you into the two-story marble lobby of one of the city's top hotels. **Pros:** easy walking distance from the El Golf business and restaurant area; concierge; heated indoor pool. **Cons:** bad traffic congestion around the hotel; fee for Wi-Fi. [$] *Rooms from: 108000 pesos* ✉ *Av. Vitacura 2885* ☎ *2/2394–2000* 🌐 *www.intercontisantiago.com* 🛏 *281 rooms, 15 suites* 🍴 *Breakfast* [M] *Tobalaba.*

$$$$ HOTEL **Santiago Marriott Hotel.** The first 25 floors of this gleaming copper tower house the Marriott, which welcomes guests into its impressive two-story, cream marble lobby with full-grown palm trees in and around comfortable seating areas. **Pros:** excellent, friendly service; concierge. **Cons:** removed from the action in a suburban neighborhood; some rooms come with Internet, depending on customer affiliation, others pay a daily fee. [$] *Rooms from: 151000 pesos* ✉ *Av. Kennedy 5741* ☎ *2/2426–2000* 🌐 *www.santiagomarriott.com* 🛏 *220 rooms, 60 suites* 🍴 *Breakfast* [M] *No metro.*

$$$$ HOTEL **W Santiago.** Located in the heart of the fashionable El Golf business and restaurant district, South America's first W Hotel, opened in 2009, set a new standard of luxury in Santiago. **Pros:** excellent location; heated outdoor pool; great shops inside the hotel (clothing, jewelry, crafts). **Cons:** expensive; not everyone is comfortable with the bath and shower integrated into the bedroom; Internet is free in lobby and some common areas, but there's a charge for in-room usage. [$] *Rooms from: 175000 pesos* ✉ *Isidora Goyenechea 3000* ☎ *2/2770–0000* 🌐 *www.starwoodhotels.com/whotels* 🛏 *196 rooms* 🍴 *Breakfast* [M] *El Golf.*

PROVIDENCIA

$ HOTEL **Chilhotel.** Good midrange hotels are few and far between in Santiago, and this small hotel is one of the few. **Pros:** family-owned, excellent service closely supervised by owners; a 10-minute metro ride from downtown; free Wi-Fi. **Cons:** small rooms; no elevator. [$] *Rooms from: 45000 pesos* ✉ *Cirujano Guzmán 103* ☎ *2/2235–0713* 🌐 *www.chilhotel.cl* 🛏 *17 rooms, 3 apartments* 🍴 *Breakfast* [M] *Manuel Montt.*

$$$ HOTEL **Four Points by Sheraton.** The heart of Providencia's shopping district is just steps away from this hotel, a favorite with savvy business visitors to the city. **Pros:** excellent value for money. **Cons:** free Internet only in the lobby, hourly charge in rooms. [$] *Rooms from: 87000 pesos* ✉ *Av. Santa Magdalena 111* ☎ *2/750–0300* 🌐 *www.fourpoints.com* 🛏 *112 rooms, 16 suites* 🍴 *Breakfast* [M] *Los Leones.*

$$$ B&B/INN **Hotel Carménère.** In a serene house on a quiet street, this eco-friendly hotel (really a B&B) does what it can to minimize its impact. **Pros:** lots of care taken with decorations, plants, and food. **Cons:** on occasion the whole property is rented out, leaving no rooms for other guests. [$] *Rooms from: 108000 pesos* ✉ *María Luisa Santander 0292* ☎ *2/2204–6372* 🌐 *www.hotelcarmenere.com* 🛏 *5 rooms* 🍴 *Breakfast.*

$$ HOTEL Fodor's Choice ★ **Hotel Orly.** A treasure like this in such a convenient location in the middle of Providencia is a real find. **Pros:** attractively decorated; excellent maintenance; free Wi-Fi. **Cons:** difficult to get a room on short notice. [$] *Rooms from: 84000 pesos* ✉ *Av. Pedro de Valdivia 027*

☎ *2/2231–8947* 🌐 *www.orlyhotel.com* 🛏 *25 rooms, 3 suites* 🍴 *Breakfast* [M] *Pedro de Valdivia.*

$ B&B/INN 🏨 **Italia Suite Bed & Breakfast.** Stay in one of Santiago's most interesting design neighborhoods at this cozy B&B in Barrio Italia, a newly vibrant part of Providencia known for its design shops and antique stores. **Pros:** neighborhoody feeling; attentive hosts; free Wi-Fi. **Cons:** not on the main metro line in Providencia, though still metro-accessible. [$] *Rooms from: 36000 pesos* ✉ *Tegualda 1846* ☎ *2/2505–9530* 🌐 *www.italiasuite.com* 🛏 *8 rooms, 1 suite* 🍴 *Breakfast* [M] *Irrarazaval.*

$$$ HOTEL 🏨 **Le Rêve.** This classic French house from the 20th century has been turned into a fine boutique hotel in Santiago's Providencia neighborhood. **Pros:** self-serve snacks in the kitchen until 1 am. **Cons:** some noise from nearby restaurants. [$] *Rooms from: 109000 pesos* ✉ *Orrego Luco 023* 🌐 *www.lereve.cl* 🛏 *28 rooms, 3 suites* 🍴 *Breakfast* [M] *Los Leones or Pedro de Valdivia.*

$$ B&B/INN Fodor's Choice ★ 🏨 **Meridiano Sur Petit Hotel.** This small family-run hotel is a welcome addition to Santiago's limited range of mid-priced lodgings. **Pros:** five-minute walk from metro; restful atmosphere and friendly service; great collection of books about Chile to browse. **Cons:** rooms in basement have natural light but are very small, so it's worth the extra few thousand pesos per night for an upstairs room. [$] *Rooms from: 59400 pesos* ✉ *Santa Beatriz 256* ☎ *2/2235–3659* 🌐 *www.meridianosur.cl* 🛏 *8 rooms* 🍴 *Breakfast* [M] *Manuel Montt.*

$$$$ HOTEL 🏨 **San Cristóbal Tower and Sheraton Santiago.** Two distinct hotels stand side by side at this lovely property that for the most part functions as a single entity, as nearly all amenities are shared by guests of both hotels. **Pros:** impeccable service; concierge. **Cons:** on the north side of the Mapocho River, a taxi ride away from the nearest metro station and from business, restaurant, and shopping areas; Wi-Fi is free only in the lobby and there is a minimum three-hour charge in rooms. [$] *Rooms from: 210000 pesos* ✉ *Av. Santa María 1742* ☎ *2/233–5000* 🌐 *www.starwoodhotels.com* 🛏 *127 rooms, 12 suites* 🍴 *Breakfast* [M] *No metro.*

$$$ HOTEL 🏨 **Santiago Park Plaza.** Although this hotel bills itself as English in style, it's removed the formerly opressive dark furnishings, making the lobby and restaurant larger and airier. **Pros:** in the heart of Providencia with a metro station at the doorstep. **Cons:** breakfast not impressive. [$] *Rooms from: 88000 pesos* ✉ *Av. Ricardo Lyon 207* ☎ *2/2372–4029* 🌐 *www.parkplaza.cl* 🛏 *101 rooms, 3 suites* 🍴 *Breakfast* [M] *Los Leones.*

VITACURA

$$ HOTEL 🏨 **Hotel Kennedy.** This glass tower may seem impersonal, but small details show the staff cares about keeping guests happy. **Pros:** Aquarium restaurant, with its good international cuisine and a cellar full of excellent Chilean wines; free Wi-Fi. **Cons:** now 20 years old, the hotel is showing its age. [$] *Rooms from: 85000 pesos* ✉ *Av. Kennedy 4570* ☎ *2/2290–8100* 🌐 *www.hotelkennedychile.com* 🛏 *123 rooms, 10 suites* 🍴 *Breakfast* [M] *No metro.*

NIGHTLIFE AND PERFORMING ARTS

Although it can't rival Buenos Aires or Rio de Janeiro, Santiago buzzes with increasingly sophisticated bars and clubs. Santiaguinos often meet for drinks during the week, usually after work when most bars have happy hour. Then they call it a night, as most people don't really cut loose until Friday and Saturday, unless it's before a long weekend, when Thursday is dubbed "*viernes chico.*" Weekends commence with dinner beginning at 9 or 10 and then a drink at a pub. (This doesn't refer to an English beer hall; a pub here is a bar with loud music and a lot of seating.) No one thinks of heading to the dance clubs until 1 am, and they stay until 4 or 5 am.

NIGHTLIFE

Bars and clubs are scattered all over Santiago, but a handful of streets have such a concentration of establishments that they resemble block parties on Friday and Saturday nights. Pub crawls along Avenida Pío Nono and neighboring streets in Bellavista yield venues aimed at a young crowd (the drinking age is 18). Across the river and further west, Lastarria also has a lot of lively little bars. To the east in Providencia, the area around the Manuel Montt metro station and the Tobalaba station attract a slightly older and better-heeled crowd.

What you should wear depends on your destination. Bellavista has a mix of styles ranging from blue jeans to basic black and, in general, the dress gets smarter the farther east you move, but remains casual.

Note that establishments referred to as "nightclubs" are almost always female strip shows. The signs in the windows usually make it quite clear what goes on inside. The same is true for certain cafés with blacked-out windows, called "cafés con piernas" (literally: coffee with legs).

CENTRO

BARS AND CLUBS

El Rincón de las Canallas. A secret meeting place during the Pinochet regime, El Rincón de las Canallas still requires a password to get in (it's *Chile libre,* meaning "free Chile"). The walls are painted with political statements such as "Somos todos inocentes" ("We are all innocent"). It's a two-story affair, with loads of graffiti and business cards on the walls and ceiling. ⊠ *Tarapacá 810* ☎ *2/2632–5491* ⊕ *www.canallas.cl.*

CUECA CLUBS

El Huaso Enrique. This classic of Barrio Yungay predates the current immigration of hipsters and the revitalization of the neighborhood. For nearly 60 years, the kitchens have turned out Chilean specialties such as the heavy-hitting *chorrillana,* a plate of French fries covered in stewed onions and sausage, and topped with a fried egg. They also teach classes in the stompiest style of Chile's national dance, the *cueca brava.* Classes are Tuesday through Saturday at 7:30 pm and cost 3,000 pesos. Given the timing, it's best to dance first, then eat. ⊠ *Maipú 462* ☎ *2/681–5257* ⊕ *www.elhuasoenrique.cl* Ⓜ *Quinta Normal.*

Fodor'sChoice **La Chiminea.** Hidden on a side street downtown, you might be forgiven
★ to for thinking that La Chiminea was just a hole in the wall. Besides
towering plates of french fries and happy-hour specials, this place has
an undying love of all things Chilean, especially *cueca*, the national
dance. Come here with nothing but a competitive spirit and a hanky
(yes, a hanky), which is essential to the dance. Classes run Monday
and Thursday at 8 pm and cost 2,500 pesos. ☒ *Principe de Gales 90*
☎ *2/2697–0131* ⊕ *www.lachimenea.cl* Ⓜ *La Moneda.*

SALSA CLUBS
Klub Mangosta. Live music accompanies dancers at Klub Mangosta.
There are salsa and bachata classes every night from Wednesday to
Saturday from 9 to 11. Entry is 3,500 pesos for men and 2,500 pesos
for women. ☒ *Av. Vicuña Mackenna 1603* ☎ *2/2424–7228.*

LASTARRIA AND BELLAS ARTES
BARS AND CLUBS
El Diablito. Identifiable by the leering devil on the sign, El Diablito is one
of the only divey places left in Bellas Artes/Lastarria. It's filled with spurs
and stirrups and other metal items. If you want to see what this area
felt like about 10 years ago, before gentrification, this is a good spot to
try. It's popular for drinks after work or late at night. ☒ *Merced 336,
Parque Forestal* ☎ *2/2638–3512.*

PARQUE FORESTAL
BARS AND CLUBS
Fodor'sChoice **Catedrál.** At the base of Cerro Santa Lucía, partially in a former conve-
★ nience store (not that you'd notice), Catedrál is one of three establishments with the same owners. They are all connected but have three
different entrances. Occasional live music and a heated-in-winter
upstairs terrace make the Catedrál's bar popular among the 30 and up
crowd (but there is no happy hour). Ópera is an upmarket restaurant
serving food from some far-flung places, such as fish wrapped in phyllo,
veal, pork, and other oven-cooked meats with slightly fussy presentation. Around the corner, on the street Merced is the café with Belgian
sandwiches, large portions of cake, soup, and most importantly, what
is probably the creamiest ice cream in all of Santiago. ☒ *José Miguel
de la Barra 407* ☎ *2/2664–3048* ⊕ *www.operacatedral.cl* ☉ *Catedrál
and Ópera closed Sun.*

BELLAVISTA
BARS AND CLUBS
Bar Constitución. The popular Bar Constitución has hosted hot Chilean
musical groups in a cozy atmosphere with good drinks for many years.
However, in July of 2014, it lost their cabaret license, meaning there is
no longer live music and that now, like other bars, they close at 2 or 3
am, depending on the night. The bar still sees lots of customers in their
20s and 30s and specializes in shared appetizer plates and *limacuya,*
a drink with vodka, lime juice, and passion fruit. ☒ *Constitucón 61*
☎ *2/2244–4569* ⊕ *www.facebook.com/bar.constitucion.5.*

Bokhara. On Bellavista's main drag, Bokhara is one of the city's largest and most popular gay discos. Men arriving before 11:30 with a
printed flyer from the website enter free. There are two floors, each

2

with different DJs, but the music tends toward electronic and house. There are two shows nightly, one at 11:30 upstairs and another at 2:30 downstairs, but there is closed circuit TV, so you can watch the show on the other floor if you like. ✉ *Pío Nono 430* ☎ *2/2732–1050* ⊕ *www.bokhara.cl.*

El Toro. This restaurant touts itself as being gay-centered, but groups, families, and everyone in between feels comfortable in this cozy spot. It is packed every night except Sunday, and the tables are spaced close enough to eavesdrop on the conversations of the models and other members of the "*farandula*" (Chilean celebrities) who frequent the place. Lunch is less expensive, with offers like eggplant lasagna or a Peruvian chicken stew. It functions as a bar-restaurant until 2 am, but may close earlier on quieter nights like Monday or Tuesday. ✉ *Loreto 33* ☎ *2/2737–5937.*

Etniko. For a modern, minimalist fusion sushi bar, this is a good choice. The interior is mostly wood, enhanced by dramatic lighting, with long tables. Etniko also has good drinks and music ranging from electro house to lounge and techno, with local and international DJs. ✉ *Constitución 172* ☎ *2/2732–0119* ⊕ *www.etniko.cl.*

La Casa en el Aire. La Casa en el Aire is a great place to listen to live bands. The Constitución location is in the Patio Bellavista; the Antonia López location is larger. If your Spanish is good, you can listen to storytelling and standup, too, or even perform. ✉ *Constitución 40* ☎ *2/2436–9002* ⊕ *www.lacasaenelaire.cl.*

Fodor'sChoice **Vox Populi.** Vox Populi is a longtime favorite in Bellavista in an old
★ house on a quiet corner. The bar has several rooms, including a basement down a spiral staircase, and an outdoor patio that's perfect for a nighttime drink. It's gay-owned (and gay-friendly), and the bar makes a mean pisco sour to go with its small plates. ✉ *Ernesto Pinto Lagarrigue 364, Bellavista* ☎ *2/2738–0562* ⊕ *www.barvoxpopuli.cl.*

SALSA CLUBS

Havana Salsa. If you're itching to dance salsa or merengue, come to this club any night between Thursday and Saturday. It starts with an all-you-can-eat buffet (11,900 pesos; 6,000 pesos without) of Cuban specialties, and at midnight, there's a 40-minute show with professional dancers. Only after that does the dance floor open to the public. ✉ *Dominica 142* ☎ *2/2737–1737* ⊕ *www.havanasalsa.cl* Ⓜ *Baquedano.*

Maestra Vida. This small club gets full quickly, but salsa dancers say it's the best in Santiago. There are classes from Wednesday to Sunday, except Saturday. Classes for beginners to advanced start at 9 pm and go to 10:30, except on Sunday, when they start at 8 and end at 10. Come alone or with a partner; Maestra Vida is gay-friendly. ✉ *Pío Nono 380* ☎ *2/2777–5325* ⊕ *www.maestravida.cl.*

LAS CONDES

BARS AND CLUBS

Flannery's. Flannery's, close to the main drag of Avenida El Bosque Norte, is an honest-to-goodness pub serving Irish food and beer. The upstairs, downstairs, and outside area often fill with expats and their friends. ✉ *Encomenderos 83* ☎ *2/2233–6675* ⊕ *www.flannerys.cl.*

PERFORMING ARTS

From the dozens of museums scattered around the city, it's clear Santiaguinos also have a strong love of culture. Music, theater, and other artistic endeavors supplement weekends spent dancing the night away.

DANCE

Ballet Nacional Chileno. The venerable Ballet Nacional Chileno, founded in 1945, performs at the Teatro Universidad de Chile near Plaza Baquedano. ⊠ *Av. Providencia 043, Providencia* ☎ *2/2978–2480* ⊕ *www. ceacuchile.com/ballet-nacional-chileno.*

Ballet de Santiago. The Teatro Municipal has its own company, the Ballet de Santiago, which performs regularly, often with guest soloists. ⊠ *Plaza Alcalde Mekis, Agustinas 789, Santiago Centro* ☎ *2/2463–1000* ⊕ *www.balletdesantiago.com.*

FILM

Santiago's many cinemas screen movies in English with Spanish subtitles. Movie listings are posted in El Mercurio and other dailies. Admission is generally between 3,000 and 4,000 pesos, with reduced prices for matinees. The newest multiplexes—with mammoth screens, plush seating, and fresh popcorn—are in the city's malls, but don't overlook the offerings at the Centro Cultural Palacio La Moneda or el Biografo if you want more artsy or themed films.

Cine Hoyts Parque Arauco. Cine Hoyts Parque Arauco is the city's most modern cinema, with 3D and deluxe seating. Be sure to check to see if movies are subtitled (*subtitulada*) or dubbed (*doblada*), especially for kids' movies. The website shows the current listings. ⊠ *Parque Arauco mall, Av. Kennedy 5413, Las Condes* ☎ *600/500–0400* ⊕ *www. cinehoyts.cl.*

Cinemark Alto Las Condes. Among the best theaters in town is the Cinemark Alto Las Condes. Its dozen screens, some of which are 3D or XD, show the latest releases. The most expensive seats, in the premier class (for selected screenings), come with their own lounge, recline like spacious airline seats, and have a leg rest. ⊠ *Alto Las Condes mall, Av. Kennedy 9001, Las Condes* ☎ *600/586–0058* ⊕ *www.cinemark.cl/ theatres/alto-las-condes.*

El Biógrafo. Most of the city's art cinemas tend to screen international favorites. The old standby is El Biógrafo, which shows foreign films on its single screen in the cute, cobblestoned neighborhood of Lastarria. There is a café upstairs with a nice rooftop deck, passable food, and good drinks for pre- and postscreening. ⊠ *José Victorino Lastarria 181, Santiago Centro* ☎ *2/2633–4435* ⊕ *www.elbiografo.cl/wordpress* Ⓜ *Universidad Católica or Bellas Artes.*

MUSIC

Club de Jazz de Santiago. This club has been in operation since 1943 and hosted jazz greats like Louis Armstrong and Herbie Hancock, as well as Chilean national performers. Performances take place Wednesday and Thursday at 9:30 pm for 3,000 pesos, and Friday and Saturday at 10:30 pm for 5,000 pesos. It's inside a restaurant called La Fábrica, which serves pizza, pasta, and other Italian dishes. ✉ *Ossa 123, La Reina* ☎ *2/2830–6208* ⊕ *www.clubdejazz.cl* Ⓜ *Plaza Egaña.*

La Peña de Nano Parra. This brightly colored house in Bellavista is a great place to take in local music with a down-to-earth and generally young, local crowd. Peñas are traditional watering holes where *la nueva canción chilena*, a kind of Latin American resistance folk music, was first popularized. Due to their historically political nature, peñas became clandestine during the dictatorship. ✉ *Ernesto Pinto Lagarrigue 80, Bellavista* ☎ *9/6586–6832* ⊕ *www.lapeña.cl.*

Movistar Arena. Movistar Arena, a covered stadium inside Parque O'Higgins, is a frequent venue for concerts by popular singers and groups, principally those on international tours. It has seating for 12,000, though seats to the side of the stage have poor acoustics. ✉ *Av. Beaucheff 1204, Santiago Centro* ☎ *2/2770–2300* ⊕ *www. movistararena.cl.*

Parque de las Esculturas. This lovely little sculpture park is tucked in between the Mapocho River and Cerro San Cristóbal. Arrive there by walking over the bridge from Pedro de Valdivia, which also hosts several sculptures. In the park there is a map identifying dozens of trees and sculptures. It's a lovely place to spend an hour or two in the afternoon. The park hosts numerous open-air concerts in the early evenings in summer, including the Festival Internacional de Jazz de Providencia. ✉ *Av. Santa María between Av. Pedro de Valdivia Norte and Padre Letelier, Providencia.*

Fodor'sChoice   **Teatro Municipal.** The Teatro Municipal, Santiago's 19th-century theater, ★   presents excellent classical concerts, opera, and ballet by internationally recognized artists from March to December. Opened in 1857, it was designed by French architects and has had several major renovations since. The Renaissance-style building hosts one of the city's most refined monuments with a lavish interior that deserves a visit. The cobblestone path around the building completes the picture. ✉ *Plaza Alcalde Mekis, Agustinas at San Antonio, Santiago Centro* ☎ *2/463–1000* ⊕ *www. municipal.cl.*

Teatro Oriente. Following a lengthy closure, the Teatro Oriente reopened and once again hosts dance, music, theater for all ages, and special programming for children and senior citizens. ✉ *Pedro de Valdivia 099, Providencia.*

Teatro Universidad de Chile. The Coro Sinfónico and the Orquesta Sinfónica, the city's highly regarded chorus and orchestra, perform near Plaza Baquedano at the Teatro Universidad de Chile. Other functions such as ballet and quartets and solo vocal performances take place throughout the year. Your best bet is to drop by the ticket office and see what's on while you're in town. ✉ *Av. Providencia 043, Providencia* ☎ *2/2978–2480* ⊕ *www.teatro.uchile.cl.*

THEATER

Provided that you understand at least a little Spanish, you may want to take in a bit of Chilean theater. Performances take place all year, mainly from Thursday to Sunday around 8 pm.

Festival Internacional Teatro a Mil. In January, the year's best plays are performed at the Estación Mapocho and other venues in a program called the Festival Internacional Teatro a Mil. The name refers to the admission price of 1,000 pesos (just under $2), though some spectacles, particularly the often large-scale opening and closing events near the Moneda Palace, are free. Some events, like those at theaters, cost considerably more. ☎ 2/2925–0300 ⊕ www.santiagoamil.cl.

Matucana 100. Over the past several years, Matucana 100, a converted train warehouse, has become one of the main anchors of the area surrounding Quinta Normal Park. On weekends there are outdoor dance events, and Matucana 100 frequently host fairs, art installations, and film festivals. New in 2014, Cafe 100 sells specialty coffee and coconut water, a good complement to the nearby Soul Kitchen food truck, which serves a hearty Sunday brunch until 4 pm. ⊠ Matucana 100, Quinta Normal ☎ 2/2964–9240 ⊕ www.m100.cl Ⓜ Quinta Normal or Estación Central.

Sala La Comedia. The well-respected theater company by the name of ICTUS performs in the Sala la Comedia, a theater just outside the Lastarria neighborhood. The company's been around for more than 50 years and is considered the most important independent theater group in the country. ⊠ Merced 349, Santiago Centro ☎ 2/2639–1523 ⊕ www. teatroictus.cl.

SPORTS AND THE OUTDOORS

Sunday is the day for sports. In the prosperous eastern part of the city, jogging and bicycling are popular, and inline skating is catching on. Some streets are closed to traffic for the latter. People also take *fútbol* (soccer) games quite seriously. Head to an open park to check out some local pick-up games, and try Parque de Los Reyes (near Barrio Brasil) if you want to see *futbolito* (soccer played on a mini-pitch) at play.

BICYCLING

Santiago has no shortage of public parks, and they provide good opportunities to see the city. If you're ambitious you can even pedal up Cerro San Cristóbal, the city's largest hill.

Fodor'sChoice **La Bicicleta Verde.** This has become one of the top indie tour providers in
★ Santiago. From their storefront just across the river from Bellas Artes, you can rent singles and tandems, starting at 5,000 pesos for a half day, and join different thematic (historical, political, wine-based) bike tours. ⊠ Loreto 6 ☎ 2/2570–9338 ⊕ www.labicicletaverde.com.

SOCCER

Chile's most popular spectator sport is soccer, but a close second is watching the endless bickering among owners, trainers, and players whenever a match isn't going well.

Estadio Nacional. First-division fútbol matches, featuring the city's handful of local teams, are held in the Estadio Nacional, southeast of the city center in Ñuñoa. Soccer is played year-round, with most matches taking place on weekends. It is also a major concert venue, and its history of use as a detention center during the dictatorship does not prevent its continued popularity. It was declared a national monument in 2003. ✉ *Av. Grecia 2001, Ñuñoa* ☎ *2/2238–8102.*

> ### WHAT TO LOOK FOR
>
> All manner of fine woolen items, carvings, lapis lazuli, and other handicrafts can be acquired at street markets in the Pueblito Los Dominicos—a craft "village" at the end of the red line metro, in an old cloister. Look for the shop run by Artesanías de Chile, a foundation that selects top-quality work and ensures artisans receive a fair price. An hour's drive from Santiago, the quaint village of Pomaire is famous for its brown greda, the earthenware pottery that is a common feature of Chilean tables.

SHOPPING

Vitacura is, without a doubt, the destination for upscale shopping. Lined with designer boutiques with SUVs double-parked out front, Avenida Alonso de Córdova is Santiago's equivalent of 5th Avenue in New York or Rodeo Drive in Los Angeles. "Drive" is the important word here, as nobody strolls from place to place. Although buzzing with activity, the streets are strangely empty. Here you'll see names like Emporio Armani, Louis Vuitton, and Hermès. Other shops are found on nearby Avenidas Vitacura and Nueva Costanera.

Providencia, another of the city's most popular shopping districts, has rows of smaller, less luxurious boutiques. Avenida Providencia slices through the neighborhood, branching off for several blocks into the parallel Nueva Providencia. The shops continue east to Tobalaba, after which Avenida Providencia changes its name to Avenida Apoquindo and the neighborhood becomes Las Condes. Or to be on the cutting edge, head south to Avenida Italia (close to Salvador), where there are several blocks of shops stretching south from Bilbao. Converted row houses and workshops have been given over to (mostly) home design stores, cafés, and restaurants with courtyards in back. The street Girardi also has several antiques dealers.

Bohemian Bellavista attracts those in search of the perfect thick woolen sweater or the right piece of lapis lazuli jewelry. Santiago Centro is much more down to earth while the Mercado Central just to the north of Parque Forestal is where anything ocean-related is sold, and nearby markets like Vega Chica and Vega Central sell cheese, fruit, meat, eggs, vegetables, cleaning supplies, signs, and many other items. The shops are grouped together by type.

Shops in Santiago are generally open weekdays 10–7 and Saturday 10–2. Malls are usually open daily 10–10.

CENTRO

ANTIQUES

Antiguedades Balmaceda. West of Estación Mapocho and at the end of Avenida Brasil, this complex also known as Anticuarios Parque de Los Reyes is filled with antiques dealers, each with different numbered shops, some of which have websites. They are used to foreigners coming and poking around, some of whom have been known to fill entire containers with jewelry, chandeliers, ceramics, and crystalware to bring back home. ■ TIP→ Take a quick peek across the street to the skate park at Parque de Los Reyes, where some of the best skateboarders in Chile practice on weekends. ⊠ *Av. Brasil at Balmaceda, Santiago Centro.*

CLOTHING

Donde Golpea El Monito. In the countryside, men often wear *texanos* (cowboy hats), *paños* (formal hats), and *chupallas* (flat-brimmed hats). If you've ever wondered where to buy these proper toppers, head to Donde Golpea El Monito. At this downtown shop, in business for nearly a century, the friendly staff shows the differences between each hat and how to wear them. Also for sale are spurs, ponchos, and other *huaso* (Chilean cowboy) essentials. ⊠ *21 de Mayo 707, Santiago Centro* ☎ *2/638–4907* ⊕ *www.dondegolpeaelmonito.cl.*

FOOD

L'atelier del Cioccolato. If you can make even the briefest visit to this boutique chocolate shop in the small Espacio M mall, built behind the facade of what was once a palace, then do so. In addition to the usual bonbons are a few flavors specific to Chile, such as piney-tasting *boldo,* lemony *cedrón,* or ones with basil, oregano, and *merquén,* a smoked spice from the indigenous Mapuche people. Themed gift sets include Pablo Neruda boxes. ⊠ *Inside Espacio M, Compañía de Jesús 1214, local 113-4, Santiago Centro* ☎ *2/2733–8049.*

SHOPPING MALLS

Mall VIVO del Centro. Santiago's downtown mall includes sporting goods stores, a food court with fast food restaurants, and public bathrooms. It's close to the Mercado Central and has free Wi-Fi in the rest areas and food court. ⊠ *Puente 689, Santiago Centro* ☎ *2/2598–1433* ⊕ *vivoelcentro.mallvivo.cl* ⊗ *Mon.–Sat. 10–9, Sun. 11–9.*

LA ALAMEDA

MARKETS

Centro Artesanal Santa Lucía. This souvenir market just across the Alameda from the base of Cerro Santa Lucía has some indigenous and locally made crafts, including some (not the finest quality) lapis lazuli items. Get your ears or navel pierced as well. It's open daily 10–7. As in all crowded and touristy areas, keep an eye on valuables. ⊠ *Alameda and Diagonal Paraguay, La Alameda.*

LASTARRIA AND BELLAS ARTES

BOOKS

La Tienda Nacional. For independent books from local authors, including kids' books and locally designed toys, head here. There are also postcards and posters with historical Chilean motifs, indie rock and folk bands from the 1970s, and today's music, films, and documentaries for sale. ⊠ *Merced 369, Lastarria* ☎ *2/2638–4706* ⊕ *www.latienda nacional.cl* Ⓜ *Bellas Artes.*

WINE

Fodor's Choice **Santiago Wine Club.** Take your most finicky wine-loving friends to this
★   small storefront in Barrio Lastarria to try its highly rated, indie, terroir, and signatures wines, many of which are fairly hard to find elsewhere. ⊠ *Rosal 386, Lastarria* ☎ *2/2632–6596* ⊕ *www.santiagowineclub.cl* Ⓜ *Bellas Artes or Universidad Católica.*

BELLAVISTA

MARKETS

Feria Artesanal Pío Nono. Bellavista's colorful Feria Artesanal Pío Nono, held in the park at the start of Avenida Pío Nono, comes alive every night of the week. The area, particularly the south end of Pio Nono, is even busier on weekends, when vendors gather in Parque Domingo Gómez, in the shadow of the Universidad de San Sebastian Building to display their handicrafts. It's a bit hit or miss for quality, but you can't beat it for convenience. ⊠ *Corner of Pío Nono and Bellavista, Bellavista.*

PROVIDENCIA

GIFTS

Manao. This leather goods shop sells colorful, one-of-a-kind purses, bags, and accessories with material from Chile, Argentina, and Brazil. The craftsmanship is all Chilean though, with owner Paola Vidal behind all the designs and much of the handiwork. She can make custom items, though these will take a few days to stitch together. ⊠ *Condell 1447, Providencia* ☎ *9/9987–9984* ⊘ *Closed Mon.*

JEWELRY

Blue Stone. This is one of the top-end stores in which to buy lapis lazuli, the blue stone for which Chile is famous. Unlike other stores that have dozens of the same items, each piece of jewelry here is unique as are decorative items for the table, including sets of cutlery inlaid with lapis lazuli, and home furnishings such as copper vessels from replicas of original designs by indigenous peoples of Chile. ⊠ *Los Araucanos 2020, at Los Conquistadores, Providencia* ☎ *2/2232–2581* ⊕ *www.bluestone.cl.*

LAS CONDES

JEWELRY

Chantal Bernsau. For truly original jewelry using local materials, visit the shop of Chantal Bernsau, on the first floor of the W Hotel. She sells mainly chunky pendants with large beads made mostly of local stones (but does not specialize in lapiz lazuli). The items are pricey, but the work is top-quality. ⊠ *Inside W Hotel main lobby, Isidora Goyenechea 3000, shop 106-B, Las Condes* ☎ *2/2245–1984* ⊕ *www.chantal bernsau.cl/tiendas.*

MARKETS

Fodor's Choice **Pueblito Los Dominicos.** This "village" inside a former cloister sports some
★ 150 shops filled with crafts made of fine leather and wool, semiprecious stones (including lapis lazuli), and *greda* (Chile's version of terra-cotta). There's also a wonderful display of cockatoos and other live birds. It's a nice place to visit, especially on weekends when traveling musicians entertain the crowds. It's open daily 10–8 in summer and 10–7 in winter, and there are two restaurants serving traditional Chilean food. Next door is an attractive whitewashed church dating from the late 18th century. The complex is a bit far afield, but easily accessed by the metro of the same name. ■ TIP➔ **If you can find one of the old (paper, not plastic) 2,000 peso bills, the church is on it.** ⊠ *Av. Apoquindo 9085, Las Condes* ☎ *2/289–69841* ⊕ *www.culturallascondes.cl/home/centro-artesanal.html* Ⓜ *Los Dominicos.*

SHOPPING MALLS

Alto Las Condes. This mall has more than 200 shops, three department stores, a multiplex cinema, interior food court, and an outside patio lined with restaurants. Also here is an American-style upmarket supermarket, appropriately named Jumbo, that carries excellent Chilean wines. ⊠ *Av. Kennedy 9001, Las Condes* ☎ *2/2299–6965* ⊕ *www.alto lascondes.cl* Ⓜ *No metro.*

Costanera Center. This mall organizes stores by type and has 12 movie screens, free Wi-Fi, and a wide variety of food. You can't miss the building, which stands 62 stories high. The mall occupies the first six floors. ⊠ *Andres Bello 2425, Las Condes* ☎ *2/2916–9200* ⊕ *www. costaneracenter.cl* Ⓜ *Tobalaba.*

Parque Arauco. This North American–style shopping center with outdoor plazas and fountains has an eclectic mix of designer boutiques, including clothing outlets like Benetton, Ralph Lauren, and Laura Ashley. Chile's three largest department stores—Falabella, Ripley, and Almacenes París—sell everything from perfume to plates. The trendiest shops are mostly in the outdoor boulevard, which also has a wide selection of restaurants. There's free shuttle service from several Santiago hotels, which is handy, as it is not metro-accessible. ■ TIP➔ **The view of the mountains from this mall's upper floors and plazas are spectacular, especially after a rain.** ⊠ *Av. Kennedy 5413, Las Condes* ☎ *600/500-0011* ⊕ *www.parquearauco.cl.*

WINE

El Mundo del Vino. This world-class store has an international selection, in-store tastings, wine classes, and books for oenophiles. In addition to this shop in the W Hotel, there are also branches in the Alto Las Condes, Parque Arauco, and Costanera Center shopping malls. ⊠ *Av. Isidora Goyenechea 3000, Las Condes* ☎ *2/2584–1173* ⊕ *www. elmundodelvino.cl.*

VITACURA

ANTIQUES

Centro Comercial Lo Castillo. Some nice antiques shops are found in the basement of the Centro Comercial Lo Castillo, which is quite small and, apart from a cinema and the antiques shops, sells mostly women's clothes and jewelry. It's one block up from the corner of Avenida Alonso de Córdova. The indoor shopping arcade is from the 1980s and *caracol-,* or snail-like, in its spiral layout. Le Fournil restaurant, just across Avenida Vitacura in Paseo Mañío, is a good place for a coffee or light meal. ⊠ *Candelaria Goyenechea 3820, Vitacura* ☎ *2/2228–0432* ⊕ *www.plazalocastillo.cl* ☽ *Closed Sun.*

CLOTHING

Alfombras Wool. This shop sells a wide variety of wool carpets and other weavings designed and produced in Chile. ⊠ *Av. Kennedy 7308, Vitacura* ☎ *2/2870–0022* ⊕ *alfombraswool.com.*

Casimires Ingleses Matilde Medina. Yards and yards of cashmere fill the window of Casimires Ingleses Matilde Medina. The owner imports her beautiful scarves and sweaters from England and sells fine dress shirts, which are also imported. ⊠ *Av. Vitacura 3660, Vitacura* ☎ *2/220–7146* ⊕ *www.casimiresingleses.com.*

Hermès. Looking a bit like a fortress, Hermès occupies some prime real estate on Alonso de Córdoba, Santiago's main upscale international brand shopping drag. ⊠ *Av. Alonso de Córdova 2526, Vitacura* ☎ *2/2374–1576* ⊕ *vb.com/hermes/santiago* ☽ *Closed Sun.*

GALLERIES

Galleries are scattered around the city, and admission is usually free. The newspaper El Mercurio lists current exhibitions in its Saturday supplement *Vivienda y Decoración.* Bellavista, which is full of small galleries and where restaurants often put on exhibitions, is the place to scout the work of young artists, but it is Vitacura that is the heart of the more consolidated gallery scene.

Galería Animal. See works by local artists at Galería Animal, a spacious, luminous gallery in Vitacura. The large-scale pieces include sculpture and other types of installations. ⊠ *Nueva Costanera 3731, Vitacura* ☎ *2/2371–9090* ⊕ *www.galeriaanimal.cl.*

Galería Isabel Aninat. International artists hold exhibitions in this Vitacura gallery, which has two rooms and a sculpture garden. ⊠ *Espoz 3100, Vitacura* ☎ *2/2481–9870* ⊕ *Galería Isabel Aninat.*

HANDICRAFTS

Pura. The staff at Pura has picked out the finest handicrafts from around the region. Here you can find expertly woven blankets and throws, colorful pottery, cushions, housewares, and fine leather goods. Most items are handmade. ⊠ *Av. Kennedy 5413, 3rd fl., local 14, Vitacura* ☎ *2/2211–7875* ⊕ *www.purartesanos.cl.*

SHOPPING STREETS

Avenida Alonso de Córdova. In Vitacura, you can wrap yourself in style on and near Avenida Alonso de Córdova. This wide street, home to high end chain stores, is where the well-heeled shop for more expensive items. Make sure to ring the bell at these shops, as they usually keep their doors locked (not just anybody gets in).

WINE

La Vinoteca. Proudly proclaiming itself Santiago's first fine wine shop, La Vinoteca stocks vintages from all over Chile and abroad, as well as beer and liquor. There is an outlet at the airport for last-minute purchases and another shop 14 blocks down Manuel Montt from Providencia. ⊠ *Av. Nueva Costanera 3955, Vitacura* ☎ *2/2953–6290* ⊕ *www. lavinoteca.cl* ☾ *Closed Sun.*

SIDE TRIPS FROM SANTIAGO

For more than a few travelers, Santiago's main attraction is its proximity to the continent's best skiing. The snowcapped mountains to the east of Santiago have the largest number of runs, not just in Chile or South America, but in the entire Southern Hemisphere. The other attraction is that the season lasts from June to September and, in some places, October, so savvy skiers can take to the slopes in Chile when people back home are hitting the beach. It's no wonder that skiing aficionados and pros from around the world head to Chile.

The wineries around Santiago make for interesting day- or multiday trips. These winemakers provide the majority of the country's excellent exports, and you might find the source of your favorite Chilean wine back home just a short jaunt from the capital. The Casablanca Valley, west of Santiago, on the road to Valparaíso, is where some of the country's best white wines are produced.

The Cajón del Maipo in the Andes makes for a relaxing trip to soak in hot springs, take a hike, or wander through the crafts village of Pomaire, 70 km (43 miles) west of Santiago.

CENTRAL MAIPO

Talagante is 40 km (25 miles) southwest of Santiago.

The Central Maipo Valley is home to some of the most traditional wineries in Chile, like Viña Undurraga. In the lowest part of the valley, close to the coast, are the newcomers, producing lighter red wines from grapes cooled by sea breezes, as well as some Sauvignon Blancs.

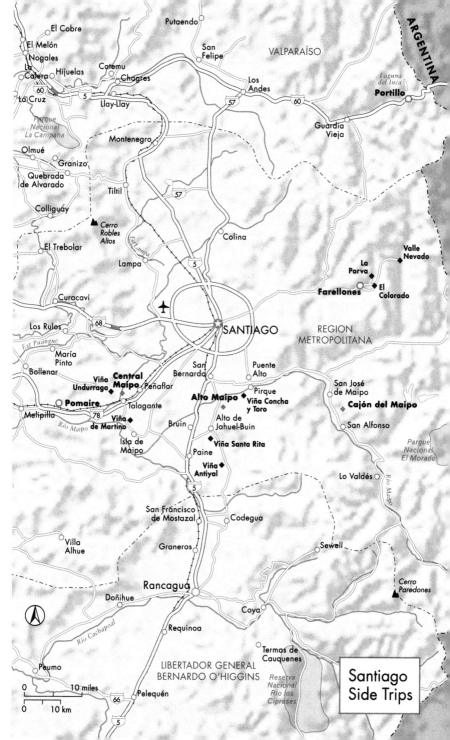

ARGENTINA

El Cobre
El Melón
Nogales
La Calera
Hijuelas
La Cruz
60

Putaendo
San Felipe
VALPARAÍSO
Los Andes
57   60
Catemu
Chagres
Llay-Llay
5

Guardia Vieja
Laguna del Inca
Portillo

Olmué
Granizo
Quebrada de Alvarado
Colliguay
El Trebolar

Montenegro
Tiltil
57

Cerro Robles Altos
Lampa

Colina

Valle Nevado
La Parva
Farellones
El Colorado

Curacaví
Los Rulos
68
Est. Puangue
María Pinto
Bollenar

5

SANTIAGO

REGION METROPOLITANA

Viña Undurraga
Central Maipo
Peñaflor
Pomaire
78
Talagante
Viña de Martino
Metipilla
Río Maipo
Isla de Maipo

San Bernardo
Alto Maipo
Bruin
Alto de Jahuel-Buin
Viña Santa Rita
Paine
Viña Antiyal

Puente Alto
Pirque
Viña Concha y Toro

San José de Maipo
Cajón del Maipo
San Alfonso

Lo Valdés
Río Maipo
Parque Nacional El Morado

Villa Alhue

San Fráncisco de Mostazal
Graneros

Codegua

Sewell

Cerro Paredones

Rancagua
Doñihue
Río Cachapoal
Requínoa

Coya

Termas de Cauquenes

Peumo
66
5
Pelequén

LIBERTADOR GENERAL BERNARDO O'HIGGINS
Reserva Nacional Río los Cipreses

0   10 miles
0   10 km

Santiago Side Trips

GETTING HERE AND AROUND

The Autopista del Sol (Ruta 78) from Santiago to the port of San Antonio runs through the heart of the Maipo Valley, but vineyards are too far off the highway to be reached by public transport. Drive to these vineyards, take an organized tour, or combine local transportation with taxis or colectivos (shared taxis) to get to your destination.

WINERIES

Viña De Martino. The De Martino family has been making wine in Isla de Maipo since the 1930s and were the first in Chile to bottle Carménère, now Chile's signature grape. The winery is a strong proponent of organic viticulture. Its winemaking team has done groundbreaking work in seeking out the country's finest terroirs. Tours and tastings are run at a variety of price points and interest levels, and there's an elegant lunch for a minimum seven people and buffet for less. Several vegetarian entrée options are available alongside meat and seafood. ⊠ *Manuel Rodríguez 229, Isla de Maipo* ☎ *2/2577–8837* ⊕ *www.demartino.cl* ⊠ *From 10,000 pesos* ⌂ *Reservations essential* ⊙ *Tours by appointment: weekdays 9–6, Sat. 10:30–1:30.*

Viña Undurraga. Don Francisco Undurraga Vicuña founded this winery in 1885 in the town of Talagante, 34 km (21 miles) southwest of Santiago. Today you can tour the gardens—designed by Pierre Dubois, who planned Santiago's Parque Forestal—or take a look at the facilities and enjoy a tasting. Reserve ahead for a spot on a tour in English or Spanish. Viña Undurraga is along the way to Pomaire, so you might visit both in the same day. Private tours for a minimum of two participants begin weekdays at noon and must be reserved two days in advance at cost of 28,000 pesos per person. ⊠ *Camino a Melipilla Km 34, Talagante* ☎ *2/2372–2850* ⊕ *www.undurraga.cl* ⊠ *8,000 pesos for group tours; 28,000 pesos for private* ⊙ *Tours weekdays at 10:15, noon, 2, and 3:30; weekends at 10:15, noon, and 1:30 with 24-hrs notice.*

ALTO MAIPO

Pirque is 39 km (24 miles) southeast of Santiago. Buin is 35 km (22 miles) south of Santiago.

Some of Chile's finest red wines hail from the Alto Maipo, the eastern sector of the Casablanca Valley. There are a number of wineries—old and new, big and small—snuggled up into the foothills of the Andes Mountains.

GETTING HERE AND AROUND

The only easy ways to reach the Antiyal and Santa Rita vineyards in the Alto Maipo are by car or on an organized wine tour. Pirque can be reached by taking Línea 4 of the metro to Puente Alto; from there, it is only a short taxi ride, and there are also frequent colectivos (shared taxis).

WINERIES

Fodor'sChoice **Viña Antiyal.** Chilean winemaker Alvaro Espinoza and his wife, Marina
★ Ashton, harvested their first organically grown grapes from biodynamically managed vines in their own front yard back in 1998 and

thus was born Chile's first ultra-premium "garage wine." They've grown a bit since then and have more land higher in the mountains but still produce just 25,000 bottles (each numbered by hand) of their red-blend Antiyal. Tours are personalized, with emphasis on environmentally friendly and biodynamic winegrowing. Llamas, alpacas, geese, and the family dog wander the vineyards. Visits should be arranged at least a week in advance. Antiyal has also opened a small bed and breakfast on-site. Contact them through the winery to arrange a stay. ⊠ *Padre Hurtado 68, Buin* ☎ *9/319–6345* ⊕ *www.antiyal.com* ✉ *From 20,000 pesos* ⚓ *Reservations essential.*

One of Viña Santa Rita's current wine cellars played an important role in Chile's battle for independence. Legend has it that in 1814 then-owner Doña Paula Jaraquemada saved the lives of revolutionary hero Bernardo O'Higgins and his 120 soldiers by hiding them in a basement, and refusing to let the Spanish enter. Santa Rita's 120 label commemorates the event.

Fodor's Choice ★ **Viña Concha y Toro.** Chile's largest producer is consistently good in every price range, from the most inexpensive table wines to some of Chile's finest—and priciest—labels. Melchor de Concha y Toro, who once served as Chile's minister of finance, built the *casona,* or manor house, in 1875. He was among the first to import French vines, making this a cutting-edge winery since its foundation in 1883. The typical hour-long tour includes a stroll through the century-old gardens and vineyards, a look at the modern facilities, and a visit to the Casillero del Diablo, the famed cellar where Don Melchor kept his finest stock. There is a sound-and-light show in the dark here that appeals to lovers of kitsch. Tastings of three wines are provided as part of the tour. Reserve tours a few days ahead for weekdays or a week ahead for popular weekend hours. With the extension of the metro to Puente Alto, the vineyard is easy reach by private or shared taxi (*colectivo*) from the end of the line, though the complimentary wine glass is unlikely to survive the way home. ⊠ *Av. Virginia Subercaseaux 210, Pirque* ☎ *2/2476–5269* ⊕ *www.conchaytoro.com* ✉ *Regular tour 9,000 pesos; Marqués de Casa Concha tour 19,000 pesos* ⚓ *Reservations essential* ☉ *Daily 10–5:10; regular English tours at 10:20, 11:30, 1, 2:30, 3:10, 3:40, and 4. Spanish tours are more frequent. Marqués de Casa Concha tour (includes more tastings with a sommelier) in English daily at 4 pm, and more frequently in Spanish.*

Fodor's Choice ★ **Viña Santa Rita.** Chile's third-largest winery, on a sprawling estate with an impressive museum, dates to 1880, when everything from vines to winemakers was brought from France. The Pompeiian-style manor now houses the pricey 16-room Casa Real Hotel, owned by, but operated separately from, the winery. The house, its neogothic chapel, and the park that surrounds them are strictly off limits to all but the hotel's guests, though on tours you get a good peek. The on-site Andean Museum, with its small collection of pre-Columbian artifacts and textiles, is open to the public free of charge and highly recommended. Winery tours take you down into the musty fan vault cellars, now national monuments, which were built by French engineers in 1875 using a limestone-and-egg-white stone masonry technique called *cal y canto*. Stop in for a lunch at Doña Paula for a formal meal, or stick to the snack bar for lighter fare. There are six different types of tours including winemaker, picnic, bike, and wine. You must reserve a week ahead for tours. ✉ *Camino Padre Hurtado 0695, Alto Jahuel-Buin* ☎ *2/2362–2594 weekdays or 2/362–2590 weekends* 🌐 *www.santarita.com* 🎫 *Tour 10,000 pesos; tours of the grounds, but not the wine cellars free with lunch at Casa de Doña Paula. Deluxe tour 35,000 pesos, includes premium wines and a cheese platter* 🕒 *Tours Tues.–Fri. at 11:30, 12:15, 2, and 4, weekends at 12:15 and 2.*

WHERE TO EAT

$$$$ CHILEAN 🍴 **La Casa de Doña Paula.** A century-old colonial building with thick adobe walls houses Viña Santa Rita's restaurant. Beneath the exposed beams of the peaked wooden ceiling, the restaurant is decorated with old religious sculptures and portraits, including one of Paula Jaraquemada, who owned the land at the time of the revolution. If you plan to lunch here, arrive in time to join the winery's 12:15 tour so you're not rushing through lunch to make the 2 pm tour. Locally raised meats are the draw here; try the delicious *costillar de cerdo* (pork ribs). For dessert, the house specialty is *ponderación,* a crisp swirl of fried dough atop vanilla ice cream with caramel syrup. The minimum charge for lunch is 16,500 pesos, so you might as well tuck in. [$] *Average main: 15000 pesos* ✉ *Viña Santa Rita, Camino Padre Hurtado 0695, Alto Jahuel-Buin* ☎ *2/2362–2590* 🌐 *www.santarita.com/chile/restaurant-dona-paula* ✍ *Reservations essential* 🕒 *Closed Mon. No dinner.*

POMAIRE

70 km (43 miles) west of Santiago.

You can easily spend a morning or afternoon wandering around the quaint village of Pomaire, a former settlement of indigenous people comprising nothing more than a few streets of single-story adobe dwellings. On weekends Pomaire teems with people wandering around, shopping, and having lunch in one of the country-style restaurants with red-and-white checked tablecloths and clay ovens that specializes in empanadas and other typical Chilean foods.

Pomaire is famous for its brown *greda,* or earthenware pottery, which is ubiquitous, in one form or another, throughout Chile. Order pastel de choclo and it is nearly always served in a round, simple clay dish—they're heavy and retain the heat, so the food is brought to the table piping hot.

The village bulges with bowls, pots, and plates of every shape and size, not to mention piggy banks, plant pots, vases, and the unmissable "*chanchito de la suerte,*" three-legged pigs that make great souvenirs. Most of the shops at the top of the main street sell the work of others; walk farther down or into the side streets and find the workshops from which they buy. Prices are cheaper there.

GETTING HERE AND AROUND

Pomaire is easy to find. It's clearly signposted to the right off the Autopista del Sol (Ruta 78). You can also take the Ruta Bus 78 buses, which depart frequently from Terminal San Borja in downtown Santiago and leave you at the turnoff to Pomaire, 2 km (1 mile) from the village. Once you get to the tiny village, it's small enough to get around on foot. To return to Santiago, simply walk back to the highway and hail the first bus, or in the late afternoon, wait at the church and take a bus back to Santiago (earlier in the day you have to make a connection in Melipilla).

EXPLORING

FAMILY **Granja Educativa Alfafera Greda.** You can take a course in pottery-making at this workshop, run by local artisans especially for visitors. Suitable for both children aged five and up and adults, the two-hour course starts with a video in English, followed by instruction in the use of a pottery wheel, and winds up with an insight into the techniques used by the area's indigenous peoples. ✉ *San Antonio 355, corner of Arturo Prat* ☎ *9/9879–3533* 🎟 *3,000 pesos* 🕒 *Times vary so call a day in advance to reserve or confirm.*

WHERE TO EAT

$$ CHILEAN 🍴 **La Greda.** Named for the earthenware pottery that made this village famous, La Greda is a great place for grilled meats. Try the *filete de la greda,* a steak covered with a sauce of tomatoes, onions, and mushrooms, and topped with cheese. Or try a complete *menú,* with drink, main, side, and coffee included. The expansive outdoor dining room has vines winding around the thick wood rafters. If the weather is cool, the staff lights a fire in the woodstove to keep things toasty. [$] *Average main: 10000 pesos* ✉ *Manuel Rodríguez 251, at Roberto Bravo* ☎ *2/831–1166* 🕒 *No dinner.*

$$ CHILEAN FAMILY 🍴 **San Antonio.** The food here is much the same as elsewhere in Pomaire, but, particularly for families with children, it offers a number of perks. There's a children's menu and, on weekends, everyone who eats here can take the free pottery course at the Granja, just across the road. Diners can also use the nearby swimming pool for a modest fee or sprawl under the fig tree for a postlunch nap. [$] *Average main: 7000 pesos* ✉ *Roberto Bravo 320* ☎ *2/2831–9307* 🌐 *www.restaurantsanantonio.cl* [$] *Average main: 7000 pesos* ✉ *San Antonio 298* ☎ *2/831–9307* 🌐 *www.restaurantsanantonio.cl/.*

CAJÓN DEL MAIPO

San Alfonso is 60 km (37 miles) southeast of Santiago.

The Cajón del Maipo, a narrow valley deep in the Andes, is irresistible for those who want to soak in natural hot springs; stroll through picturesque mountain towns, where low adobe houses line the roads; or just take in the stark but majestic landscape. In summertime, *humitas,* or fresh corn (unfilled) tamales are a popular snack or meal. There are hot springs at Baños Morales, just below the Refugio Lo Valdés, and higher up the valley at Baños de Colina. The dirt road is rough (and impassable in winter), but the pools of steaming water and the spectacular setting are well worth the effort when the weather is in your favor.

GETTING HERE AND AROUND

To reach Cajón del Maipo, head south on Avenida José Alessandri until you reach the Rotonda Departamental, a large traffic circle. There you take Camino Las Vizcachas (aka Camino Cajón del Maipo), following it south into the valley.

Expediciones Manzur sells round-trip tickets from Santiago to Lo Valdés Mountain Center in Cajón del Maipo, Baños Morales, and the Baños de Colina hot springs. Buses run Saturday, Sunday, and Wednesday, leaving at 7:30 am from Ramón Carnicer 5 (near Baquedano). A round-trip ticket (going and coming in one day) to Baños Morales costs 12,000 pesos; it's 18,000 pesos for Baños de Colina. Prior booking is essential and you should sit on the right side of the van for a good view of the river on the ascent.

ESSENTIALS

Bus Information Expediciones Manzur ⊠ *Sótero del Río 475, Suite 507, Santiago Centro, Santiago* ☎ *2/2643–5651.*

EXPLORING

Baños de Colina. These hot springs high in the mountains are a series of natural pools down which water drops, cooling gradually. The road is rough and often impassable in winter and there is little infrastructure, but the view is spectacular. Rustic lodging and camping is available. Do not confuse these rustic springs with Termas de Colina, which are similarly named but located north of the city. ⊠ *Camino Cajón del Maipo, 104 km (65 miles) from Santiago, Baños de Colina.*

Baños Morales. Two pools in the tiny village of Baños Morales, where the Morales and Volcán rivers meet, are pleasantly warm, not hot, and rich in iodine and other minerals. You can hike from this area as well. Be warned that surprise winter storms can trap you here. The village has some rustic lodging, but many people prefer to come for the day. ⊠ *Camino Cajón del Maipo, 92 km (57 miles) from Santiago, Villa Baños Morales.*

FAMILY **Cascada de las Animas.** This small tourist complex in the shadow of the mountains has a swimming pool and picnic area for short stays, as well as lodgings for longer sojourns. This is also a great base for exploring the Cajón. Accommodations come in several forms, including campsites, lodge suites, and free-standing cabins with rustic wood furniture. From here, multiday horse-back-riding trips, guided hikes, and rafting excursions are available, as is transportation from Santiago. ⊠ *Camino al Volcán 31087, San Alfonso* ☎ *2/2861–1303* ⊕ *www.cascada.net* 🖃 *12,000 pesos for admission to swimming pool and picnic area in high season; 10,000 in low season.*

Refugio Lo Valdés. The Lo Valdés Mountain Center, built in 1932, and also called the Refugio Alemán, provides simple lodgings and organizes activities such as trekking and horse riding in the mountains. It is open year-round and has a restaurant that also serves day visitors until 8 pm. If you'd prefer to do your own hike, the center can give you a map and instructions as well. ⊠ *Km 77, Camino Cajón del Maipo, Lo Valdés* ☎ *9/9230–5930* ⊕ *www.refugiolovaldes.com.*

FARELLONES SKI AREA

32 km (20 miles) east of Santiago.

Three world-class ski resorts (El Colorado, La Parva, and Valle Nevado) lie just outside Santiago near the village of Farellones. They have a total of 48 lifts that can carry you to the top of the 1,260 acres of groomed runs. Farellones, with some unremarkable shops, restaurants, and hotels, lies at the base of the Cerro Colorado mountain. Shorten your drive by parking at the Curva 17 parking lot of Valle Nevado and taking the gondola up to mid-mountain from there. All ski areas rent equipment, for about 25,000 (basic) to 37,000 (professional) pesos per day.

GETTING HERE AND AROUND

It can take up to two hours to reach these ski resorts, which lie 48–56 km (30–35 miles) from Santiago. The road is narrow, winding, and full of Chileans racing to get to the top. If you decide to drive, make sure you have a four-wheel-drive vehicle or snow chains, which you can rent along the way or before you leave Santiago from international car rental agencies (such as Hertz or Avis). The chains are installed for about 10,000 pesos. Don't think you need them? There's a police checkpoint just before the road starts to climb into the Andes, and if the weather is rough they make you turn back.

To reach these areas by car, follow Avenida Kennedy or Avenida Las Condes eastward until you leave Santiago. Here, you begin an arduous journey up the Andes, making 40 consecutive hairpin turns. The road forks when you reach the top, with one road taking the relatively easy 16-km (10-mile) route east to Valle Nevado, and the other following a more difficult road north to Farellones and La Parva.

Several bus companies run regularly scheduled service to the Andes in winter. Skitotal buses depart from the company's office on Avenida Apoquindo and head to all of the ski resorts. Buses depart as they fill, starting at 7:30 am; and the last trip up departs at 8:30. A round-trip ticket costs 13,000 pesos to Farellones, La Parva, and El Colorado, and 15,000 pesos to Valle Nevado. You can arrange for private transfer with them as well, which varies in price for round-trip from 120,000 for one to three passengers, to 170,000 for 6 to 10 passengers. Skitotal also offers hotel-to-slopes or airport-to-slopes service. Expediciones Manzur leaves daily at 8:30 from Ramon Carnicer 5 (near Plaza Baquedano) for 12,000 round-trip in a shared van, or 120,000 for up to 10 people in a private van.

ESSENTIALS

Bus Contacts Skitotal ⊠ *Apoquindo 4900, Las Condes, Santiago* ☎ *2/2246-0156* ⊕ *www.skitotal.cl.*

WHERE TO STAY

EL COLORADO

$$$$ **La Cornisa.** This quaint old inn on the road to Farellones gives you
HOTEL   easy access to the slopes, as there's a free shuttle to and from the nearby ski areas. **Pros:** cozy, intimate ambience; outdoor hot tub. **Cons:** not as close to the slopes as the ski resorts themselves. $ *Rooms from: 147000*

pesos ✉ *Av. Los Cóndores 636, Farellones* 🕾 *2/2321–1172* ⊕ *www. lacornisa.cl* 🍴 *10 rooms* 🍽 *Some meals.*

VALLE NEVADO

Three hotels dominate Valle Nevado; staying at one gives you access to the facilities at the other two. The larger two—Puerta del Sol and Valle Nevado—are part of the same complex. The three hotels share restaurants, which serve almost every type of cuisine. Rates include lift tickets, breakfast, and dinner. Peak season is July and August; you can find deals in June and September.

$$$$
RESORT **Puerta del Sol.** The largest of the Valle Nevado hotels, Puerta del Sol can be identified by its signature sloped roof. **Pros:** only 160 feet from the ski slopes; interconnecting rooms good for families. **Cons:** rooms are quite small. $ *Rooms from: 318000 pesos* ✉ *13 km (8 miles) beyond La Parva, El Colorado* 🕾 *2/2477–7000, 800/669–0554 toll-free in U.S.* ⊕ *www.vallenevado.com* 🍴 *124 rooms* ⊗ *Closed Oct.–May* 🍽 *Some meals.*

$$$$
RESORT **Tres Puntas.** It bills itself as a hotel for young people, and Tres Puntas may indeed remind you of a college dormitory. **Pros:** the Pub Tres Puntas is a fun place to meet friends after a day on the slopes, which are only a two-minute walk away; free Wi-Fi. **Cons:** for the price, rooms are very cramped. $ *Rooms from: 290000 pesos* ✉ *13 km (8 miles) beyond La Parva, Farrellones, La Parva* 🕾 *2/2477–7000, 800/669–0554 toll-free in U.S.* ⊕ *www.vallenevado.com* 🍴 *82 rooms* ⊗ *Closed Oct.–May* 🍽 *Some meals.*

$$$$
RESORT **Valle Nevado.** The resort's most extravagantly priced lodge provides ski-in–ski-out convenience. **Pros:** ski-in, ski-out; free Wi-Fi. **Cons:** expensive, particularly if you plan to be out on the slopes all day. $ *Rooms from: 194000 pesos* ✉ *13 km (8 miles) beyond La Parva, Farellones* 🕾 *2/2477–7000, 800/669–0554 toll-free in U.S.* ⊕ *www. vallenevado.com* 🍴 *53 rooms* 🍽 *Some meals.*

SPORTS AND THE OUTDOORS

SKIING

El Colorado. The closest ski area to Santiago, El Colorado has 568 acres of groomed runs—the most in Chile. There are 19 ski lifts here and 101 runs for beginners through to experts, as well as the best snowpark in South America, which has six jumps. The beginner runs are at the base of the mountain near the village of Farellones. Sled tracks and a few other activities for nonskiers opened in 2014. There are a few restaurants and pubs nearby, but most are down in the village of Farellones. The ski season here runs from mid-June through September, depending on snowfall. ✉ *On road between Farellones and La Parva, El Colorado* 🕾 *2/2353–6760* ⊕ *www.elcolorado.cl* 🎿 *Lift tickets 34,000–42,000 pesos* ⊗ *Mid-June–late Sept.*

La Parva. This colorful conglomeration of private homes set along a handful of mountain roads with stunning views of Santiago is home to a resort with 16 ski lifts, most leading to runs for intermediate skiers. The more adventurous (and advanced) can take part in heliskiing on the resort's 1,800-plus acres. ✉ *3 km (2 miles) up road from Farellones,*

La Parva ☎ 2/2964–2100 ⊕ *www.laparva.cl* ✑ *29,000–40,000 pesos* ⊘ *June–Sept.*

Valle Nevado. Chile's largest ski region is a luxury resort area with 17 ski lifts that connect to 46 runs covering 7,000 acres. Intended for skiers who like a challenge, this resort has few beginner slopes. Two of the extremely difficult runs from the top of Cerro Tres Puntas are called Shake and Twist. If that doesn't intimidate you then you might be ready for some heliskiing. The helicopter whisks you to otherwise inaccessible peaks where you can ride a vertical drop of up to 2,500 meters (8,200 feet). A ski school at Valle Nevado gives pointers to everyone from beginners to experts. Many of the visitors here are European, as are the ski instructors, though in recent years more Brazilians have been coming to Chile for the skiing as well. ✉ *13 km (8 miles) beyond La Parva, El Colorado* ☎ *2/2477–7000* ⊕ *www.vallenevado.com* ✑ *38,000–43,000 pesos* ⊘ *Mid-June–Sept.*

PORTILLO SKI AREA

160 km (100 miles) northwest of Santiago.

Numerous world speed records have been broken on the renowned slopes of Portillo, close to the Argentine border. It also has the best views of any of the area's ski resorts. It's a three-hour drive from the city, so a day trip would be exhausting. The only accommodation is Hotel Portillo and its two nearby lodges, which requires a minimum one-week stay.

GETTING HERE AND AROUND
Portillo is three hours north of Santiago. Call the hotel there ahead of time to find out about road conditions.

By car from Santiago, take the Américo Vespucio beltway north and exit onto the Los Libertadores Highway to Los Andes. From Los Andes, take the International Highway (Ruta 60) east until you reach the resort. International car rental agencies (such as Hertz and Avis) in Santiago can provide vehicles equipped with snow chains for climbs to the Andes.

Skitotal has service to Portillo; buses depart from the company's office on Avenida Apoquindo on Wednesdays and Saturdays only. Buses depart as they fill starting at 7:30 am; a round-trip ticket (same day) costs 23,000 pesos. Private transfers cost from 150,000 pesos (one to three people) to 210,000 (7 to 10 people). The company also offers hotel and airport-to-slopes service. Expediciones Manzur runs mini-buses to Portillo on Sunday for 28,000 pesos. Buses leave at 8:30 am from Ramón Carnicer 5, just off Plaza Baquedano. Prior booking is essential.

ESSENTIALS
Bus Contacts Expediciones Manzur ✉ *Sotero del Rio 475, Suite 507, Santiago Centro, Santiago* ☎ *2/2643-5651* ⊕ *www.expedicionesmanzur.cl.* **Skitotal** ✉ *Apoquindo 4900, Las Condes, Santiago* ☎ *2/2246-0156* ⊕ *www.skitotal.cl.*

WHERE TO STAY

$$$$
HOTEL
ALL-INCLUSIVE

🏨 **Hotel Portillo.** Situated high in the Andes, this is a boutique resort with big skiing. Pros: with few day visitors, runs and lifts are never crowded; friendly international atmosphere. Cons: minimum seven-night stay; in bad weather, the road can become blocked, cutting off transport from Santiago. $ *Rooms from: 352000 pesos* ⊠ *Ruta 60 (Camino a Mendoza), Portillo* ☎ *2/2361–7000 hotel, 2/2263–0606 office in Santiago, 800/829–5325 toll-free in U.S.* ⊕ *www.skiportillo.com* ⇆ *120 rooms and family apartments, 6 suites* ❂ *All-inclusive.*

SPORTS AND THE OUTDOORS

SKIING

Portillo. The slopes here were discovered by engineers building the now-defunct railroad that linked Chile to Argentina. After the railroad was inaugurated in 1910, skiing aficionados headed here despite the fact that there were no facilities available. Hotel Portillo, the only accommodation in the area, opened its doors in 1949, making Portillo the country's first ski resort, and went on to host the World Ski Championships in 1966. Today, it has 35 runs—the longest of these, Juncalillo, stretches 3.2 km (2 miles)—for beginners through to experts, as well as 14 lifts. The most famous run is the very steep Roca Jack, used for training by Olympic ski teams. Day visitors can dine in the *auto-servicio* (cafeteria-style) restaurant, at Tío Bob's restaurant, in the main dining room (most formal option), or at the Ski Box for on-slope snacks. Equipment rentals are available for around 20,000 pesos per day. ⊠ *Ruta 60 (Camino a Mendoza), Portillo* ☎ *2/2263–0606, 800/829–5325 toll-free in U.S.* ⊕ *www.skiportillo.com* ⛷ *29,000–39,000 pesos* ☾ *Mid-June–mid-Oct.*

THE CENTRAL
COAST

WELCOME TO THE CENTRAL COAST

TOP REASONS TO GO

★ **Riding the ascensores:** Valparaíso's steep hills are smoothed out a bit by the *ascensores*, or funiculars, that shuttle locals between their jobs near the port and their homes in the hills.

★ **Beautiful beaches:** Thousands of Santiaguinos flock to the Central Coast's beaches every summer, where dozens and dozens of seafood shacks serve the masses.

★ **Superb shopping:** The streets of Cerro Alegro and Cerro Concepción in Valparaíso are lined with shops selling everything from finely wrought jewelry to hand-tooled leather, while Viña has everything from large department stores and outlet malls to trendy shops and boutiques.

★ **Seafood straight from the net:** Almost every town on the Central Coast has its own wharf where fishermen land with last night's catch. Bustling with shoppers, the *caleta* offers an excellent biology lesson on the diversity of sea life in addition to, of course, many a gastronomic treat.

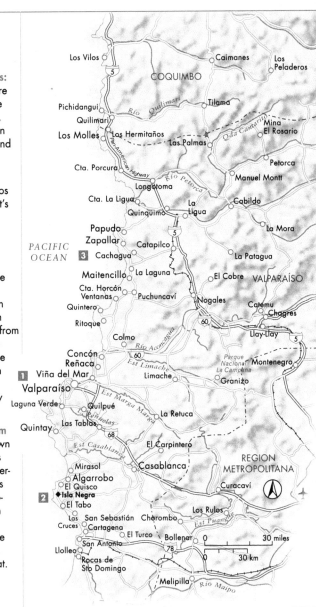

CAR TRAVEL

Since it's so easy to get around in Valparaíso and Viña del Mar, there's no need to rent a car unless you want to travel to other towns on the coast.

TRAIN TRAVEL

The bright, spacious Merval commuter train links Valparaíso with Viña del Mar. It runs every 12 minutes from 6 am to 11:30 pm on weekdays, and from 8 am to 10 pm on weekends and holidays. Check out the website to plan your trip: ⊕ *www.metro-valparaiso.cl.*

RESTAURANTS

Dining is one of the great pleasures of visiting the Central Coast. It's not rare to see fishermen bringing the day's catch straight to the restaurants that inevitably line the shore. Your server will be happy to share with you which fish were caught fresh that day. Try *corvina a la margarita* (sea bass in shellfish sauce) or *ostiones a la parmesana* (scallops served with melted Parmesan cheese). The more daring can also try a batch of raw shellfish bought direct from the fishermen's nets and served with a dash of lemon. With the exception of major holidays or fancier restaurants, reservations are almost never required here. Many restaurants still close between lunch and dinner: from 3 or 4 to 7 or 8.

HOTELS

Because the central beach resorts were developed by and for the Santiago families who summer here, they are dominated by vacation homes and apartments, although new, often upmarket hotels have been built especially around Valparaíso, Viña del Mar, Reñaca, and Concón. Cabañas, somewhat rustic cabins with a kitchenette and one or more bedrooms, are designed to accommodate families on tighter budgets. An even more affordable option is a *residencial* (guesthouse), often just a few rooms for rent in a private home. *Hotel reviews have been shortened. For full information, visit Fodors.com.*

WHAT IT COSTS IN CHILEAN PESOS (IN THOUSANDS)			
$	$$	$$$	$$$$
Under 6	6–8	9–11	over 11
Under 46	46–75	76–105	over 105

nts

Restaurant prices are the average cost of a main course at dinner or, if dinner is not served, at lunch. Hotel prices are the lowest cost of a standard double room in high season, excluding tax.

PARAÍSO AND VIÑA DEL MAR

Viña del Mar and Valparaíso (Vineyard of the Sea and Paradise Valley, respectively) each maintain an aura that warrants their dreamy appellations. Only minutes apart, these two urban centers are nevertheless as different as twin cities can be. Valparaíso won the heart of poet Pablo Neruda, who praised its "cluster of crazy houses," and it continues to

1 Valparaíso and Viña del Mar. The twin cities of Chile's Central Coast could not be more different. The winding streets of Valparaíso, a once great port, are filled with historic monuments recalling their 19th-century glory. Thanks to a tourism boom and UNESCO's naming of the city as a World Heritage Site, a cultural renaissance is underway. Neighboring Viña del Mar has the country's largest casino, some of Chile's most elegant hotels, and a sharp nightlife scene that make it an excellent place to blow off some steam.

2 The Southern Beaches. Isla Negra, the oceanside retreat of Pablo Neruda, South America's most famous poet, is the main attraction south of Valparaíso. Along the way, don't miss the relaxed charms of Algarrobo or Quintay, a forgotten former whaling station.

3 The Northern Beaches. The beaches north of Viña have something for every type of traveler, from the beautiful young crowd at Reñaca and the summer bustle of Concón to easygoing Maitencillo and stunning Zapallar, an exclusive seaside resort for Santiago's rich and powerful.

GETTING ORIENTED

3

The Central Coast lies two hours west of Santiago, across the Coastal mountains. Dominated by the overlapping cities of Valparaíso and Viña del Mar, this is where stressed Santiaguinos come to sunbathe, party, and gorge on seafood every moment they can. In the summer, even the smallest resort can heave with visitors, but outside of January and February they can be quiet. Two of Neruda's three homes—La Sebastiana, nestled in the hills of Valparaíso, and his beach-side abode in small-town Isla Negra—are found along Chile's Central Coast. The sundry objects he collected in his vast travels around the globe inhabit his former residences and give each one a life of their own.

Updated by Anthony Esposito

Most people head to the Central Coast for a single reason: the beaches. Yes, some may be drawn by the rough grandeur of the windswept coastline, with its rocky islets inhabited by sea lions and penguins, yet this stretch of coastline west of Santiago has much more than sun and surf. The biggest surprise is the charm of Valparaíso, Chile's second-largest city. It shares a bay with Viña del Mar but the similarities end there. Valparaíso is a bustling port town with a jumble of colorful cottages nestled in the folds of its many hills. Viña del Mar has lush parks surrounding neoclassical mansions and a long beach lined with luxury high-rises. Together they form an interesting contrast of working class and wealth at play.

The *balnearios* (small beach towns) to the north and south of the twin cities have their own character, often defined by coastal topography. You can take a long stroll along the stone path built between the mansions and rocks that jut out into the Pacific in Zapallar; watch or join the surfers in Maitencillo; indulge yourself in the culinary delights of Concón; gawk at the sculpted bodies that strut around Reñaca's hip beach; visit a former whaling station in quaint Quintay; discover Neruda's infatuation with the sea in Isla Negra; and take a dip in clear-blue and, yes, chilly water in Algarrobo's El Canelillo.

Proximity to Santiago has resulted in their development—in some cases overdevelopment—as summer resorts. At the beginning of the 20th century, Santiago's elite started building vacation homes. Soon after, when trains connected the capital to beaches, middle-class families started spending their summers at the shore. Improved highway access in recent decades has allowed Chileans of all economic levels to enjoy the occasional beach vacation.

Late December through mid-March, when schools let out for summer vacation and Santiago becomes torrid, the beaches are packed. Vacationers frolic in the chilly sea by day and pack the restaurants and bars at night. The rest of the year, the coast is relatively deserted and, though often cool and cloudy, a pleasantly tranquil place to explore. Local *caletas*—literally meaning "coves," where fishing boats gather to unload their catch, usually the site of local fishing cooperatives—are always colorful and lively.

PLANNING

WHEN TO GO

It seems that all of Chile heads to the coast i of January and February. This can be a great weather at its warmest and the nightlife hopping time to find a room, especially on weekends. Ma in advance as possible. Spring (September, Octobe fall (March, April, and May) can be perfect times are warm and breezy, and the nights cool. Consid shoulder months of December and March, whic but also provide relative solitude in which to exp

FESTIVALS AND SEASONAL EVENTS

The annual Festival Internacional de la Canción Festival) takes place during a week in mid-Febru The concerts are broadcast live on television. Mos processions on Día de San Pedro (June 29). A statu saint of fishermen, is typically hoisted onto a fishin a coastal procession. When the clock strikes midi Eve, the bay that runs from Valparaíso to Concón the world's most spectacular fireworks shows.

PLANNING YOUR TIME

Plan to spend at least two days in Valparaíso, wher funiculars and explore the cobbled streets. While y day trip is an excursion to Pablo Neruda's waterfr Isla Negra. You'll want to take a day or so to stroll beach town of Viña del Mar. After that you can dr coastal highway, stopping for lunch in either Con From there you can return to Viña del Mar or con night in Zapallar.

GETTING HERE AND AROUND

AIR TRAVEL

The Central Coast is served by LAN Airlines, and a riers, via Santiago's Aeropuerto Comodoro Arturo I hour and a half drive from either Viña del Mar or V

BUS TRAVEL

There is hourly bus service between Santiago and bo Viña del Mar. Tur-Bus, Pullman, and other companie tiago's Terminal Alameda, or take buses from metr and avoid most of the capital's traffic. Smaller comp other beach resorts depart from Santiago's Terminal

To get to nearby Reñaca or Concón you can take a *mic* bus) from Viña del Mar, or from Valparaíso to get to L your best bet for getting to the smaller beach towns south of the twin cities is from Valparaíso's bus term as the buses may fill up, especially in summer.

Restaura

Hotels

VAL

CLOSE UP

Beachgoing in Chile

To the vast majority of Chileans, summer holiday means one thing: heading to the beach. Whether on the banks of a southern lake, one of the north's deserted coves, or one of the pleasant towns of the Central Coast, from late December to early March, the beaches are packed. Even where the water is safe enough to enter, the icy Humboldt Current, rushing up from Antarctica, means only the young, the brave, and typically the locals can bear more than a few seconds up to their chests.

There is little reason to move when lying on the beach. Wandering salesmen constantly appear, plying ice cream, drinks, *palmeras* (a heart-shape puff pastry), and other goodies. And watch out for the *promotoras*, scantily clad young women, and increasingly men, promoting everything from batteries to beer. Where permitted, Chileans will set up a *parrilla* for one of their famous *asados*, grilling meat and sausages over a charcoal fire. The athletic may go for a game of *paleta*, batting a tennis ball back and forth with a small wooden racket, or the occasional *pichanga* (pick-up soccer game). If you want to escape the crowds, try walking along to the next beach, which may be surprisingly empty though just a few hundred meters away. The southern end of Maitencillo or the north of Papudo are particularly suitable for exploration.

Strong sun protection in Chile is essential, due to the nearby hole in the ozone layer. Even if the day begins in a fog, the mist quickly burns off, leaving you vulnerable to the sun's rays. Be sure to pack a hat, strong sunblock, and something to cover you up. You might even consider a beach umbrella, often available to rent right on the beach. Once the sun goes down, temperatures can fall quickly as sea breezes pick up, so bring a light jacket or sweater as well.

be a disorderly, bohemian, charming town. Valparaíso's lack of beaches keeps its mind on matters more urban, if not urbane.

Viña del Mar, Valparaíso's glamorous sibling, is a clean, orderly city with miles of beige beach, a glitzy casino, manicured parks, and shopping galore. Viña, together with nearby Reñaca, is synonymous with the best of life for vacationing Chileans. Its beaches gleam, its casino rolls, and its discos sizzle.

VALPARAÍSO

Fodor'sChoice ★ *10 km (6 miles) south of Viña del Mar via Avenida España, 120 km (75 miles) west of Santiago via Ruta 68.*

Valparaíso's dramatic topography—45 *cerros*, or hills, overlooking the ocean—requires the use of winding pathways and wooden *ascensores* (funiculars) to get up many of the grades. The slopes are covered by candy-color houses—there are almost no apartments in the city—most of which have exteriors of corrugated metal peeled from shipping containers decades ago. Valparaíso has served as Santiago's port for centuries. Before the Panama Canal opened, Valparaíso was the busiest port in South America. Harsh realities—changing trade routes, industrial decline—have diminished its importance, but it remains one of Chile's principal ports.

Most shops, banks, restaurants, bars, and other businesses cluster along the handful of streets called *El Plan* (the flat area) that are closest to the shoreline. *Porteños* (which means "the residents of the port") live in the surrounding hills in an undulating array of colorful abodes. At the top of any of the dozens of stairways, the *paseos* (promenades) have spectacular views; many are named after prominent Yugoslavian, Basque, and German immigrants. Neighborhoods are named for the hills they cover.

With the jumble of power lines overhead and the hundreds of buses that slow down—but never completely stop—to pick up agile riders, it's hard to forget you're in a city. Still, walking is the best way to experience Valparaíso. Be careful where you step, though—locals aren't very conscientious about curbing their dogs.

GETTING HERE AND AROUND

By car from Santiago, take Ruta 68 west through the coastal mountains and the Casablanca Valley as far as you can go, until the road descends into Valparaíso's Avenida Argentina, on the city's eastern edge. If you don't have a car, Tur-Bus, Pullman, and Condor buses leave several times an hour for Valparaíso and Viña del Mar from Santiago. Tur-Bus and Pullman both leave from Terminal Alameda (the Universidad de Santiago Metro station), while Condor and Sol del Pacífico use Terminal Santiago (Estación Central station). Alternatively, you can save yourself a crawl through Santiago by catching a bus from the Pajaritos Metro station on the city's western edge.

If you're using Valparaíso as your hub, you can use Pullman Bus to get to most coastal towns south of the city. Tur-Bus heads north to Cachagua, Zapallar, Papudo, and other towns. Sol del Pacífico also runs buses to the northern beaches. Valparaíso has two information booths: one at Muelle Prat that is supposedly open daily 10–2 and 3–6 (although in real life the hours vary wildly).

TIMING AND PRECAUTIONS

You need a good pair of shoes to fully appreciate Valparaíso. Walking past all the sights, exploring the museums, and enjoying a meal and drinks makes for a long, full day. You might visit La Sebastiana the next morning to give yourself more time to linger. Definitely bring sunblock or a hat. Even if it's cloudy when you start, the sun often comes out by afternoon.

TOURS

Fodor'sChoice **Tours 4 Tips.** Undoubtedly, the best way to explore Valparaíso's twist-
★ ing streets is on foot. The Tours 4 Tips walking tour leaves from Plaza Sotomayor every day at 10 am and 3 pm; simply look for an individual in a striped shirt that resembles the popular "Where's Waldo" character. This three-hour tour gives you a premier introduction to the port city's history, unique culture, culinary delights, and street art. There is no charge up front, but a generous tip is expected (10,000 Chilean

pesos or more). ⊠ *Plaza Sotomayor* ⊕ *www.tours4tips.com* ⊠ *Free, but tips are expected.*

ESSENTIALS

Bus Contacts Condor Bus ☎ *32/259-4682* ⊕ *www.condorbus.cl.* **Pullman Bus** ☎ *32/225-3125, 32/259-6690* ⊕ *www.ventapasajes.cl.* **Sol del Pacífico** ☎ *32/221-3776, 32/279-5700.* **Tur-Bus** ☎ *32/221-2028* ⊕ *www.turbus.cl.* **Valparaíso Bus Depot** ⊠ *Av. Pedro Montt 2800* ☎ *32/223-7209.*

Rental Cars Rosselot ⊠ *Victoria 2675* ☎ *32/235-2365* ⊕ *www.rosselot.cl/rent-a-car.*

Visitor Information Tourism Office ⊠ *Condell 1490* ☎ *32/293-9262* ⊕ *www.ciudaddevalparaiso.cl.* **Valparaíso Muelle Prat office** ⊠ *Muelle Prat.*

EXPLORING

TOP ATTRACTIONS

Ascensor El Peral. The steep El Peral funicular, constructed in 1902 and considered a national monument, runs 52 meters from the Palacio de Justicia (court house) on the edge of Plaza Sotomayor, up to the gorgeous Paseo Yugoslavo on Cerro Alegre, where the Palacio Baburizza houses a fine arts museum. ⊠ *Plaza Sotomayor, Cerro Alegre.*

Ascensor Reina Victoria. This funicular, dating from 1902, is often toted as Valparaíso's most beautiful. The 40-meter ride, mostly vertical, connects Avenida Elías near Plaza Aníbal Pinto with Cerro Concepción. Once atop the hill, you'll come out to a small plaza where you can swoosh down a small metallic slide if your inner child so desires. ⊠ *Elías, Cerro Concepción.*

Fodor's Choice ★ **Cerro Concepción.** Ride the Ascensor Concepción to this hilltop neighborhood covered with houses and cobblestone streets. The greatest attraction is the view, which is best appreciated from Paseo Gervasoni, a wide promenade to the right when you exit the ascensor, and Paseo Atkinson, one block to the east. Over the balustrades that line the promenades are amazing vistas of the city and bay. Nearly as fascinating are the narrow streets above them, some of which are quite steep. Continue uphill to Cerro Alegre, which has a bit of a bohemian flair. ⊠ *Ascensor Concepción, Prat.*

Fodor's Choice ★ **La Sebastiana.** People come to La Sebastiana to marvel at the same ocean that inspired so much of Pablo Neruda's poetry. The house is named for Sebastián Collado, a Spanish architect who began to construct it as a home for himself but died before it was finished. The incomplete building stood abandoned for 10 years before Neruda finished it, revising the design (he had no need for the third-floor aviary or the helicopter landing pad) and adding curvaceous walls, narrow stairways, a tower, and a polymorphous character. A maze of twisting stairwells leads to an upper room where a video shows Neruda enunciating the five syllables of the city's name over and again as he rides the city's ascensores. The upper berth contains his desk, books, and some original manuscripts. What makes the visit to La Sebastiana memorable, however, is Neruda's nearly obsessive delight in physical objects. The house is a shrine to his many cherished things, such as the beautiful orange-pink bird he brought back embalmed from Venezuela. His lighter spirit is here

Valparaíso

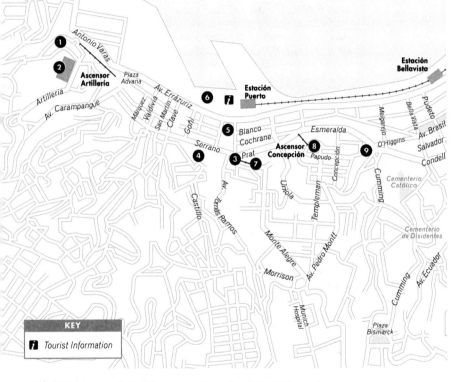

Bahía de Valparaíso

Estación Bellavista

Ascensor Artillería

Plaza Advana

Estación Puerto

Plaza Sotomayor

Ascensor Concepción

Cementerio Católico

Cementerio de Disidentes

Munich Hospital

Plaza Bismarck

KEY

i *Tourist Information*

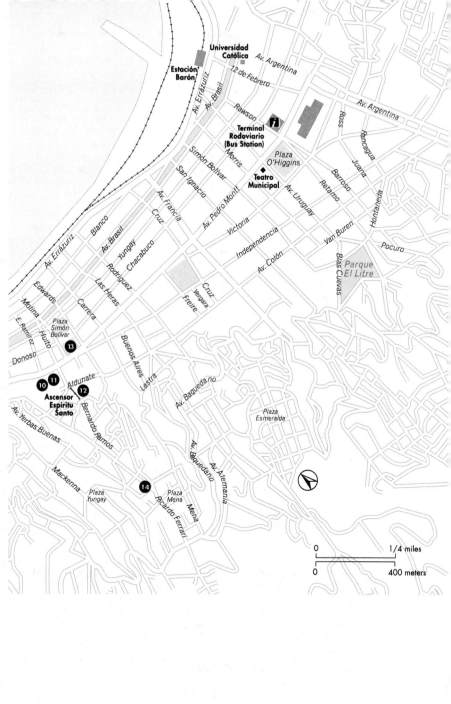

also, in the carousel horse and the pink-and-yellow barroom stuffed with kitsch. ✉ *Ferrari 692* ☎ *32/225–6606* ⊕ *www.fundacionneruda. org* 🎫 *5,000 pesos* 🕙 *Jan. and Feb., Tues.–Sun. 10:30–6:50; Mar.–Dec., Tues.–Sun. 10:10–6.*

Muelle Prat. Though its name translates as Prat Dock, the muelle is actually a wharf with steps leading to the water. Sailors from the ships in the harbor arrive in *lanchas* (small boats), or board them for the trip back to their vessels. It's a great place to enjoy the port buzz and watch ships anchored in the harbor. To get a closer look, you can board one of the lanchas—it costs 1,000 pesos for a trip out to a ship and back, or 20,000 pesos for a 60-minute tour of the bay. Here you'll also find the tourist information office and a row of souvenir shops. ✉ *Av. Errázuriz at Plaza Sotomayor.*

Museo a Cielo Abierto (*The Open Sky Museum*). This museum is a winding walk past 20 official murals (and a handful of unofficial ones) by some of Chile's best painters. There's even one by the country's most famous artist, Roberto Matta. The path is not marked—there's no real fixed route—as the point is to get lost in the city's history and culture. ✉ *Ascensor Espíritu Santo up to Cerro Buenavista.*

Fodor's Choice ★   **Museo de Bellas Artes.** The Art Nouveau Palacio Baburizza, built in 1916, houses the city's fine-arts museum. Former owner Pascual Baburizza donated this large collection of European paintings to the city. The fanciful decorative exterior is reminiscent of the style of Spanish architect Antoni Gaudí—note the bronze children dancing around the portico. The paintings and the impressive mansion itself take you on a historical journey through Chile's past. ✉ *Ascensor El Peral to Paseo Yugoslavo, Paseo Yugoslavo 176, Cerro Alegre* ☎ *32/225–2332* ⊕ *www. museobaburizza.cl* 🎫 *2,000 Chilean pesos* 🕙 *Tues.–Sun. 10:30–5:30.*

Plaza Sotomayor. Valparaíso's most impressive square, Plaza Sotomayor, serves as a gateway to the bustling port. **Comandancia en Jefe de la Armada,** headquarters of the Chilean navy, is a grand, gray building that rises to a turreted pinnacle over a mansard roof. At the north end of the plaza stands the **Monumento de los Héroes de Iquique,** which honors Arturo Prat and other heroes of the War of the Pacific. In the middle of the square (beware of traffic—cars and buses come suddenly from all directions) is the **Museo del Sitio.** Artifacts from the city's mid-19th-century port, including parts of a dock that once stood on this spot, are displayed in the open under glass. ✉ *Av. Errázuriz at Cochrane.*

WORTH NOTING

Galería Municipal de Arte. This crypt in the basement of the Palacio Lyon is the finest art space in the city. Temporary exhibits by top-caliber Chilean artists are displayed on stone walls under a series of brick arches. It's easy to miss the entrance, which is on Calle Condell just beyond the Museo de Historia Natural de Valparaíso. ✉ *Condell 1550* ☎ *32/293–9568, 32/293–9667* ⊕ *www.munivalpo.cl/cultura* 🎫 *Free* 🕙 *Mon.–Sat. 10–7.*

Museo de Historia Natural de Valparaíso. Within the Palacio Lyon, one of the few buildings to survive the devastating 1906 earthquake is this rather outdated natural history museum. Among the more unusual exhibits are a pre-Columbian mummy, newborn conjoined twins in formaldehyde, and stuffed penguins. ⊠ *Condell 1546* ☎ *32/254–4840* ⊕ *www.mhnv.cl* 🎟 *Free* ⊙ *Tues.–Sat. 10–6, Sun. 10–2.*

Museo Lord Cochrane. There's a small collection of naval paraphernalia here, but the real reason for a visit is to see the house itself, constructed for Lord Thomas Cochrane. The colonial-style house, with its red-tile roof and stately wood columns, is one of the most beautiful in Valparaíso. As you might expect for an admiral's abode, it has wonderful views of the port. ⊠ *Merlet 195* ☎ *32/293–9558* 🎟 *Free* ⊙ *Tues.–Sun. 10–6.*

Museo Naval y Marítimo de Valparaíso. Atop Cerro Artillería is the large neoclassical mansion that once housed the country's naval academy. It now contains a maritime museum, with displays that document the history of the port and the ships that once defended it. Cannons positioned on the front lawn frame the excellent view of the ocean. ⊠ *Ascensor Artillería up to Paseo 21 de Mayo 45, Paseo 21 de Mayo 45* ☎ *32/243–7651* 🎟 *1,000 pesos* ⊙ *Tues.–Sun. 10–5:30.*

Paseo 21 de Mayo. Ascensor Artillería pulls you uphill to Paseo 21 de Mayo, a wide promenade surrounded by well-tended gardens and stately trees from which you can survey the port and a goodly portion of the city through coin-operated binoculars. A gazebo—a good place to escape the sun—seems to be hanging in midair. Paseo 21 de Mayo is in the middle of Cerro Playa Ancha, one of the city's more colorful neighborhoods. ⊠ *Ascensor Artillería at Plaza Advana.*

FAMILY **Plaza Victoria.** The heart of the lower part of the city is this green plaza with a lovely fountain bordered by four female statues representing the seasons. Two black lions at the edge of the park look across the street to the neo-Gothic cathedral and its unusual freestanding bell tower. ⊠ *Condell at Molina.*

BEACHES

If it's beaches you're after, head to Viña del Mar or one of the other resort towns along the coast.

Laguna Verde. A short bus ride south of the city is Laguna Verde, a largely uncrowded stretch of shore that is absolutely gorgeous. There are no eateries, so make sure to pack a picnic. **Amenities: none. Best for:** swimming; solitude; sunset.

Playa Las Torpederas. Valparaíso has only one notable beach, Playa Las Torpederas, a sheltered crescent of sand east of the port. Though less attractive than the beaches up the coast, it does have very calm water. **Amenities:** food and drink; parking. **Best for:** sunset; swimming.

WHERE TO EAT

$ ✕ **Bar Restaurant San Carlos.** If you were to ask a local to take you to a
CHILEAN traditional restaurant, chances are you would wind up here. The family-owned establishment features a long wooden bar, older gentlemen playing dominos, and the star dish: *causeo* (cow feet cut into squares and cooked till the fat melts away, mixed with onions, chili, beans, and vineger and served cold.) It's tastier than it sounds, and besides,

Chilean Coastal Cuisine

"In the turbulent sea of Chile lives the golden conger eel," wrote Chilean poet Pablo Neruda in a simple verse that leaves the real poetry for the dinner table. To many, dining is the principal pleasure of a trip to the Central Coast. Along with that succulent conger eel, *congrio*, menus here typically have *corvina* (sea bass), a whitefish called *reineta*, and the mild *lenguado* (sole). The appetizer selection, which is invariably extensive, usually includes *ostiones* (scallops), *machas* (razor clams), *camarones* (shrimp), and *jaiba* (crab). Because lobster is extremely rare in Chilean waters, it's more expensive here than just about anywhere in the world.

Fish and meat dishes are often served alone, which means that if you want french fries, mashed potatoes, a salad, or *palta* (avocado), you have to order it as an *agregado* (side dish). Bread, a bowl of lemons, and a sauce called *pebre* (a mix of tomato, onion, coriander, parsley, and often chili) are always brought to the table. Valparaíso is known for a hearty, cheap meal called *chorillana*—a mountain of minced steak, onions, cheese, and eggs on a bed of french fries.

you only live once. $ *Average main: 5000 pesos* ⊠ *Las Heras 684, on corner of Colón* ☎ *32/223–4043.*

$$
SEAFOOD
✕ **Bote Salvavidas.** This restaurant on Muelle Prat has great views of the harbor from its glass-walled dining room. As you might guess, it specializes in seafood. Dishes such as *congrio margarita* (conger eel with shellfish sauce), *caldillo de marisco* (shellfish chowder), and *pastel de jaiba* (crab pie) are among the popular specialties. $ *Average main: 7500 pesos* ⊠ *Muelle Prat* ☎ *32/225–1477* ⊕ *www.restaurantbotesalvavidas.cl.*

$$
ECLECTIC
✕ **Brighton.** Nestled on the edge of Cerro Concepción, this popular restaurant has an amazing view from its black-and-white-tiled balcony. Vintage advertisements hang on the walls of the intimate dining room. A limited menu includes standards such as *machas a la parmesana* (razor clams with Parmesan) and ceviche, as well as several kinds of crepes and hearty Chilean sandwiches. An extensive wine list and cocktail selection make it a popular night spot, especially on weekends, when there's live music. $ *Average main: 7500 pesos* ⊠ *Paseo Atkinson 151* ☎ *32/222–3513* ⊕ *www.brighton.cl.*

$$$$
SEAFOOD
Fodor's Choice
★
✕ **Café Turri.** Near the top of Ascensor Concepción, this 19th-century mansion commands some of the best views of Valparaíso. It holds one of the city's best-known restaurants, and the menu has a French twist: onion soup with Gruyère and foie gras sits alongside excellent seafood. In the newspaper-cum-menu, you can read about local art shows and upcoming concerts. Outside there's a terrace, and inside are two floors of dining rooms. $ *Average main: 12500 pesos* ⊠ *Templeman 147, at Paseo Gervasoni* ☎ *32/225–2091, 32/236–5307* ⊕ *www.turri.cl.*

$$$
CHILEAN
✕ **Café Vinilo.** Serving traditional Chilean cuisine with a contemporary touch, Café Vinilo prides itself on making its own beer, bread, and desserts. They also work directly with their food suppliers, so you can rest assured the rock fish ceviche on your plate was likely caught that same

morning by a diver in Quintero, an hour's drive north along the coast. [$] *Average main: 9000 pesos* ✉ *Almirante Montt 448, Cerro Alegre* ☎ *32/223–0665.*

$$ CHILEAN 🍴 **Casino Social J. Cruz M.** This eccentric restaurant is a Valparaíso institution, thanks to its legendary status for inventing the *chorillana* (minced beef with onions, cheese, and an egg atop french fries), which is now served by most local restaurants. There is no menu—choose either a plate of *chorillana* for two or three, or *carne mechada* (stewed beef), with a side of french fries, rice, or tomato salad. Glass cases choked with dusty trinkets surround tables covered with plastic cloths in the cramped dining room. You may have to share a table. The restaurant is at the end of a bleak corridor off Calle Condell. [$] *Average main: 7000 pesos* ✉ *Condell 1466, Casa 11* ☎ *32/221–1225* 🌐 *www.jcruz.cl* 💳 *No credit cards.*

$ CHILEAN 🍴 **El Desayunador.** If you're in the mood for breakfast in the morning or the afternoon, this restaurant, with a name that roughly translates as "the breakfast hall," is perfect. In the heart of one of Cerro Alegre's main drags, El Desayunador not only serves up a great coffee and eggs, but also tasty sandwiches and salads. This cozy spot has quickly become a favorite among tourists. [$] *Average main: 3500 pesos* ✉ *Almirante Montt 399, Cerro Alegre* ☎ *32/236–5933.*

$$$$ SEAFOOD 🍴 **La Colombina.** This restaurant is in an old home on Cerro Alegre, in one of the city's most beautiful hilltop neighborhoods. Dining rooms on two floors are notable for their elegant furnishings, stained-glass windows, and impressive views of the city and sea. Seafood dominates the menu, with such inventive dishes as breaded sea bass with lentils, bacon, and anchovies, or Magellanic lamb roasted with orange-and-red-wine sauce. Choose from a list of 80 national wines. [$] *Average main: 12500 pesos* ✉ *Paseo Apolo 91, off Paseo Yugoslavo, Cerro Alegre* ☎ *32/223–6254* 🌐 *www.restaurantlacolombina.cl.*

$$$ ITALIAN Fodor's Choice ★ 🍴 **Pasta y Vino.** One of the hippest spots on fashionable Cerro Concepción, Pasta y Vino is usually packed, and the hosts look like they have escaped from a fashion magazine. The imaginative Italian food is just as attractive. Try gnocchi made from beetroot, chestnuts, or aubergine, or ravioli stuffed with salmon in curry sauce. The wine list, focusing on local vintages, is impressive. The hip young staff in floor-length black aprons couldn't be more accommodating. [$] *Average main: 10000 pesos* ✉ *Papudo 427, Cerro Concepción* ☎ *32/249–6187* 🌐 *pastaevinoristorante.cl* ✍ *Reservations essential* ⏲ *Closed Mon.*

$$ SEAFOOD 🍴 **Sabor Color.** This trendy restaurant in a turn-of-the-century home has a rotating collection of art (for sale) hanging on its brightly colored walls, which is evocative of Valparaíso's hills. There's also a small stage on the second floor for live music on the weekends. But the real allure is its dishes, such as *congrio del huerto* (country conger eel) cooked over asparagus and sauteéd tomatoes with a touch of bacon in a light butter and seafood broth. The cocktail bar, with its myriad preparations of piscos, is also impressive. [$] *Average main: 8000 pesos* ✉ *Templeman 561, Cerro Concepción* ☎ *32/259–8472* 🌐 *www.saborcolor.cl.*

WHERE TO STAY

$$$$
B&B/INN
Fodor$Choice
★

🏨 **Casa Higueras.** The hills of Valparaiso have enjoyed a boom of boutique hotels in the last decade, but this one is a cut above the rest. **Pros:** a rare spot of luxury in Valparaiso. **Cons:** the rest of the street could benefit from a paint job. $ *Rooms from: 197000 pesos* ✉ *Higueras 133, Cerro Alegre* ☎ *32/249–7900* ⊕ *www.casahigueras.cl* ⬎ *20 rooms, including 3 suites* ⑩ *Breakfast.*

$$$
B&B/INN
Fodor$Choice
★

🏨 **Casa Thomas Somerscales.** Perched high atop Cerro Alegre, between ascensores El Peral and Reina Victoria, this palm-shaded mansion has an unobstructed view of the sea. **Pros:** light, bright rooms in the heart of hip Valpo. **Cons:** a steep climb back to your room at night. $ *Rooms from: 79000 pesos* ✉ *San Enrique 446, Cerro Alegre* ☎ *32/233–1379* ⊕ *www.hotelsomerscales.cl* ⬎ *8 rooms* ⑩ *Breakfast.*

$$
B&B/INN

🏨 **Fauna Hotel.** As the name suggests, Fauna stays true to its natural surroundings: the floors, stairs, and handrails are made from recycled native wood, adobe is used generously in the architecture, and the span of the hotel's interior street-side wall, extending some two floors, is actually the exposed containment wall originally constructed to keep Cerro Alegre standing. **Pros:** incredible views of the bay; centrally located. **Cons:** a bit boisterous. $ *Rooms from: 70000 pesos* ✉ *Pasaje Dimalow 166, Cerro Alegre* ☎ *32/327–0719* ⊕ *www.faunahotel.cl* ⬎ *15 rooms, 2 suites* ⑩ *No meals.*

$$
B&B/INN
Fodor$Choice
★

🏨 **Gran Hotel Gervasoni.** Set in a sprawling Victorian mansion that spreads across five floors, the Gervasoni is a chance to step back in time into Valparaíso's past. **Pros:** a chance to imagine life in Valparaíso's Victorian apogee. **Cons:** steep stairs may not suit all legs, and the views are rather spoiled by a concrete office block. $ *Rooms from: 59000 pesos* ✉ *Paseo Gervasoni 1, Cerro Concepción* ☎ *32/223–9236* ⊕ *www.hotelgervasoni.com* ⬎ *14 rooms* ⑩ *Breakfast.*

$
B&B/INN
Fodor$Choice
★

🏨 **Hotel Brighton B&B.** This bright-yellow Victorian house enjoys an enviable location at the edge of tranquil Cerro Concepción. **Pros:** unmatched views across Valpo and the bay. **Cons:** some of the rooms are a bit noisy. $ *Rooms from: 45000 pesos* ✉ *Paseo Atkinson 151, Cerro Concepción* ☎ *32/222–3513* ⊕ *www.brighton.cl* ⬎ *8 rooms, 1 suite* ⑩ *Breakfast.*

$$
B&B/INN

🏨 **Hotel Manoir Atkinson.** One of the first boutique hotels to spring up on fashionable Cerro Concepción and Cerro Alegre, this cozy house lies at the end of Paseo Atkinson, near many local attractions. **Pros:** many of Valparaíso's best restaurants are just a block or two away. **Cons:** despite location, many of the rooms lack sea views. $ *Rooms from: 65000 pesos* ✉ *Paseo Atkinson 165, Cerro Concepción* ☎ *32/327–5425* ⊕ *www.hotelatkinson.cl* ⬎ *6 rooms, 1 suite* ⑩ *Breakfast.*

$$$$
B&B/INN

🏨 **Palacio Astoreca Hotel.** Complete with a piano bar, wine cellar, spa, massage room, indoor heated swimming pool, wood-fire heated Jacuzzi, and indoor garden, this hotel seeks to please. **Pros:** a beautiful setting in a renovated Victorian mansion. **Cons:** a bit pricey, but well worth it. $ *Rooms from: 189000 pesos* ✉ *Calle Montealegre 149, Cerro Alegre* ☎ *32/327–7700* ⊕ *www.hotelpalacioastoreca.com* ⬎ *17 rooms, 6 suites* ⑩ *No meals.*

$$$$
B&B/INN

🏨 **Zerohotel.** Perched on one of the quieter corners of bustling Cerro Alegre, this former Dutch diplomat's residence dating to to the 1880s, has been transformed into a chic boutique hotel. **Pros:** a quiet, relaxing corner on Cerro Alegre's normally bustling streets. **Cons:** no restaurant. [$] *Rooms from: 135000 pesos* ✉ *Lautaro Rosas 343, Cerro Alegre* ☎ *32/211–3113* 🌐 *www.zerohotel.com* 🛏 *9 rooms* 🍴 *Breakfast.*

NIGHTLIFE AND PERFORMING ARTS

Valparaíso has an inordinate number of nocturnal establishments, which run the gamut from pubs to tango bars and salsa dance clubs. Thursday through Saturday nights most places get crowded between 11 pm and midnight and young people stay out until dawn. The main concentrations of bars and clubs are on Subida Ecuador, near Plaza Anibal Pinto, and a block of Avenida Errázuriz nearby. Cerro Concepción, Alegre, and Bellavista have quieter options, many with terraces perfect for admiring the city lights.

3

BARS

It's not surprising that there are a handful of bars surrounding the dock. The rougher ones west of Plaza Sotomayor are primarily patronized by sailors, whereas those to the east welcome just about anybody.

Bar de Pisco. True to its name, this venue specializes in pisco, the national drink distilled from muscat grapes. There are more than 30 different available brands here. The bartenders in this cramped bar serve up delicious cocktails, such as *el apiado* (pisco, lime juice, celery, and lemon juice), or shots of *aguardiente* (various distilled spirits) that have been infused with vanilla, cinnamon, or basil. ✉ *Almirante Montt 484, Cerro Alegre* ☎ *32/319–2161.*

Bar La Playa. The huge antique mirrors of Bar La Playa, just west of Plaza Sotomayor, give it a historic feel. It becomes packed with party animals after midnight on weekends in January and February. ✉ *Serrano 567* ☎ *32/225–2838* 🌐 *www.barlaplaya.cl.*

Bar Victoria. Fishing nets hanging from the ceiling, brightly polished wood floors, and black-and-white photos on the walls give this bar-restaurant an old-fashioned feel. Patrons come for a bite to eat, from *chorrillana* (french fries topped with eggs, onions, and beef) to ceviche, and then stay for the beer on tap. ✉ *Salvador Donoso 1540* ☎ *32/245–9387.*

Cassot Bar. On busy Subida Ecuador street, where a good chunk of the port's nightlife resides, Cassot Bar is perfect for an early casual conversation or a late romping party. The DJ plays indie, new wave, Britpop, and electronic music. ✉ *Subida Ecuador 110* ☎ *9/8954–1659.*

El Viaje Bar. Take a trip to this late-night haunt and have a seat on a trolley bus that has been outfitted with tables. There is live music on certain nights. ✉ *Subida Cumming 93* ☎ *9/7488–9513.*

LIVE MUSIC

Tango dancing is so popular in Valparaíso that you might think you were in Buenos Aires.

Brighton. On Cerro Concepción, Brighton has live bolero music on Friday and tango on Saturday, starting at 11 pm. Its black-and-white tile terrace overlooks the city's glittering lights. ✉ *Paseo Atkinson 151, Cerro Concepción* ☎ *32/222–3513.*

Cinzano. Dance to live tango music weekends at Cinzano, an old-fashioned watering hole facing Plaza Anibal Pinto. The walls above the bar are decorated with scenes of old Valparaíso, including some notable shipwrecks. ⊠ *Anibal Pinto 1182* ☎ *32/221–3043.*

Color Café. On Cerro Concepción, tiny Color Café serves up live Latin music on weekends and brunch and sandwiches throughout the week. ⊠ *Papudo 526* ☎ *32/222–6687.*

La Colombina. On Cerro Alegre, La Colombina has live Latin music during the weekend. ⊠ *Paseo Yugoeslavo 15, Cerro Alegre* ☎ *32/223–6245, 32/317–8151* ⊕ *www.restaurantlacolombina.cl.*

Fodor's Choice
★
La Piedra Feliz. A classic in this port city, concert fans should check out La Piedra Feliz, which hosts performances by Chile's best bands Tuesday through Saturday. The music starts at 9 pm on weeknights and 11 pm on weekends. Wednesday is jazz night. ⊠ *Av. Errázuriz 1054* ☎ *32/225–6788, 9/8921–3389* ⊕ *www.lapiedrafeliz.cl.*

PERFORMING ARTS VENUE

Teatro Municipal de Valparaíso. Off Plaza O'Higgins, the lovely old Teatro Municipal de Valparaíso hosts symphonies, ballet, and opera May through November. ⊠ *Uruguay 410* ☎ *32/225–7480.*

SPORTS AND THE OUTDOORS

BOATING

Muelle Prat Boat Tours. Informal boat operators at Muelle Prat take groups on a 30-minute circuit of the bay. If you have several people, consider hiring your own boat for 30,000 pesos. ▧ *From 3,000 Chilean pesos.*

SOCCER

Estadio Municipal. Valparaíso's first-division soccer team is the Santiago Wanderers. Home matches are usually held at the Estadio Municipal in Playa Ancha. ⊠ *Independencia 2061* ☎ *32/221–7210* ⊕ *www. santiagowanderers.cl.*

SHOPPING

Outside of Santiago, there are more shops in Valparaíso than anywhere else in Chile. If it's handicrafts you're looking for, head to the bohemian neighborhoods of Cerro Concepción and Cerro Alegre. There are dozens of workshops where you can watch artisans ply their crafts.

Feria de Antigüedades. The weekend flea market, Feria de Antigüedades, has an excellent selection of antiques. ⊠ *Av. Argentina at Plaza O'Higgins.*

Ripley. The country's major department store chain, Ripley, is across from Plaza Victoria. The fifth floor has a food court. ⊠ *Condell 1646* ☎ *600/600–0202* ⊕ *www.ripley.cl.*

Taller Arte en Plata. Taller Arte en Plata displays necklaces, bracelets, and rings, almost all made from silver. ⊠ *Lautaro Rosas 449A, Cerro Alegre* ☎ *32/222–2963* ⊕ *www.silverworkshop.cl.*

VIÑA DEL MAR

130 km (85 miles) northwest of Santiago.

Viña del Mar has high-rise apartment buildings that tower above its excellent shoreline. Here are wide boulevards lined with palms, lush parks, and mansions. Miles of beige sand are washed by heavy surf. The town has been known for years as Chile's tourist capital (a title currently being challenged by several other hot spots) and is currently in the midst of some minor refurbishment.

Viña, as it's popularly known, has the country's oldest casino, excellent hotels, and an extensive selection of restaurants. To some, all this means that Viña del Mar is modern and exciting; to others, it means the city is lacking in character. But there's no denying that Viña del Mar has a little of everything—trendy boutiques, beautiful homes, interesting museums, a casino, varied nightlife, and, of course, one of the best beaches in the country.

GETTING HERE AND AROUND

From Santiago, take Ruta 68 west through the coastal mountains, turning off to Viña del Mar as the vineyards of the Casablanca Valley give way to eucalyptus forests. The spectacular twisting access road (Agua Santa), through hills dotted with Chilean palm trees, drops you on Avenida Alvarez, just a couple of blocks from downtown Viña del Mar. Tur-Bus, Condor, Pullman, and Sol del Pacífico all run buses to Viña del Mar. Tur-Bus leaves from its Alameda terminal. Viña del Mar has the best tourist office on the coast, offering fistfuls of helpful maps and brochures.

ESSENTIALS

Visitor Information Viña del Mar main office ⊠ *Arlegui 715* ☎ *32/218–5710* ⊕ *www.visitevinadelmar.cl* ☼ *Weekdays 9–2 and 3–7; weekends 10–2 and 3–7.*

EXPLORING
TOP ATTRACTIONS

Club Viña del Mar. It would be a shame to pass up a chance to see this private club's magnificent interior. The neoclassical building, constructed in 1901 of materials imported from England, is where wealthy locals come to play snooker, a British variant of billiards. Nonmembers are usually allowed to enter only the grand central hall, but there are often tours of the building during the week. The club hosts occasional concerts during which you may be able to circumambulate the second-floor interior balcony. ⊠ *Plaza Sucre at Av. Valparaíso* ☎ *32/268–0016* ⊕ *www.clubvina.cl.*

Museo de Arqueológico e Historia Francisco Fonck. A 500-year-old stone *moai* (a carved stone head) brought from Easter Island guards the entrance to this archaeological museum. The most interesting exhibits are the finds from Easter Island, which indigenous people call Rapa Nui, such as wood tablets displaying ancient hieroglyphics. The museum, named for groundbreaking archaeologist Francisco Fonck—a native of Viña del Mar—also has an extensive library of documents relating to the island. ⊠ *4 Norte 784* ☎ *32/268–6753* ⊕ *www.museofonck.com* 🎫 *2,500 pesos* ☼ *Mon. 10–2 and 3–6, Tues.–Fri. 10–6, weekends 10–2.*

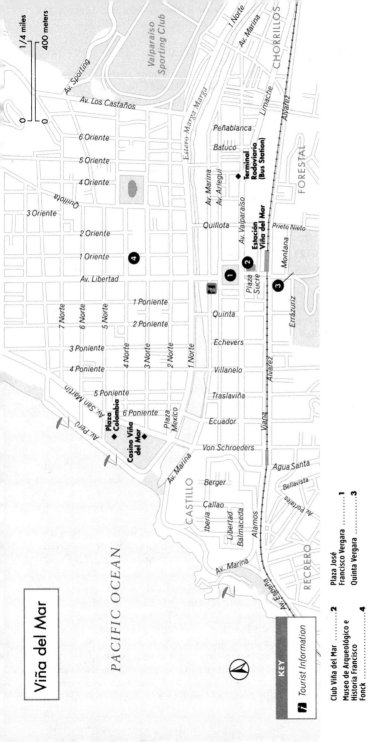

Viña del Mar

PACIFIC OCEAN

Valparaíso Sporting Club

1/4 miles
400 meters

Av. Sporting
Av. Los Castaños

6 Oriente
5 Oriente
4 Oriente
3 Oriente
2 Oriente
1 Oriente

Quillota

Av. Libertad

1 Poniente
2 Poniente
3 Poniente
4 Poniente
5 Poniente
6 Poniente

7 Norte
6 Norte
5 Norte
4 Norte
3 Norte
2 Norte
1 Norte

Av. San Martín
Av. Perú
Av. Marina

Plaza Colombia
Casino Viña del Mar
Plaza México

Estero Marga Marga

Peñablanca
Batuco
Av. Marina
Av. Arlegui
Av. Valparaíso
Quillota
Quinta
Echevers
Villanelo
Traslaviña
Ecuador
Von Schroeders
Berger
Callao
Iberia
Libertad
Balmaceda
Álamos

Terminal Rodoviario (Bus Station)
Estación Viña del Mar
Plaza Sucre
Prieto Nieto
Montana
Errázuriz
Alvarez
Viana

CHORRILLOS
FORESTAL
Limache

1 Norte
Av. Marina

CASTILLO

Av. Marina
Av. España
Av. Portales

Agua Santa
Bellavista

RECRERO

KEY

Tourist Information

Plaza José Francisco Vergara	**1**
Club Viña del Mar	**2**
Quinta Vergara	**3**
Museo de Arqueológico e Historia Francisco Fonck	**4**

3

Plaza José Francisco Vergara. Viña del Mar's central square, Plaza Vergara is lined with majestic palms. Presiding over the east end of the plaza is the patriarch of coastal accommodations, the venerable Hotel O'Higgins, which has seen better days. Opposite the hotel is the neoclassical Teatro Municipal de Viña del Mar, where you can watch a ballet, theater, or music performance. To the west on Avenida Valparaíso is the city's main shopping strip, a one-lane, seven-block stretch with extra-wide sidewalks and numerous stores and sidewalk cafés. You can hire a horse-drawn carriage to take you from the square past some of the city's stately mansions.

QUICK BITES

Mercado Del Mar. In search of a great place to watch the sunset? Head to Mercado Del Mar, an ultramodern restaurant right on the beach. Locals eschew the food and come instead for coffee and a view of the sky turning various shades of pink, purple, and green. ✉ ***Av. Perú 100*** ☎ ***32/284–6421.***

Quinta Vergara. Lose yourself on the paths that wind amid soaring eucalyptus trees on the grounds that contain one of Chile's best botanical gardens. An amphitheater here holds an international music festival, *Festival Internacional de la Canción de Viña del Mar,* in February. ✉ *Av. Errázuriz 563* ☎ *32/226–9435* 🎫 *Free* 🕑 *Tues.–Sun. 7–6.*

BEACHES

Las Salinas. A short drive north of town is the tiny Las Salinas, a crescent of sand that has the calmest water in the area. **Amenities:** food and drink; toilets; parking. **Best for:** walking; sunset; swimming.

Playa Caleta Abarca. One of Viña's most visited beaches, smack in the center of town, Playa Caleta Abarca is crowded with worshippers in mid-summer, making it a great place for people-watching. It lies between the hotel Sheraton Miramar and Cerro Castillo. **Amenities:** food and drink. **Best for:** swimming.

Fodor's Choice ★ **Playa El Sol.** Just north of the rock wall along Avenida Peru is a stretch of sand that draws throngs of people December through March. Viña del Mar really has just one main beach, bisected near its southern end by an old pier, though its parts have been given separate names: Playa El Sol and Playa Blanca. **Amenities:** food and drink; parking; toilets; showers. **Best for:** walking; sunset.

WHERE TO EAT

$$$ STEAKHOUSE 🍴 **Armandita.** Meat-eaters need not despair in this city of seafood saturation. This rustic restaurant half a block west of Avenida San Martín serves almost nothing but grilled meat, including various organs. The menu includes popular dishes such as *lomo a lo pobre* (flank steak served on a bed of french fries and topped with a fried egg). The *parrillada especial,* a mixed grill of steak, chicken, ribs, pork, and sausage, serves two or three people. [$] *Average main: 9000 pesos* ✉ *6 Norte 119* ☎ *32/268–1607* 🌐 *www.armandita.cl.*

$$$ SEAFOOD Fodor's Choice ★ 🍴 **Delicias del Mar.** Former television chef Raúl Madinagoitía presides over the kitchen at Delicias del Mar. The menu abounds with seafood delicacies, such as Peruvian-style ceviche and *centolla magallánica* (king crab from southern Patagonia). Oenophiles are impressed by the extensive, almost exclusively Chilean wine list. Save room for one of the

excellent desserts, maybe crème brûlée, chocolate mousse, or cheesecake with a raspberry sauce. $ *Average main: 9000 pesos* ⊠ *Av. San Martín 459* ☎ *32/290–1837* ⊕ *www.deliciasdelmar.com.*

$$$ ✕ **San Marco.** More than five decades after Edoardo Melotti emigrated
ITALIAN here from northern Italy, the restaurant maintains a reputation for first-class food and service. A modern dining room with abundant foliage and large windows overlooks busy Avenida San Martín. Farther inside, the two dining rooms in the house that the restaurant originally occupied are elegant and more refined. The menu includes traditional gnocchi, as well as *pansotti del bosco* (spinach pasta filled with turkey and puréed chestnuts) and *bistecca alla toscana* (strip steak). Complement your meal with a bottle from the extensive wine list. $ *Average main: 10000 pesos* ⊠ *Av. San Martín 597* ☎ *32/297–5304* ⊕ *www. ristorantesanmarco.cl.*

$$ ✕ **Shitake.** With so much fresh fish available, it's a wonder that it took
JAPANESE so long for sushi and sashimi to catch on with locals. Now that it has, it's hard to find a block downtown that lacks a Japanese restaurant. A favorite with locals is Shitake, which occupies a few gold and beige rooms on Avenida San Martín. The tempura is flavorful, especially when it incorporates juicy Ecuadorean shrimp. Sushi here is a group activity—you can order platters of anywhere from 18 to 103 pieces. $ *Average main: 7500 pesos* ⊠ *Av. San Martín 419* ☎ *32/290–1458* ⊕ *www.shitake.cl.*

WHERE TO STAY

$$ 🏨 **Cap Ducal.** Inspired by transatlantic ocean liners, this ship-shape
B&B/INN building on the waterfront has oddly shape rooms that are nicely decorated with plush carpets and pastel wallpaper. **Pros:** unique architecture. **Cons:** noise of traffic can spoil the great views. $ *Rooms from: 71000 pesos* ⊠ *Av. Marina 51* ☎ *32/262–6655* ⊕ *www.capducal.cl* ⇥ *23 rooms, 3 suites* ⦿ *Breakfast.*

$$$$ 🏨 **Hotel Del Mar.** A rounded facade, echoing the shape of the adjacent
RESORT Casino Viña del Mar, means that almost every room at this oceanfront
Fodor's Choice hotel has unmatched views. **Pros:** notable in-house restaurant. **Cons:**
★ constant chiming of gaming machines may grate on your nerves, but there are ways to escape. $ *Rooms from: 240000 pesos* ⊠ *Av. San Martín 199* ☎ *32/284–6300* ⊕ *www.enjoy.cl* ⇥ *50 rooms, 10 suites* ⦿ *Breakfast.*

$$$$ 🏨 **Hotel Gala.** Modern, spacious, light-filled rooms in this upscale
HOTEL 14-story hotel have panoramic views of the city. **Pros:** great views in the heart of downtown Viña. **Cons:** the staff seems stretched a bit thin. $ *Rooms from: 106000 pesos* ⊠ *Arlegui 273* ☎ *32/232–1500* ⊕ *www. galahotel.cl* ⇥ *64 rooms, including 13 suites* ⦿ *Breakfast.*

$$$$ 🏨 **Hotel Oceanic.** Built on the rocky coast between Viña and Reñaca,
B&B/INN this boutique hotel has luxurious rooms with gorgeous ocean views. **Pros:** watch the waves on the rock from your hotel terrace. **Cons:** a long way out of Viña. $ *Rooms from: 106000 pesos* ⊠ *Av. Borgoño 12925, north of town* ☎ *32/283–0006* ⊕ *www.hoteloceanic.cl* ⇥ *18 rooms, 12 suites* ⦿ *Breakfast.*

$$$$ RESORT Fodor's Choice ★ **Sheraton Miramar.** This sophisticated city hotel certainly earns it name, as you can do almost everything here while you gaze at the sea. **Pros:** first-class city hotel with spectacular views. **Cons:** area around the hotel is blighted by one of Viña's main access roads. [$] *Rooms from: 150000 pesos* ✉ *Av. Marina 15* ☎ *32/238–8600* 🌐 *www.sheraton.cl* 🛏 *142 rooms, 4 suites* 🍴 *Breakfast.*

$$ B&B/INN **Tres Poniente.** Come for the personalized service and for many of the same amenities you'll find at larger hotels at a fraction of the cost. **Pros:** good value on a quiet backstreet. **Cons:** a long walk from the beach or Viña's main attractions. [$] *Rooms from: 49000 pesos* ✉ *3 Poniente 70, between 1 and 2 Norte* ☎ *32/247–8576* 🌐 *www.hotel3poniente.com* 🛏 *11 rooms* 🍴 *Breakfast.*

3

NIGHTLIFE AND PERFORMING ARTS

Viña's nightlife varies considerably according to the season, with the most glittering events concentrated in January and February. There are nightly shows and concerts at the casino and frequent performances at Quinta Vergara. During the rest of the year, things get going only on weekends. Aside from the casino, late-night fun is concentrated in the area around the intersection of Avenida San Martín and 4 Norte, the shopping strip on Avenida Valparaíso, and the eastern end of the alley called Paseo Cousiño. Viña residents tend to go to Valparaíso for live music, since it has a much better selection.

BARS

Margarita. Margarita is a popular watering hole late at night, with live music and karaoke on weekends. The namesake cocktail is a killer. ✉ *Av. San Martín 501* ☎ *32/269–6737.*

CASINO

Casino Viña del Mar. With a neoclassical style that wouldn't be out of place in a classic James Bond movie, Casino Viña del Mar has a restaurant, bar, and cabaret, as well as roulette, blackjack, and 1,500 slot machines. It's open nightly until the wee hours of the morning most of the year. There's a 3,800-peso cover charge and keep in mind that people dress up to play here, especially in the evening. ✉ *Av. San Martín 199* ☎ *32/250–0600* 🌐 *www.enjoy.cl/enjoy-vina-del-mar.*

DANCE CLUBS

Club Divino. Club Divino is one of the hottest and most vibrant discos on the Central Coast. It's a bit out of town, so it's best to drive or take a cab. ✉ *Camino Internacional 537, Reñaca Alto* ☎ *9/5708–4660* 🌐 *www.clubdivino.cl.*

THEATER

Teatro Municipal de Viña del Mar. A lovely neoclassical auditorium in the center of the city, Teatro Municipal de Viña del Mar hosts frequent theatrical productions, as well as music and dance performances. ✉ *Plaza José Francisco Vergara s/n* ☎ *32/218–5426.*

SPORTS AND THE OUTDOORS

GOLF

Granadilla Country Club. You can play 18 holes Tuesday through Sunday at the Granadilla Country Club. It's an established course in Santa Inés—a 10-minute drive from downtown. The greens fees are 65,000 pesos, and they rent clubs for 15,000 pesos, but you need to make a reservation. ✉ *Camino Granadilla s/n* ☎ *32/268-9249* ⊕ *www.granadilla. cl* 🖃 *65,000 Chilean pesos* 🏌 *18 holes, 6,443 yards, par 72.*

HORSE RACING

Valparaíso Sporting Club. Valparaíso Sporting Club hosts horse racing every Wednesday. The Clásico del Derby, Chile's version of the Kentucky Derby, takes place the first Sunday in February. Rugby, polo, cricket, and other sports are also played here. ✉ *Av. Los Castaños 404* ☎ *32/265-5610* ⊕ *www.sporting.cl.*

SHOPPING

Avenida Valparaíso. Viña's main shopping strip is Avenida Valparaíso between Cerro Castillo and Plaza Vergara, where wide sidewalks accommodate throngs of shoppers. Stores here sell everything from shoes to cameras, and there are also sidewalk cafés, bars, and restaurants.

Centro Artesanal Calle Quinta. Local crafts are sold at the Centro Artesanal Calle Quinta. ✉ *Quinta 232, between Viana and Av. Valparaíso* ☎ *32/268-7162.*

Espacio Urbano. For one-stop shopping, locals head to the mall. Espacio Urbano, on the north end of town, is a longtime favorite. ✉ *Av. 15 Norte at 2 Norte* ☎ *32/238-8200* ⊕ *www.espaciourbano.cl/15norte.*

Falabella. Falabella is a popular department store south of Plaza Vergara. ✉ *Sucre 250* ☎ *600/380-5000* ⊕ *www.falabella.com.*

Feria Artesanal Muelle Vergara. On the beach, near the pier at Muelle Vergara, the Feria Artesanal Muelle Vergara is a crafts fair open daily in summer and on weekends the rest of the year.

CASABLANCA WINE VALLEY

Don't miss the chance to stop at the many wineries along the road between Santiago and the coast. As you come out of the Zapata tunnel (at Km 60 on Ruta 68), the importance of wine production to the local economy will be obvious. Vineyards carpet the floor of the Casablanca Valley for as far as the eye can see. Just 30 years ago most winemakers considered this area inhospitable for wine grapes, yet today it is at the forefront of the country's wine industry. Experts have come to recognize the valley's proximity to the sea as its main asset, because cooler temperatures give the grapes more time to develop flavor as they ripen.

Almost all wineries are open to visitors. Choices for activities might include a tour, a tasting, lunch at an on-premises restaurant, or even an overnight stay (all for a price, of course). Although most offer tours on a daily basis, call ahead to ensure someone is available to show you around.

3

GETTING HERE AND AROUND

Most of the vineyards are a bit of a trek from the main highway, so having a bus drop you off on the side of the road probably isn't the best way to go. If you drive there, plan to spend several hours touring and tasting the wines, and give yourself time for the alcohol to leave yours system as police have enforced a "zero-tolerance" policy on drinking and driving. Alternately indulge and spend the night, or take one of many guided tours.

TOURS

If you want to visit more than one winery, the **Casablanca Valley Wine Producers Association** (☎ 32/274–3755 or 32/274–3933 ⊕ *www.casablanca valley.cl*) runs one-day and two-day visits.

WINERIES

Casas del Bosque. Nestled among rolling vine-covered hills just outside the town of Casablanca, Casas del Bosque offers a ride through the vineyard in an old wagon, a tour of the winemaking facilities, and a tasting. During March and April, the main harvest months, you can learn even more about the production process with the chance to pick your grapes and take them for selection and pressing. Like many wineries in the valley, Casas del Bosque has its own restaurant, Tanino. ✉ *Fundo Santa Rosa, Hijuela No. 2, Casablanca* ☎ 2/2480–6940 ⊕ *www.casasdelbosque.cl*.

House of Morande. Even if you don't have time to take a tour, at least make time to stop at the restaurant here, just off the highway as you hit the valley floor from the Zapata tunnel. Pablo Morande was one of the first to recognize Casablanca's potential for producing world-beating grapes back in the late 1970s and uses the ultrastylish restaurant, which combines unusual local fare and modern techniques, to showcase the wines from his winery (actually located in the neighboring Maipo Valley). Try the five-course *maridaje* menu with dishes that are chosen to match the wine. ✉ *Ruta 68, at Km 61, just past Viñedos Organicos Emiliana, Valparaíso* ☎ 32/275–4701, 9/7979–2734 ⊕ *www.morande.cl*.

Viña Matetic. Viña Matetic, which straddles the border between the Casablanca Valley and the adjacent San Antonio Valley, may take the prize for the region's most stunning bodega. Set into a ridge overlooking vines on both sides, it resembles a futuristic bunker worthy of a James Bond villain, with sloping passageways revealing glimpses into the barrels stored below. A couple of kilometers away, the winery's octagonal restaurant looks out over beautifully manicured gardens, in the middle of which is a recently restored guest house with seven elegantly decorated rooms available to rent. ✉ *Fundo Rosario, Lagunillas, Casablanca* ☎ 2/2595–2661, 2/2611–1501 ⊕ *www.mateticvineyards.com*.

THE SOUTHERN BEACHES

Once a dominion of solitude and sea, the stretch of coastline south of Valparaíso has seen much development, not all of it well planned, over the past few decades. A succession of towns here caters to the

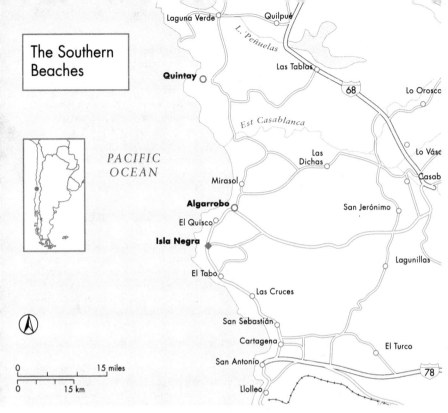

The Southern Beaches

PACIFIC OCEAN

0 — 15 miles
0 — 15 km

beach-bound hordes January and February, and become a sleepy retreat for most of the rest of the year. Though none of the towns are terribly attractive, a few of the beaches are quite nice and the towns, especially in the off-season, give you a good feel for rural life in this neck of the woods. The main reason to visit—and it's a great one—is to take a look at poet Pablo Neruda's hideaway at Isla Negra. Here you can see the various treasures he collected during his lifetime.

Because large waves create dangerous undertows at some southern beaches, pay attention to warning flags: red means swimming is prohibited, whereas green, usually accompanied by a sign reading "playa apta para nadir" (beach suitable for swimming), is a go-ahead signal.

QUINTAY

30 km (19 miles) south of Valparaíso.

Not too long ago, migrating sperm whales could still be seen from the beaches at Quintay. The creatures were all but exterminated by the whaling industry that sprang up in Quintay in 1942. Whaling was banned in 1967, and Quintay returned to being a quiet fishing village. If you wonder what the coast used to be like before condos began springing up, head to this charming spot.

GETTING HERE AND AROUND

From Valparaíso, follow Ruta 68 back to Santiago and after 23 km (14 miles), turn onto Ruta G-28, which winds down through the hills to Quintay. From Santiago, follow Ruta 68, turn off at Km 92 at the exit named "Quintay-Tunquen," and follow the road for approximately 23 km (14 miles) to the fishing harbor. Everything is crowded around the narrow bay except the museums, which are located in a school at the entrance to the village and next to the wharf.

EXPLORING

Escuela San Pedro de Quintay. The town's elementary school serves as a makeshift museum dedicated to Quintay's whaling past. Jose Daniel Barrios, a former whaler, maintains the humble display; his whaling contract is among the exhibits. Others include photos of the plant, a whale gun, whale teeth, and a harpoon. Also here are some pottery and skeletons from the indigenous Aconcagua people, who inhabited the region around 1300. ⊠ *Escuela San Pedro s/n* 🖅 *Donation* ⊗ *Jan. and Feb., daily 10–noon and 2–6; Mar.–Dec., hrs vary.*

Quintay Whaling Factory. Fundación Quintay, a former whaling station that operated from 1943 to 1967, has been converted into a quaint museum that gives you a window into this coastal town's past. The museum, along with the skeletal remains of a whale, are just a stone's throw away from the handful of brightly colored fishing boats at the wharf. ⊠ *Caleta Quintay* ⊕ *www.fundacionquintay.cl* 🖅 *600 pesos* ⊗ *Daily 9–7.*

BEACHES

Playa Grande. Vacation apartments have replaced the pine forest surrounding Playa Grande, which gets its fair share of sun worshippers in summer. There are two ways to reach the beach: through the town, following Avenida Teniente Merino, or through the gated community of Santa Augusta. **Amenities:** food; toilets; parking (fee). **Best for:** surfing; sunset; walking; swimming.

WHERE TO EAT

$$ ✕ **Pezcadores.** Echoing the colors of the fishing boats below, this seafood
SEAFOOD restaurant is painted vivid shades of yellow, green, and red. The restaurant's proximity to the *caleta* (cove) means the fish on your plate was probably pulled from the water early that morning. The sea bass here is about the freshest around. Attentive servers will help you choose from the good wine selection. $ *Average main: 7500 pesos* ⊠ *Costanera s/n* ☎ *32/236–2068* ⊕ *www.pezcadores.cl.*

SPORTS AND THE OUTDOORS

DIVING

Chile's coastline has several interesting shipwrecks. Two are off the shores of Quintay, including Indus IV, a whaling ship that went down in 1947.

Austral Divers. Austral Divers offers diving courses and trips from its beachside office. ⊠ *Caleta Quintay, Quintay, Quintay, Santiago* ☎ *9/9885–5099, 2/2492–7975* ⊕ *www.australdivers.cl.*

ALGARROBO

35 km (22 miles) south of Quintay.

The largest town south of Valparaíso, Algarrobo is the first in a string of towns spread along the coast to the south. Though Algarrobo isn't the prettiest, it has a winding coastline with several yellow-sand beaches, and consequently attracts throngs of sun worshippers. The pine forest behind two of its more popular beaches, El Canelo and Canelillo, is also worth exploring.

GETTING HERE AND AROUND

From Valparaíso, follow Ruta 68 back to Santiago and turn off onto Ruta F90 just before Casablanca. From there it is approximately 35 km (22 miles) to Algarrobo. Pullman and Tur-Bus travel regularly to Algarrobo from the Alameda Terminal (Universidad de Santiago Metro station) in Santiago. Most of Algarrobo's main beaches lie within easy walking distance of the town. Regular buses run from here along the coast to El Quisco and Isla Negra farther south.

ESSENTIALS

Visitor Information Municipal Tourist Office ⊠ *Avenida Peñablanca 250* ☎ *35/220–0100* ⊕ *www.municipalidadalgarrobo.cl.*

EXPLORING

Club de Yates Algarrobo. Next to Playa San Pedro is this private yacht club. In February, boats from all over the country participate in one of Chile's most important nautical events here: the Regata Mil Millas Náuticas. ⊠ *Carlos Alessandri 2447* ☎ *35/248–3438* ⊕ *www.cya.cl.*

Cofradía Náutica. A private marina at the end of a point south of town harbors some of the country's top yachts. ⊠ *Av. Almirante José Toribio Merino 3877* ☎ *35/248–1180* ⊕ *www.cofradianautica.cl.*

Isla de los Pájaros Niños. Just offshore from the Cofradía Náutica is this tiny island and penguin sanctuary that shelters more than 300 Humboldt and Magellan penguins. The upper crags of the island are dotted with hundreds of little caves dug by the penguins using their legs and beaks. Though only members are allowed in the marina, a path leads to the top of a nearby hill from which you can watch the flightless birds through binoculars.

BEACHES

El Quisco. South of Algarobbo, El Quisco is nothing but a long beach of pale sand guarded on either end by stone jetties. In the middle of the beach is a boulder with a 15-foot-high, six-pronged cactus sculpture perched atop it. South of the beach is the blue-and-yellow cove, where boats anchored offshore create a picturesque composition. In summer, the beach is packed on sunny days, as visitors outnumber *quisqueños* (locals) about 10 to 1. **Amenities:** food and drink. **Best for:** walking; sunset; swimming.

Playa Canelillo. If you want seclusion, follow the trail that leads southwest from Playa El Canelo, past the guano-splotched outcropping called Peñablanca, to the smaller Playa Canelillo. **Amenities:** parking; toilets. **Best for:** swimming; sunset; surfing; snorkeling.

Fodor's Choice
★

Playa El Canelo. Algarrobo's nicest beach is Playa El Canelo, in a secluded cove south of town. It's an idyllic spot of fine yellow sand, calm blue-green water, and a backdrop of pines. Though quiet most of the year, it can get crowded in January and February. Follow Avenida Santa Teresita south to Avenida El Canelo and the pine forest of Parque Canelo. Guarded parking there costs 4,000 to 5,000 pesos. **Amenities:** parking (fee); food and drink. **Best for:** swimming; surfing; sunset.

Playa Grande. The beige sand of this nice beach stretches northward from town for several miles. There's usually rough surf, which can make it dangerous for swimming. Massive condominium complexes on either end of this beach spill thousands of vacationers onto it every summer. **Amenities:** none. **Best for:** sunset; walking.

Playa Las Cadenas. On the north end of town, Playa Las Cadenas has a waterfront promenade. The name, "Chain Beach," refers to the thick metal links lining the sidewalk, which were recovered from a shipwreck off Algarrobo Bay. **Amenities:** food and drink; toilets. **Best for:** swimming; sunset.

Playa San Pedro. The most popular beach in town is tiny Playa San Pedro; a statue of Saint Peter in the sand next to the wharf marks the spot. It's small, but the waters are surrounded by a rocky barrier that keeps them calm and good for swimming. **Amenities:** food and drink. **Best for:** swimming; sunset; walking.

WHERE TO EAT AND STAY

$$
SEAFOOD
✕ **Algarrobo.** The only waterfront restaurant in Algarrobo has an expansive terrace overlooking the beach. The extensive menu is almost exclusively seafood, including half a dozen types of fish served with an equal number of sauces. Ostiones *pil pil* (spicy scallop scampi) and *loco apanado* (fried abalone) are popular starters. Finish with sole or sea bass steamed, grilled, or served *a lo pobre* (topped with a fried egg). $ *Average main: 6000 pesos* ⊠ *Av. Carlos Alessandri 1505* ☎ *35/248–1078.*

$$
B&B/INN
🛏 **Hotel Pacífico.** This older hotel in the heart of town, a block from Playa Las Cadenas, has bland but comfortable rooms. **Pros:** spacious rooms with views over the ocean. **Cons:** hotel is looking its age, with some rooms rather worn. $ *Rooms from: 73000 pesos* ⊠ *Av. Carlos Alessandri 1930* ☎ *35/248–2855* ⊕ *www.hotel-pacifico.cl* ↷ *74 rooms* ⦿ *Breakfast.*

$$
B&B/INN
🛏 **Pao Pao.** The octagonal pine cabanas here range from cozy studios that sleep two, to two-bedroom apartments complete with wooden decks and hot tubs. **Pros:** rural setting makes it ideal for families. **Cons:** the adjacent restaurant opens only during January and February. $ *Rooms from: 60000 pesos* ⊠ *Camino Mirasol 170* ☎ *35/248–1264* ⊕ *www.turismopaopao.cl* ↷ *22 cabins* ⦿ *No meals.*

$$$
RENTAL
🛏 **San Alfonso del Mar.** If you want to swim in the sea but aren't keen to brave the polar temperatures of Chilean waters, try this set of imposing apartment buildings on Algarrobo's northern edge with its eight-hectare, one-thousand-meter, turquoise-blue seawater pool that stretches the length of the complex. **Pros:** avoid the chilly Humboldt Current in style. **Cons:** if you do feel the need to stray, it's a long walk to town. $ *Rooms*

from: 100000 pesos ✉ *Camino Mirasol 866* ☎ *35/248–1636* ⊕ *www. sanalfonso.cl* ⟳ *160 apartments* ⊟ *No credit cards* ⦿ *No meals.*

SPORTS AND THE OUTDOORS
DIVING
Pablo Zavala. Pablo Zavala runs boat dives to half a dozen spots from the Club de Yates. ✉ *Av. Carlos Alessandri 2447* ☎ *9/9435–4835.*

ISLA NEGRA

6 km (4 miles) south of El Quisco; 71 km (44 miles) south of Valparaíso.

"I needed a place to work," Chilean poet and Nobel laureate Pablo Neruda wrote in his memoirs. "I found a stone house facing the ocean, a place nobody knew about, Isla Negra." Neruda, who bought the house in 1939, found much inspiration here. "Isla Negra's wild coastal strip, with its turbulent ocean, was the place to give myself passionately to the writing of my new song," he wrote.

GETTING HERE AND AROUND
From Algarrobo, head out as if returning to Santiago but turn southward at the crossroads on the road marked El Quisco. Follow the coast road through El Quisco for 20 minutes to reach the small village of Isla Negra. The path leading down to Neruda's house begins from the main road just after a row of stores selling handicrafts and souvenirs. Buses run regularly along the coast road from San Antonio to Algarrobo.

EXPLORING
Fodor's Choice ★ **Casa-Museo Isla Negra.** A shrine to his life, work, and many passions, this is a must-see for Pablo Neruda's ardent admirers. Perched on a bluff overlooking the ocean, the house displays the treasures—from masks and maps to seashells and a narwhal tusk—he collected over the course of his remarkable life. Although he spent much time living and traveling abroad, Neruda made Isla Negra his primary residence later in life. He wrote his memoirs from the upstairs bedroom; the last pages were dictated to his wife here before he departed for the Santiago hospital where he died of cancer. Neruda and his wife are buried in the prow-shaped tomb area behind the house.

Just before Neruda's death in 1973, a military coup put Augusto Pinochet in command of Chile. He closed off Neruda's home and denied all access. Neruda devotees chiseled their tributes into the wooden gates surrounding the property. In 1989 the Neruda Foundation, started by his widow, restored the house and opened it as a museum. Here his collections are displayed as they were while he lived. The living room contains—among numerous other oddities—a number of bowsprits from ships hanging from the ceiling and walls. Neruda called them his "girlfriends."

You can visit the museum with an audio guide tour, available in English, on a first-come, first-served basis. The tour helps you understand Neruda's many obsessions, from the positioning of guests at the dinner table to the east–west alignment of his bed. Objects had a spiritual and symbolic life for the poet, which the tour makes evident. ✉ *Poeta*

CLOSE UP

Neruda's Inspiration

First, let's clear up one thing: Isla Negra may mean "Black Island," but this little stretch of rugged coastline is not black, and it is not an island. This irony must have appealed to Nobel Prize–winning poet Pablo Neruda, who made his home here for more than three decades.

Of his three houses, Pablo Neruda was most attached to Isla Negra. "Ancient night and the unruly salt beat at the walls of my house," he wrote in one of his many poems about his home in Isla Negra. It's easy to see how this house, perched high above the waves crashing on the purplish rocks, could inspire such reverie.

Neruda bought this house in 1939. Like La Sebastiana, his house in Valparaíso, it had been started by someone else and then abandoned. Starting with the cylindrical stone tower, which is topped by a whimsical weather vane shaped like a fish, he added touches that could only be described as poetic. There are odd angles, narrow hallways, and various nooks and crannies, all for their own sake.

What is most amazing about Isla Negra, however, is what Neruda chose to place inside. There's a tusk from a narwhal in one room, and figureheads from the fronts of sailing ships hanging overhead in another. There are huge collections ranging from seashells to bottles to butterflies. And yet it is also just a house, with a simple room designed so he could gaze down at the sea when he needed inspiration.

Neruda s/n ☎ *35/246–1284* 🌐 *www.fundacionneruda.org* 🎟 *5,000 pesos* 🕒 *Mar.–Dec., Tues.–Sun. 10–6; Jan. and Feb., Tues.–Sun. 10–8.*

WHERE TO EAT AND STAY

$$ SEAFOOD 🍴 **El Rincón del Poeta.** Inside the entrance to the Neruda museum at Isla Negra, this small restaurant has a wonderful ocean view, with seating both indoors and on a protected terrace. The name translates as the Poet's Corner, a theme continued in the small but original menu. One of the house specialties is *oda al caldillo de congrio Nerudiano* (literally, Neruda's ode to conger eel stew). Neruda, who had a penchant for transforming the mundane into the beautifully poetic, wrote of the Chilean culinary dish: "In Chile's stormy sea lives the rosy conger eel, giant eel of snowy meat. And in Chile's stewpots, on the coast, is where the stew, thick and succulent, useful, was born." You might also try Reineta Especial *Garcia Lorca,* a Patagonian bream fillet, abundant in this part of the Pacific. There are lighter dishes as well such as a chicken sandwich. [$] *Average main: 8000 pesos* ✉ *Casa-Museo Isla Negra, Poeta Neruda s/n* ☎ *35/246–1774* 🌐 *www.elrincondelpoeta.cl* 🕒 *Closed Mon.*

$$ B&B/INN 🏨 **La Candela.** During your stay at La Candela, you can wander along the same rocky Pacific shore that Neruda once explored. **Pros:** seaside coziness a short walk from Neruda's house. **Cons:** not somewhere to stay if you need to stay connected. [$] *Rooms from: 70000 pesos* ✉ *De la Hostería 67* ☎ *35/246–1254* 🌐 *www.candela.cl* 🛏 *20 rooms* 🍽 *Breakfast.*

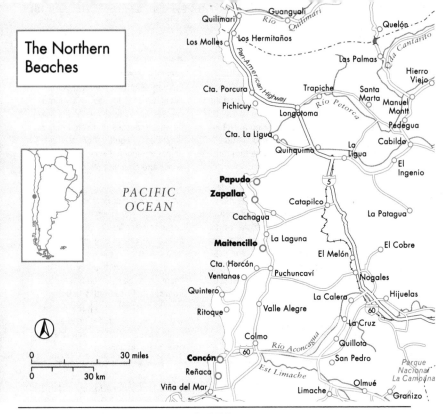

PACIFIC
OCEAN

0 ——————————— 30 miles
0 ——————————— 30 km

THE NORTHERN BEACHES

To the north of Viña del Mar, the Pacific collides with the rocky offshore islands and a rugged coastline broken here and there by sandy bays. The coastal highway runs from Viña del Mar to Papudo, passing marvelous scenery along the way. Between Viña and Concón, it winds along steep rock faces, turning inland north of Concón, where massive sand dunes give way to expanses of undeveloped coastline, reminiscent of northern California's coastline. The farther north you drive, the greater the distance between towns, each of which is on a significantly different beach. Whether as a day trip from Viña or on a series of overnights, this stretch of coast is well worth exploring.

CONCÓN

16 km (10 miles) north of Viña del Mar, along Avenida Borgoño.

How to explain the lovely name Concón? In the language of the Changos, *co* meant "water," and the duplication of the sound alludes to the confluence of the Río Aconcagua and the Pacific. When the Spanish arrived in 1543, Pedro de Valdivia created an improvised shipyard here that was destroyed by natives, leading to one of the first clashes between indigenous and Spanish cultures in central Chile.

Today, the town that holds the name is packed with high-rise apartment buildings, though it does have decent ocean views and great seafood restaurants. The attraction lies to the north and south: the rugged coastal scenery along the road that connects it to Reñaca, and the sand dunes that rise up behind the beaches north of town.

GETTING HERE AND AROUND

Concón, occupying a long stretch of coast on the south bank of the mouth of the Aconcagua river, lies 16 km (19 miles) north of Viña del Mar along the spectacular Avenida Borgoño (check out the houses built into the cliffs), passing through Reñaca. If coming direct from Santiago, take Ruta 5 north until Km 109 and take the turn to Quillota all the way to the coast. Buses from Viña del Mar leave regularly from Plaza Francisco Vergara.

EXPLORING

Isla de Lobos. North of town across from a large wooden restaurant is a small rocky island that shelters a permanent population of sea lions, which can be viewed from shore. ⊠ *Costanera, 9 km (5½ miles) north of Concón.*

Roca Oceánico. This massive promontory covered with scrubby vegetation has footpaths winding throughout that afford excellent views of Viña del Mar and Valparaíso—and of the sea churning against black volcanic rock below. ⊠ *Costanera, 1 km (½ mile) north of Isla de Lobos.*

BEACHES

Playa La Boca. At the north end of town is the gray-sand Playa La Boca. It was named "Mouth Beach" because the Río Aconcagua flows into the Pacific here, which makes the water murky. **Amenities:** food and drink; water sports. **Best for:** walking; sunset; surfing.

Playa Las Bahamas. Just beyond the wharf is Playa Las Bahamas, the beach favored by surfers and windsurfers. **Amenities:** none. **Best for:** surfing; windsurfing.

Playa Los Lilenes. The southernmost beach in Concón, Playa Los Lilenes is a tiny yellow-sand cove with calm waters. **Amenities:** none. **Best for:** swimming.

Fodor'sChoice ★ **Playa Ritoque.** Concón's nicest beach is Playa Ritoque, a long, wide golden strand that starts several miles north of town and stretches northward for several miles. Access is good at Punta de Piedra, 5 km (3 miles) north of town, where guarded parking costs 2,000 pesos per day. About 1 km (½ mile) north of here, vast sand dunes rise up behind the beach. **Amenities:** parking (fee). **Best for:** walking; solitude; sunset; surfing.

WHERE TO EAT AND STAY

$$
SEAFOOD
Fodor'sChoice ★
✕ Aquí Jaime. Owner Jaime Vegas is usually on hand here, seating customers and scrutinizing the preparation of such house specialties as *ensalada de mariscos Aquíjaime* (a seafood salad mix of abalone, crab meat, shrimp, scallops, fried calamari, and clams with melted Parmesan cheese), *arroz a la valenciana* (paella packed with seafood), and *ceviche de centolla* (king crab ceviche). Perhaps this is why the small restaurant perched on a rocky promontory next to Caleta Higuerillas

has one of the best reputations in the region. Large windows let you watch the waves crashing just below, passing boats and pelicans, and the coast that stretches northward. [$] *Average main: 6000 pesos* ✉ *Av. Borgoño 21303* ☎ *32/281–2042* 🌐 *www.aquijaime.cl* ⊗ *No dinner Sun. and Mon.*

$$$$ RENTAL 🏨 **Bahía Bonita.** Perched on a hilltop overlooking Concón, this all-suites hotel has rooms with flower-filled terraces—some more than one—overlooking the crashing waves. **Pros:** apartments have plenty of space to spread out. **Cons:** a steep climb from the beach. [$] *Rooms from: 132000 pesos* ✉ *Av. Borgoño 22040, Subida San Fabián, Con-Con* ☎ *32/281–8757* 🌐 *www.aparthotelbahiabonita.cl* 🛏 *13 suites* 🍴 *Breakfast.*

$$$$ B&B/INN 🏨 **Radisson Acqua Hotel & Spa Concón.** Rising out of a craggy headland with spectacular views up and down the coast, this hotel blends almost seamlessly into its surroundings. **Pros:** escape the summer crowds of larger towns, while still just a walk from the beach. **Cons:** hard floors and a cool atmosphere make this less than ideal for children. [$] *Rooms from: 110000 pesos* ✉ *Av. Borgoño 23333, Concón* ☎ *32/254–6400* 🌐 *www.radisson.cl* 🛏 *57 rooms, 9 suites* 🍴 *Breakfast.*

SPORTS AND THE OUTDOORS

HORSEBACK RIDING

Sol y Mar. Sol y Mar has horseback excursions on the beach or to the sand dunes that can be combined with kayaking or boat trips on a nearby lake. ✉ *Camino a Quintero, Km 5* ☎ *32/281–3675* 🌐 *www.solymar.cl.*

MAITENCILLO

20 km (12 miles) north of Quintero.

This town is a string of cabanas and eateries spread along the 4-km (2½-mile) Avenida del Mar. Two long beaches are separated by an extended rocky coastline that holds the local caleta. To complement the abundant sand and surf, there is a decent selection of restaurants, bars, and accommodations. The windswept coast south of the town is almost completely undeveloped and a magnet for seabirds; it's also ideal for paragliding.

GETTING HERE AND AROUND

From Concón, follow Ruta F30 E north turning inland from the coast past Quintero until signs show the turnoff for Maitencillo and La Laguna. If coming from Santiago, take Ruta 5 Norte and exit at the turn for Catapilco (just after the El Melón tunnel) and follow the road to the coast.

ESSENTIALS

Visitor Information **Municipal Tourism Office of Maitencillo** ✉ *Av. Bernardo O'Higgins 70, Puchancavi* ☎ *32/279–1085.*

EXPLORING

Monumento Nacional Isla Cachagua. Off the coast from Cachagua, several miles north of Maitencillo, is the protected island inhabited by Magellan and Humboldt penguins. No one is allowed on the island, but you can ride around in a small boat that can be hired at the Caleta de La

Laguna or Caleta de Zapallar. You can also view the island from the beach below Cachagua, though you need binoculars to watch the penguins wobble around.

BEACHES

Playa Aguas Blancas. The light-gray sand of Playa Aguas Blancas lies to the south of a rock outcropping, protected from the swells, and consequently is good for swimming. A constant stiff breeze and the cliffs leading down to the beach also make it ideal for paragliding **Amenities:** none. **Best for:** walking; swimming; sunset; solitude.

Playa Durazno. If you follow Avenida 21 de Mayo to its end, you come to Playa Durazno, a small, unattractive gray-sand beach that does have calm water. **Amenities:** none. **Best for:** sunset; solitude.

Playa El Caleuche. Playa El Caleuche, beyond the rocks at the end of Playa Durazno, is safe for swimming. **Amenities:** none. **Best for:** swimming.

Playa El Libro. Surfing is popular at Playa El Libro, which is reached from Hermanos Carrera or Balmaceda via concrete stairs. Swimming is prohibited here, but kids play in the little pools that form behind the rocks. **Amenities:** none. **Best for:** surfing; sunset.

Playa Larga. On the north side is the largest beach in town, the extra-wide Playa Larga. It's often pounded by big surf. **Amenities:** food and drink. **Best for:** surfing; walking; sunset.

WHERE TO EAT AND STAY

$$
MEDITERRANEAN
✕ **La Canasta.** Serpentine bamboo tunnels connect rooms through La Canasta, and slabs of wood suspended by chains serve as tables: the scene could be straight from *The Hobbit*. A small menu changes regularly, but includes dishes such as *cordero a la ciruela* (lamb with a cherry sauce) and *corvina queso de cabra* (sea bass with goat cheese). Although it's across from the beach, there's no view. $ *Average main: 6000 pesos* ✉ *Av. del Mar 592* ☎ *32/277–1028* ⊕ *www.hermansen.cl.*

$$$
B&B/INN
Altamar Aparthotel. All the rooms in this brick-red building with a vaguely New England feel have ocean views, though those on the third floor have the best ones. **Pros:** enjoy breakfast on your terrace overlooking the ocean. **Cons:** no restaurant. $ *Rooms from: 92000 pesos* ✉ *Av. del Mar 3600* ☎ *32/277–2440* ⊕ *www.altamaraparthotel.cl* 🛏 *18 apartments* ❘⊙❘ *Breakfast.*

$$$
B&B/INN
Cabañas Hermansen. Set in an overgrown garden, these cabanas feel far away from everything. **Pros:** the best place to escape the crowds without leaving Maitencillo. **Cons:** like almost everywhere in Maitencillo, you have to cross a busy road to reach the beach. $ *Rooms from: 77000 pesos* ✉ *Av. del Mar 592* ☎ *32/277–1028* ⊕ *www.hermansen.cl* 🛏 *16 cabins* ❘⊙❘ *No meals.*

$$$$
RESORT
Marbella. Golf fairways, pine trees, and ocean vistas surround this four-story white-stucco resort building; the spacious, colorful rooms are decorated with original art and have large terraces with views of Maitencillo Bay. **Pros:** stunning setting; plenty to do. **Cons:** distance from the beach—you need a car if you also want to explore the coast. $ *Rooms from: 144000 pesos* ✉ *Carretera Concón–Zapallar, Km 35* ☎ *32/279–5900, 02/2438–5300* ⊕ *www.marbella.cl* 🛏 *68 rooms, 16 suites, 6 penthouse* ❘⊙❘ *Multiple meal plans.*

SPORTS AND THE OUTDOORS

GOLF

Marbella Country Club. The Marbella Country Club has 27 holes of golf—without a doubt some of the best on the coast—in an exclusive environment. The tennis and paddle-tennis courts are available only to members and to guests of the Marbella resort. Greens fees for hotel guests are 22,000 pesos, whereas nonguests pay 42,000 pesos during the week and 52,000 pesos on weekends. ⊠ *Carretera Concón–Zapallar, Km 35* ☎ *32/277–2402* ⊕ *www.marbellacountryclub.cl.*

HANG GLIDING

Parapente Aventura. *Parapente,* a seated version of hang gliding, is popular here. Parapente Aventura has classes and two-person trips for beginners. ⊠ *Cerro Tacna, Calle Los Laureles 22-9* ☎ *9/7919–9292, 9/9547–5955* ⊕ *www.parapenteaventura.cl.*

HORSEBACK RIDING

Club Ecuestre Cachagua. In Cachagua, Club Ecuestre Cachagua runs horseback tours to scenic overlooks. ⊠ *Costanera s/n, Cachagua* ☎ *33/277–1596, 9/9199–6194.*

ZAPALLAR

Fodor'sChoice   *48 km (30 miles) north of Concón along the Camino Concón-Zapallar.*
★

An aristocratic enclave for the past century, Zapallar doesn't promote itself as a vacation destination. In fact, it has traditionally been reluctant to receive outsiders. The resort is the brainchild of Olegario O'Valle, who owned property here. In 1893, following an extended stay in Europe, O'Valle decided to recreate the Riviera on the Chilean coast. He allotted plots of land to friends and family with the provision that they build European-style villas. Today the hills above the beach are dotted with these extravagant summer homes. Above them are the small, tightly packed adobes of a working-class village that has developed to service the mansions.

GETTING HERE AND AROUND

From Maitencillo, follow Ruta F30 E north over the clifftops until signs indicate the turn for Zapallar. If coming from Santiago, take Ruta 5 Norte, exit at the turnoff for Catapilco, and follow the road to the coast.

EXPLORING

Caleta de Zapallar. At the south end of Playa Zapallar is a rocky point that holds Caleta de Zapallar, where local fisherfolk unload their boats, sell their catch, and settle in for dominoes. The view of the beach from the caleta is simply gorgeous. On the other side of the point, a trail leads over the rocks to rugged but equally impressive views.

FAMILY   **Plaza del Mar Bravo.** Up the hill from Caleta de Zapallar is this plaza. Rough Sea Square has a park with an ocean view and a large playground. In January and February, there are usually mule rides for kids.

BEACHES

Fodor'sChoice   **Playa Zapallar.** Zapallar's raison d'être is a crescent of golden sand
★   kissed by blue-green waters, with a giant boulder plopped in the middle. Cropped at each end by rocky points and backed by large pines

and rambling flower gardens, it may well be the loveliest beach on the Central Coast. **Amenities:** food and drink. **Best for:** swimming; sunset; snorkeling.

WHERE TO EAT AND STAY

$$$$
SEAFOOD
Fodor'sChoice
★

✕ **El Chiringuito.** Pelicans, gulls, and cormorants linger among the fishing boats anchored near this remarkable seafood restaurant. Since it's next door to the fishermen's cooperative, the seafood is always the freshest. For starters choose from *machas* (razor clams), *camarones* (shrimp), or *ostiones* (scallops) cooked *al pil pil* (with chili sauce and garlic), *a la parmesana* (with cheese), or *a la crema* (with a cream sauce). Then sink your teeth into any of half a dozen types of fish, served with different sauces. The dining room—with a floor of crushed shells and hand-carved chairs resembling sea creatures—is a delight. $ *Average main: 11500 pesos* ⊠ *Caleta de Zapallar s/n* ☎ *33/274–1024* ⊗ *No dinner weekdays Mar.–Nov.*

$$$
B&B/INN
Fodor'sChoice
★

📷 **Isla Seca.** Bougainvillea and cypress trees surround two identical moss-green buildings with well-appointed, spacious rooms. **Pros:** quiet; feels secluded. **Cons:** not all rooms have ocean view. $ *Rooms from: 90000 pesos* ⊠ *Camino Costero Ruta F-30-E No. 31* ☎ *33/274–1224* ⊕ *www.hotelislaseca.cl* ⇆ *32 rooms, 10 suites* ⊚ *No meals.*

PAPUDO

11 km (7 miles) north of Zapallar.

In a letter dated October 8, 1545, Spanish conquistador Pedro Valdivia wrote: "Of all the lands of the New World, the port of Papudo has a goodness above any other land. It's like God's Paradise: it has a gentle temperate climate; large, resounding mountains; and fertile lands."

Today a jumble of apartment buildings and vacation homes detracts from the view Valdivia once admired, but the beaches and coast north of town remain quite pleasant. For years Papudo was connected to Santiago by a train that no longer runs. You can still find bits of that history in the quiet resort town.

GETTING HERE AND AROUND
From Zapallar, follow Ruta F30 E for 11 km (7 miles) north over the cliff tops until the road winds down into Papudo.

EXPLORING
Iglesia Parroquial de Papudo. Near the south end of town is this lovely 19th-century church. It was once part of a convent that has been replaced by vacation apartments. ⊠ *Costanera s/n* ⊗ *Open Jan. and Feb., weekends.*

Palacio Recart. A block from the beach sits this yellow building, built in 1910, which now holds municipal offices and hosts occasional art and history exhibitions. ⊠ *Costanera s/n.*

BEACHES
Chileans migrate to Papudo from Santiago every summer to play on its beaches.

Playa Chica. A small beach on the south end of town, Playa Chica is well protected and safe for swimming. **Amenities:** food and drink. **Best for:** swimming.

Playa Durazno. You have to do a bit of walking to reach Playa Durazno. It's an attractive beach north of Playa Grande—past the condominiums—that is lined with pine trees and protected by a rocky barrier offshore. **Amenities:** none. **Best for:** sunset; solitude.

Playa Grande. Papudo's most popular beach is Playa Grande, a wide strand that stretches northward from the Barco Rojo for more than a mile. **Amenities:** food and drink; parking. **Best for:** walking; swimming; sunset.

WHERE TO STAY

$$ B&B/INN 🏨 **Hotel Carande.** The only respectable hotel in town, Carande has rooms devoid of charm but just a short walk from the beach. **Pros:** great views down to the beach. **Cons:** lacks personality. [$] *Rooms from: 48000 pesos* ✉ *Chorillos 89* ☎ *33/279–1105* 🌐 *www.hotelcarande.cl* 🛏 *29 rooms, plus 1 suite* 🍴 *Breakfast.*

4

EL NORTE CHICO

WELCOME TO EL NORTE CHICO

TOP REASONS TO GO

★ **Sugar-sand beaches:** Soft sand, turquoise water, and warm breezes make El Norte Chico's beaches among Chile's best. In summer (January and February) you may have to fight for a place in the sun.

★ **Starry skies:** Thanks to some of the clearest skies in the world, Chile's northern desert is a top destination for international stargazers and scientists. A number of astronomical observatories in El Norte Chico arrange tours.

★ **Nature reserves:** Explore Parque Nacional Fray Jorge with its ghost-like fog, the petrified forest of Monumento Nacional Pichasca, and the barren desert landscape of the Parque Nacional Pan de Azúcar.

★ **Wine and pisco:** Any trip to El Norte Chico is incomplete without sampling its most famous export, *pisco*. The liquor's muscat grapes flourish in this temperate climate, which is also ideal for wine-grape-growing (particularly pinot noir), making this an up-and-coming wine producing region.

1 The Elqui Valley. Hot sun, cool pisco sours, and a heaven full of stars every night. Only an hour's drive from La Serena but a world apart from the bustling regional capital, the Elqui Valley is an inspirational place. It's easy to see where Chilean Nobel Prize–winning poet Gabriela Mistral, raised in the Valley, got her inspiration.

2 The Limarí Valley. This verdant valley is perfect for grape-growing and the source of some of Chile's newest and most exciting wines. It is also home to the only lapis lazuli mine in the country. The valley's main town, Ovalle, makes for a nice stop-off between Santiago and La Serena.

3 The Copiapó Valley. Copiapó itself is a hot, inland town where the mining industry's newly minted wealthy is building hotels and homes. Nevertheless, just 15 minutes outside of Copiapó is the desert, where quail and lizards scamper beneath the shadows of cacti, and rocks bear mysterious carvings.

ANTOFAGASTA

Parque Nacional
Pan de Azúcar

Chañaral

El Salvador

Salar de
Pedernales

PACIFIC
OCEAN

Diego de
Almagro

Potrerillos

La Ola

Inca
del Oro

Cerro
Ermitanno

31

Bahía Inglesa

5

3

Salar de
Maricunga

Copiapó

Cta. del
Medio

Tierra
Amarilla

Los Azules

La Guardia

ATACAMA

Los Loros

Río Copiapó

Algarrobal

Las Juntas

Huasco

Freirina

5

Cta. Sarco

Domeyko

Gonay

Cerro del
Toro

Cta. Chañaral

La Higuera
Los Hornos

Las Breas

El Romeral

Cerro Las
Tortolas

La Serena

41

Vicuña

Coquimbo

Tongoy

Pisco
Elqui

Quebrada
Seca

2

Ovalle

Monte
Patria

Río Elqui

Parque
Nacional
Fray Jorge

5

Punitaque

Central
Los Molles

Cta
Morritos

San Marcos

Tulahuén

Puerto
Oscuro

COQUIMBO

Combarbalá

Illapel

ARGENTINA

Río Choapa

Salamanca

0   50 miles

Quilimari

0   75 km

VALPARAÍSO

A N D E S

4

GETTING
ORIENTED

El Norte Chico is a vast
region spreading some 700
km (435 miles) between
Río Aconcagua and Río
Copiapó. Ideally, you need
more than one base to
explore the entire area. In the
south, La Serena is a good
place to start if you're going
to the Elqui Valley. The Limarí
Valley is where you want
to be if your destination is
Valle del Encanto. Copiapó,
near the region's northern
border, is a convenient stop
if you're headed to Parque
Nacional Pan de Azúcar.

Updated by
Sam Edwards

Between the fertile central valley to the south and the vast expanse of the Atacama Desert to the north, El Norte Chico—or Chile's Little North—hosts a fantastically eclectic range of climates, landscapes, and activities in a compact area. Among the burnt hills, stargazers and wine buffs rub shoulders with adrenaline seekers in a region known equally for its white-sand beaches and towering mountains as its world-class research telescopes and vineyards.

These varied landscapes and ecosystems, unsurprisingly, are home to a diverse range of flora and fauna. Visitors with the will to tear themselves away from the beaches can tour rocky offshore islands that shelter colonies of penguins and sea lions or cruise the clear, cool waters of the marine reserves where sperm whales and bottlenose dolphins flourish. Shimmering mountain lakes are home to huge flocks of flamingos. Even the parched earth flourishes twice a decade in a phenomenon called el desierto florido, or the flowering desert. During these years, the bleak landscape gives way to a riot of colors—flowers of every hue imaginable burst from the normally infertile soil of the plain.

In a land where water is so precious, it's not surprising that the people who migrated here never strayed far from its rivers. In the south, La Serena sits at the mouth of the Elqui River. El Norte Chico's most important city, La Serena is the region's cultural center as well, with colonial architecture and a European flavor. Nearby, in the fertile Elqui Valley, farmers in tiny villages grow grapes to make pisco, the potent brandy that has become Chile's national drink. Those in search of archaeological wonders head to Valle del Encanto, a large collection of ancient petroglyphs.

On El Norte Chico's northern frontier is the Río Copiapó. This is the region that grew up and grew rich during the silver boom. The town of Copiapó, this area's most important trade center, makes an excellent jumping off point for exploring the hinterland. Heading toward the ocean, you come to Parque Nacional Pan de Azúcar, where some of El Norte Chico's most stunning coastal scenery is.

PLANNER

WHEN TO GO
During the summer months of January and February, droves of Chileans and Argentines flee their stifling hot cities for the relative cool of El Norte Chico's beaches. Although it is an exciting time to visit, prices go up and rooms are hard to find. Make your reservations at least a month in advance. For a little tranquillity, it is better to visit when the high season tapers off in March. Moving inland, the weather is mild all year. The almost perpetually clear skies explain why the region has

the largest concentration of observatories in the world, although the temperatures drop quite a bit when you head to the mountains.

PLANNING YOUR TIME

Five days should give you time for a quick road trip to see the best the region has to offer. Start by visiting the Valle del Encanto near Ovalle to see the petroglyphs, and then go to nearby Viña Tabalí vineyard, ending the day with a relaxing dip in the hot springs at the Termas de Socos. The next morning, head toward the coast to La Serena and spend the day exploring the whitewashed churches and lively markets of this quaint colonial town. On the third day, journey to the idyllic and mystical village of Pisco Elqui to relax with a massage and obligatory pisco sour, before spending the evening stargazing. The following morning, head north to Bahía Inglesa to sunbathe on some of the region's most beautiful and deserted beaches, finishing on day five in Copiapó after a visit to the Parque Nacional Pan de Azúcar.

GETTING HERE AND AROUND

AIR TRAVEL

While El Norte Chico lacks an international airport, both LAN and Sky operate several flights daily from Santiago to La Serena and Copiapó. Round-trip flights to El Norte Chico can be as cheap as 40,000 pesos if booked in advance but much more expensive in high season and for late availability.

BUS TRAVEL

Every major city in El Norte Chico has a bus terminal, and there are frequent departures to other cities as well as smaller towns in the area. Keep in mind that there may be no bus service to the smallest villages or more remote national parks.

CAR AND TAXI TRAVEL

Because of the distances between cities, a car is the best way to truly see El Norte Chico. Many national parks can be visited only by car, preferably a four-wheel-drive vehicle. Without one, taxis are the most efficient way to get around any city. Most have meters, but for those that don't, check the price with the operator before setting out. A cheaper alternative is a *colectivo*, a taxi that picks up several people going in the same direction. Colectivos charge a fixed rate per person regardless of the number of passengers and run very regularly during business hours. Fares begin at around 500 pesos per person for inter-city trips, increasing up to around 2,500 for traveling longer distances between towns.

RESTAURANTS

Although El Norte Chico is not known for gastronomy, the food here is simple, unpretentious, and often quite good. Along the coast, you'll find abundant seafood. Don't pass up the *merluza con salsa margarita* (hake with a butter sauce featuring almost every kind of shellfish imaginable) or *choritos al vapor* (mussels steamed in white wine). Inland you come across country-style *cabrito* (goat), *conejo* (rabbit), and *pichones escabechados* (baby pigeons). Don't forget to order a pisco sour, the frothy concoction made with a grape-based brandy distilled in the Elqui Valley.

People in El Norte Chico generally eat a heavy lunch around 2 pm that can last two hours, followed by a light dinner around 10 pm.

Reservations are seldom needed, except in the fanciest restaurants. Leave a 10% tip if you enjoyed the service.

HOTELS

The good news is that lodging in El Norte Chico is relatively inexpensive. Your best bet is often the beach resorts, which have everything from nice cabanas to high-rise hotels. Farther inland, the region is experiencing a boom in boutique hotels and innovative rental properties, meaning lodging in style in beautiful surroundings is more affordable than ever. Almost all lodging options listed offer breakfast included in the price. *Hotel reviews have been shortened. For full information, visit Fodors.com.*

WHAT IT COSTS IN CHILEAN PESOS (IN THOUSANDS)			
$	$$	$$$	$$$$
Restaurants Under 6	6–9	10–13	over 13
Hotels Under 51	51–85	86–115	over 115

Restaurant prices are the average cost of a main course price at dinner or, if dinner is not served, at lunch. Hotel prices are the lowest cost of a standard double room in high season, excluding tax.

HEALTH AND SAFETY

Naturally, in the desert, drinking plenty of nonalcoholic fluids is crucial, as is protecting your face and body from the sun's powerful rays. Get a good pair of sunglasses for driving, as the glare can be intense. Keep in mind that pisco sours, though they may go down as smooth as lemonade, are a powerful drink, so a moderate intake is recommended.

TOURS

You're welcome to tour many of the region's pisco distilleries. Several of them are more than 100 years old, with the oldest distillery in Pisco Elqui in the Elqui Valley. The Solar de Pisco Elqui has been entirely renovated since it began operations, but you can still take a tour of the old plant and learn how pisco is made. This is where the famous Tres Erres brand is distilled. In Pisco Elqui you also find Los Nichos, a quaint 130-year-old distillery open to the public, whereas nearby Vicuña is home to Chile's most popular brand, Capel. To escape the crowds, head to the Pisquera Aba distillery near Vicuña or ask at your hotel about less frequently visited distilleries in the Limarí Valley.

THE ELQUI VALLEY

It's hard to believe that hidden by the dusty brown hills of El Norte Chico is a sliver of land as lush and green as the Elqui Valley. The people who live along the Río Elqui harvest everything from olives to avocados. The most famous crop is the grape variety distilled to make Chile's national drink—pisco. A village named after this lovely elixir, Pisco Elqui, sits high up in the valley.

The Elqui Valley is renowned not only for its grapes, but also for its unusually clear skies, which have brought scientists from around the world to peer through the telescopes of the area's many observatories. The stars also attract many new agers, who believe the planet's spiritual center has shifted from the Himalayas to the Elqui Valley. Many who came here to check out the vibes decided to stay.

The Elqui Valley has been inhabited for thousands of years. First came the Diaguitas, whose intricate pottery is among the most beautiful of pre-Columbian ceramics, then the

> ## MYSTICISM AND MEDITATION
>
> Considered the geomagnetic center of the world, the Elqui Valley is renowned as a place for reflection and relaxation. In tranquil Pisco Elqui, spa treatments and esoteric sessions like Reiki are commonplace on the list of hotels' additional services.

Molles. The Incas, who came here 500 years ago in search of gold, are relative newcomers. The clues these cultures left behind are part of what makes the Elqui Valley so fascinating.

LA SERENA

Fodor's Choice ★ *480 km (300 miles) north of Santiago.*

Steeped in history, Chile's second-oldest city, La Serena, wears two distinct faces today. On one hand, it charms visitors with its European-style old quarter. On the other, it dazzles with a dash of modern pomp and convenience through its upmarket beachfront—a great place to indulge in sunshine and luxurious hotels and restaurants. The city's location within easy striking distance of many top regional attractions makes it a good base to explore the budding astronomy, viticulture, and wildlife of El Norte Chico.

One of the most stunning features amid the pleasant streets and hidden plazas of La Serena is the number of churches: there are more than 30, and many date as far back as the late 16th century. Most have survived fires, earthquakes, and pirate attacks, all common threats in the turbulent decades after conquistador Pedro de Valdivia founded the city in 1544.

The preservation of colonial architecture, and its continuance, is thanks to Gabriel González Videla, who was president of Chile from 1946 to 1952. ■ TIP➔ **Take care of banking or medical needs in La Serena, as there are fewer services in other towns in the area.**

GETTING HERE AND AROUND

La Serena is almost exactly 300 miles north of Santiago via Ruta 5, the Pan-American Highway. A bus trip takes about six hours from the capital, often with a stop in Ovalle (from which it's an hour or less to La Serena). La Serena's bus terminal on Avenida Amunátegui is a 15-minute walk or a 5-minute ride from downtown (colectivos 21 and 44 make the trip for less than a dollar). Daily flights from Santiago take about an hour to reach La Serena's La Florida Airport, which is 20 to 30 minutes from downtown via car or taxi. The Pan-American Highway runs right through town if you follow Avenida Francisco de

Aguirre toward the ocean. The Elqui Valley is just an hour to the east of La Serena via Route 41.

TOURS

From La Serena, tours can be arranged for regional highlights including the Elqui Valley, several observatories, and the nature reserve on Isla Damas, where you can spot penguins, whales, and dolphins. Historical tours of La Serena and adjacent Coquimbo are available from almost all local operators.

Elqui Valley Tour. This operator runs regular tours to the Isla Damas marine nature reserve, La Serena's historical center, Mamalluca Observatory, and the Elqui Valley. When there is sufficient demand, Elqui Valley Tours also leads excursions to areas of Parque Nacional Fray Jorge and Valle de Encanto, as well as the nearby town of Andacollo. ⊠ *Arturo Prat 567, Interior Patio* ☎ *51/214–846, 9/7374–2208* ⊕ *www.elquivalleytour.cl* ✉ *From 20,000 pesos.*

Ingservtur. This local tour operator organizes visits to sites of historical interest in La Serena, nearby observatories, the Elqui Valley, and the Isla Damas marine reserve. ☎ *51/248–4008* ⊕ *www.ingservtur.cl* ✉ *From 20,000 pesos.*

Itravel. The holder of a national tourism service seal of quality, Itravel leads excursions to Isla Damas and the surrounding areas of marine interest: the Elqui Valley and Fray Jorge National Park. As well as organizing visits to the tourist-friendly Mamalluca Observatory, this company goes to the more remote research observatories not serviced by public transport. Private tours to other destinations can also be arranged. ⊠ *Eduardo de la Barra 657* ☎ *51/222–4350, 51/9–6190–7045* ⊕ *www.itravel.cl* ✉ *From 19,000 pesos.*

Talinay. Trekking in the Andes, scuba diving, rock climbing, and paintballing are among the activities available through this adventure tourism specialist. You can also organize visits to the popular regional attractions, including the Isla Damas reserve, Mamalluca Observatory, and Elqui Valley. ⊠ *Parcela 52, Hortencia Bustamante* ☎ *9/8360–6464* ⊕ *www.talinaychile.com* ✉ *From 24,000 pesos.*

ESSENTIALS

Air Contacts La Florida Airport (LSC) ⊠ *Ruta 41* ☎ *51/227-0236.* **LAN** ⊠ *Balmaceda 406* ☎ *600/526-2000* ⊕ *www.lan.com.*

Bus Contacts La Serena Bus Station ⊠ *Av. El Santo and Amunátegui* ☎ *51/222-4573.* **Tur-Bus** ☎ *600/660-6600* ⊕ *www.turbus.cl.*

Car Rental Contacts Avis ⊠ *Av. Francisco de Aguirre 063* ☎ *51/254-5300* ⊕ *www.avis.cl.* **Budget** ⊠ *Av. Francisco de Aguirre 063* ☎ *51/254-5300* ⊕ *www.budget.cl.* **Hertz** ⊠ *Av. Francisco de Aguirre 0409A* ☎ *2/2360-5770* ⊕ *www.hertz.com* ⊠ *La Florida Airport* ☎ *51/256-0432* ⊕ *www.hertz.cl.*

Taxi Contacts Pacífico ⊠ *Los Carreras 572* ☎ *51/2218-000, 9/8337-7133.* **Radio Taxi El Libertador** ⊠ *Baquedano 2405* ☎ *51/225-2777, 51/225-2727.*

Visitor Information Sernatur ⊠ *Los Carrera 691, Copiapó* ☎ *52/221-2838, 52/223-1510* ⊕ *www.sernatur.cl.*

EXPLORING
TOP ATTRACTIONS

Fodor's Choice ★ **Museo Arqueológico de La Serena.** Housing many fascinating artifacts—including an impressive collection of Diaguita pottery—this museum is a must-see for anyone interested in the history of the region. The Archaeology Museum contains one of the world's best collections of precolonial ceramics. Also here is a *moai* (carved stone head) from Easter Island. ⊠ *Cordovez and Cienfuegos* ☎ *51/267–2243 tickets, 51/267–2210 central desk* ⊕ *www.museoarqueologicolaserena.cl* ⊠ *600 pesos (includes Museo Histórico Gabriel González Videla)* ⊙ *Tues.–Fri. 9:30–5:50, Sat. 10–1 and 4–7, Sun. 10–1.*

Museo Mineralógico. One of the most complete mineral collections in the world is on display here. Exhibits highlight fossils and minerals from the surrounding region. ⊠ *University of La Serena, Benavente 980, Faculty of Engineering* ☎ *51/220–4096* ⊠ *500 pesos* ⊙ *Mon.–Wed. 9:30–2:30.*

WORTH NOTING

Iglesia Catedral. The largest church in La Serena, this imposing cathedral faces the beautiful Plaza de Armas and is open to the public. French architect Jean Herbage built this behemoth using stone from the Soldado mine in 1844 in the so-called Serena style of arches and columns, but it wasn't until the turn of the 20th century that the bell tower was added. ⊠ *Cordovez and Balmaceda.*

Iglesia San Francisco. One of La Serena's oldest churches, Iglesia San Francisco has a Baroque facade and thick stone walls. The exact date of the church's construction is not known, as the city archives were destroyed in 1680, but it's estimated that the structure was built sometime between 1585 and 1627. The church is open to the public. ⊠ *Balmaceda 640.*

Iglesia Santo Domingo. This impressive church was built in 1673 and then rebuilt after a pirate attack in 1755. Its Italian Renaissance–style facade is eye-catching and its best feature is the elegant bell tower. ⊠ *Pedro Pablo Muñoz and Cordovez.*

Memorial en Homenaje a los Detenidos Desaparecidos y Ejecutados Políticos de la IV Región. A reminder of Chile's recent tragic past—a troubled and frightening era—the Memorial to the Disappeared Prisoners and Executed Politicians of the IV Region is dedicated to the "disappeared" of this area of Chile, who were killed during the Pinochet regime in the 1970s and '80s. More than 60 persons, many of whom died in their early twenties, are listed on the large stone monument. ⊠ *Adjacent to Parque Japonés on steps leading up to Pedro Pablo Muñoz street.*

Museo Histórico Gabriel González Videla. The former president's home has exhibits about him as well as works by Chilean artists. ⊠ *Matta 495* ☎ *51/221–7189* ⊕ *www.museohistoricolaserena.cl* ⊠ *600 pesos (includes Museo Arqueológico)* ⊙ *Weekdays 10–6, Sat. 10–1.*

Parque Japonés. A Japanese garden in the heart of Latin America, this park is a pleasant place to pass an afternoon. Here you will find koi-filled ponds, intricate bridges, and a network of paths. A mining company built the park as a goodwill gesture to its Japanese trading partners. ⊠ *Eduardo de la Barra s/n (at bottom of staircase)*

☎ *51/221–7013* 🎟 *1,000 pesos* ⏲ *Mar.–Dec., Tues.–Sun. 10–5:40; Jan. and Feb., daily 10–8.*

BEACHES

La Herradura. Well-sheltered within a small cove, La Herradura—or The Horseshoe—is a small but attractive beach, which enjoys calm waters and lies within easy striking distance of Coquimbo. These days it is best known as a holiday destination or as a prime spot for diving and windsurfing, but the area's history as a fishing cove can still be seen in the brightly colored boats tethered out in the calm waters of the bay. **Amenities:** food and drink; parking (fee). **Best for:** swimming; sunset; surfing; windsurfing; snorkeling.

Playa Peñuelas. Stretching along the city's coastline up until neighboring Coquimbo, this sandy city beach is La Serena's star attraction and a popular spot for families, surfers, and couples, who come to enjoy the great views over the bay at sunset. Like many city beaches, though, it suffers from mild trash problems in parts and is overrun with tourists during the summer high season. The large waves favored by surfers also mean swimming is prohibited in places. **Amenities:** food and drink; lifeguards (summer only); parking (fee); toilets. **Best for:** walking; sunset; surfing.

Fodor's Choice ★ **Playa Totoralillo.** Even though it's a bit of a trek, this stunning package of bleach-white sand, turquoise water, and rocky desert scenery is worth the trip. The 17-km (10-mile) trip south from Coquimbo is more than made up for by the natural advantages of the beach and the perfect conditions for swimming, diving, fishing, and snorkeling. **Amenities:** food and drink (summer only); parking (fee). **Best for:** snorkeling; sunset; surfing; swimming; walking.

WHERE TO EAT

$$ CHILEAN 🍴 **Donde el Guatón.** Popular with locals, this European-style steak house serves everything from shish kebab to steak with eggs. The early republic-themed decor and waiters clad in the traditional garb of the Chilean cowboy, or *huaso,* narrowly avoid coming off as contrived, but ultimately present a fitting backdrop for the plethora of hearty local fare. With its several intimate dining areas off the main salon and good selection of wines from the nearby Elqui Valley, this is a good place to enjoy a romantic, candlelit meal. On weekends there is live folk guitar music. [$] *Average main: 7500 pesos* ✉ *Brasil 750* ☎ *51/221–1519* ⏲ *No dinner Sun.*

$$ ITALIAN 🍴 **La Mía Pizza.** Just across the road from the beach and with great views across the bay, this pizza parlor serves a range of tasty pasta classics appealing to holidaymakers and the business lunch crowd alike. The extensive menu includes locally sourced delights such as *cordero* Sebastián (lamb in a red wine and mushroom sauce, served with potatoes and polenta), as well as traditional Italian staples, and for dessert a papaya split. [$] *Average main: 8000 pesos* ✉ *Av. Del Mar 2100* ☎ *51/221–2891, 51/221–2232* ✍ *Reservations not accepted* ⏲ *No dinner Sun. Mar.–Dec.*

WHERE TO STAY

$$$ HOTEL **Costa Real.** Centrally located and replete with all the modern touches you might expect from an executive-class hotel—business center, meeting rooms, and Wi-Fi access throughout—Costa Real is an eminently efficient, practical option for any visit to La Serena. **Pros:** modern and clean. **Cons:** on a busy thoroughfare; far from beach. [$] *Rooms from: 90000 pesos* ✉ *Av. Francisco de Aguirre 170* ☎ *51/222–1010* 🌐 *www.costareal.cl* 🛏 *49 rooms, 2 suites* 🍴 *Breakfast.*

$$$ HOTEL FAMILY **Hotel Club La Serena.** Defining itself in opposition to its more luxurious, high-end rivals, this hotel offers a professional but somewhat understated, four-star setting for business delegations in the off-season before letting its hair down for a few months each summer to cater to the die-hard beachcombers, who descend on the conveniently located complex. **Pros:** near the beach; nice pool. **Cons:** rooms are rather small. [$] *Rooms from: 90000 pesos* ✉ *Av. del Mar 1000* ☎ *51/222–1262* 🌐 *www.clublaserena.com* 🛏 *54 rooms, 44 suites* 🍴 *Breakfast.*

$$$ HOTEL **Hotel de la Bahía.** Every room has a sea view at this hotel that towers over the far end of the Avenida del Mar. **Pros:** a sea view from every room; top-tier facilities and service. **Cons:** can be noisy at night; out-of-the-way location. [$] *Rooms from: 100000 pesos* ✉ *Av. Peñuelas Norte 56* ☎ *51/242–3000* 🌐 *www.enjoy.cl* 🛏 *111 rooms, 10 suites* 🍴 *Breakfast.*

$$ B&B/INN **Hotel del Cid.** A good option for those keen to explore the history of Chile's second oldest city, this welcoming B&B in a colonial-style building provides personalized service and a homey atmosphere. **Pros:** family atmosphere; personalized service. **Cons:** far from the beach. [$] *Rooms from: 55000 pesos* ✉ *Av. Bernardo O'Higgins 138* ☎ *51/221–2692* 🌐 *www.hoteldelcid.cl* 🛏 *25 rooms* 🍴 *Breakfast.*

NIGHTLIFE

Ovo Lounge. Vast, modern, and unashamedly generic, Ovo Lounge is a decent option for mainstream music until late every Thursday through Saturday. This chain club tends to attract a slightly more affluent crowd in the 25–35 age range. ✉ *Av. Peñuales Norte 56* 🎟 *7,000 pesos including cover.*

Rapsodia. A huge palm dominates the central courtyard at Rapsodia, a small coffee shop and pub in the center of town, which carries on late into the evening on Thursday and Friday. This is a great place to grab a snack and listen to live jazz and blues. ✉ *Arturo Prat 470, interior courtyard* ☎ *51/221–2695.*

SHOPPING

Mall Plaza La Serena. This sprawling, modern, 70-store mall is home to coffee and wine shops, music stores, and two movie theaters. ✉ *Alberto Solari 1400* ☎ *2/2585–7000* 🌐 *www.laserena.mallplaza.cl.*

Mercado La Recova. On the corner of Cienfuegos and Cantournet, this modern market housed in a pleasant neoclassical building sells dried fruits, handicrafts, and lapis lazuli jewelry. The Diaguita-style ceramics and the trinkets made from *combarbalita*, the locally mined marblelike rock, are particularly stunning. ✉ *Cantournet and Cienfuegos.*

VICUÑA

62 km (38 miles) east of La Serena via Ruta 41.

As you head into the Elqui Valley, the first town you come to is Vicuña, famous as the birthplace of one of Chile's most important literary figures, Gabriela Mistral. Her beautiful, haunting poetry often looks back on her early years in the Elqui Valley. Mistral's legacy is unmistakable as you wander through town. In the Plaza de Armas, for example, there is a chilling stone replica of the poet's death mask.

GETTING HERE AND AROUND

Vicuña is about an hour's drive or bus ride from La Serena, a straight shot on Route 41. Enjoy the views of the vineyards as you make the slight climb from the coast. The tiny bus terminal in Vicuña is serviced by a number of regular buses, vans, and colectivos.

Colectivos run 24 hours and can be flagged down at designated stops. To take the colectivo from La Serena to Vicuña, go to the main office at Domeyko 565 or flag the colectivo from the corner of Cienfuegos and Cantournet, outside La Recova market.

ESSENTIALS

Bus Contacts **Bus Station** ⊠ *Av. Bernardo O'Higgins, near corner of Arturo Prat.* **Vicuña and Valle de Elqui colectivo** ☎ *51/241-695.*

Visitor Information **Vicuña Tourist Information** ⊠ *At bottom of Torre Bauer, opposite Plaza de Armas* ☎ *51/267-0308.*

EXPLORING
TOP ATTRACTIONS

Centro Tursitico Capel. Visiting a pisco vineyard is a great way to learn about the history of the product that has come to define the Elqui Valley, not to mention the perfect excuse to enjoy a relaxing glass of this tasty, fruity, aromatic drink in beautiful surroundings. At Centro Turistico Capel, just across the Elqui River from Vicuña, tour the bottling facility, well-groomed gardens, and artisan's gallery, before tasting several piscos. ⊠ *Camino a Peralillo s/n* ☎ *51/255-4337* 🎟 *Standard tour 2,500 pesos* ۞ *Mar.–Dec., daily 10–6; Jan. and Feb., daily 10–7.*

Gran Observatorio Solar de Chile. This new project of the Pangue Observatory claims to be the only solar tourist observatory in South America. Using a specialized Lunt Solar System Telescope—one of only seven in the world—visitors can observe phenomena such as sunspots, the equatorial bulge, and solar flares. Tours run all day and throughout the year, though observations are often hampered by overcast weather June to August. ⊠ *San Martín 233* ☎ *51/241-2584* 🎟 *2,500 pesos* ۞ *Daily 10–5:30.*

Museo Gabriela Mistral. An expansive tribute to Vicuña's favorite daughter, the Gabriela Mistral Museum gathers a wide array of artifacts from the writer's life, including handwritten letters, poems, and a signed copy of Canto General given to her by her compatriot and fellow Nobel Prize winner, Pablo Neruda. A pleasant garden behind the main salon pays tribute to Mistral's love of nature. ⊠ *Gabriela Mistral 759* ☎ *51/241-1223* ⊕ *www.dibam.cl/sdm_mgm_vicuna* 🎟 *600 pesos* ۞ *Jan. and*

STARRY NIGHTS

With some of the clearest skies in the Southern Hemisphere, El Norte Chico is home to many of the world's most powerful telescopes, several of which give guided tours by appointment. A boom in tourist-friendly observatories in the Elqui Valley means visitors have ample opportunity to peer into the depths of the universe for themselves. Of these, Observatorio Cerro Mamal-luca (Vicuña) is the original and most popular, but the newer Observatorio del Pangue (Vicuña) now boasts the best facilities, while recently opened Gran Observatorio Solar de Chile (Vicuña) is the only place in South America where tourists can observe the sun.

Cerro Tololo Observatory. Perched at 2,200 meters (7,200 feet), Cerro Tololo Observatory runs free tours of its two principal telescopes on Saturday. During January and Febru-ary, priority is given to nonspecial-ist visitors—although high demand means it's worth reserving at least a month in advance—while the rest of the year the observatory tours cater principally to delegations. Tours should first be requested by phone or email, then, once the reservation has been made, permission certifica-tion can be picked up at the obser-vatory's offices in Las Serena on the corner of avenidas Huanhalí and J. Cisternas. Tours may be canceled in bad weather. ⊠ *Rte. 41, 80 km (50 miles) east of La Serena, Colina El Pino, Vicuña* ☎ *51/220–5200* ⊕ *www.ctio.noao.edu.*

Gemini South Observatory. With one of the largest telescopes in the world, an 8.1-meter Cassegrain, this observatory 10 km (6 miles) from Cerro Tololo is operated by a consortium of six nations. Tours of the telescope are free of charge on Friday mornings May through September and can be catered to the interests of the group (usually 10–25 people). Email at least a month in advance to request a place on the tour. Priority is given to student and scientific delegations. ⊠ *Rte. 41, 90 km (55 miles) east of La Serena, Cerro Pachón, Vicuña* ☎ *51/220–5600* ⊕ *www.gemini.edu.*

Las Campanas Observatory. This observatory of the Carnegie Institute of Washington, 100 km (62 miles) north of La Serena, has twin 6.5-meter Magellan telescopes, which can be visited on free tours of the facilities Saturday 10–2:30. Due to demand visitors are advised to make reservations several weeks in advance. Preference is given to school groups and delegations. ⊠ *Rte. 41, 80 km (50 miles) east of La Serena, Colina El Pino, Vicuña* ☎ *51/220–7301* ⊕ *www.lco.cl.*

La Silla Observatory. Adminis-tered by the 15-member European Southern Observatory (ESO), La Silla Observatory is one of the largest and most important observatories in the Southern Hemisphere. Free tours are available of the three principal telescopes each Saturday at 2 pm, except during July and August, due to the risk of snowstorms in this period. Note that bookings are only accepted if made via the online visitor form. ⊠ *Pan-American Hwy., about 130 km (80 miles) north of La Serena, signposted just after turnoff for Incahuasi and before reaching Vallenar, Vallenar* ☎ *2/2463–3100* ⊕ *www.ls.eso.org.*

*Feb., Mon.–Sat. 10–7, Sun. 10–6; Mar.–Dec., weekdays 10–5:45, Sat.
10:30–6, Sun. 10–1.*

Observatorio Cerro Mamalluca. The most welcoming of the Elqui Valley
observatories and the one that attracts the most visitors, Mamalluca
is 9 km (5½ miles) north of Vicuña. On the Basic Astronomy tour,
visitors are given an introductory talk before stargazing on the terrace
and taking turns looking through a 12-inch digital telescope at sights
including the moons of Jupiter and the rings of Saturn. Another tour
focuses more on the Andean interpretation of the constellations. You
can either make your own way to the observatory or contract transport from the tour office in Vicuña at 3,000 pesos per person. ⊠ *Tour
office, Gabriela Mistral 260* ☎ *51/267–0330* 💴 *Each tour 4,500 pesos*
🕙 *Basic Astronomy tour daily at 8:30 pm, 10:30 pm, 12:30 am, and
2:30 am; Andean Cosmology tour daily at 7:30 pm, 9:30 pm, 11:30
pm, 1:30 am, and 3:30 am.*

Fodor'sChoice   **Pangue Observatory.** One of the many tourist observatories to pop up
★   across the region catering to the growing numbers of visitors keen to
catch their own glimpse of the mysteries of the universe, Pangue—17
km (11 miles) south of Vicuña—boasts more firepower than most,
with arguably the most powerful telescope in the region. Through the
16- and 25-inch telescopes are solar systems, planets, galaxies, and
nebulae. The standard tour allows enough time to see eight to 10 such
phenomena, while budding stargazers are welcome to bring their own
list of sites, and tour guides help you find them. Tours can be organized
from the tour office at San Martín 233 in Vicuña and are available
in English, French, and Spanish. Note that tours do not run for the
week around each full moon. ⊠ *17 km north of Vicuña, Ruta Antakari
D445* ☎ *51/241–2584* ⊕ *observatoriodelpangue.blogspot.com* 💴 *From
21,000 pesos.*

Viña Cavas del Valle. A pleasant stop along the drive between Vicuña
and Pisco Elqui, this boutique vineyard uses natural processes to produce several much-praised wines. Production is limited, and the wine
is sold only here at the vineyards. Tours include a visit of the original
ancestral home, which now houses the cellar. ⊠ *Ruta R-485, at Km
14.5; 1 km before Montegrande from Vicuña* ☎ *9/6842–5592* ⊕ *www.
cavasdelvalle.cl* 💴 *Free* 🕙 *Jan. and Feb., daily 10–8; Mar.–Dec., daily
10–6:30.*

WORTH NOTING

Cerro de la Virgen. Devotees of the Virgen de Lourdes, the town's patron
saint, consider this hill a place of pilgrimage. Overlooking the city,
it affords a great view of Vicuña. It's a 2-km (1-mile) hike north of
the city via a path on Baquedano between Independencia and Yungay.
■ TIP→ Head up in the evening to see the surrounding hills in the Elqui
Valley bathed in deep reds and oranges by the setting sun.

Iglesia de la Inmaculada Concepción. A huge steeple tops this 1909 church
facing the central square. It has some pretty ceiling paintings and an
image of the Virgin del Carmen carried by Chilean troops during the
War of the Pacific. The wooden, fire-engine-red Torre Bauer, next to
the church, was prefabricated in Germany. ⊠ *Gabriela Mistral 315.*

Pisquera Aba. Just off the road that leads from Vicuña to Pisco Elqui is a small, family-run distillery known for producing several premium piscos. The free 40-minute tour includes tastings. ✉ *Fundo San Juan, sector El Arenal, Km 66 Ruta 41* ☎ *51/241–1039* 🌐 *www.pisquera-aba.cl* 🎟 *Free* 🕒 *Mar.–Dec., daily 9–6; Jan. and Feb., daily 10–7.*

Solar de los Madariaga. Built between 1870 and 1875 and maintained as a historic, colonial-era home of the region, this museum is complete with antique furnishings, including ornate furniture and pictures of the Madariaga family. ✉ *Gabriela Mistral 683* ☎ *51/241–1220* 🎟 *900 pesos* 🕒 *Mar.–Dec., Wed.–Mon. 11–2 and 4–6; Jan. and Feb., Wed.–Mon. 10:30–2:30 and 4–7.*

4

WHERE TO EAT AND STAY

$$ LATIN AMERICAN 🍴 **Restaurant Halley.** With open-air dining under a straw roof, this restaurant gives you the feeling that you're having a picnic. The menu focuses on hearty country fare, and the *cabrito* (roasted goat) is especially succulent. If you've got a sweet tooth, the *velo de novia* (a milk flan with pineapple and meringue) is a delicious house specialty. [$] *Average main: 7000 pesos* ✉ *Gabriela Mistral 404* ☎ *51/241–1225* 🌐 *www.turismohalley.cl.*

$ B&B/INN 🏨 **Hostal Valle Hermoso.** Set in a beautiful turn-of-the-century house that seeps history and has some of the most reasonable rates in town, it's no wonder that Hostal Valle Hermoso has become a favorite with visiters. **Pros:** beautiful building; comfy; great-value lodging; near museums. **Cons:** no garden; Wi-Fi signal can be patchy in rooms. [$] *Rooms from: 31300 pesos* ✉ *Gabriela Mistral 706* ☎ *51/241–1206* 🌐 *www.hostalvallehermoso.com* 🛏 *9 rooms* 🍽 *Breakfast.*

$ B&B/INN 🏨 **Hotel Halley.** In a pretty colonial house with wood trim and white walls, this inn has carefully decorated rooms filled with authentic circa-1950s radios and more doilies than you could possibly imagine. **Pros:** garden is a great place to escape the usually warm weather; quaint; central location. **Cons:** small pool; old-fashioned. [$] *Rooms from: 36500 pesos* ✉ *Gabriela Mistral 542* ☎ *51/241–2070* 🌐 *www.turismohalley.cl* 🛏 *11 rooms, 1 suite* 🍽 *Breakfast.*

NIGHTLIFE

Antawara Restobar. While it admittedly has little competition, Antawara has cemented its position as Vicuña's principal spot for evening entertainment. Andean food and traditional Chilean fare are on the menu, then later on, regular live music and a wide selection of locally produced piscos keep things lively in the only real nightlife spot in this otherwise permanently sleepy town. ✉ *Gabriela Mistral 107.*

PISCO ELQUI

43 km (27 miles) east of Vicuña.

This idyllic village of fewer than 600 residents has two pisco plants. Once known as La Unión, the town, perched on a sun-drenched hillside, received its current moniker in 1939. Gabriel González Videla, at that time the president of Chile, renamed the village in a shrewd maneuver to ensure that Peru would not gain exclusive rights over the term "pisco." The Peruvian town of Pisco also produces the heady brandy.

GETTING HERE AND AROUND

From Vicuña, take Ruta 41 east to the turn for Paihuano (Ruta D-485). Follow this serpentine, narrow road south about 12 km (7½ miles) into Pisco Elqui. Buses and colectivos run with frequency between La Serena, Vicuña, and Pisco Elqui. A bus or colectivo between Vicuña and Pisco Elqui costs about 1,500 pesos. The small bus lines Via Elqui and Sol de Elqui make the 30-minute trip between La Serena and Pisco Elqui with 20-passenger buses.

ESSENTIALS

Bus Contacts Sol de Elqui ☏ *51/231-7499.* **Valle de Elqui colectivo** ☏ *51/222-4517.* **Via Elqui** ☏ *51/231-2422.*

TOURS

Elqui Enduro. Renting out motorbikes, with or without guides, Elqui Enduro explores the Elqui Valley and more remote Andean landscapes in a fresh way. Among the sites you can visit are glaciers, the high altitude Agua Negra mountain pass, and various mountain lakes. ⊠ *Arturo Pratt s/n* ☏ *9/7979-0830* ⊕ *www.elquienduro.com* 🖾 *From 30,000 pesos.*

Turismo Dagaz. With a wide range of specialized tours around Pisco Elqui, Turismo Dagaz is part of the town's booming adventure tourism sector. Visits to Elqui Valley and the high Andean scenery of Agua Negra, close to the Argentine border, round out stargazing evenings and trekking activities. ⊠ *Arturo Prat s/n* ☏ *9/7399-4105* ⊕ *www. turismodagaz.com* 🖾 *From 15,000 pesos.*

Turismo Migrantes. Trekking, bicycle hire, horse-riding, and astronomical tours are organized by this operator based close to Pisco Elqui's central plaza. ⊠ *Av. Libertador Bernardo O'Higgins s/n* ☏ *51/245-1917* ⊕ *www.turismomigrantes.cl* 🖾 *From 13,000 pesos.*

EXPLORING

Casa Escuela. Gabriela Mistral, born in nearby Vicuña, grew up in Montegrande and considered the tiny village her hometown. Her family lived in the schoolhouse where her elder sister taught. This was later turned into a museum and displays some relics of the poet's life. Visitors can also visit the Nobel Prize–winning poet's tomb on a nearby hillside. ⊠ *Central plaza, Montegrande* 🖾 *500 pesos* ⊙ *Tues.–Sun. 10–1 and 3–6.*

Fodor's Choice **Destilería Mistral.** In the older section of this plant, maintained strictly for
★ show, you can see the antiquated copper cauldrons and wooden barrels formerly used to distill this famous brand. The distillery arranges daily tours, followed by tastings of pisco sour. ⊠ *Av. Libertador Bernardo O'Higgins 746* ☏ *51/245-1358* ⊕ *www.piscomistral.cl* 🖾 *Tours 6,000 pesos* ⊙ *Tours by request (when you arrive) Jan. and Feb., daily noon–7; Mar.–Dec., daily 11–5.*

Los Nichos. About 4 km (2½ miles) past Pisco Elqui lies this operational pisco distillery. Guided tours show you around its workings and culminate in the basement, where the original owner and his partners

CLOSE UP

Chile's National Drink

Distilled from muscat grapes grown in the sunbaked river valleys of El Norte Chico, pisco is indisputably Chile's national drink. This fruity, aromatic brandy is enjoyed here in large quantities—most commonly in a delightful elixir known as a pisco sour, which consists of pisco, lemon juice, and sugar. A few drops of bitters on top is optional. Some bars step it up a notch by adding whipped egg white to give the drink a frothy head. Another concoction made with the brandy is piscola—the choice of many late-night revelers—which is simply pisco mixed with soda. Tea with a shot of pisco is the Chilean answer to the common cold, and it may just do the trick to relieve a headache and stuffy nose. Whichever way you choose to take your pisco, expect a pleasant, smooth drink.

Chileans have enjoyed pisco, which takes its name from *pisku*, the Quechuan word for "flying bird," for more than 400 years. The drink likely originated in Peru—a source of enmity between the two nations. In 1939, Chilean President Gabriel González Videla went so far as to change the name of the town of La Unión to Pisco Elqui in an attempt to gain exclusive rights over the name pisco, but Peru already had its own town south of Lima named Pisco. The situation is currently at a standoff, with both countries claiming they have the better product.

The primary spot for pisco distillation is the Elqui Valley, which is particularly renowned for the quality of its grapes. The 300 days of sunshine per year here make it perfect for cultivating muscat grapes. The distillation process has changed very little in the past four centuries. The fermented wine is boiled in copper stills, and the vapors are then condensed and aged in oak barrels for three to six months—pisco makers call the aging process "resting." The result is a fruity but potent brandy with between 30% and 50% alcohol.

would raid the stock for prolonged, secretive drinking sessions. More clear-headed visitors note that he and his friends also found time to amass a rather morbid collection of epithets, now displayed on the walls. ■TIP→ **Instead of taking the bus, try hiring a bicycle and doing the comfortable three-minute ride to the vineyard on your own steam, taking in views of the valley as you go.** ⊠ *Camino Público Pisco Elqui Horcón, at Km 3.5* ☎ *51/245–1085* 🖘 *1,000 pesos (includes tour and tasting)* ⊗ *Mar.–Dec., daily 10:30–6; Jan. and Feb., daily 11–7.*

WHERE TO STAY

$$ 🏠 **Elqui Domos.** Though the walls of these modern pods are made from
RENTAL   heavy, translucent material, this is far from camping. **Pros:** stargazing seclusion in a unique setting; unbeatable valley views. **Cons:** public transport required if you don't arrive by car. 💲 *Rooms from: 85500 pesos* ⊠ *Camino Público Pisco Elqui Horcón, at Km 3.5* ☎ *9/7709–2879* ⊕ *www.elquidomos.cl* 🖘 *7 domes, 4 cabins* ⑩ *Breakfast.*

$ 🏠 **El Tesoro de Elqui.** Beautiful gardens with flowers of every imaginable shape and size surround this hotel's cabanas, which have gleaming
B&B/INN   pine floors and furniture and adobe walls. **Pros:** rooms with views of

the stars; quiet. **Cons:** hard to navigate paths at night to reach rooms. $ *Rooms from: 34000 pesos* ✉ *Arturo Prat s/n* ☎ *51/245–1069* 🌐 *www.tesoro-elqui.cl* 🛏 *11 rooms, 2 apartments* 🍴 *Breakfast.*

$$ RESORT 🏨 **Refugio Misterios de Elqui.** The mountainside slopes up dramatically immediately behind these cabanas, making for dramatic views. **Pros:** a great spot to unwind; mini golfing green; on-site restaurant with extensive menu. **Cons:** only some rooms have fridges; footpaths a bit steep; no Wi-Fi in rooms $ *Rooms from: 75000 pesos* ✉ *Arturo Prat s/n* ☎ *51/245–1126* 🌐 *www.misteriosdeelqui.cl* 🛏 *6 cabanas, 1 suite* 🍴 *Breakfast.*

NIGHTLIFE

There isn't much to do at night in Pisco Elqui but lie on your back and enjoy the brilliant stars.

La Terraza. Craft beers, an exhaustive array of piscos, and tasty sandwiches are served at this late-night terrace bar, which is a great place to take in the clear night skies over an evening drink. ✉ *Opposite plaza.*

Los Jugos. Although now serving a full menu, Los Jugos is still known best for the signature delicious fruit juices that gave it its name. Particularly good are the slightly off-beat combinations such as *zanahoria y naranja* (carrot and orange). The plaza-front location and late opening hours also make this a good bet for a casual bite and drink in the evenings. ✉ *At plaza.*

SHOPPING

You can also head to the pisco distilleries to pick up a bottle of freshly brewed pisco.

Frutos de Elqui. Fresh fruit marmalade and preserves are sold at Frutos del Elqui, opposite the town's main plaza. ✉ *Av. Libertador Bernardo O'Higgins, Local 1* ☎ *9/9011–9192.*

THE LIMARÍ VALLEY

The fertile Limarí Valley is a nice break after the bleak desert stretches of the Pan-American Highway, and you pass plenty of signs for *queso de cabra* (goat cheese), field after field of muscat grapes (used for pisco), and acre upon acre of avocado, creating a rich tapestry of greens as you travel inland. As one of the regions with the least annual rainfall, the valley has three dams to ensure it stays fertile and that the vineyards can cultivate the Pinot Noir, Viognier, Sangiovese, and Carménère for which it is becoming famous.

The Limarí Valley also has the country's only lapis lazuli mine (lapis lazuli is a semiprecious stone found exclusively in Chile and Afghanistan), and is known for its production of combarbalita (a marblelike rock), which is fashioned into everything from jewelry boxes to chess pieces.

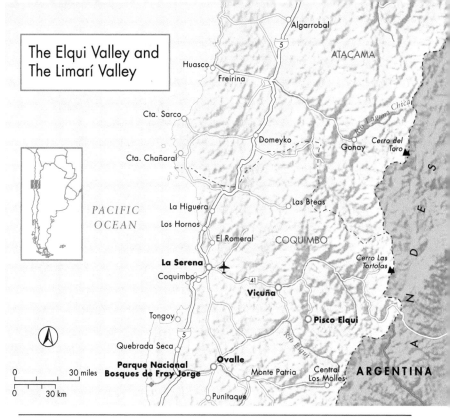

The Elqui Valley and
The Limarí Valley

ATACAMA

Algarrobal

Huasco
Freirina

Cta. Sarco

Domeyko

Río Laguna Chica

Gonay
Cerro del
Toro

Cta. Chañaral

PACIFIC
OCEAN

La Higuera

Las Breas

Los Hornos

El Romeral

COQUIMBO

La Serena

Cerro Las
Tortolas

Coquimbo

Vicuña

Tongoy

Pisco Elqui

Río Elqui

ANDES

Quebrada Seca

Ovalle

ARGENTINA

Parque Nacional
Bosques de Fray Jorge

Monte Patria

Central
Los Molles

0   30 miles
0   30 km

Punitaque

OVALLE

88 km (55 miles) south of La Serena via Ruta 43.

Ovalle always suffers in comparison to its fairer sister to the north, La Serena, as it has no beaches or breezes. However, it can be a good base for trips to Monumento Natural Pichasca and Valle del Encanto or a stopping-off point between Santiago and La Serena for lunch.

GETTING HERE AND AROUND

Ovalle is about an hour from La Serena via Ruta 43. A 15-minute drive on Ruta 45 out of Ovalle takes you to Valle del Encanto; just beyond that to the west, it intersects with the Pan-American Highway (Ruta 5). Many buses make daily trips between Ovalle and Santiago (five hours) or La Serena (one hour).

ESSENTIALS

Bus Contacts Medialuna Terminal ✉ *Ariztía 769* ☎ *53/262–6612.*

EXPLORING

Iglesia San Vicente Ferrer. On the Plaza de Armas, this church, constructed in 1849, is worth a visit if religious tourism is your thing. Its bells were made in the Chilean port town of Valparaíso in 1877 and, although damaged by an earthquake in 1997, the church was completely restored in 2002 and remains open. ✉ *Libertad 260.*

Monumento Natural Pichasca. Heading toward the Andes you come across this nature reserve covered with a forest of petrified tree trunks imprinted with dozens of leaf and animal fossils. Nearby is a cave beneath a stone overhang that housed indigenous peoples thousands of years ago. Inside are some cave paintings by the Molle people. ⊠ *50 km (31 miles) northeast of Ovalle on Camino Ovalle–Río Hurtado* ☎ *51/224–4306* 🔖 *2,500 pesos* ☉ *Wed.–Sun. 9–4:30.*

Plaza de Armas. The town's shady central plaza is a pleasant place to pass an afternoon. ⊠ *Bordered by Libertad, Miguel Aguirre, Av. Benjamín Vicuña Mackenna, and Victoria.*

Termas de Socos. A tourist complex cut from the rough land, this hot spring is said to have waters with incredible healing powers, spouting from the earth at 28°C (82°F). Curative or not, a thermal bath here is extremely relaxing, even if the experience is the same as being in the tub in your bathroom at home (you sit in a bathtub in a private room indoors). Massages and use of the Jacuzzis are also available at an extra cost. ⊠ *Pan-American Hwy. at Km 370; 24 km (15 miles) west of Ovalle on Ruta 45* ☎ *53/198–2505, 2/2236–3336* ⊕ *www.termasocos. cl* 🔖 *4,500 pesos for ½ hr* ☉ *Daily 8:30–7.*

Fodor'sChoice **Valle del Encanto.** En route to the Valle del Encanto (Valley of Enchant-
★ ment), the herds of goats and their caretakers charm, but true enchantment arrives in the stillness of the valley, where you feel like you've stepped back in time while searching out the petroglyphs left by hunters almost 4,000 years ago. Unlike geoglyphs, which are large-scale figures chiseled into the landscape, petroglyphs are small pictures carved onto the rock surface. One of Chile's densest collections of petroglyphs can be found here. The 30 images were most likely etched by the Molle culture between 100 and 600 AD. The figures wear ceremonial headdresses hanging low over large, expressive eyes. On occasion a guide waits near the petroglyphs and can show you the best of the carvings for a small fee. To reach the site, take Ruta 45 west from Ovalle. About 19 km (12 miles) out of town, head south for 5 km (3 miles) on a rough, dry road. ⊠ *24 km (15 miles) west of Ovalle* ☎ *51/224–4306* 🔖 *2,500 pesos* ☉ *Wed.–Sun. 9–4:30.*

Viña Tabalí. One of Chile's newer vineyards is on the same unpaved road that leads to the Valle del Encanto and a perfect place to relax after exploring the petroglyphs. Tours, which must be reserved at least one day in advance, include a tasting session in the impressive underground cellar. ⊠ *Hacienda Santa Rosa de Tabalí s/n, Camino Monumento Histórico de Valle del Encanto; about 2 km (1 mile) after turnoff from Ruta 45, on right* ☎ *2/2477–5535, 2/2477–5530* ⊕ *www.tabali.cl* 🔖 *10,000 pesos, includes tasting and admission to Valle del Encanto* ☉ *Weekdays 10–6.*

WHERE TO EAT AND STAY

$$ ✗ **Neus.** Local engineering entrepreneur Nelson La Torre ("Neus") runs
ECLECTIC this joint and whips up a mean bowl of fettuccine. If you're lucky, he'll have some freshly arrived fish from the coast to grill or fry. If he turns on the karaoke machine later in the evening—fasten your safety

EL NORTE CHICO WILDLIFE

Situated between the mountains and the sea, the Central Valley has a host of wildlife, despite its barren appearance. Look for the Andean fox (*zorro andino*) in Parque Fray Jorge, or the California quail (*cordoniz*) hopping along the desert floor of Valle del Encanto. Just an hour's cruise from La Serena is the national reserve of the Chaplinesque Humboldt penguin, also home to a host of sea lions (*lobos marinos*) and other sea creatures, such as the brown pelican. If you're very lucky, and you keep still long enough, you may even spot a puma at night in the Elqui Valley. CONAF (Corporación Nacional Forestal de Chile 🌐 *www.conaf.cl*) maintains Chile's national parks and forests, and can provide information on El Norte Chico's more remote regions. In La Serena check with tour companies for tours to national parks and the interior. In Copiapó you can arrange trips to Altiplano, Chile's far north, with Turismo Atacama. The website of *Jacobita* magazine (🌐 *www.jacobita.cl*) has a large listing and photo gallery of plants, rodents, insects, birds, and mammals that subsist in El Norte Chico.

4

belts. *Average main: 8000 pesos* ✉ *Coquimbo 347* ☎ *53/2623–393* *Closed weekends.*

$$ B&B/INN Fodor's Choice ★ **Hacienda Santa Cristina.** One of the Limarí Valley's best-kept secrets, this homestead is a rural oasis just a few kilometers from the Pan-American Highway as it heads north from Ovalle toward La Serena. **Pros:** personalized attention; beautiful, tranquil location. **Cons:** access by unpaved road. *Rooms from: 60000 pesos* ✉ *Ruta D-505, Quebrada Seca-Ovalle, at Km 4* ☎ *53/262–2335* 🌐 *www.haciendasantacristina.cl* *12 rooms* *Breakfast.*

$$ HOTEL **Hotel Limarí.** By far the best option in Ovalle, this ranch-style hotel with only two floors opened in 2009 at the forefront of a renewed effort to attract tourists to the area. **Pros:** a wide range of programs and activities to get to know the region better. **Cons:** outside town center. *Rooms from: 75300 pesos* ✉ *Camino Sotaqui at Km 5* ☎ *53/266–1400* 🌐 *www.hotellimari.cl* *40 rooms* *Breakfast.*

PARQUE NACIONAL BOSQUES DE FRAY JORGE

110 km (68 miles) south of La Serena.

Seemingly defying the logic of El Norte Chico's otherwise barren landscapes, Parque Nacional Fray Jorge is a lush cloud forest formed by a unique microclimate. Calling this desert oasis home are the chungungo, a South American sea otter, Humboldt penguins, and the Andean fox as well as almost 300 endemic plant species.

GETTING HERE AND AROUND

From the Pan-American Highway at Km 387, turn off onto an unpaved road and follow the signs to the park, which is 27 km (11 miles) west. Public transport to the park is not available.

EXPLORING

Parque Nacional Fray Jorge. A patch of land so rich in vegetation and animal life in the heart of El Norte Chico's dry, desolate landscape defies logic. But Parque Nacional Fray Jorge, a UNESCO world biosphere reserve since 1977, has a small cloud forest similar to those found in Chile's damp southern regions. The forest, perched 600 meters (1,968 feet) above sea level, receives its life-giving nourishment from the *camanchaca* (fog) that constantly envelops it. Within this forest, come across ferns and trees found nowhere else in the region. A slightly slippery boardwalk leads you on a 20-minute tour. Budget time for the park as part of a longer day—the idea of "national park" in Chile is different from the concept in North America, and the "park" part of Fray Jorge is rather small. Although interesting, Fray Jorge will not take a lot of time to see, but there is a picnic table where you can lunch and watch the fog drift over the Pacific Ocean below. ⊠ *Pan-American Hwy. at Km 387* ☎ *9/9346–2706* ⊕ *www.conaf.cl* 🖂 *2,500 pesos* ☉ *Thurs.–Sun. 9–4:30.*

THE COPIAPÓ VALLEY

The region once known as Copayapu, meaning "cup of gold" in the Andean Quechua language, was first inhabited by the Diaguitas around 1000 BC. The Incas arrived several hundred years later in search of gold. Conquistador Diego de Almagro, who passed this way in 1535, was the first European to see the lush valley.

During the 19th century, the Copiapó Valley proved to be a true cup of gold when prospectors started large-scale mining operations in the region. But today, the residents of the valley make their living primarily from copper.

The northernmost city in the region, Copiapó, lies at the end of the world. Here the semi-arid El Norte Chico gives way to the Atacama Desert. Continuing north from Copiapó there is little but barren earth for hundreds of miles.

COPIAPÓ

145 km (90 miles) north of Vallenar.

Copiapó was officially founded in 1744 by Don Francisco Cortés, who called it Villa San Francisco de La Selva. Originally a *tambo,* or resting place, Copiapó was where Diego de Almagro recuperated after his grueling journey south from Peru in 1535. The 19th-century silver strikes solidified Copiapó's status as an important city in the region. The town has a lovely central park, Plaza Prat, lined with 100-year-old pepper trees.

GETTING HERE AND AROUND

Copiapó's Desierto de Atacama Airport (DAT) is a bit more than one hour's flying time from Santiago and connects to other points in El Norte Chico and El Norte Grande via Sky and LAN airlines. The DAT is about an hour from Copiapó but more like 30 minutes from Caldera—think of it as a big triangle. Several car rental companies have branches

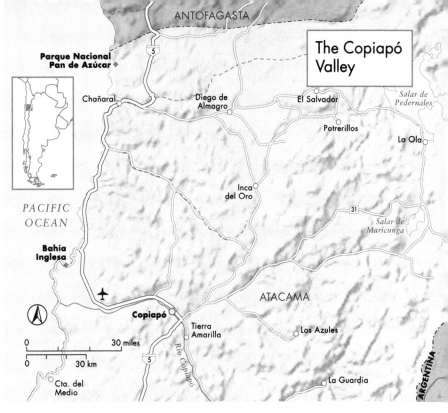

at DAT airport. Copiapó's bus terminal is serviced by all major bus lines. To the north (about 45 minutes via Ruta 5) lie the beaches of Caldera and Bahía Inglesa.

ESSENTIALS

Air Contacts LAN ✉ *Colipí 484, local 102-A* ☎ *600/526–2000* ⊕ *www.lan.com.* **Sky** ✉ *Bernardo O´Higgins 460* ☎ *600/600-2828* ⊕ *www.skyairline.cl.*

Bus Contacts Copiapó Bus Station ✉ *Chañarcillo 680* ☎ *52/223-8612.*

Taxi Contacts Radio Taxi San Francisco ✉ *Santiago Watt 856* ☎ *52/221-8788.*

Visitor and Tour Information Sernatur ✉ *Matta 461, La Serena* ☎ *51/222-5199, 51/222-5138* ⊕ *www.turismoregiondecoquimbo.cl.* **Turismo Atacama** ✉ *Los Carrera 716* ☎ *52/221-4767.*

EXPLORING

Iglesia Catedral Nuestra Señora del Rosario. English architect William Rogers built this neoclassical church facing the central square in the middle of the 19th century. Check out the silver tabernacle and image of the Virgin del Rosario at the altar. ✉ *Chacabuco at Av. Libertador Bernardo O'Higgins.*

Iglesia San Francisco. This red-and-white candy cane of a church was built in 1872, and although it looks as if it's made of cement, it's actually constructed of Oregon pine. The adjacent Plaza Godoy has a statue of goat-herder Juan Godoy, who accidentally discovered huge silver deposits in nearby Chañarcillo. ✉ *Juan Godoy 65.*

Museo Mineralógico. This museum offers a geological history of the region and what is perhaps the country's largest collection of rocks and minerals. There are close to 2,500 samples, including some found only in the Atacama Desert. The museum even displays a few meteorites that fell in the area. ✉ *Colipí and Manuel Rodriguez* ☎ *52/220–6606* 🌐 *www.unap.cl/museomin* 🎟 *500 pesos* 🕒 *Weekdays 10–1 and 3:30–7, Sat. 10–1.*

Museo Regional de Atacama. A historic home that once belonged to the wealthy Matta family now houses this museum. The house, built by mining engineer Felipe Santiago Matta between 1840 and 1850, shows the history of the region through its reconstructions of 19th-century rooms. The exhibits themselves are dedicated to mining and archaeology. ✉ *Atacama 98* ☎ *52/221–2313* 🌐 *www.museodeatacama.cl* 🎟 *600 pesos* 🕒 *Tues.–Sat. 9–6.*

WHERE TO STAY

$$$ HOTEL 🏨 **Hotel Chagall.** Located half a block from the Copiapó's central plaza, this well-equipped business hotel has clean, homey, modern, and spacious rooms, with colorful woven comforters in local designs. **Pros:** located right in the center of the city; good facilities. **Cons:** some rooms on street side may be noisy. [$] *Rooms from: 91000 pesos* ✉ *Av. Bernardo O'Higgins 760* ☎ *52/235–2900* 🌐 *www.chagall.cl* 🛏 *88 rooms* 🍴 *Breakfast.*

$$$ HOTEL 🏨 **Hotel Diego de Almeida.** Enjoying a privileged spot on the city's main square, this hotel has comfortable and elegantly decorated rooms. **Pros:** excellent location. **Cons:** can be noisy; parking is limited. [$] *Rooms from: 104500 pesos* ✉ *Av. Bernardo O'Higgins 640* ☎ *52/220–7700* 🌐 *www.hoteldiegodealmeida.com* 🛏 *136 rooms* 🍴 *Breakfast.*

$ B&B/INN 🏨 **Hotel La Casona.** Beautiful gardens surround this quaint country inn with a red facade. **Pros:** friendly service; homey. **Cons:** not in the center of town; rooms very hot in summer and only some have fans. [$] *Rooms from: 50000 pesos* ✉ *Av. Bernardo O'Higgins 150* ☎ *52/221–7277* 🌐 *www.lacasonahotel.cl* 🛏 *12 rooms* 🍴 *Breakfast.*

BAHÍA INGLESA

68 km (42 miles) northwest of Copiapó.

Some of the most beautiful beaches in El Norte Chico are at Bahía Inglesa, which was originally known as Puerto del Inglés because of the number of English buccaneers using the port as a hideaway. It's not just the beautiful white sand that sets these beaches apart, however: it's also the turquoise waters, fresh air, and fabulous weather. Combine all this with the fact that the town has yet to attract large-scale development and you can see why so many people flock here in summer. If you are fortunate enough to visit during the low season, you can experience a tranquility rarely felt in Chile's other coastal towns.

GETTING HERE AND AROUND

Follow the Pan-American Highway about one hour north until the small towns of Caldera and Bahía Inglesa come into view: you may smell the salty Pacific before you see the buildings. Buses big and small, as well as taxi colectivos, service Caldera, 5 km (3 miles) north of Bahía Inglesa. From Caldera it's a 10-minute cab ride to Bahía Inglesa. To the north lies Antofagasta, about six hours from both Caldera and Bahía Inglesa by car or bus on the Pan-American Highway.

BEACHES

FAMILY **Playa La Piscina.** Stunningly pretty, impossibly calm, and perfect for swimming, Playa La Piscina is in many ways the ideal town beach. Bordering Bahía Inglesa's main drag, this beach—which translates as "the swimming pool"—enjoys perfect white sand and bright blue waters, all a short walk from most hotels and restaurants. Unsurprisingly, it gets very busy in the summer high season. **Amenities:** food and drink; water sports; toilets; lifeguards (summer only); parking. **Best for:** swimming.

Playa Las Machas. Stretching from the southernmost tip of Bahía Inglesa right around the bay, Playa Las Machas has escaped the attention of the majority of tourists and is a relaxing alternative to the more crowded beaches in the town proper. Whether you decide to explore the long shoreline on foot, taking in the dramatic scenery as you go, or find yourself a secluded spot for sunbathing and to get away from it all, this white-sand beach is a great place to while away a lazy afternoon. **Amenities:** none. **Best for:** walking; surfing; solitude; sunset.

WHERE TO EAT AND STAY

$$ ⨉ **El Plateao.** With ocean views and the region's best food, this bohemian bistro is a must for anyone staying in the area. The innovative, contemporary menu lists such culinary non sequiturs as curry dishes and *tallarines con mariscos* (a pan-Asian noodle concoction served with shellfish and topped with cilantro). On the sand-covered, two-tiered porch, you can sit in a comfy chair and watch the sunset. $ *Average main: 9000 pesos* ⊠ *Av. El Morro 756* ☎ *09/826–0007.*

ECLECTIC
Fodor's Choice
★

$$ ⌂ **Apart Hotel Playa Blanca.** If you are tired of indistinguishable chain hotels, a condo at Playa Blanca, complete with comfortable living room and full kitchen, may just do the trick. **Pros:** right on the water; you hear the waves crash from your bed. **Cons:** location means a dark walk home from the action at night. $ *Rooms from: 64800 pesos* ⊠ *Camino de Martín 1300* ☎ *9/5011–1235* ⊕ *www.aparthotelplayablanca.com* ⇨ *10 condos, 1 apartment* ⊟ *No credit cards* |○| *No meals.*

RENTAL
FAMILY

$$ ⌂ **Hotel Rocas de Bahía.** This sprawling modern hotel has rooms with huge windows facing the sea. **Pros:** can't beat the views. **Cons:** on same road as main disco in town, which is open until dawn on weekends. $ *Rooms from: 72200 pesos* ⊠ *Av. El Morro 888* ☎ *52/231–6005* ⊕ *www.rocasdebahia.cl* ⇨ *36 rooms* |○| *Breakfast.*

HOTEL

SPORTS AND THE OUTDOORS

WATER SPORTS

Morro Ballena Expediciones. There are all types of water sports in the area. Morro Ballena Expediciones arranges fishing, kayaking, and scuba-diving trips as well as sealife tours on which, if you're lucky, you might spot whales or dolphins. ⊠ *El Morro s/n, south end of Playa La Piscina* ☎ *9/9886–3673* ⊕ *www.morroballena.cl* ✉ *From 15,000 pesos.*

PARQUE NACIONAL PAN DE AZÚCAR

175 km (109 miles) north of Copiapó.

Some of the best coastal scenery in the country can be found at Parque Nacional Pan de Azúcar. Imposing cliffs give way to deserted white-sand beaches in this captivating reserve, which stretches for 40 km (25 miles) along the coast and is home to dolphins, cormorants, sea lions, and pelicans.

GETTING HERE AND AROUND

You can take Route C-120 north from Chañaral for 29 km (18 miles) directly into the park, or take the Pan-American Highway north of Chañaral to Km marker 1,410, then cut toward the coast onto Route C-110 to the park.

ESSENTIALS

Turismo Atacama in Copiapó has tours to the park, and Sernatur in Copiapó is a good source of information.

EXPLORING

Fodor'sChoice   **Parque Nacional Pan de Azúcar.** This national reserve stretching for 40 ★   km (25 miles) along the coast north of the town of Chañaral has some of Chile's most spectacular coastal scenery. Steep cliffs fall into the crashing sea, their ominous presence broken occasionally by white-sand beaches. These isolated stretches of sand make for excellent picnicking. Be careful if you decide to swim, as there are often dangerous currents. Within the park is an incredible variety of flora and fauna. Pelicans can be spotted off the coast, as can sea lions, dolphins, sea otters, cormorants, and plovers. There are some 20 species of cacti in the park, including the rare copiapoa, which resembles a little blue pincushion. The park also shelters rare predators like the desert fox. From the tiny fishing village of Caleta Pan de Azúcar, you can hire local fisherfolk to take you to a large colony of Humboldt penguins on a nearby island. ⊠ *An unpaved but signposted road north of cemetery in Chañaral leads to park* ☎ *52/221–3404* ⊕ *www.conaf.cl* ✉ *4,000 pesos* ☉ *Park daily, ranger kiosk daily 8:30–12:30 and 2–6.*

WHERE TO STAY

$ ⌂ **Lodge Pan de Azúcar.** Surrounded by the imposing "Sugar Loaf" RENTAL   mountain range to the rear and the crashing waves of the Pacific in front, you'd be hard pressed to find a more remote location to stay. **Pros:** gloriously remote and beyond reach of even the most nagging boss; unbeatable views. **Cons:** no power other than lighting and kitchen; few dining alternatives available in the only nearby village; hard to get to without your own car. ⓢ *Rooms from: 48600 pesos* ⊠ *Camino C-120, on left after passing park ranger's kiosk* ☎ *9/9280–3483* ⊕ *www. pandeazucarlodge.cl* ⏎ *5 cabanas* ⦿ *No meals.*

EL NORTE
GRANDE

WELCOME TO
EL NORTE GRANDE

TOP REASONS
TO GO

★ **San Pedro de Atacama:** This unassuming town in the middle of the desert is a world-class destination for the beautiful outdoor excursions nearby. Visit magical moonlike landscapes, large sand dunes, lush valleys filled with 900-year-old cactus plants, salt flats with blue lagoons and pink flamingos, and surreal geysers with steam and bubbling water at dawn break.

★ **Flora and fauna:** Yes, the Atacama Desert is one of the driest places on earth. But head to the Chilean Altiplano, just a few hours east of Arica, and you'll find an abundance of fauna and, depending on the season, flora. Pink flamingos dot the edges of volcanic lakes like Lago Chungará on the Bolivian border, and slender brown vicuñas—treasured for their fur, the finest of the American camelids—run in small herds through the sparse grasslands.

★ **Pristine beaches:** Pristine sands line the shore near Arica and Iquique. The beaches are packed during summer months, but in the off season you just might have the beach to yourself.

1 The Nitrate Pampa. Snowcapped volcanoes dominate the landscape to the east, making mornings in this region especially memorable. The vast lunar landscapes around San Pedro de Atacama make for days' worth of fascinating trekking. Just watching the sun—or moon—rise over the dunes is worth the trip itself. And bird lovers will find the Reserva Nacional Los Flamencos well worth the high-altitude adjustment for a chance to see hundreds of pink flamingos against the backdrop of shimmering blue and green lakes.

2 San Pedro and the Atacama Desert. If you get beyond the hype and the hippies, San Pedro is a great place. The range of outdoor activities, from sandboarding to hiking to biking, and the breathtaking sights, including moonlike landscapes, volcanoes, flamingos, and Incan graveyards, make it a must-see stop in the North. Spend your mornings hiking, biking, and boarding, afternoons swimming, and nights beside a blazing outdoor fire in the patio of one of San Pedro's down-home but delicious eateries, gazing up at the star-filled heavens.

3 Iquique and Nearby. The port of Iquique is the world's largest exporter of fish meal, but its heyday was as a nitrate center in the 19th century. Fading mansions remain, and this regional capital is still a popular destination. From here you can do a day trip to the hot springs of Mamiña, also glimpsing the ghost town of Humberstone, while getting to the petroglyph Gigante de Atacama—Chile's largest—in time for the sunset.

4 Arica and Nearby. Arica, at the intersection of Chile, Bolivia, and Peru, is part of the "land of eternal spring" and its pedestrian-mall eateries can ease even the most impatient traveler into a chair for a day. Sights to see include mummies dating to 6000 BC, Aymara markets, and national parks with alpine lakes and herds of vicuña.

GETTING ORIENTED

San Pedro de Atacama is one of the continent's hotspots, a hotspot for outdoor-sports enthusiasts, birdwatchers, and sand-boarders. If you miss the human touch, board a 4 am van full of fellow travelers heading out to the steaming geysers. Resting between two giant branches of the Andean mountains is the *altiplano*, or high plains, where you'll see natural marvels such as crystalline salt flats, geysers, and volcanoes. You'll also spot flocks of flamingos and herds of vicuña, a cousin to the llama.

5

Updated
by Amanda
Barnes

The Norte Grande is as vast as it is remote, but don't be fooled by this seemingly empty landscape: the Atacama Desert is filled with natural wonders that make it one of most breathtaking destinations in the world. With a striking desert and volcano-lined horizon as your backdrop, you can discover otherworldly landscapes like salt-crusted white valleys, burnt-orange sand formations, stunning blue lagoons, lush oases, and picture-perfect beach destinations. Exhilarating hikes up volcanoes or through cactus-laden creeks and adrenaline-boosting bike rides attract outdoor sports enthusiasts, while relaxing thermal pools, a plethora of wildlife, calming beaches, and colorful native culture keeps tamer travelers charmed.

Spanning some 1,930 km (1,200 miles), Chile's Great North stretches from the Río Copiapó to the borders of Peru and Bolivia. Here you will find the Atacama Desert, the driest place on Earth—so dry that in many parts no rain has ever been recorded.

Yet people have inhabited this desolate land since time immemorial. Indeed, the heart of El Norte Grande lies not in its geography but in its people. The indigenous Chinchorro people eked out a meager living from the sea more than 8,000 years ago, leaving behind the magnificent Chinchorro mummies, the oldest in the world. High in the Andes, the Atacameño tribes traded livestock with the Tijuanacota and the Inca. Many of these people still cling to their ways of life, though much of their culture was lost during the colonial period and by the abandonment of small villages as mining in the region boomed.

When huge deposits of nitrates were found in the Atacama region in the 1800s, the "white gold" brought boom times to towns like Pisagua, Iquique, and Antofagasta. Because most of the mineral-rich region lay beyond its northern border, Chile declared war on neighboring Peru and Bolivia in 1878. Chile won the five-year battle and annexed the land north of Antofagasta, a continuing source of national pride for many Chileans. With the invention of synthetic nitrates, the market for these fertilizers dried up and the nitrate barons abandoned their opulent mansions and returned to Santiago. El Norte Grande was once again left on its own.

What you'll see today is a land of both growth and decay. The glory days of the nitrate era are gone, but copper has stepped in to help fill that gap (the world's largest open-pit copper mine is here). El Norte Grande is still a land of opportunity for fortune-seekers, as well as for tourists looking for a less-traveled corner of the world. It is a place of beauty and dynamic isolation, a place where the past touches the present in a troubled yet majestic embrace.

PLANNER

WHEN TO GO

In the height of the Chilean summer, January and February, droves of Chileans and Argentines mob El Norte Grande's beaches. Although this is a fun time to visit, prices go up and finding a hotel can be difficult. Book your room a month or more in advance. The high season tapers off in March, an excellent time to visit if you're looking for a bit more tranquillity. If you plan to visit the altiplano, bring the right clothing. Winter can be very cold, and summer sees a fair amount of rain. San Pedro is sunny year-round and pleasant to visit, but the best seasons are spring and fall when the crowds are gone and the days are not too hot, nor the nights too cold.

FESTIVALS

Every town in the region celebrates the day honoring its patron saint. Most are small gatherings attended largely by locals. One fiesta not to be missed takes place in La Tirana from July 12 to 18. During this time some 80,000 pilgrims converge on the town to honor the Virgen del Carmen with dancing in the streets.

PLANNING YOUR TIME

You'll have to hustle to see much of El Norte Grande in less than a week. You can spend at least two days in San Pedro de Atacama, visiting the incredible sights such as the bizarre moonscape of the Valle de la Luna and the desolate salt flats of the Salar de Atacama. For half a day soak in the hot springs in the tiny town of Pica, then head to the nitrate ghost town of Humberstone. On the way to Iquique, take a side trip to the Gigante de Atacama, the world's largest geoglyph. After a morning exploring Iquique, head up to Arica, the coastal town that bills itself as the "land of eternal spring." Be sure to visit the Museo Arqueológico de San Miguel de Azapa to see the Chinchorro mummies. Stop in Putre to catch your breath before taking in the flamingos at Parque Nacional Lauca or the vicuñas, llamas, and alpacas of Reserva Nacional Las Vicuñas.

GETTING HERE AND AROUND

AIR TRAVEL

There are no international airports in El Norte Grande, but from Santiago you can transfer to a flight headed to Antofagasta, Calama, Iquique, or Arica. Round-trip flights can run up to 300,000 pesos or more. The cities within El Norte Grande are far apart, so flying between them can save you time and provide more comfort. Principal Airlines, Sky Airline, and LAN offer services with prices ranging from 40,000 to 200,000 pesos.

BUS TRAVEL

Travel between the larger towns and cities in El Norte Grande is easy, but there may be no bus service to some smaller villages or the more remote national parks. No bus company has a monopoly, so shop around for the best price and note there are often several bus stations in each city.

CAR TRAVEL

A car is definitely the best way to see El Norte Grande. Driving in the cities can be a little hectic, but highway travel is usually smooth sailing and the roads are generally well maintained. Ruta 5, more familiarly known as the Pan-American Highway, bisects all of northern Chile. Ruta 1, Chile's answer to California's Highway 101, is a beautiful coastal highway running between Antofagasta and Iquique.

RESTAURANTS

The food of El Norte Grande is simple but quite good. Along the coast you can enjoy fresh seafood and shellfish, including *merluza* (hake), *corvina* (sea bass), *ostiones* (scallops), and *machas* (similar to razor clams but unique to Chile), to name just a few. Ceviche (a traditional dish made with raw, marinated fish) is a Chilean (and Peruvian) specialty found in much of El Norte Grande, but make sure you sample it in a place where you are confident that the fish is fresh. Fish may be ordered *a la plancha* (grilled in butter and lemon) or accompanied by a sauce such as *salsa margarita* (a butter-based sauce comprising almost every shellfish imaginable). As you enter the interior region you'll come across heartier meals such as *cazuela de vacuno* (beef stew served with corn on the cob and vegetables) and *chuleta con arroz* (porkchop with rice).

People in the north generally eat a heavy lunch around 2 pm that can last two hours, followed by a light dinner around 10 pm. Reservations are seldom needed, except in the poshest of places. Leave a 10% tip if you enjoyed the service.

HOTELS

The Atacama has seen a boom in luxury accommodations in recent years. San Pedro, in particular, hosts more than half a dozen luxury lodgings that range from lavish desert resorts to tasteful boutiques. Luxury hotels usually are full board with activities included and transfers to the airport. Otherwise, opt for one of the smaller hotels in town that offer reasonable prices. The gamut of hotels outside of San Pedro are less exciting, and be warned that some accommodations bill themselves as "luxury" despite not having seen a lick of clean paint for years. In rural towns, accommodation is relatively inexpensive and hotels are few and far between so you might have to make do with guesthouses with basic rooms and shared bathrooms. *Hotel reviews have been shortened. For full information, visit Fodors.com.*

| WHAT IT COSTS IN CHILEAN PESOS (IN THOUSANDS) | | | |
	$	$$	$$$	$$$$
Restaurants	Under 6	6–9	10–13	over 13
Hotels	Under 51	51–85	86–115	over 115

Restaurant prices are the average cost of a main course price at dinner or, if dinner is not served, at lunch. Hotel prices are the lowest cost of a standard double room in high season, excluding tax.

HEALTH AND SAFETY

The main concern you should have in the North is the sun: A hat and sunblock are always a good idea, and be sure to drink plenty of fluids during any outdoor activity. The altitude can also be a problem for some, so take the first day slow and acclimatize.

Use common sense: Don't be flashy with cash or expensive cameras. The North is relatively tranquil, but when venturing out from the center of any town into other neighborhoods, it's always safer to take a cab than to walk (ask an employee to call one for you). The main industry in El Norte Grande is mining, which means there is an inflated population of men. Foreign women attract more than a few wandering gazes, and while the attention is usually harmless, if you want to avoid extra admirers you should dress more conservatively.

THE NITRATE PAMPA

The vast *pampa salitrera* is an atmospheric introduction to Chile's Great North. Between 1890 and 1925 this region was the site of more than 100 *oficinas de salitre,* or nitrate plants. For a glorious period, Chile was the king of production of the fertilizer saltpeter (sodium nitrate), led by the "Father of Nitrate," Englishman James Humberstone. The Dover-born chemist applied James Shanks' method of producing sodium nitrate, and soon it was used throughout Chile. The War of the Pacific fought by Chile, Peru, and Bolivia was caused at least in part by the desire for these rich deposits beneath the Atacama Desert. The invention of synthetic nitrates spelled the end for all but a few plants. Crumbling nitrate works lay stagnant in the dry desert air, some disintegrating into dust, others remaining a fascinating testament to the white gold that, for a time, made this one of Chile's richest regions.

ANTOFAGASTA

565 km (350 miles) north of Copiapó.

Antofagasta is the most important—and the richest—city in El Norte Grande. It was part of Bolivia until 1879, when it was annexed by Chile in the War of the Pacific. The port town became an economic powerhouse during the nitrate boom. With the rapid decline of nitrate production, copper mining stepped in to keep the city's coffers filled.

Many travelers end up spending a night in Antofagasta on their way to the more interesting destinations like San Pedro de Atacama, Iquique,

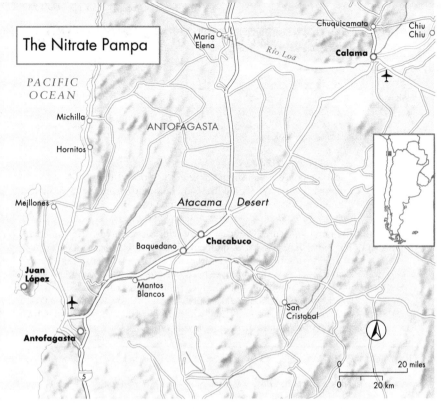

The Nitrate Pampa

PACIFIC
OCEAN

Michilla

Hornitos

Mejillones

Juan
López

Antofagasta

5

Maria
Elena

Río Loa

ANTOFAGASTA

Atacama / Desert

Baquedano   Chacabuco

Mantos
Blancos

San
Cristobal

Chuquicamata   Chiu
                 Chiu

Calama

0   20 miles
0   20 km

and Arica, but a few sights here are worth a look. Around two in the afternoon the city shuts down most of the streets in the center of town, making for pleasant afternoon shopping and strolling.

GETTING HERE AND AROUND

Antofagasta's airport, 30 minutes from downtown, is a regular stop on Sky Airline's northern run, about a two-hour flight from Santiago. From Caldera in the south, it's a six- to seven-hour ride up the Pan-American Highway by bus or car, but at least on this stretch you'll see some of the ocean. The bus terminal on LaTorre is just a short walk from downtown. Regular buses leave to Calama (3 hours), San Pedro (4½ hours), and Iquique (6 hours). The beaches of Juan Lopez are 45 minutes up the coast road, and the famous "La Portada" a mere 16 km (10 miles) from downtown—minibuses run there from LaTorre 2723 frequently. The Tur-Bus terminal, one of the bigger bus lines serving all of Chile, is just down the street on LaTorre. Desertica Expediciones arranges trips into the interior, including excursions to Parque Nacional Pan de Azúcar in El Norte Chico.

ESSENTIALS

Air Travel Cerro Moreno Airport (Antofagasta) (CNF) ☎ 55/225-4998
🌐 www.aeropuertoantofagasta.cl. LAN ☎ 600/526-2000 🌐 www.lan.com. Sky
Airline ☎ 55/245-9090 🌐 www.skyairline.cl.

Bus Contacts **Pullman** ✉ *Latorre 2805* ☎ *600/320–3200* ⊕ *www.pullman.cl.*
Tur-Bus ✉ *Latorre 2751* ☎ *600/660–6600* ⊕ *www.turbus.cl.*

Rental Car Contacts **Avis** ✉ *Av. Baquedano 364* ☎ *55/256–3140, 600/368–
2000* ⊕ *www.avis.com.* **Budget** ✉ *Aeropuerto* ☎ *600/441–0000* ⊕ *www.budget.
cl.* **Hertz** ✉ *Pedro Aguirre Cerda 15030, Parque Industrial La Portada* ☎ *55/242–
8042* ⊕ *www.hertz.cl.*

Visitor Information **Sernatur Antofagasta** ✉ *Prat 384, 1st fl.* ☎ *55/245–
1818/9* ⊕ *www.sernatur.cl* ⊘ *Weekdays 10–6, Sat. 10–2.*

EXPLORING

Museo Regional de Antofagasta. Inside the historic customs house, this
museum is the town's oldest building, dating back to 1866. It displays
clothing and other bric-a-brac from the nitrate era. ✉ *Balmaceda 2786*
☎ *55/222–7016* ⊕ *www.museodeantofagasta.cl* 🖼 *600 pesos (free Sun.)*
⊘ *Tues.–Fri. 9–5, weekends 11–2.*

Torre Reloj. High above Plaza Colón is this clock tower whose face is a
replica of London's Big Ben. It was erected by British residents in 1910.
✉ *Plaza Colon.*

WHERE TO EAT

$$$ ✕ **Club de Yates.** This seafood restaurant with nice views of the port
SEAFOOD caters to yachting types, which may explain why the prices are a bit
higher than at other restaurants in the area. The food is quite good,
especially the *ostiones a la parmesana* (oysters with Parmesan cheese).
The maritime theme is taken to the extreme—the plates, curtains,
tablecloths, and every decoration imaginable come in the mandatory
navy blue. The service is excellent. 💲 *Average main: 10000 pesos* ✉ *Av.
Balmaceda 2705* ☎ *55/248–5553* ⊕ *www.clubdeyatesantofagasta.cl*
⌁ *Reservations essential.*

$ ✕ **Don Pollo.** This rotisserie restaurant prepares some of the best roasted
FAST FOOD chicken in Chile—a good thing, because it's the only item on the menu.
The thatched-roof terrace is a great place to kick back after a long day of
sightseeing. 💲 *Average main: 1500 pesos* ✉ *Ossa 2594* ▤ *No credit cards.*

$$ ✕ **Restaurant Arriero.** Serving up traditional dishes from Spain's Basque
SPANISH country, Arriero is the place to go for delicious barbecued meats. A
healthy selection of national wines supplements the menu. The restaurant is in a pleasant Pyrenees-style inn decorated with traditional
cured hams hanging from the walls. The owners play jazz on the piano
almost every evening. 💲 *Average main: 8000 pesos* ✉ *Condell 2644*
☎ *55/226–4371* ⊕ *www.arrieroafta.cl* ⊘ *No dinner Sun.*

WHERE TO STAY

$$$ 🛏 **Enjoy Hotel del Desierto.** Although you may be sharing the spa and
HOTEL gym with many guests, you will get a spacious room to yourself and a
comfortable big bed. **Pros:** big rooms; modern. **Cons:** service could be
more attentive. 💲 *Rooms from: 115000 pesos* ✉ *Av. Angamos 01455*
☎ *55/265–3000* ⊕ *www.enjoy.cl/enjoy-antofagasta* ⇆ *92 rooms, 8
suites* ⏆ *Breakfast.*

$$ 🛏 **Hotel Antofagasta.** Part of the Panamericana Hoteles chain, this high-
HOTEL rise on the ocean comes with first-class views and a lovely kidney-shape
pool. **Pros:** nice beachfront location. **Cons:** no Wi-Fi in rooms; a bit

sterile. [$] *Rooms from: 83000 pesos* ✉ *Av. Balmaceda 2575* ☎ *55/222–8811* 🌐 *www.hotelantofagasta.cl* 🛏 *145 rooms, 8 suites* 🍴 *Breakfast.*

JUAN LÓPEZ

38 km (24 miles) north of Antofagasta.

Those turned off by the hustle and bustle of Antofagasta will likely be charmed by Juan López, a hodgepodge of pastel-color fishing shacks and a picturesque *caleta* (cove). In high season, January and February, the beaches are crowded and dirty. The rest of the year you may have the white, silken sand to yourself for a nice stroll or swim.

GETTING HERE AND AROUND

Juan López is just a hop up the coastal road from Antofagasta, and in the busy season there are plenty of minibuses and *colectivos* (shared taxis) making the trip. It takes about 30 to 40 minutes.

EXPLORING

La Portada. On the coast about 13 km (8 miles) south of Juan López lies this offshore volcanic rock that the sea has carved into an arch. It's one of the most photographed natural sights in the country. Many local travel agencies include La Portada as part of area tours.

BEACHES

People come to Juan López for the beaches, and there are plenty from which to choose, both around town and within a short drive.

Balneario Juan López. The most popular beach is Balneario Juan López, a small strip of light sand near the center of town. It can get uncomfortably crowded in summer, but the water is warm and tranquil. **Amenities:** food and drink; parking; toilets. **Best for:** swimming.

Playa Acapulco. For a relaxed, uncrowded experience, head to the beaches outside town. Picturesque Playa Acapulco is in a small cove north of Balneario Juan López that is popular with snorklers. **Amenities:** food and drink. **Best for:** snorkeling.

Playa Rinconada. About 5 km (3 miles) south of Juan López, Playa Rinconada is lauded by locals for its warm water and strong winds that make it popular for windsurfing. **Amenities:** food and drink; toilets. **Best for:** windsurfing.

CHACABUCO

70 km (43 miles) northeast of Antofagasta.

There are many ghost towns left from the nitrate boom in the early 20th century, and Chacabuco is one of them, although, this deserted town has a darker history than most. Augusto Pinochet used the abandoned town, originally founded in 1924 for saltpeter plain exploitations, during his dictatorship as a concentration camp for almost 2,000 people between 1973 and 1974. The small town was surrounded by landmines to ensure no one attempted escape. Nowadays you can visit this unsettling place and see a display in the theater about life in Chacabuco when it was a nitrate plant, and get more information about its days as a concentration camp.

GETTING HERE AND AROUND

To reach Chacabuco from Antofagasta, head east through the coastal range until you hit the Panamerican Highway (Ruta 5 Norte) and follow it northeast in the direction of Calama.

EXPLORING

Chacabuco. A mysterious dot on the desert landscape, the ghost town of Chacabuco is a decidedly eerie place. More than 7,000 employees and their families lived here when the Oficina Chacabuco (a company mining town that was made a national monument in 1971) was in operation between 1922 and 1944.

During the first years of Augusto Pinochet's military regime, Chacabuco was used as a prison camp for political dissidents. The artwork of prisoners still adorns many of the walls. Do not walk around the town's exterior, as land mines from this era are still buried here.

Today you'll find tiny houses, their tin roofs flapping in the wind and their walls collapsing. You can wander through many of the abandoned and restored buildings and take a look inside the theater, which has been restored to its previous appearance as a boomtown. ⊠ *70 km (43 miles) northeast of Antofagasta on Pan-American Hwy.* ▧ *1,000 pesos* ⊙ *Daily 7 am–8 pm.*

CALAMA

215 km (133 miles) northeast of Antofagasta.

The discovery of vast deposits of copper in the area turned Calama into the quintessential mining town, and therein lies its interest. People from the length of Chile flock to this dusty spot on the map in hopes of striking it rich in "the land of sun and copper"—most likely working for Codelco, Chile's biggest company, which has three mines in the surrounding area. A modern-day version of the boomtowns of the 19th-century American West, Calama is rough around the edges, but it does possess a certain energy.

Founded as a *tambo,* or resting place, at the crossing of two Inca trails, Calama still serves as a stopover for people headed elsewhere. Some people traveling to San Pedro de Atacama end up spending the night here, and the town does have a few attractions of its own.

GETTING HERE AND AROUND

Daily flights from Santiago via Sky, AirComet, and LAN arrive 20 minutes from downtown at Calama's El Loa airport (CJC). Bus service to neighboring San Pedro is frequent and fast—it's about an hour between the two towns. To points north, you can fly to Iquique and Arica in an hour (if you can avoid the puddle-jumper service that adds a few stops), but a bus or car will take you seven and nine hours, respectively. Be very careful when passing the mining company trucks that may slow your journey. Mining companies own all the bright red pick-ups you'll no doubt notice around town.

ESSENTIALS

Air Travel El Loa Airport (CJC) ⊠ *Ruta 25.* **LAN** ☎ *600/526–2000* ⊕ *www.lan. com.* **Sky Airline** ☎ *600/600–2828* ⊕ *www.skyairline.cl.*

Rental Car Contacts Avis ⊠ *Parque Industrial Apiac, Km 2, Sitio 25–26* ☎ *55/256-3153* ⊕ *www.avis.com.* **Budget** ⊠ *Parque Industrial Apia B, Sitio 1-C* ☎ *55/236-1072* ⊕ *www.budget.cl.* **Hertz** ⊠ *Granaderos 1416* ☎ *55/234-1380* ⊕ *www.hertz.cl.*

Visitor Information Municipal Tourism Office ⊠ *Latorre 1689* ☎ *55/253-1707* ⊕ *www.calamacultural.cl* ⊙ *Weekdays 8-1, 2-6.*

EXPLORING

Catedral San Juan Bautista. The gleaming copper roof of this cathedral on Plaza 23 de Marzo, the city's main square, testifies to the importance of mining in this region. ⊠ *Ramírez at Av. Granaderos.*

Museo Historia Natural de Calama. This small museum in El Loa Park has artifacts from Calama's history and pre-Colombian times. ⊠ *Parque El Loa (O'Higgins)* 💲 *500 pesos.*

WHERE TO EAT AND STAY

$$
CHILEAN
✕**Patagonia.** Decked with historic memorabilia, Patagonia is best known for its steak—large slices of steaming beef, cooked on the grill. Most people don't stray too far from the classics and it's probably best not to, as this is what Patagonia does best. Order a bottle of good Cabernet and a steak, and experience a carnivore's dream. 💲 *Average main: 9000 pesos* ⊠ *Granaderos 2549* ☎ *55/234-1628.*

$$
B&B/INN
🛏**Hotel El Mirador.** This friendly bed-and-breakfast around the corner from Plaza 23 de Marzo is set in a colonial-style house built in the 19th century. **Pros:** homey feel; short walk to shopping and restaurants. **Cons:** some street noise; some rooms are darker than others. 💲 *Rooms from: 55000 pesos* ⊠ *Sotomayor 2064* ☎ *55/234-0329* ⊕ *www.hotelmirador. cl* ⇌ *15 rooms* ⊙ *Dec. 24–26, Dec. 31–Jan. 2* ❯❮*Breakfast.*

$$$
HOTEL
🛏**Park Hotel Calama.** It's easy to see why international mining consultants frequent this top-notch hotel. **Pros:** nice swimming pool; relaxing lounge. **Cons:** nothing within walking distance. 💲 *Rooms from: 95000 pesos* ⊠ *Alcalde Jose Lira 1392* ☎ *55/271-5800* ⊕ *www.parkcalama.cl* ⇌ *104 rooms, 4 suites* ❯❮*Breakfast.*

$$
HOTEL
🛏**Sonesta.** This modern hotel has all the conveniences you need for a night's stay in the middle of town, with a pool and fitness center. **Pros:** central location. **Cons:** mediocre service. 💲 *Rooms from: 55000 pesos* ⊠ *Av. Balmaceda 2634* ☎ *55/268-1100* ⊕ *www.sonesta.com* ⇌ *148 rooms, 1 suite* ❯❮*Breakfast.*

SAN PEDRO AND THE ATACAMA DESERT

The most popular tourist destination in El Norte Grande (and perhaps all of Chile), San Pedro de Atacama sits in the heart of the Atacama Desert and in the midst of some of the most breathtaking scenery in the country. A string of towering volcanoes, some of which are still active, stands watch to the east. To the west is La Cordillera de Sal, a mountain range composed almost entirely of salt. Here you'll find such marvels as the Valle de la Luna (Valley of the Moon) and the Valle de la Muerte (Valley of Death), part of the Reserva Nacional Los Flamencos. The desolate Salar de Atacama, Chile's largest salt flat, lies to the south. The number of attractions in the Atacama area does not end there: alpine

CHUQUICAMATA

Chuquicamata. The trucks never stop rolling and the machinery never stops grinding at Chuquicamata, the world's biggest open-pit mine, located just outside of Calama. Nine-hundred workers split three eight-hour shifts, digging, transporting, and processing the metal on which Chile runs.

Chuquicamata is part of Codelco's operation, the state-owned cooperative that is a legacy of President Salvador Allende's nationalization of copper in 1970 (with four mines and one metallurgic division, it's the country's largest company).

One is dwarfed by the sheer scale of "Chuqui," as locals call it: it's 5 km long, 2 km wide, and 1 km deep. It takes any of the 96 trucks, some of which have beds 12 meters wide, a half hour to navigate the winding road to the bottom of the pit. The monstrous German-made trucks cost a pretty penny, about $4 million, and are refueled by pressure-hoses in the same way Formula One cars are gassed up. After all, a 4,000-liter (1,000-gallon) tank could take a while to fill the conventional way. Even the tires cost about $20,000 apiece. Because they run night and day, the trucks require constant maintenance and generally only about 80 are in operation at any one time. The most modern cranes can shovel out up to 50 tons of rock at a time and require a single operator, while in years gone by 20-ton cranes required a crew of 12.

Copper goes through a three-stage separation process, beginning with the rocks being crushed, milled, and "floated" through water. This results in about 33% pure copper, and an intense smelting process refines that to 99%. Cathodes, operating like giant magnets, separate the copper from the remaining impurities, including gold and silver, resulting in a final product that is 99.9% pure copper. A byproduct of the process, molybdenum, is even more precious than copper because of its high melting point, and is set aside for later sale.

Stare into the vast pit of Chuquicamata and you'll be convinced that Chile uncovered untold riches below the barren Atacama Desert. In 2008, Codelco profits totaled more than $9 billion. But after decades of mining, production has fallen sharply due to structural problems and lower copper content. As the mine becomes too deep to exploit profitably, Codelco is looking to develop an underground operation at Chuquicamata, which could begin later this decade. But with 70 years of reserves and demand in China and India booming, copper looks set to remain the "master beam" of the Chilean economy for decades to come.

There is a small museum at the mine's entrance where you can get a close-up view of the machinery used to make such big holes. Tours are in Spanish and English. Reserve in advance by phone or by email. It's about a 20-minute taxi ride (5,000 pesos) from downtown Calama. ⊠ *16 km (10 miles) north of Calama* ☎ *55/232–2122* ⊕ *www.codelco.cl* ✉ *By donation* ⊙ *Tours weekdays at 1 pm.*

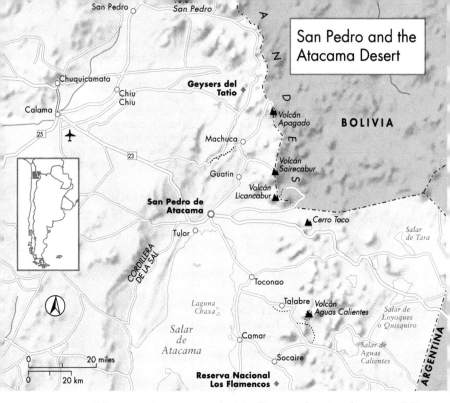

San Pedro and the
Atacama Desert

San Pedro

San Pedro

Chuquicamata

Chiu
Chiu

Geysers del
Tatio

BOLIVIA

Volcán
Apagado

Calama

25

Machuca

23

Volcán
Sairecabur

Guatin

Volcán
Licancabur

San Pedro de
Atacama

Tulor

Cerro Toco

CORDILLERA
DE LA SAL

Salar
de Tara

Toconao

Talabre

Volcán
Aguas Calientes

Salar de
Loyoques
o Quisquiro

Laguna
Chaxa

Salar
de
Atacama

Camar

Salar de
Aguas
Calientes

Socaire

ARGENTINA

0   20 miles

0   20 km

Reserva Nacional
Los Flamencos

lakes, steaming geysers, colonial villages, and ancient fortresses all lie
within easy reach.

The area's history goes back to pre-Columbian times, when the Atacameño people scraped a meager living from the fertile delta of the
San Pedro River. By 1450 the region had been conquered by the Incas,
but their reign was cut short by the arrival of the Europeans. Spanish
conquistador Pedro de Valdivia, who eventually seized control of the
entire country, camped here in 1540 while waiting for reinforcements.
By the 19th century San Pedro had become an important trading center
and was a stop for llama trains on their way from the altiplano to the
Pacific coast. During the nitrate era, San Pedro was the main resting
place for cattle drives from Argentina.

SAN PEDRO DE ATACAMA

Fodor's Choice   *100 km (62 miles) southeast of Calama.*

★   It is not an exaggeration to call San Pedro de Atacama a once-in-a-
lifetime destination. After all, there's nowhere else quite like it. Otherworldly landscapes surround the quiet town of San Pedro, which is a
real oasis in the desert in the literal and metaphorical sense: greenery
and rushing irrigation channels give life to this dusty town, and the

intriguing community of travelers, artisans, and natives have created a stress-free oasis far removed from the burdens of normal life. Over the last decade San Pedro has exploded in tourism, now offering more than 100 accommodation options, three dozen restaurants, and more tourism operators than you'll care to count.

What is so attractive about San Pedro? For adventurists, it is the opportunity to do high-altitude climbing, sandboarding, and mountain biking. For sightseers, it is the volcano-lined horizon, the salt-shaken valleys, the clear blue salt lakes teeming with flamingos, and the steam-spitting geysers. And for pleasure seekers, it is simply soaking in the beautiful Atacama sun and landscapes while moving to the San Pedro pace: nice and slow.

GETTING HERE AND AROUND

San Pedro is an hour's bus or car ride from Calama. You can either take the private (65,000 pesos) or shared (12,000 pesos) shuttle services from the airport, or the cheaper option of a bus ride (1,500). There's no need to book in advance. You'll find two shuttle companies as you arrive at the baggage claim in the airport. If you want to take the public bus you'll need to travel into Calama bus station first. Tur-Bus and a few other companies serve San Pedro, and the bus terminal is just a few blocks from downtown at the intersection of Lincacabur and Domingo Atienz. If planning other trips around Chile, there's a Tur-Bus ticket window here.

SAFETY AND PRECAUTIONS

Take good care driving on the road between Calama and San Pedro as many accidents happen around sundown, when the blinding altiplano sun hits the horizon, hindering visibility.

ESSENTIALS

There is an emergency clinic in San Pedro on the main plaza, but the nearest proper hospital is in Calama. There are no international banks, but there are four ATMS in the town and money-changing houses are easy to find.

Visitor Information Sernatur San Pedro de Atacama ⊠ *Toconao at Gustavo LePaige* ☎ *55/285–1420* ⊕ *www.chile.travel* ⊙ *Daily 9–9.*

TOURS

Every corner you turn in San Pedro, someone is offering a tour. Most of them offer the same classic routes—geysers, flamingos, Valle de la Luna—and all seem to have surprisingly low prices. But if it seems too good to be true, it probably is.

Make sure to ask how many people will be on the tour and how long you will spend at each place. Avoid unlicensed companies or agencies that sell into other company's tours. Try to stick with reputable companies that employ guides who have been in San Pedro long enough to know the best lookout points.

If you don't want to go with a group, hire a private driver and guide. A car and chauffeur should cost around 50,000 pesos per half-day, excluding gas. Ask the tourism office or your hotel for their recommendations.

Atacama Mistica. Focusing on volcano treks, Atacama Mistica takes small groups up volcanoes to peer into craters and enjoy the sweeping views of the desert beneath. Half-day, full-day, and even two-day treks are on their agenda. They also offer trips to Uyuni in Bolivia, stopping at lagoons, hot springs, and salt flats along the way. ⊠ *Caracoles 238* ☎ *55/285–1966* ⊕ *www.atacamamistica.cl* 🖃 *From 90,000 pesos.*

Cosmo Andino Expediciones. Operating for more than 28 years, Cosmo is one of the most established and reliable tour operators. All guides and drivers are contracted (not freelance) and the vehicles are their own. The classic tours are all covered, although Cosmo prides itself on beating the crowd with earlier start times and spending longer in each location than the other companies. They offer multiple hiking options, but their newest addition is the full-day Tara tour enjoying volcanos, llamas, and spectacular views. ⊠ *Caracoles s/n, corner of Tocapilla* ☎ *55/285–1069* ⊕ *www.cosmoandino.cl* 🖃 *From 12,000 pesos.*

TurisTour. This reliable chain has the biggest fleet of vehicles in San Pedro. It offers classic group tours (up to 35 people) that show you to the highlights of San Pedro—the geysers, the salar, Valle de la Luna, and Laguna Cejar. The company also offers a less common half-day Archaeological Tour, which visits small settlements and a typical farm. Another option is to hire a driver to head into the desert. ⊠ *Caracoles, corner of Calama* ☎ *55/242–4748* ⊕ *www.turistour.cl* 🖃 *From 44,000 pesos.*

EXPLORING

Iglesia San Pedro. To the west of the square is one of the altiplano's largest churches. It was miraculously constructed in 1744 without the use of a single nail—the builders used cactus sinews to tie the roof beams and door hinges. The new refurbishment (to be completed early 2015) maintains the same original structure but should reinforce the church for centuries to come. ⊠ *Gustavo Le Paige s/n* ⊙ *Daily 9–2 and 3–8.*

Pukara de Quitor. Just 3 km (2 miles) north of San Pedro lies this ancient fortress at the entrance to the Valle de Catarpe, which was built in the 12th century to protect the Atacameños from invading Incas. It wasn't the Incas but the Spanish who were the real threat, however. Spanish conquistador Pedro de Valdivia took the fortress by force in 1540. The crumbling buildings were carefully reconstructed in 1981 by the University of Antofagasta. ⊠ *On road to Valle Catarpe* 🖃 *3,000 pesos* ⊙ *Daily 9:15–5:30.*

Tulor. This archaeological site, 9 km (5½ miles) southwest of San Pedro, marks the remains of the oldest known civilization in the region. Built around 800 BC, the village of Tulor was home to the Linka Arti people, who lived in small mud huts resembling igloos. The site was uncovered only in the middle of the 20th century, when Jesuit missionary Gustavo Le Paige excavated it from a sand dune. Archaeologists hypothesize that the inhabitants left because of climatic changes and a possible sand storm. Little more about the village's history is known, and only one of the huts has been completely excavated. As one of the well-informed guides will tell you, even this hut is sinking back into the obscurity of the Atacama sand. ⊠ *9 km (5½ miles) southwest of San Pedro, then 3 km (2 miles) down road leading to Valle de la Luna* 🖃 *3,000 pesos* ⊙ *Daily 9–7.*

WHERE TO EAT

$$ CHILEAN Fodor's Choice ★ 🍴 **Baltinache.** Offering "indigenous fusion" food, Baltinache is a unique option in San Pedro. Its daily menu incorporates native ingredients as well as typically Chilean preparations like *curanto, merkin,* and *la patasca*. They also offer grilled fish and meat (including *guanaco* and wagyu beef), too. This intimate restaurant has a lot of charm, with brightly colored paintings on the wall alongside children's drawings, and local music piping out of the open-plan kitchen. A couple blocks out of town on a mud road, it's not the easiest to find, but it's worth the trip. [$] *Average main: 8000 pesos* ✉ *Domingo Atienza, Allyu de Larache* ☎ *9/7658–2677* ✍ *Reservations essential* ⏲ *Closed Mon.*

$$ LATIN AMERICAN 🍴 **Café Adobe Restaurante.** One of the most popular restaurants in San Pedro, Adobe gets extra points for its atmospheric fire pit and local Andean band. The food reflects international and local tastes with quesadillas, salads and pizzas, alongside the calorific Chilean favorite of steak *a la pobre* (topped with fried egg, onions and fries) and more tasteful Atacama-inspired fusion dishes like Patagonian lamb kofte with local broad bean hummous and rica rica (a local herb) raita. Don't leave without trying a coca leaf or *rica rica* pisco sour! [$] *Average main: 7000 pesos* ✉ *Carcoles 211* ☎ *55/285–1132* 🌐 *www.cafeadobe.cl.*

$$ CHILEAN 🍴 **Casa Piedra.** This rustic stone structure (*piedra* means "stone") affords views of the cloudless desert skies from its central courtyard. As at most San Pedro eateries, it can be a hit or miss—the blazing fire and outdoor garden is a hit, but the typical Chilean and international cuisine can swing either way depending on how busy it is. Stick to the classics and enjoy the ambience. [$] *Average main: 8000 pesos* ✉ *Caracoles 225* ☎ *9/7984–4148* ⏲ *Closed Mon.*

$$ PIZZA 🍴 **Charrua.** While you may not have come to San Pedro to eat pizza, this busy little joint serves respectable thin-crust pies. Service is speedy and friendly. The restaurant itself is not classy, but if you are looking for a bit of home comfort or takeout for your hotel patio, Charrua is the place. Note that they don't have an alcohol license. [$] *Average main: 7000 pesos* ✉ *Tocopilla 442* ☎ *55/285–1443* 💳 *No credit cards.*

$$ CHILEAN 🍴 **Delicias de Carmen.** Carmen has managed to attract locals and tourists alike with her immensely popular restaurant that serves affordable, typically Chilean home-style dishes, ranging from soups and stews to roast meats and fish. Warm bread is served with a killer *pebre* (spicy salsa) and the lunch specials are the best value in San Pedro. [$] *Average main: 7000 pesos* ✉ *Calama 360* ☎ *9/089–5673.*

WHERE TO STAY

$$$$ RESORT Fodor's Choice ★ 🏨 **Alto Atacama Desert Lodge & Spa.** Surrounded by the Salt Mountains Range (Cordillera de la Sal) in the midst of Chile's Atacama Desert, this 42-room luxury retreat is an unlikely oasis in a landscape that seems to extend endlessly in every direction. **Pros:** one-of-a-kind desert escape; excellent facilities. **Cons:** expensive. [$] *Rooms from: 250000 pesos* ✉ *Camino Pukará, Sector Suchor* ☎ *02/2912–3945* 🌐 *www.altoatacama.com* 🛏 *42 rooms* 🍽 *Multiple meal plans.*

$$$$
RESORT

Cumbres San Pedro de Atacama. This attractive, widespread resort has 60 rooms, each with its own private patio looking onto the gardens planted with native flora. **Pros:** massive beds; great breakfast buffet; lots of outdoor areas. **Cons:** spa can get full; not-so-personalized service. *Rooms from: 150000 pesos ✉ Av. Las Chilcas s/n Lote 10, Parcela 2 ☎ 55/285–2136 ⊕ www.cumbressanpedro.com ⤴ 60 rooms ⊚ Multiple meal plans.*

$$$$
HOTEL
ALL-INCLUSIVE
Fodor's Choice
★

explora Atacama. The hotel delivers the best service and amenities of any lodging in northern Chile—and it makes a statement while doing so, housed in a sleek, modern building that has won architectural awards. **Pros:** top-notch service; four pools; excellent food. **Cons:** expensive; Wi-Fi spotty in evenings. *Rooms from: 490000 pesos ✉ Domingo Atienza s/n, Ayllu de Larache ☎ 2/2395–2800 in Chile, 866/750–6699 in U.S. ⊕ www.explora.com/explora-atacama ⤴ 50 rooms, 4 suites ⊚ All-inclusive.*

$$$$
HOTEL
FAMILY

Hotel Altiplánico. This hotel village outside the center of San Pedro has the look and feel of a pueblo: a labyrinth of walkways lead you from room to room, which are each constructed with typical mud-color adobe and adorned with private terraces and often outdoor showers. **Pros:** refreshing pool; privacy; great stars at night. **Cons:** long walk from town (no provided transfers); rooms quite dark, but cool. *Rooms from: 150000 pesos ✉ Domingo Atienza 282 ☎ 55/285–1212 ⊕ www.altiplanico.cl ⤴ 32 rooms ⊚ Breakfast.*

$$$$
HOTEL

Lodge Andino Terrantai. Right behind the main plaza, Terrantai is a real gem combining the historical and modern: the historical part is a 200-year-old colonial house with high cane ceilings supported by entire tree trunks, and the modern part (constructed in 1996) opens out into a maze of river-stone walls with secret fountains and gardens. **Pros:** unique design; great location for walking to the plaza; attention to details. **Cons:** noise travels; rooms are basic; Wi-Fi slow. *Rooms from: 130000 pesos ✉ Tocopilla 411 ☎ 55/285–1045 ⊕ www.terrantai.com ⤴ 21 rooms ⊚ Breakfast.*

$$$$
RESORT
ALL-INCLUSIVE
Fodor's Choice
★

Tierra Atacama. One of the most stylish hotels in the North, Tierra has an imaginative take on design, services, and excursions to give it a touch of luxury and originality without losing that atacameño feel or respect for local places, people, and traditions. **Pros:** luxury masquerading as roughing it; excellent spa; good service; great tours. **Cons:** a little far the action but that's the idea; expensive. *Rooms from: 215000 pesos ✉ Calle Séquitor s/n, Ayllú de Yaye in San Pedro de Atacama ☎ 55/555–975 ⊕ www.tierraatacama.com ⤴ 32 suites ⊚ All-inclusive.*

NIGHTLIFE

The bohemian side of San Pedro gets going after dinner and generally ends around midnight. Afterward, locals move to the outskirts for clandestine raves. There is an increasing problem with trafficked cocaine from Bolivia through San Pedro, so be careful if anyone tries to offer you some. Back in the legal sphere, most of the bars and small cafés are on Caracoles and it is all pretty mellow. Your choices are pretty much limited to whether you want to sit outside by a fire or inside, where it's a bit warmer.

Café Export. Café Export is smaller and more intimate than the other bars in town. There's a pleasant terrace out back, although during high season you'll be hard-pinched to find some space between tourists and locals. ✉ *Caracoles at Toconao* ☎ *55/851-547.*

La Estaka. La Estaka is a hippie bar with funky decor, and a local feel. Reggae music rules, and the international food isn't half bad either. ✉ *Caracoles 259B* ☎ *55/285–1286* ⊕ *www.laestaka.cl.*

SPORTS AND THE OUTDOORS

San Pedro is an outdoors lover's dream. There are great places for biking, hiking, and horseback riding in every direction. Extreme-sports enthusiasts can try their hand at sandboarding on the dunes of the Valle de la Muerte. Climbers can take on the nearby volcanoes, which provide an exhilarating high-altitude ascent; the only trouble is the crowds. At the Valle de la Luna, for example, sunset at the large dune is somewhat spoiled by the large tourist vans that dump a couple hundred sightseers there for the renowned sundown. The number of tour agencies and outfitters in San Pedro can be a bit overwhelming: shop around, pick a company you feel comfortable with, ask questions, and make sure the company is willing to cater to your needs.

Whatever your sport, keep in mind that San Pedro lies at 2,400 meters (7,900 feet) above sea level. If you're not acclimated to the high altitude, you'll feel tired much sooner than you might expect, so save excursions to the altiplánico or geysers until your last days. Also, remember to slather on the sunscreen and drink plenty of water.

BIKING

An afternoon ride to the Valle de la Luna is unforgettable, as is a quick trip to the ruins of Tulor, or the Laguna Cejar. Bike rentals can be arranged at most hotels and tour agencies. A bike can be rented for a half day for 3,000 pesos and for an entire day for 5,000 pesos.

HIKING

There is fantastic hiking throughout San Pedro, whether you want to spend a half-day trekking the Valle de Lune, an afternoon in the Cactus Valley, or a full day hiking up a volcano.

HORSEBACK RIDING

Atacama Horse. San Pedro has the feeling of a Wild West town, so why not hitch up your horse and head out on an adventure? Although the sun is quite intense during the middle of the day, sunset is a perfect time to visit Pukara de Quitor or Tulor. You can do day rides or multiple day rides and crossings. ✉ *Tocopilla 406* ☎ *55/285–1956* ⊕ *www. atacamahorseadventure.com* ✉ *From 50,000 pesos.*

SANDBOARDING

It's like snowboarding, only hotter. Many agencies offer a three-hour sandboarding excursion into the Valle de la Muerte from 4 pm to 9 pm—the intelligent way to beat the desert heat. These tours run about 7,000 pesos and include an instructor. If you're brave and have your own transportation, you can rent just the board for 4,000 pesos. There is also a combination sandboarding-and-sunset tour for 15,000 pesos, which closes the day with a desert sunset over the Valle de la Luna.

Since a fall on the sand can be hard, you should wear a helmet and board with caution.

Atacama Inca Tour. For sandboarding, Atacama Inca Tour takes you out to the Valley de los Muertos with an instructor to surf the dunes on their pro boards. You can combine sandboarding with a hike and sunset visit to the Valle de la Luna followed by a pisco sour at sundown. ⊠ *Tocanao (s/n)* ☎ *55/285–1062* ✉ *From 15,000 pesos.*

Turismo Teckara. In the center of San Pedro, Teckara rent boards and offer tours to Valle de la Muerte. ⊠ *Tocanao 455* ☎ *55/285–1623* ✉ *From 8,000 pesos.*

STARGAZING

The Atacama Desert is one of the best places for star gazing in the world due to its clear skies, high altitude, and isolation from light pollution. So good is the star gazing here that San Pedro de Atacama is home to one of the world's biggest space ventures, the international ALMA observatory (not open to the public yet).

While the naked eye is perfectly good for spotting constellations, planets, and shooting stars (there's an average visibility of four every hour here), you shouldn't miss out on an opportunity to look through one of the many powerful telescopes here. Luxury hotels sometimes have their own telescopes and outdoor observatories.

SPACE. SPACE offers one of the best astronomical tours in San Pedro. The complete darkness allows you to observe the night sky with the naked eye and through a dozen powerful telescopes. The tour finishes with an astronomy chat over hot chocolate. Popular with backpackers, tours are nightly (weather depending) and depart from the city center with native English-speaking specialist guides. ⊠ *166 Caracoles* ☎ *55/285–1935* ⊕ *www.spaceobs.com* ✉ *From 18,000 pesos (includes transport).*

SHOPPING

Just about the entire village of San Pedro is an open-air market. Shopping here is fun, but prices are probably about 20% to 30% higher than in neighboring areas, and you'll find many of the same products: the traditional altiplano ponchos (aka serapes), jewelry, and even musical instruments. If you are taking a tour out to some of the smaller villages you might find the same products being sold at a much lower price.

Feria Artesenal. The Feria Artesanal, just off the Plaza de Armas, is bursting at the seams with artisan goods. Here, you can buy high-quality knits from the altiplano, such as sweaters and other woolen items. ⊠ *Off plaza.*

Galería Cultural de Pueblos Andinos. Galería Cultural de Pueblos Andinos is an open-air market selling woolens and crafts. ⊠ *Caracoles s/n, east of town.*

Mallku. Mallku is a pleasant store carrying traditional altiplano textiles, some up to 20 years old. ⊠ *Caracoles 190c* ☎ *55/285–1417.*

GEYSERS DEL TATIO

Fodor'sChoice *95 km (59 miles) north of San Pedro.*

★ Witnessing the fumaroles at daybreak here is one of the best experiences Chile has to offer. The geysers pump out boiling water throughout the day, and seeing the steam rise against the stark landscapes is breathtaking.

GETTING HERE AND AROUND
El Tatio is open all day for visits, but nearly everyone arrives just before sunrise, when the cold night air gives the steaming geysers an imposing presence. Tour groups depart San Pedro around 4 or 5 am, depending on the time of year. Most tours start with a walk through the geyser field and end with a simple breakfast and the chance for a quick dip in the nearby thermal pools. Tours usually return to San Pedro at midday.

EXPLORING

Fodor'sChoice **Geysers del Tatio.** The world's highest geothermal field, the Geysers del
★ Tatio is a breathtaking natural phenomenon. The sight of dozens of *fumaroles,* or geysers, throwing columns of steam into the air is unforgettable. A trip to El Tatio usually begins at 4 am, on a guided tour, when San Pedro is still cold and dark (any of the tour agencies in San Pedro can arrange this trip). After a two-hour bus trip on a relentlessly bumpy road, you reach the high plateau about daybreak. (The entrance fee is covered if you are on a tour, otherwise it is 5,000 pesos.) The jets of steam are already shooting into the air as the sun slowly peeks over the adjacent cordillera. The rays of light illuminate the steam in a kaleidoscope of chartreuses, violets, reds, oranges, and blues. The vapor then silently falls onto the sulfur-stained crust of the geyser field. As the sun heats the cold, barren land, the force of the geysers gradually diminishes, allowing you to explore the mud pots and craters formed by the escaping steam. Be careful, though—the crust is thin in places and people have been badly burned falling into the boiling-hot water. ⊠ *Geysers El Tatio, San Pedro de Atacama* 🎫 *5,000 pesos*

Termas de Puritama. On your way back to San Pedro, you may want to stop at the Termas de Puritama hot springs. A hot soak may be just the thing to shake off that early morning chill. A relaxing daytrip in itself, the termas are a series of 8 pools each one connected by wooden platforms and surrounded by foliage in the middle of this natural valley. If you don't have your own transport, you can book a transfer or group tour from many agencies in San Pedro. If you are staying at Hotel Explora, you'll have exclusive access to the first (and warmest) spring. ⊠ *Termas de Puritama, San Pedro de Atacama* 🎫 *15,000 pesos.*

RESERVA NACIONAL LOS FLAMENCOS

Fodor'sChoice *10 km (6 miles) south and east of San Pedro.*

★ In the middle of one of the largest salt flats in the world, crowds of pink flamingos flock to a couple pretty lagoons. While the flamingos often get the most attention, the whole setting is stunning, with volcanoes in the backdrop and vast, white stretches of land that paint a beautiful picture at sunset.

Nearly all San Pedro tour companies take you to the Reserva, but if you're in your own vehicle, take the road toward Toconao for 33 km (20½ miles) to the park entrance.

ESSENTIALS

CONAF. You can get information about the Reserva Nacional Los Flamencos at the station run by CONAF, the Chilean forestry service. ⊠ *CONAF station near Laguna Chaxa* ⊕ *www.conaf.cl* ⚏ *2,500 pesos* ☉ *Daily 8–8.*

EXPLORING

Altiplanico Lakes: Miscanti and Miñeques. At more than a 4,000-meter altitude, these lakes are in a completely different climate to San Pedro below. The altiplanico is much more humid and while that means you are likely to experience rain and snow in certain seasons, the area is also alive with color and wildlife. The pastel-color backdrop is picture perfect with the large blue lagoons and volcanoes in the distance. The largest of the lagoons is Miscanti, at 4,350-meter-high (14,270-foot-high), which merits a few moments of contemplation and is one of the prettiest spots in Atacama (on a sunny day). Miñeques is home to many birds, occasionally flamingos, and is perfect for some wildlife spotting. The altiplanico lakes are usually a full day excursion from San Pedro. ⊠ *Laguna Miscanti, San Pedro de Atacama* ⚏ *2,500 pesos.*

Laguna Miñeques. Here you will find vicuña and huge flocks of flamingos. It is a smaller lake, adjacent to Laguna Miscanti, that is absolutely spectacular.

Fodor's Choice ★ Reserva Nacional Los Flamencos. Many of the most astounding sights in El Norte Grande lie within the boundaries of the protected Reserva Nacional Los Flamencos. This sprawling national reserve to the south and east of San Pedro encompasses a wide variety of geographical features, including alpine lakes, salt flats, and volcanoes.

Fodor's Choice ★ Salar de Atacama. About 10 km (6 miles) south of San Pedro you arrive at the edge of Chile's largest salt flat. The rugged crust measuring 3,000 square km (1,158 square miles) formed when salty water flowing down from the Andes evaporated in the stifling heat of the desert. Unlike other salt flats, which are smooth surfaces of crystalline salt, the Salar de Atacama is a jumble of jagged rocks that look rather like coral. **Laguna Chaxa,** in the middle of Salar de Atacama, is a very salty lagoon that is home to three of the New World's four species of flamingos. The elegant pink-and-white birds are mirrored by the lake's glassy surface. Near Laguna Chaxa, beautiful plates of salt float on the calm surface of **Laguna Salada.** Visiting the salar is a half-day excursion from San Pedro and often better at sunset when the sky can paint pretty pink colors, reflected in the mirrorlike lagoons. Bring your binoculars for flamingo observing. ⊠ *Laguna Chaxa, San Pedro de Atacama.*

Salar de Tara. This salar, growing in popularity, appeals for its extreme wilderness and beauty, and it's high in the altiplánico on the road to Bolivia—with Licancabur Volcano in full view. Over 4,440 meters high, Tara has some similarities to the Altiplánico Lakes, however, what makes it unique is the unusual rock formations that appear like castles in the sky, surreal sculptures among the sand flats, and flamingo-spotted lagoons. It is a full day from San Pedro, and involves a long and bumpy road both ways. ⊠ *Salar de Tara, San Pedro de Atacama.*

Fodor's Choice
★ **Valle de la Luna.** This surreal landscape of barren ridges, soaring cliffs, sand dunes, and pale valleys could be from a canvas by Salvador Dalí. Originally a small corner of a vast inland sea, the valley rose up with the Andes. The water slowly drained away, leaving deposits of salt and gypsum that were folded by the shifting of the Earth's crust and then worn away by wind and rain. The vastness and grandeur of some of the formations is quite breathtaking, and listening carefully to the cracking of the salt crystals as the sun warms up and cools down the surfaces is quite awe-inspiring. Visiting the Valle de la Luna is fabulous at sunset, although this is also when truck loads of tourists arrive, so if you want the valley to yourself visit in the morning when there is barely a soul there. You can visit by car, by bike (bring a big hat for shade!), or horseback. ⊠ *14 km (9 miles) west of San Pedro, San Pedro de Atacama* 🕮 *2,500 pesos.*

Valle de la Muerte. Not far from the Valle de la Luna, just on the other side of Ruta 98 leading to Calama, are the reddish rocks of the Valle de la Muerte (Death Valley). Jesuit missionary Gustavo Le Paige, who in the 1950s was the first archaeologist to explore this desolate area, discovered many human skeletons. These bones are from the indigenous Atacameño people, who lived here before the arrival of the Spanish. He hypothesized that the sick and the elderly may have come to this place to die. The name of the valley comes from its Mars-like, red appearance and was originally called Valle de Martes (Mars Valley), but Gustavo's foreign pronounciation of Martes (Mars) soon became heard as Muerte (dead). ⊠ *San Pedro de Atacama* 🕮 *Free.*

OFF THE
BEATEN
PATH **Salar de Uyuni.** It's possible to take a three- to five-day, four-wheel-drive organized tour from San Pedro into Bolivia's massive and mysterious salt flat, the largest in the world. Beware: the accommodations—usually clapboard lodgings in small oasis towns—are rustic to say the least, but speeding along the Salar de Uyuni, which is chalkboard flat, is a treat. Nearby are geysers, small Andean lagoons, and islands of cactus that stand in sharp contrast to the sealike salt flat.

IQUIQUE AND NEARBY

The waterside town of Iquique itself is rather dreary, but the area holds many sights that merit a visit. Wander down to the port and *muelles* (fishing piers) and watch the fishing boats come in; while you're there, imagine the key battle of the War of the Pacific being waged offshore in 1879, or Sir Francis Drake and his gang of brigands arriving to sack the town in 1577. You can find out more about this history at the Museo Naval.

A stone's throw from Iquique, nitrate ghost towns like Humberstone sit in eternal silence. Farther inland you encounter the charming hot-spring oases of Pica and Mamiña and the enigmatic Gigante de Atacama, the world's largest geoglyph.

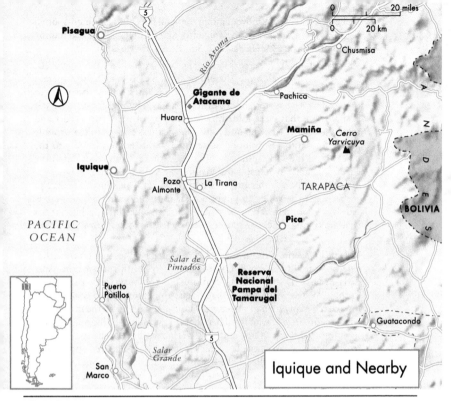

Iquique and Nearby

IQUIQUE

390 km (242 miles) northwest of Calama.

Iquique is the capital of Chile's northernmost region, but it wasn't always so important. For hundreds of years it was a tiny fishing community. After the arrival of the Spanish the village grew slowly into a port. The population, however, never totaled more than 100. It was not until the great nitrate boom of the 19th century that Iquique became a major port. Many of those who grew rich on nitrate moved to the city and built opulent mansions, almost all of which still stand today. Many of the old mansions are badly in need of repair, however, giving the city a rather worn-down look. The boom went bust, and those who remained turned again to the sea to make a living. Today Iquique is the world's largest exporter of fish meal.

At the base of a coastal mountain range, Iquique is blessed with year-round good weather. This may explain why it's popular with vacationing Chilean families, who come for the long stretches of white beaches as well as the *zona franca,* or duty-free zone.

y gets going after dark. Young vacationers stay out all night nd the next day lazing around on the beach.

f which feature folk and jazz performances, get crowded ight.

is bar is popular with a wide range of ages for dancing and d *Vivar 1406* ☎ *57/242–1373.*

s caters to the 30-plus crowd with live bands playing the Eagles and Kiss, and sometimes provides an all-you-can- fet. ⊠ *Arturo Prat 2996* ☎ *57/234–6497* ☉ *Closed Sun.*

S

am, the beachfront discos start filling with a young, ener . Check out the dance clubs along Playa Brava and jus n.

rt of a popular chain of discos, Kamikaze is jam-packed s with young people dancing to salsa music. ⊠ *Bajo Molle* w.kamikaze.cl.

G

Many Chileans come to Iquique with one thing on their pping. About 3 km (2 miles) north of the city center is the a—known to locals as the Zofri—the only duty-free zone try's northern tip. This big, unattractive mall is stocked cigarettes, alcohol, and electronic goods. Remember that ses, such as personal computers, are taxable upon leaving , ⊠ *Av. Salitrera Victoria* ☎ *57/251–5600* ⊕ *www.zofri.c* . *11–9.*

miles) east of Iquique.

t from the brown desert, the tiny village of Mamiña has hot springs. Renowned throughout Chile for their curative se springs draw people from around the region. Every hote the thermal water pumped into its rooms, so you can enjo e privacy of your own *tina,* or bathtub. The valley also ha lic pools fed by thermal springs. The town itself is perched cliff above a terraced green valley where locals grow alfalfa

ERE AND AROUND

125 km (78 miles) from Iquique proper: go back to Ruta d south briefly before taking Ruta A-65 directly east into you'd also like to see Tambillo (a resting spot on the Inca the turnoff for Ruta A-651. For the adventurous and hard there are minivans that head to Mamiña from Iquique.

NG

tions in town are given in relation to the Mamiña bottling produces the popular mineral drinking water sold in many ops.

GETTING HERE AND AROUND

Iquique's Diego Aracena airport (IQQ) is about 45 minutes from downtown proper (35 km [22 miles]; 16,000 pesos in taxi fare) and is served by the three major airlines: Sky, Air Comet, and LAN. Iquique is about seven hours via bus or car from Calama (400 km [249 miles]); once you've turned off the Pan-American Highway it's a narrow, serpentine road down to the town, so don't try passing any of the big trucks or other vehicles that may be slowing you down.

The tourist sights of Mamiña, Pica, and the Gigante de Atacama can all be done in one day's driving, and if you don't want to drive yourself, two tour companies in town offer all-inclusive tours. There are two official taxi stands, one on Plaza Prat and one on the pedestrian street of Baquedano. Both will quote you rates to and from the airport, as well as day tours to nearby sites like the Gigante de Atacama, Humberstone, and Mamiña. To get to Pica, La Tirana, and the surrounding sights from Iquique, head south on Ruta 5 (Pan-American Highway) to Km 1,800 (Cruce Sara). Then head east on Ruta 685. As for rental cars, the best deals are in Iquique, but cars rented here can't be taken out of the area.

ESSENTIALS

Air Travel Diego Aracena Airport (IQQ) ☎ 57/247-3473. **LAN** ☎ 600/526-2000 ⊕ www.lan.com. **Sky Airline** ☎ 58/225-1816 ⊕ www.skyairline.com.

Rental Car Contacts Avis ⊠ Manuel Rodriguez 730 ☎ 57/257-4330 ⊕ www.avis.com. **Hertz** ⊠ Aníbal Pinto 1303 ☎ 57/251-0432 ⊕ www.hertz.com.

Taxi Contacts Taxi Aeropuerto ⊠ Baquedano 302, corner of Wilson ☎ 57/241-9004, 57/241-5916.

Visitor Information Sernatur Iquique ⊠ Aníbal Pinto 436 ☎ 57/241-9241 ⊕ www.sernatur.cl ☉ Weekdays 9-6, Sat. 10-2.

TOURS

Avitours. Offering full- or multiday tours to local attractions like Isluga Volcano, the Pampa Calichera, and Humberstone, Avitours can also organize paragliding over Iquique. ⊠ Baquedano 997 ☎ 57/241-3334 ⊕ www.avitours.cl 🎫 From 25,000 pesos.

EXPLORING

Calle Baquedano. Leading out from Plaza Prat is this pedestrian mall with wooden sidewalks. This is a great place for an afternoon stroll past some of Iquique's *salitrera*-era mansions or for a leisurely cappuccino in one of the many sidewalk cafés. An antique trolley runs the length of the mall.

Museo Naval. Located in the old customs house, the museum has displays about the Battle of Iquique in 1879, when the Chileans claimed Iquique from their neighbors to the north. Here you can get a glimpse of what the soldiers wore during the war and the antiquated English arms used by the Chilean army. A well-hidden corridor displays photos and descriptions of two-dozen bird species of the Chilean seashore. ⊠ Sotomayor and Anibal Pinto ☎ 57/251-7138 ☉ Tues.–Sat. 10–1, 3-6, Sun. 11–2

5

Geoglyphs of the Atacama Desert

In addition to the Gigante de Atacama, the world's largest geoglyph at 86 meters (282 feet) high, there are geoglyphs throughout El Norte Grande. The rock art at Cerros Pintados comprises the largest collection of geoglyphs in South America. More than 400 images adorn this hill in Reserva Nacional Pampa del Tamarugal. Figures representing birds, animals, people, and geometric patterns appear to dance along the hill. Farther north, the Tiliviche

geoglyphs decorate a hill sitting not far from the modern-day marvel of the Pan-American Highway. These geoglyphs, most likely constructed between AD 1000 and 1400 during the Inca reign, depict a large caravan of llamas. All of these llamas are headed in the same direction—toward the sea—a testament, perhaps, to the geoglyphs' navigational use during the age when llama trains brought silver down to the coast in exchange for fish.

Museo Regional. Along the historic Calle Baquedano is this natural-history museum of the region. It showcases pre-Columbian artifacts such as deformed skulls and arrowheads, as well as an eclectic collection from the region's nitrate heyday. ⊠ Baquedano 951 ☎ 57/254–4719 🖅 2,000 pesos ⏱ Tues.–Fri. 9–5:30, Sat. 9:30–6.

Fodor's Choice ★ **Palacio Astoreca.** For a tantalizing view into the opulence of the nitrate era, visit this Georgian-style palace. Built in 1903, it includes highlights such as the likeness of Dionysus, the Greek god of revelry; a giant billiard table; and a beautiful skylight over the central hall. An art- and natural-history museum on the upper level houses modern works by Chilean artists and artifacts such as pottery and textiles. ⊠ Av. Bernardo O'Higgins 350 ☎ 57/242–5600 ⏱ Tues.–Sat. 9–6, Sun. 11–2.

Plaza Prat. Life in the city revolves around this plaza, where children ride bicycles along the sidewalks and adults chat on nearly every park bench. The 1877 **Torre Reloj**, with its gleaming white clock tower and Moorish arches, stands in the center of the plaza.

Teatro Municipal. Unlike most cities, Iquique does not have a cathedral on the main plaza. Instead, you'll find the sumptuous Teatro Municipal, built in 1890 as an opera house. The lovely statues on the Corinthian-columned facade represent the four seasons. If you're lucky you can catch one of the infrequent plays or musical performances here. ⊠ Plaza Prat ☎ 57/241–1292 🖅 From 1,500 pesos ⏱ Daily 10–6.

BEACHES

Playa Blanca. Thirteen km (8 miles) south of the city center on Avenida Balmaceda, Playa Blanca is a sandy spot that you can often have all to yourself and enjoy the active sealife. **Amenities:** parking; food and drink. **Best for:** swimming; snorkeling.

Playa Brava. If you crave privacy, head south on Avenida Balmaceda to Playa Brava, a pretty beach that's often deserted except for young people lighting bonfires in the evening. The currents here are quite

strong, so swim...
and drink; toilets...

FAMILY
Fodor's Choice ★ **Playa Cavancha.** J...
Playa Cavancha,...
families and ofte...
touch the llamas...
through aquariu...
inhabit the rivers...
and drink; toilets...

WHERE TO EA...

$$ SPANISH ✕**Casino Español.**...
transformed into...
architecture that...
good, though rat...
Andalucian style...
of sauces that acc...
Carolina, sea bas...
of pure catalan (...
pers). $ Average...

$$ SEAFOOD ✕**Club Nautico Ca**...
seafood restaurar...
ish, right down t...
the sole in Cleopa...
style sautéed shri...
waiters. $ Averag...
⚭ Reservations e...

$$ SEAFOOD ✕**Neptuno.** When...
lovers' paradise f...
che, mussels in g...
selection of Chile...
phernalia on disp...
$ Average main:...
restauranteneptu...

WHERE TO ST...

$$$ HOTEL 🏨**Hotel Terrado A**...
of Iquique's histo...
location; friendly...
others. $ Rooms...
0500 ⊕ www.ter...

$$ HOTEL 🏨**Sunfish.** On Pla...
many with views...
1970s in style. [...
☎ 57/254–1000 ...

$$$$ HOTEL 🏨**Terrado Suites.**...
the Terrado is Iq...
need in one place...
in Chile. $ Room...
0500 ⊕ www.terr...

NIGHT...
Iquique...
and then...

BARS
Bars, mo...
around...

Bar Sovia...
live musi...

Runas. R...
likes of t...
eat sushi...

DANCE C...
At about...
getic cro...
south of...

Kamikaze...
on weeke...
Km 7 ⊕...

SHOPPI...
Zona Fran...
minds—s...
Zona Fra...
in the co...
with che...
large pur...
the coun...
⏱ Mon.–...

MAMIÑA

125 km (...

An oasis...
hundreds...
powers, t...
in town h...
a soak in...
several p...
on a rock...

GETTING...
Mamiña...
5, and he...
Mamiña....
trail), tak...
of-bottom...

EXPLOR...
Most dir...
plant, wh...
Chilean s...

Baños Ipla. Ipla is the hottest of the termas with a direct channel of thermal water practically going straight to the large public tinas, surrounded by plenty of greenery. There are basic changing facilities, showers, and a snack bar. ✉ *Near Mamiña bottler* 🎟 *2,000 pesos.*

Barros El Chino. If you'd like to wallow in the mud, try a soothing mud bath in a secluded setting at Barros El Chino. After your bath, you can bake in the sun on a drying rack and then leap into one of the plunge pools to wash the stinky brown stuff off your skin. ✉ *Near Mamiña bottler* 🎟 *2,000 pesos.*

Iglesia Nuestra Señora del Rosario. This simple and charming church in the central plaza dates to 1632. The church's twin bell towers are unique in Andean Chile. A garish electric sign mars the front of the building.

Vertiente del Radium. This fountain near the Baños Ipla with slightly radioactive spring water, is said to cure every type of eye malady.

5

WHERE TO STAY

$ HOTEL 🏨 **Hotel los Cardenales.** Two highlights of this hotel are its lovely garden and its pool, which is covered by an awning to protect you from the fierce rays of the sun. **Pros:** nice views. **Cons:** a bit dated in every sense. [$] *Rooms from: 40000 pesos* ✉ *Camino Barros El Chino s/n* ☎ *57/257–5639* 🌐 *www.loscardenales.cl* 🛏 *41 rooms* 💳 *No credit cards* 🍴 *Multiple meal plans.*

PICA

114 km (71 miles) southeast of Iquique.

From a distance, Pica appears to be a mirage. This oasis cut from the gray and brown sand of the Atacama Desert is known for its fruit—the limes used to make pisco sours are grown here. A hint of citrus hangs in the air, because the town's chief pleasure is sitting in the Plaza de Armas and sipping a *jugo natural,* fresh-squeezed juice of almost any fruit imaginable, including mangoes, oranges, pears, and grapes. You can buy a bag of any of those from a vendor for the bus trip back to Iquique.

EXPLORING

Cocha Resbaladero. Most people come to Pica not for the town itself but for the incredible hot springs at Chocha Resbaladero. Tropical green foliage surrounds this lagoonlike pool cut out of the rock, and nearby caves beckon to be explored. It is quite a walk, about 2 km (1 mile) north of town, but well worth the effort. You can also drive here. ✉ *Gen. Ibañez* 🎟 *2,000 pesos* 🕒 *8–8* 🕒 *Closed Wed.*

WHERE TO EAT AND STAY

$ LATIN AMERICAN 🍴 **Los Naranjos.** This is a popular place among the locals because of the inexpensive lunch specials, usually featuring a meat or fish dish. It's nothing fancy, with long tables in a low-slung dining room. [$] *Average main: 3500 pesos* ✉ *Barboza 200, at Esmeralda* ☎ *57/274–1318* 💳 *No credit cards.*

$ B&B/INN 🏨 **Hotel los Emelios.** Birds chirping in the garden and a refreshing plunge pool make this comfortable, homey, family-owned B&B your best bet in Pica. **Pros:** friendly staff. **Cons:** feels more like a hostel than a hotel, since baths are shared. 🏷 *Rooms from: 20000 pesos* ✉ *L. Cochrane 213* ☎ *57/274–1126* 💬 *5 rooms* 🚫 *No credit cards* ⦿ *Breakfast.*

RESERVA NACIONAL PAMPA DEL TAMARUGAL

96 km (60 miles) southeast of Iquique.

This large forest in the middle of the desert is a unique sight. One of the highlights of the Reserva is the enormous geoglyphs that were created 500–1,500 years ago in the Cerros Pintados.

GETTING HERE AND AROUND

From Iquique, drive to the Pan-American Highway and head south. The entrance, which is two kilometers east of the highway, lies 24 km (15 miles) south of Pozo Almonte.

EXPLORING

Reserva Nacional Pampa del Tamarugal. The tamarugo tree is an anomaly in the almost lifeless desert. These bushlike plants survive where most would wither because they are especially adapted to the saline soil of the Atacama. Over time they developed extensive root systems that search for water deep beneath the almost impregnable surface. Reserva Nacional Pampa del Tamarugal has dense groves of tamarugos, which were almost wiped out during the nitrate era when they were felled for firewood. At the entrance to this reserve is a CONAF station. ✉ *24 km (15 miles) south of Pozo Almonte on Pan-American Hwy.* ☎ *57/275–1055* 🖥 *Free.*

Fodor's Choice ★ **Cerros Pintados** (*Painted Hills*). The amazing Cerros Pintados within the Reserva Nacional Pampa del Tamarugal are well worth a detour. Here you'll find the largest group of geoglyphs in the world. These figures, which scientists believe helped ancient peoples navigate the desert, date from AD 500 to 1400. They are also enormous—some of the figures are decipherable only from the air. Drawings of men wearing ponchos were probably intended to point out the route to the coast to the llama caravans coming from the Andes. More than 400 figures of birds, animals, and geometric patterns adorn this 4-km (2½-mile) stretch of desert. There is a CONAF kiosk on a dirt road 2 km (1 mile) west of the Pan-American Highway. ✉ *45 km (28 miles) south of Pozo Almonte* ☎ *57/275–1055* 🖥 *1,500 pesos* 🕐 *Mon.–Sun. 9–5.*

GIGANTE DE ATACAMA

84 km (52 miles) northeast of Iquique.

Although there are more than 5,000 geoglyphs in the Atacama, this one is the most iconic. The Gigante de Atacama is an 86-meter depiction of a giant man (or perhaps Pachamama) that looks like a computer-game character from the 1980s. Of course, this geoglyph is far older—most likely dating back to 900 AD—and was created by the area's indigenous peoples.

GETTING HERE AND AROUND

To get here from Iquique, head north on Ruta 5, take Ruta A-483 toward Chusmiza (east), then turn west at Huara and travel for 14 km (8 miles).

EXPLORING

Fodor's Choice ★ **Gigante de Atacama.** The world's largest geoglyph, the Gigante de Atacama, measures an incredible 86 meters (282 feet). The Atacama Giant, thought to represent a chief of an indigenous people or perhaps created in honor of Pachamama (Mother Earth), looks a bit like a space alien. It is adorned with a walking staff, a cat mask, and a feathered headdress that resembles rays of light bursting from his head. The exact age of the figure is not known, but it certainly hails from before the arrival of the Spanish, perhaps around AD 900. The geoglyph, which is on a hill, is best viewed just before dusk, when the long shadows make the outline clearer. ⊠ *Cerro Unita, 14 km (8 miles) west of turnoff to Chusmiza* ✆ *Free.*

5

PISAGUA

168 km (104 miles) north of Iquique.

Pisagua, one of the region's most prominent ports during the nitrate era, at one time sustained a population of more than 8,000 people. Many of the mansions built at that time are still standing, although others have fallen into disrepair. During Pinochet's regime, Pisagua was the site of a prison, which was later used as a hotel and has since closed. Today, there are only around 100 inhabitants in Pisagua—fisherfolk and guano harvesters primarily. The echoes of the Pinochet massacres and the bygone era of decadence still haunt the oceanfront village.

GETTING HERE AND AROUND

Follow Ruta 5 north from Iquique for around 2½ hours before turning west and beginning the descent down to the coast. The village lies 168 kilometers north of Iquique.

EXPLORING

Teatro Municipal. This theater testifies to the wealth the town once possessed. Built in 1892 at the height of the nitrate boom, it has lavish touches, such as the painted cherubs dancing across the ceiling. The theater sits right on the edge of the sea, and waves crash against its walls, throwing eerie echoes through the empty, forgotten auditorium. You can get the key, and a very informative free tour, from a woman in the tourist kiosk opposite the theater.

Torre Reloj. The town's most famous sight, this clock tower, built in 1887 from Oregon pine, stands on a hill overlooking the city; its blue and white paint peeling in the hot coastal sun. Constructed by Alexandre Gustave Eiffel, it is an excellent place to catch views of the town and its port.

WHERE TO EAT

$ SEAFOOD ✕**Restaurant La Picada de Don Gato.** This terrace restaurant, recommended by locals, serves simple but exquisite seafood. The shellfish dishes, especially the *locos mayo*, tasty Chilean abalone awash in mayonnaise,

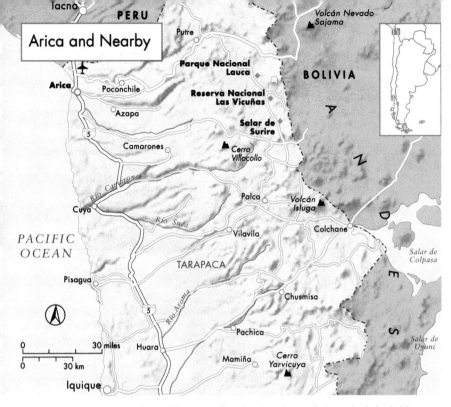

PERU

Tacna

Putre

Volcán Nevado
Sajama

Parque Nacional
Lauca

BOLIVIA

Arica

Poconchile

Reserva Nacional
Las Vicuñas

Azapa

Salar de
Surire

Camarones

Cerro
Villacollo

Río Carbrones

Palca

Volcán
Isluga

Cuya

Río Suca

Colchane

Salar de
Colpasa

PACIFIC
OCEAN

Vilavila

TARAPACA

ANDES

Pisagua

Río Aroma

Chusmisa

Salar de
Uyuni

Pachica

0   30 miles
0   30 km

Huara

Mamiña

Cerro
Yarvicuya

Iquique

are particularly delicious. Don't let the plastic chairs, which look like they belong in a bus station, distract you from the great food. $ *Average main: 3800 pesos* ✉ *Arturo Prat 127* ☎ *57/273–1511* ▭ *No credit cards.*

ARICA AND NEARBY

At the very tip of Chile, Arica is the country's northernmost city. This pleasant community on the rocky coast once belonged to Peru. In 1880, during the War of the Pacific, Chilean soldiers stormed El Morro, a fortress set high atop a cliff in Arica. Three years later, much of the land north of Antofagasta that was once part of Peru and Bolivia, belonged to Chile. Though the Arica of today is fervently Chilean, you can still see the Peruvian influence in the streets and market stalls of the city. Indigenous women still sell their goods and produce in the town's colorful markets.

Inland from Arica, the Valle Azapa cuts its way up into the mountains, a strip of green in a land of brown. Here, the excellent Museo Arqueológico de San Miguel de Azapa contains the world's oldest mummies. They were left behind by the Chinchorro people who inhabited Chile's northern coast during pre-Hispanic times. Ascending farther up the mountains toward the Bolivian border you pass through the pleasant indigenous communities of Socoroma and Putre. These towns, though far from picturesque, are good resting points if you're planning to make the journey to the 4,000-meter-high (13,120-foot-high) Parque Nacional Lauca and the neighboring Reserva Nacional Las Vicuñas. The beautiful Lago Chungará, part of Parque Nacional Lauca, lies near Bolivia, creating what is probably the country's most impressive border crossing.

ARICA

301 km (187 miles) north of Iquique.

Arica boasts that it is "the land of the eternal spring," but its temperate climate and beaches are not the only reason to visit this small city. Relax for an hour or two on the Plaza 21 de Mayo. Walk to the pier and watch the pelicans and sea lions trail the fishing boats as the afternoon's catch comes in. Walk to the top of the Morro and imagine battles of days gone by, or wonder at the magnitude of modern shipping as Chilean goods leave the port below by container ship.

GETTING HERE AND AROUND

Arica is a true international crossroads: planes arrive daily from Santiago (Sky, LAN, Air Comet), buses pull in from La Paz, and colectivos laden with four passengers head in both directions for Tacna and the Peruvian border. The airport is about 15 minutes north of town (a taxi fare is about 7,000 pesos). The bus terminal is a quick five-minute taxi ride to downtown. Vans leave in the morning from Patricio Lynch if you want a local's experience of getting to Putre; you can also take colectivos there for a bargain rate (about US$1) to the museum out on Azapa Valley (15- to 20-minute ride). Arica is about four or five hours north of Iquique by auto or bus (300 km [187 miles]).

ESSENTIALS

Air Travel Arica Chacalluta Airport (ARI). LAN ☎ *600/526–2000* ⊕ *www.lan. com.* **Sky Airline** ☎ *600/600–2828* ⊕ *www.skyairline.cl.*

Rental Car Contacts Budget ✉ *Colón 996* ☎ *58/225–8911* ⊕ *www.budget.cl.* **Hertz** ✉ *Baquedano 999* ☎ *58/223–1487* ⊕ *www.hertz.cl.*

Taxi Contacts Taxi Tarapaca ☎ *58/222–1000, 58/242–4000.*

Visitor Information Sernatur, Chilean Tourism ✉ *San Marcos 101* ☎ *58/225–2054* ⊗ *Closed Sun.*

TOURS

Geotour. This well-respected agency arranges trips from Arica to Parque Nacional Lauca, the Salar de Surire, and the Reserva Nacional Las Vicuñas. ✉ *Bolognesi 421* ☎ *58/225–3927* ⊕ *www.geotour.cl* ⌖ *From 50,000 pesos.*

EXPLORING

Aduana de Arica. Across from the Parque General Baquedano, the Aduana de Arica, the city's former customs house, is one of Eiffel's creations. It currently contains the town's cultural center, where you

CLOSE UP

Eiffel's Other Tower

An extremely ambitious man, Alexandre Gustave Eiffel designed buildings and bridges all over the world, so when Peruvian president José Balta invited him to construct a new church, Eiffel leaped at the chance. (Before the War of the Pacific, much of what is now northern Chile was part of Peru or Bolivia.) The structure was originally intended for the coastal town of Ancón, but when a great earthquake felled Arica's cathedral in 1868, the parts that had already been fabricated in Eiffel's Parisian workshop were rerouted.

Eiffel took advantage of new building materials—for example, iron—in constructing the Iglesia de San Marcos, a job that took five years. The plates and girders were cast in an iron foundry in Paris and transported to Arica, where they were carefully assembled. The only part of this marvel of Gothic-style architecture that is wood is the massive front door. Eiffel's structure withstood a harrowing test just two years after completion, when an earthquake and storm surge pummeled the town. In 2001, it stood tall again when parts of Arica succumbed to yet another temblor.

In addition to the church and customs house in Arica, Eiffel designed a clock tower in the Chilean town of Pisagua. In neighboring Peru you can see the cathedral—made of more traditional stone—that Eiffel designed for the town of Tacna in 1870 and the bridge he designed for Arequipa in 1882. All this happened before his famed Parisian tower was built in 1889.

can find exhibits about northern Chile, old photographs of Arica, and works by local painters and sculptors. ⊠ *Free* ☉ *Daily 10–6.*

El Morro de Arica. Hanging over the town, this fortress is impossible to ignore. This former Peruvian stronghold was the site of one of the key battles in the War of the Pacific. The fortress now houses the **Museo de las Armas,** which commemorates that battle. As you listen to the proud drum roll of military marches, you can wander among the uniforms and weapons of past wars. ⊠ *Reached by footpath from Calle Colón* ⊠ *600 pesos* ☉ *Daily 8–8.*

Estacion Ferrocarril. North of Parque General Baquedano is the defunct train station for the Arica–La Paz railroad. Though trains no longer run across the mountains to the Bolivian capital, there are round-trip journeys four times a week to the altiplano. The 1913 building houses a small museum with a locomotive and other remnants of the railroad. ⊠ *Free* ☉ *Daily 10–6.*

Iglesia de San Marcos. Located on the Plaza Colón, the Iglesia de San Marcos was erected in 1876 and was constructed entirely from iron. Alexandre Gustave Eiffel, designer of that famed eponymous Parisian tower, had the individual pieces cast in France before bringing them to Arica.

Fodor's Choice ★ **Museo Arqueológico de San Miguel de Azapa.** A visit here is a must for anyone who travels to El Norte Grande. In an 18th-century olive-oil refinery, this museum houses an impressive collection of artifacts from the cultures of the Chinchorros (a coastal people) and Tijuanacotas (a group that lived in the antiplano). Of particular interest are the Chinchorro mummies, the oldest in the world, dating to 6000 BC. The incredibly well-preserved mummies are arranged in the fetal position, which was traditional in this area. To look into their wrinkled, expressive faces is to get a glimpse at a history that spans more than 8,000 years. The tour ends at an olive press that functioned until 1956, a reminder of the still-thriving industry in the surrounding valley. The museum is a short drive from Arica. You can also make the 20-minute journey by colectivo from Patricio Lynch for about 1,200 pesos. ⊠ *12 km (7 miles) south of town on route to Putre* ☎ *58/220–5555* ⊕ *www. uta.cl/masma* ⊠ *2,000 pesos* ☉ *Jan. and Feb., daily 10–7; Mar.–Dec., daily 10–6.*

Fodor'sChoice
★
Museo del Mar. This museum houses a well-maintained and colorful collection of more than 1,000 seashells and oceanic oddities from around the world. The owner has traveled the globe for more than 30 years to bolster his collection, which includes specimens from Africa, Asia, and you guessed it—Arica. ⊠ *Sangra 315* ☎ *09/8225–4949* ⊕ *www. museodelmardearica.cl* ⊠ *2,000 pesos* ☉ *Weekdays 11–7, Sat. 11–2:30.*

BEACHES

Part of the reason people flock to Arica is the beaches. The surf can be quite rough in some spots, so look for—and heed—signs that say "no apta para bañarse" ("no swimming").

Playa Brava. The long stretch of Playa Brava is renowned for its consistent waves (which are too strong for swimming) and beautiful sunsets. **Amenities:** parking. **Best for:** solitude; surfing; sunset.

FAMILY **Playa Chinchorro.** The white sands of Playa Chinchorro, 2 km (1 mile) north of the city are popular with families and swimmers. You can also rent Jet Skis in high season. **Amenities:** parking; food and drink; toilets. **Best for:** swimming.

FAMILY **Playa El Laucho.** South of El Morro, Playa El Laucho is the closest to the city, and thus the most crowded. It's also a bit rocky at the bottom but waters are calm and inviting. **Amenities:** parking; food and drink; toilets; showers; lifeguards. **Best for:** swimming.

WHERE TO EAT

$$
SEAFOOD
✕**Club de Deportes Náuticos.** This old yacht club with views of the port serves succulent seafood dishes in a relaxed terrace setting. One of the friendliest restaurants in town, this former men's club is a great place to meet the old salts of the area. Bring your fish stories. $ *Average main: 6400 pesos* ⊠ *Isla Alacran s/n* ☎ *58/222–4396* ☉ *Closed Mon. No dinner.*

$$
SEAFOOD
✕**El Rey de Mariscos.** Locals love this seafood restaurant, and for good reason. The *corvina con salsa margarita* (sea bass in a seafood-based sauce) is a winner, as is the *paila marina,* a hearty soup stocked with all manner of fish. The dreary fluorescent lights and faux-wood paneling give this restaurant on the second story of a concrete-block building an undeserved down-at-the-heels air. $ *Average main: 8500 pesos* ⊠ *Colon 565* ☎ *58/222–9232.*

$

SEAFOOD

Fodor's Choice

★

✕**Maracuyá.** Wicker furniture enhances the cool South Pacific atmosphere of this pleasant, open-air restaurant that literally sits above the water on stilts. The international menu focuses on fish. The seafood, lauded by locals, is always fresh; ask the waiter what the fishing boats brought in that day. House specialties include octopus grilled in lemon and olive oil, salmon in an orange sauce, and sea bass in the pineapple-flavored *salsa amazonia*. $ *Average main: 12000 pesos* ⊠ *Av. Comandante San Martin 0321* ☎ *58/222-7600* ⊕ *www.restaurantmaracuya.cl.*

WHERE TO STAY

$$

HOTEL

FAMILY

Hotel Arica. Sitting on the ocean between Playa El Laucho and Playa Las Liseras, this hotel has a sense of somewhat faded grandeur with elegant but dated rooms, although the views of the ocean are top notch and the staff are courteous and attentive. **Pros:** beautiful setting; nice restaurant. **Cons:** somewhat dated; far from downtown. $ *Rooms from: 85800 pesos* ⊠ *Av. Comandante San Martin 599* ☎ *58/225-4540* ⊕ *www.panamericanahoteles.cl* ⤳ *114 rooms, 14 suites, 20 cabanas* ⍥ *Breakfast.*

$$

HOTEL

Hotel Aruma. This modern boutique hotel is located in the city center and has minimalist furnishings with a splash of color in the comfortable communal spaces and outdoor sun terrace and pool. **Pros:** central location; modern; comfy beds. **Cons:** rooms are a little small. $ *Rooms from: 65000 pesos* ⊠ *Calle Patricio Lynch 530* ☎ *58/225-0000* ⊕ *www.aruma.cl* ⤳ *16 rooms* ⍥ *Breakfast.*

NIGHTLIFE

You can join the locals for a beer at one of the cafés lining the pedestrian mall of 21 de Mayo. These low-key establishments, many with outdoor seating, are great places to spend afternoons watching the passing crowds. An oddity in Arica is the attire of the servers in various tranquil cafés and tea salons (usually called "café con piernas" or "cafés with legs"): women serve coffee and tea dressed in lingerie.

Discoteca SoHo. Discoteca SoHo, near Playa Chinchorro, livens things up on weekends with the sounds of pop and cumbia. ⊠ *Buenos Aires 209* ⊕ *www.discosoho.com.*

SHOPPING

Calle 21 de Mayo. Calle 21 de Mayo is a good place for window-shopping. ⊠ *21 de Mayo.*

Calle Bolognesi. Calle Bolognesi is crowded with artisan stalls that sell handmade goods. ⊠ *Bolognesi.*

Calle Chacabuco. The length of Calle Chacabuco is closed to traffic on Sunday for a market featuring everything from soccer jerseys to bootleg CDs. ⊠ *Chacabuco.*

Feria Internacional. The Feria Internacional on Calle Máximo Lira sells everything from bowler hats (worn by Aymara women) to blankets to batteries. The Terminal Pesquero next door offers an interesting view of fishing, El Norte Grande's predominant industry. ⊠ *Maximo Lira.*

Poblado Artesenal. Located outside the city in the Azapa Valley, the Poblado Artesenal is an artisan cooperative designed to resemble an altiplano community. This is a good place to pick up traditionally styled ceramics and leather. ✉ *Hualles.*

PARQUE NACIONAL LAUCA

47 km (29 miles) southeast of Putre.

The Parque Nacional Lauca offers dramatic landscapes and eye-catching wildlife. Stunning volcanic landscapes and colorful desert scrubland are dotted with llamas, flamingos, and all sorts of flora.

GETTING HERE AND AROUND

Follow the CH-11 International Highway out of Arica toward Bolivia. Just after the town of Putre, take the right-hand turning towards Palca. The park entrance lies 47 kilometers southeast of Putre.

TOURS

Raíces Andinas. As well as full-day trips, Raíces Andinas offers longer 2- and 14-day trips between Chile and Argentina. Most tours include lunch and guides. ✉ *Héroes del Morro 632, Arica* ☎ *58/223–3305* ⊕ *www.raicesandinas.com* ✍ *From 25,000 pesos.*

EXPLORING

Lago Chungará. This lake sits on the Bolivian border at an amazing altitude of 4,600 meters (15,100 feet) above sea level. Volcán Parinacota, at 6,330 meters (20,889 feet), casts its shadow onto the lake's glassy surface. Hundreds of flamingos make their home here. There is a CONAF-run office at Lago Chungará on the highway just before the lake. ✉ *From Ruta 11, turn north on Ruta A-123* ⊕ *www.conaf.cl* ✍ *Free* ☉ *CONAF office daily 8–8.*

Lagunas Cotacotani. About 8 km (5 miles) east of Parinacota are the beautiful Laguna Cotacotani, which means "land of many lakes" in the Quechua language. This string of ponds—surrounded by a desolate moonscape formed by volcanic eruptions—attracts many species of bird, including Andean geese.

Parinacota. Within Parque Nacional Lauca, off Ruta 11, is the altiplano village of Parincota, one of the most beautiful in all of Chile. In the center of the village sits the whitewashed **Iglesia Parinacota,** dating from 1789. Inside are murals depicting sinners and saints and a mysterious "walking table," which parishioners have chained to the wall for fear that it will steal away in the night. An interesting Aymara cultural commentary can be found in the Stations of the Cross, which depict Christ's tormenters not as Roman soldiers, but as Spanish conquistadors. Opposite the church you'll find crafts stalls run by Aymara women in the colorful shawls and bowler hats worn by many altiplano women. Only 18 people live in the village, but many more make a pilgrimage here for annual festivals such as the Fiesta de las Cruces, held on May 3, and the Fiesta de la Virgen de la Canderlaria, a three-day romp that begins on February 2.

Fodor'sChoice ★ **Parque Nacional Lauca.** On a plateau more than 4,000 meters (13,120 feet) above sea level, the magnificent Parque Nacional Lauca shelters flora and fauna found in few other places in the world. Cacti, grasses, and a brilliant emerald-green moss called *llareta* dot the landscape.

Playful *vizcacha*—rabbitlike rodents with long tails—laze in the sun, and llamas, graceful vicuñas, and alpacas make their home here as well. About 10 km (6 miles) into the park is a CONAF station with informative brochures. ⊠ *Off Ruta 11* ☎ *58/225–0570 in Arica* ⊕ *www. conaf.cl* ✉ *Free.*

RESERVA NACIONAL LAS VICUÑAS

121 km (75 miles) southeast of Putre.

This 100 km (62 mile) reserve is filled with vicuñas that graze in the high plains near the blue alpine lakes. There are also volcanoes in the distance and salt flats in the forefront.

GETTING HERE AND AROUND
From the town of Putre, follow the international highway to Bolivia for a few kilometers, then take the turn southeast on a unpaved road that leads to the Lauca National Park. The entrance to the Las Vicuñas National Reserve lies 121 kilometers past Putre.

EXPLORING

Fodor'sChoice ★ **Reserva Nacional Las Vicuñas.** Although it attracts far fewer visitors than neighboring Parque Nacional Lauca, Reserva Nacional Las Vicuñas contains some incredible sights—salt flats, high plains, and alpine lakes. And you can enjoy the vistas without running into buses full of tourists. The reserve, which stretches some 100 km (62 miles), has a huge herd of graceful vicuñas. Although quite similar to their larger cousins, llamas and alpacas, vicuñas have not been domesticated. Their incredibly soft wool, among the most prized in the world, led to so much hunting that these creatures were threatened with extinction. Today it is illegal to kill a vicuña. Getting to this reserve, unfortunately, is quite a challenge. There is no public transportation, and the roads are passable only in four-wheel-drive vehicles. Many people choose to take a tour out of Arica. ⊠ *From Ruta 11, take Ruta A-21 south to park headquarters* ☎ *58/225–0570 in Arica* ⊕ *www.conaf.cl.*

SALAR DE SURIRE

126 km (78 miles) southeast of Putre.

EXPLORING
Salar de Surire. After passing through the high plains, where you'll spot vicuña, alpaca, and the occasional desert fox, you'll catch your first glimpse of the sparkling Salar de Surire. Seen from a distance, the salt flat appears to be a giant white lake. Unlike its southern neighbor, the Salar de Atacama, it's completely flat. Three of the four New World flamingos (Andean, Chilean, and James') live in the nearby lakes. ⊠ *South from Reserva Nacional Las Vicuñas on Ruta A-235* ☎ *58/225–0570 in Arica* ⊕ *www.conaf.cl* ✉ *Free.*

THE CENTRAL VALLEY

WELCOME TO THE CENTRAL VALLEY

TOP REASONS TO GO

★ **Wine tasting:** The Central Valley is the heart of Chile's wine country. Vineyards for both table and wine grapes cover the landscape—in fact, the Pan-American Highway runs through some of the longest continuous vineyards in the world. There is ample opportunity to taste the delicious product, too, from full-bodied reds at BBQs to crisp whites by the pool.

★ **Rowdy rodeos:** The Central Valley is also home to the *huaso*, a cousin of the Argentine *gaucho*. *Huasos*, in their typical flat-topped, wide-brimmed hats, are a common sight around Rancagua, where they flock to the national *Medialuna* (rodeo arena) for their favorite sport.

★ **Scenic countryside:** The Central Valley is not limited to vineyards. Rivers and lakes lie between hillsides dotted with cactus and fruit trees. Venture east into the Andes countryside and the dirt roads weaving the high mountaintops pass pretty waterfalls and swimming holes, perfect for exploring on foot, bike, or horseback.

1 Maipo Valley. Take a breather from the fast pace of the capital and ease into the calm and charm of rural life. Only a short drive south of Santiago, these Andes highlands and their many vineyards make a great day trip. Use Maipo as the starting point for a longer multi-valley side trip.

2 Rapel Valley. Chile's agricultural heartland is the rodeo country home of the *huaso*, known for their wide-brimmed hat and jaunty smile. There's some mighty fine wine, too. The valley is divided into two wine appellations, Cachapoal and Rancagua to the north and Santa Cruz and Colchagua to the south.

3 Curicó Valley. Dormant volcanoes make a gorgeous backdrop for the valley's extensive vineyards, and Curicó city's charming plaza fills with excitement and grape stomping each April for one of the country's most traditional wine fests. If wine's not your thing, try the upscale resorts on Vichuquén Lake near the coast or camping at Radal Siete Tazas National Park.

4 Maule Valley. Scratch any surface and find plenty of rural tradition and natural beauty. The O'Higginiano Museum and the Villa Huilquilemu in Talca beautifully portray the area's cultural heritage, and Chile's only local train still makes daily runs to the coast. Vineyards old and new pepper the stunning countryside.

PACIFIC OCEAN

Constitución
Chanco
Cobquecura
Quirihue
Coelemu
Tomé
Talcahuano
Concepción
Isla Santa María
San Pedro
Lota
Arauco
La Laja
Curanilahué
Lebú
Nacimiento
Parque Nacional Nahuelbuta
Angol
Cañete
Contulmo
Collipulli
Puren

GETTING ORIENTED

Geographically speaking, the Central Valley isn't really a valley at all, but rather an "Intermediate Depression" between two mountain ranges—the Andes to the east, and Coastal Range to the west. The two separate just north of Santiago, leaving a fertile flatland between them that runs south to the Bío Bío, where the Coastal Mountains gradually descend into the Pacific Ocean. The large Central Valley is divided into the four subregions: the Maipo Valley (Santiago sits in its center), the Rapel Valley (divided into Cachapoal and Colchagua), the Curicó Valley (around the city of Curicó), and the Maule Valley (south from Talca).

6

Updated
by Amanda
Barnes

The Central Valley is the most abundant valley in Chile, not just for fruit and grape production, but also for the wealth of adventure: hiking the Andes, steaming in thermal pools, scaling rocks, or heli-skiing down snowy slopes. At the coast, you can tan on the lovely beaches, surf world-class waves, and nosh on outstanding seafood. In between, indulge in some of the finest wines South America has to offer while enjoying the laidback charm of rural life.

The Central Valley is Chile's agricultural heartland. The rich soil benefits from ample spring melt-water for irrigation and long, warm, and dry summers. Grapes especially thrive, and wine has been an important product in much of the Central Valley for the past four centuries.

The Central Valley is a straight shot down the Pan-American Highway between the volcanic cones of the Andes on the west and the lower Coastal Mountains to the east. As you head south, the relatively dry foliage of the short, scrubby indigenous bushes gives way to verdant pastures and thick pine and eucalyptus forests.

It's about a five-hour drive straight south from Santiago to Chillán and nearly another hour east to Concepción, but plan to stop and explore along the way. Most valleys have Wine Route (Ruta del Vino) associations, which are happy to help visitors plan tours of the wineries, as are most hotels.

PLANNING

WHEN TO GO

Timing your visit to the Central Valley really depends on what you want to do there. January and February are peak summer vacation months in Chile, so parks are open and beaches full. The weather is clear and sunny—cool on the mountains and coast, and quite hot in between, making this the best time for many outdoor activities. If winter sports are on the bucket list, it's best to come from June to August, although the snow may last into September.

If wineries draw you to the Central Valley, however, consider that grapes are picked from late February through early May, depending on the varietal and area. This is certainly the best time to visit area vineyards, since you can see everything from crushing to bottling. Visit on a weekend, and there's a good chance of joining one of the many harvest festivals that take place throughout the region at this time of year. But don't overlook a visit another time of year, as wineries offer tastings and fun activities year-round.

FESTIVALS

The harvest season, or *crush* as it is often called, is the most important time of the year in wine country. Most of Chile's wine-producing regions mark the moment with a *Fiesta de la Vendimia*, or harvest festival, which take place in March and April. The biggest and most spectacular events are held in Colchagua and Curicó, including grape-stomping competitions and harvest-queen contests. Maule, another notable festival, kicks off the year with its Carmenère Festival in January, in honor of the very Chilean red wine grape.

Not every fiesta is wine related, of course. Catholic roots run deep here, and many traditional religious festivals remain, such as those in honor of San Pedro and San Pablo, the patron saints of fishermen (on June 29 in fishing villages all along the coast). San Sebastian, the much persecuted, arrow-pierced saint, draws thousands of devotees to Yumbel (108 km [68 miles] from Concepción) on January 20. And during the fiesta de San Francisco, held October 4 in the small colonial-era village of Huerta de Maule, 38 km (24 miles) southwest of Talca, more than 200 huasos gather from all over Chile for a day of horseback events, including races around the central square.

GETTING HERE AND AROUND

BUS TRAVEL

The two big bus companies in the region, Pullman Bus and Tur-Bus, offer regular departures that leave precisely on time from Santiago's Alameda Terminal bound for Rancagua, Talca, Curicó, Chillán, and Concepción. One-way fare from Santiago to Chillán runs about 8,000 pesos.

CAR TRAVEL

Traveling by car is often the most convenient way to see the region. The Central Valley is sliced in half by Chile's major highway, the Pan-American Highway, also called Ruta 5, which passes through all of the major towns in the region. Be sure to have cash on hand for the frequent tolls, which are rather high and increase on weekends and holidays. Keep your receipt; some smaller exits have toll booths, and you can avoid the fare by showing your paid ticket.

TRAIN TRAVEL

The train remains an excellent way to travel through the Central Valley. Express trains from Estación Central in Santiago to the cities of Rancagua, Curicó, Talca, Chillán, and Concepción are comfortable and faster than taking the bus or driving.

RESTAURANTS

No matter where or when you eat in the Central Valley, a good bottle of local wine is likely to be on the table, so a handful of wine-related words doubtless come in handy. *Vino* is the Spanish word for wine; red is *tinto* (never *rojo*) and white is *blanco*. Drink them by the *copa*, or wine glass, or take part in more formal wine tasting called *desgustación* and *cata*.

Central Valley cuisine consists of hearty fare based on locally raised beef and pork, served with local vegetables and followed by fruit-based desserts. These are always accompanied by regional—usually red—wine. Most Chileans eat a big lunch around 1 pm and have a light dinner late in the evening. If you want to try real, home-style Chilean cooking, your best bet is to follow suit and look for lunch at the same time. Afterward you may need to adopt the local siesta habit as well.

In the summer look for popular favorites such as *porotos granados* (fresh cranberry beans with corn, squash, and basil), *humitas* (Chilean tamales) with fresh-sliced tomatoes, or *pastel de choclo* (a savory ground-beef base served in a clay bowl, sometimes with a piece of chicken, and always generously slathered with a rich grated corn topping). Desserts are often simply fresh fruits served in their own juice. Do watch for the refreshing *mote con huesillo* served cold as a drink or dessert. Begin by eating the *mote,* a type of wheat hominy; then slurp up the juice from the *huesillo,* a large dried peach, which serves as the final act of this three-course treat.

HOTELS
Accommodation ranges from simple B&Bs, beautiful old estancias, rustic-chic mountain lodges, and basic hotels in between. While in wine country, you might want to opt for lodgings at the wineries themselves, whether in resorts, guesthouses, or boutique hotels. *Hotel reviews have been shortened. For full information, visit Fodors.com.*

WHAT IT COSTS IN CHILEAN PESOS (IN THOUSANDS)				
	$	$$	$$$	$$$$
Restaurants	Under 6	6–9	10–13	over 13
Hotels	Under 51	51–85	86–115	over 115

Restaurant prices are the average cost of a main course at dinner or, if dinner is not served, at lunch. Hotel prices are the lowest cost of a standard double room in high season, excluding tax.

TOURS
With most wineries in the Central Valley, you can make your own direct booking and the relatively easy-to-navigate road network makes renting a car a good option to get around yourself. However, Chile has a zero tolerance law for drunk driving, so booking a taxi for the day is often preferable, and safer. Alternatively, each of the agencies below organizes private and group tours to the different wine regions.

Ruta Valle de Luz. This alternative wine tourism company organizes visits to garage wineries and organic producers. The day often starts with a tasting in its excellent boutique garage wine store on the main road to Santa Cruz. An artisan route to see the local craftsmen can also be incorporated into the tour. Hearty lunches exploring local cuisine are an added highlight. If you want to get away from the big producers, this is the tour agency for you. ⊠ *La Vino Garage, Carretera del vino, Km 30(between Nancagua and Santa Cruz), Santa Cruz* ☎ *09/9234-3434* ⊕ *www.turismorutavalledeluz.com* ✉ *From 45,000 pesos* ☼ *Daily 11–7.*

Santiago Adventures. This tourism outfitter organizes wine tours from Santiago to the different wine routes either in full- or multiday trips. Visits usually come with premium wine pours, your own bilingual guide,

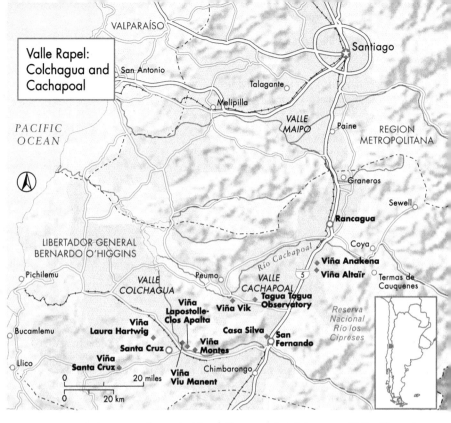

Valle Rapel:
Colchagua and
Cachapoal

private transfer, and pick-up from your hotel doorstep. ⊠ *Dr. Manuel Barros Borgoño 198, Piso 2, Providencia, Santiago* ☎ *2/244-2750* ⊕ *www.santiagoadventures.com* ✉ *From 193,000 pesos* ⊙ *Weekdays 9–6.*

VALLE RAPEL: COLCHAGUA AND CACHAPOAL

RANCAGUA

87 km (54 miles) south of Santiago along Pan-American Hwy.

In 1814, the hills around Rancagua were the site of a battle in the War of Independence known as the *Desastre de Rancagua* (Disaster of Rancagua). Chilean independence fighters, including Bernardo O'Higgins, held off the powerful Spanish army for two days before surrendering, but escaping to fight another day. In the resulting blaze, much of the town was destroyed.

Despite its historical significance and current importance as a regional commercial center, the city has relatively little to offer in terms of tourism. By all means, visit the historic area around the central plaza or take in a rodeo in the national *Medialuna,* or rodeo arena, but otherwise skip the city and head straight for one of the more interesting attractions outside of town such as a copper mine, hot spring, nature reserve, or winery.

GETTING HERE AND AROUND

Rancagua is a one-hour hop due south from Santiago by car or bus. It's a bit faster by train and much too close to justify flying. Wheeled transport takes the Pan-American Highway, while rail options go beside it. Traffic heading out of Santiago is often sluggish, and delays due to roadwork are frequent, but the highway is generally in good condition and allows for speeds of 120 kph (75 mph) for most of the route.

ESSENTIALS

Bus Contacts Rancagua Terminal al Sur ⊠ *Ocarrol 1175* ☎ *72/223–6938.* **Rancagua Terminal de Buses** ⊠ *Av. Libertador Bernardo O'Higgins 0484* ☎ *72/222–5425* ⊕ *www.terminalohiggins.cl.* **Tur Bus** ⊠ *O Higgins 0484* ☎ *600/660–6600* ⊕ *www.turbus.cl.*

Visitor and Tour Information Sernatur Rancagua ⊠ *German Riesco 350* ☎ *72/223–0413* ⊕ *www.sernatur.cl* ⏱ *Weekdays 8:30–6.*

EXPLORING

TOP ATTRACTIONS

Viña Altaïr. Inspired by the brightest star in the Aquila constellation, this French-Chilean joint venture was formed to produce one excellent wine: Altaïr. Today the winery offers a second celestial bottling called Sideral. Both are red blends from grapes grown in the foothills of the Andes. The winery runs three different types of tours, ranging from a straightforward winery tour and tasting to horseback riding through the vineyards and high into the hills. There's even a spectacular nocturnal version that includes a moonlight ride on horseback through the vineyards and a tasting under the stars. All tours include tastings of one or both house wines. ⊠ *Fundo Totihue, Camino Pimpinela s/n, Requinoa* ☎ *97/518–6554* ⊕ *www.altairwines.com* 🍷 *18,000–72,000 pesos* ⚲ *Reservations essential* ⏱ *Mon.–Sat. 10–3.*

Viña Anakena. Based in the Andean sector of the Cachapoal Valley known as "Alto Cachapoal," this winery has properties in a number of Chilean wine regions to ensure the finest results for each variety. Their labels include symbols inspired by the motifs found in Chile's various indigenous cultures. Visits include a tour of the vineyards, cellars, varietal garden, and scenic overlook, along with tastings of *reserva* or premium lines. You can also reserve ahead for lunch, horseriding, or wine- and food-pairing classes. ⊠ *Camino Pimpenela s/n, Requinoa* ☎ *02/2433–8600* ⊕ *www.anakenawines.cl* 🍷 *From 10,000 pesos* ⚲ *Reservations essential* ⏱ *Mon.–Sat. 10:30–4:30, Sun. 10:30–noon.*

WORTH NOTING

Casa del Pilar de la Esquina. Located across the street from the Museo Regional de Rancagua, Casa del Pilar de la Esquina once belonged to Fernando Errázuriz Aldunate, who helped draft the country's constitution. In addition to displays on the area's history and indigenous cultures, there are often modern-art exhibits on the first floor. ⊠ *Estado 682, at Ibieta* ☎ *72/222–1524* 🍷 *Free* ⏱ *Tues.–Fri. 10–6.30, Sat. 9–1.*

Iglesia de la Merced. A block north of the plaza along Calle Estado is this 18th-century church that was declared a national monument for its beauty and significance in the city's fateful history. It was in this bell tower that O'Higgins waited in vain for reinforcements during the Battle of Independence. The somber, neoclassical twin spires are a fitting memorial. Sadly parts of the church were damaged in the 2010 earthquake, although reconstruction work continues. ⊠ *Corner of Cuevas and Estado.*

Mina El Teniente and Sewell. High in the mountains north of Termas de Cauquenes, 60 km (37 miles) northeast of Rancagua, the El Teniente Mine is the world's largest subterranean copper mine, in operation since colonial times. In 1905 the city of Sewell, known as the "city of stairs," was constructed at 2,130 meters (6,988 feet) above sea level to house miners. Abandoned in the early 1970s, Sewell was declared a UNESCO World Heritage Site in 2006. Rancagua tour operator VTS offers guided tours of both the mine and the city every Saturday, Sunday, and public holiday, with transport from Santiago or Rancagua. ⊠ *Millán 1020* ☎ *72/295–2692 VTS* ⊕ *www.vts.cl* ⊠ *From 30,000 pesos.*

Museo Regional de Rancagua. This three-room museum re-creates a typical 18th-century home, complete with period furniture and religious artifacts. A small collection of 19th-century weaponry is the type that would have been used in the momentous Battle of Rancagua. Dioramas illustrate this dramatic moment in the country's quest for independence. The whitewashed colonial building is a few blocks south of Plaza de los Héroes. ⊠ *Estado 685, at Ibieta* ☎ *72/221–524* ⊕ *www.museorancagua.cl* ⊠ *1000 pesos, includes Casa de Pilar de Esquina* ⊙ *Tues.–Sat. 10–6.*

Plaza de los Héroes. Today's Rancagüinos enjoy relaxing in the city's central square, the Plaza de los Héroes. A statue of the valiant war hero and future first president Bernardo O'Higgins on horseback stands proudly in the center of the plaza. Although each side of the statue base contains one of his famous sayings, curiously enough, there is nothing to indicate who the statue is to visitors and newcomers. ⊠ *Plaza de los Heroes.*

Reserva Nacional Río los Cipreses. Numerous trails lead through thick forests of cypress trees at this 92,000-acre national reserve 50 km (31 miles) east of Rancagua. Occasionally, some come to clearings where you are treated to spectacular views of the mountains above. CONAF, the national parks service, has an office here with informative displays and maps. Hiking, swimming, and horseback riding are all available, and you can camp overnight for 5,000 pesos per group. Just south of the park is the spot where a plane carrying Uruguayan university students crashed in 1972. The story of the group, part of whom survived three months in a harsh winter by resorting to cannibalism, was told in the book and film *Alive.* ⊠ *Carretera del Cobre s/n* ☎ *72/297–505* ⊕ *www.conaf.cl* ⊠ *2,200 pesos* ⊙ *Daily 8:30–5:30.*

WHERE TO EAT AND STAY

$$ ✕ **Juan y Medio.** On the north-bound side of the Pan-American Highway,
CHILEAN between the towns of Requinoa and Rosario, this well-loved Chilean
FAMILY diner caters to hearty appetites. It began as a humble truck stop in 1946

and established a tremendous reputation for its trucker-size portions of Chilean favorites—whopping steaks and ribs grilled over a wood fire, slow-cooked *cazuelas,* and stews that leave you wanting nothing more than a hammock and a long nap. The original eatery burned in 2006, and Chilean travelers mourned the loss until it reopened, much bigger and a bit splashier, a year later. It seats up to 500 people and fills fast on busy weekends. Stop in at noon or 6 to beat the local crowd, which tends to eat much later. One of the dining rooms overlooks a simple children's play area, which has a very large bird cage with many attractive species. [$] *Average main: 8000 pesos* ✉ *Ruta 5, Km 109, Rosario* ☎ *72/252–1726* 🌐 *www.juanymedio.cl.*

$$$$ **HOTEL** 🏨 **Puma Lodge.** This large mountain lodge is set right in the middle of the Andes and in winter (June–September) operates the most dedicated heli-ski service in South America. **Pros:** peaceful location; heli-ski access. **Cons:** remote location requires 4x4 in winter; expensive. [$] *Rooms from: 280000 pesos* ✉ *Reserva Nacional Rio Los Cipreses, Fundo Sierra Nevada, Km 22* ☎ *09/6308–2492* 🌐 *www.noihotels.com* 🛏 *24 rooms* 🍴 *Breakfast.*

SPORTS AND THE OUTDOORS

RODEO

National Rodeo Arena. One of the great highlights of life in Rancagua includes excursions to the National Rodeo Arena: the *Medialuna Monumental,* especially in late March, when it hosts the national championship. This is a great opportunity to glimpse *huaso* tradition in its full glory: horsemanship, riding and cow-herding skills, traditional foods, crafts, music, and dance. ✉ *Av. Germán Ibarra s/n, at Av. España* 🌐 *www.caballoyrodeo.cl.*

SAN FERNANDO AND NEARBY

152 km (94 miles) south of Santiago.

San Fernando is surrounded by popular wineries, handsome hotels, colonial estancias, and beautiful nature spots. The city is a convenient stopping point alongside Ruta 5. The gateway to Colchagua Valley, San Fernando city has an attractive plaza and all the necessary conveniences, although the main attractions lie in the surrounding rural areas, vineyards, and fruit plantations. Streets are colorfully lined with fruit stands selling eye-catching citrus fruits, melons, and ripe avocados. West of San Fernando is where the wine route to Santa Cruz begins, but there is much to discover toward the Andes, too.

GETTING HERE AND AROUND

San Fernando is almost two hours by car, over two hours by bus, and a bit faster by train. If you are moving further south by public transport, chances are you might have to stop off in San Fernando first to change buses at the terminal.

ESSENTIALS

Bus Contacts San Fernando Terminal de Buses ✉ *Manso de Velasco (corner of Rancagua)* ☎ *72/271–3912.*

EXPLORING

TOP ATTRACTIONS

Casa Silva. Casa Silva is one of the most convenient wineries to visit in the area, as it is just a five-minute detour from the main Ruta 5. The atmospheric wine cellar is one of the oldest in Colchagua and the colonial architecture has been tastefully refurbished throughout the winery and production rooms, where a tour shows the main facilities as well as the family's collection of classic cars. Finish up with a tasting in the modern tasting room and wine shop, or cycle, drive, or walk through the vineyards to the excellent restaurant overlooking the polo fields. ✉ *Hijuela Norte(El Tambo exit from Ruta 5)* ☎ *72/291–3117, 72/271–6519* 🌐 *www.casasilva.cl* 🕓 *Daily 10–5.*

Viña Vik. This holistic vineyard in the middle of its own private 11,000-acre valley doesn't do anything by half measures. With stylish design and sensitive sustainability measures, this is one of the most high-end wineries in the country. A visit includes a barrel tasting of different red varieties before a taste of the final blend. You can make a day of your visit with horseback riding in the stunning estate and lunch. ✉ *Millahue s/n, San Vincente de Tagua Tagua* ☎ *09/9534–9437* 🌐 *www.vinavik.com* 🎟 *Reservations required.*

6

WORTH NOTING

Tagua Tagua Observatory. On a clear night, the Colchagua Valley can be excellent for stargazing. Eccentric expat Ian Hutcheon runs an observatory just outside of Tagua Tagua, where family-friendly events begin with a welcome glass of wine (made with meteorites in the barrel), after which there is entertaining discussion, presentation, and observation through advanced telescopes. During the day, Hutcheon leads nature hikes in the area with a buried treasure surprise. ✉ *Observatorio Tagua Tagua, Tunca Arriba s/n, San Vicente de Tagua Tagua* ☎ *9/228–5005* 🌐 *www.centroastronomico.cl* 🎟 *5,000 pesos.*

WHERE TO EAT AND STAY

$$$ CHILEAN Fodor's Choice ★

🍴 **Casa Silva Restaurant.** Among the vineyards and polo fields of Casa Silva winery, this is one of the region's best restaurants. It serves a gourmet menu of irresistible delicacies including tuna ceviche, wagu beef on the BBQ, seafood salads, beef jerky empanadas, an eclectic mix of tapas dishes, and indulgent Chilean desserts. The wine list is all from the Casa Silva winery, of course, but it's an enormous portfolio of varieties and the prices carry attractive discounts. Whitewashed walls, large windows, and balconies overlooking the estate and colorful flower arrangements make this one of the most pleasant places to dine in the Colchagua Valley. [$] *Average main: 10000 pesos* ✉ *Hijuelas Norte* ☎ *9/6847–5786* 🌐 *www.casasilva.cl.*

$$ INTERNATIONAL

🍴 **Hydro.** On the road into San Fernando, this fusion restaurant-bar is a great spot for some creative cuisine. While you can order Chilean classics here, the chef's flair is for fusion dishes. More unusual concoctions, which are all named after genres of music, are recommended, as well as the interesting ceviches, delicious octopus tacos, and the best sushi in the region. Good cocktails, artisanal beers, and friendly service complete the experience. [$] *Average main: 6000 pesos* ✉ *Av. Bernardo O'Higgins Sur 0280* ☎ *72/271–6663* 🌐 *www.hydrorestobar.cl* 🕓 *Closed Sun.*

$$$$ HOTEL Fodor's Choice ★ **Hacienda Los Lingues.** This beautifully restored 17th-century hacienda is one of the oldest in Chile, and its sweeping 20,000-acre estate overflows with charm. **Pros:** history is handsomely restored; beautiful estate; Wi-Fi in bedrooms. **Cons:** service is a bit stuffy. [$] *Rooms from: 190000 pesos* ✉ *Ruta 5 S, Km 124.5 s/n* ☎ *22/431–0510* 🌐 *www.loslingues.com* 🛏 *14 rooms, 2 suites* 🍴 *Breakfast.*

$$$$ HOTEL Fodor's Choice ★ **Viña Vik Hotel.** This state-of-the-art art hotel on the grounds of the Viña Vik winery offers perhaps the most beautiful views of the Central Valley. **Pros:** beautiful private valley location; great outdoor activities; quirky art design. **Cons:** expensive; yoga studio next to playroom gets noisy. [$] *Rooms from: 800000 pesos* ✉ *Millahue s/n, San Vincente de Tagua Tagua* ☎ *09/9534–9437 cell phone* 🌐 *www.vinavik.com* 🛏 *17 suites, 5 master suites, 1 family cabin* 🍴 *Multiple meal plans.*

SANTA CRUZ

Fodor's Choice ★ *180 km (112 miles) southwest of Santiago; 104 km (65 miles) southwest of Rancagua via the Pan-American Highway to San Fernando, then southwest on I–50.*

This once sleepy village has become the height of rural chic in recent years, due, in large part, to the booming Colchagua Valley wine industry, which produces many of Chile's award-winning red wines. It has an attractive central plaza surrounded by a mix of modern and traditional architecture, including the town hall, the Colchagua Museum, the Wine Route office, and the grand Hotel Santa Cruz Plaza. The Church still stands on the Plaza although little of the 19th-century building survived the 2010 earthquake; it has been completely refurbished and rebuilt since.

Santa Cruz is the perfect home base for visiting the Colchagua wineries that extend out to the east and west, mostly along Route I–50.

GETTING HERE AND AROUND

Getting to Santa Cruz is easiest by car. After reaching San Fernando on Ruta 5 you need to pass the first exit north of the city and continue another 2 km (1 mile) to the exit marked "Santa Cruz, Carretera del Vino, Pichilemu." This is I–50, the "Wine Highway," which takes you west through wine country along the coast to Pichilemu, surf capital of Chile. It is very easy to visit most of the valley's wineries by car; in fact, you see a number of them along the way on this aptly named route.

If using public transportation, take a bus or train to San Fernando and then the local bus or *colectivo* (a shared taxi with a fixed route) to Santa Cruz.

ESSENTIALS

Bus Contacts **Santa Cruz Terminal** ✉ *Rafael Casanova 480, Santa Cruz* ☎ *72/282–2191.*

EXPLORING

TOP ATTRACTIONS

Museo de Colchagua. One of the best museums in Chile if not Latin America, this attractive museum, built in colonial style at the end of the 20th century, focuses on the history of the region back to prehistory It's

HISTORY OF CHILEAN WINE

Fans of Chilean wines owe a debt to missionaries who arrived here in the 16th century. Spanish priests, who needed wine to celebrate the Catholic Mass, planted the country's first vineyards from Copiapó in the north to Concepción in the south. Of course, not all the wine was intended for religious purposes, and vines were quickly sent north and planted in the Maipo Valley around Santiago to fill the "spiritual void" experienced by the early Spanish settlers—many of whom were soldiers and sailors.

With the rise of cross-Atlantic travel and trade that began in the 19th century, some Chileans made fortunes in the mining industry. They returned from Europe with newfound appreciation for French food, dress, architecture, and lifestyles. Many began building their own Chilean-style chateaux, particularly on the outskirts of Santiago. French varietals such as Cabernet Sauvignon, Malbec, and Carmenère thrived in

the Central Valley's rich soils and the near-perfect climate, and thus Chile's second "wine boom" was launched.

Chilean wineries did not keep pace with the rest of the world and stagnated throughout much of the 20th century. However, the introduction of modern equipment such as stainless steel tanks in the late 1980s caught the country some global attention. Fresh national and international investment in the industry made Chilean wine a tasty and affordable option. Continued advances in growing techniques and wine-making methods throughout the 1990s and into the early 21st century have resulted in the production of exceedingly excellent wines of premium and ultrapremium quality, with increasingly hefty price tags. Wine exports increase annually, and since 2010 Chile has been one of the top five wine exporters worldwide, shipping their wine to more than 90 countries around the globe.

6

the largest private natural-history collection in the country, and second only in size to Santiago's Museo Nacional de Historia Natural. Exhibits include pre-Columbian mummies; extinct insects set in amber viewed through special lenses; the world's largest collection of silver work by the indigenous Mapuche; and the only known original copy of Chile's proclamation of independence. A few early vehicles and wine-making implements surround the building. The museum is the creation of Santa Cruz native and international businessman Carlos Cardoen. Expect to spend around four hours here. ⊠ *Av. Errázuriz 145, Santa Cruz* ☎ *72/282–1050* ⊕ *www.museocolchagua.cl* 🎟 *7,000 pesos* 🕐 *Mar.–Sept., daily 10–6; Oct.–Feb., daily 10–7.*

Museo San José del Carmen de El Huique. Here you can look into the lifestyle of Chile's 19th-century rich and famous. Construction began on the current house in 1829 and was completed with the inauguration of the chapel in 1852. The Errázuriz family, who can trace the 2,600-acre estate back through family lines to 1756, donated it to the Chilean Army in 1975. It was reopened as a museum in the 1990s and is now the only remaining preserved, intact estate of its kind in Chile open to the public. Inside, sumptuous suites are filled with opal glass, lead crystal, bone china, antique furniture, and family portraits evoking Chile's aristocratic past. Servants' quarters are also part of the tour, as are the kitchens and 16 working patios, each dedicated to a specific household chore, such as laundry, butchering, or cheese making. Guides are knowledgeable and have tales to tell, as many grew up hearing family stories about working at the estate. The tour ends with a visit to the chapel, which has Venetian blown-glass balustrades around the altar and the choir loft. Visits are by prior reservation only, and English-speaking guides are available with sufficient notice. ⊠ *26 km (16 miles) north of Santa Cruz to Palmilla, turn left to Estación Colchagua, then turn right and follow signs to museum, Santa Cruz* ☎ *09/733–1105 cell phone* ⊕ *www.museoelhuique.cl* ⊡ *2,000 pesos* ⊙ *Tues.–Sun. 10–11:30 and 2:30–4:30.*

Ruta del Vino de Colchagua. The Colchagua Valley wineries had the good sense to band together back in the 1990s, when Chile's latest wine boom was just starting. Founding the Ruta del Vino de Colchagua has paid off handsomely, not only for marketing but organizing world-class wine tourism. The Wine Route's office, next to the Santa Cruz Plaza Hotel on the main square, provides basic information about its 13 member wineries and arranges guided tours in English to most. Though most wineries have their own guides, few of them speak English, and some only accept visits arranged by Ruta del Vino. The office arranges tours to two or three vineyards, with or without lunch, starting from 49,000 pesos per person and up, depending on the complexity of the tour. The harvest season—March and April—kicks off with the *Fiesta de la Vendimia* (Grape Harvest Festival) and is always a great time to visit. ⊠ *Plaza de Armas 298, Santa Cruz* ☎ *72/282–3199* ⊕ *www.colchaguavalley.cl* ⊙ *Weekdays 9–8, weekends 10–8.*

Viña Lapostolle-Clos Apalta. Lapostolle's showcase winery is one of the most attractive pieces of architecture in Chile: the barrel-stave-shape beams rising impressively above the vineyards create a wooden nest for the winery which is built into a hillside to facilitate the gravity-flow process. The prized grapes are picked from the biodynamic vineyards and taken to the top floor, where they are separated by hand, dropped into tanks on the floor below, then racked to barrels on the floor below, and so on until the grapes are six floors down into the hillside, where they are finally trucked out and shipped around the world. Join one of the three daily tours with tastings, or stay for a fabulous lunch at the Lapostolle Residence with a fresh and organic menu picked straight from their own garden. ⊠ *Apalta, Km 4, Santa Cruz* ☎ *72/295–3350* ⊕ *www.closapalta.com* ⊡ *From 20,000 pesos* ⤷ *Reservations essential* ⊙ *Tours at 10, 12:30, and 4 (and 5:30 in summer).*

Viña Laura Hartwig. Viña Laura Hartwig is a small winery on lands where grapes have been grown for more than a century. The likeness of Laura Hartwig, the elegant owner of the estate, is beautifully drawn on the winery's labels by the famous Chilean artist Claudio Bravo. After a tour of the facilities, sample the Carmenère, a type of grape grown only in Chile. It has more character than Merlot but is not as full-bodied as Cabernet Sauvignon. Also worth trying is the Malbec, which has a lasting finish, a sensation compared by a winery guide to "kissing

Sean Connery." ⊠ *Camino Barreales s/n, Santa Cruz* ☎ *72/282–3179* ⊕ *www.laurahartwig.cl* ☉ *Daily 9–6 winter, 9:30–7:30 summer.*

Fodor's Choice
★

Viña Montes. Founded in 1987 in the Curicó Valley as Discover Wine, this highly successful premium wine producer has since moved its center of operations to the renowned Apalta sector of Colchagua and changed its name to Montes, after its star winemaker and owner. Known for its deep, rich, concentrated, oaky red wines and crisp whites (most also oaked), every bottle has a stylized angel on the label. The new gravity-flow winery—launched in 2004—was designed according to feng shui principles. If you are feeling light-headed after the tasting, their restaurant Bistro Alfredo serves typical Chilean cuisine overlooking water features and the hillside. There is also a more active wine tour, which involves a mountain hike followed by a picnic and wine tasting at the summit. ⊠ *Parcela 15, Millahue de Apalta, Santa Cruz* ☎ *72/281–7815* ⊕ *www.monteswines.com* 🗋 *12,000 pesos* ⚲ *Reservations essential* ☉ *Tours at 10:30, noon, 3, and 5.*

Viña Santa Cruz. Chilean businessman Carlos Cardoen not only owns the Santa Cruz Plaza Hotel but the winery of the same name as well. This relatively new project is dedicated to producing premium red wines in the Lolol sector of the Colchagua Valley. If you've seen the hotel, you already know that Cardoen does not do things halfway, and the winery confirms that observation. In addition to the usual vineyards, stainless-steel tanks, and oak barrels, a cable car gives visitors get a bird's-eye view of the valley. On top of the hill is a replica "indigenous village," which represents three separate Chilean native cultures: Aymará, Mapuche, and Rapa Nui. There is also an astronomical center, gastronomical center, and a wine and gift shop. ⊠ *Carretera I–72, Km 25, Lolol* ☎ *72/637–5330* ⊕ *www.vinasantacruz.cl* 🗋 *From 9,500 pesos* ⚲ *Reservations essential.*

Viña Viu Manent. Each visit to this traditional family winery starts with a horse-drawn carriage ride through the vineyards. Afterward, you work your way to the beautiful colonial-style house, which is used for events and wine tasting. Focusing mainly on red wines from the Colchagua Valley, Viu also includes a couple of coastal wines from Casablanca and even a Malbec from Argentina. Pick wines to taste after the tour or over lunch at their excellent Rayuela restaurant, which keeps live oysters in freezing cold Jacuzzis out back. ⊠ *Carretera del Vino, Km 37, Santa Cruz* ☎ *72/285–8350 general, 2/2840–3181 tours and wine shop* ⊕ *www.viumanent.cl* 🗋 *From 10,000 pesos* ☉ *Tours: 10:30, noon, 3, and 4:30 all year (and 11 and 1 Sept.–Mar.).*

WORTH NOTING

Iglesia Parroquial. Facing the central square is this imposing, fortress-like, white stucco structure. Originally built in 1817, the church has been refurbished and renovated many times since, after damaging earthquakes. ⊠ *Plaza de Armas 28, Santa Cruz* ⊕ *www.parroquialasantacruz.cl.*

Plaza de Armas. In the center of the palm-lined Plaza de Armas is a colonial-style bell tower with a carillon that chimes every 15 minutes. Inside the tower is a tourism kiosk with information leaflets. ⊠ *Plaza de Armas, Santa Cruz.*

WHERE TO EAT

$ CHILEAN 🍴 **Club Social de Santa Cruz.** This simple restaurant overlooking the town's main square is known for its meat dishes. The house specialties are *conejo guisada con finas hierbas* (rabbit stewed with herbs) and *codorniz con salsa cazador* (quail in a bacon-mushroom sauce), but there are also plenty of typical beef, chicken, and fish dishes as well. In summer, the courtyard fills with locals lunching under the shady pergola. [$] *Average main: 4000 pesos* ✉ *Plaza de Armas 178, Santa Cruz* ☎ *72/282–2529.*

$$ CHILEAN 🍴 **Los Varietales.** The restaurant at the Hotel Santa Cruz Plaza is by far the best in town. The menu features typical Chilean dishes prepared with flair and paired well with the extensive list of Colchagua Valley wines available by glass or bottle. In warmer months, the trellised terrace in back is a great spot for lunch. [$] *Average main: 9500 pesos* ✉ *Plaza de Armas 286, Santa Cruz* ☎ *72/220–9600* 🌐 *www.hotelsantacruzplaza.cl.*

$$ CHILEAN 🍴 **Pan Pan Vino Vino.** On the wine road, this old bakery has been converted into a beautiful restaurant turning local products into sophisticated fare, such as curried duck, eggplant casserole with polenta, and steak drizzled in red wine reduction. Traditional displays and rustic-chic design nod to the old bakery that once supplied the daily bread for the Cunaco Hacienda. A charming delicatessen on the same site sells locals products like cheeses, jams, and wine. You can even find vintages from the '80s and '90s, although quality is not assured. [$] *Average main: 8000 pesos* ✉ *Camino San Fernando a Santa Cruz, Km 31 s/n, Cunaco, Cunaco* ☎ *72/285–8059* 🌐 *www.panpanvinovino.cl* 🕒 *No dinner Sun.–Thurs.*

$$ MODERN ITALIAN 🍴 **Vino Bello.** For a taste of Italy in the wine region, head to Vino Bello, where an impressive range of pizzas, pastas, salads, antipasti, grilled meat, and fish dishes beg to be sampled with one of the many local wines on offer. Don't miss out on the cocktail offerings either, in particular the chili-laced version of a pisco sour. Smooth music, attractive surroundings, and some nice twists on the classics make Vino Bello a taste of *la dolce vita* in Colchagua. [$] *Average main: 7500 pesos* ✉ *Barreales (s/n), Santa Cruz* ☎ *72/282–2755* 🌐 *www.vino-bello.com.*

WHERE TO STAY

$$$$ HOTEL 🏨 **Hotel Santa Cruz Plaza.** This beautiful, colonial-style hotel on the Plaza de Armas may look historic, but it was actually built in 2000 with all the comforts you expect from a modern hotel in a historic style. **Pros:** great location; handsome decor; quirky museum displays. **Cons:** rooms can be small; some street noise in back rooms; labyrinthine layout makes some rooms hard to find. [$] *Rooms from: 214200 pesos* ✉ *Plaza de Armas 286, Santa Cruz* ☎ *72/220–9600, 2/2470–7474 in Santiago* 🌐 *www.hotelsantacruzplaza.cl* 🛏 *107 rooms, 9 suites* 🍽 *Breakfast.*

$$ HOTEL 🏨 **Hotel TerraViña.** This pretty Spanish-style boutique hotel is only minutes outside of Santa Cruz, yet peacefully surrounded by its own vineyards and gardens. **Pros:** buffet breakfast; late check-out; convenient location. **Cons:** small bathrooms; noise travels between rooms. [$] *Rooms from: 89000 pesos* ✉ *Camino Los Boldos (s/n), Barreales,*

Santa Cruz ☎ *72/282–1284* ⊕ *www.terravina.cl* ⇆ *18 rooms, 1 suite* ⦿ *Breakfast.*

$$ | ⊡ **Hotel Vino Bello.** This countryside B&B is in a charming family house
B&B/INN with six en suite bedrooms comfortably decorated in a homey style with handpainted wash basins. **Pros:** convenient location; homey atmosphere. **Cons:** a bit worn in places; some road noise in bedrooms. **$** *Rooms from: 71400 pesos* ⊠ *Camino Los Boldos (s/n), Santa Cruz* ☎ *72/282–5788* ⊕ *www.vino-bello.com* ⇆ *6 rooms* ⦿ *Breakfast.*

$$$$ | ⊡ **Lapostolle Residence.** Overlooking the stunning Apalta Valley and
RESORT Lapostolle winery, the Lapostolle Residence is one of the most upscale
ALL-INCLUSIVE wine residences in South America. **Pros:** excellent chef; beautiful valley;
Fodor's Choice fantastic service. **Cons:** expensive; limited activities. **$** *Rooms from:*
★ *750000 pesos* ⊠ *Camino Apalta, Km 4, Santa Cruz* ☎ *72/295–3360* ⊕ *www.lapostolle.com* ⇆ *4 suites* ⦿ *All-inclusive.*

$$ | ⊡ **Posada Colchagua.** This cheerful family posada in the rural Isla de
B&B/INN Yaquil area offers both good value and a peaceful stay in the Col-
FAMILY chagua Valley. **Pros:** good value; kind hospitality; experience of rural Chile. **Cons:** car required. **$** *Rooms from: 60000 pesos* ⊠ *Isla de Yaquil, Santa Cruz* ☎ *72/2293–3606* ⊕ *www.posadacolchagua.cl* ⇆ *10 rooms* ⦿ *Breakfast.*

SPORTS AND THE OUTDOORS
HORSEBACK RIDING
Cabalgatas Santa Cruz. Expat Ian Garrett organizes three-hour horseback rides at his 1,500-acre family farm near Santa Cruz. The 40 horses bear riders up the foothills to a vantage point over the valley, where a picnic spread of cheese and wine from the family vineyard awaits. ⊠ *Rafael Casanova 445, Santa Cruz* ☎ *9/7667–2595 cell, 72/282–3630 home* ⊕ *www.cabalgatassantacruz.com* ⧆ *From 30,000 pesos (hotel or Santa Cruz transfer included).*

SHOPPING
Alpaca Artesania Chilena. If you want authentic Chilean leather goods, alpaca wool, huaso hats, and colorful artisan products, this small shop on the main square carries them all—and more. ⊠ *Plaza de Armas 276, Santa Cruz* ☎ *9/8348–8983.*

La Lajuela. For a souvenir you can't find elsewhere, head to La Lajuela, a hamlet 8 km (5 miles) southeast of Santa Cruz. Residents here weave *chupallas,* straw hats made from a fiber called *teatina* that is cut, dyed, dried, and braided by hand. ⊠ *La Laguela, Santa Cruz.*

VALLE CURICÓ

CURICÓ

113 km (71 miles) south of Rancagua along Pan-American Hwy.

Curicó, which means "black water" in Mapudungún, the native Mapuche language, was founded in 1743. Today this agro-industrial center is the provincial capital and the gateway to the Curicó wine valley. The Plaza de Armas is one of the most attractive in the Central Valley; it is a center of activity year-round but fills to capacity for the Fiesta de la Vendimia (Wine Harvest Festival) each March. Most of the wineries are south of the city and easily reached from the Pan-American Highway. Other points of interest are found toward the Andes or on the coast.

GETTING HERE AND AROUND

Return to the Pan-American Highway and head south for just a short 50 km (31 miles) to Curicó. You can also take an inter-urban bus to Curicó, or head back to San Fernando and hop the train for the very quick trip south. Once you're in Curicó, you can get around by local bus, taxi, or *colectivo*. If visiting wineries, be sure to contact the Ruta del Vino de Curicó, which can help make arrangements for visits and transport to other sights, such as Radal Siete Tazas or Vichuquén.

ESSENTIALS

Bus Contacts **Curicó Terminal** ⊠ *Arturo Prat 780* ☎ *75/255–8119.* **Pullman del Sur** ⊠ *Camilo Henríquez 253* ☎ *75/231–0387* ⊕ *www.pdelsur.cl.*

Visitor Information **Curicó Tourism Office** ⊠ *Manso de Velasco 449* ☎ *75/254–3026* ⊕ *www.curico.cl.*

EXPLORING

TOP ATTRACTIONS

Viña Miguel Torres. Just south of Curicó and immediately off the Pan-American Highway is one of Chile's most visitor-savvy vineyards. The tour begins with an orientation video that provides a glossy overview of the winery—its roots in the family winery in Catalonia, Spain, and Miguel Torres's choice to set up shop in Chile while his sister opted for California. Torres was a leader in Chile's wine revolution and is credited as the first in the country to use a stainless-steel tank, now de rigueur. He also brought another tradition from his native Iberia: the annual Wine Harvest Festival that takes place in Curicó's main plaza. Be sure to visit the restaurant, definitely one of the finest in the area, and the overnight guest house welcomes the public. ⊠ *Ruta 5 S, Km 195* ☎ *75/256–4121* ⊕ *www.migueltorres.cl* ⊠ *5,000 pesos* ☉ *Daily 10–6.*

Viña San Pedro. The vineyard that surrounds Viña San Pedro in the Molina sector of the valley is one of the largest and oldest in Latin America. The first vines were planted here in 1701. The winery is also among the most modern, with 28 half-million-liter stainless-steel tanks producing more wine than any other competitor except Concha y Toro. San Pedro's top of the line is the premium Cabo de Hornos (which is Spanish for Cape Horn), followed by 1865 (the year the winery was founded), and Castillo de Molina. The bottling plant has a sleek glass dome and a second-floor viewing platform. There's also a great little wine shop just off the highway where you can pick up some bargains. Tours can be arranged through the Ruta del Vino office in Curicó. ⊠ *Ruta 5 S, Km 205, exit to Lontue* ☎ *75/249–1517* ⊕ *www.sanpedro.cl* ⊠ *9,000–40,000 pesos* ☉ *Mon.–Sat. 10–5.*

WORTH NOTING

Parque Nacional Radal Siete Tazas. This 10,000-acre national reserve, 70 km (43 miles) southeast of Curicó, is famous for the unusual "Seven Teacups," a series of pools created by waterfalls along the Río Claro

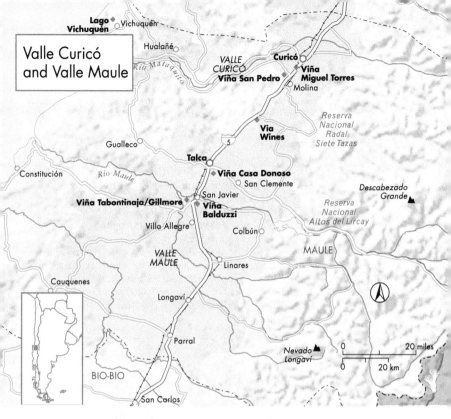

Valle Curicó and Valle Maule

(although sadly less water-abundant since the 2010 earthquake). The falls are a short hike from the park entrance, where you'll find a CONAF station. Farther along the trail are two other impressive cascades: the *Salto Velo de la Novia* (Bridal Veil Falls) and *Salto de la Leona* (Lioness Falls). Black woodpeckers, hawks, and eagles are common throughout the park, and condors nest in the highest areas. If you're lucky, you might glimpse the scarce *loro tricahue,* an endangered species that is Chile's largest and most colorful parrot. Camping is permitted in the park, which is snowed over in winter. October–March is the best time to visit. ⊠ *Camino Molina–Parque Inglés* ☎ *71/222–4461 CONAF* ⊕ *www.conaf.cl* ⊠ *4,000 pesos* ⊘ *Daily 8:30–6:30.*

Plaza de Armas. The lovely Plaza de Armas has a pretty fountain ringed by statues of dancing nymphs. Nearby is an elaborate bandstand constructed in New Orleans in 1904. ⊠ *Plaza de Armas.*

LAGO VICHUQUÉN

112 km (69 miles) west of Curicó.

An hour's drive from Curicó, this lake is a popular place for water sports such as sailing and water-skiing. The town itself, about 8 km (5 miles) away, is worth a visit for its museum but has little to offer in terms of dining or lodging. Black-necked swans are a common sight on meandering Lago Vichuquén and nearby Laguna Torca, which is a protected area.

EXPLORING

Museo Colonial de Vichuquén. Ceramics, stone tools, and other artifacts collected from pre-Hispanic peoples are on display. ⌧ *Av. Manuel Rodríguez s/n* 🖂 *1,500 pesos* ☉ *Daily 10–1, 3–5.*

WHERE TO STAY

$$ 🏨 **La Hostería.** This two-story structure, constructed entirely of native
HOTEL woods, affords unparalleled views of Lago Vichuquén, with many rooms overlooking the lake from private decks. **Pros:** beautiful location; spacious rooms. **Cons:** lack of attention to detail; no insect screens; thin walls means noise travels. $ *Rooms from: 65000 pesos* ⌧ *Sector Aquelarre, Lago Vichuquén* ☎ *9/6830–3000* ⊕ *www.lagovichuquen.cl* ⤶ *13 rooms* ▭ *No credit cards* ¶❍¶ *Breakfast.*

$$$ 🏨 **Marina Vichuquén.** The comfortable Marina Vichuquén has an envi-
HOTEL able location right on the shore and makes use of it with its own marina.
Fodor's Choice **Pros:** plenty to do here; well-kept; good restaurant. **Cons:** somewhat
★ remote location; no beach. $ *Rooms from: 95200 pesos* ⌧ *Sector Aquelarre, Lago Vichuquén* ☎ *75/240–0265* ⊕ *www.marinavichuquen.cl* ⤶ *18 rooms* ¶❍¶ *Breakfast.*

VALLE MAULE

Talca is the capital of Maule, Chile's largest wine valley. Dozens of wineries are scattered throughout the region, which begins north of Talca in San Rafael and extends south to the regional border at the Perquilauquén River, just south of Parral. Most are roughly grouped into two areas: east of the highway around San Clemente, or slightly west of the highway around San Javier and Villa Alegre. Long ignored as backward, Maule is now an up-and-coming region as insightful winemakers have discovered its value in producing excellent red wines with some of the oldest vines in the Americas.

TALCA

56 km (35 miles) south of Curicó on Ruta 5.

Straddling the banks of the Río Claro, Talca is not only Maule's most important industrial center; it is also one of the most appealing towns in the Central Valley. It was founded in 1692 and intelligently designed on a regimented grid pattern divided into quadrants—*poniente* means west, *oriente* east, *sur* south, and *norte* north—centered around the pretty Plaza de Armas. Be sure to take some time to check out its native and exotic trees.

GETTING HERE AND AROUND

No surprises here; once again it's back to the Ruta 5 (Pan-American Highway) for an easy ride to Talca, about 65 km (40 miles) south of Curicó.

ESSENTIALS

Bus Contacts Talca Terminal ⊠ *2 Sur 1920* ☎ *71/224–3270.*

Rental Car Contacts Rosselot ⊠ *Av. San Miguel 2710, Cruce Varoli* ☎ *71/224–7979* ⊕ *www.rosselot.cl.*

Visitor Information Sernatur ⊠ *1 Oriente 1150, 1st fl.* ☎ *71/223–3669, 71/222–6940* ⊕ *www.sernatur.cl.*

EXPLORING

TOP ATTRACTIONS

Via Wines. Via Wines, the northernmost winery in the Maule Valley, in San Rafael, is a company with a sense of humor. Its most recognizable brand, "Oveja Negra," means black sheep. A visit takes you through the modern winery and gorgeous vineyards with the Andes as a backdrop. Make reservations through the Ruta del Vino office. ⊠ *Fundo Las Chilcas, San Rafael* ☎ *71/241–5500* ⊕ *www.viawines.com/via_experience* ⚲ *Reservations essential.*

Viña Balduzzi. Albano Balduzzi, descended from 200 years of Italian winemakers, built this 40-acre estate in San Javier in 1900. Today his great-grandson, Jorge López-Balduzzi, is in charge and pumps out a million liters of wine each year. The premium label features varietals such as Cabernet Sauvignon, Sauvignon Blanc, Carmenère, Merlot, and a sweet late-harvest Chardonnay. Tours include a peek at the cellars that stretch underneath the property, and a collection of antique machinery, as well as a tasting. Within the estate is a beautiful expanse of oak and cedar trees perfect for a picnic, and if you want to get a bird's eye view of the estate you can take a flying tour of the vineyards in a private airplane. ⊠ *Av. Balmaceda 1189, San Javier* ☎ *73/232–2138* ⊕ *www.balduzzi.cl* ⚲ *From 3,000 pesos* ☉ *Mon.–Sat. 9–6.*

Viña Casa Donoso. Ten minutes east of Talca along a dirt road are the massive iron gates that mark the entrance to this red hacienda with barrel-tile roof. The estate was once called Domain Oriental, because it is east of the city, but today it bears the name of the family who owned it for generations before it was purchased by four Frenchmen in 1989. The vineyards themselves climb up into the Andean foothills. The oenological work is performed by a skilled Chilean staff, and the results are superb. Make reservations through the Ruta del Vino office. ⊠ *Fundo La Oriental, Camino a Palmira, Km 3.5* ☎ *71/234–1400* ⊕ *www.casadonoso.cl* ⚲ *6,000 pesos* ⚲ *Reservations essential.*

FAMILY
Fodor'sChoice
★
Viña Tabontinaja/Gillmore. The Gillmores, who own this winery, are a creative bunch. In addition to making truly fine red wines (sold as Viña Gillmore), they have created a fun place to stop and spend a couple of hours or stay on for a night or two. There's an impressive zoo on-site that includes a pair of puma, a rare Chilean deer called a *pudu*, and a raucous group of peacocks. An adobe chapel has been turned into a museum. This is a great place to stay while on the way south. Its odd-looking guest houses made from ancient recycled fermentation tanks provide all the comforts of home, as well as a wood-burning hot tub and great food. Take the Pan-American Highway to the "Camino a Constitución" turnoff, south of San Javier. Head east over the Loncomilla

River and through the rolling hills of the Coastal Mountains for 20 km (12½ miles); Tabontinaja is on the right. ✉ *Camino a Constitución, Km 20, San Javier* ☎ *73/197–5539* 🌐 *www.gillmore.cl* 🎟 *From 5,000 pesos* ✍ *Reservations essential.*

WORTH NOTING

Avenida Bernardo O'Higgins. A cedar-lined boulevard popular with joggers, skaters, and strolling couples, the Avenida Bernardo O'Higgins is a pleasant stretch of green. At its western tip is the Balneario Río Claro, where you can hire a boat to paddle down the river.

Cerro de la Virgen. You can make out the city's orderly colonial design from this hill that affords a panoramic view of Talca and the vineyards in the distance.

Ramal Talca–Constitución. There may be no better way to get to know the Central Valley than by taking a ride on Chile's only remaining *ramal* (branch-line railroad), which runs from Talca to the coastal city of Constitución. The 88-km (55-mile) Ramal Talca–Constitución makes a slow trip to the coast—3 hours and 20 minutes each way—stopping for about 15 minutes at each of the small towns en route. In Constitución, admire the coastal cliffs and rock formations. The train departs Talca's Estación de Tren daily at 7:30 am and returns at 4:45. A good option is to arrange a tour on which you take the train to Constitución, then board a van to nearby sand dunes and other natural attractions. ✉ *11 Oriente 1000* 🌐 *www.tmsa.cl* 🎟 *2,100 pesos.*

San Clemente. This town 16 km (10 miles) southeast of Talca, hosts the best rodeo in the region from September to April, with riding, roping, dances, and beauty-queen competitions. The events take place weekends 11–6. The national championship selections are held here near the end of the season. ✉ *San Clemente.*

WHERE TO STAY

$ HOTEL 🏨 **Hostal del Puente.** This quiet, family-run hotel, at the end of a dusty street two blocks west of the Plaza de Armas, is quite a bargain. **Pros:** good budget option. **Cons:** no frills. [$] *Rooms from: 28000 pesos* ✉ *1 Sur 407* ☎ *71/2220–930* 🌐 *www.hostaldelpuente.cl* 🛏 *18 rooms* 💳 *No credit cards* 🍴 *Breakfast.*

$$ HOTEL 🏨 **Hotel Terrabella.** Half a block west of the Plaza de Armas, this hotel has rooms that although neither especially bright nor spacious, are tasteful and spotless. **Pros:** central location. **Cons:** no frills. [$] *Rooms from: 59000 pesos* ✉ *1 Sur 641* ☎ *71/2227–132* 🛏 *21 rooms* 🍴 *Breakfast.*

$$$ HOTEL 🏨 **Tabonko.** This boutique wine hotel right in the Gillmore vineyard is designed to look like two large wine barrels. **Pros:** personally attended by the owners; vineyard setting. **Cons:** closed in winter; a bit remote. [$] *Rooms from: 100000 pesos* ✉ *Camino a Constitucion, Km 20, San Javier* ☎ *73/2197–5539* 🌐 *www.tabonko.cl* 🛏 *15 rooms* 🕒 *Closed Apr.–Oct.* 🍴 *Breakfast.*

THE LAKE
DISTRICT

WELCOME TO THE LAKE DISTRICT

TOP REASONS TO GO

★ **Volcanoes:** Volcán Villarrica and Volcán Osorno are the conical, iconic symbols of the northern and southern Lake District, respectively, but some 50 other volcanoes loom and fume in this region. Not to worry; eruptions are rare.

★ **Stunning summer nights:** Southern Chile's austral summer doesn't get more glorious than January and February, when sunsets don't fade until well after 10 pm, and everyone is out dining, shopping, and enjoying the outdoors.

★ **Lakes and rivers:** The region may sport a long Pacific coastline, but everyone flocks to the inland lakes to swim, sunbathe, kayak, sail, and more. The region also hosts numerous wild rivers that are, among other things, excellent for fly-fishing.

★ **Soothing hot springs:** Chile counts some 280 thermal springs, and a good many of the well-operated ones are in the Lake District, the perfect place to pamper yourself after a day of outdoor adventure and sightseeing.

1 La Araucanía. This region contains some of Chile's most spectacular lake scenery. Several volcanoes, among them Villarrica and Llaima, two of South America's most active, loom over the region. Burgeoning Pucón, on the shore of Lago Villarrica, has become the tourism hub of southern Chile. Other quieter alternatives exist, however. Lago Calafquén, farther south, begins the *Siete Lagos* (Seven Lakes) chain that stretches across the border to Argentina.

2 Los Lagos. The southern half of the Lake District is a land of snowcapped volcanoes, rolling farmland, and the shimmering lakes that give the region its name. This landscape is literally a work in progress, as it's part of the so-called Ring of Fire encircling the Pacific Rim. Most of Chile's 55 active volcanoes are here.

GETTING ORIENTED

Throughout the Lake District, volcanoes burst into view alongside large lakes and winding rivers. Architecture and gastronomy here are unlike anywhere else in Chile, much of it influenced by the large-scale German colonization of the 1850s and '60s. The Pan-American Highway (Ruta 5) runs down the middle, making travel to most places in the region relatively easy. It connects the cities of Temuco, Osorno, and Puerto Montt but bypasses Valdivia by 50 km (30 miles). A drive from Temuco to Puerto Montt should take less than four hours. Flying between the hubs is a reasonable option. The region now has a passenger train connecting Temuco and Puerto Montt, plus many towns in between.

Updated
by Jimmy
Langman
As you travel the winding roads of the Lake District, the snowcapped shoulders of volcanoes emerge, mysteriously disappear, then materialize again, peeping through trees or towering above broad valleys. You might be tempted to belt out "The hills are alive...," but this is southern Chile, not Austria. With densely forested national parks, a dozen large lakes, vastly improved hotels and restaurants, and easy access to roads and public transportation, Chile's Lake District has come pretty close to perfecting tourism. It's great for adventure travel and outdoor sports, but also has outstanding local cuisine, especially seafood, and a rich cultural past.

The Lake District is the historic homeland of Chile's indigenous Mapuche people, who revolted against the early Spanish colonists in 1598, driving them from the region. The Mapuche kept foreigners away for nearly three centuries. Though small pockets of the Lake District were controlled by Chile after it won its independence in 1818, most viewed the forbidding region south of the Río Bío Bío as a separate country.

Eventually, an 1881 treaty ended the Mapuche control over the territory, and in the middle of the 18th century Santiago began to recruit waves of German, Austrian, and Swiss immigrants to settle the so-called empty territory. The Lake District quickly took on the Bavarian-Tyrolean sheen that is still evident today.

PLANNER

WHEN TO GO
Most Chileans head here during southern Chile's glorious summer, between December and March. For fishermen, the official season commences the second Friday of November and runs through the first Sunday of May. Visiting during the off-season is no hardship, though, and lodging prices drop dramatically. An increasing number of Santiaguinos flee the capital in winter to enjoy the Lake District's brisk, clear air or to ski and snowboard down volcanoes and Andean hills.

FESTIVALS AND SEASONAL EVENTS
Summer means festival season in the Lake District. Communities across the region hold their own festivals in January and February, but the Festival Costumbrista in Castro, Chiloé, held the third week of February, is the can't-miss event. In late January and early February, Semanas Musicales de Frutillar brings together the best in classical music. Verano en Valdivia is a two-month-long celebration centered on the February 9

anniversary of the founding of Valdivia. During the first week of October, Valdivia also hosts a nationally acclaimed international film festival. Puerto Varas hosts an entertaining and fun Rain Festival each June.

GETTING HERE AND AROUND

AIR TRAVEL

None of the Lake District's airports—Osorno, Puerto Montt, Temuco, and Valdivia—receives international flights; flying here from another country means connecting in Santiago. Of the five cities, Puerto Montt has the greatest frequency of domestic flights.

BUS TRAVEL

There's no shortage of bus companies traveling the Pan-American Highway (Ruta 5) from Santiago south to the Lake District. The buses, which are very comfortable, have assigned seating and aren't too crowded. Tickets may be purchased in advance. If you are traveling overnight, consider spending extra dough on a "cama" bus; the seats are wider, fold back like a bed, and thus are much more comfortable.

CAR TRAVEL

It's easier to see more of the Lake District if you have your own vehicle. The Pan-American Highway through the region is a well-maintained four-lane toll highway. Bring plenty of small bills for the frequent toll booths.

RESTAURANTS

Meat and potatoes are popular in the cuisine of southern Chile. The omnipresent *cazuela* (a plate of rice and potatoes with beef or chicken) and *pastel de choclo* (a corn, meat, and vegetable casserole) are solid, hearty meals. But it is the seafood that most sets this region apart from other places. In Puerto Montt, tourists regularly fall in love with the local shellfish offerings, especially when served in traditional plates like *curanto* and *paila marina.*

Among the greatest gifts from the waves of German immigrants were their tasty *küchen,* rich fruit-filled pastries. (Raspberry and local *murta* berries are a special favorite here.) Sample them during the late-afternoon *onces,* the coffee breaks locals take to tide them over until dinner. The Germans also brought their beer-making prowess to the New World; Valdivia, in particular, is where the popular Kunstmann brand got its start.

HOTELS

Many hotels, even the newly built ones, are constructed in Bavarian-chalet style echoing the region's Germanic heritage. Central heating is a much-appreciated feature whenever it's available in lodgings here in winter and on brisk summer evenings. If not, you grow to appreciate the wood-heated stoves that abound all over the region. Air-conditioning is uncommon, but then it's rarely necessary this far south. Rates usually include a continental breakfast of coffee, cheese, bread, and jam. Although most of the places listed here stay open all year, call ahead to make sure the owners haven't decided to take a well-deserved vacation during the April–October off-season. *Hotels reviews have been shortened. For full information, visit Fodors.com.*

WHAT IT COSTS IN CHILEAN PESOS (IN THOUSANDS)			
$	**$$**	**$$$**	**$$$$**
Restaurants	Under 6	6–8	9–11	over 11
Hotels	Under 46	46–75	76–105	over 105

Restaurant prices are the average cost of a main course price at dinner or, if dinner is not served, at lunch. Hotel prices are the lowest cost of a standard double room in high season, excluding tax.

TOURS

Awash in rivers, mountains, forests, gorges, and its namesake lakes, this part of the country is one of Chile's outdoors capitals. Outfitters traditionally are concentrated in the northern resort town of Pucón and the southern Puerto Varas, but firms up and down this 400-km-long (240-mile-long) swath of Chile can rent you equipment or guide your excursions.

The increasing popularity of such excursions means that everybody wants a slice of the adventure pie. Quality varies widely, especially in everybody's-an-outfitter destinations such as Pucón. Ask questions about safety and guide-to-client ratios. (A few unscrupulous businesses might take 20 climbers up the Villarrica Volcano with a single guide.) Also, be brutally frank with yourself about your own capabilities: Are you really in shape for rappelling? Or is bird-watching more your style? This is nature at its best and sometimes most powerful.

LA ARAUCANÍA

La Araucanía is the historic home of the Araucano, or Mapuche, culture. The Spanish both feared and respected the Mapuche. This nomadic society, always in search of new terrain, was a moving target that the Spaniards found impossible to defeat. Beginning with the 1598 battle against European settlers, the Mapuche kept firm control of the region for almost 300 years. After numerous peace agreements failed, a treaty signed near Temuco ended hostilities in 1881 and paved the way for the German, Swiss, and Austrian immigration that would transform the face of the Lake District.

TEMUCO

675 km (405 miles) south of Santiago on Pan-American Hwy. (Ruta 5).
This northern gateway to the Lake District acquired a bit of pop-culture cachet as the setting for a segment in *The Motorcycle Diaries,* a film depicting Che Guevara's prerevolutionary travels through South America in the early 1950s. But with its office towers and shopping malls, today's Temuco would hardly be recognizable to Guevara. The city has a more Latin flavor than the communities farther south. (It could be the warmer weather and the palm trees swaying in the pleasant central park.) It's also an odd juxtaposition of modern architecture and indigenous markets, with traditionally clad Mapuche women darting across

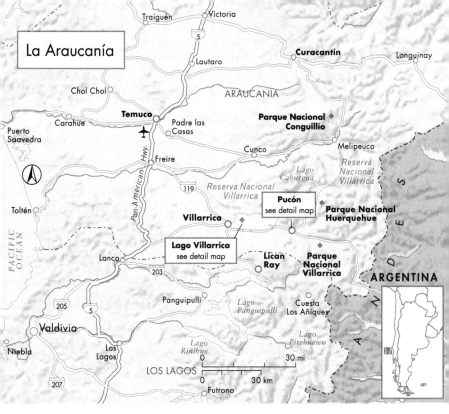

La Araucanía

the street and business executives talking on cell phones, but oddly enough it all works. It warrants a day in town if you have the time.

GETTING HERE AND AROUND

At least a dozen bus lines serve Temuco; it's an obligatory stop on the long haul between Santiago and Puerto Montt. The city also hosts Manquehue Airport, 6 km (4 miles) southwest of town, which has daily connections to Santiago and other Chilean cities. At the airport, in addition to taxis, there are several transfer services that can take you into town. If going to Villarrica or Pucón, you probably come through here as well. The Pan-American Highway, Ruta 5, runs through the city and is paved, but several of the outlying roads connecting Temuco to smaller, rural towns are two-lanes and unpaved. Be careful on such roads, as the Chilean auto accident rate due to passing cars is high.

ESSENTIALS

Bus Contacts Buses JAC ✉ Centenario 01259 ☎ 45/246–5500 ⊕ www.jac.cl. **Cruz del Sur** ✉ Terminal de Buses, Av. Vicente Pérez Rosales 1609 ☎ 45/273–0310 ⊕ www.busescruzdelsur.cl. **Tur-Bus** ✉ Av. Diego Portales, Puerto Montt ☎ 65/225–9320 ⊕ www.turbus.cl.

Rental Car Contacts Avis ✉ San Martín 755 ☎ 45/246–5280 ⊕ www.avis. cl. **Budget** ✉ Concepcion 127, Puerto Montt ☎ 65/228–6277 ⊕ www.budget.

cl ✉ *Airport, El Tepual, Puerto Montt* ☎ *65/229–4100* ⊕ *www.budget.cl.* **Hertz** ✉ *Andres Bello 792* ☎ *45/231-8585* ⊕ *www.hertz.cl.*

Visitor Information Sernatur ✉ *Antonio Varas 415, Puerto Montt* ☎ *65/222–3016* ⊕ *www.sernatur.cl.* **Temuco Tourist Office** ✉ *Mercado Municipal* ☎ *45/220-3345.*

EXPLORING
TOP ATTRACTIONS

Cholchol. The experience of visiting this small village 29 km (18 miles) northwest of Temuco begins the moment you board the bus. Expect to share space with Mapuche vendors and their enormous sacks and baskets of fruits and vegetables, all returning from market. A trip in your own vehicle is much less wearing but infinitely less colorful. Regardless of your chosen mode of transport, you arrive in Cholchol to the sight of *rucas,* traditional indigenous thatch huts, plus claptrap wooden houses, horse-drawn carts, and artisan vendors lining the dusty streets—all of whom sell their wares from 9 until about 6. Photo opportunities are plentiful, but be unobtrusive and courteous with your camera. Locals dislike being treated as merely part of the scenery.

Monumento Natural Cerro Ñielol. This imposing hillside site is where the 1881 treaty between the Mapuche and the Chilean army was signed, allowing the city of Temuco to be established. Trails bloom with bright red *copihues* (a bell-like flower with lush green foliage), Chile's national flower, in autumn (March–May). The monument, not far from downtown, is part of Chile's national park system. ✉ *Av. Arturo Prat, 5 blocks north of Plaza Teodoro Schmidt* ☎ *45/229–8222* 📷 *1,200 pesos* ⊙ *Jan.–Mar., daily 8:30–11; Apr.–Nov., daily 8:30–12:30 and 2:30–6.*

Fodor's Choice   **Museo Nacional Ferroviario Pablo Neruda.** Author Pablo Neruda was ★   Chile's most famous train buff. (Neruda spent his childhood in Temuco, and his father was a rail worker.) Accordingly, the city has transformed its old rail yard into this well-laid-out museum documenting Chile's rail history and dedicated it to the author's memory. Thirteen locomotives (1 diesel and 12 steam) and nine train carriages are housed in the round engine building. Scattered among the exhibits are snippets from Neruda's writings: "Trains were dreaming in the station, defenseless, sleeping, without locomotives," reads one. Exhibits are labeled in Spanish, but an English-speaking guide is on hand if you need translation. The museum lies a bit off the beaten path, but if trains fascinate you, as they did Neruda, it's worth the short taxi ride from downtown. Twice-monthly tourist rail excursions to Valdivia, using the museum's restored 1940 steam locomotive, are worth an afternoon of your time. ✉ *Av. Barros Arana 565* ☎ *45/973–940* 📷 *1,000 pesos* ⊙ *Tues.–Sun. 9–6.*

Museo Regional de la Araucanía. Housed in a 1924 mansion, this museum covers the history of the area. It has an eclectic collection of artifacts and relics, including musical instruments, utensils, and the country's best collection of indigenous jewelry. Upstairs, exhibits document the Mapuche people's three-century struggle to keep control of their land. The presentation could be more evenhanded: the rhetoric glorifies the Central European colonization of this area as the *pacificación de la Araucanía* (taming of the Araucanía territories). But the museum gives you a reasonably good Spanish-language introduction to Mapuche history, art, and culture. ⊠ *Av. Alemania 84* ☎ *45/274–7948* ⊕ *www. museoregionalaraucania.cl* 🔤 *600 pesos* ⊙ *Tues.–Fri. 9:30–5:30, Sat. 11–5, Sun. 11–2. Closed Mon.*

Plaza Aníbal Pinto. Temuco's bustling central square is ringed with imported palm trees—a rarity in this part of the country. A monument to the 300-year struggle between the Mapuche and the Spaniards sits in the center.

WORTH NOTING

Catedral de Temuco. The city's modern cathedral sits on the northwest corner of the central square, flanked by an office tower emblazoned with a cross.

Museo de Chol Chol. This small museum in Temuco exhibits a collection of animal-shaped ceramics and textiles with bold rhomboid and zigzag designs—both are distinctively Mapuche specialties—as well as old black-and-white photographs. A *fogón,* the traditional cooking pit, graces the center of the museum. ⊠ *Balmaceda s/n* ☎ *45/261–3350* 🔤 *300 pesos* ⊙ *Tues.–Sun. 9–6.*

WHERE TO EAT

$
CAFÉ
✕ **Confitería Central.** Coffee and homemade pastries are specialties of this café, but old-school sandwiches, hot dogs, and other simple dishes are also available. Steaming hot empanadas are served on Sunday and holidays, and during the week it seems all of Temuco stops by for a quick lunch among the clattering of dishes and the army of waitresses maneuvering their way around the tables. 🔢 *Average main: 4000 pesos* ⊠ *Manuel Bulnes 442* ☎ *45/221–0083* ⊕ *www.confiteriacentral.cl.*

$$
STEAKHOUSE
✕ **La Pampa.** Wealthy local professionals frequent this upscale modern steak house for its huge, delicious cuts of beef and the best *papas fritas* (french fries) in Temuco. Although most Chilean restaurants douse any kind of meat with a creamy sauce, this is one of the few exceptions: the entrees are served without anything but the simplest of seasonings. 🔢 *Average main: 7500 pesos* ⊠ *Caupolicán 0155* ☎ *45/232–9999* ⊕ *www.lapampa.cl* 🔖 *Reservations essential* ⊙ *No dinner Sun.*

$
CHILEAN
✕ **Las Muñecas del Ñielol.** This 37-year-old institution in Temuco has attained legendary status for its homemade food. The kitchen puts its own tasty spin on traditional Chilean dishes like *guatitas a la española,* a stew of cow's stomach, bacon, sausage, and tomato cooked in wine. The interior is simple, clean, and basic; it's all about the food here. 🔢 *Average main: 3500 pesos* ⊠ *Caupolicán 1347* ☎ *45/223–7368* ⊙ *Closed Sun.*

$
CHILEAN
✕ **Mercado Municipal.** In the central market around the produce stalls are small stands offering such typical Chilean meals as cazuela and pastel de choclo. Many have actually taken on the trappings of sit-down restaurants, and a few even have air-conditioning. The complex closes at 8 in summer and 6 the rest of the year, so late-night dining is not an option. 🔢 *Average main: 3500 pesos* ⊠ *Manuel Rodríguez 960* ☎ *45/297–345* ▭ *No credit cards.*

$$$
SPANISH
✕ **Toro Bravo.** The eclectic decor, with a mix of deer skins and odd photos on the walls, may not be the most coherent, but the food is simply

The People of the Land

The Mapuche profoundly affected the history of southern Chile. For almost 300 years this indigenous group fought to keep colonial, then Chilean powers out of their land. The Spanish referred to these people as the Araucanos, from a word in the Quechua language meaning "brave and valiant warriors." In their own Mapudungun language, today spoken by some 400,000 people, the word *Mapuche* means "people of the land." In colonial times only the Spanish missionaries, who were in close contact with the Mapuche, seemed to grasp what this meant. "There are no people in the world," one of them wrote, "who so love and value the land where they were born."

Chilean schoolchildren learning about the Mapuche are likely to read about Lautaro, a feared and respected young chief whose military tactics were instrumental in driving out the Spanish. He cunningly adopted a know-thy-enemy strategy that proved tremendously successful in fending off the colonists. Students are less likely to hear about the tightly knit family structure or nomadic lifestyle of the Mapuche. Even the region's two museums dedicated to Mapuche culture, in Temuco and Valdivia, traditionally focused on the three-century war with the Spaniards. They toss around terms like *pacificación* (meaning "to pacify" or "to tame") to describe the waves of European immigrants who settled in the Lake District at the end of the 1800s, the beginning of the end of Mapuche dominance in the region.

Life has been difficult for the Mapuche since the signing of a peace treaty in 1881. Their land was slowly usurped by the Chilean government. Some 200,000 Mapuche today are living on small settlements known as reducciones (literally meaning "reductions"). Other Mapuche have migrated to the cities, in particular fast-growing Temuco, in search of employment. Many have lost their identity in the urban landscape, assimilating to the popular Chilean way of life.

A resurgence in Mapuche pride these days takes several forms, some peaceful, some militant. Mapuche demonstrations in Temuco are now commonplace, many calling attention to deplorable living conditions. Some are seeking the return of their land, while others are fighting against the encroachment of power companies damming the rivers and logging interests cutting down the forests. News reports occasionally recount attacks and counterattacks between indigenous groups and police in remote rural areas far off the beaten tourist path. The courts have become the newest battleground as the Mapuche seek legal redress for land they feel was wrongfully taken.

Awareness of Mapuche history is increasing. (Latest census figures show that about 1 million of Chile's population of 17 million can claim some Mapuche ancestry.) There is also a newfound interest in the Mapuche language and its seven dialects. Mapudungun poetry movingly describes the sadness and dilemma of integration into modern life and of becoming lost in the anonymity of urban life. Never before really understood by others who shared their land, the Mapuche may finally make their cause known.

fantastic. Steaks are big, and there's a variety of seafood and pasta dishes on the menu. Upon arrival, start it all off with a pisco sour. Weekends get crowded, so reserve your table ahead of time. $ *Average main: 9000 pesos* ⊠ *San Martín 468* ☎ *45/232–0161.*

WHERE TO STAY

$$
B&B/INN

Goblin's House Hotel. Situated above an Irish bar and restaurant of the same name, this boutique hotel is a fun spot for your overnight stay in Temuco. **Pros:** attentive service from the owner; relaxed environment; pool table in the bar. **Cons:** beyond the great bar, no gym or other services. $ *Rooms from: 47000 pesos* ⊠ *Pirineos 0841* ☎ *45/232–0044* ⊕ *www.hotelgoblin.cl* ⇄ *13 rooms* ¡○¡ *Breakfast.*

$$
HOTEL

Hotel Don Eduardo. This orange, classic nine-story hotel is close to the city center and has rooms that are clean, pleasant, and mostly spacious. **Pros:** central location; clean; parking. **Cons:** no gym; restaurant closed on weekends. $ *Rooms from: 50000 pesos* ⊠ *Andres Bello 755* ☎ *45/221–4133* ⊕ *www.hoteldoneduardo.cl* ⇄ *46 rooms* ¡○¡ *Breakfast.*

$$
HOTEL

Hotel Frontera. This lovely old hotel is really two in one, with *nuevo* (new) and *clásico* (classic) wings facing each other across Avenida Bulnes in the city center. **Pros:** centrally located; good restaurant; includes parking. **Cons:** service slow at times; no air-conditioning. $ *Rooms from: 60000 pesos* ⊠ *Av. Bulnes 733–726* ☎ *45/220–0400* ⊕ *www.hotelfrontera.cl* ⇄ *90 rooms, 1 suite* ¡○¡ *Breakfast.*

$$
HOTEL
FAMILY

Hotel RP. In a central location with reasonable prices, the hotel has fine rooms, attentive service, and closed parking on-site. **Pros:** comfortable, ample rooms; central location; good service. **Cons:** no restaurant; breakfasts could be better. $ *Rooms from: 55000 pesos* ⊠ *Diego Portales 779* ☎ *45/297–7777* ⊕ *www.hotelrp.cl* ⇄ *23 rooms, 1 suite* ¡○¡ *Breakfast.*

$
B&B/INN

Posada Selva Negra. This bed-and-breakfast run by a German-Chilean couple is a good option. **Pros:** safe neighborhood; great breakfast. **Cons:** 18 blocks from the center. $ *Rooms from: 34000 pesos* ⊠ *Tirzano 110* ☎ *45/223–6913* ⊕ *www.hospedajeselvanegra.cl* ⇄ *7 rooms* ▭ *No credit cards* ¡○¡ *Breakfast.*

NIGHTLIFE

Caravan. This bar has more than 50 beers available and excellent food. It's also open for lunch. ⊠ *Alemania 0740* ☎ *45/224–0666* ⊕ *caravan-temuco.cl.*

Sanseacabó. There's live music here every night, from blues to Latin rock, and generous cocktail drinks. ⊠ *Hoschtetter 435* ☎ *45/224–1010.*

Taberna del Bucanero. This pub and disco has a pirate theme as well as karaoke and especially good mixed drinks. ⊠ *Manuel Bulnes 315* ☎ *9/7619–2670.*

SHOPPING

Temuco is ground central for the Mapuche Nation. Here you will find the gamut of Mapuche Indian handicrafts, from carpets to sweaters to sculpture.

Casa de la Mujer Mapuche. This indigenous women's center lets you shop for textiles, ponchos, and jewelry in a display room, with a minimum of fuss (the organization even handles catalog sales). Proceeds support social development programs. It's open weekdays 9 to 1. ⊠ *Arturo Prat 289* ☎ *45/223–3886.*

Farmacia Herbolaria Mapuche Makewe Lawen. This shop sells ancestral Mapuche remedies for everything from simple head colds to cancers and improving sexual performance. ⊠ *Aldunate 245* ☎ *45/252–0888.*

Feria Libre. At the Feria Libre, you can bargain hard with the Mapuche vendors, who sell their crafts and produce in the blocks surrounding the railroad station and bus terminal. Leave the camera behind, as the vendors aren't happy about being photographed. It's open from about 7 to 2, Monday through Saturday. ⊠ *Barros Arana at Miraflores.*

Fodor'sChoice **Mercado Municipal.** This market is one of the best places in the country ★ to find Mapuche woolen ponchos, pullovers, and blankets. The interior of the 1930 structure has been extensively remodeled and is quite open and airy. The low-key artisan vendors share the complex with butchers, fishmongers, and fruit sellers. There is no bargaining, but the prices are fair. It opens daily at 8, but closes around 3 on Sunday. ⊠ *Manuel Rodríguez 960.*

Padre Las Casas. Across the Río Cautín from Temuco is the suburb of Padre Las Casas, a Mapuche community whose center is populated by artisan vendors selling locally crafted woodwork, textiles, and pottery under the auspices of the town's rural development program. You can purchase crafts here weekdays 9 to 5. ⊠ *2 km (1 mile) southeast of Temuco.*

PARQUE NACIONAL CONGUILLÍO

126 km (78 miles) northeast of Temuco.

One of southern Chile's most beautiful and oldest tree species, the araucaria tree thrives in the native forest that blankets one of Chile's best national parks. This natural paradise is a wonderful place for hiking, with lakes surrounded by forest and steep mountains. It's also home base for Llaima Volcano, one of Chile's most active.

GETTING HERE AND AROUND

About 126 km (78 miles) northeast of Temuco, the roads are paved until the town of Curacautín; from there it's 40 km (25 miles) on gravel and dirt roads, marked with signs, to the park.

ESSENTIALS

CONAF. Chile's national parks are administered by CONAF, which provides maps and other information about them. In summer the organization arranges hikes in Parque Nacional Conguillío. The agency is strict about permits to ascend the nearby volcanoes, so expect to show evidence of your climbing ability and experience. ⊠ *Bilbao 931, Temuco* ☎ *45/229–8148.*

EXPLORING

Parque Nacional Conguillío. Volcán Llaima, which has shown constant, but not dangerous levels of activity since 2002, is the brooding centerpiece of Parque Nacional Conguillío. One of Chile's most active volcanoes, the 3,125-meter (10,200-foot) monster has created the moonscape of hardened laval flow that characterizes the park's southern portion. In the 610-square-km (235-square-mile) northern sector, there are thousands of umbrella-like araucaria pines, also known as monkey puzzle trees. The Sierra Nevada Trail is the most popular for short hikes. The three-hour trek begins at park headquarters on Laguna Conguillío and continues northeast to Laguna Captrén. Heavy snow can cut off the area in winter, so November to March is the best time to visit the park's eastern sector. Conguillío's western sector, Los Paraguas, comes into its own in winter because of a small ski center.

The main entrance to the park is in the Melipeuco sector, which is reached from Temuco via a paved road that passes through the towns of Cunco and Melipeuco before becoming a gravel road over its final section. In Melipeuco, a private company, Sendas Conguillio, administers excellent cabins and camping facilities. ✉ *Parque Nacional Conguillo, Melipeuco* ☎ *45/273–6200* 🎫 *4,500 pesos* ⏲ *Dec.–Mar., daily 8 am–10 pm; Apr.–Nov., daily 8–5.*

WHERE TO STAY

$$$ B&B/INN Fodor's Choice ★ 🏨 **Sendas Conguillio.** The official lodging concession at the park, Sendas Conguillo rents 11 rustic but comfortable cabins in the spectacular Araucaria forest. **Pros:** quality cabins in the middle of stunning nature; hot tub. **Cons:** off-the-beaten track; you need a vehicle and patience to arrive. [$] *Rooms from: 90000 pesos* ✉ *Parque Nacional Conguillo, Melipeuco* ☎ *65/297–2336* 🌐 *www.parquenacionalconguillio.cl* 🛏 *11 cabins, 1 mountain hut* 🍴 *Multiple meal plans.*

CURACAUTÍN AND NEARBY

90 km (56 miles) northeast of Temuco.

The ancient homeland of the proud indigenous Pehuenche people, Curacautín province is one of the most spectacular places in southern Chile for adventuring into wild nature, with the ever-present Llaima and Lonquimay volcanoes towering over the landscape. Here you find several reserves and parks, hot springs, and increasing tourism activities, which are beginning to rival the more well-known area to the south around Villarrica and Pucón.

GETTING HERE AND AROUND

You can get to Curacautin via Temuco, going north from Temuco on Ruta 5 for about 30 km (18 miles) until you reach the Lautaro exit. From there it's about 60 km (37 miles) on a paved road through hilly, scenic countryside landscape before arriving to the small town of Curacautín, the starting point for adventures at the many nature parks and reserves in the zone.

WHERE TO STAY

$$$ RESORT 🏨 **Lodge Nevados de Sollipulli.** This extraordinary lodge at the base of Sollipulli Volcano, whose crater is filled with a massive glacier, is located 130 km (81 miles) from Temuco inside Reserva Nacional Villarrica. **Pros:** surrounded by nature; unique accommodations; excursions. **Cons:** remote location; road is unpaved. [$] *Rooms from: 82500 pesos* ✉ *Fundo el Carmen, Sector Laguna Carilafquen, Melipeuco*

☎ 45/227–6000 🌐 *www.sollipulli.cl* 🛏 *8 rooms* ⏲ *Closed May and June* 🍴 *Multiple meal plans.*

$$$$ B&B/INN 🏨 **Ñamku Lodge.** This small, exclusive lodge is in the middle of a luxurious forest on the road to Lonquimay Volcano and Reserva Malalcahuello. **Pros:** personalized service; hiking trails nearby; comfortable beds. **Cons:** expensive; the two larger suites have less privacy if traveling as a family or larger group, as several beds share the same room. [$] *Rooms from: 210000 pesos* ✉ *Ruta 89, Km 91, Malalcahuello* ☎ *9/6675–5738* 🌐 *www.namkulodge.com* 🛏 *3 suites* 🍴 *Multiple meal plans.*

$$$$ RESORT 🏨 **Valle Corralco Hotel & Spa.** This modern, spiffy hotel and spa is in a privileged mountain setting with some of the best skiing in the Southern Hemisphere during winter months. **Pros:** great skiing; abundant views; modern facilities. **Cons:** no Wi-Fi in rooms; expensive in relation to services, especially the package deals. [$] *Rooms from: 166000 pesos* ✉ *Reserva Nacional Forestal Malalcahuello, Malalcahuello* ☎ *45/294–0310* 🌐 *www.corralco.com* 🛏 *54 rooms, 4 suites* 🍴 *Breakfast.*

VILLARRICA

87 km (52 miles) southeast of Temuco via Pan-American Hwy. or Ruta 199 southeast from Freire.

Villarrica was founded in 1552, but the Mapuche wars prevented extensive settlement of the area until the early 20th century. Founded by the Spanish conqueror Pedro de Valdivia, it was a Spanish fortress built primarily to serve as a base for gold mining in the area. The fortress's mission succeeded until 1599, when the Mapuche staged an uprising and destroyed the original town. On December 31, 1882, a historic meeting between more than 300 Mapuche chiefs and the Chilean government was held in Putue, a few kilometers outside of the town. The next day, the town was refounded.

Today this pleasant town of about 49,000 people, situated on the lake of the same name, is in one of the loveliest, least-spoiled areas of the southern Andes and has stunning views of the Villarrica and Llaima volcanoes. To Villarrica's eternal chagrin, it lives in the shadow of Pucón, a flashier neighbor several miles down the road. Many travelers drive through without giving Villarrica a glance, but it has some wonderful hotels that don't give you a case of high-season sticker shock. Well-maintained roads and convenient public transportation make the town a good base for exploring the area.

GETTING HERE AND AROUND

Located southeast of Temuco, Villarrica can be reached by a paved, two-lane road, from the town of Freire, or farther to the south, from Loncoche. Several bus lines serve the town. For about 2,000 pesos, buses leave every hour from the Temuco bus terminal and arrive in Villarrica about one hour later.

ESSENTIALS

Bus Contacts **Buses JAC** ✉ *Bilbao 610* ☎ *45/246–7777.*

Rental Car Contacts **Hertz** ✉ *Picarte 640* ☎ *45/221–8316* 🌐 *www.hertz.cl.*
Renta Car Castillo ✉ *Anfion Muñoz 415* ☎ *45/241–1618.*

OUTDOOR ADVENTURES AT A GLANCE

Pucón. Just 20 minutes from the 2,847-meter-high (9,341-foot) Villarrica Volcano, Pucón is one of Chile's top spots for adventure travel. The active volcano has itself become an obligatory climb for the many nature- and adventure-seeking tourists who come to Chile. In winter, the volcano is a favorite spot for skiing and snowboarding. Nearby Trancura River is a rafting, kayaking, and fishing paradise. Villarrica and Caburgua lakes are outstanding for fishing, swimming, kayaking, and water-skiing. There are several worthy nature hikes close to Pucón, featuring some of the most beautiful forests in Chile, including the El Cani Sanctuary and Huerquehue National Park.

Puerto Varas. This small, tranquil town on the edge of Lake Llanquihue has become a capital of sorts for travel in the southern Lake District. The lake itself frequently boasts strong winds suitable for first-class windsurfing and sailing. At Canopy Lodge of Cascadas, the largest canopy area in Chile, not far from Puerto Varas, you can zip line 70 meters (230 feet) above canyons and forest. The Petrohué River offers the opportunity for rafting, and along with numerous other rivers in the area, great fishing. Biking alongside the lake is a popular trip, too. Vicente Pérez Rosales Park and Alerce Andino Park have good trails for hiking and camping, while Osorno Volcano excels for treks, skiing, and snowboarding. Some two hours from Puerto Varas is Cochamó Valley, a fantastic spot that has drawn comparisons to Yosemite Park in California for its high granite mountain cliffs, waterfalls, and overall landscape. This is a rock climber's paradise and a hiker's dream, with exceptional horseback-riding trails, too. Just south from Cochamó is Puelo, a river valley in the shadow of the Andes Mountains. It's the launching point for some of Chile's best fly-fishing, in addition to great hiking and other outdoors action.

Valdivia. A complex network of 14 rivers cuts through the landscape in and around this southern Chilean city, forming dozens of small islands. About 160 km (99 miles) of the river system are navigable in waters ranging from 5 to 20 meters (16½ to 66 feet) deep. That makes ideal territory for kayaking, canoeing, and sailing, among other water sports. Valdivia is also near the Pacific coast. Curiñanco beach, 25 km (15½ miles) from Valdivia, is considered a prime spot for fishing. Then there are the intact coastal temperate rainforests on the outskirts of town, secluded areas with beautiful scenery for long hikes and camping trips. At the private Oncol Park, 22 km (14 miles) from Valdivia, are hiking trails and an 870-meter (2,854-foot) tree-top canopy course.

Osorno. No outdoor wonder, this city is within an hour's drive of Puyehue National Park, one of Chile's best hiking areas, and several lakes for fishing and boating, such as Rupanco. To the west, there is horseback riding, fishing, and hiking along the Pacific coast and at the indigenous network of parks, Mapu Lahual, which is managed by Huilliche native communities.

Lago Villarrica

TO TEMUCO

0   10 mi
0   10 km

Melipeuco

Cunco   Villa García

Río Allipén

ARAUCANÍA

Reserva Nacional Villarrica

Río Curaco

119

Río Tolten

199

Reserva Nacional Villarrica

Lago Colico

Lago Caburgua

Parque Nacional Huerquehue

Reigolil

Termas de Huife

Villarrica

Lago Villarrica

Pucón

Río Pucón

199

Cararrehua

Carén

Sector Rucapillán

Volcán Villarrica

Parque Nacional Villarrica

Volcán Quetrupillán

Lican Ray

Lago Calafquén

Coñaripe

Termas Geométricas

Puesco

Calafquén

Pullinque

Panguipulli

LOS LAGOS

Cuesta Los Añiques

ARGENTINA

Lago Panguipulli

Visitor Information Villarrica Tourist Office ✉ *Pedro de Valdivia 1070* ☎ *45/220–6618.*

TOURS

Amity Tours. This tour company runs several worthy day trips around Villarrica, including a Villarrica Volcano buggy tour and a full-day family rafting trip and barbecue on the mild but pretty Tolten River, which runs alongside the town. ✉ *Geronimo de Alderete 283, Pucón* ☎ *45/244–4574* ⊕ *www.amity-tours.com* 🏷 *From 55,000 pesos per person, with a minimum of 4 people.*

EXPLORING

Museo Histórico y Arqueológico de Villarrica. The municipal museum displays an impressive collection of Mapuche ceramics, masks, leather, and jewelry. A replica of a *ruca* hut graces the front yard. It's made of thatch so tightly entwined that it's impermeable to rain. ✉ *Pedro de Valdivia 1050* ☎ *45/241–5706* 🏷 *300 pesos* ☉ *Weekdays 9:30–1 and 3:30–7.*

WHERE TO EAT

$$
CAFÉ

✕ **Café 2001.** For a filling sandwich, a homemade *küchen* cake, and an espresso or cappuccino brewed from freshly ground beans, this is the place to stop in Villarrica. Pull up around a table in front or slip into one of the quieter booths by the fireplace in the back. The *lomito completo* sandwich—with a slice of pork, avocado, sauerkraut, tomato, and mayonnaise—is one of the best in the south. [$] *Average main: 6000 pesos* ✉ *Camillo Henríquez 379* ☎ *45/241–1470* 🌐 *www.cafebar2001.cl.*

$$$ BARBECUE Fodor's Choice ★ 🍴 **Fuego Patagon.** On the outskirts of town near the lake, this stellar restaurant serves exceptional steaks. The menu has good and generous barbeque plates (including wild boar, goat, and lamb); there is a nice variety of seafood and pasta dishes, too. Desserts like homemade ice cream and tiramisu are worth the extra splurge. Service, which includes the involvement of the owner, is also friendly and prompt. [$] *Average main: 10000 pesos* ✉ *Pedro Montt 40* ☎ *45/241–2207* 🌐 *www.fuegopatagon.cl* 🕒 *No dinner Sun.*

$$$ SEAFOOD FAMILY 🍴 **Mesa del Mar.** This upscale restaurant in the center of town specializes in gourmet seafood. The menu also includes other diverse offerings, but it is the colorful, exquisitely prepared fish and shellfish that deserve your close attention. They also have a special kids' menu. [$] *Average main: 9000 pesos* ✉ *Geronimo de Alderete 835* ☎ *45/241–9515* 🌐 *www.mesadelmar.cl.*

$$ ECLECTIC 🍴 **The Travellers.** Martín Golian and Juan Pereira met by happenstance and decided to open a place serving food from their homelands—and a few other countries. The result is a place that serves one or two dishes from Germany, Thailand, China, Italy, Mexico, and many countries in between. While you chow down on an enchilada, your companions might be having spaghetti with meatballs or sweet-and-sour pork. Dining on the front lawn under umbrella-covered tables is the best option on a summer evening when the Travellers also turns into a bar playing retro dance music. [$] *Average main: 6000 pesos* ✉ *Valentín Letelier 753* ☎ *45/241–3617* 🌐 *www.thetravellers.cl.*

7

WHERE TO STAY

$ B&B/INN 🏨 **Hostal & Turismo Don Juan.** This is an inexpensive option in the center of Villarrica that gives you all you need; rooms are simply furnished, but clean, with Wi-Fi, cable, and parking on-site. **Pros:** central location; helpful staff; cheap. **Cons:** rooms are simple. [$] *Rooms from: 35000 pesos* ✉ *General Korner 770* ☎ *45/241–1833* 🌐 *www.hostaldonjuan.cl* 🛏 *20 rooms* 🍽 *No meals.*

$$$ B&B/INN 🏨 **Hostería de la Colina.** Attentive service as well as special little touches like homemade ice cream and bountiful breakfasts give this place an edge over others. **Pros:** friendly service; lovely ambience; scenic views. **Cons:** TV only in the bar. [$] *Rooms from: 81000 pesos* ✉ *Las Colinas 115, Casilla 382* ☎ *45/241–1503* 🌐 *www.hosteriadelacolina.com* 🛏 *10 rooms, 2 cabins* 🍽 *Multiple meal plans.*

$$$ B&B/INN 🏨 **Hotel El Ciervo.** Villarrica's oldest hotel is an unimposing house on a quiet street, but inside are elegant details such as wrought-iron fixtures and wood-burning fireplaces. **Pros:** friendly, attentive service; good food. **Cons:** some rooms are small; price is a bit high. [$] *Rooms from: 88000 pesos* ✉ *General Körner 241* ☎ *45/241–1215* 🌐 *www.hotelelciervo.cl* 🛏 *13 rooms, 1 suite* 🍽 *Breakfast.*

$$$$ HOTEL FAMILY 🏨 **Villarrica Park Lake Hotel.** This classic, European-styled hotel and spa with modern touches is the perfect mix of old-world plush and clean, uncluttered design. **Pros:** lake view; activities on-site. **Cons:** understaffed; no Wi-Fi in rooms, must pay extra for wired Internet access.

$ *Rooms from: 118000 pesos* ⊠ *13 km (8 miles) east of Villarrica on road to Pucón* ☎ *45/245–0000* ⊕ *www.villarricaparklake.coma* ⇥ *70 rooms, 11 suites* ◯ *Breakfast.*

SPORTS AND THE OUTDOORS

Fodor'sChoice

★

Aurora Austral. Spectacular dog-sledding trips pulled by huskies are run by this tour agency, from one-day dog sledding below Villarrica Volcano to seven days crossing the Andes from Chile to Argentina. In summer, the dogs pull carriages. ⊠ *Casilla 310* ☎ *9/8901–2574* ⊕ *www.auroraaustral.com.*

SHOPPING

Feria Mapuche. This market features some of the best local artisans that make all manner of Mapuche handicrafts, from sweaters and ponchos to wooden figurines. ⊠ *Corner of Pedro de Valdivia with Julio Zegers* ☉ *Jan. and Feb., daily 9–noon.*

PUCÓN

Fodor'sChoice

★

25 km (15 miles) east of Villarrica.

The resort town of Pucón, on the southern shore of Lago Villarrica, attracts Chileans young and old. By day, there are loads of outdoor activities in the area. The beach on Lago Villarrica feels like one of Chile's popular coastal beach havens near Viña del Mar. By night, young people flock to the major nightspots and party until dawn. The older crowd has a large array of fine restaurants and trendy shops to visit. Pucón has many fans, though some lament the town's meteoric rise to fame. Still, this is the place to have fun 24 hours a day in southern Chile. Be warned, however, that accommodations are hard to come by in February, which is easily the busiest month. Outside of summer, most stores, restaurants, and pubs here close down.

With Volcán Villarrica looming south of town, a color-coded alert system on the Municipalidad (city hall) on Avenida Bernardo O'Higgins signals volcanic activity, and signs around town explain the colors' meanings: green—that's where the light almost always remains—signifies "normal activity," indicating steam being let off from the summit with sulfuric odors and constant, low-level rumblings; yellow and red indicate more dangerous levels of activity. Remember: The volcano sits 15 km (9 miles) away, and you are scarcely aware of any activity. Indeed, ascending the volcano is the area's most popular excursion.

GETTING HERE AND AROUND

Pucón has only a small air strip 2 km (1 mile) outside of town for private planes, but national airlines such as LAN and Sky fly regularly to Temuco. From Temuco, Buses JAC has frequent service to Pucón. Roads that connect Pucón to Ruta 5, the Pan-American Highway, are paved from Loncoche and Freire. In Pucón, there are several taxis that can move you about, but the town itself is small and in most cases you just need your two feet.

Pucón

Lago Villarrica
Playa Grande
La Peninsula
Clemente Holzapfel
Carlos Ansorena
Pasaja Luck
Pedro de Valdivia
Alderete
Mapuche Museuo
General Urrutia
Caupolican
Lincoyan
Fresia
O'Higgins
Camino Internacional
Brasil
Chile
Miguel Ansorena
Palguin
Arauco
Colo Colo
Uruguay
Peru
Paraguay
Peru
TO ARGENTINA
TO VILLARRICA
Ecuador
Sebastian Engler
KEY
Restaurants
Hotels

Restaurants

- Cassis 2
- Empanadas y Hamburguesas Lleu-Lleu 4
- La Maga 1
- Latitude 39 3
- Pizza Cala 6
- Trawen Restaurant 7
- Viva Perú 5

Hotels

- Apart Hotel Del Volcán 6
- Hostal Geronimo 4
- Hotel Antumalal 8
- Hotel Boutique CasaEstablo 7
- Hotel Malalhue 9
- Hotel O Gudenschwager 3
- Hotel Posada del Rio 5
- Mirador los Volcanes 2
- Peumayen Lodge & Termas Boutique 1

ESSENTIALS

Bus Contacts **Buses JAC** ✉ *Corner of Palguín and Uruguay* ☎ *45/299–0880* 🌐 *www.jac.cl.* **Tur-Bus** ✉ *General Pedro Lagos 538, Temuco* ☎ *45/227–8161* 🌐 *www.turbus.cl.*

Rental Cars **Hertz** ✉ *Gerónimo de Alderete 324* ☎ *45/244–1664* 🌐 *www.hertz.cl.***Kilometro Libre** ✉ *Gerónimo de Alderete 480* ☎ *45/244–4399* 🌐 *www.rentacarkilometrolibre.com.* **Pucón Rent A Car** ✉ *Av. Colo Colo 340* ☎ *45/244-3052* 🌐 *puconrentacar.cl.*

Visitor Information **Pucón Tourist Office** ✉ *Av. Bernardo O'Higgins 483* ☎ *45/229–3002.*

EXPLORING

Mapuche Museo. This small, private museum houses an array of Mapuche artifacts, including musical instruments, masks, rock sculptures, pipes, and other items representative of Mapuche culture and history. ✉ *Capoulican 243* ☎ *45/244–1963* 🌐 *www.pucononline.cl/museo* 🎫 *1,500 pesos* ⏲ *Jan. and Feb., daily 11–1 and 6–10; Mar.–Dec., daily 11–1 and 3–7.*

Parque Cuevas Volcánicas. Halfway up Volcán Villarrica, you find this cave right next to a very basic visitor center. It first opened up in 1968 for spelunkers to explore, but eventually tourism proved more lucrative. A short tour takes you deep into the electrically illuminated cave via wooden walkways that bring you close to the crystallized basalt formations. Your tour guide may make occasional hokey references to witches and pumas hiding in the rocks, but it's definitely worth a visit—especially if uncooperative weather prevents you from partaking of the region's other attractions and activities. ✉ *Volcán Villarrica National Park* 🌐 *www.cuevasvolcanicas.cl* 🎫 *12,000 pesos* ⏲ *Daily 10–6.*

Fodor's Choice ★ **Termas Geométricas.** Chile's volcanoes have endowed the area around Pucón with numerous natural hot springs. Located 3 km (2 miles) south of Villarrica National Park, about a two-hour drive from Pucón, this is one of the best and most beautiful. Seventeen natural hot-spring pools, many of them secluded, dot the dense native forest. Each thermal bath has its own private bathrooms, lockers, and deck. ✉ *3 km (2 miles) south of Villarica National Park* ☎ *9/7477–1708* 🌐 *www.termasgeometricas.cl* 🎫 *24,000 pesos* ⏲ *Jan.–Mar., daily 10 am–11 pm; Apr.–Dec., daily 11–8.*

WHERE TO EAT

$ CAFÉ 🍴 **Cassis.** This wonderful café and restaurant is dessert heaven, with assorted pastries baked fresh every day, chocolates galore, and an excellent selection of ice cream. The restaurant also has a varied menu of sandwiches, pizza, and more, and an extensive wine list. In summer, sit at one of the tables outside on the sidewalk. This place stays quite lively until about 3 am on summer nights. [$] *Average main: 4500 pesos* ✉ *Fresia 223* ☎ *45/244–9088* 🌐 *www.chocolatescassis.com.*

$ FAST FOOD 🍴 **Empanadas y Hamburguesas Lleu-Lleu.** This is the place in Pucón to eat Chile's famous empanadas, filled with a variety of ingredients like cheese, meat, and chicken. The vegetarian empanada is chock full of healthy goodies including corn, tomatoes, spinach, and mushrooms.

Giant hamburgers can also be had. The place is open every day 10 am to 7 am, which makes it a popular destination for the late-night bar crowd. [$] *Average main: 2500 pesos* ✉ *520 General Urrutia* 💳 *No credit cards.*

$$$$ STEAKHOUSE 🍴 **La Maga.** Argentina claims to prepare the best *parrillada,* or grilled beef, but here's evidence that Uruguayans are no second best. Watch the beef cuts turn slowly over the wood fire at the entrance. Wood, rather than charcoal, is the key, says the owner, Emiliano Villanil, a transplant from Punta del Este. The product is a wonderfully smoked, natural taste, accented with a hint of spice in the mild *chimichurri* (a tangy steak sauce). Portions are big. [$] *Average main: 12000 pesos* ✉ *Geronimo de Alderete 276* ☎ *45/244–4277* 🌐 *www.lamagapucon.cl.*

$$ ECLECTIC 🍴 **Latitude 39.** Inventive hamburgers, sandwiches, burritos, tacos, and all-day breakfast are served at this California-inspired restaurant. Check out the Buddha burger, which is topped with popcorn shrimp and spicy sriracha sauce, the beer-battered fish tacos, or the delicious *huevos rancheros,* fried eggs on Mexican tortillas. As it's often packed, especially in summer, be prepared to wait. [$] *Average main: 6100 pesos* ✉ *Gerónimo de Alderete 324* ☎ *9/7430–0016* 🌐 *latitude39.cl* 🕓 *Closed Sun.*

$$ PIZZA 🍴 **Pizza Cala.** The excellent pizza here is cooked in a wood-fired oven, making for exquisite crust. A host of great toppings are exactly the way Italy meant a pizza to be. Combine with a fresh tossed salad and a local microbrew beer and you can't go wrong. In summer, take a seat outside if you can. [$] *Average main: 8500 pesos* ✉ *Lincoyan 361* ☎ *45/246–3024.*

$$ CONTEMPORARY Fodor's Choice ★ 🍴 **Trawen Restaurant.** This solar-powered, creative restaurant features fresh and organic ingredients. Breakfasts include homemade yogurt, free-range eggs, and Italian coffee, while lunch and dinner present everything from over-size empanadas and sandwiches to meat to fish to pasta, plus dishes found few other places, like gnocchi stuffed with chickpeas and feta cheese. Vegetarians unite for the great salads and vegan plates, too. [$] *Average main: 6500 pesos* ✉ *O'Higgins 311* ☎ *45/244–2024* 🌐 *www.trawen.cl.*

$$$ PERUVIAN 🍴 **Viva Perú.** As befits the name, Peruvian cuisine reigns supreme at this restaurant with rustic wooden tables. Try the *ají de gallina* (hen stew with cheese, milk, and peppers), ceviche, or the splendid *saltado nikkei*, a Japanese-style dish of fish, shrimp, squid, and stir-fried vegetables. You can dine on the porch, a nice option for a pleasant summer night—and take advantage of the two-for-one pisco sours nightly until 9 pm. [$] *Average main: 10000 pesos* ✉ *Lincoyan 372* ☎ *45/244–4025* 🌐 *www.vivaperudeli.cl.*

WHERE TO STAY

$$$ HOTEL 🏨 **Apart Hotel Del Volcán.** In keeping with the region's immigrant heritage, the furnishings of this chalet-style hotel look like they come straight from Germany. **Pros:** kitchen; central location; large apartments. **Cons:** no restaurant. [$] *Rooms from: 86000 pesos* ✉ *Fresia 420* ☎ *45/244–2055* 🌐 *www.aparthoteldelvolcan.cl* 🛏 *18 rooms* 🍽 *Breakfast.*

$$ HOTEL 🏨 **Hostal Geronimo.** This hotel is a solid choice and well-located in the town, an easy walk to everything yet on a quiet street. **Pros:** central location; good value; excellent service. **Cons:** small rooms. [$] *Rooms*

7

from: 55000 pesos ✉ *Geronimo Alderete 665* ☎ *45/244–3762* 🌐 *www.geronimo.cl* 🛏 *34 rooms* 🍴 *Breakfast.*

$$$$ B&B/INN Fodor's Choice ★ 🏨 **Hotel Antumalal.** A young Queen Elizabeth stayed here in the 1950s, as did actor Jimmy Stewart—and the Antumalal hasn't changed much since. **Pros:** secluded location and views; fireplace in room; unique architecture. **Cons:** no covered parking. [$] *Rooms from: 190000 pesos* ✉ *Km 2, Camino Pucón-Villarica* ☎ *45/244–1011* 🌐 *www.antumalal.com* 🛏 *16 rooms, 3 suites* 🕒 *Closed June* 🍴 *Multiple meal plans.*

$$$$ B&B/INN 🏨 **Hotel Boutique CasaEstablo.** A true boutique hotel, with 10 rooms, the CasaEstablo is personally managed by the owners and their two lovely dogs, who provide service above and beyond. **Pros:** personalized service; location; meals with a view. **Cons:** road to hotel is steep; extra free to use the wood-fired hot tub. [$] *Rooms from: 120000 pesos* ✉ *Camino Villarrica–Pucón, Km 20* ☎ *45/244–3084* 🌐 *www.casaestablo.cl* 🛏 *10 rooms* 🍴 *Multiple meal plans.*

$$$ B&B/INN 🏨 **Hotel Malalhue.** Dark wood and volcanic rock were used in building this hotel at the edge of Pucón, on the road to Calburga. **Pros:** rooms are comfortable; cozy sitting room. **Cons:** 15-minute walk to town. [$] *Rooms from: 92000 pesos* ✉ *Camino Internacional 1615* ☎ *45/244–3130* 🌐 *www.malalhue.cl* 🛏 *24 rooms* 🍴 *Breakfast.*

$$ B&B/INN 🏨 **Hotel O Gudenschwager.** The Chilean-born, Los Angeles–raised owner of this property, Pablo Guerra, has taken one of Pucón's oldest lodgings and given it a complete overhaul, turning this old dame into one of the town's finest B&Bs. **Pros:** prime location; attentive service. **Cons:** no TV in rooms; can get cold at night. [$] *Rooms from: 80000 pesos* ✉ *Pedro de Valdivia 12* ☎ *45/244–9073* 🌐 *www.hogu.cl* 🛏 *15 rooms* 🍴 *Breakfast.*

$$ B&B/INN FAMILY 🏨 **Hotel Posada del Río.** This hotel has good quality rooms and cabins on its beautiful, 4-hectare (10-acre) private park, Metreñehue, which is covered with native forest and skirts along the Trancura River. **Pros:** good facilities; secluded riverside location near Pucón; spacious cabins. **Cons:** no air-conditioning in summer; weak and sometimes unavailable Wi-Fi. [$] *Rooms from: 70000 pesos* ✉ *Km 11, Camino Pucón-Calburga* ☎ *9/5821–5306* 🌐 *www.parquemetrenehue.com* 🛏 *6 rooms, 7 cabins* 🍴 *Breakfast.*

$$$$ B&B/INN 🏨 **Mirador los Volcanes.** In a gorgeous, rural setting, complete with sheep outside your spacious cabin, this is an idyllic spot to relax and stay close to several of the best sights in the Pucón area, like Lake Caburga, Huerquehue National Park, and numerous natural hot springs. **Pros:** tranquil, beautiful countryside setting; nearby lake and park; pools. **Cons:** 18 km (11 miles) from Pucón. [$] *Rooms from: 110000 pesos* ✉ *Km 17.5, Camino Pucón-Caburgua* ☎ *9/8189–8801* 🌐 *www.miradorlosvolcanes.com* 🛏 *10 cabins* 🍴 *Breakfast.*

$$ B&B/INN Fodor's Choice ★ 🏨 **Peumayen Lodge & Termas Boutique.** This hotel is truly a sight to behold, set on a stunning, 48-hectare (119-acre) property dominated by native forests and biking and hiking trails. **Pros:** attention to detail; wonderful food; beautiful surroundings. **Cons:** hot springs are sometimes more lukewarm than hot. [$] *Rooms from: 75000 pesos* ✉ *Camino Pucón Huife, Km 28* ☎ *9/7778–0285* 🌐 *www.termaspeumayen.cl* 🛏 *9 rooms, 4 suites* 🕒 *Closed Aug.* 🍴 *Multiple meal plans.*

NIGHTLIFE

Pucón has a fantastic nightlife in summer. There are several bars south of Avenida Bernardo O'Higgins.

Krater Pub. This veteran pub is open all year. A steak house by day, it fills up at night as a social gathering place for drinks, tapas, music, and karaoke. ☒ *Bernardo O'Higgins 447 B* ☏ *9/6628–9724.*

Mamas & Tapas. A local favorite is the friendly Mamas & Tapas, which is de rigueur among the expat crowd. Light Mexican dining morphs into DJ-generated or live music at night, which lasts into the wee hours. ☒ *Bernardo O'Higgins 597* ☏ *45/244–9002.*

Sala Murano. This discotheque chain in Chile has one of the liveliest party centers in Pucón, with fiestas and drink specials throughout the year. ☒ *Pasaje Las Rosas 175* ☏ *9/7604–0056* ⊕ *www.salamurano.cl.*

SPORTS AND THE OUTDOORS

At first glance Pucón's myriad outfitters look the same and sell the same slate of activities and rentals; quality varies, however. The firms listed below get high marks for safety, professionalism, and friendly service. Although a given outfitter might have a specialty, it usually offers other activities as well. Pucón is the center for rafting expeditions in the northern Lake District, with Río Trancura 15 minutes away, making for easy half-day excursions on Class III–V rapids.

FLY-FISHING

Mario's Fishing Zone. This operator guides fly fishing day trips on the Trancura and Liucura rivers near Pucón. Transport, boat, and food are included. ☒ *580 Av. Bernardo O'Higgins* ☏ *9/760–7280* ⊕ *www.flyfishingpucon.com* ☒ *From 70,000 pesos.*

HORSEBACK RIDING

Huepilmalal. This operator arranges horseback riding in the nearby Cañi mountain range, with everything from half-day to six-day excursions. ☒ *Km 27, Carretera a Huife* ☏ *9/643–2673* ⊕ *www.huepilmalal.cl.*

MULTISPORT OPERATORS

Aguaventura. Friendly, French-owned Aguaventura outfits for rafting, as well as canoeing, kayaking, snowshoeing, and snowboarding. They specialize in trekking up the volcano for a ski descent, although you should be an expert skier if you want to join them. ☒ *Palguín 336* ☏ *45/244–4246* ⊕ *www.aguaventura.com* ☒ *From 15,000 pesos.*

Captura Chile. This adventure tour operator specializes in heli-skiing and heli-fishing, but also provides individuals and private groups with overflights of the Pucón area, as well as overland excursions in 4x4 vehicles around Villarrica Volcano. ☒ *General Urrutia 615, Local 103* ☏ *9/699–3686* ⊕ *www.capturachile.com.*

Politur. This tour operator can take you rafting on the Río Trancura, trekking in nearby Parque Nacional Huerquehue, hiking up Volcán Villarrica, skiing, and skydiving. ☒ *Av. Bernardo O'Higgins 635* ☏ *45/244–1373* ⊕ *www.politur.com* ☒ *From 25,000 pesos.*

Sol y Nieve. For rafting trips, canyoning, hiking, and skiing expeditions, sign up with this tour operator. It takes groups up Villarrica Volcano.

✉ *Lincoyan 361* ☎ *45/244–4761* ⊕ *www.solynievepucon.cl* ✉ *From 50,000 pesos.*

Summit Chile. The experienced guides at Summit Chile rent gear and lead treks to the Villarrica Volcano summit; they also offer other outdoor adventures. It's the only agency with rock-climbing excursions in Pucón. ✉ *Urrutia 585* ☎ *45/244–3259* ⊕ *www.summitchile.org* ✉ *From 45,000 pesos.*

PARQUE NACIONAL HUERQUEHUE

35 km (21 miles) northeast of Pucón.

Unless you have a four-wheel-drive vehicle, this 124-square-km (48-square-mile) park is accessible only in summer (even then, a jeep isn't a bad idea). It's worth a visit for the two-hour hike on the Lago Verde trail beginning at the ranger station near the park entrance. You head up into the Andes through groves of araucaria pines, eventually reaching three startlingly blue lagoons with panoramic views of the whole area, including distant Villarrica Volcano.

GETTING HERE AND AROUND

Take the Caburga road from Pucón, following the signs to Huerquehue, which is about 22 km (14 miles) northeast of Pucón.

WHERE TO STAY

$$$$ 🏨 **Termas de Huife.** Just outside Parque Nacional Huerquehue, this resort
B&B/INN   lets you relax in three steaming pools set beside an icy mountain stream. **Pros:** access to hot springs and park. **Cons:** price is steep. 💲 *Rooms from: 134000 pesos* ✉ *33 km (20 miles) from Pucón on road to Calburga, Pucón* ☎ *45/244–1222* ⊕ *www.termashuife.cl* 🛏 *5 rooms, 9 cabins* ❉ *Breakfast.*

PARQUE NACIONAL VILLARRICA

15 km (9 miles) south of Pucón.

EXPLORING

Parque Nacional Villarrica. The main draw of this popular 610-square-km (235-square-mile) national park, which has skiing, hiking, and many other outdoor activities, is the volcano. Happily, you don't need to have any climbing experience to reach the 3,116-meter (9,350-foot) summit, but a guide is a good idea. The volcano sits in the park's Sector Rucapillán, a Mapuche word meaning "house of the devil." That name is apt, as the perpetually smoldering volcano is one of South America's most active. CONAF closes off access to the trails at the slightest hint of volcanic activity deemed out of the ordinary. It's a steep uphill walk to the snow line, but doable any time of year. All equipment is supplied by any of the Pucón outfitters that organize daylong excursions for about 50,000 pesos per person. Your reward for the six-hour climb is the rare sight of an active crater, which continues to release clouds of sulfur gases and explosions of lava. You're also treated to superb views of the nearby volcanoes, the less-visited Quetrupillán and Lanín. ☎ *45/244–3781 CONAF in Temuco* ✉ *4,000 pesos* ❉ *Daily 8–6.*

Fodor's Choice **Santuario El Cañi.** Chile's first private nature preserve, this park hosts one
★ of the last remaining, extensive Araucaria forests, a magnificent tree species that can live up to 2,000 years and that is oft nicknamed "monkey
puzzle" because of its tangled branches which swirl around its tree top.
With about 500 hectares (1,235 acres) altogether, this is one of the best
treks you can do in southern Chile. The hike to El Cañi's highest ground
(1,600 meters), called El Mirador, is a three- to four-hour steep climb,
but rewards you with some of the most beautiful views to be found of
the region's lakes and volcanoes. The sanctuary can provide a guide
(required in winter) and prices start at 45,000 pesos. There are camping
sites and a *refugio* for overnight stays. Located about 20 km (12 miles)
east of Pucón, the park is accessible via the road to Lago Caburgua
(take the turnoff at Km 14). Then turn on the paved road with the sign
"Termas Huife" and drive until you reach El Cañi. It is also possible to
arrive by bus. ⊠ *Santuario El Cañi, Pucón* ☎ *9/837–3928, 9/931–3846*
⊕ *www.santuariocani.cl* ⬜ *4,000 pesos.*

SPORTS AND THE OUTDOORS
SKIING
Ski Pucón. This popular ski resort, in the lap of Volcán Villarrica, has
17 runs of varying levels of expertise, but they're mostly for beginners
and intermediate skiers. There are seven ski lifts, but note: These lifts
are slow going. There's also equipment rental and good snowboarding, too. The ski season usually begins early July and sometimes runs
through mid-October. High-season rates are 30,000 pesos per day and
25,000 pesos per half day. There is also a restaurant, coffee shop, and
boutique for skiing accessories, as well as skiing and snowboarding
classes. ⊠ *Parque Nacional Villarrica, Pucón* ☎ *45/244–1901* ⊕ *www.
skipucon.cl.*

LICAN RAY

30 km (18 miles) south of Villarrica.

In the Mapuche language, Lican Ray means "flower among the stones."
This pleasant, unhurried little resort town of 1,688 inhabitants is on
Lago Calafquén, the first of a chain of seven lakes that spills over into
Argentina. You can rent rowboats and sailboats along the shore, which
is also a fine spot to soak up sun.

GETTING HERE AND AROUND
You can reach Lican Ray via the paved Ruta 199 from Temuco and
Villarrica. From Valdivia and points south, take Ruta 203 to Panguipulli, then travel on dirt and gravel roads north to Lican Ray. There
is daily and frequent bus service to the town from nearby locales such
as Villarrica.

ESSENTIALS
Visitor Information Lican Ray Tourist Office ⊠ *General Urrutia 310*
☎ *45/243-1201.*

WHERE TO EAT AND STAY

$$ ITALIAN 🍴 **Cábala Restaurant.** Impeccable service is the hallmark of this Italian restaurant on Lican Ray's main street. The brick-and-log building has indoor and outdoor seating, perfect to watch the summer crowds stroll by as you enjoy pizza and pasta. [$] *Average main: 7500 pesos* ✉ *General Urrutia 201* ☎ *9/8448–3199* 🕒 *Closed Apr.–Nov.*

$$ B&B/INN 🏨 **Harris Hotel.** After more than two decades in operation, this modern, rustic hotel on the lakefront has become a top lodging option for Lican Ray. **Pros:** terrace views of lake; clean and comfortable. **Cons:** rooms are simply furnished; small. [$] *Rooms from: 60000 pesos* ✉ *Cacique Manquel 105* ☎ *45/243–1553* 🌐 *www.hotelharris.cl* 🛏 *8 rooms, 2 cabins* 🍽 *Breakfast.*

$ B&B/INN FAMILY 🏨 **Hostal Hofmann.** The bright, airy rooms at this house outside town are built for extra comfort with lots of pillows and thick, colorful quilts on the beds. **Pros:** comfy rooms; hearty breakfast. **Cons:** no restaurant. [$] *Rooms from: 45000 pesos* ✉ *Camino a Coñaripe 100* ☎ *45/243–1109* 🌐 *www.hostalhoffmann.cl* 🛏 *11 rooms* 🍽 *Breakfast.*

LOS LAGOS

Some of Chile's oldest cities are in Los Lagos, yet you may be disappointed if you come looking for colonial grandeur. Wars with indigenous peoples kept the Spaniards, then Chileans, from building here for 300 years. An earthquake of magnitude 9.5, the largest recorded in history, was centered near Valdivia and rocked the region on May 22, 1960. It destroyed many older buildings in the region and produced a tsunami felt as far away as Japan.

Still, eager to fill its tierras baldías (uncultivated lands) in the 19th century, Chile worked tirelessly to promote the country's virtues to German, Austrian, and Swiss immigrants looking to start a new life. The newcomers quickly set up shop, constructing breweries, foundries, shipyards, and lumberyards. By the early part of the 20th century, Valdivia had become the country's foremost industrial center, aided in large part by the construction of a railroad from Santiago. To this day the region retains a distinctly Germanic flair, and you might swear you've taken a wrong turn to Bavaria when you pull into towns such as Frutillar or Puerto Octay.

VALDIVIA

120 km (72 miles) southwest of Villarrica.

One of Chile's most scenic cities, it gracefully combines Chilean wood-shingle construction with the architectural style of the well-to-do German settlers who colonized the area in the late 1800s. The historic appearance is a bit of an illusion, as the 1960 earthquake destroyed all but a few old riverfront structures. The city painstakingly rebuilt its downtown area, seamlessly mixing old and new buildings. Today you can enjoy evening strolls through its quaint streets and along two rivers, the Valdivia and the Calle-Calle.

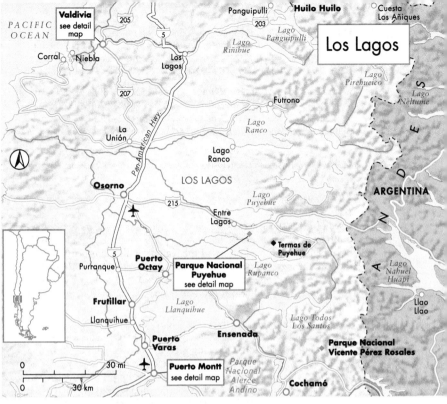

Various tour boats leave from the docks at Muelle Schuster along the Río Valdivia for a one-hour tour around nearby Isla Teja. Expect to pay about 5,000 pesos. If you have more time, a five-hour excursion takes you to Niebla near the coast for a visit to the colonial-era forts. A four-hour tour north transports you to Punucapa, the site of a 16th-century Jesuit church and a nature sanctuary at San Luis de Alba de Cruces. Most companies charge around 22,000 pesos for either of the longer tours (depending on whether the tour includes a meal). Each tour company offers all three excursions daily during the December–March high season, and you can always sign on to one at the last minute. Most will not operate tours for fewer than 15 passengers, however, which makes things a bit iffy during the rest of the year.

GETTING HERE AND AROUND

Like most other major cities in the Lakes District, Valdivia is served by Ruta 5, the Pan-American Highway. The city also has an airport with frequent flights by national airlines such as LAN, and the nation's bus lines regularly stop here as well. Valdivia's bus terminal is by the river at the cross section of Muñoz and Prat. Some outlying towns and sites around Valdivia you may want to visit, however, are only connected by dirt roads.

ESSENTIALS

Bus Contacts Buses JAC ⊠ *Anfión Muñoz 360* ☎ *63/233-3343.* **Cruz del Sur**
⊠ *Anfión Muñoz 360* ☎ *63/221-3840* ⊕ *www.busescruzdelsur.cl.* **Valdivia Bus
Depot** ⊠ *Anfión Muñoz 360* ☎ *63/222-0498.*

Rental Car Contacts Assef y Méndez ⊠ *General Lagos 1335* ☎ *63/221-3205*
⊕ *www.assefymendez.cl.* **Autovald** ⊠ *Vicente Pérez Rosales 660* ☎ *63/221-
2786* ⊕ *www.autovald.cl.* **Avis** ⊠ *Beauchef 619* ☎ *63/233-3561* ⊕ *www.avis.cl.*
Budget ⊠ *San Martin 755, Temuco* ☎ *45/223-2715* ⊕ *www.budget.cl.*

Visitor Information Sernatur ⊠ *Bulnes 586, Temuco* ☎ *45/231-2857,
211-969* ⊕ *www.sernatur.cl.* **Valdivia Tourist Office** ⊠ *Terminal de Buses,
Anfión Muñoz 360* ☎ *63/227-8748.*

EXPLORING
TOP ATTRACTIONS

Catedral de Nuestra Señora del Rosario. Valdivia'a imposing modern cathedral faces the west side of the central plaza. A small museum inside
documents the evangelization of the region's indigenous peoples from
the 16th through 19th centuries. ⊠ *Independencia 514* ☎ *63/223-2040*
⊡ *Free* ⊘ *Masses: weekdays 7 am and noon, Sat. 8 am and 7 pm, Sun.
10:30 am, noon, and 7 pm. Museum: weekdays 10:30-7, weekends
10:30-8.*

Cervecería Kunstmann. Valdivia has a long history of producing beer
and this brewery brews the country's beloved lager. The Anwandter
family immigrated from Germany a century-and-a-half ago, bringing
along their beer-making know-how. The *cervecería* (brewery), on the
road to Niebla, hosts interesting guided tours by prior arrangement.
There's also a small museum and a souvenir shop where you can buy the
requisite caps, mugs, and T-shirts; plus a pricey restaurant serving German fare. ⊠ *Ruta 350 No. 950* ☎ *63/229-2969* ⊕ *www.lacerveceria.cl*
⊡ *Free* ⊘ *Restaurant and museum: daily noon-midnight.*

Mercado Fluvial. This awning-covered market in the southern shadow
of the bridge leading to Isla Teja is a perfect place to soak up the atmosphere of a real fish market. Vendors set up early in the morning; you
hear the thwack of fresh trout and the clatter of oyster shells as they're
piled on the side of the market's boardwalk fronting the river. If the
sights, sounds, and smells are too much for you, fruit and vegetable
vendors line the other side of the walkway opposite the river. ⊠ *Av.
Arturo Prat at Libertad* ⊘ *Mon.-Sat. 8-3.*

Museo de Arte Contemporáneo. Fondly known around town as the
"MAC," this is one of Chile's foremost modern-art museums. The
complex on Isla Teja was built on the site of the old Anwandter brewery destroyed in the 1960 earthquake. The minimalist interior, for-
merly the brewery's warehouses, contrasts sharply with a modern glass
wall fronting the Río Valdivia, completed for Chile's bicentennial. The
museum has no permanent collection; it's a rotating series of temporary
exhibits by contemporary Chilean artists. ⊠ *Los Laureles, Isla Teja*
☎ *63/222-1968* ⊕ *www.macvaldivia.uach.cl* ⊡ *Jan. and Feb., 1,200
pesos; Mar.-Dec., free* ⊘ *Daily 10-2 and 4-8.*

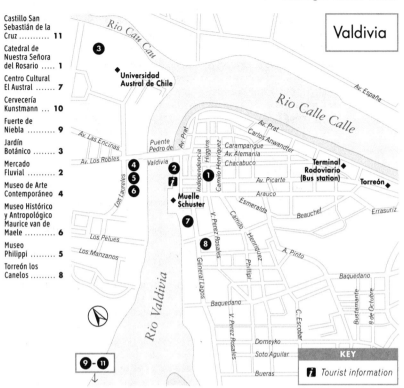

Valdivia

Museo Histórico y Antropológico Maurice van de Maele. For a historic overview of the region visit this museum on neighboring Isla Teja. The collection focuses on the city's colonial period, during which time it was settled by the Spanish, burned by the Mapuche, and invaded by Dutch corsairs. Downstairs, rooms recreate the interior of the late 19th-century Anwandter mansion that belonged to one of Valdivia's first immigrant families; the upper floor delves into Mapuche art and culture. ✉ *Los Laureles, Isla Teja* ☎ *63/221–2872* 💰 *1,500 pesos* ☉ *Daily 10–8.*

WORTH NOTING

Castillo San Sebastián de la Cruz. Across the estuary from the Fuerte de Niebla is this large and well-preserved fort from 1645. In the January through February summer season, historic reenactments of Spanish military maneuvers take place daily at 4 and 6. To get there, you need to rent a small boat, which costs only about 700 pesos at the marina near Fuerte de Niebla. ✉ *1 km (½ mile) north of Corral* ☎ *63/247–1828* 💰 *1,000 pesos* ☉ *Jan. and Feb., Tues.–Sun. 10–7; Mar.–Dec., Tues.–Sun. 11–6.*

Centro Cultural El Austral. A walk south of downtown on Yungay and General Lagos takes you through a neighborhood of late-19th- and early-20th-century houses that were spared the ravages of the 1960 earthquake. One of these houses dates to 1870 and accommodates the

Centro Cultural El Austral. It's worth the stop if you have an interest in period furnishings. ⊠ *Yungay 733* ☎ *63/2213–6588* ⊕ *www. macvaldivia.uach.cl* 🖾 *Free* ☉ *Tues.–Sun. 10–1 and 4–7.*

Fuerte de Niebla. To protect the all-important city of Valdivia, the Spanish constructed a series of strategic fortresses at Niebla, where the Valdivia and Tornagaleones rivers meet. Portions of the 1671 Fuerte de Niebla and its 18 cannons have been restored. The ground on which the cannons sit is unstable; you can view them from the ramparts above. The old commander's house serves as a small museum documenting the era's military history. ⊠ *1 km (½ mile) west of entrance to Niebla* ☎ *63/228–2084* 🖾 *600 pesos; free Wed.* ☉ *Jan. and Feb., Tues.–Sun. 10–7; Mar.–Dec., Tues.–Sun. 11–6.*

Jardín Botánico. North and west of the Universidad Austral campus, this garden is awash with 1,000 species of flowers and plants native to Chile. It's a lovely place to wander among the alerce, cypress, and laurel trees whatever the season. If you can't make it to Conguillío National Park to see the monkey puzzle trees, this is the place to see them. It's particularly enjoyable in spring and summer. ⊠ *Isla Teja* ☎ *63/222–1313* 🖾 *Free* ☉ *Dec.–Feb., daily 8–8; Mar.–Nov., daily 8–4.*

FAMILY **Museo Philippi.** Behind the history and anthropology museum, this museum bears the name of 19th-century Chilean explorer and scientist Rudolph Amandus Philippi and is designed to foster an interest in science among young people. ⊠ *Los Laureles, Isla Teja* ☎ *63/221–2872* 🖾 *1,300 pesos* ☉ *Daily 10–1 and 2–8.*

Torreón Los Canelos. Just south of the Centro Cultural El Austral lies one of two fortress towers constructed in 1774 to defend Valdivia from constant indigenous attacks. Both towers—the other sits on Avenida Picarte between the bus terminal and the bridge entering the city over the Río Calle Calle—were built in the style of those that guarded the coasts of Andalusia, in southern Spain. A wall and moat connected the two Valdivia towers in the colonial era, effectively turning the city into an island. ⊠ *General Lagos at Yerbas Buenas.*

EN
ROUTE

Isla Huapi. Some 20% of Chile's one million Mapuche live on *reducciones,* or reservations. One of the most welcoming communities is on Isla Huapi, a leafy island in the middle of deep-blue Lago Ranco. It's out of the way—about 80 km (48 miles) southeast of Valdivia—but worth the trip for those interested in Mapuche culture. A boat departs from Futrono, on the northern shore of the lake, at 7 am Monday, Wednesday, and Friday, returning at 5 pm. The pastoral quiet of Isla Huapi is broken once a year in January or February with the convening of the island council, in conjunction with the Lepún harvest festival. You are welcome during the festival, but be courteous and unobtrusive with your camera.

WHERE TO EAT

$ ╳ **Café Haussmann.** The excellent *crudos* (steak tartare), German-style
GERMAN sandwiches, and delicious *küchen* cakes here are testament to the fact that Valdivia was once a mecca for German immigrants. The place is small—a mere four tables and a bar—but it's that rarest of breeds in Chile: a completely nonsmoking restaurant. 🖫 *Average main: 4500*

pesos ✉ *Bernardo O'Higgins 394* ☎ *63/221–3878* 🌐 *www.haussmann.cl* ⏲ *Closed Sun.*

$$$ STEAKHOUSE Fodor's Choice ★ 🍴 **La Parrilla de Thor.** This riverfront institution is constantly packed with locals, which is always a good sign that you've come to the right restaurant. The Argentine owner Teodoro Poulsen serves beef and chicken in fine Argentine *parrilla* style. This is perhaps the finest steak house in Chile's Lake District. Though the restaurant bills itself as the "king of steak," you might consider the chicken (*milanesa de pollo*) instead. To do it right, order a bottle of wine from their excellent wine list to accompany your meal. [$] *Average main: 10000 pesos* ✉ *Arturo Prat 653, Costanera* ☎ *63/227–0767.*

$ CAFÉ 🍴 **La Ultima Frontera.** The creative and wide variety of sandwiches in this bohemian café have made it a national legend. Inhabiting a restored mansion, the place has colorful art on the walls and a popular outdoor terrace. On first glance, La Ultima Frontera appears to be nothing more than a college hangout, or a trendy place for the artsy crowd, but the abundant, reasonably priced, and delicious food attracts young and old. The many locally brewed beers on tap provide the perfect complement. [$] *Average main: 3500 pesos* ✉ *Perez Rosales 787* ☎ *63/223–5363* ⏲ *Closed Sun.*

$$ CAJUN 🍴 **New Orleans.** Louisiana Cajun cooking in southern Chile is far from common, but this place pulls it off and has become a must stop on the tourist trail. Excellent meats and seafood with a spicy, Cajun twist populate the extensive menu, like *filete Mardi Gras* or red curry shrimp. As noteworthy as the food, the service and ambience contribute positively to the whole experience. It's definitely worth checking out. [$] *Average main: 8000 pesos* ✉ *Esmeralda 682* ☎ *63/221–8771.*

$$ CAFÉ 🍴 **Salón de Té Entrelagos.** This swanky café caters to Valdivian business executives, who come here to make deals over sandwiches (try the Isla Teja—with grilled chicken, tomato, artichoke hearts, asparagus, olives, and red peppers), decadent crepes, and desserts. In the evenings, the atmosphere feels less formal—the menu is exactly the same—as the Entrelagos becomes a place to meet friends, who converse well into the night. Next door is the Entrelagos chocolate store, which is a good place to buy a gift or splurge. [$] *Average main: 6500 pesos* ✉ *Vicente Pérez Rosales 640* ☎ *63/221–2039* 🌐 *www.entrelagos.cl.*

WHERE TO STAY

$$$ HOTEL 🏨 **Hotel Diego de Almagro Valdivia.** A good value in a superb location on the riverfront and near the city center, this hotel is part of a national chain. **Pros:** near the city center; good nightlife nearby. **Cons:** no pool; nonsmoking hotel. [$] *Rooms from: 79700 pesos* ✉ *Arturo Prat 433, Costanera* ☎ *2/235–59250* 🌐 *www.dahoteles.com* 🛏 *105 rooms* 🍽 *Breakfast.*

$$$$ HOTEL Fodor's Choice ★ 🏨 **Hotel Dreams Valdivia.** This swanky hotel is the tallest in Valdivia and thus has tremendous views no matter the vantage point. **Pros:** rooms with a view; modern comforts; near the action. **Cons:** not much local charm. [$] *Rooms from: 110000 pesos* ✉ *Carampangue 190* ☎ *2/2346–4300, 600/626–0000* ✎ *reservas@mundodreams.com* 🛏 *100 rooms, 16 suites* 🍽 *No meals.*

$$ B&B/INN 🏨 **Hotel El Castillo.** This grand 1920s German-style house sits at Niebla's main intersection on the riverfront and has been converted into a lovely bed-and-breakfast with lots of knickknacks, antiques, and cuckoo clocks in the common areas. **Pros:** nice ambience; good views from rooms. **Cons:** no restaurant. [$] *Rooms from: 49000 pesos* ✉ *Antonio Ducce 750* ☎ *63/228–2061* 🌐 *www.hotelycabanaselcastillo.com* 🛏 *13 rooms* 🍴 *Breakfast.*

$$ HOTEL 🏨 **Hotel Naguilán.** Located on the banks of the Río Valdivia, this is an entertaining and pretty spot, and the hotel itself is overall one of good quality. **Pros:** attentive service; river location. **Cons:** 15-minute walk to downtown; older wing. [$] *Rooms from: 75000 pesos* ✉ *General Lagos 1927* ☎ *63/221–2851* 🌐 *www.hotelnaguilan.com* 🛏 *33 rooms, 3 suites* 🍴 *Breakfast.*

$$$$ HOTEL 🏨 **Hotel Puerta del Sur.** In a near perfect location, on a secluded spot on Isla Teja, yet only eight blocks from downtown Valdivia, this highly regarded four-star lodging has spacious, pleasant rooms, decorated in soft lavender tones, and views of the river. **Pros:** location; great service; lots of activity options. **Cons:** maintenance issues due to advancing age. [$] *Rooms from: 115000 pesos* ✉ *Los Lingues 950, Isla Teja* ☎ *63/222–4500* 🌐 *www.hotelpuertadelsur.com* 🛏 *40 rooms, 5 suites* 🍴 *Breakfast.*

$$ HOTEL 🏨 **Hotel Villa del Rio.** This classic Valdivia hotel is located next to Rio Calle-Calle on a well-maintained site with green areas and gardens. **Pros:** riverside location; facilities; amenities. **Cons:** older hotel; a hike to downtown. [$] *Rooms from: 75000 pesos* ✉ *Espana 1025* ☎ *63/221–6292* 🌐 *www.hotelvilladelrio.com* 🛏 *82 rooms, 2 suites* 🍴 *Breakfast.*

NIGHTLIFE

Here in the hometown of Austral University of Valdivia, a major Chilean university, the nightlife is lively and fun, particularly in and around the downtown area known as Calle Esmeralda. Bars, discos, and pubs are not just student-oriented, though; there are also many establishments in Esmeralda and elsewhere in the city that cater to older folks.

Carre Social Club. This fun club with an outdoor terrace, indoor pub, and disco has generous happy hour specials before 11 pm. ✉ *Esmeralda 677* ☎ *63/223–9288.*

Rio Music Bar. This vibrant bar is popular with the twentysomething crowd, with live music and good food. ✉ *Alemania 290* ☎ *63/221–1229.*

XS Disco. This is where the dance party is in Valdivia, especially on Friday evening. ✉ *Carampangue 190* ☎ *600/626–0000* 🌐 *www.clubxs.cl.*

SPORTS AND THE OUTDOORS

Numerous rivers, lush coastal temperate rain forests, and the Pacific coastline are some of the attractions for sports lovers in and around Valdivia. This is a great place for anything related to the river. Birdwatching is a joy, particularly when you witness the rare black-necked swans, one of the world's smallest, which have made the Valdivia area their main habitat despite pollution problems from a nearby pulp mill.

Pueblito Expediciones. This Valdivia-based tour operator organizes marvelous rafting, kayaking, and nature-appreciation trips on nearby rivers.

✉ *San Carlos 188* ☎ *63/224–5055* ⊕ *www.pueblitoexpediciones.cl* 💲 *From 29,000 pesos.*

Turismo Hua Hum. This veteran tour operator runs city tours, bike rentals, and hiking excursions to nearby Parque Oncol and the Coastal Alerce Reserve. ✉ *Carelmapu 2133* ⊕ *www.huahum.cl* 💲 *From 19,000 pesos.*

SHOPPING

Entrelagos. Affiliated with the restaurant of the same name next door, Entrelagos has been whipping up sinfully rich chocolates for decades and arranging them with great care in the storefront display windows. Most of what is sold here is actually made at Entrelagos's factory outside town, but a small army of chocolate makers is on-site to let you see, on a smaller scale, how it's done, and to carefully package your purchases for your plane ride home. ✉ *Vicente Pérez Rosales 622* ☎ *63/221–2047.*

Mercado Municipal. The city's 1918 Mercado Municipal barely survived the 1960 earthquake intact, but it thrives again after extensive remodeling and reinforcement as a shopping-dining complex. A few restaurants, mostly hole-in-the-wall seafood joints, but some quite nice, share the three-story building with artisan and souvenir vendors. ✉ *Block bordered by Av. Arturo Prat, Chacabuco, Yungay, and Libertad* ☎ *63/222–0353* ⊙ *Dec.–Mar., daily 8 am–10 pm; Apr.–Nov., daily 8–8.*

HUILO HUILO

Fodor's Choice ★ *165 km east of Valdivia.*

At this private nature reserve, which spans nearly 120,000 hectares (300,000 acres), you find some of the last and best stands of Chile's native evergreen forest, a temperate rainforest ecosystem rich in plants and unique wildlife like the world's smallest deer, the pudu, and the monito del monte, the only surviving member of an otherwise extinct marsupial order. In addition, Huilo Huilo has undergone an ambitious project to restore the endangered huemul deer to the landscape. The reserve is home to rivers ideal for rafting and fishing, plus the spectacular Lake Pirihueico, which can be crossed by ferry to get to Argentina's tourist resort San Martin de Los Andes. Snow at the top of the park's Mocho Volcano is year-round, making it one of the country's best destinations for snowboarding. In the nearby town of Neltume and at the park store, you can purchase unique local handicrafts based on forest mythological characters known as *duendes* and *hadas*.

GETTING HERE AND AROUND

Travel east from Valdivia by car, pass by picturesque country farms along Ruta 5, going through Lanco until you reach the town of Panguipulli. From there, pick up the Panguipulli–Puerto Fuy International Highway, which becomes gravelly and narrow, with wicked curves, over the last stretch of 10 km (6 miles) leading into Huilo Huilo.

WHERE TO STAY

$$$
RESORT
FAMILY
🏨 **Huilo Huilo.** This massive ecotourism complex boasts four hotels, numerous cabins, and several camping sites amid the beautiful temperate forest, rivers, and lakes at the Huilo Huilo Biological Reserve.

CLOSE UP

Hier ist alles so Deutsch

In the Lake District, you meet people with names like María Schmidt or Pablo Gudenschwager. At first, such juxtapositions sound odd, but, remember, this melting pot of a country was liberated by an Irishman man named Bernardo O'Higgins.

The Lake District's Germanic origins can be traced to one Vicente Pérez Rosales. (Every town and city in the region names a street for him, and one of Puerto Montt's more fabulous lodgings carries his name.) Armed with photos of the region, Don Vicente, as everyone knew him in his day, made several trips on behalf of the Chilean government to Germany, Switzerland, and Austria in the mid-19th century to recruit waves of European immigrants to settle the Lake District and end 300 years of Mapuche domination in the region once and for all.

Thousands signed on the dotted line and made the long journey to start a new life in southern Chile. It was a giant leap of faith for the original settlers, but it didn't hurt that the region looked just like the parts of Central Europe that they'd come from. The result was an old-fashioned Germanic work ethic mixed with a Latin spirit. But don't bother to dust off that high-school German for your trip here; few people speak it these days.

Pros: nature; architecture; spa. **Cons:** no Wi-Fi in rooms; customer service is inconsistent. $ *Rooms from: 86275 pesos* ✉ *Camino Internacional, Huilo Huilo, between Netulme and Puerto Fuy* ☎ *63/267–2020, 2/2887–3500* 🌐 *www.huilohuilo.com* 🛏 *102 rooms, 19 cabins* 🍴 *Breakfast.*

OSORNO

107 km (65 miles) southeast of Valdivia, via Ruta 5, Pan-American Hwy.

Although the least visited of the Lake District's four major cities, Osorno is one of the oldest in Chile, but the Mapuche prevented foreigners from settling here until the late 19th century. Like other communities in the region, it bears the imprint of the German settlers who came here in the 1880s. The 1960 earthquake left Osorno with little historic architecture, but a row of 19th-century houses miraculously survived on Juan Mackenna between Lord Cochrane and Freire. Their distinctively sloped roofs, which allow adequate drainage of rain and snow, are replicated in many of Osorno's newer houses. Situated in a bend of the Río Rahue, the city makes a convenient base for exploring the nearby national parks.

GETTING HERE AND AROUND

Osorno is about a 1½-hour flight from Santiago. By car, Osorno is reached by the paved Ruta 5, or Pan-American Highway. There is also passenger train service via Temuco. All the main bus lines serve Osorno on a frequent basis.

ESSENTIALS

Bus Contacts **Buses Vía Octay** ✉ *Errázuriz 1400* ☎ *64/223-7043.* **Osorno Bus Depot** ✉ *Errázuriz 1400* ☎ *64/223-4149.*

Visitor Information **Sernatur** ✉ *Av. Arturo Prat 555, Valdivia* ☎ *63/223-9317* ⊕ *www.sernatur.cl.*

TOURS

Osorno Tourist Office. The friendly people at the tourist office arrange free daily tours in summer. Each day has a different focus, including walks around the city, fruit orchards, or nearby farms. ✉ *North side of Plaza de Armas, Mackenna and Freire* ☎ *64/221-8740* ⚏ *Free* ⊘ *Office: Dec.–Feb., daily 9–8; Mar.–Nov., weekdays 9–1 and 2:30–6. Tours: daily 10:30.*

EXPLORING

Catedral de San Mateo Apostol. This modern cathedral fronts the Plaza de Armas and is topped with a tower resembling a bishop's mitre. "Turn off your cell phone," the sign at the door admonishes those who enter. "You don't need it to communicate with God." ✉ *Plaza de Armas* ⊘ *Mass: Mon.–Sat. 7:15 pm, Sun. 10:30, noon, and 8:15.*

Fodor's Choice ★ **Mapu Lahual.** On the Pacific coast, about a three-hour drive from Osorno, is a network of indigenous parks spread over nine Huilluiche Indian communities amid 50,000 hectares of pristine temperate rainforest. Day trips include a sail up the coast to visit a Huilluiche settlement. The eight-person boat leaves from Bahía Mansa, but keep an eye on the weather as the boat won't run if it's really windy. Exploring the indigenous parks by land is a more intrepid trip, although trekking, horseback rides, and homestays (simple, basic accommodations) with descendants of the Huilluiche, are possible. Nature lovers will appreciate the native alerce forest as you cross the Chilean Coastal Range, home to 30 different bird species and an equal number of mammals, including the Molina's hog-nosed skunk, mountain monkeys, and pumas. A highlight for those going by water is the beautiful, white-sand Condor Beach. ✉ *Freire 585, Osorno* ☎ *9/8731-3418* ⊕ *www.mapulahual.cl.*

Museo Municipal Osorno. This museum contains a decent collection of Mapuche artifacts, Chilean and Spanish firearms, and exhibits devoted to the German settlement of Osorno. Housed in a pink neoclassical building dating from 1929, this is one of the few older structures in the city center. ✉ *Manuel Antonio Matta 809* ☎ *64/223-8615* ⊕ *www.osornomuseos.cl* ⚏ *Free* ⊘ *Mon.–Thurs. 9:30–5:30, Fri. 9:30–4:30, Sat. 2–7.*

WHERE TO EAT

$ ✕ **Café Central.** You can dig into a hearty American-style breakfast in the morning and burgers and sandwiches the rest of the day at this diner on the Plaza de Armas. It's most famous around town for its *completos*—Chilean hot dogs topped with gobs of mayo, guacamole, and whatever else you desire. The friendly, bustling staff speaks little English, but if it's clear you're foreign, an English menu is presented to you with great fanfare. ⚏ *Average main: 2500 pesos* ✉ *O'Higgins 610* ☎ *64/225-7711.*

CAFÉ

$$$ BARBECUE Fodor's Choice ★ 🍴 **El Galpón.** This is a good place to eat barbecue, steaks, and chicken (and only that: it's meat only here). There are not a lot of good dining options in Osorno, but this is probably the best. The design intrigues as well, resembling a *galpón,* which means "barn" in English. [$] *Average main: 9500 pesos* ✉ *Lord Cochrane 816* ☎ *64/223–4098* ⌚ *Closed Mon. No dinner Sun.*

WHERE TO STAY

$$ HOTEL 🏨 **Hotel García Hurtado de Mendoza.** Long one of Osorno's better lodgings, this stately hotel built in 1988 is a good option in the center of town, just two blocks from the Plaza de Armas. **Pros:** excellent location; friendly service. **Cons:** hotel restaurant closed on weekends; no gym. [$] *Rooms from: 72000 pesos* ✉ *Juan Mackenna 1040* ☎ *64/223–7111* 🌐 *www.hotelgarciahurtado.cl* 🛏 *31 rooms* 🍽 *Breakfast.*

$$$ HOTEL 🏨 **Hotel Waeger.** In operation for nearly seven decades, this German hotel has seemingly become synonymous with travel to Osorno. **Pros:** best restaurant in town; close to center. **Cons:** classic decor and atmosphere is not for everyone. [$] *Rooms from: 81000 pesos* ✉ *Lord Cochrane 816* ☎ *64/223–3721* 🌐 *www.hotelwaeger.cl* 🛏 *45 rooms* 🍽 *Breakfast.*

$$$ HOTEL Fodor's Choice ★ 🏨 **Sonesta Hotel Osorno.** Until this hotel opened in 2010, Osorno was truly bereft of a modern, high-quality hotel. **Pros:** spacious rooms; high-quality facilities; next to casino and shops. **Cons:** service is sometimes slow. [$] *Rooms from: 103000 pesos* ✉ *Ejercito 395* ☎ *64/255–5000* 🌐 *www.sonesta.com/osorno* 🛏 *106 rooms, 1 suite* 🍽 *Breakfast.*

SHOPPING

Centro de Artesanía Local. Osorno's city government operates this complex of 46 artisan vendors' stands built with steeply sloped roofs. Woodwork, leather, and woolens abound. Prices are fixed but fair. It's open January and February, daily 9 am–10 pm, and March–December, daily 10–8. ✉ *Juan MacKenna at Ramón Freire.*

EN ROUTE

Auto Museum Moncopulli. An Osorno business executive's love for tailfins and V-8 engines led him to establish this auto museum. His particular passion is the little-respected Studebaker, which accounts for 50 of the 80 vehicles on display. Elvis and Buddy Holly bop in the background to put you in the mood. ✉ *Ruta 215, 25 km (16 miles) east of Osorno, Puyehue* ☎ *64/221–0744* 🌐 *www.moncopulli.cl* 🎟 *2,500 pesos* ⌚ *Dec.–Mar., daily 10–8; Apr.–Nov., daily 10–6.*

PARQUE NACIONAL PUYEHUE

81 km (49 miles) east of Osorno, via Ruta 215

One of Chile's most popular national parks, Parque Nacional Puyehue draws crowds who come to bask in its famed hot springs. Most never venture beyond them, and that's a shame. A dozen miles east of the Aguas Calientes sector lies a network of short trails leading to spectacular moonlike volcanic landscapes and evergreen forests with dramatic waterfalls.

GETTING HERE AND AROUND

From Osorno, the park is about 80 km (50 miles) to the east off Highway 215. There are also several buses and travel agencies in Osorno that can help with transport to the park.

EXPLORING

Volcán Puyehue. Truly adventurous types attempt the five-hour hike to the summit of 2,240-meter (7,350-foot) Volcán Puyehue. As with most climbs in this region, CONAF rangers insist on ample documentation of experience before allowing you to set out. Access to the 1,070-square-km (413-square-mile) park is easy; head east from Osorno on the highway leading to Argentina. ✉ *Ruta 215* ☎ *65/248–6101* 🎫 *800 pesos* 🕐 *Dec.–Feb., daily 8 am–9 pm; Apr.–Oct., daily 8–8.*

WHERE TO STAY

$$$$ B&B/INN Fodor's Choice ★ 🏨 **Cantarias Lodge & Spa.** An exclusive boutique lodge on the south shore of Lake Puyehue, Cantarias combines friendly, personalized service and the best restaurant in the region with outdoor excursions like fly-fishing, kayaking, trekking, and skiing. **Pros:** excellent service; superior restaurant; impeccable location. **Cons:** lodge is oriented toward longer stays; often booked solid. [$] *Rooms from: 292262 pesos* ✉ *Km 63.5, Ruta Internacional 215* ☎ *64/261–2320* 🌐 *www.cantarias.com* 🛏 *5 suites* 🍴 *Multiple meal plans.*

$$$ RESORT 🏨 **Termas Aguas Calientes.** The triangular-shape cabins at this hotel are surprisingly well-equipped, with kitchens, Internet, cable TV, and phone. **Pros:** thermal pools; kitchen; cheap option for families or groups. **Cons:** lack of privacy, the other cabins are in close proximity. [$] *Rooms from: 81000 pesos* ✉ *Camino Antillanca, Km 4, Puyehue National Park* ☎ *64/223–6988, 2/2957–0300* 🌐 *www.termasaguascalientes.cl* 🛏 *26 cabins* 🍴 *Breakfast.*

$$$$ RESORT ALL-INCLUSIVE FAMILY 🏨 **Termas Puyehue Wellness and Spa Resort.** This grand stone-and-wood hot springs resort sits on the edge of Parque Nacional Puyehue. **Pros:** near Puyehue Park; thermal pools; all-inclusive. **Cons:** some of the older rooms could benefit from upgrading; pools can get crowded. [$] *Rooms from: 137000 pesos* ✉ *Ruta 215, Km 76, Puyehue* ☎ *64/233–1400, 2/2293–6000 in Santiago* 🌐 *www.puyehue.cl* 🛏 *107 rooms, 16 suites* 🍴 *All-inclusive.*

PUERTO OCTAY

50 km (30 miles) southeast of Osorno, via Ruta 5, Pan-American Hwy.

The story goes that a German merchant named Ochs set up shop in this tidy community on the northern tip of Lago Llanquihue. A phrase uttered by customers looking for a particular item, "*¿Ochs, hay . . . ?*" ("Ochs, do you have . . . ?"), gradually became "Octay." With spectacular views of the Osorno and Calbuco volcanoes, the town was the birthplace of Lake District tourism. A wealthy Santiago businessman constructed a mansion (now the famed Hotel Centinela) outside town in 1912, using it as a vacation home to host his friends.

GETTING HERE AND AROUND

Puerto Octay is easily accessible on paved roads from Ruta 5, the Pan-American Highway. It's about an hour north of Puerto Montt.

WHERE TO EAT AND STAY

$$$$ BARBECUE 🍴 **Rancho Espantapajaros.** Midway between Puerto Octay and Frutillar, this countryside restaurant has an all-you-can eat buffet for 12,000 pesos, which includes the tasty, rarely offered *carne de jabali,* or wild boar meat. But the entire menu is worthy, including homemade integral bread, organic fruits and vegetables, and other meat and chicken dishes done up with regional flavors like quinoa and merquen, plus a plethora of cakes and desserts. You are likely to be stuffed to the gills upon leaving. [$] *Average main: 12000 pesos* ✉ *Quilanto, Km 6* ☎ *65/233–0049* 🌐 *www.espantapajaros.cl* ✍ *Reservations essential* 🕒 *Closed Apr.–Nov. No dinner Mon.–Thurs.*

$$$ B&B/INN FAMILY 🏨 **Hotel Centinela.** Simple and elegant, the venerable 1912 Hotel Centinela has seen better days but remains one of Chile's best-known accommodations. **Pros:** historic; dramatic views. **Cons:** facilities need some TLC; inconsistent service. [$] *Rooms from: 82000 pesos* ✉ *Península de Centinela, 5 km (3 miles) south of Puerto Octay* ☎ *64/239–1326* 🌐 *www.hotelcentinela.cl* 🛏 *11 rooms, 1 suite, 16 cabins* 🍽 *Multiple meal plans.*

$ B&B/INN 🏨 **Zapato Amarillo.** This modern alerce-shingled house with wood-paneled rooms affords a drop-dead gorgeous view of Volcán Osorno outside town. **Pros:** good food; fantastic views. **Cons:** neighbor noise through thin walls. [$] *Rooms from: 34000 pesos* ✉ *Ruta U-55, Km 2.5* ☎ *64/221–0787* 🌐 *www.zapatoamarillo.cl* 🛏 *6 rooms, 4 with bath* 💳 *No credit cards* 🕒 *Closed June–Aug.* 🍽 *Multiple meal plans.*

7

FRUTILLAR

30 km (18 miles) southwest of Puerto Octay.

Halfway down the western edge of Lago Llanquihue lies the small town of Frutillar, a destination for European immigrants in the late 19th century and, today, arguably the most picturesque Lake District community. The town—actually two adjacent hamlets, Frutillar Alto and Frutillar Bajo—is known for its perfectly preserved German architecture. Don't be disappointed if your first sight of the town is the nondescript neighborhood (the Alto) on the top of the hill; head down to the charming streets of Frutillar Bajo that face the lake, with their picture-perfect view of Volcán Osorno. The town has rapidly developed its touristic infrastructure, and it is worth a stop.

GETTING HERE AND AROUND

The town is about 45 minutes north of Puerto Montt, on Ruta 5, the Pan-American Highway. Several bus lines make stops here on Santiago–Puerto Montt routes.

ESSENTIALS

Visitor and Tour Information **Informacion Turistica** ✉ *Costanera Philippi in front of boat dock.* **Secretaria Municipal de Turismo** ✉ *Av. Philippi 753* ☎ *65/242–1685.*

EXPLORING

Fodor's Choice ★ **Museo Colonial Alemán.** Step into the past at one of southern Chile's best museums. Besides displays of 19th-century agricultural and household implements, this open-air museum has full-scale reconstructions of buildings—a smithy and barn, among others—used by the original German settlers. Exhibits at this complex administered by Chile's Universidad Austral are labeled in Spanish and German, but there are also a few signs in English. A short walk from the lake up Avenida Arturo Prat, the museum also has beautifully landscaped grounds and great views of Volcán Osorno. ✉ *Av. Vicente Pérez Rosales at Av. Arturo Prat* ☎ *65/242–1142* 🎟 *1,500 pesos* 🕒 *Dec.–Feb., daily 10–1 and 2–8; Mar.–Nov., daily 10–1 and 2–6.*

WHERE TO EAT

$ CAFÉ 🍴 **Café Capuccini.** Sink into one of the plush couches here and write some postcards while nursing a gourmet coffee. If the couches are taken—they are in demand—grab one of the small tables adorned with a musical-score lampshade. All have astounding lake and volcano views out the curving, sweeping picture window. This café in the Teatro de Lagos serves light fare (sandwiches, küchen, and desserts) throughout the day. It's also possible to purchase some of the art or photos on display in the regular expositions held here. [$] *Average main: 4000 pesos* ✉ *Philippi 1000* ☎ *65/242–2900* 🕒 *Closed Sun.*

$$ GERMAN 🍴 **Club Alemán.** One of the German clubs that dot the Lake District, this is probably the best restaurant in the center of town. Open every day, there is an ample menu, but most regulars opt for one of their four or five rotating prix-fixe menus (just 5,000 pesos on week days). There is always a meat and seafood option—often steak and salmon—with soup, salad, and dessert. Don't forget the *küchen* cake. [$] *Average main: 7000 pesos* ✉ *Philippi 747* ☎ *65/242–1249.*

$$$ CONTEMPORARY Fodor's Choice ★ 🍴 **Se Cocina.** The gourmet meals at Se Cocina, made from fresh local ingredients from the organic garden on-site, are excellent, but it's almost worth coming here for the experience alone. The food is prepared right in front of you at the open kitchen, which is next to the dining room tables. There are big windows with views out to the green hills and the lake, and the fireplace roars in winter. The stoves, one of which is a 1932 brick oven, are constantly in operation. Don't miss the exceptional microbrew made here. This is an event, not just a meal. [$] *Average main: 9500 pesos* ✉ *Camino a Tortal Km 2, sector Quebrada Honda* ☎ *9/8972–8195* ✍ *Reservations essential.*

WHERE TO STAY

$$$ B&B/INN Fodor's Choice ★ 🏨 **Hotel Ayacara.** This attractive yellow-and-green house built at the turn of the 19th century has tasteful design and tremendous views of the lake and Osorno Volcano. **Pros:** historic, remodeled home; views. **Cons:** limited parking. [$] *Rooms from: 86000 pesos* ✉ *Philippi 1215* ☎ *65/242–1550, 2/2430–7000 in Santiago* 🌐 *www.hotelayacara.cl* 🛏 *8 rooms* 🍽 *Breakfast.*

$$$ B&B/INN 🏨 **Hotel Elun.** From just about every vantage point at this hillside lodging just south of town—the lobby, the library, and, of course, the guest rooms—you have a spectacular view of Lago Llanquihue. **Pros:** great views; attentive service. **Cons:** food options are limited. [$] *Rooms from:*

88500 pesos ✉ *Camino Punta Largo, Km 0.2* ☎ *65/242–0055* 🌐 *www.hotelelun.cl* 🛏 *14 rooms, 3 suites* 🍴 *Breakfast.*

$$$ B&B/INN 🏨 **Hotel Frau Holle.** This 1940s German colonial house, remodeled into a boutique hotel, is surrounded by lush gardens and has a privileged location on a hill with stunning views close to the lakeshore and Teatro del Lago. **Pros:** excellent service; attention to detail. **Cons:** slightly more expensive than other similar boutique hotels in the area. [$] *Rooms from: 105000 pesos* ✉ *Antonio Varas 54* ☎ *65/242–1345* 🌐 *frauholle-frutillar.cl* 🛏 *7 rooms, 2 apartments* 🍴 *Multiple meal plans.*

$$$ B&B/INN 🏨 **Hotel Serenade de Franz Schubert.** The names of the guest rooms here reflect musical compositions—like Fantasia and Wedding March—and each door is painted with the first few sheet-music bars of the work it's named for. **Pros:** quiet, historic home; good breakfasts. **Cons:** rooms have an old, formal decor. [$] *Rooms from: 100000 pesos* ✉ *Pedro Aguirre Cerda 50* ☎ *65/242–0332* 🌐 *www.hotelserenade.cl* 🛏 *6 rooms* 🍴 *Breakfast.*

$$ B&B/INN 🏨 **Playa Maqui Lodge.** In the countryside, this excellent lodging combines quiet nights, great views, and private access to a lakeside beach. **Pros:** secluded location with private lake front; excellent rooms; great service. **Cons:** off the beaten track; you may feel isolated without your own vehicle. [$] *Rooms from: 59000 pesos* ✉ *Km 6, Ruta V155* ☎ *65/233–0000* 🌐 *www.playamaqui.cl* 🛏 *7 rooms, 2 apartments* 🍴 *Multiple meal plans.*

$$ B&B/INN 🏨 **Salzburg Hotel & Spa.** Rooms at this Tyrolean-style lodge command excellent views of the lake. **Pros:** great view; spa; brewery on-site. **Cons:** no TV in rooms. [$] *Rooms from: 59000 pesos* ✉ *Costanera Norte* ☎ *65/242–1589* 🌐 *www.salzburg.cl* 🛏 *31 rooms, 9 cabins, 5 bungalows* 🍴 *Breakfast.*

PERFORMING ARTS

Semanas Musicales de Frutillar. Each year, in late January and early February, the town hosts an excellent series of mostly classical concerts (and a little jazz) at Teatro del Lago and the lakeside Centro de Conciertos y Eventos, a semi-outdoor venue. Ticket prices are a reasonable 8,000 pesos. ✉ *Av. Philippi 777* ☎ *65/242–1290* 🌐 *www.semanasmusicales.cl.*

Fodor's Choice ★ **Teatro del Lago.** Culture in Frutillar, and the southern Lake District in general, nowadays follows the lead of Teatro del Lago, which hosts a year-round schedule of concerts, art shows, and film. Events take place every week. The building itself is state-of-the-art, and worth a look when walking along the lakefront in Frutillar. ✉ *Av. Philippi 1000* ☎ *65/242–2954* 🌐 *www.teatrodellago.cl.*

SPORTS AND THE OUTDOORS

Playa Frutillar. Packed with summer crowds, the gray-sand Playa Frutillar stretches for 15 blocks along Avenida Philippi. From this point along Lago Llanquihue you have a spectacular view due east of the conical Volcán Osorno, as well as the lopsided Volcán Puntiagudo.

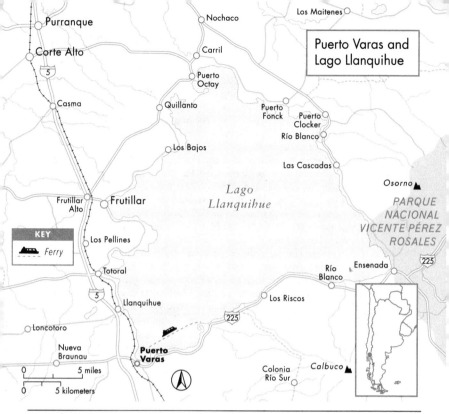

Puerto Varas and
Lago Llanquihue

Los Maitenes

Nochaco

Purranque

Corte Alto

5

Carril

Casma

Puerto
Octay

Quillanto

Puerto
Fonck

Puerto
Clocker

Río Blanco

Los Bajos

Las Cascadas

Osorno

*Lago
Llanquihue*

PARQUE
NACIONAL
VICENTE PÉREZ
ROSALES

Frutillar
Alto

Frutillar

KEY

Los Pellines

Ferry

Totoral

Río
Blanco

Ensenada

225

5

Llanquihue

Los Riscos

225

0   5 miles

Loncotoro

Nueva
Braunau

**Puerto
Varas**

Colonia
Río Sur

Calbuco

0   5 kilometers

PUERTO VARAS

Fodor's Choice   *27 km (16 miles) south of Frutillar via Ruta 5, Pan-American Hwy.*

★   A fast-growing resort town on the edge of Lago Llanquihue, Puerto
Varas is renowned for its view of both the Osorno and Calbuco volcanoes. Stunning rose arbors and Germanic-style architecture grace the
many centuries-old houses and churches that dot this tranquil town.
Well-situated, it's not far to Chiloé, Puerto Montt, Vicente Pérez Rosales
National Park, Cochamó, and other regional hot spots. With literally
dozens of big hotels and smaller B&Bs added in recent years, as well as
several cafés and trendy restaurants, a modern casino, and an interesting bar scene, the town is now an honest rival to Pucón as the region's
top vacation spot.

GETTING HERE AND AROUND

Puerto Varas is only about a 20-minute drive from the center of nearby
Puerto Montt. You can get to the Puerto Montt airport via a 40-minute
drive south on Ruta 5. Most of the bus lines that serve Puerto Montt
make obligatory stops in Puerto Varas on their way north or south.
Around town, there are numerous taxis and several minivan buses,
which make several stops, the most prominent being on Avenida Salvador near the corner of Santa Rosa. Both taxis and buses can take

you to countryside locations such as Ensenada and Puerto Montt for a minimal cost. You can cross to Argentina via bus or boat.

ESSENTIALS

Bus Contacts Buses JAC ⊠ *Walker Martínez 227* ☎ *65/238–800* ⊕ *www.jac.cl.* **Cruz del Sur** ⊠ *San Francisco 1317* ☎ *65/223–6969* ⊕ *www.busescruzdelsur.cl.* **Tur-Bus** ⊠ *Palguín 383, Pucón* ☎ *45/244–3564* ⊕ *www.turbus.cl.*

Rental Car Contacts Hunter Rent-a-Car ⊠ *San José 130* ☎ *65/223–7950.*

Visitor and Tour Information Casa del Turista ⊠ *Piedra Plen, in front of Plaza de Armas* ☎ *65/223–7956.* **Oficina de Turismo** ⊠ *San Francisco 441* ☎ *65/223-2437.*

WHERE TO EAT

$ ✕ **Café Danes.** This friendly café-restaurant next to Santa Isabel Super-
CHILEAN market on Puerto Varas's main drag, Calle del Salvador, serves a set lunch menu and a range of plates in the Chilean way, from sandwiches to beef and chicken dishes. The large beef and vegetarian empanadas and the illustrious *küchen* cakes are not to be missed. $ *Average main: 5000 pesos* ⊠ *Del Salvador 441* ☎ *65/223–2371.*

$$$ ✕ **Casa Valdes.** Start your dinner off right with a pisco sour at this
SEAFOOD relaxed, lakeside seafood restaurant. Better yet, sit at a table outside on
Fodor's Choice the terrace. The ambience here is near perfect. This restaurant is mostly
★ known for its seafood, but there are several other options on the menu. The cooking style is influenced in part by Basque cuisine, with its fish and other plates often accompanied by peppers, beans, and potatoes. The restaurant fills up fast for dinner, so patience with servers is often needed. Come early or reserve a table ahead of time. $ *Average main: 9000 pesos* ⊠ *Santa Rosa 040* ☎ *9/9079–3938* ☼ *Closed Sun.*

$$$ ✕ **La Marca.** For quality steaks, this is the top spot in town. Located just
STEAKHOUSE up the hill from the town plaza, service is attentive and the portions just right. The menu has a variety of other dishes, but the main draw is the *parrilla*-style grilled meats. Start it all off with a pisco sour and *sopaipillas*, a sort of sweet fried bread, before moving on to the *bife chorizo* or *lomo vetado*—both are tasty cuts of meat. $ *Average main: 10000 pesos* ⊠ *Santa Rosa 539* ☎ *65/223–2026* ⊕ *www.lamarca.cl.*

$$ ✕ **La Olla.** This Puerto Varas institution serves the best fish in Chile,
SEAFOOD according to its legion of fans. The specialties of the house also include a variety of seafood plates, empanadas, and Chilean-style beef dishes. The restaurant, located just past Puerto Chico at the beginning of the Camino Ensenada road, is big, with two dining rooms. Still, on weekends, it's almost always full during peak hours, so reserve a table ahead of time. $ *Average main: 8500 pesos* ⊠ *R-225, Km 1 (Camino a Ensenada)* ☎ *65/223–4605* ⊕ *www.laolla.cl.*

$$$$ ✕ **Mercado 605.** This is Puerto Varas's best fine-dining restaurant, serv-
INTERNATIONAL ing gourmet cuisine best described as international fusion that uses
Fodor's Choice local ingredients. The presentation of the food is beautiful; there is a
★ pleasant ambience; and the service is friendly. This is both a place to eat lightly from a wide selection of appetizers and tapas, or choose a main course served in generous portions like ravioli stuffed with boar meat or red wine braised short ribs. For wine lovers, there is a store on-site, so choose your favorite and uncork it at the table. $ *Average main:*

7

11500 pesos ✉ Imperial 605 ☎ 65/223–1980 🌐 www.mercado605.cl ⏲ Closed Sun. No lunch.

WHERE TO STAY

$$ B&B/INN 🏨 **Estancia 440.** In a beautiful, restored German colonial mansion less than a 10-minute walk from downtown Puerto Varas, this B&B pays close attention to detail throughout. **Pros:** ambience; restored home; clean and comfortable. **Cons:** in a residential area; the street is not the most attractive. [$] *Rooms from: 70000 pesos ✉ Decher 440 ☎ 65/223–3921 🌐 www.estancia440.cl 🛏 7 rooms 🍴 Breakfast.*

$$ B&B/INN 🏨 **The Guest House.** In a restored 1926 mansion just a couple of blocks from downtown, period furnishings and antiques fill the cheery rooms here. **Pros:** southern Chile character; excellent breakfasts; comfortable rooms. **Cons:** street noise. [$] *Rooms from: 59000 pesos ✉ O'Higgins 608 ☎ 65/223–1521 🌐 www.theguesthouse.cl 🛏 10 rooms 🍴 Breakfast.*

$$$ HOTEL FAMILY Fodor's Choice ★ 🏨 **Hotel Cabañas del Lago.** Encompassing a large swath of the western end of the Puerto Varas waterfront, this is the biggest hotel in the city and has an unparalleled proximity to the lake. **Pros:** great views; close to the lake; diverse services. **Cons:** some rooms in the older wing are smallish. [$] *Rooms from: 90000 pesos ✉ Luis Wellmann 195 ☎ 65/220–0100 🌐 www.hotelcabanadellago.cl 🛏 157 rooms, 19 suites 🍴 Breakfast.*

$$$$ HOTEL 🏨 **Hotel Dreams de Los Volcanes.** In the center of town next to the casino, this hotel has exceptional rooms with all the latest amenities including iPod docking stations. **Pros:** lake views; spa and pool; downtown location. **Cons:** casino environment. [$] *Rooms from: 109000 pesos ✉ Del Salvador 21 ☎ 65/249–2000 🛏 50 rooms, 4 suites 🍴 Breakfast.*

$$$$ HOTEL 🏨 **Hotel Patagónico.** This relaxing, comfortable hotel has a privileged location close to downtown with commanding views of the lake and volcanoes. **Pros:** spacious rooms; tranquil location. **Cons:** service is inconsistent; some rooms lack lake views. [$] *Rooms from: 106000 pesos ✉ Klenner 349 ☎ 65/220–1000 🌐 www.hotelpatagonico.cl 🛏 91 rooms, 2 suites 🍴 Breakfast.*

$$$ HOTEL 🏨 **Hotel Puelche.** The exterior of this quiet, laid-back hotel resembles a mix of hotel and mountain lodge, which is apt because Puelche combines a large hotel's amenities and services with the more intimate feel and personalized attention seen in a mountain lodge. **Pros:** lovely ambience; excellent service. **Cons:** no gym. [$] *Rooms from: 85000 pesos ✉ Imperial 695 ☎ 65/223–3600 🌐 www.hotelpuelche.com 🛏 21 rooms 🍴 Breakfast.*

$$$ B&B/INN Fodor's Choice ★ 🏨 **Los Caiquenes Hotel Boutique.** This high-end boutique hotel on the shore of Lake Llanquihue is just outside of Puerto Varas. **Pros:** maximum comfort; big, luxurious rooms; lakeside location. **Cons:** hotel is on the outskirts of town. [$] *Rooms from: 105000 pesos ✉ Camino Ensenada, Km 9.5 ☎ 9/8159–0489 🌐 www.hotelloscaiquenes.cl 🛏 8 suites ⏲ Closed June 🍴 Breakfast.*

NIGHTLIFE

Puerto Varas has a diverse array of bars and clubs scattered through the downtown area and the Costanera waterfront.

Bravo Cabrera. This lively bar-restaurant packs a nice local crowd most nights, with music from the 1980s and 1990s getting louder as the night goes on. But do not underestimate the excellent restaurant here as well. The pizzas are the most popular choice by the locals, but the menu also includes soups, salads, sandwiches, ribs, pasta, and more—all for a reasonable price. ⊠ *Vicente Perez Rosales 1071* ☎ *65/223-3441* ⊕ *www.bravocabrera.cl.*

Casino Dreams Puerto Varas. The flashy Casino Dreams Puerto Varas has the most prestigous address in town, facing the center of the waterfront. For a small town casino, it's actually a modern, well-done place, with all the Vegas-style trappings, from slot machines to roulette, along with a restaurant, bar, weekly music, comedy, and other entertainment. ⊠ *Del Salvador 21* ☎ *65/249-2000.*

Club Orquidea. Near the center of town, this is the trendiest nightlife spot in Puerto Varas, with drinks constantly flowing at the long bar, two outdoor seating areas for smokers, karaoke or live music on most evenings, and good pizza and bar food. ⊠ *San Pedro 537.*

La Buena Vida Bistró. Most nights, this club has the best live music in town, with jazz, blues, rock, and Latin music. There's also acceptable international cuisine on tap. In summer, take your drink on their outdoor terrace overlooking Lake Llanquihue. ⊠ *Vicente Perez Rosales 1290* ☎ *9/9700-8842.*

SPORTS AND THE OUTDOORS

Puerto Varas has a plethora of outdoor options. Fly-fishing is prominent in the region, with many rivers and the huge Lago Llanquihue making attractive targets. The region has still more to offer, including mountain biking, canyoning, wind surfing, sailing, hiking in Vicente Pérez Rosales Park, or just enjoying the lake by kayak. You can also hike up the nearby volcanoes. With so much attractive nature in its backyard, it's no wonder Puerto Varas has become a global destination for outdoor-adventure enthusiasts.

BIRD-WATCHING

Birds Chile. Go on bird-watching excursions throughout the Lake District with Birds Chile. ⊠ *Santa Rosa 131* ☎ *9/9235-4818* ⊕ *www.birdschile.com* ⊠ *From 18,000 pesos.*

FLY-FISHING

Saltos del Maullín. Go exclusive fly-fishing on the Maullín River, located about 24 km (15 miles) outside of Puerto Varas. Take lessons, go boating on the river, take a guided hike in the nearby forest, and enjoy a Patagonian barbecue. ⊠ *Fundo la Isla, Rio Maullín, Nueva Branau* ☎ *9/9325-9490* ⊕ *www.saltosdelmaullin.cl* ⊠ *From 160,000 pesos.*

Tres Piedras. This longtime fly-fishing agency in Puerto Varas organizes day- and multiday trips at nearby lakes and rivers. ☎ *65/233-0157, 9/7618-7826* ⊕ *www.trespiedras.cl* ⊠ *From 150,000 pesos.*

MULTISPORT OPERATORS

Al Sur Expediciones. This operator runs a variety of excursions in Puerto Varas and the Lake District, including sea kayaking, trekking, and rafting. ⊠ *Aconcagua 8* ☎ *65/223-2300* ⊕ *www.alsurexpeditions.com* ⊠ *From 32,000 pesos.*

Chile Backcountry. Ski, snowboard, and mountain bike on trips to Osorno Volcano and other areas around Puerto Varas and the Lake District. The ski tours are especially noteworthy. ☎ *9/9458–3722* 🌐 *www.chilebackcountry.com* 🎫 *From 60,000 pesos.*

Miralejos. This operator organizes trekking, kayaking, mountaineering, and horseback-riding trips in both Cochamó and Puelo. ✉ *San Pedro 311, Puerto Varas* ☎ *65/223–4892* 🌐 *www.miralejos.cl* 🎫 *From 85,000 pesos.*

TREKKING

Huella Andina Expeditions. These experts guide excursions to the major volcanoes of southern Chile, including trekking to the summit of Osorno Volcano. ☎ *9/7548–7967* 🌐 *www.huellandina.com* 🎫 *From 165,000 pesos.*

ENSENADA

47 km (28 miles) east of Puerto Varas.

A drive along the southern shore of Lago Llanquihue to Ensenada takes you through the heart of Chile's *murta*-growing country. Queen Victoria is said to have developed a fondness for these tart red berries, and today you find them used as ingredients in syrups, jams, and küchen. Frutillar, Puerto Varas, and Puerto Octay might all boast about their views of Volcán Osorno, but you can really feel up close and personal with the volcano when you arrive in the town of Ensenada, which also neighbors the jagged Volcán Calbuca. The lake drive to Ensenada is also without doubt one of the prettiest in southern Chile.

GETTING HERE AND AROUND

By car, it's a beautiful scenic ride about 48 km (30 miles) east of Puerto Varas on the Camino Ensenada. In Puerto Varas, a regular, hourly minibus (until 9 pm) also provides transport to Ensenada.

WHERE TO EAT AND STAY

$$$ CAFÉ Fodor'sChoice ★ 🍴 **Onces Bellavista.** If traveling by car near Ensenada in the late afternoon on a weekend, be sure to stop here. From 4 pm to 8 pm, they serve *onces,* which is a sort of Chilean teatime. For 9,200 pesos you get great küchen, cake, bread, cheese, salami, coffee, tea, chocolate, and more. A panoramic view of the volcanoes and lake provides the backdrop. There is also a mini-zoo with animals such as llamas and guanaco, a tennis court, and private lakeside beach. Six well-equipped cabins are available if you want to stay overnight. In summer, onces are served every day, but the rest of the year only on weekends and holidays. [$] *Average main: 9200 pesos* ✉ *Km 34, Camino Ensenada* ☎ *65/233–5323* 🌐 *www.oncesbellavista.cl* 💳 *No credit cards.*

$ B&B/INN 🏨 **Casa Ko.** This B&B has friendly, warm hosts from France, who make fantastic breakfasts and meals and provide exceptional service. **Pros:** friendly hosts; good breakfast; volcano views. **Cons:** vehicle required to get here; some rooms do not have private bath. [$] *Rooms from: 35000 pesos* ✉ *Km 37, Camino Ensenada* ☎ *9/7703–6477* 🌐 *www.casako.com* 🛏 *6 rooms, 1 cabin* 🍽 *Multiple meal plans.*

$$$$ 🛏 **Yan Kee Way Lodge.** This luxury lodge is tucked up close to Lake
HOTEL Llanquihue and Osorno Volcano. **Pros:** excellent restaurant; spacious
suites; near volcano and park. **Cons:** an hour drive from Puerto Varas.
$ *Rooms from: 205000 pesos* ✉ *Km 42, Camino Ensenada* ☎ *866/881–*
9215, 65/221-2030 ⊕ *www.southernchilexp.com* 🛏 *19 rooms, 13*
suites 🍽 *Breakfast.*

PARQUE NACIONAL VICENTE PÉREZ ROSALES

3 km (2 miles) east of Ensenada.

GETTING HERE AND AROUND
Take a one-hour drive along Ruta 224, Camino a Ensenada, from
Puerto Varas. Several agencies in Puerto Varas run guided trips and
transport to the park.

EXPLORING
Parque Nacional Vicente Pérez Rosales. Chile's oldest national park
was established in 1926. South of Parque Nacional Puyehue, the
2,538-square-km (980-square-mile) preserve includes the Osorno and
lesser-known Puntiagudo volcanoes, as well as the deep-blue Lago
Todos los Santos. The Volcán Osorno appears in your car window soon
after you drive south from Osorno and doesn't disappear until shortly
before your arrival in Puerto Montt. (The almost-perfectly conical volcano has been featured in a Samsung television commercial shown in
the United States.) The visitor center opposite the Hotel Petrohué provides access to some fairly easy hikes. The Rincón del Osorno trail
hugs the lake; the Saltos de Petrohué trail runs parallel to the river of
the same name. Rudimentary campsites are available for 10,000 pesos
per person. ☎ *65/248–6101* 🎟 *1,500 pesos* ☉ *Dec.–Feb., daily 9–8;*
Mar.–Nov., daily 9–6.

WHERE TO STAY
$$$$ 🛏 **Petrohué Lodge.** The common areas in this rustic orange chalet have
B&B/INN vaulted ceilings and huge fireplaces. **Pros:** inside Vicente Pérez Rosales
Park; organized outdoor excursions. **Cons:** room furniture outdated;
pool not heated. $ *Rooms from: 157080 pesos* ✉ *Parque Nacional*
Vicente Perez Rosales, Petrohue ☎ *65/221-2025* ⊕ *www.petrohue.com*
🛏 *20 rooms, 4 cabins* 🍽 *Multiple meal plans.*

SPORTS AND THE OUTDOORS
Canopy Chile. Make like Tarzan and swing through the treetops in the
shadow of Volcán Osorno with Canopy Chile. A helmet, a very secure
harness, 2 km (1 mile) of zip line strung out over 12 platforms (the
second-longest in South America), and experienced guides give you
a bird's-eye view of the forest below. ✉ *Ruta U99-V, Camino Casca-*
das Km 60, Cascadas ☎ *9/6333–8293* ⊕ *www.canopychile.cl* 🎟 *From*
27,000 pesos.

Cruce Andino. This all-day crossing of the spectacular Andean mountain lakes between Puerto Varas and Bariloche is the classic trip of
the area and worth doing. It leaves out of Lake Todos Los Santos in
Vicente Perez Rosales National Park at 10 am every day. There is a stop
for lunch at an island lake called Peulla before eventually arriving in

7

Bariloche at around 9 pm. The operator can also pick you up at your hotel if in Puerto Varas or Bariloche. ⊠ *Del Salvador 72, Puerto Varas* 🕾 *65/243–7127* ⊕ *www.cruceandino.com* ✉ *From 165,000 pesos.*

Ski & Outdoor Volcán Osorno. About 60 km (37 miles) from Puerto Varas, Volcán Osorno is the setting for entertaining skiing with breathtaking vistas of the Lake District. The Ski & Outdoor Center on the volcano has two ski lifts, 12 ski trails with varied levels of difficulty, and a store which rents equipment and provides ski and snowboard lessons. The Mirador restaurant has a hot lunch and coffee. Daily ski passes are 24,000 pesos on weekends and 17,000 on weekdays. In summer, the volcano is a great spot for hiking and mountain biking. ⊠ *Volcán Osorno, Puerto Varas* 🕾 *65/223–3445, 9/6679–2284* ⊕ *www.volcan osorno.com.*

PUERTO MONTT

20 km (12 miles) south of Puerto Varas via Ruta 5, Pan-American Hwy.

For most of its history, windy Puerto Montt was the end of the line for just about everyone traveling in the Lake District. Now the Carretera Austral carries on southward, but for all intents and purposes Puerto Montt remains the region's last significant outpost, a provincial city that is the hub of local fishing, textile, and tourist activity.

Today the city center is full of malls, condos, and office towers—it's the fastest-growing city in Chile—but away from downtown, Puerto Montt consists mainly of low clapboard houses perched above its bay, the Seno de Reloncaví. If it's a sunny day, head east to Playa Pelluco or one of the city's other beaches. If you're more interested in exploring the countryside, drive along the shore for a good view of the surrounding hills.

GETTING HERE AND AROUND

Puerto Montt is a main transit hub in the region. Buses from Santiago and all points in southern Chile ramble through here at some point, while many cruise ships dock at the port. Puerto Montt's El Tepual Airport has daily air traffic from all the major airlines that serve Chile. The Pan-American Highway also stops here, while the mostly unpaved Carretera Austral, which winds it ways through Chilean Patagonia, begins south of the city. To cross over into Argentina by boat, buses leave from here and from Puerto Varas. Chiloé Island is less than two hours' drive from Puerto Montt. Take the last part of Ruta 5, or the Pan-American Highway, to Pargua, where two ferries cross the Chacao Channel every hour.

CRUISE TRAVEL TO PUERTO MONTT

The many large cruise ships that arrive to the public port of Puerto Montt, the most important in southern Chile, must anchor offshore and use smaller tender boats to carry passengers to the dock. The port is located at the western end of the city at Caleta Angelmo, which conveniently for travelers is also the best place to shop for local handicrafts and try local seafood in numerous small restaurants at the tail end of the waterfront.

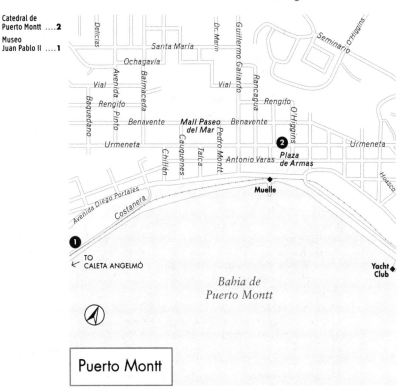

Catedral de
Puerto Montt **2**

Museo
Juan Pablo II **1**

Puerto Montt

Downtown Puerto Montt, where all the malls, office buildings, and hubbub is located, is about 9 blocks, or one mile away. You can walk there in about 20 minutes or so, but buses or cheap taxis (usually about 1,500 pesos per person) are prevalent near the port and can whisk you to the city center within minutes. Moreover, many of the taxis and local tour operators are often waiting at the port to offer you deals on day trips in the city or nearby tourism destinations like Puerto Varas, Volcan Osorno, and Frutillar.

ESSENTIALS

Bus Contacts Cruz del Sur ⊠ *Av. Diego Portales* ☎ *65/225-4731* ⊕ *www. busescruzdelsur.cl/.* **Puerto Montt Bus Depot** ⊠ *Av. Diego Portales* ☎ *65/228-3000.* **Tur-Bus** ⊠ *Del Salvador 1093, Puerto Varas* ☎ *65/223-2678* ⊕ *www. turbus.cl.*

Rental Car Contacts Avis ⊠ *Diego Portales 701, Oficina 2* ☎ *65/2367-840* ⊕ *avis.cl* ⊠ *Airport, El Tepual* ☎ *65/225-6668* ⊕ *www.avis.cl.* **Hertz** ⊠ *Calle de Servicio 1431, Parque Industrial Tyrol* ☎ *65/226-8944* ⊕ *https://www.hertz.cl* ⊠ *Airport, El Tepual* ☎ *65/226-8944* ⊕ *www.hertz.cl.*

Visitor and Tour Information Puerto Montt Tourist Office ⊠ *Plaza de Armas* ☎ *65/226-1823.* **Sernatur** ⊠ *Bernardo O'Higgins 667, Osorno* ☎ *64/223-7575* ⊕ *www.sernatur.cl.*

EXPLORING

Beaches at Maullín. About 70 km (43 miles) southwest of Puerto Montt, at this small town near Pargua—the ferry crossing to Chiloé—the Maullín River merges with the Pacific Ocean in spectacular fashion. Be sure to visit the expansive Pangal Beach, with large sand dunes teeming with birds. If staying overnight, there are cabins and a campground. ⊠ *Ruta 5 south from Puerto Montt, about a 1-hr drive.*

Fodor's Choice ★ **Caleta Angelmó.** About 3 km (2 miles) west of downtown along the coastal road lies Puerto Montt's fishing cove. This busy port serves small fishing boats, large ferries, and cruisers carrying travelers and cargo southward through the straits and fjords that form much of Chile's shoreline. On weekdays, small launches from Isla Tenglo and other outlying islands arrive early in the morning and leave late in the afternoon. The fish market here has one of the most varied selections of seafood in all Chile.

Catedral de Puerto Montt. Latin America's ornate church architecture is nowhere to be found in the Lake District. More typical of the region is Puerto Montt's stark 1856 Catedral. The alerce-wood structure, modeled on the Pantheon in Paris, is the city's oldest surviving building. ⊠ *Plaza de Armas* ☉ *Mass: Mon.–Sat. noon and 7 pm; Sun. 8:30, 10, and noon.*

Museo Juan Pablo II. This museum, east of the city's bus terminal, has a collection of crafts and relics from the nearby archipelago of Chiloé. Historical photos of Puerto Montt give a sense of the area's slow and often difficult growth, plus the impact of the 1960 earthquake, which virtually destroyed the port. Pope John Paul II celebrated Mass on the grounds during his 1987 visit. One exhibit documents the event. ⊠ *Av. Diego Portales 991* ☎ *65/222–3029* ⊠ *Free* ☉ *Weekdays, 9–7, weekends 10–6.*

OFF THE BEATEN PATH **Parque Nacional Alerce Andino.** Barely a stone's throw from Cochamó, the mountainous 398-square-km (154-square-mile) Parque Nacional Alerce Andino, with more than 40 small lakes, was established to protect some 20,000 endangered alerce trees. Comparable to California's hardy sequoia, alerce grow to average heights of 40 meters (130 feet) and can reach 4 meters (13 feet) in diameter. Immensely popular as a building material for houses in southern Chile, they are quickly disappearing from the landscape. Many of these are 3,000 to 4,000 years old. ⊠ *Carretera Austral, 35 km (21 miles) east of Puerto Montt* ☎ *65/248–6401* ⊠ *2,000 pesos* ☉ *Daily 9–6.*

WHERE TO EAT

$$ ITALIAN ✕ **Azzurro.** This great Italian restaurant serves mouthwatering pizzas and pasta, but also on the menu are some beef and fish plates if you prefer something else. The restaurant is housed in a modest blue building, with a rustic wooden interior and informal atmosphere. $ *Average main: 7000 pesos* ⊠ *Liborio Guerrero 1769, Balneario Pelluco* ☎ *65/231–8989* ⊕ *www.azzurro.cl* ☉ *No dinner Sun.*

$ CAFÉ ✕ **Café Haussmann.** Its pale-wood and chrome decor might make this place seem trendy, but this restaurant is actually a classic Germanic dining spot in southern Chile, with great sandwiches and light meals of crudos, cakes, and küchen. [$] *Average main: 4950 pesos* ✉ *San Martín 185* ☎ *65/229–3390* 🌐 *www.haussmann.cl* ⏲ *Closed Sun.*

$ CHILEAN 🍴 **Caleta Angelmó.** More than a dozen small kitchens and eateries at this enclosed market 3 km (2 miles) west of Puerto Montt along the coast road prepare southern Chilean seafood favorites like *curanto,* a potpourri of shellfish, meat, and potatoes, and *paila marina,* a hearty seafood stew with mainly shellfish. Each kitchen has separate tables and counters. Don't expect set hours, but most open around 11 am for lunch and serve for about three hours. Every day in the January to March high season, they reopen 6–9 pm for dinner. The rest of the year, most of the kitchens close some days of the week. In the same complex is a colorful fish market and stores selling local handicrafts. [$] *Average main: 3500 pesos* ✉ *Caleta Angelmó* 💳 *No credit cards.*

$$$ STEAKHOUSE Fodor's Choice ★ 🍴 **Cotelé.** This is a top steak house not just for Puerto Montt, but for Chile. On a hill overlooking the Puerto Montt bay, it has the look and feel of a typical *quincho,* with wooden walls and tables with the grill in the middle. Here, it is strictly about meticulously preparing the best possible steaks. The waiter takes your order by showing you cuts of raw meat and asking you to choose from either a tender fillet, sirloin, or rib-eye steak. While you munch on a delicious *sopaipillas con pebre* (fried bread) and sip your pisco sour or red wine, the meat is cooked on a grill in front of you and then served with salad and potatoes. The result is a steak of world-class distinction, and indeed a restaurant that has built a legion of fans the world over. [$] *Average main: 9000 pesos* ✉ *Juan Soler Manfredini 1661* ☎ *65/227–8000* 🌐 *www.cotele.cl* ✍ *Reservations essential* ⏲ *Closed Sun.*

7

$$$ STEAKHOUSE 🍴 **El Fogón de Pepe.** If you need a change of pace from the ubiquitous seafood in Puerto Montt, this is a great option. Roast beef plates, roasted ribs, chicken, and steaks are all exquisite. Service is friendly, but be aware that it is normally packed on weekends. [$] *Average main: 10000 pesos* ✉ *Rengifo 845* ☎ *65/227–1527* ⏲ *Closed Sun. No lunch Sat.*

$$$ SEAFOOD 🍴 **Restaurant Kiel.** Hospitable German-born proprietor Helga Birkir stands guard at this Chilean-Teutonic seafood restaurant on the coast about 15 minutes west of Puerto Montt. Helga serves a little bit of everything, but it's her curanto that draws crowds. Fresh produce from her well-kept garden makes lunch here a delight. [$] *Average main: 9000 pesos* ✉ *Camino Chinquihue, Km 8, Chinquihue* ☎ *65/225–5010* ⏲ *No dinner Sun.*

$ CAFÉ 🍴 **Sanito.** "Simple, tasty, ready" is the motto of this lively eatery with a menu that emphasizes healthy salads and sandwiches in addition to great coffee. The ambience is hip and trendy, with the latest, greatest music on display. Take note that lunchtime fills up with workers. Feel free to ask for delivery to your hotel. [$] *Average main: 4000 pesos* ✉ *Copiapó 66* ☎ *65/225–9032* 🌐 *www.sanito.cl* ⏲ *Closed weekends.*

WHERE TO STAY

$$ HOTEL 🏨 **Holiday Inn Express.** Stunning views of Puerto Montt Bay and the city make this place an excellent choice. **Pros:** amazing views; walking distance to city center. **Cons:** few extras like a pool. [$] *Rooms from: 73000 pesos* ✉ *Av. Costanera, above Mall Paseo Costanera* ☎ *65/256–6000* 🌐 *www.holidayinnexpress.cl* 🛏 *105 rooms* 🍽 *Breakfast.*

$ HOTEL **Hotel Central.** Close to the bus station, this is a good, low-priced option for a night or two in Puerto Montt. **Pros:** excellent service; cheap; central location. **Cons:** decor is old-fashioned. [$] *Rooms from: 40000 pesos* ✉ *Juan José Mira 1092* ☎ *65/225–7516* 🌐 *www.hotelcentral.cl* 🛏 *29 rooms* 🍴 *Breakfast.*

$$$ HOTEL **Hotel Don Luis.** In an excellent location down the street from the cathedral and city plaza and near the big shopping mall in town, this hotel also boasts many rooms with panoramic vistas of Reloncaví Sound. **Pros:** central location; breakfast; helpful staff. **Cons:** slightly expensive compared to similar hotels in the city. [$] *Rooms from: 82000 pesos* ✉ *Urmeneta at Quillota* ☎ *65/225–9001* 🌐 *www.hoteldonluis.cl* 🛏 *60 rooms, 1 suite* 🍴 *Breakfast.*

$$ HOTEL **Manquehue Hotel Puerto Montt.** Mainly set up to be the premier business hotel in Puerto Montt, this hotel goes above and beyond by offering travelers good value and comfort. **Pros:** value for cost; pool; safer part of town. **Cons:** outside of the city center. [$] *Rooms from: 64000 pesos* ✉ *Seminario 252* ☎ *65/233–1000* 🌐 *www.hotelpuertomont.cl* 🛏 *142 rooms, 2 suites* 🍴 *Breakfast.*

NIGHTLIFE AND PERFORMING ARTS

NIGHTLIFE

Puerto Montt is a big city with a bustling nightlife. Most of the better bars and discos are in Pelluco or the Rengifo neighborhood. If you do venture out late at night, be careful where you walk, as the city's growth in size has fueled a growth in street crime.

Boulebar. This is a fun bar in the city center for music, tapas, and drinks. There's a second, more modern branch at Rengifo 920. ✉ *Benavente 435, 2nd fl.* ☎ *65/234–8973* 🌐 *www.boulebar.cl.*

Souk Multiespacio. This music club and discotheque at Balneario Pelluco often hosts national performing artists and big crowds. ✉ *Las Toninas 2011 (Balneario Pelluco)* ☎ *9/7683–7712.*

Taytao. This longtime bar and disco at Pelluco beach is a lively night spot, with four dance floors, six rooms, karaoke, a restaurant, and live music. ✉ *Juan Soler Manfredini* ☎ *65/225–1818.*

PERFORMING ARTS

Casa del Arte Diego Rivera. A gift of the government of Mexico, this art center commemorates the famed muralist of the same name. It hosts art exhibitions in the gallery, as well as evening theater productions and occasional music and film festivals. ✉ *Quillota 116* ☎ *65/248–2638.*

SHOPPING

Feria Artesanal Angelmó. An excellent selection of handicrafts is sold at the best prices in the country at the Feria Artesanal Angelmó, on the coastal road near Caleta Angelmó. Chileans know there's a better selection of crafts from Chiloé for sale here than in Chiloé itself. Baskets, ponchos, figures woven from different kinds of grasses and straw, and warm sweaters of raw, hand-spun, and hand-dyed wool are all for sale. Much of the merchandise is geared toward tourists, so look carefully for more authentic offerings. Haggling is expected. It's open daily 9–dusk.

COCHAMÓ

94 km (59 miles) southwest of Puerto Varas via Ruta 225, Camino a Ensenada, following the signs south to Ralun, which is 15 km (9 miles) north of Cochamó.

The small fishing villages of Cochamó are blessed with friendly people but little infrastructure. Only a few farms dot the countryside. In short, nature with a capital "N" is the real reason to come here. Civilization has barely touched these great, vast nature areas, some of Chile's (and the world's) last. Think of Yosemite National Park in California without the crowds. Granite walls and domes are prevalent throughout the valley. At Río Puelo, the emerald-blue water seems like a dream amid the rare, ancient alerce forests and Andean mountain scenery. An old frontier cattle trail in Cochamó Valley, once used as a hideout by Butch Cassidy and the Sundance Kid, reminds the visitor that the only way through this natural wonderland is by foot or horse. You don't find any cars or roads here.

GETTING HERE AND AROUND

There are few cars in Cochamó, and even fewer gas stations (though you can get gas by the container). Walking is probably the most efficient way to get around. Nearby Puelo is even smaller than Cochamó. If you must, rent a car in Puerto Montt or Puerto Varas. Roads in the region are mostly gravel and dirt, so four-wheel drive would be good. Buses do service these towns, however. If you take the bus, arrange with a travel agency or outfitter beforehand to help with transport to the nature areas on your wish list.

ESSENTIALS

Visitor Information **Cochamó Municipalidad** ✉ *Calle Santiago Bueras, Puelo* ☎ *65/235–0271* 🌐 *www.cochamo.cl.*

WHERE TO STAY

$$$$ B&B/INN 🏨 **Andes Lodge.** Billed as a fly-fishing and outdoors lodge, the Andes Lodge has earned a favorable reputation among its many visitors. **Pros:** great for those focused on fly-fishing; a top hotel in the area. **Cons:** expensive daily rate for what you get; simply furnished rooms. [$] *Rooms from: 165000 pesos* ☎ *9/9234–6003* 🌐 *www.andeslodgechile.com* 🛏 *8 rooms* 🍴 *Multiple meal plans.*

$$$ HOTEL FAMILY Fodor's Choice ★ 🏨 **Mítico Puelo Lodge.** It feels like you have the Patagonia Andes all to yourself at this rustic Puelo Valley retreat that was built in 1991 as a private getaway for fly-fishing enthusiasts. **Pros:** exclusive location; lots of expert-led excursions; good for families; passionate service. **Cons:** two hours from closest airport; only satellite phone service (extra charge); excursions are extra (except for all-inclusive plans). [$] *Rooms from: 84000 pesos* ✉ *Lago Tagua Tagua* ☎ *65/223–4892* 🌐 *www.miticopuelo.com* 🛏 *6 standard rooms, 12 superior rooms, 1 family apartment* 🍴 *Multiple meal plans.*

$ B&B/INN 🏨 **Posada Martin Pescador.** In the middle of pristine nature, this small but cozy lodge on the shores of Lago Totoral in the Puelo area is an ideal base for exploration. **Pros:** pristine nature; quiet and tranquil; rustic charm. **Cons:** remote location, organize carefully how to get here.

[$] *Rooms from: 42000 pesos* ✉ *Km 2, Llanada Grande, Puelo, Llanada Grande* ☎ *9/731–7178, 9/884–6555* 🌐 *www.posadamartinpescador.cl* 🛏 *2 rooms* 🍴 *Breakfast.*

SPORTS AND THE OUTDOORS

Cochamó and Río Puelo's vast forests, fast-flowing rivers, and mountains are an outdoors-lover's mecca. Before you pursue any of the myriad activities available, though, be sure to get your bearings. Unlike national parks, these areas are not formally protected and maintained, and therefore often lack well-marked trails. Check with a local outfitter or travel agency to get more information on where to go and how.

Andes Patagonia. For horseback-riding, boating, hiking, and kayaking trips throughout the Río Puelo area, including ascents of Volcán Yates and hikes to ancient alerce forests and glaciers, check with Andes Patagonia. ✉ *Río Puelo Alto* ☎ *9/9549–1069* 🌐 *www.andespatagonia.cl* 🎫 *From 40,000 pesos.*

Cochamó Aventura. Cochamó Aventura runs trekking, rafting, kayaking, and biking trips in Cochamó and Puelo but specializes in 1- to 14-day horseback-riding excursions. ☎ *9/9289–4314* 🌐 *www.campoaventura.cl* 🎫 *From 50,000 pesos.*

CHILOÉ

WELCOME TO CHILOÉ

TOP REASONS TO GO

★ **Charming churches:** Within Chile, Chiloé is known for the simply elegant churches that dot Isla Grande. Almost all are open to the public, and a visit is essential.

★ **Traditional crafts:** Chiloé's sweaters, ponchos, blankets, and rugs are a defining feature of the island. There's nothing warmer, woollier, or more wonderful anywhere else in Chile.

★ **Nature:** Chiloé's close proximity to breeding grounds for blue whales, a globally endangered species, makes it one of the planet's top destinations for whale-watching. Many other animals call Chiloé home, too; there's spectacular bird-watching, including massive penguin colonies and rare birds like the Chucao Tapaculo.

★ **Fantastic folklore:** Spirits of all stripes haunt Chiloé—or at least populate its colorful folklore, which is full of trolls, witches, mermaids, and ghost ships.

1 Ancud and Nearby. Your ferry may arrive on Chiloé at Chacao, but Ancud is the area's main transportation hub and the island's second-largest city. Explore here the otherworldly wetlands at Chepu, the fog- and folklore-steeped towns of Quemchi and Quicaví, and northeastern Chiloé's famous churches. If you venture to Isla Quinchao, stop in Achao, a busy fishing town.

2 Castro and Nearby. Castro is the capital and the larger more cosmopolitan answer to Ancud. You can see a lot from here, including Chonchi's brightly painted houses and the Parque Nacional Chiloé. Other small towns dot the east coast down to Quellón, home to nearby Parque Tantauco and where you can take ferries to Chaitén and the mainland.

GETTING ORIENTED

Most people explore Chiloé by car. Major towns and landmarks are no more than an hour or two apart. The Pan-American Highway (Ruta 5) that meanders through northern Chile ends at the Golfo de Ancud and continues again on Isla Grande. It connects the cities of Ancud, Castro, and Chonchi before ending in Quellón. Paved roads connect the Pan-American to Quemchi and Dalcahue, and Achao on Isla Quinchao. There are plans to pave the coastal route connecting the village of San Antonio de Chacao with Dalcahue. A more scenic route leads from Chacao to Caulín and Ancud, via Huicha. The road west from Ancud every year is paved farther and pavement should eventually extend to the lighthouse at Corona Point.

8

Updated
by Jimmy
Langman

Steeped in magic, shrouded in mist, the 41-island archipelago of Chiloé is that proverbial world apart, isolated not so much by distance from the mainland as by the quirks of history. It's also fast becoming one of Chile's favorite travel destinations. Chiloé is packed with fascinating nature, from wild beaches to thick, temperate forests. Opportunities abound for trekking, horseback riding, kayaking, bird-watching, whale-watching, and more. Much of the island's 200,000 residents are descendants of blended colonial and indigenous cultures with fascinating traditions in farming, fishing, and devout Catholicism, not to mention finely crafted woolen sweaters, rich seafood stews, unique wooden churches, and *palafito,* or houses poised on stilts.

Originally inhabited by the indigenous Chono people, Chiloé was gradually taken over by the Huilliche. Though Chiloé was claimed as part of Spain's empire in the 1550s, colonists dismissed the archipelago as a backwater despite its strategic importance. The 1598 rebellion by the Mapuche people on the mainland drove a contingent of Spanish settlers to the isolated safety of Chiloé. Left to their own devices, Spaniards and Huilliche lived and worked side by side. Their society was built on the concept of *minga,* a help-thy-neighbor spirit resembling traditions of pioneer America, such as barn raisings and quilting bees. The outcome was a culture neither Spanish nor indigenous, but Chilote—a quintessential mestizo society.

Isolated from the rest of the continent, islanders had little interest in or awareness of the revolutionary fervor sweeping Latin America in the early 19th century. In fact, the mainland Spaniards recruited the Chilote to help put down rebellions in the region. When things got too hot in Santiago, the Spanish governor took refuge on the island, just as his predecessors had done two centuries earlier. Finally defeated, the Spaniards abandoned Chiloé in 1826, surrendering their last outpost in South America, and the island soon joined the new nation of Chile.

Nowadays, the isolation is more psychological than physical. Chiloé is just over 2 km (1 mile) from the mainland at its nearest point, and dozens of buses and frequent ferries every day make the half-hour crossing between Chiloé and Pargua, near Puerto Montt in the Lake District on the mainland. As well, a modern airport was inaugurated in Castro in 2013. In recent years, the island's tourism offerings have taken a giant leap forward with several luxury hotels and sophisticated gourmet restaurants opening in the Castro area and the massive private park

Tantauco drawing droves of trekkers near Quellon. Today, Chiloé is embracing the world while firmly preserving its cultural past.

PLANNER

WHEN TO GO

Chiloé is increasingly a year-round destination, but like the rest of southern Chile, the ideal time to go is during the summer months, from December to March. Summer is sunnier and the prime time for cultural festivals all over the island. Although Chiloé is known to be rainy—some parts receive more than 150 inches annually—periods of sunshine regularly break the spells. Year-round, however, mist and fog prevail and deepen the mystery of the islands, while the crisp, breezy air is refreshing.

FESTIVALS AND SEASONAL EVENTS

Like elsewhere in southern Chile, most of Chiloé's festivals take place in summer. Fiestas Costumbritsas, which celebrate Chilote customs and folklore, take place over several weekends between December and February in Ancud, Castro, and other towns. There are still other special events, such as a biodiversity fair in Castro the third week of February and a small open-air film festival in Ancud during the first few days of February.

PLANNING YOUR TIME

After crossing the Golfo de Ancud on the morning ferry on your first day, drive south to Ancud. Soak up the port town's atmosphere, but do try to visit the colony of penguins at nearby Puñihuil. Head to Dalcahue the next day, and have lunch at the colorful artisans' market. Then, take the short ferry ride to Isla Quinchao and visit the colorful church of Santa María de Loreto. Back on Isla Grande, proceed to Castro. Spend the next day relaxing, shopping, or visiting the capital's museums and the lovely church, then head south to tour Chonchi, known to locals as the "City of Three Stories." From there it's just a one hour drive to the Pacific coast to visit the Parque Nacional Chiloé, where you can enjoy a hike through the forest and go horseback riding on the beach. If you have another day or two, consider going to Parque Tantauco near Chiloé's southernmost town, Quellón.

GETTING HERE AND AROUND

AIR TRAVEL

In November 2012, Chiloé added the modern Mocopulli Airport near Castro that connects the island with national and international flights four times a week via Aeropuerto El Tepual in Puerto Montt. Chiloé also has several small airports for regional flights and private planes.

BOAT AND FERRY TRAVEL

Since Chiloé is an archipelago, the only way to arrive by car is to take one of the frequent ferries across the eastern end of the Chacao Channel. Both Cruz del Sur and Transmarchilay operate the frequent ferry service that connects mainland Pargua with Chacao.

BUS TRAVEL
Cruz del Sur and its subsidiary Transchiloé operate some 30 buses per day between Ancud and the mainland, usually terminating in Puerto Montt. Many routes continue north to Temuco, and a few travel all the way to Santiago. Buses arriving from the mainland provide local service once they reach the island, making frequent stops.

CAR TRAVEL
Rather than terminating in Puerto Montt, the Pan-American Highway skips over the Golfo de Ancud and continues through Ancud, Castro, and Chonchi before stopping in Quellón. Paved roads also lead to Quemchi, Dalcahue, and Achao on Isla Quinchao. There are rental car agencies in Castro and Ancud.

RESTAURANTS
As befits an island culture, seafood reigns in Chiloé. The signature Chilote dish is the *curanto,* a hearty stew of shellfish, chicken, sausages, and smoked pork ribs. It's served with plenty of potato-and-flour patties, known as *milcao* and *chapaleles. Salmón ahumado* (smoked salmon) is another favorite, though salmon are not native to this area. Avoid any uncooked shellfish unless you're certain you can trust the chef.

Breakfast here is often a humble menu of instant Nescafe coffee with warm bread rolls, jam, and butter. Like the rest of Chile, most residents take their lunch between 1 pm and 3 during the week and often do so with gusto. In addition to seafood, Chilotes enjoy empanadas—baked or fried bread stuffed with meat, chicken, seafood, and other fillings. Roasted lamb is another favorite, with sheep raising still a common livelihood throughout the island.

The archipelago is also known for its tasty fruit liqueurs, usually from the central Chiloé town of Chonchi. Islanders take berries and apples and turn them into the *licor de oro* that often awaits you at your hotel.

HOTELS
Over the past five years, Chiloé's hotel offerings have taken a quantum leap, with world-class luxury lodgings beginning to appear on the mainland. But the islands are still mostly dominated by smaller, more reasonably priced hotels. Castro and Ancud have the most choices; Chonchi, Achao, and Quellón less so. Central heating and a light breakfast are standard in better hostelries. Not all places, especially in rural towns, take credit cards, but ATMs are more readily available than you might expect.

Outside the major cities, *hospedaje* (lodgings) are few and far between. But in summer, they seem to sprout in front of every other house in Castro and Ancud, as homeowners rent rooms to visitors. Quality varies, so inspect the premises before agreeing to take a room from someone who greets you at the bus station. *Hotel reviews have been shortened. For full information, visit Fodors.com.*

Chiloé's Chapels

More than 150 wooden churches are scattered across the eastern half of Chiloé's main island and the smaller islands nearby. Jesuit missionaries came to the archipelago after the 1598 Mapuche rebellion on the mainland, and the chapels they built were an integral part of the effort to convert the indigenous peoples. Pairs of missionaries traveled the region by boat, making sure to celebrate Mass in each community at least once a year. Franciscan missionaries continued the tradition after Spain expelled the Jesuits from its New World colonies in 1767.

The architectural style of the churches calls to mind those in rural Germany, the home of many of the missionaries.

The complete lack of ornamentation is offset only by a steep roof covered with wooden shingles called *tejuelas* and a three-tier hexagonal bell tower. An arched portico fronts most of the churches. Getting to see more than the outside of many of the churches can be a challenge. Many stand seemingly forlorn in their solitude on the coast and remain locked most of the year; others are open only for Sunday services. There are two main exceptions: Castro's orange-and-lavender Iglesia de San Francisco, dating from 1906—it's technically not one of the Jesuit churches but built in the same style—opens its doors to visitors; and Achao's Iglesia de Santa María de Loreto gives daily guided Spanish-language tours.

WHAT IT COSTS IN CHILEAN PESOS (IN THOUSANDS)			
$	$$	$$$	$$$$
Restaurants	Under 6	6–8	9–11	over 11
Hotels	Under 46	46–75	76–105	over 105

Restaurant prices are the average cost of a main course at dinner or, if dinner is not served, at lunch. Hotel prices are for the lowest cost of a standard double room in high season.

ANCUD AND NEARBY

Although it's the second-largest city in Chiloé, Ancud feels like a small town. With its hills, irregular streets, and commanding ocean views, it gets raves for its quiet charm.

Raw nature is on tap at Chepu, while Chiloé's tranquil and mystical heart is at Quemchi and Quicaví. It's also worth spending a day on Isla Quinchao, reached via ferry from Dalcahue.

ANCUD

90 km (54 miles) southwest of Puerto Montt.

The village of Chacao (where your ferry arrives) was actually the site of one of the first Spanish shipyards in the Americas, but it was moved in 1769 to Ancud, which was deemed a more defensible location.

Ancud was repeatedly attacked during Chile's war for independence and remained the last stronghold of the Spaniards in the Americas—as well as the seat of their government-in-exile after they fled from Santiago, until 1826—when the island was finally annexed by Chile.

GETTING HERE AND AROUND

Boats leave Pargua, on the mainland, every 15 minutes from 7 am until late in the evening. Trips take about 30 minutes. An additional 30 minutes down the road from Chacao, Ancud is the first real stop on Chiloé Island for most visitors. Roads from Chacao to Ancud are paved, but if you venture north or west of town to visit attractions such as the lighthouse at Faro Corona or the penguin colony at Puñihuil, the road eventually turns into gravel. There are several bus lines that serve Chiloé cities, particularly Ancud and Castro. Most visitors board buses in Puerto Montt, which is about 2½ hours from Ancud. Add another hour to get to Castro. The main bus line serving Chiloé, Cruz del Sur, has frequent service throughout the island, including Chonchi and Quellón.

ESSENTIALS

Bus Contacts Cruz del Sur ⊠ *Los Carrera 850* ☎ *65/262-2506* ⊕ *Bus.* **Terminal Interurbano Ancud** ☎ *65/262-0370.*

Ferry Service Cruz del Sur ⊠ *Los Carrera 850* ☎ *65/262-2506* ⊕ *www.busescruzdelsur.cl/.*

Rental Car Contacts Chiloe Rent A Car ⊠ *Antonio Burr 887* ☎ *65/262-0868* ⊕ *www.chiloerentacar.cl.*

Visitor Information Sernatur ⊠ *Libertad 665* ☎ *65/262-2800* ⊕ *www.sernatur.cl/.*

EXPLORING

Fuerte de San Antonio. Northwest of downtown Ancud, the 16 cannon emplacements of this fort are nearly all that remain of Spain's last outpost in the New World. Constructed in 1786, the fort was a key component in the defense of the Canal de Chacao, especially after the Spanish colonial government fled to Chiloé during Chile's war for independence. ⊠ *Lord Cohrane at San Antonio* 🖭 *Free* ☉ *Open 24 hrs.*

Museo Regional de Ancud. Statues of mythical Chilote figures, such as the Pincoya and Trauco, greet you on the terrace of this fortresslike museum, just uphill from the Plaza de Armas. The replica of the schooner *La Goleta Ancud* is the museum's centerpiece; the ship carried Chilean settlers to the Strait of Magellan in 1843. Inside is a collection of island handicrafts. ⊠ *Libertad 370* ☎ *65/262-2413* ⊕ *www.museoancud.cl* 🖭 *600 pesos* ☉ *Jan. and Feb., daily 10–7; Mar.–Dec., Tues.–Fri., 10–5:30, weekends 10–2.*

Fodor's Choice   **Puñihuil.** One of the best nature excursions on Chiloé is at Puñihuil.
★   Located 29 km (18 miles) southwest of Ancud, the three small islets here are home to an abundant colony of Humboldt and Magellanic penguins, along with a variety of other birds and wildlife. From December to May, a local tour operator, Ecomarine Puñihuil (⊕ *www.ballenaschiloe.cl*), takes out up to eight people in the mornings to search for blue

whales, which have been extensively tracked in the area by scientists. ☎ *9/8174–7592 mobile* 🌐 *www.pinguineraschiloe.cl.*

WHERE TO EAT

$$ CHILEAN
🍴 **Kuranton.** This intimate establishment specializes in *curanto,* available at both dinner and lunch (most restaurants only have it for lunch). A variety of other dishes fill out the menu, from standard Chilote seafood to pizza, beef, chicken, and sandwiches. The walls of the restaurant are lined with curious photos, statues, and other Chiloé memorabilia. The wood-burning stove in the center of the dining room is much appreciated on the often cold and rainy nights. [$] *Average main: 7000 pesos* ✉ *94 Arturo Prat* ☎ *65/262–3090.*

$ SEAFOOD
🍴 **Mascaron de Proa Restaurant.** For excellent seafood and sea views, this is the place. Founded in 1992 in front of Arena Gruesa beach on the northern end of the coastal road (behind Cabanas Las Golondrinas), the restaurant serves its food against the backdrop of volcanoes emerging in the horizon on a clear day. Try a seafood platter for starters, and for the main course, consider the outstanding fresh fish, such as *merluza austral* (hake). [$] *Average main: 5000 pesos* ✉ *Baquedano 560* ☎ *65/262–1979* 💳 *No credit cards* 🕒 *No dinner Sun.*

$$ SEAFOOD Fodor's Choice ★
🍴 **Ostras Caulin.** Just 12 miles outside of Ancud, this now classic spot cracks open some of the world's best oysters, taken each day from the coast in front of the small, wooden restaurant. Oysters come in multiple forms: fried, poached, creamed, and raw. Fish dishes, baked veal, and wine round out the menu, as does the special children's menu. Combine your meal with bird-watching at nearby Caulin Bay. [$] *Average main: 7000 pesos* ✉ *Caulin (9 km from Chacao)* ☎ *9/643–7005* 🌐 *www.ostrascaulin.cl* 🕒 *No dinner.*

8

WHERE TO STAY

$ HOTEL
🏨 **Faros del Sur.** This rustic, wooden hotel that bills itself as a "boutique hostal" is a worthy choice for the views alone. **Pros:** grand views; friendly service. **Cons:** rooms are basic; no-frills. [$] *Rooms from: 37000 pesos* ✉ *Costanera Norte 320* ☎ *65/262–5799* 🌐 *www.farosdelsur.cl* 🛏 *14 rooms* 🍽 *Breakfast.*

$ B&B/INN
🏨 **Hotel Balai.** Facing the town plaza, this hotel has an ideal location in the center of town. **Pros:** location; ambience; friendly service. **Cons:** paper-thin walls make for difficult sleeping if neighbors snore; parking is two blocks away; small bathrooms. [$] *Rooms from: 32000 pesos* ✉ *Pudeto 169* ☎ *65/262–2541* 🌐 *www.hotelbalai.cl* 🛏 *12 rooms* 🕒 *Closed on some holidays* 🍽 *Breakfast.*

$$ HOTEL
🏨 **Hotel Don Lucas.** This attractive, navy blue–and-gold hotel is conveniently located near downtown and the plaza, yet also on the waterfront with great views of the bay. **Pros:** waterfront views; good location. **Cons:** can get noisy; small rooms. [$] *Rooms from: 69600 pesos* ✉ *Av. Costanera 906* ☎ *65/262–0950* 🌐 *www.hoteldonlucas.cl* 🛏 *19 rooms* 🍽 *Breakfast.*

$ HOTEL
🏨 **Hotel Galeón Azul.** On a bluff overlooking Ancud's waterfront, this older hotel is a smart choice for the price. **Pros:** waterfront views; proximity to downtown; ample private parking. **Cons:** thin walls; street noise. [$] *Rooms from: 42000 pesos* ✉ *Libertad 751* ☎ *65/262–2567*

🌐 *www.hotelgaleonazul.cl/galeon* 🛏 *15 rooms* 💳 *No credit cards* 🍴 *Breakfast.*

$$ HOTEL **Panamericana Hotel Ancud.** A solid choice for your stay, the venerable Panamericana Hotel Ancud has long been one of Chiloé's top hotels. **Pros:** privileged views of Ancud Bay; good restaurant. **Cons:** rooms are on the small side. [$] *Rooms from: 55000 pesos* ✉ *San Antonio 30* ☎ *65/262–2340* 🌐 *www.panamericanahoteles.cl/ancud* 🛏 *24 rooms* 🍴 *Breakfast.*

NIGHTLIFE

Ancud has some good bars. Chilotes are friendly, upbeat sorts, known to enjoy a night of drinking. Most of the bars are in the downtown shopping district, but a few nightspots are closer to the waterfront.

Lumiere Bar. The large square-shape bar inside this inviting place is popular with the locals. Good bar food is served late into the evening. ✉ *Eldiberto Ramirez 28* ☎ *65/262–1980.*

Retro's Pub. Bar tunes blare loudly at the smoky, crowded Retro's Pub. Its Mexican food offerings—burritos, fajitas, and nachos—are a nice change of pace from Chiloé's ubiquitous seafood. ✉ *Maipu 615* ☎ *65/262–6410.*

SPORTS AND THE OUTDOORS

Water sports such as sailing or sea kayaking are popular in Ancud. There are several fishing and trekking possibilities as well. Along the coastline you can see dolphins, penguins, and often whales from the safety of the area's picturesque beaches.

MULTISPORT OPERATORS

Austral Adventures. Austral Adventures arranges bilingual, tailor-made kayaking, trekking, and bird-watching trips. ☎ *65/262–5977* 🌐 *www.austral-adventures.com.*

Chiloé Indomito. This agency leads hiking and naturalist trips in northern Chiloé as well as tours of old Spanish forts and historic churches. ☎ *9/9509–3741* 🌐 *www.chiloeindomito.cl.*

Turismo Pehuén. A pioneer on the island, the leading tourism operator on Chiloé has long been Turismo Pehuén. It runs a variety of top-notch nature and culture excursions of Castro, Ancud, and the surrounding region. ✉ *Latorre 238, Castro* ☎ *65/263–5254* 🌐 *www.turismopehuen.cl.*

SHOPPING

Feria Municipal Rural y Artesanal. Shopping in Ancud is nothing extraordinary, though there's a fine artisans' market just below the town plaza and a few blocks up from the waterfront. There you find woolen blankets, sweaters, dolls, wooden figurines, and other items by Chiloé artisans. ✉ *Corner of Libertad and Dieciocho.*

CHEPU

38 km (24 miles) southwest of Ancud.

This is a stop for hardcore nature lovers. Here at a confluence of three rivers, the Chepu River valley forms before merging finally into the Pacific Ocean. Along the way it passes through wetlands and sunken forest created by the 1960 earthquake, the most powerful quake on record. This area is overflowing with 128 species of birds and is a great spot for kayaking and hiking along the shoreline.

GETTING HERE AND AROUND

Take Route 5 south from Ancud, and look for the sign "Camino a Chepu" at Km 25. Here, turn onto the gravel road, which goes straight before you are forced to turn left at Coipomó. The road goes approximately 13 km (8 miles) before reaching Chepu. Altogether, it takes approximately 45 minutes by car from Ancud.

WHERE TO STAY

$$ **⌂ Chepu Adventures Ecolodge.** An extraordinary eco-sustainable lodge,
B&B/INN this is more than just a place to sleep, but a starting point for kayaking, bird-watching, and hiking the Chepu River and Pacific coast. **Pros:** environmentally friendly; kayak at dawn; private cabins **Cons:** remote location. [$] *Rooms from: 54000 pesos* ⊠ *Camino a Chepu, Km 32, Chepu, Chiloe* ☎ *9/9379–2481* ⊕ *www.chepu.cl* ⤳ *6 rooms* ❚❶❚ *Multiple meal plans.*

QUEMCHI

62 km (37 miles) southeast of Ancud.

On the protected interior of the Golfo de Ancud, Quemchi is a small, tranquil fishing village that makes for a good stopover when visiting churches and other tourist sites in northeastern Chiloé. There are several historic churches and scenic islands nearby.

GETTING HERE AND AROUND

You can reach Quemchi via paved roads from Ancud in less than an hour by car. To get to nearby tourist sites, be prepared for gravelly, dusty country roads that require careful driving, preferably in a four-wheel-drive vehicle. Additionally, there are a few small islands nearby worth seeing. You can hire a boat at the town port, where there is usually a handful of captains on hand ready to negotiate a fee for the service.

EXPLORING

Isla de Aucar. This tiny forested islet 6 km (4 miles) south of Quemchi is reached by walking across a stunning wooden bridge some 510 meters (1,673 feet) long. Black-necked swans and other birds frequent the area. The island hosts a botanical garden and Jesuit chapel and cemetery that date to 1761. ⊠ *Isla de Aucar.*

Morro Lobos. Reached by a 45-minute boat ride from the port of Quemchi, this immense rock outcrop juts out of the sea off the coast of Caucahue Island. Hundreds of sea lions and marine birds call it home. Boats at the port can be hired for about 12,000 pesos.

WHERE TO EAT

$ ✕ **El Chejo.** The guestbook at this small, waterfront restaurant is jammed
CHILEAN with raves and compliments about its Chiloé seafood dishes, but it's the dozen types of empanadas—filled with beef, cheese, clams, salmon, or crab meat, to name a few—that impress most. [$] *Average main: 4090 pesos* ⊠ *Diego Bahmonde 251* ☎ *65/269–1490* ▭ *No credit cards.*

QUICAVÍ

25 km (15 miles) southeast of Quemchi.

The center of all that is magical and mystical about Chiloé, Quicaví sits forlornly on the eastern coast of Isla Grande. Superstitious locals strongly advise against going anywhere near the coast to the south of town, where miles of caves extend to the village of Tenaún. They believe that witches, and evil ones at that, inhabit them. On the beaches, local lore says, are mermaids that lure fishermen to their deaths. (These are not the beautiful and benevolent Pincoya, also a legendary kelp-covered mermaid. A glimpse of her is thought to portend good fishing for the day.) Many Quicaví denizens claim to have glimpsed Chiloé's notorious ghost ship, the *Caleuche,* roaming the waters on foggy nights, searching for its doomed passengers. Of course, a brief glimpse of the ship is all anyone dares admit, as legend holds that a longer gaze could spell death.

GETTING HERE AND AROUND

From Ancud, Quicaví is reached by going first to Quemchi, then driving south along a two-lane dirt road through the Chiloé countryside for about 40 minutes.

EXPLORING

Iglesia de San Pedro. In an effort to win converts, the Jesuits constructed this enormous church on the Plaza de Armas. The original structure survives from colonial times, though it underwent extensive remodeling in the early 20th century. It's open for services on the first Sunday of every month at 11 am, which is your best bet for getting a look inside.

DALCAHUE

44 km (27 miles) southwest of Quicaví; 74 km (44 miles) southeast of Ancud; 20 km (12 miles) northeast of Castro.

Most days travelers in the laid-back port town of Dalcahue stop only long enough to board the ferry that deposits them 15 minutes later on Isla Quinchao. But the artisan market here is a worthy stop, if only to sample the local food. Dalcahue is a pleasant coastal town—one that deserves a longer visit.

GETTING HERE AND AROUND

Dalcahue is about an hour from Ancud along paved roads. There is also frequent bus service, particularly from Castro, which is about a 15-minute drive from Dalcahue. Dalcahue Expreso buses can be caught at Castro's bus terminal (at the corner of Freire and O'Higgins) or at several bus stops along the road between Dalcahue and Ancud.

EXPLORING

Iglesia de Nuestra Señora de los Dolores. This 1850 church, modeled on the churches constructed during the Jesuit era, sits in the main square (Plaza de Armas). A portico with nine arches, an unusually high number for a Chilote church, fronts the structure. The church holds a small museum with historic town and church documents and old church ornaments. ☎ 65/264–1456 ✉ *Free* ⌚ *Church and museum Tues.–Sun. 10–1 and 3–6.*

Museo Histórico Etnográfico de Dalcahue. A *fogón*—a traditional indigenous cooking pit—sits in the center of the small *palafito* (a shingled house built on stilts and hanging over the water) housing this museum that displays historical exhibits about the indigenous peoples of Chiloé—the Chonos and Huilluiche. ⊠ *Pedro Montt 40* ☎ *65/264–2379* 🖾 *Free* ⊗ *Daily 9–6.*

WHERE TO STAY

$ 🖼 **Hotel La Isla.** A friendly attitude greets you at this wood-shingled hotel
B&B/INN with a cozy sitting room and big fireplace off the lobby. **Pros:** comfortable; friendly service. **Cons:** pricey for what you get. Ⓢ *Rooms from: 45000 pesos* ⊠ *Mocopulli 113* ☎ *65/264–1241* ⊕ *www.hotellaisla.cl* ⤹ *19 rooms* ⚏ *Breakfast.*

$ 🖼 **Residencial La Fiera.** This is an inexpensive, fine option in town, with
B&B/INN basic but modern rooms. **Pros:** cheap; near waterfront. **Cons:** few private rooms; shared bathrooms. Ⓢ *Rooms from: 25000 pesos* ⊠ *Manuel Rodriguez 154* ☎ *65/264–1293* ⊕ *www.residenciallafiera.cl* ⤹ *32 rooms, 5 with bath* ⚏ *Breakfast.*

SHOPPING

Feria Artesanal in Dalcahue. Dalcahue's Sunday-morning crafts market, near the waterfront municipal building, draws crowds who come to shop for Chilote handicrafts, woolens, baskets, and woven mythical figures. Things get under way about 8 am and begin to wind down by mid-day, just in time to eat lunch at the lively food stalls at the Cocineria behind the market. Bargaining is expected, though the prices are already quite reasonable. ⊠ *Av. Pedro Montt.*

ISLA QUINCHAO

1 km (½ mile) southeast of Dalcahue.

For many visitors, the elongated Isla Quinchao, the easiest to reach of the islands in the eastern archipelago, defines Chiloé. Populated by hardworking farmers and fisherfolk, Isla Quinchao provides a glimpse into the region's past. Head to Achao, Quinchao's largest community, to see the *alerce*-shingle (a wood native to Chile) houses, busy fishing pier, and colonial church.

GETTING HERE AND AROUND

The roads from Dalcahue, and the main road through Isla Quinchao, are paved. About two hours from Ancud, Achao is a 30-minute journey from Dalcahue, the town from which you catch the ferry to cross Ayacara Bay. The ride is a mere five minutes, and there are frequent departures from 7 am to midnight. It's free for pedestrians and 2,000 pesos each way for cars. Once on the island, the road to Achao winds its way through verdant countryside, often with tremendous views of the surrounding sea.

EXPLORING

Iglesia de Nuestra Señora de Gracia. About 10 km (6 miles) south of Achao is the archipelago's largest church. As with many other Chilote churches, the 200-foot structure sits in solitude near the coast. The church has no tours but may be visited during Sunday Mass at 11 am. ⊠ *7 km (4 miles) north of Castro, Nercon.*

Fodor'sChoice **Iglesia de Santa María de Loreto.** Achao's centerpiece is this 1730 church,
★ the oldest remaining house of worship on the archipelago. In addition to the alerce wood so commonly used to construct buildings in the region, the church also uses cypress and *mañío* trees. Its typically unadorned exterior contrasts with the deep-blue ceiling embellished with gold stars and rich Baroque carvings on the altar inside. Mass is celebrated Sunday at 11 am and Tuesday at 7 pm, but docents give guided tours while the church is open. An informative Spanish-language museum behind the altar is dedicated to the period of Chiloé's Jesuit missions. All proceeds go to much-needed church restoration. ⊠ *Plaza de Armas, Delicias at Amunategui, Achao* 🕾 *65/266–1881* 🎫 *500 pesos* 🕙 *Daily 10:30–1 and 2:30–7.*

WHERE TO EAT AND STAY

$ ✕ **Hostería La Nave.** Inside this rambling beachfront building that arches
SEAFOOD over the street, this restaurant serves seafood, beef, and other dishes. Try the oysters or *merluza margarita,* hake fish in a shellfish sauce. Above the restaurant is a *hostería* (small hotel) with 30 rooms. The rooms are nothing special, but they're clean and serve as a fine option in a pinch. 💲 *Average main: 6000 pesos* ⊠ *Arturo Prat at Sargento Aldea, Achao* 🕾 *65/266–1219* 🖃 *No credit cards.*

$$ ✕ **Mar y Velas.** Scrumptious oysters and a panoply of other gifts from the
SEAFOOD sea are served on the top floor of this big wooden house at the foot of Achao's dock (accessible via a side stairway). Many in town maintain the food here is the best around. That said, service can be slow at times. 💲 *Average main: 7000 pesos* ⊠ *Serrano 2, Achao* 🕾 *65/266–1375.*

$ 🏨 **Hospedaje Sol y Lluvia.** If you plan to stay in Isla Quinchao over-
B&B/INN night, this is the best option. **Pros:** clean; pleasant; secure parking. **Cons:** not close to the beach. 💲 *Rooms from: 24000 pesos* ⊠ *Ricardo Jara 9* 🕾 *65/266–1383* 🛏 *8 rooms, 3 with bath* 🖃 *No credit cards* ⦿❙ *Breakfast.*

CASTRO AND NEARBY

With a population of 42,000, Castro is now Chiloé's largest city. Though hardly an urban jungle, this is big-city life Chiloé-style. Residents of more rural parts of the island, who visit the capital no more often than necessary, return home with tales of traffic so heavy that it has to be regulated with stoplights.

South of Castro, Chonchi's colorful wooden houses climb the hillside. Parque Nacional Chiloé, one of the island's main attractions, is a great place to spend the night before the ferry ride back to the mainland from Quellón.

CASTRO

45 km (28 miles) west of Achao, 88 km (55 miles) south of Ancud.

Founded in 1567, Castro is Chile's third-oldest city. Its history has been one of destruction, with three fires and three earthquakes laying waste to the city over four centuries. The most recent disaster was in 1960, when a tidal wave caused by an earthquake on the mainland engulfed the city.

Castro's future as Isla Grande's governmental and commercial center looked promising after the 1598 Mapuche rebellion on the mainland drove the Spaniards to Chiloé, but then Dutch pirates sacked the city in 1600. Many of Castro's residents fled to the safety of more isolated parts of the island. It wasn't until 1982 that the city finally became Chiloé's administrative capital.

Next to its wooden churches, *palafitos,* shingled houses on stilts in the water along the coast, are the best-known architectural symbol of Chiloé. Avenida Pedro Montt, which becomes a coastal highway as it leads out of town, is the best place to see palafitos in Castro. Many of these ramshackle structures have been turned into restaurants and artisan markets.

GETTING HERE AND AROUND

In the center of the Isla Grande de Chiloé, Castro is only about one hour's drive from Ancud along Ruta 5, the Pan-American Highway. For a more interesting journey, consider the unpaved coastal road to Castro via Quemchi, which takes twice as long but passes numerous tourist sites.

In late 2012, Castro opened Mocupulli Airport, which four days a week receives commercial flights from the mainland. There is also regular and frequent bus service from the terminal in Puerto Montt to Castro, which takes almost four hours. Buses Arroyo has routes throughout Chiloé and the Lake District. Queilén and Gallardo operate on Chiloé Island only. Dalcahue Expreso is a local bus between Castro and Dalcahue. Cruz del Sur and Tur-Bus are long-distance buses that have routes throughout the country and into Argentina. Reserve ahead for buses.

ESSENTIALS

Boat Contacts Ferry dock ⊠ *Pedro Montt 48.*

Bus Contacts Buses Arroyo ⊠ *San Martin s/n* ☎ *65/263–5604.* **Buses Gallardo** ⊠ *San Martin 667* ☎ *65/263–4521.* **Cruz del Sur** ⊠ *San Martin 486* ☎ *65/263–2389* ⊕ *www.busescruzdelsur.cl.* **Dalcahue Expreso** ⊠ *Ramirez 233* ☎ *65/263–5164.* **Queilén Bus** ☎ *65/263–2173.* **Terminal de Buses Rurales** ⊠ *San Martin 667* ☎ *65/263–2594.* **Tur-Bus** ⊠ *Pedro Montt 39* ☎ *65/232–1252* ⊕ *www.turbus.cl.*

Rental Car Contacts ADS Rent-a-Car ⊠ *Esmeralda 260* ☎ *65/263–7777.* **Salfa Sur Rent-a-Car** ⊠ *Gabriela Mistral 499* ☎ *65/263–0422.*

Visitor Information Tourism Office of the Castro Municipality ⊠ *Blanco Encalada 273* ☎ *65/254–7706.*

EXPLORING

Fodor's Choice ★ **Iglesia de San Francisco.** Any tour of Castro begins with this much-photographed 1906 church, constructed in the style of the archipelago's wooden churches, only bigger and grander. Depending on your perspective, terms like "pretty" or "garish" describe the orange-and-lavender exterior colors chosen when the structure was spruced up before Pope John Paul II's 1987 visit. It's infinitely more reserved on the inside. The dark-wood interior's centerpiece is the monumental carved crucifix hanging from the ceiling. In the evening, a soft, energy-efficient external illumination system makes the church one of Chiloé's most impressive sights. ✉ *Plaza de Armas, corner of Freire and Caupolican* ⏲ *Dec.–Feb., daily 9–12:30 and 3–11:30; Mar.–Nov., daily 9–12:30 and 3–9:30.*

Museo de Arte Moderno de Chiloé. Housed in five refurbished barns in a city park northwest of downtown, this modern-art complex—referred to locally as the MAM—exhibits works by Chilean artists. The museum opens to the public only when there are exhibitions or special events. ✉ *Pasaje Díaz 181* ☎ *65/263–5454* 🌐 *www.mamchiloe.cl* 🎟 *Free* ⏲ *Jan.–Mar., daily 10–6; Apr.–Dec., daily 10–5.*

Museo Regional de Castro. This museum, one block from the Plaza de Armas, gives a good (Spanish-only) introduction to the region's history and culture. Packed into a fairly small space are artifacts from the Huilliche era (primarily farming and fishing implements) through the 19th century (looms, spinning wheels, and plows). One exhibit displays the history of the archipelago's wooden churches; another shows black-and-white photographs of the damage caused by the 1960 earthquake that rocked southern Chile. The museum has a collection of quotations about Chiloé culture by outsiders. "The Chilote talks little, but thinks a lot. He is rarely spontaneous with outsiders, and even with his own countrymen he isn't too communicative," wrote one ethnographer. ✉ *Esmeralda 205* ☎ *65/263–5967* 🎟 *Free* ⏲ *Jan. and Feb., Mon.–Sat. 9:30– 7, Sun. 10:30–1; Mar.–Dec., weekdays 9:30–1 and 3–6:30, Sat. 9:30–1.*

WHERE TO EAT

$ CAFÉ 🍴 **Cafe del Puente.** There is outstanding cake and coffee with scenic views at this popular café located at the start of Castro's Gamboa district. They also offer excellent breakfasts and sandwiches. But do not miss the *kuchen,* a type of German pie, especially the one filled with blueberries and *murta* berries. [$] *Average main: 4500 pesos* ✉ *Ernesto Riquelme 1180* ☎ *65/263–4878.*

$$ CONTEMPORARY Fodor's Choice ★ 🍴 **El Mercadito.** With a fresh, creative approach to traditional Chilote cuisine, this restaurant is a nice change of pace in the island's restaurant scene—and, most importantly, it serves up really good food. El Mercadito is in a restored house overlooking the waterfront in the historic Pedro Montt barrio. Exciting dishes include "Mi Borrachito," a spicy conger eel stew with *choritos* and fried native potatoes, and "Bombas de Jaiva," a fried, breaded appetizer stuffed with *chupe de jaiba,* a typical crab stew in Chiloé. Be sure to start your meal off with an icy pisco sour. [$] *Average main: 7000 pesos* ✉ *Pedro Montt 210* ☎ *65/253–3866* 🌐 *www.elmercaditodechiloe.cl* ⏲ *Closed Tues.*

$$$ CONTEMPORARY 🍴 **Mar y Canela.** With a charming ambience, Mar y Canela is an intimate dining experience that features inventive food made with fresh, often

organic, local ingredients. Take the classic local fish plate, *merluza austral,* which is served here with a curry sauce flavored with native rhubarb berries and accompanied by sautéed Chilote potatoes with country cheese wrapped in chard. ■ **TIP→ The restaurant shares the premises with Pura Isla, a store for top-quality Chiloé handicrafts and clothing.** $ *Average main: 9000 pesos* ✉ *Ernesto Riquelme 1212* ☎ *65/253–1770* 🌐 *www.marycanela.cl.*

$$ SEAFOOD 🍴 **Sacho Restaurant.** Going strong since the late 1970s, Sacho is the place to go for the favorite seafood plates Chiloé is known for, cooked in the traditional style, from fish and curanto to *chupe de jaiba* (crab stew). Service is friendly and mostly prompt, even when it fills up at lunchtime with locals. Though there is a nice bay view, it's not the ambience you're here for; it's for the Chiloé seafood. There are chicken and beef plates for nonseafood lovers. $ *Average main: 6000 pesos* ✉ *Thomson 213* ☎ *65/263–2709* 🌐 *www.sachorestaurant.cl* ⏲ *Closed Mon.*

WHERE TO STAY

$$ HOTEL 🏨 **Hotel de Castro.** Looming over downtown near the estuary, this hotel has a sloped chalet-style roof with a long skylight, which makes the interior seem bright and airy even on a cloudy day. **Pros:** central location; bay views; spa. **Cons:** older building is dated; weak Wi-Fi signal on some floors. $ *Rooms from: 54000 pesos* ✉ *Chacabuco 202* ☎ *65/263–2301* 🌐 *www.hoteldecastro.cl* 🛏 *49 rooms, 20 suites* 🍽 *Breakfast.*

$$$ HOTEL 🏨 **Hotel de la Isla Enjoy Chiloé.** This five-star hotel, part of Chile's Enjoy casino chain, rents a mix of rooms and self-catering apartments that tastefully blend into the landscape. **Pros:** views; entertainment on-site; spa. **Cons:** Chiloé culture is secondary here. $ *Rooms from: 105000 pesos* ✉ *Ruta 5 Sur 2053* ☎ *65/258–4500* 🛏 *72 rooms, 4 suites* 🍽 *Breakfast.*

8

$$$$ HOTEL 🏨 **Hotel Parque Quilquico.** Across the Dalcahue Channel at Rilan Peninsula, Hotel Parque Quilquico charmingly incorporates the colorful style of Chiloé architecture into a hotel with a green conscience. **Pros:** countryside setting; trail; terraces. **Cons:** Wi-Fi connection spotty in places; some rooms are small. $ *Rooms from: 167445 pesos* ✉ *Quilquico Rural s/n* ☎ *65/2297–1000* 🌐 *www.hpq.cl* 🛏 *21 rooms, 8 palafito suites* 🍽 *Breakfast.*

$$$$ B&B/INN Fodor's Choice ★ 🏨 **Noi Centro de Ocio Chiloé.** A tremendous place to disconnect and relax while exploring Chiloé, this beautiful, countryside hotel rents various types of lodging. **Pros:** privacy; views; luxurious setting. **Cons:** Wi-Fi only in common area. $ *Rooms from: 250000 pesos* ✉ *Península de Rilán* ☎ *65/297–1911* 🌐 *www.centrodeocio.cl* 🛏 *15 rooms, 3 suites* 🍽 *Some meals.*

$$ B&B/INN 🏨 **Palafito 1326 Hotel Boutique.** A renovated *palafito* (traditional stilt house) in the Gambo neighborhood, this hotel inside Castro is a small, quiet alternative to the bigger, luxury options in the area. **Pros:** views from the terrace; central heating; quiet. **Cons:** often sold out; no TV; limited parking. $ *Rooms from: 68000 pesos* ✉ *Ernesto Riquelme 1326* ☎ *65/253–0053* 🌐 *www.palafito1326.cl* 🛏 *12 rooms* 🍽 *Breakfast.*

$$ B&B/INN 🏨 **Palafito del Mar.** One of the best of the many *palafito* hotels on stilts popping up in Castro nowadays, this modern boutique hotel has rooms done right, with blonde wood paneling and earthy-toned furnishings.

Pros: lots of light; location; friendly staff. **Cons:** price is high for this type of hotel. $ *Rooms from: 60000 pesos* ✉ *Pedro Montt 567* ☎ *65/263–1622* ⊕ *www.palafitodelmar.cl* ⇨ *11 rooms, 4 suites* �‖ *Breakfast.*

$$$$
HOTEL
ALL-INCLUSIVE
Fodor'sChoice
★

☷ **Tierra Chiloé.** This stunning 12-room lodge on the Rilan Peninsula combines nature, high design, and verdant countryside like a fine art painting. **Pros:** impressive building; attentive service; tasty meals; secluded, countryside setting. **Cons:** occasional salmon farming pens amid the sea views; most of the excursions are group trips. $ *Rooms from: 341411 pesos* ✉ *San José Playa, Castro, Casilla* ☎ *2/2207–8861* ⊕ *www.tierrachiloe.com* ⇨ *12 rooms* �‖ *All-inclusive.*

SPORTS AND THE OUTDOORS

Sea kayaking around the outlying islands near Castro has become one of Chiloé's main draws. There are also interesting options for fishing, horseback riding, and hiking in the surrounding countryside, particularly in and around Chiloé National Park.

KAYAKING

Altue Sea Kayaking. Altue Sea Kayaking is one of Chile's oldest adventure travel operators. From December to March, the outfitter leads five-day/four-night trips around the Chiloé archipelago, departing from its seakayaking center near Dalcahue. ✉ *Dalcahue* ☎ *9/419–6809* ⊕ *www.seakayakchile.com.*

MULTISPORT OPERATOR

Chiloetnico. This agency runs a variety of nature and culture tours throughout Chiloé, with both day-trip and multiday options, including trekking, cycling, kayaking, city tours, and visits to historical churches. ✉ *Ernesto Riquelme 1228* ☎ *65/263–0951* ⊕ *chiloetnico.cl* ⬚ *From 52,000 pesos.*

SHOPPING

Feria Artesanal Castro. The city's Feria Artesanal, a lively, often chaotic crafts market, is regarded by most as the best place on the island to pick up the woolen sweaters, woven baskets, and straw figures for which Chiloé is known. Prices are already quite reasonable, but vendors expect some bargaining. The stalls share the place with several food vendors. It's open daily 9–dusk though the best time to come is Saturday morning, when artisans from all over the island come to sell their wares. ✉ *Eusebio Lillo s/n.*

CHONCHI

23 km (14 miles) south of Castro.

The colorful wooden houses of Chonchi are on a hillside so steep that it's known in Spanish as the Ciudad de los Tres Pisos (City of Three Stories). The town's name means "slippery earth" in the Huilliche language, and if you tromp up the town's steep streets on a rainy day you can understand why. Arranged around a scenic harbor, Chonchi wins raves as one of Chiloé's most picturesque towns.

GETTING HERE AND AROUND

Chonchi is 15 minutes south of Castro via the Pan-Amercan Highway, Ruta 5.

EXPLORING

Fodor's Choice ★ **Iglesia de San Carlos.** The town's centerpiece, this church on the Plaza de Armas was started by the Jesuits in 1754 but left unfinished until 1859. Rebuilt in the neoclassical style, the church is now a national monument. An unusually ornate arcade with five arches fronts the church, and inside are an intricately carved altar and wooden columns. The church contains Chonchi's most prized relic, a statue of the Virgen de la Candelaria. According to tradition, this image of the Virgin Mary protected the town from the Dutch pirates who destroyed neighboring Castro in 1600. Townspeople celebrate the event every February 2 with fireworks and gunpowder symbolizing the pirate attack. The building is open for mass Sunday at 11 am. ✉ *Plaza de Armas, at Centenario and Francisco Corral.*

Museo de las Tradiciones Chonchinas. This small museum documents life in Chonchi through furnishings and photos in a 19th-century house. ✉ *Centenario 116* ☎ *65/267–2802* 🎟 *500 pesos* 🕒 *Tues.–Sun. 10–1:30 and 3–6:45.*

WHERE TO EAT AND STAY

$ SEAFOOD 🍴 **Mercado Chonchi.** In a tidy building, this market with four restaurants is a great spot for an informal lunch, though it's also open for dinner. The restaurants, in a food court overlooking the water, mainly serve standard Chiloé fare such as curanto and assorted seafoods. A favorite is the restaurant Ballena Azul, which makes great pizza. [$] *Average main: 5000 pesos* ✉ *Irarrázabal 47* 💳 *No credit cards.*

$$$$ B&B/INN 🏨 **Espejo de Luna.** About a 40-minute drive south of Castro, this hotel has astounding vistas of the Gulf of Corcovado with volcanoes and mountains crowning the horizon. **Pros:** excellent restaurant; privacy; natural beauty. **Cons:** poor Internet connection. [$] *Rooms from: 155000 pesos* ✉ *Pan-American Hwy., Km 35; just south of Castro and town of Altyuy, Queilén* ☎ *974/313–091* 🌐 *www.espejodeluna.cl* 🛏 *5 rooms, 3 cabins* 🍽 *Some meals.*

$ B&B/INN 🏨 **Hotel & Cabanas Huildin.** Built in 1945, this building was originally a private home, then for many years a restaurant, until becaming a hotel in 1992. **Pros:** historic building; views of the bay; cozy ambience. **Cons:** some rooms are small; no restaurant; room service ends at 2 pm. [$] *Rooms from: 24000 pesos* ✉ *Centenario 102* ☎ *65/267–1388* 🌐 *www.hotelhuildin.com* 🛏 *12 rooms, 10 cabins* 🍽 *Breakfast.*

PARQUE NACIONAL CHILOÉ

35 km (21 miles) west of Chonchi.

The Parque Nacional Chiloé comprises a huge swath of Chiloé's Pacific coast. It's a wonderful mix of broad beaches, rolling sand dunes, lush temperate rain forest, and, to the north, extensive wetlands, that come together to form one of the country's most visually compelling parks. It's a draw for eco-tourists. But even though the climate is often windy and rainy, this is also just a spectacular place to roam the beautiful beach.

8

GETTING HERE AND AROUND

To get to Chiloé National Park, take the Pan-American Highway, or Ruta 5, south from Ancud or Castro. A paved side road from the highway leading to the park is found at Notuco, near the town of Chonchi, which is only 22½ km (14 miles) south of Castro.

EXPLORING

Fodor'sChoice **Parque Nacional Chiloé.** This 430-square-km (166-square-mile) park hugs
★ Isla Grande's sparsely populated Pacific coast. The park's two sectors differ dramatically. Heavily forested with evergreens, Sector Anay, to the south, is most easily entered from the coastal village of Cucao. A road heads west to the park from the Pan-American Highway at Notuco, just south of Chonchi. Popular among backpackers is its short, woody Tepual Trail, which begins at the Chanquín Visitor Center, 1 km (½ mile) north of the park entrance and winds through a rare, intact forest of tepu trees (*Tepualia stipularis*), whose large, twisted trunks are visible above and below your walking path. Along the path as well are signs explaining the significance of the forest and what it holds. The longer Dunas Trail leads through the forest to the beach dunes near Cacao. Keep an eye out for the Chiloé fox, native to Isla Grande; more reclusive is the *pudú*, a miniature deer. Some 3 km (2 miles) north of the Cucao entrance is a Huilliche community on the shore of Lago Huelde. Unobtrusive visitors are welcome. At the southern end of the park is one of Chile's best beaches, Cucao Beach, where dunes extend along the unusually wide sand. Camping is permitted. The northern Sector Chepu contains primarily wetlands and a large bird population (most notably penguins) and sea-lion colony. Get there via Ruta 5, but take the crossroad toward Rio Chepu, then continue west on a gravel road until Puerto Anguay. ⊠ *North of Cucao and south of Chepu, Parque Nacional Chiloe* ☎ *65/253-2501* 🖼 *1,500 pesos* ☉ *Daily 9–8:30.*

WHERE TO STAY

$ 🏨 **El Fogon de Cucao.** Founded in 1997 by a former newspaper reporter
B&B/INN in Chile, El Fogon de Cucao has a homey atmosphere with rustic decor and big beds. **Pros:** excellent service; lakeside. **Cons:** few rooms so bookings must be made in advance. 💲 *Rooms from: 30000 pesos* ⊠ *Within Chiloé National Park, near Cucao entrance at southern end of park, Chiloe National Park* ☎ *9/946–5685* ⊕ *elfogondecucao.cl* 🛏 *9 rooms, 1 cabin* 🚫 *No credit cards* ❗️◯❗ *Breakfast.*

$$ 🏨 **Palafito Cucao Hostel.** With nine rooms, each with private bathroom
B&B/INN and a view of Cucao Lake, this is an excellent option for overnight visits to Chiloé National Park. **Pros:** lake views; heating. **Cons:** no restaurant. 💲 *Rooms from: 50000 pesos* ⊠ *Chiloe National Park, Cucao* ☎ *65/297–1164* ⊕ *www.hostelpalafitocucao.cl* 🛏 *9 rooms* 🚫 *No credit cards* ❗️◯❗ *Breakfast.*

QUEILÉN

47 km (29 miles) southeast of Chonchi.

This town named for the red cypress trees that dot the area sits on an elongated peninsula and, as such, is the only town on Isla Grande with two seafronts. Though Chiloé's windy, rainy, and cold climate is mostly unfavorable for typical beach activities, the beauty of the unspoiled seaside is unquestionable. Two of Isla Grande's best beaches are the **Playa de Queilén**, in the center of town, and the **Playa Lelbun**, 15 km (9 miles) northwest of the city.

GETTING HERE AND AROUND

From Castro, go south on Ruta 5 until you get to the Chonchi exit; from Chonchi a gravel road heads southeast to Queilén.

EXPLORING

Mirador. Uphill on Calle Presidente Kennedy, this scenic overlook has stupendous views of the Golfo de Ancud, the smaller islands in the archipelago, and, on a clear day, the Volcán Corcovado on the mainland. ⊠ *Calle Presidente Kennedy*.

Refugio de Navegantes. The town's cultural center contains a small museum with artifacts and old black-and-white photographs. Nothing is very colorful here—the muted tones of the pottery, fabrics, and farm implements reflect the stark life of colonial Chiloé. ⊠ *Pedro Aguirre Cerda s/n* ☎ *65/236–7149* 💲 *Free* ⊙ *Weekdays 9–12:30 and 2:30–6.*

QUELLÓN

99 km (60 miles) south of Castro.

The Pan-American Highway, which begins in Alaska and stretches for most of the length of North and South America, ends without fanfare here in Quellón, Chiloé's southernmost city. Quellón was the famed "end of Christendom" described by Charles Darwin during his 19th-century visit. Just a few years earlier it had been the southernmost outpost of Spain's empire in the New World. For most visitors today, Quellón is also the end of the line. But for hikers and nature lovers, Parque Tantauco is nearby. It's also the starting point for ferries that head to the Southern Coast.

8

GETTING HERE AND AROUND

Quellón is about a one-hour drive south of Castro, on the paved Ruta 5. From Quellón, you can also catch a ferry with Naviera Austral to Chaitén (Thursday), Puerto Cisnes (Tuesday), or Chacabuco (Wednesday and Saturday) along the Carretera Austral.

ESSENTIALS

Ferry Information Ferry dock ⊠ *Pedro Montt 48* ☎ *65/268–2207.*

EXPLORING

Museo Inchin Cuivi Ant. Taking its name from a Huilliche phrase meaning "from our past," the Inchin Cuivi Ant Museum stands apart from other museums in Chiloé because of its "living" exhibitions: Chilote women spin woolens on their looms, make empanadas in a traditional fogón, and cultivate a botanical garden with herbs, plants, and trees native to Chiloé. ⊠ *Ladrilleros 225* 💲 *500 pesos* ⊙ *Jan.–Mar., weekdays 10–1 and 2–8.*

OFF THE
BEATEN
PATH
Parque Tantauco. This vast, 118,000-hectare (300,000-acre) park founded by former Chile President Sebastián Piñera has added an attractive guesthouse, campground with modern bathrooms, and a series of hiking trails and overnight shelters for those who wind their way through the park's thick Valdivian temperate rainforests and rocky coastline. Serious hiking and camping enthusiasts should consider the five-day, 32-mile Transversal Trail from Chaiguata (also reachable by bus from Quellón) to Caleta Inío, the park headquarters, where you can get a boat back to Quellón. En route, you can sleep at four simple shelters, complete with bunks, cooking facilities, and latrines. Park entrance for adults costs 3,500 pesos and children 500 pesos. Trekking shelters run 8,000 pesos per night, while Caleta Ines Guesthouse has rooms for 40,000 pesos per night. The park also rent tents and kayaks to visitors. ⊠ *La Paz 034* ☎ *65/277–3100* ⊕ *parquetantauco.cl.*

WHERE TO EAT AND STAY

$
FAST FOOD
✕ **Sandwicheria Mitos.** The giant sandwiches here have obtained mythical status in these parts. The restaurant also has an extensive daily menu featuring a variety of traditional Chilean dishes like cazuela, roasted chicken, lentejas, and more. This is a good break from the ubiquitous seafood establishments on the waterfront. $ *Average main: 6000 pesos* ⊠ *Jorge Vivar 235* ☎ *9/120–6585.*

$$
HOTEL
Hotel Patagonia Insular. This seven-year-old hotel is the most modern lodging in Quellón by a good margin. **Pros:** the views; four-star amenities; friendly owner. **Cons:** no gym or spa; unstable Wi-Fi signal. $ *Rooms from: 56000 pesos* ⊠ *Av. Juan Ladrilleros 1737* ☎ *65/268–1610* ⊕ *www.hotelpatagoniainsular.cl* ⌐ *32 rooms, 2 suites* ⦿ *Breakfast.*

$
B&B/INN
Hotel Tierra del Fuego. This rambling alerce-shingle house, dating from the 1920s, is on Quellón's waterfront. **Pros:** great location; good restaurant; cheap. **Cons:** rooms vary in quality. $ *Rooms from: 20000 pesos* ⊠ *Av. Pedro Montt 445* ☎ *65/268–2079* ⌐ *23 rooms, 2 suites; 14 with bath* ⊟ *No credit cards* ⦿ *Breakfast.*

SPORTS AND THE OUTDOORS

Ana Villosa Sea Tours. Quellón is considered one of the best starting points for whale-watching, most notably for the blue whale. Also present in the canals and islands off the spectacular coast here are a plethora of marine birds and Peale's and Chilean dolphins. On board the *Ana Villlosa,* Ana Jaramillio, a Chilean who's lived much of her life in the United States, runs day tours to view these charismatic animals. The tour culminates with a visit (and lunch) on the scenic Cailin Island. ☎ *9/824–67340* ✎ *amjaramillobecker@yahoo.com.*

SHOPPING

Feria Artesanal Llauquil. Quellón's market doesn't have the hustle and bustle of similar ones in Castro and Dalcahue, but there are some good buys on woolens and straw folkloric figures. Don't bother to bargain; the prices are already extremely reasonable. ⊠ *Av. Gómez García* ⦿ *Dec.–Feb., daily 9–7; Mar.–Nov., Mon.–Sat. 9–6.*

THE SOUTHERN COAST

WELCOME TO
THE SOUTHERN COAST

TOP REASONS
TO GO

★ **Scenery:** The Carretera Austral, a dusty dirt road that was blazed through southern Chile in the 1970s and '80s, has opened up one of the most beautiful places in the world to tourists. Rent a car, preferably a four-wheel-drive truck or jeep, and soak it all in.

★ **Glaciers:** To watch a chunk of ice break off the glaciers near Mount San Valentín and fall with a thundering splash into the sea below is reason enough for a trip along the southern coast to Laguna San Rafael National Park.

★ **Fishing:** Fly-fishing fanatics were among the first to explore this area thoroughly. At any number of lodges, you can step right outside your door for great fishing. A short boat trip brings you to isolated spots where you won't run into another soul for the entire day.

★ **Rafting and kayaking:** The Futaleufú River is Class V-plus. That's raft speak for very fast-moving water. In fact, this river is considered one of the fastest in the world.

1 Chaitén, Futaleufú, and Puerto Puyuhuapi. Chaitén is the beginning point for most journeys down the Carretera Austral. From there, head to Futaleufú, located next to a world-class river for rafting and fishing, and Puerto Puyuhuapi, a scenic Patagonian town near Queulat National Park.

2 Coyhaique and Nearby. Where Río Simpson and Río Coyhaique come together is Coyhaique, the only community of any size on the Carretera Austral. Calling itself "the capital of Patagonia," Coyhaique has some 59,000 residents—more than half of the region's population.

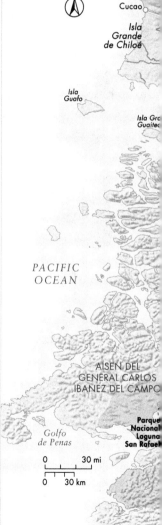

Parque Nacional Chiloé

Cucao

Isla Grande de Chiloé

Isla Guafo

Isla Gr
Guaitec

PACIFIC OCEAN

AISÉN DEL GENERAL CARLOS IBÁÑEZ DEL CAMPO

Parque Nacional Laguna San Rafael

Golfo de Penas

0   30 mi
0   30 km

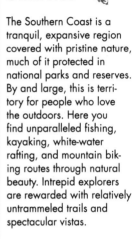

GETTING ORIENTED

The Southern Coast is a tranquil, expansive region covered with pristine nature, much of it protected in national parks and reserves. By and large, this is territory for people who love the outdoors. Here you find unparalleled fishing, kayaking, white-water rafting, and mountain biking routes through natural beauty. Intrepid explorers are rewarded with relatively untrammeled trails and spectacular vistas.

9

Updated by Jimmy Langman

The sliver of land known as the Southern Coast stretches for more than 1,000 km (620 miles), from the southernmost part of the Lakes District through southernmost Aysén. For travelers driving along the Carretera Austral, or Southern Highway, it's like a seemingly boundless tour through a natural playground. Many of its wondrous places are preserved in numerous national parks and reserves, making the region a growing, global hotspot for outdoors sports and ecotourism.

In the Southern Coast, forested mountains dominate the landscape, some of which rise dramatically from the shores of shimmering lakes. Slender waterfalls and nearly vertical streams, often seeming to emerge from the rock itself, tumble and slide from neck-craning heights. Some dissipate into misty nothingness before touching the ground, while others flow into innumerable rivers—large and small, wild and gentle—heading westward to the sea.

With the expansion of the Carretera Austral, migration has increased to the region. Still, this is one of the least-populated areas in South America, with a population density said to be lower than the Sahara Desert. The infrequent hamlets scattered along the low-lying areas of this rugged region subsist mainly as fishing villages or small farming centers. Coyhaique, the only town here of any size, has lots of dining and lodging options. Several intrepid entrepreneurs have also established world-class accommodations in remote locations throughout the region, near spectacular rivers, mountain peaks, lakes, volcanoes, and glaciers.

Planning a visit to the region's widely separated points of interest can be challenging, as getting from place to place is often difficult. Creating a logical itinerary in southern Chilean Patagonia is as much about choosing how to get here as it is about choosing where you want to go. The most rewarding mode of transport through this area is a combination of boat and plane, with an occasional car rental if you want to journey a little deeper into the hinterlands.

PLANNER

WHEN TO GO

Late spring through summer—late November to mid-March—is considered high season in this part of southern Chile. It's highly recommended that you make advance reservations if your intention is to stay at high-end hotels or resorts during this time. Although the weather is likely to be cooler and rainier in the spring (September into November) and fall (March to May), it's also a fine time for travel here.

PLANNING YOUR TIME

On your first day head straight to Futaleufú, home to one of the world's fastest and most spectacular rivers and situated among breathtaking Patagonian mountain valleys. After a few nights there, spend a day going down the Carretera Austral, or Southern Highway, to Puerto Puyuhuapi, preferably in a rented, four-wheel-drive truck or jeep to give you more flexibility. A stay at Puyuhuapi Lodge & Spa, a resort accessible only by boat, is a great way to relax and recharge for the next phase of your journey. While in Puyuhuapi, consider spending an extra day there to visit the "hanging glacier" at Parque Nacional Queulat. Afterward, go to Coyhaique, located about five hours south. The largest city in the region, Coyhaique will be a good place for shopping and eating a nice meal before heading to nearby Puerto Chacabuco, where you can board a boat bound for the unforgettable glaciers at Parque Nacional Laguna San Rafael. If you lack the time to continue farther south to see still more of Patagonia's incredible landscape, return to Puerto Montt by a ferry boat that departs from Puerto Chacabuco.

GETTING HERE AND AROUND

AIR TRAVEL

LAN has flights to the region from Santiago, Puerto Montt, and Punta Arenas. They arrive at the Southern Coast's only major airport, 55 km (34 miles) south of Coyhaique, in the town of Balmaceda. Other carriers serving southern Chile include Sky Airlines, Aerocord, and Pewen Servicios Aéreos

BOAT AND FERRY TRAVEL

Be warned that ferries in southern Chile are slow and not always scenic, particularly if skies are the least bit cloudy, but they are reliable. If you're touring the region by car, the ferry is a good choice. The main companies serving this area are Navimag, Naviera Austral, and Transmarchilay.

BUS TRAVEL

Service between Puerto Montt and Cochrane is by private operators such as Tur-Bus. Travel along the Carretera Austral is often agonizingly and inexplicably slow, so don't plan on getting anywhere on schedule.

CAR TRAVEL

You can drive the northern part of the Southern Coast without the aid of a ferry, but you need to spend some time in Argentina along the way, eventually crossing back into Chile near Futaleufú. The best route takes you to Bariloche, crossing over the Argentina border near Osorno and Puyehue, just north of Puerto Montt.

Along the Carretera Austral, the road that runs through the southern coast, Chile's southernmost reaches seem to disintegrate into a tangle of sounds, straits, channels, and fjords. The road struggles valiantly along this route, connecting tiny fishing towns and farming villages all the way from Puerto Montt to Villa O'Higgins.

Navigating the Carretera Austral requires some planning, as communities along the way are sometimes few and far between. Some parts of the highway, especially in the southernmost reaches, are deserted. Check out your car thoroughly, especially the air in the spare tire. Make sure you have a jack and jumper cables. Plan your refueling stops ahead of time and bring along food in case you find yourself stuck far from the nearest restaurant.

RESTAURANTS

All manner of fish, lamb, beef, and chicken dishes are available in the Southern Coast. By and large, entrées are simple and hearty. Given the area's great distance from Chile's Central Valley, where most of Chile's fruits and vegetables are grown, most things that appear on your plate probably grew somewhere nearby. Many dishes are prepared from scratch when you order.

HOTELS

This region offers a surprisingly wide choice of accommodations. What you don't find is the blandness of chain hotels. Most of the region's establishments reflect the distinct personalities and idiosyncrasies of their owners.

Some of the most humble homes in villages along the Carretera Austral are supplementing their family income by becoming bed-and-breakfasts. A stay in one of these *hospedajes* is an ideal way to meet the people and experience the culture. These accommodations are not regulated, so inquire about the availability of hot water and confirm that breakfast is included. Don't hesitate to ask to see the room—you may even get a choice. *Hotel reviews have been shortened. For full information, visit Fodors.com.*

WHAT IT COSTS IN CHILEAN PESOS (IN THOUSANDS)			
$	**$$**	**$$$**	**$$$$**
Restaurants	Under 6	6–8	9–11	over 11
Hotels	Under 46	46–75	76–105	over 105

Restaurant prices are the average cost of a main course at dinner or, if dinner is not served, at lunch. Hotel prices are the lowest cost of a standard double room in high season, excluding tax.

TOURS

Nomads of the Seas. This small, luxury ship cruises along the northern Chilean Patagonian coast on three one-week, all-inclusive programs: heli-skiing, fly-fishing, and wildlife adventures, which includes whale- and bird-watching, trekking, kayaking, rafting, snorkeling, jet boating, and hydrospeeding. Everything on board *The Atmosphere* is top-of-the-line, from the helicopters to the gourmet meals. It's expensive, yes, but this is a trip of a lifetime. ✉ *Del Inca 4446, Santiago* ☎ *2/2414–4690* ⊕ *www.nomads.cl* 💲 *From US$12,805.*

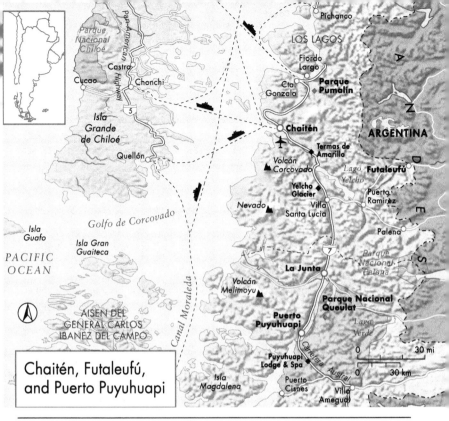

CHAITÉN, FUTALEUFÚ, AND PUERTO PUYUHUAPI

CHAITÉN

201 km (125 miles) south of Puerto Montt.

If you are traveling by ferry to and from Chiloé or Puerto Montt, you will likely pass through Chaitén. In May 2008, a volcano erupted near the town, forcing its residents to evacuate. Today, however, many have returned and Chaitén is springing back to life, with the remnants of the disaster a tourist attraction in its own right. It's an interesting and pleasant place to stay for a night or two. You can also buy food and other supplies in town before your southbound journey.

GETTING HERE AND AROUND

Four days a week (Sunday, Monday, Thursday, and Friday), Naviera Austral (⊕ *www.navieraustral.cl*) operates a ferry service between Chaitén and Puerto Montt in the Lake District and Quellón on Chiloé. Flying is also an option; a few small airlines like Aerocord, CieloMarAustral, and Pewen Servicios Aéreos run flights between Chaitén and Puerto Montt.

It's also possible to drive to Chaitén from Puerto Montt via the Carretera Austral, but you have to make use of two car ferries run by Transportes Austral (🌐 *www.taustral.cl*). It's about a six-hour journey. You must reserve your ticket ahead of time through the website or a travel agency.

EXPLORING

Lago Yelcho. One of the best places in the region to fish, this lake is constantly packed with brown trout. It runs along the Carretera Austral south of Chaitén, and there are several fishing lodges nearby catering to anglers.

Termas del Amarillo. These natural hot springs about 31 km (19 miles) southeast of Chaitén provide a nice respite for weary muscles. Situated along a river running through a heavily forested valley, the springs are warmed by Michimahuida Volcano. In addition to the natural baths, there are dressing rooms, cabins, a sauna, and pool on-site. ✉ *Off Carretera Austral, 6 km (4 miles) inland from Puerto Cardenas* 🎟 *3,600 pesos* ⏲ *Daily 8 am–9 pm.*

Yelcho Glacier. Just 2 km (1 mile) past the village of Puerto Cárdenas is Puente Ventisquero Yelcho (Glacier Bridge), the beginning of a challenging two-hour hike to Ventisquero Cavi (Hanging Glacier). The trail is clearly marked but Chaitur Excursions (🌐 *www.chaitur.com*) also organizes group treks to the glacier. ✉ *Carretera Austral*

WHERE TO STAY

$$$$ B&B/INN ALL-INCLUSIVE 🏨 **Chucao Lodge.** Focused on the serious fly-fisherman, Chucao Lodge is a high-end way to experience Lago Yelcho and other top fishing spots in the Palena area. **Pros:** fishing at diverse spots; all-inclusive. **Cons:** a long journey to get here. [$] *Rooms from: 250000 pesos* ✉ *Lago Yelcho, Puerto Cardenas* ☎ *801/415–9617* 🌐 *www.chucaolodge.com* 🛏 *5 rooms* 💳 *No credit cards* ⏲ *Closed May–mid-Oct.* 🍴 *All-inclusive.*

$$$ RESORT 🏨 **El Pangue Lodge.** Midway between La Junta and Puyuhuapi is this lodge located on the northern shore of Lake Risopatrón. **Pros:** lake setting; cabins; ideal spot for fishing. **Cons:** remote location. [$] *Rooms from: 99000 pesos* ✉ *Carretera Austral Km 240, Puerto Puyuhuapi* ☎ *67/252–6906* 🌐 *www.elpangue.com* 🛏 *12 cabins* ⏲ *Closed June and July* 🍴 *Multiple meal plans.*

$ B&B/INN 🏨 **Hospedaje and Cabanas Pudu.** This warm and inviting place, open year-round, takes you in while you wait for the ferry boat out of Chaitén. **Pros:** big and comfortable beds; friendly owners. **Cons:** often booked solid; no breakfast included. [$] *Rooms from: 45000 pesos* ✉ *Corcovado 668* ☎ *9/8227–9602, 65/273–1336* ✉ *puduchaiten@hotmail.com* 🛏 *3 rooms, 8 cabins* 🍴 *No meals.*

$$ B&B/INN 🏨 **Hotel Schilling.** For more than 40 years, Hotel Schilling has been the reliable, go-to hotel in Chaitén. **Pros:** centrally located; Wi-Fi and cable; parking. **Cons:** some rooms have dated furniture; quality of beds varies. [$] *Rooms from: 50000 pesos* ✉ *Corcovado 230* ☎ *65/273–1295, 9/6826–0680* ✉ *hotelschilling@hotmail.com* 🛏 *10 rooms* 💳 *No credit cards* 🍴 *Breakfast.*

CLOSE UP

The Carretera Austral: Chile's Road to Riches

The Pan-American Highway, which snakes its way through the northern half of Chile, never quite makes it to the Southern Coast. To connect this remote region with the rest of the country, former President Augusto Pinochet proposed a massive public works project to construct a highway called the Carretera Austral. But the $300 million venture had another purpose as well. Pinochet was afraid that without a strong military presence in the region, neighboring Argentina could begin chipping away at Chile's territory. The highway would allow the army easier access to an area that until then was accessible only by boat.

Ground was broken on the Carretera Austral in 1976, and in 1982 the first section, running from Chaitén to Coyhaique, opened to great fanfare. The only trouble was that you still couldn't get there from the mainland. It took another five years for the extension from Chaitén north to Puerto Montt to be completed. An extension from Coyhaique south to Cochrane was finished the following year.

The word "*finished*" is misleading, as construction continues to this day. Although the Carretera Austral is nicely paved near Puerto Montt, it soon reveals its true nature as a two-lane gravel surface that crawls inexorably southward for 1,156 km (718 miles) toward the outpost of Villa O'Higgins. Nor is the highway contiguous. In places the road ends abruptly at water's edge—ferries link these broken stretches of highway. The segment from Chaitén to Coyhaique is mostly gravel road, but every year the paved sections grow longer.

The Carretera Austral is lauded in tourism brochures as "a beautiful road studded with rivers, waterfalls, forests, lakes, glaciers, and the occasional hamlet." This description is accurate—you may live the rest of your life and never see anything half as beautiful as the scenery. However, the highway itself is far from perfection. The mostly unpaved road has dozens of single-lane, wide-board bridges over streams and rivers. Shoulders are nonexistent or made of soft, wheel-grabbing gravel. Periodically, traffic must wend its way through construction, amid heavy equipment and workers.

What the Carretera Austral gives adventurous travelers is a chance to see a part of the world where few have ventured. The views from the highway are truly amazing, from the conical top of Volcán Corcovado near Chaitén to the sprawling valleys around Coyhaique. Here you find national parks, where the trails are virtually deserted, such as Parque Nacional Queulat and Reserva Nacional Río Simpson.

9

EN ROUTE

🏨 **Yelcho en la Patagonia.** On the shore of Lake Yelcho, one of the best fishing spots in the world, Yelcho en la Patagonia provides a multitude of lodging and excursion options. **Pros:** location on the shore of the lake; world-class fly-fishing; cabins ideal for families. **Cons:** Wi-Fi connectivity issues. $ *Rooms from: 108000 pesos* ✉ *Lago Yelcho, Puerto Cardenas* ☎ *65/257–6005* 🌐 *www.yelcho.cl* 🛏 *8 rooms, 6 cabins* 🕓 *Closed May–Nov.* 🍴 *Multiple meal plans.*

PARQUE PUMALÍN

56 km (35 miles) north of Chaitén.

The world's largest privately owned nature preserve, Parque Pumalín in northern Chaitén hosts a pristine set of mountains, temperate rain forests, volcanoes, lakes, and rivers. Kayaking around the park's coastal fjords is a popular activity, as is hiking through some of the last intact alerce forest anywhere. The park also has excellent camping facilities, first-class cabins, and a superb café and restaurant at its headquarters in Caleta Gonzalo.

GETTING HERE AND AROUND

Caleta Gonzalo, headquarters of Pumalín Park, is about 60 km (37 miles) north of Chaitén. The road from Chaitén to Caleta Gonzalo is well maintained but not paved. You can also reach Caleta Gonzalo by ferry. To venture to the northernmost areas of the park, such as Cahuelmo hot springs, you need to rent a boat in Hornopirén, a small town about 110 km (68 miles) southeast of Puerto Montt.

TOURS

Alsur Expeditions. This longtime tour operator in Puerto Varas runs tours to the park, including treks, horseback riding, and sea kayaking. Prices vary depending on group size. ⊠ *Puerto Varas* ☎ *65/223–2300, 9/871–8827* ⊕ *www.alsurexpeditions.com.*

Chaitur. This agency in Chaitén knows the park better than almost anyone, outside of the park administrators. Tours include an inexpensive, one-day hike at three trails (Sendero los Alerces, Sendero Cascadas Escondidas, and Sendero el Volcán). ⊠ *O'Higgins 67, Chaitén* ☎ *9/7468–5608* ⊕ *www.chaitur.com* ⊠ *From 10,000 pesos.*

Yak Expediciones. This reputable tour operator in Puerto Varas runs sea kayaking trips off the fjordal coast of the northern section of Pumalín Park, with camping along the way and visits to the natural hot springs at Cahuelmo. ⊠ *Puerto Varas* ☎ *9/8332–0574* ⊕ *www.yakexpediciones.cl* ⊠ *From 440,000 pesos.*

EXPLORING

Parque Pumalín. Funded and organized by conservationist Douglas Tompkins, this park covers nearly 375,000 hectares (800,000 acres) and shelters the largest—and one of the few remaining—intact alerce forests in the world. Alerces, the world's second-longest-living tree species at up to 4,000 years, are often compared to the equally giant California redwood. Tompkins, founder of the clothing companies ESPRIT and the North Face, owns two strips of land that stretch from one side of the country to the other. He tried to buy the parcel between the two halves that would have connected them, but the sale was fiercely opposed by some officials at the time who questioned why a foreigner should own so much of Chile. The Pan-American Highway, which trundles all the way north to Alaska, is interrupted here, though the government is pushing to expand the highway through Pumalín sometime over the next decade. Meanwhile, there does exist a well-maintained road stretching 60 km (37 miles) from Chaitén to the northern entrance of the park at Caleta Gonzalo.

Parque Pumalín encompasses some of the most pristine landscape in the region, if not the world. There are a dozen trails that wind past lakes and waterfalls. Stay in excellent wooden cabins, or at one of the 17 campsites, or put up your tent on one of the local farms scattered across the area that welcome travelers. After the Chaitén Volcano eruption here in 2008, the main entrance to the park was moved to El Amarillo, some 30 km (18 miles) south of Chaitén. But one can still arrive via the more developed Caleta Gonzalo entrance to the north, where a ferry from Hornopiren can drop you off, and where the cabins and a park restaurant are located. ☒ *Information center:, Klenner 299, Puerto Varas* ☏ *65/225–0079* ⊕ *www.parquepumalin.cl* ⊡ *Free* ☉ *Daily*

Chaitur Excursiones. This tour agency in Chaitén can help you with transport to and from the park. ⊕ *www.chaitur.com.*

WHERE TO STAY

$$$
B&B/INN

🏠 **Cabañas Caleta Gonzalo.** Seven gray-shingled cabanas, each designed to be distinct from its neighbor, sit high on stilts against the backdrop of the misty mountains. **Pros:** unique; close to nature. **Cons:** remote. Ⓢ *Rooms from: 85000 pesos* ☒ *Caleta Gonzalo, Parque Pumalín* ☏ *65/225–0079* ✎ *reservas@parquepumalin.cl* ⟿ *9 cabins* ¡◎¡ *Breakfast.*

FUTALEUFÚ

159 km (99 miles) east of Chaitén.

Near the town of Villa Lucia, Ruta 231 branches east from the Carretera Austral and winds around Lago Yelcho. About 159 km (99 miles) later, not far from the Argentine border, it reaches the tiny town of Futaleufú. Despite being barely five square blocks, Futaleufú is on many travelers' itineraries. World-class adventure sports await here, where the Río Espolón and the Río Futaleufú collide. It's the staging center for serious river and sea kayaking, white-water rafting, mountain biking, fly-fishing, canyon hiking, and horseback riding. Day trips for less-experienced travelers are available.

GETTING HERE AND AROUND

The road from Chaitén to Futaleufú, which takes about four hours to drive, is almost entirely unpaved, and conditions are spotty at times. However, it's also possible to enter Futaleufú from Argentina, which is about 190 km (118 miles) southwest of Esquel. From Bariloche, Argentina, drive south for about five hours through pleasant Argentine tourist towns like El Bolson and Esquel. After Esquel you come upon the road that leads to Futaleufú. The roads are paved throughout the Argentine portion of the trip, and a car rented in Puerto Montt costs less than 40,000 pesos, although better deals can be had in Santiago. Some bus companies offer service to Futaleufú from Puerto Montt and Osorno. In Chaitén, Chaitur Excursiones (☏ *746–85608* ⊕ *www.chaitur. com*) runs mini-van service to Futaleufú.

ESSENTIALS

Visitor Information Tourist Office ☒ *Av. Bernardo O'Higgins 334* ☏ *65/272–1241.*

TOURS

Patagonia Elements. Recognized for its experience and professionalism on the Futaleufú, this Chilean-owned outfitter offers rafting, floating, fly-fishing, trekking, and kayaking. Rafting day trips are an especially inexpensive way to experience the river. ⊠ *Pedro Aguirre Cerda 549* ☎ *9/7499–0296* ⊕ *www.patagoniaelements.com* ⊠ *From US$99.*

WHERE TO EAT

$$
CHILEAN
✕ **Martin Pescador.** The restaurant's fireplace and library supply ambience along with some of the finest food on the Carretera Austral. Chilean and regional dishes like grilled trout and roasted lamb are prepared with style and mostly organic ingredients. An added benefit is that the restaurant is run by a longtime American rafting guide, who can give inside info on outdoor activities in the area. The restaurant's bar is also somewhat of a local hangout, so it's a good place to meet people. Call in advance to get the best table. $ *Average main: 8000 pesos* ⊠ *Balmaceda 603* ☎ *65/272–1279* ✉ *restaurantemartinpescador@yahoo.com.*

$
CAFÉ
✕ **Sur Andes.** This coffee shop and restaurant serves good, authentic coffee and fresh-squeezed orange juice along with tempting pastries, chocolates, sandwiches, vegetarian plates, and traditional Chilean dishes such as *pastel de choclo,* a sort of corn and meat pie. It also has lodging and trip options. $ *Average main: 6000 pesos* ⊠ *Pedro Aguirre Cerda 308* ☎ *65/272–1405* ⊕ *www.surandeschile.cl* ⊟ *No credit cards.*

WHERE TO STAY

$$
B&B/INN
☷ **Hostería Río Grande.** Guest rooms are simply decorated with carpeting, wood-paneled walls, big cozy beds, and lots of sunlight coming in through several windows. **Pros:** modern facilities; central location. **Cons:** breakfast options could be better. $ *Rooms from: 69000 pesos* ⊠ *Bernardo O'Higgins 397* ☎ *65/272–1320* ⊕ *www.pachile.com* ⇆ *12 rooms* ☉ *Breakfast.*

$$$$
B&B/INN
☷ **Hotel El Barranco.** This hotel stands out for its first-class rooms and facilities, including a pool, gym, sauna, and bikes for guests. **Pros:** good food; in-house pool, which is a rarity in these parts; central location. **Cons:** Wi-Fi unstable. $ *Rooms from: 123000 pesos* ⊠ *Bernardo O'Higgins 172* ☎ *65/272–1314* ⊕ *www.elbarrancochile.cl* ⇆ *10 rooms* ☉ *Closed May–July* ☉ *Multiple meal plans.*

$$
B&B/INN
☷ **La Gringa Carioca.** This small, rustic B&B within walking distance of the town plaza provides a countryside homey ambience with picturesque views of the surrounding mountains and Espolon River. **Pros:** central location; homelike atmosphere. **Cons:** rooms get cold at night. $ *Rooms from: 69000 pesos* ⊠ *Sargento Aldea 498* ☎ *65/272–1260* ⊕ *hostallagringacarioca.cl* ⇆ *5 rooms* ☉ *Breakfast.*

$$$$
HOTEL
Fodor'sChoice
★
☷ **Uman Lodge.** This exceptional five-star lodge in the middle of some of Patagonia's most beautiful scenery has 16 large suites, with, despite the remote location, all the amenities of a high end hotel, including cable TV, sofas, and impeccable design. **Pros:** views of the Futaleufú River; luxurious rooms; five-star amenities in a remote setting. **Cons:** a long trip to get here. $ *Rooms from: 206000 pesos* ⊠ *Fundo La Confluencia* ☎ *65/272–1700* ⊕ *www.umanlodge.cl* ⇆ *16 suites* ☉ *Closed mid-Apr.–mid-Oct.* ☉ *Multiple meal plans.*

SPORTS AND THE OUTDOORS

The main reason to visit Futaleufú is to partake in the plethora of sports and outdoor options in the area.

Earth River Expeditions. This popular eco-conscious river outfitter offers eight-day rafting trips down the Futaleufú. Earth River owns four "wilderness camps" along the river, each decked out with hot tubs and access to a variety of other sports in addition to the rafting. ☎ *800/643–2784* 🌐 *www.earthriver.com* 🎟 *From US$3,150.*

Expediciones Chile. This tour company is led and founded by former Olympic kayaker, Chris Spelius. He pioneered rafting excursions in Futaleufú, and was one of the first ever to kayak the entire river. Rafting itineraries range from three days to two weeks. Mountain-biking and horse-riding trips are available, too. ✉ *Gabriela Mistral 296* ☎ *888/488–9082* 🌐 *www.exchile.com* 🎟 *From US$1,495.*

H2O Patagonia. If you're looking for luxury and high-powered rafting, then consider H2O Patagonia, which offers eight-day rafting trips combined with a stay at their exclusive ranch, with meals cooked by an "international chef," fine wines, hot tub, and spa. Rates begin at US$3,600. ☎ *828/333–4615* 🌐 *www.h2opatagonia.com.*

LA JUNTA

150 km (93 miles) south of Chaitén.

If you're traveling by car or jeep down Carretera Austral, this small town of approximately 1,200 residents is a good place to stop for gas, meals, or an overnight rest. The town itself doesn't offer much more in terms of touristic value, but it is within close proximity to top fishing and eco-tourism spots, such as the Palena River and the 12,725-hectare (31,444-acre) Reserva Nacional Lago Rosselot.

9

GETTING HERE AND AROUND

There is only one road in and out of La Junta, the Carretera Austral. There are several minibus transport options to La Junta, leaving from Chaitén and Coyhaique.

WHERE TO STAY

$$ B&B/INN 🏨 **Espacio y Tiempo.** This is a great find after a long day driving down the Carretera Austral. **Pros:** telephone service in rooms; modern comforts; excellent in-house restaurant. **Cons:** Internet connection can be slow. [$] *Rooms from: 66000 pesos* ✉ *Carretera Austral 399* ☎ *67/231–4141* 🌐 *www.espacioytiempo.cl* 🛏 *9 rooms* 🍴 *Breakfast.*

$$$$ B&B/INN FAMILY 🏨 **Fundo Los Leones.** This lodge provides a stunning, quiet place to relax and engage in outdoor excursions, such as fishing, bird-watching, and hiking in pristine natural surroundings. **Pros:** natural beauty; quiet; friendly service. **Cons:** remote location; Internent connection is slow. [$] *Rooms from: 129000 pesos* ✉ *58 km west of La Junta, near small fishing village called Raúl Marín Balmaceda* ☎ *9/7898–2956* 🌐 *www.fundolosleones.cl* 🛏 *4 rooms* 💳 *No credit cards* 🍴 *Breakfast.*

PUERTO PUYUHUAPI

196 km (123 miles) south of Chaitén.

This mossy fishing village of about 500 residents is one of the oldest along the Carretera Austral. It was founded in 1935 by German immigrants fleeing the economic ravages of post–World War I Europe. As in much of Patagonia, Chile offered free land to settlers with the idea of making annexation by Argentina more difficult. Those early immigrants ventured into the wilderness to clear the forests and make way for farms.

Today this sleepy town near Queulat National Park and Termas de Puyuhuapi is a convenient stopover for those headed farther south in the region. It has a few modest guesthouses, as well as some markets and a gas station.

GETTING HERE AND AROUND

The mostly unpaved 210-km (130 miles) drive from Coyhaique along the Carretera Austral can be undertaken by car or bus. Patagonia Connection (🌐 *www.patagonia-connection.com*), a Santiago tour company, also gets you here in five hours by boat if you plan to stay at their Puyuhuapi Lodge. A small landing strip nearby serves private planes only.

WHERE TO STAY

$ B&B/INN 🏨 **Casa Ludwig.** This hotel provides a friendly atmosphere in an historic home with a big fireplace and living room. **Pros:** friendly service; great atmosphere. **Cons:** can be difficult to get a room during summer months. [$] *Rooms from: 40000 pesos* ✉ *Otto Uebel 202* ☎ *67/232–5220* 🌐 *www.casaludwig.cl* 🛏 *10 rooms, 6 with bath* 💳 *No credit cards* 🕒 *Closed Apr.–Sept.* 🍴 *Breakfast.*

$ B&B/INN 🏨 **Hostería Alemana.** The home of Ursula Flack, the last of the town's original German settlers, is a great choice for budget-minded travelers who want to explore the beautiful countryside. **Pros:** hotel has local character; clean. **Cons:** located just outside of town. [$] *Rooms from: 35000 pesos* ✉ *Otto Uebel 450* ☎ *67/232–5118* 🌐 *www.hosteriaalemana.cl* 🛏 *9 rooms* 🍴 *Breakfast.*

$$$ RESORT Fodor's Choice ★ 🏨 **Puyuhuapi Lodge & Spa.** Located 13 km (8 miles) south of Puerto Puyuhuapi, this first-class lodge takes care of your every need, whether you're in the mood for hiking and kayaking, excursions to glaciers at nearby Queulat National Park, or just relaxing with a massage and splashing in one of three indoor and outdoor hot-spring pools. **Pros:** quality spa treatments; including outdoor mud baths; three pools; incredible views of the bay and mountains. **Cons:** no phone or Internet. [$] *Rooms from: 89000 pesos* ✉ *Bahia Dorita s/n* ☎ *67/232–5103, 2/2225–6489 in Santiago* 🌐 *www.puyuhuapilodge.com* 🛏 *30 rooms* 🍴 *Breakfast.*

SPORTS AND THE OUTDOORS

More than 50 rivers are within easy driving distance of Puerto Puyuhuapi, making this a cherished destination among fishing enthusiasts. Poles reel in rainbow and brown trout, silver and steelhead salmon, and local species such as the *robalo*. The average size is about six pounds, but it's not rare to catch twice that size. Daily trips are organized by the staff at the resort hotel, Puyuhuapi Lodge & Spa (☎ *67/325–103, 2/225–6489 in Santiago ⊕ www.patagonia-connection.com*).

SHOPPING

Alfombras de Puyuhuapi. Carpets at Alfombras de Puyuhuapi are hand-woven by three generations of women from Chiloé, who use only natural wool thread and cotton fibers. The rustic vertical looms, designed and built specifically for this shop, allow the weavers to make carpets with a density of 20,000 knots per square meter. Trained by his father and grandfather, who opened the shop in 1945, proprietor Helmut E. Hopperdietzel proudly displays the extensive stock of finished carpets of various sizes and designs. Carpets can be shipped. The shop is closed in June. ✉ *Calle Aysen s/n* ☎ *9/935–9915, 67/232–5131* ⊕ *www. puyuhuapi.com* ۞ *Closed in June.*

PARQUE NACIONAL QUEULAT

175 km (109 miles) south of Chaitén.

EXPLORING

Parque Nacional Queulat. The rugged 154,000-hectare (380,000-acre) Parque Nacional Queulat begins to rise and roll to either side of the Carretera Austral some 20 km (12 miles) south of Puyuhuapi. The rivers and streams that crisscross dense virgin forests attract fishing aficionados from all over the world. At the higher altitudes, brilliant blue glaciers can be found in the valleys between snowcapped peaks. If you're lucky, you'll spot a *pudú,* one of the diminutive deer that make their home in the forest. Less than 1 km (½ mile) off the east side of the Carretera Austral you are treated to a close-up view of the hanging glacier, Ventisquero Colgante, which slides a sheet of ice between a pair of gentle rock faces. Several waterfalls cascade down the cliffs to either side of the glacier's foot. There is an easy 15-minute walk leading to one side of the lake below the glacier, which is not visible from the overlook. A short drive farther south, where the Carretera Austral makes sharp switchback turns as it climbs higher, a small sign indicates the trailhead for the Salto Padre García. There is no parking area, but you can leave your car on the shoulder. This short hike through dense forest is worth attempting for a close-up view of this waterfall of striking proportions. There are three CONAF stations (the national forestry service), and an informative Environmental Information Center at the parking lot for the Ventisquero Colgante overlook and the southern and northern entrances to the park. ✉ *Parque Nacional Quelat, Aysen Region* ☎ *67/221–2225* ⊕ *www.conaf.cl* 🎫 *4,000 pesos* ۞ *Daily 8:30–7.*

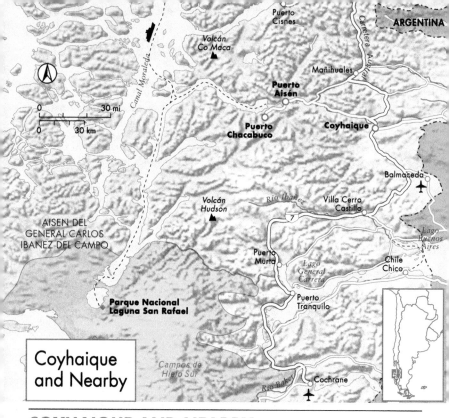

COYHAIQUE AND NEARBY

COYHAIQUE

224 km (140 miles) south of Puerto Puyuhuapi.

The hub of the Aysén region in Patagonia, this is a city in contrast, with modernity mixing with a traditionally slower rhythm in the shadow of the Andes. Within minutes of departing Coyhaique you can be fly-fishing on the Simpson River or trekking and horseback-riding amid magnificent countryside scenery. The town itself is constantly improving its shopping and cultural offerings for tourists. Throughout the year there are regular cultural festivals of all kinds, outdoor sports competitions, and surprisingly lively night spots on weekends.

GETTING HERE AND AROUND

There are regular domestic flights every day to the Southern Coast's only major airport, 55 km (34 miles) south of Coyhaique in the town of Balmaceda. Ferry lines operating in southern Chile sail the interwoven fjords, rivers, and lakes of the region. Navimag (short for "Navigación Magallanes") operates a cargo and passenger fleet throughout the region. Transmarchilay operates a cargo and passenger ferry fleet similar to that of Navimag, with ships starting in Puerto Montt and sailing to nearby Puerto Chacabuco. Tour companies often have more luxurious transport that includes stops in Chacabuco.

Renting a car, although expensive, is a worthwhile option for getting around. At Balmaceda airport there are several rental agencies. Make sure you understand the extent of your liability for any damage to the vehicle, including routine events such as a chipped or cracked windshield. If you want to visit one of the more popular parks, check out tour prices. They may prove far cheaper than driving yourself. A number of bus companies with offices in Coyhaique serve most destinations in the area.

ESSENTIALS

Bus Contacts Don Carlos ⊠ *Subteniente Cruz 63* ☎ *67/223–1981.* **Suray** ⊠ *Prat 265* ☎ *67/223–8337.* **Transfer Valencia** ⊠ *Lautaro 848* ☎ *67/223–3030.* **Tur-Bus** ⊠ *Magallanes 303* ☎ *67/223–7571.*

Rental Car Contacts AGS Rent A Car ⊠ *Av. Ogana 1298* ☎ *67/221–6711.* **Varona** ⊠ *Riquelme 438 Interior* ☎ *67/221–6674.* **Europcar** ⊠ *Aeropuerto Balmaceda* ☎ *67/267–8640* ⊕ *www.europcar.cl.* **Hertz** ⊠ *General Parra 280* ☎ *67/224–5777* ⊕ *www.hertz.cl.*

Visitor Information Sernatur ⊠ *Bulnes 35* ☎ *67/224–0290* ⊕ *sernatur.cl.*

TOURS

Geoturismo Patagonia. This veteran tour operator based in Coyhaique runs tours from five to nine nights, which include transport, guides, accommodations, breakfast, and dinner. Destinations include Capillas de Marmol, Caleta Tortel, Quelat Park, Chile Chico, and Villa O'Higgins. ⊠ *21 de Mayo 398* ☎ *67/258–3173* ⊕ *www.geoturismopatagonia.cl* ▭ *From 418,000 pesos.*

FAMILY **Patagonia Rafting Excursions.** This local tour operator is run by Marcela Rios, who knows virtually every nook and corner of Aysen and explores them through rafting, trekking, kayaking, and boating. Of particular expertise is the Lago General Carrera–Cochrane area, with trips to the Capillas de Marmol, Valle de Exploradorse, Baker River, and Mount San Lorenzo, among others. ⊠ *Paseo Horn 48* ☎ *9/9810–7791* ✎ *patagonaexcursiones@gmail.com.*

Pura Patagonia. Pura Patagonia runs diverse guided tours, including a city tour of Coyhaique and a half-day excursion devoted to bird-watching for the Andean condor, a majestic species with one of the largest wing spans of any bird. ⊠ *General Parra 202* ☎ *67/224–6000* ⊕ *www. purapatagonia.cl* ▭ *From 20,000 pesos.*

EXPLORING

TOP ATTRACTIONS

Cerro Castillo National Reserve. Just 64 km (40 miles) south of Coyhaique, this national reserve is home to one of the most beautiful mountain chains in the region, crowned majestically by the rugged Cerro Castillo. Glacier runoff fills the lakes below the mountain, and the reserve is also home to several species of deer, puma, and guanaco. Cerro Castillo could be called one of the best hikes in Patagonia, but it gets only a tiny percent of visitors compared to its more popular counterpart to the south, Torres del Paine. One excellent hiking route begins at Las

Horquetas Grandes, 8 km (5 miles) south of the park entrance. From there, go along La Lima River until Laguna Cerro Castillo, where you can begin your walk around the peak and then head toward the nearby village Villa Cerro Castillo. There is bus service from Coyhaique, but it's better to come here in your own rented vehicle. It's also preferable to hike with a guide, as trails are not always clearly marked. ✉ *Reserva Nacional Cerro Castillo, Villa Cerro Castillo* ☎ *67/221–2225* 🎟 *2,000 pesos; camping 5,000 pesos* 🕒 *Daily.*

Reserva Nacional Coyhaique. The 2,150-hectare (5,313-acre) Reserva Nacional Coyhaique, about 4 km (2½ miles) north of Coyhaique, provides hikers with some stunning views when the weather cooperates. If it's raining you can drive a 9-km (5½-mile) circuit through the park. ✉ *Reserva Nacional Coyhaique* ☎ *67/221–2139* 🎟 *1500 pesos* 🕒 *Jan. and Feb., daily 8 am–9 pm; Mar.–Dec., daily 8:30–5.*

Reserva Nacional Río Simpson. This classic fishing spot in Aysen is filled with waterfalls tumbling down steep canyon walls. A lovely waterfall called the Cascada de la Virgen is a 1-km (½-mile) hike from the information center, and another called the Velo de la Novia is 8 km (5 miles) farther. About 1 km from Coyhaique, along the banks of the Simpson River, you can also see the Piedra del Indio, a rock shaped in the profile of an indigenous individual. Get to the park via the highway that connects Coyhaique with Puerto Aysen; the park entrance is 32 km (20 miles) northeast of Coyhaique. ✉ *Reserva Nacional Rio Simpson* ☎ *67/221–2139* 🎟 *1,500 pesos* 🕒 *Jan. and Feb., daily 8 am–9 pm; Mar.–Dec., daily 8:30–5.*

WORTH NOTING

Monumento al Ovejero. The Carretera Austral leads to this monument in the northeastern corner of town. On the broad median of the Avenida General Baquedano, a solitary shepherd with his horse and his dog lean motionless into the wind behind a plodding flock of sheep. ✉ *Av. General Baquedano.*

Museo Regional de la Patagonia. This small museum has an interesting collection of black-and-white photos of early 20th-century pioneering in this region, as well as collections of household, farming, and early industrial artifacts from the same era. They also have information on the flora and fauna of the Aysen region. ✉ *J de Moraleda* ☎ *67/221–3174* 🎟 *500 pesos* 🕒 *Weekdays 8:30–1 and 3–7.*

Plaza de Armas. This is the center of town and the nexus for its attractions, including the town's cathedral and government building.

WHERE TO EAT

$$$ CHILEAN 🍴 **La Casona.** This restaurant is run by the González family—the mother cooks, her husband and son serve—and they all exude a genuine warmth to everyone who walks in the door. The design is orderly and pleasant, with fresh flowers in a vase on tables covered with white linen. There's plenty of traditional Chilean fare on the menu, including the standout *centolla* (king crab) and *langostino* (lobster), roasted lamb, and, of course, the hearty *filete casona*—roast beef with bacon, mushrooms, and potatoes. [$] *Average main: 9000 pesos* ✉ *Obispo Vielmo 77* ☎ *67/223–8894.*

$$ ✕**Mamma Gaucha.** This "Italo-Patagon" pizzeria in the heart of Patago-
PIZZA nia mixes the best of Italian cuisine with local ingredients and cooking
Fodor'sChoice methods. There is the excellent, clay-oven baked pizza (the one with
★ *cordero* meat is a running favorite), heaping salads, and inventive plates
like grilled camembert smothered in calafate sauce and homemade pan-
zotti pasta stuffed with crab. For beer lovers, Mamma makes one of the
finest microbrews in Chile, *La Tropera*. $ *Average main: 6500 pesos*
✉ *Horn 47-D* ☎ *67/221–0721* ⊘ *Closed Sun.*

$$ ✕**Restaurant Histórico Ricer.** This popular restaurant in the center of town
CHILEAN is a Coyhaique institution. The stairs in the back lead to a wooden
FAMILY dinner parlor with walls covered in fascinating sepia photos from the
town's archives. Among the most popular items on the menu are trout,
rabbit, and grilled leg of lamb. Lighter fare includes excellent empanadas filled with *locate* (a local mollusk), and varied sandwiches. There's
great homemade ice cream, too. Evenings often see local music groups,
which add to the authentic Patagonian atmosphere imbued by the pottery and crocheted hangings from the family's matriarch. $ *Average
main: 7000 pesos* ✉ *Horn 48* ☎ *67/223–2920* ⊕ *www.historicoricer.cl.*

WHERE TO STAY

$$$$ ⊡ **Cinco Rios Lodge.** This lodge gives you the best of both worlds—just
B&B/INN 8 km (5 miles) outside of Coyhaique, yet in a beautiful countryside set-
Fodor'sChoice ting. **Pros:** rural setting; fly-fishing experts; rooms with beautiful views.
★ **Cons:** primarily a place for fishermen. $ *Rooms from: 141000 pesos*
✉ *Km 5, Camino Balmaceda* ☎ *67/224–4917* ⊕ *www.cincorios.cl* ⤶ 6
rooms ⦿*| Multiple meal plans.*

$$$ ⊡ **El Reloj.** Simple, clean, wood-paneled rooms contain just the basic
B&B/INN pieces of furniture here. **Pros:** on the river; good food. **Cons:** no frills.
$ *Rooms from: 78000 pesos* ✉ *Av. General Baquedano 828* ☎ *67/223–
1108* ⊕ *www.elrelojhotel.cl* ⤶ *18 rooms* ⦿*| Breakfast.*

$$$ ⊡**Hostal Belisario Jara.** You realize how much attention has been paid
B&B/INN to detail here when the proprietor points out that the weather vane
on the peak of the single turret is a copy of one at Chilean poet Pablo
Neruda's home in Isla Negra. **Pros:** nice atmosphere; central location;
excellent service. **Cons:** some rooms are small. $ *Rooms from: 75000
pesos* ✉ *Francisco Bilbao 662* ☎ *67/223–4150* ⊕ *www.belisariojara.cl*
⤶ *8 rooms* ⦿*| Breakfast.*

$$$$ ⊡ **Nomades Hotel Boutique.** This small, boutique hotel has quickly become
B&B/INN a hot spot for visitors to Coyhaique. **Pros:** close attention to guest needs;
beautiful rooms; quiet. **Cons:** no gym or spa. $ *Rooms from: 110000
pesos* ✉ *Baquedano 84* ☎ *67/223–7777* ⊕ *www.nomadeshotel.com*
⤶ *7 rooms, 2 apartments* ⦿*| Breakfast.*

NIGHTLIFE

Coyhaique's nightlife is about what you'd expect from a city of its size.
There isn't a huge number of bars and discos, but the places they do
have are hopping at times.

Café Peña Quilantal. For music and dancing with more of a regional flair,
try Café Peña Quilantal. Admission includes a sit-down dinner and
dancing all night to the varied tunes of the Quilantal band. ✉ *Baquedano 791* ☎ *67/223–4394* ▱ *5,000 pesos* ⊘ *Fri. and Sat. 9–late.*

Piel Roja. The outrageous stylishness of this bar and disco, whose name translates as "red skin," is given a boost by its remote location. Opening relatively early, at 7 pm, it fills four levels with several bars, a large dance floor, and private nook with sculptural decor, eclectic oversize furnishings, and a mix of art nouveau and Chinese motifs. The weekend cover price of 3,000 pesos for men is credited toward drinks. ⊠ *Moraleda 495* ☏ *67/223–6635* ⊕ *www.pielroja.cl.*

SPORTS AND THE OUTDOORS
SKIING
El Fraile Ski Center. The only ski center in the Aysen region is located on Camino Lago Pollux, about 29 km (18 miles) outside of Coyhaique. There are two lifts for five slopes surrounded by native forest on the 1,600-meter (5,250-foot) Cerro Fraile. This small, government-run ski center has equipment available for rent, and there is a ski school. There are no accommodations but there is a cafeteria on-site for meals. The season runs June through September. Ski tickets begin at 15,000 pesos. ⊠ *Cerro Fraile* ☏ *67/221–3187* ⊕ *www.skielfraile.com.*

SHOPPING
Coyhaique is no shopping mecca, but as it's the largest settlement around, you should stock up on general supplies here if you're heading off on a long exploring expedition.

Feria Artesanal. This market hosts several stalls selling unique woolen clothing, small leather items, and pottery, making it a good place to search for gifts. ⊠ *Plaza de Armas between Dussen and Horn.*

PUERTO CHACABUCO AND PUERTO AISÉN

68 km (43 miles) northwest of Coyhaique.

The drive from Coyhaique to the town of Puerto Aisén and its port, Chacabuco, is beautiful. The mist hangs low over farmland, adding a dripping somnolence to the scenery. Dozens of waterfalls and rivers wend their way through mountain formations. Yellow poplars surround charming rustic lodges, and sheep and cattle graze on mossy, vibrant fields. The picture of serenity terminates at the sea, where the nondescript town of Puerto Aisén and its port Chacabuco—Coyhaique's link to the ocean—sits. This harbor ringed by snowcapped mountains is where you board the ferries that head north to Puerto Montt in the Lake District and Quellón on Chiloé, as well as boats going south to the spectacular Laguna San Rafael.

GETTING HERE AND AROUND
Puerto Chacabuco is less than an hour's drive from Coyhaique, and about 10 minutes from nearby Puerto Aisén. Several bus lines in Coyhaique serve Chacabuco. The town is also the jumping-off point for Laguna San Rafael, although the boats going to the park are almost all luxury tour vessels, which you need to contract in Coyhaique or in Santiago. Consult a travel agent beforehand if you plan to use one of these.

EXPLORING

Puerto Aisén. A hanging bridge leads from Chacabuco to Puerto Aisén, founded in 1928 to serve the region's burgeoning cattle ranches. Devastating forest fires that swept through the interior in 1955 filled the once-deep harbor with silt, making it all but useless for transoceanic vessels. Nowadays, fishing and salmon farming are the leading economic activities. The town gained some fame in February 2012, when protests here sparked a region-wide revolt over an array of social issues. The busy main street is a good place to stock up on supplies for boat trips to the nearby national parks. ✉ *Puerto Aisen.*

WHERE TO STAY

$$$$ HOTEL
🏨 **Hotel Loberías del Sur.** On a hill overlooking the modest port, this upscale four-star hotel was born because the owner, who runs a catamaran service to Parque Nacional Laguna San Rafael, needed a place to pamper foreign vacationers for the night. **Pros:** well-equipped spa; boat tours to Laguna San Rafael Park; exceptional food. **Cons:** nothing to do in port itself; pool is small. [$] *Rooms from: 128000 pesos* ✉ *Carrera 50, Puerto Chacabuco* ☎ *67/235–1112* 🌐 *www.loberiasdelsur.cl* 🛏 *60 rooms* 🍴 *Breakfast.*

$$ B&B/INN Fodor's Choice ★
🏨 **Patagonia Green.** The cabins and suites at this hotel located 400 meters (1,312 feet) from the Chacabuco side of the Ibanez bridge are extra comfortable, and the nice, attentive owner and manager can help arrange all kinds of excursions to nearby nature areas, including Laguna San Rafael Park. **Pros:** cabins well-equipped; good base for exploring the area; **Cons:** managed directly by the owner, so she is sometimes overworked. [$] *Rooms from: 72000 pesos* ✉ *Av Lago Riesco s/n, Puerto Chacabuco* ☎ *67/233–6796* 🌐 *www.patagoniagreen.cl* 🛏 *6 rooms, 4 cabins* 🕒 *Closed June and July* 🍴 *Breakfast.*

SPORTS AND THE OUTDOORS

The principal reason to come here for many travelers is to board a boat bound for the spectacular glaciers and ice at Laguna San Rafael Park. To do so, you must arrange with one of three tour operators or organize your own private boat. But given that it's a 10-hour round-trip, organizing your own transportation can be quite expensive. That said, the area around Puerto Aisén is nature-rich and worth checking out. Nearby, for example, is Parque Aiken del Sur, a small private park on the banks of Riesco Lake with excellent walks through native flora and strong fly-fishing possibilities. For fishermen, the area is bountiful in prime fishing spots at the numerous rivers and lakes.

Catamaranes del Sur. This agency arranges day trips by boat to Laguna San Rafael, part of an all-inclusive package deal including a three- or four-night stay at their Loberías del Sur Hotel in Puerto Chacabuco. There is also a half-day hike at nearby Aiken del Sur park. Rates begin at US$1,400. ✉ *Carrera 50, Puerto Chacabuco* ☎ *67/235–1112, 2/2231–1902 in Santiago* 🌐 *www.catamaranesdelsur.cl.*

Patagonia Green. This hotel can arrange all kinds of excursions to nature attractions around Puerto Aisén, including an overflight of glaciers at nearby Laguna San Rafael Park. ✉ *Puerto Chacabuco* ☎ *67/233–6796* 🌐 *www.patagoniagreen.cl.*

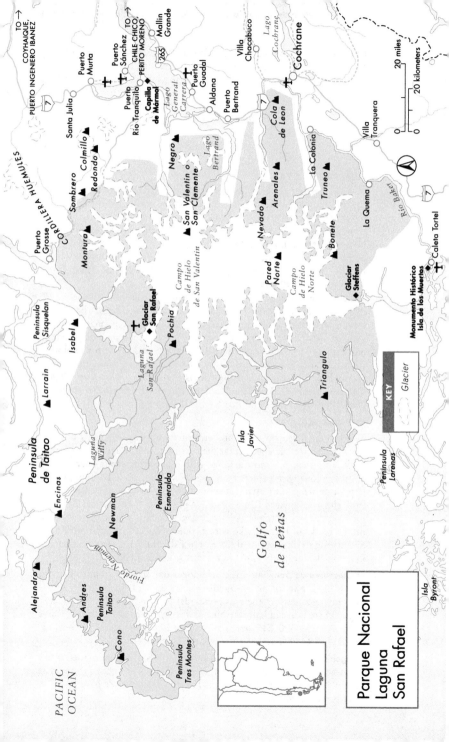

Parque Nacional
Laguna
San Rafael

PARQUE NACIONAL LAGUNA SAN RAFAEL

5 hrs by boat from Puerto Chacabuco.

One of Chile's largest parks, extending 168 square km (65 square miles), Laguna San Rafael encompasses the length of Chile's vast northern Patagonia ice fields. The main attraction at this park is the San Rafael glacier, which begins 4,056 meters (13,310 feet) above sea level at Mount San Valentín. Also located within the park, San Valentín is the highest peak in the southern Andean mountain range. While there are opportunities for serious hikers to go trekking here, it's the glacier that most visitors stop at to breathlessly watch gigantic chunks of ice continually split off its brilliant blue sides and thunderously crash into the lagoon.

GETTING HERE AND AROUND

Several different companies make the trip to Laguna San Rafael. The cheapest are Navimag and Transmarchilay, which offer two-night trips from Puerto Chacabuco and four-night trips from Puerto Montt. More luxurious are the three-night cruises from Puerto Chacabuco and the six-night cruises from Puerto Montt run by Skorpios (⊕ *www.skorpios.cl*). For those with less time, Patagonia Connection has day trips from Chacabuco on a deluxe catamaran.

EXPLORING

Parque Nacional Laguna San Rafael. Nearly all of the 1,742,000-hectare (3,832,400-acre) Parque Nacional Laguna San Rafael is inaccessible fields of ice, and only a handful of the people have ever set foot on land. Most travel by boat from Puerto Chacabuco or Puerto Montt through the maze of fjords along the coast to the expansive San Rafael Lagoon. Floating on the surface of the brilliant blue water are scores of icebergs that rock from side to side as boats pass. Most surprising is the variety of forms and colors in each iceberg, including a shimmering, translucent cobalt blue. The massive Ventisquero San Rafael glacier measures 4 km (2½ miles) from end to end but is receding about 182 meters (600 feet) a year. Paint on a bordering mountain marks the location of the glacier in past years. It's a noisy beast, roaring like thunder as the sheets of ice shift. If you're lucky, you can see huge pieces of ice calve off, causing violent waves that should make you glad your boat is at a safe distance.

Wildlife lovers can glimpse black-browed albatross and elegant black-necked swans here, as well as sea lions, dolphins, elephant seals, and *chungungos*—the Chilean version of the sea otter. ⊠ *Parque Nacional Laguna San Rafael* ☎ *67/221–2225* 🛈 *4,000 pesos.*

LAGO GENERAL CARRERA AND NEARBY

280 km (174 miles) southeast of Coyhaique.

It takes a 280-km (174-mile) drive from Coyhaique along the rutted, mostly unpaved Carretera Austral to reach Lago General Carrera—a beautiful, almost surreally blue lake, the biggest in Chile (and the second-largest in South America, after Lake Titicaca). This spectacular place is more than worth the trip. Every year, more and more travelers have been making the pilgrimage in four-wheel-drive vehicles to fish, hike, and gasp at the mountains, glaciers, and waterfalls that dot the landscape.

TOURS

Fodor's Choice ★ **Patagonia Adventure Expeditions.** Founded and led by American Jonathan Leidich, Patagonia Adventure Expeditions has been guiding in Patagonia for nearly two decades, specializing in glacier excursions to the dramatic and highly beautiful Aysén Glacier Trail and Baker River. ✉ *Cochrane* ☎ *9/8182–0608* 🌐 *www.adventurepatagonia.com* 🎫 *From US$1,800.*

EXPLORING

$$ B&B/INN 🏨 **El Mirador de Guadal.** With a spectacular location and spacious rooms, this hotel is a great base for excursions in the southern part of the Carretera Austral. **Pros:** personalized service; good and reasonably priced restaurant; spacious cabins. **Cons:** unstable Wi-Fi connection. [$] *Rooms from: 75000 pesos* ✉ *Km 2, Camino a Chile Chico, Puerto Guadal* ☎ *2/2813–7920* 🌐 *www.elmiradordeguadal.com* 🛏 *10 rooms, 3 suites* ⏲ *Closed May–Sept.* 🍴 *Breakfast.*

WHERE TO STAY

$$$ B&B/INN 🏨 **Green Baker Lodge.** Overlooking the magnificent Baker River—one of Chile's best destinations for fly-fishing and rafting—this lodge rents comfortable rooms. **Pros:** comfortable cabins; river access; service. **Cons:** excursions are expensive. [$] *Rooms from: 75000 pesos* ✉ *Puerto Bertrand* ☎ *67/241–1903* 🌐 *www.greenlodgebaker.com* 🛏 *5 rooms, 7 cabins* 🍴 *No meals.*

$$ B&B/INN 🏨 **Terra Luna Lodge.** Occupying 15 peaceful acres at the southeastern edge of the Lake General Carrera, this property boasts charming but basic redwood cabins, grazing horses, and a beautiful main lodge, where all meals are served. **Pros:** good value; location is a good base for excursions. **Cons:** quality of rooms varies. [$] *Rooms from: 60000 pesos* ✉ *Km 1.5, Camino a Mallin Grande, Puerto Guadal* ☎ *9/8449–1092 bookings, 9/6619–5590 lodge* 🌐 *www.terraluna.cl* 🛏 *23 rooms* 🍴 *Multiple meal plans.*

OFF THE BEATEN PATH

🏨 **Robinson Crusoe Deep Patagonia.** At the southernmost end of the Carretera Austral, or Southern Highway, this upscale oasis combines wooden floors and ceilings with comfortable beds and exceptional vistas. **Pros:** quality facilities and building; outdoor Jacuzzi. **Cons:** due to extreme remote location, fresh vegetables and fruit are not always available; often booked solid in summer months. [$] *Rooms from: 125000 pesos* ✉ *Carretera Austral, Km 1.240, Villa O'Higgins* ☎ *2/2334–1503* 🌐 *www.robinsoncrusoe.com* 🛏 *12 rooms* ⏲ *Closed Mon.–Thurs. Closed Apr.–Dec. 15* 🍴 *Breakfast.*

SOUTHERN CHILEAN PATAGONIA AND TIERRA DEL FUEGO

WELCOME TO SOUTHERN CHILEAN PATAGONIA AND TIERRA DEL FUEGO

TOP REASONS TO GO

★ **Natural wonders:** Patagonia has some of the most dramatic and eye-catching landscapes in the world, including milky blue lakes, dark forests, spectacular glaciers, and theatrical mountains.

★ **Mad about ornithology:** With plentiful fish food courtesy of the frosty Humboldt Current, southern Chile enjoys one of the richest populations of sea birds in the world. Perhaps most dazzling is the largest of all sea birds, the albatross, eight species of which migrate through Chilean waters.

★ **Glaciers galore:** One of the prime justifications for traveling thousands of miles via sea, air, and land is to set yourself opposite an impossibly massive wall of ice, contemplating the blue-green-turquoise spectrum trapped within.

★ **Penguin encounters:** Humboldt, Rockhopper, and Magellanic penguins congregate around the southern Patagonian coast—at the noisy, malodorous colony of Isla Magdalena you'll find a half-burned lighthouse and more than 120,000 of our waddling friends.

1 **Puerto Natales and Torres del Paine.** Puerto Natales serves as the last stop before what many consider the finest national park in South America, Parque Nacional Torres del Paine, 91 miles north. A worthy break in your journey is the city itself, commonly called Natales, which has an isolated charm to it and boasts an array of fine eateries.

2 **Punta Arenas.** Lord Byron's legendary mariner grandfather gave Chile's southernmost city its name. Situated at the foot of the Andes, monument-laden Punta Arenas faces the island of Tierra del Fuego, where the Atlantic and Pacific oceans convene—and there it thrived as a key 19th-century refueling port for maritime traffic.

3 **El Calafate, El Chaltén, and Parque Nacional los Glaciares.** The wild, icy expanse of the Hielo Continental ice-cap and the exquisite turquoise surface of Lago Argentino exist in dramatic contrast to the tourist boomtown atmosphere of El Calafate, where international visitors flock for the modern hotels and for legendary Argentine steak.

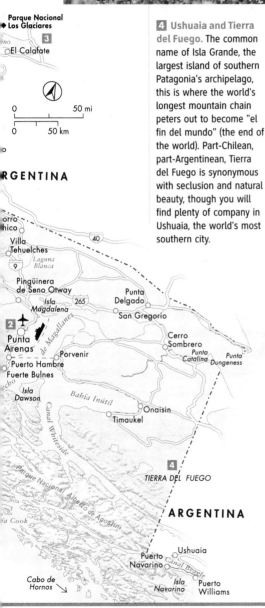

Parque Nacional Los Glaciares **3**

El Calafate

0   50 mi

0   50 km

RGENTINA

orro hico

Villa Tehuelches

Laguna Blanca **9**

Pingüinera de Seno Otway

Isla Magdalena 265

2

Punta Arenas   Porvenir

Puerto Hambre

Fuerte Bulnes

Isla Dawson

Bahía Inútil

Onaisin

Timaukel

Punta Delgado

San Gregorio

Cerro Sombrero

Punta Catalina   Punta Dungeness

4

TIERRA DEL FUEGO

ARGENTINA

Puerto Navarino   Ushuaia

Cabo de Hornos

Isla Navarino   Puerto Williams

4 **Ushuaia and Tierra del Fuego.** The common name of Isla Grande, the largest island of southern Patagonia's archipelago, this is where the world's longest mountain chain peters out to become "el fin del mundo" (the end of the world). Part-Chilean, part-Argentinean, Tierra del Fuego is synonymous with seclusion and natural beauty, though you will find plenty of company in Ushuaia, the world's most southern city.

GETTING ORIENTED

Punta Arenas, more than 2,000 km (1,360 miles) south of Santiago, is the capital of this Chilean province. The only other settlement of any size in Magallanes is Puerto Natales, 240 km (149 miles) to the northwest, a well-positioned gateway to Parque Nacional Torres del Paine. Frequent bus service links the two cities. At the bottom end of the continent, separated by the Magellan Strait and split between Chile and Argentina, lies Tierra del Fuego. It's comprised of a number of islands; Isla Grande attracts the vast bulk of visitors. The resort town of Ushuaia, Argentina, is by a long stretch the leading tourist attraction of the region.

10

Updated
by Amanda
Barnes

Patagonia is one of the most extreme and visually stunning destinations in the world. This sparsely populated region occupies the southernmost territories of the world. Here you'll find the iconic Torres del Paine and their multicolored rocky spires; the stunning Perito Moreno glacier and many surrounding ice formations in one of the biggest glacier parks on the planet; and tiny farming and fishing communities that offer plenty of stellar outdoor activities.

While the population is one of the least dense in the world, those that inhabit Patagonia have introduced exquisite cuisine and world-class activities. Cuisine is based around the natural bounty in these parts: succulent king crab; richly flavored and freely roaming Patagonian lamb; and a host of native vegetation and sea dwellers. Outdoor activities involve the sea and land, too: from trekking through deep forests, rivers, and mountain ranges, to sea-kayaking past icebergs and along fjords, to spotting wildlife like penguins and flamingos.

Although Patagonia is the most isolated part of South America (Tierra del Fuego is physically cut off from the rest of the continent by two vast ice caps and the Strait of Magellan), that doesn't stop visitors from flocking here. If you make it as far as the southernmost tip of Tierra del Fuego, you'll encounter sheep-wrangling gauchos, islands inhabited solely by elephant seals and penguin colonies, and austere landscapes that captivated everyone from Charles Darwin to Butch Cassidy and the Sundance Kid.

PLANNER

WHEN TO GO

In each season Patagonia has its own magic. November to March—summer in the Southern Hemisphere—is considered high season in Patagonia, when there is generally more sunshine and clearer skies. Demand for accommodations is highest in January and February, so advance reservations are vital. Summer weather in these latitudes is by no means warm, but rather pleasantly cool. Bring an extra layer or two; windbreakers are essential, as summer can bring the strongest winds. On or near these Antarctic waters, stiff breezes can be biting.

In spring (September to November) and fall (March to May) the weather is usually delightfully mild, but can also be downright cold, depending on clouds and the wind. These seasons do, however, bring wonderful colors to the landscape, and the population shrinks by more than half. The winter months of June, July, and August are blissfully free of tourists, although many attractions and hotels go into hibernation.

GETTING HERE AND AROUND

If you want to begin your trip in Chile, fly into Punta Arenas, the region's principal city, or drive in from Argentina—if you've been visiting El Calafate—and head directly to Puerto Natales and Torres del Paine. If you'd rather begin touring the area in Argentina, head on down to Ushuaia: many fly or cruise from Punta Arenas to Ushuaia or vice versa. Remote spots, such as Isla Magdalena or Puerto Williams, can be reached only by boat or airplane.

AIR TRAVEL

LAN (⊕ *www.lan.com*) operates flights daily between Punta Arenas and Santiago, Coyhaique, and Puerto Montt. Sky (⊕ *www.skyairline. cl*) also offer competitive fares and fly to Puerto Natales in Summer. Aerovías DAP (⊕ *www.aeroviasdap.cl*) has regularly scheduled flights exclusively in Patagonia, between Punta Arenas, Porvenir, and Puerto Williams. Aerolíneas Argentinas (⊕ *www.aerolineas.com.ar*) has service between Buenos Aires, El Calafate, and Ushuaia, Argentina.

BOAT TRAVEL

Boat tours are a popular way to see otherwise inaccessible parts of Patagonia and Tierra del Fuego.

BUS TRAVEL

The four-hour trip between Punta Arenas and Puerto Natales is serviced several times a day by small private companies. The best is Buses Fernández. To travel the longer haul between Punta Arenas, Río Gallegos, and Ushuaia, Argentina, your best bet is Tecni-Austral, based in Argentina and the only regular bus service that crosses the Magellan strait. Book your ticket in advance.

CAR TRAVEL

If you truly enjoy the call of the open road, there are few places that can rival the vast emptiness and jaw-dropping beauty of Patagonia. Be prepared for miles and miles of semi-desert steppes with no gas stations, towns, or even restrooms. Always carry plenty of water, snacks, a jack, and tire-changing tools, with at least one spare. Take extra care when driving on *ripio* (gravel roads): it's easy to flip small cars at speeds over 80 kmh (55 mph). Fill your tank at every opportunity. If you're not driving, consider simply paying for a *remis* (car with driver) for day excursions.

RESTAURANTS

Menus tend to be extensive, although two items in particular might be considered specialties: *centolla* (king crab) and moist, tender *cordero magallánico* (Magellanic lamb). Many Chilean restaurants offer salmon *a la plancha* (grilled), a satisfying local delicacy. If you hop the border into Argentina, the dining options are cheaper and similar. You'll find the same fire-roasted cordero (in Argentina it's *cordero a la cruz* or *al asador*), but you'll also get a chance to try the famous Argentine *parrillas* (grilled-meat restaurants). Many restaurants close for several hours in the afternoon and early evening (3–8).

Huge numbers of foreign visitors mean that vegetarian options are getting better; *woks de verdura* (vegetable stir-fries) are a newly ubiquitous option. Most cafés and bars serve quick bites known as *minutas*. The

10

CLOSE UP

Border Crossings

The border between Chile and Argentina is still strictly maintained, but crossing it doesn't present much difficulty beyond getting out your passport and waiting in a line to get the stamp. Most travelers end up crossing the border by bus, which means getting out of the vehicle for 30–45 minutes to go through the bureaucratic proceedings, then loading back in.

Crossing by car is also quite manageable (check with your car-rental company for restrictions on international travel), although snow chains are often required in winter. Chilean customs officers are extremely strict about bringing food into the country, especially compared to their Argentine counterparts. Always declare food products (they are usually quite flexible once items are declared), otherwise you face a hefty fine.

region is also famous for its stone fruits, which are used in various jams, preserves, sweets, and *alfajores* (a chocolate-covered sandwich of two cookies with jam in the middle). When in El Calafate, be sure to nibble on some calafate berries (or drink them in cocktails like the Calafate Sour)—legend has it if you eat them in El Calafate you are destined to return one day soon.

HOTELS

Punta Arenas has many historic hotels offering luxurious amenities and fine service. A night or two in one of them should be part of your trip, although Puerto Natales or accommodations within Torres del Paine park is where you should spend most of your time.

There aren't many budget options accommodations in Patagonia; the luxury market, on the other hand, is booming. Patagonia is a "once-in-a-lifetime" destination that most people are happy to splurge on, and the increasing cruise culture doesn't ease accommodation prices. In most cities and towns you'll find a mix of big, expensive hotels with comfortable resorts, local flavor estancias, and small B&B-style *hosterías*.

The terms *hospedaje* and *hostal* are used interchangeably in the region, so don't make assumptions based on the name. Many *hostals* are fine hotels—not youth hostels with multiple beds—just very small. By contrast, some *hospedajes* are little more than a spare room in someone's home. *Hotel reviews have been shortened. For full information, visit Fodors.com.*

WHAT IT COSTS IN CHILEAN PESOS (IN THOUSANDS)			
$	**$$**	**$$$**	**$$$$**
Restaurants	Under 6	6–9	10–13	over 13
Hotels	Under 51	51–85	86–115	over 115

Restaurant prices are the average cost of a main course price at dinner or, if dinner is not served, at lunch. Hotel prices are the lowest cost of a standard double room in high season, excluding taxes.

HEALTH AND SAFETY

Emergency services and hospitals are widely available in the cities. At Torres del Paine, there is an emergency clinic during the summer at the National Park administration office. The closest hospital is in Puerto Natales. Additionally, every park guide is trained in first aid.

Most mountains are not high enough to induce altitude sickness, but the weather can turn nasty quickly. Sunglasses and sunscreen are essential. Although tap water is safe to drink throughout the region, most travelers still choose to drink bottled water. Do not approach or let your children approach sea lions, penguins, or any other animals, no matter how docile or curious they might seem.

VISITOR INFORMATION

Sernatur, Chile's national tourism agency has offices in Punta Arenas and in Puerto Natales (⊕ *www.sernatur.cl*). The Punta Arenas office is open weekdays 8:30 to 6 and Saturday 10 to 4, and the small Puerto Natales office is open weekdays 8:30 to 5.30. You can also try the helpful folks at the Punta Arenas City Tourism Office, in an attractive kiosk (with free Internet) in the main square. It's open December to March, Monday to Saturday 8 to 8 and Sunday 9 to 2; April to November, Monday to Thursday 8 to 6 and Friday 8 to 5. Sometimes they offer last-minute specials to fill remaining seats on popular tours. Ask for complete printouts of transportation timetables; information sometimes changes on short notice.

CRUISING IN PATAGONIA

Cruising is a leisurely and comfortable way to take in the rugged marvels of Patagonia and the southernmost region of the world. Sailing through remote channels and reaching islands virtually untouched by man, you'll witness fjords, snowcapped mountains and granite peaks and their reflections dominating the glacial lakes. You'll get a close look at elephant seals and colonies of Magellanic penguins and cormorants from the comfort of your vessel and during shore excursions taken in Zodiacs (small motorized boats) led by naturalist guides. Far from the beaten path, you'll visit small fishing villages only accessible by sea, explore fantastic temperate rain forests, and enjoy the freshest seafood and local wines.

10

Most short cruises depart from Ushuaia, Argentina, or Punta Arenas, Chile, while longer and more luxurious itineraries typically depart from either Buenos Aires or Santiago.

WHEN TO GO

In the Southern Hemisphere, where the seasons are reversed, November through March is considered high season. However, the weather in Patagonia is unpredictable: strong winds and sudden storms are common. Summertime (December through February) is the best time to visit. Shoulder months—October, November, March, and April—tend to have cooler temperatures but also less wind, and far fewer cruises run in winter months.

November (early summer). The natural nesting cycle of Magellanic penguins is November to February. Penguins arrive at the rookeries at the beginning of the month. Spring flowers are in full bloom. This is the best time to catch the bird nesting of finches, sparrows, condors, albatrosses, and other species.

December and January (high summer). The warmest months see penguin chicks hatch in Tierra del Fuego. Long daylight hours also mean great photography opportunities all over Patagonia.

February and March (late summer). Receding ice allows for easier exploration farther south. Penguin colonies are very active, as the adults feed the chicks.

BOOKING YOUR CRUISE

The majority of cruisers plan their trips four to six months ahead of time. Book a year ahead if you're planning to sail on a small adventure vessel, as popular itineraries may be full six to eight months ahead.

Consider booking shore excursions when you book your cruise to avoid disappointment later. You can even book your spa services pre-cruise to have your pick of popular times, such as sea days.

Although most travel is booked over the Internet nowadays, for cruises, booking with a travel agent who specializes in Patagonia cruises is still your best bet. Agents have strong relationships with the lines, and have a better chance of getting you the cabin you want, and possibly even a free upgrade. Cruise Lines International Association (⊕ *www.cruising. org*) lists recognized agents throughout the United States.

CRUISE ITINERARIES

Choosing an itinerary is as important as choosing a cruise line or tour operator that fits your tastes and budget. We highlight possibilities that focus on specific areas, as well as typical departure points and costs, and the tour operators that can take you there.

ANTARCTIC CRUISES

Founded to promote environmentally responsible travel to Antarctica, the **International Association of Antarctica Tour Operators** (☎ *401/841–9700* ⊕ *www.iaato.org*) is a good source of information, including suggested readings. Most companies operating Antarctica trips are members of this organization and display its logo in their brochures.

Season: November–March.
Location: Most cruises depart from Ushuaia, in Argentine Patagonia.
Cost: From US$2,995 (triple-occupancy cabin) for 12 days from Ushuaia; prices can get quite high and always book in advance.
Tour Operators: Abercrombie & Kent; Adventure Center; Big Five Tours & Expeditions; ElderTreks; G.A.P. Adventures; Lindblad Expeditions; Mountain Travel-Sobek; Quark Expeditions; Travcoa; Wilderness Travel; Zegrahm Expeditions.

Overview: Ever since Lars-Eric Lindblad operated the first cruise to the "White Continent" in 1966, Antarctica has exerted an almost magnetic pull for serious travelers. From Ushuaia, the world's southernmost city, you'll sail for two (often rough) days through the Drake Passage. Most visits are to the Antarctic Peninsula, the continent's most accessible region. Accompanied by naturalists, you'll travel ashore in motorized rubber craft called Zodiacs to view penguins and nesting seabirds. Some cruises visit research stations, and many call at the Falkland, South Orkney, South Shetland, or South Georgia islands. Adventure Center and Big Five Tours & Expeditions offer sea kayaking and, at an extra cost, the chance to camp for a night on the ice.

Expedition vessels have been fitted with ice-strengthened hulls; many originally were built as polar-research vessels. It's wise to inquire about the qualifications of the onboard naturalists and historians; the maximum number of passengers carried; the ice-readiness of the vessel; onboard medical facilities; whether there is an open bridge policy, and the number of landings attempted per day.

CRUISING THE TIP OF SOUTH AMERICA
Cruising the southern tip of South America and along Chile's western coast north to the Lake District reveals fjords, glaciers, lagoons, lakes, narrow channels, waterfalls, forested shorelines, fishing villages, and wildlife. While many tour operators include a one- or two-day boating excursion as part of their Patagonia itineraries, the companies listed below offer from four to 12 nights aboard ship.

Season: September–April.
Locations: Chilean fjords; Puerto Montt and Punta Arenas, Chile; Tierra del Fuego and Ushuaia, Argentina.
Cost: From US$1,078 for a four-day, three-night cruise between Punta Arenas and Ushuaia.
Tour Operators: Abercrombie & Kent; Adventure Life; Big Five Tours & Expeditions; Cruceros Australis, International Expeditions; Lindblad Expeditions; Mountain Travel-Sobek; Wilderness Travel; Wildland Adventures.
Overview: Boarding your vessel in Punta Arenas, Chile, or Ushuaia, Argentina, you'll cruise the Strait of Magellan and the Beagle Channel, visiting glaciers, penguin rookeries, and seal colonies before heading north along the fjords of Chile's western coast. With Abercrombie & Kent and Wildland Adventures, you'll savor the mountain scenery of Torres del Paine National Park for several days before or following the cruise, while Lindblad Expeditions, Mountain Travel-Sobek, and International Expeditions visit Tierra del Fuego National Park. Cruceros Australis and some other companies also include Cape Horn National Park. Most itineraries begin or end in Santiago or Punto Arenas, Chile or Buenos Aires, El Calafate or Ushuaia, Argentina.

OCEAN CRUISES
Some ships set sail in the Caribbean and stop at one or two islands before heading south; a few transit the Panama Canal en route. West Coast (U.S.) departures might include one or more Mexican ports before reaching South America. Fourteen- to 21-day cruises are the

norm. Vessels vary in the degree of comfort or luxury as well as in what is or isn't included in the price. Guided shore excursions, gratuities, dinner beverages, and port taxes are often extra.

Season: October–April.

Locations: Many itineraries visit Argentina (Buenos Aires and Ushuaia), Brazil (Belém, Fortaleza, Rio de Janeiro, and Salvador), and Chile (Antofagasta, Arica, Cape Horn, Coquimbo, Puerto Montt, Punta Arenas, and Valparaíso).

Cost: Prices vary according to the ship, cabin category, and itinerary. Figure US$1,950 to US$4,495 for a 14-day cruise, excluding international airfare.

MAJOR CRUISE LINES

Celebrity Cruises: Fjords, glaciers, and emerald lakes are the highlight of a cruise down the west coast of Chile and back up the Atlantic Coast to Buenos Aires. The 15-day cruise is offered December, January, and February. ☎ 800/647-2251 ⊕ www.celebrity.com.

Oceania Cruises: Patagonia (Buenos Aires to Valparaíso in January, and Lima to Buenos Aires in March) voyages with Oceania are as relaxed and elegant as a private country club—mahogany decor, plush carpeting, and grand, sweeping staircases. ☎ 800/254-5067 ⊕ www. oceaniacruiseline.com.

Princess Cruises: Trips (in January and February) on this cruise line include eight ports of call in the Argentine and Chilean Patagonia region. ☎ 800/774-6237 ⊕ www.princess.com.

Seabourn Cruise Line: Patagonia cruises with Seabourn include visits to the Beagle Channel and the Chilean fjords, a couple cruises run from November through to February. ⊕ www.seabourn.com.

Silversea Cruises: Voyages with Silversea dock in Uruguay, the Falkland Islands, and Ushuaia, among others, running in November, December, and January. ☎ 877/276-6816. ⊕ www.silversea.com.

PUERTO NATALES AND TORRES DEL PAINE, CHILE

Serious hikers often come to this area and use Puerto Natales as their base for hiking the classic "W" or circuit treks in Torres del Paine, which take between four days and a week to complete. Others choose to spend a couple of nights in one of the park's luxury hotels and take in the sights during day hikes.

If you have less time, however, it's possible to spend just one day touring the park, as many people do, with Puerto Natales as your starting point. In that case, rather than drive, you'll want to book a one-day Torres del Paine tour with one of the many tour operators here. Most tours pick you up at your hotel between 8 and 9 am and follow the same route, visiting several lakes and mountain vistas, seeing Lago Grey and its glacier, and stopping for lunch in Hostería Lago Grey or one of the other hotels inside the park. These tours return around sunset. A budget option is the daily bus tour (year-round) from the bus station

Puerto Natales
and Nearby

with Transportes María José, which also offers hop-on, hop-off options
for hikers and campers.

While visiting Torres del Paine remains the most popular excursion,
nearby Parque Bernardo O'Higgins is also ripe for exploration with
popular boat tours to glaciers with companies Turismo 21 de Mayo
(year-round) and Agunsa (September through April).

Argentina's magnificent Glaciar Perito Moreno, near El Calafate, can
be visited on a popular (but extremely long) one-day tour, leaving at the
crack of dawn and returning late at night—don't forget your passport.
It's a four-hour-plus trip in each direction; some tours sensibly include
overnights in El Calafate.

PUERTO NATALES

242 km (150 miles) northwest of Punta Arenas.

Puerto Natales has become the main base for exploring a number of
southern Patagonia's top attractions, including Parque Nacional Torres
del Paine and Parque Nacional Bernardo O'Higgins. The medium-sized
fishing town offers picturesque views of the Seno Última Esperanza
(Last Hope Sound) channel, which was named by Spanish navigator

Juan Ladrillero in the 16th century as it was his last hope to reach the Straight of Magellan.

As a launching point for many touristic sites, Puerto Natales has recently seen a large increase in tourism and development with a new surge of luxury accommodation offering all-inclusive stays with excursions. The town has added a string of hip eateries, cafés, and boutique hotels recently, and is starting to challenge the more staid larger city of Punto Arenas as a hub for exploring the entire region.

GETTING HERE AND AROUND

The trip to Puerto Natales from El Calafate is a beautiful journey through color-washed Patagonian landscapes with white peaked mountains in the distance and picturesque estancias and cattle ranches dotted along the way.

Puerto Natales centers on the Plaza de Armas, a lovely, well-landscaped sanctuary. A few blocks west of the plaza on Avenida Bulnes you'll find the small Museo Histórico Municipal. On a clear day, an early morning walk along Avenida Pedro Montt, which follows the shoreline of the Seno Última Esperanza (or Canal Señoret, as it's called on some maps), can be a soul-cleansing experience. The rising sun gradually casts a glow on the mountain peaks to the west.

ESSENTIALS

Bus Contacts Buses Fernández ⊠ *Eleuterio Ramirez 399, Puerto Natales* ☎ *612/411–111* ⊕ *www.busesfernandez.com.* **Cootra** ⊠ *Baquedano 456, Puerto Natales* ☎ *612/412–785.* **Transportes María José** ⊠ *Avda. España 1455, Puerto Natales* ☎ *61/2414–312.*

Rental Cars Avis ⊠ *Eberhard 577, Puerto Natales* ☎ *612/614–388*

Visitor and Tour Information Sernatur Puerto Natales ⊠ *Av. Pedro Montt and Phillipl, Puerto Natales* ☎ *61/2412–125* ⊕ *www.patagonia-chile.com* ☾ *Summer, weekdays 8:30–7, weekends 10–1 and 2:30–6; winter, weekdays 8:30–5.*

EXPLORING

TOP ATTRACTIONS

Monumento Natural Cueva de Milodón. In 1896, Hermann Eberhard stumbled upon a gaping cave that extended 200 meters (650 feet) into the earth. Venturing inside, he discovered the bones and dried pieces of hide (with deep red fur) of an animal he could not identify. It was later determined that what Eberhard had discovered were the extraordinarily well-preserved remains of a prehistoric herbivorous mammal, *mylodon darwini,* about twice the height of a man, which they called a *milodón.* The discovery of a stone wall in the cave, and of neatly cut grass stalks in the animal's feces led researchers to conclude that 10,000 years ago a group of Tehuelche Indians captured this beast. The cave is at the Monumento Natural Cueva de Milodón. The cathedral-size space was carved out of a solid rock wall by rising waters. It was the final destination for Bruce Chatwin in research for his book *In Patagonia,* but its dusty floor and barren walls are unspectacular, and the tacky life-size fiberglass model at the cave mouth is useful only as a reference to the size of the gigantic animal that lived here. ⊠ *5 km (3 miles) off Ruta 9* *signpost, 28 km (17 miles) northwest of Puerto Natales, Puerto Natales* 🎫 *4,000 pesos* ⏲ *Oct.–Apr., daily 8–8; May–Sept., daily 8:30–6.*

Museo Historico Municipal. A highlight in the small but interesting Museo Historico Municipal is a room filled with antique prints of Aonikenk and Kaweshkar indigenous peoples. Another room is devoted to the exploits of Hermann Eberhard, a German explorer considered the region's first settler. Check out his celebrated collapsible boat. In an adjacent room you will find some vestiges of the old Bories sheep plant, which processed the meat and wool of more than 300,000 sheep a year. ✉ *Av. Bulnes 285, Puerto Natales* ☎ *61/220–9548* 🎫 *1,000 pesos* ⏲ *Weekdays 8–7, Sat. 10–1 and 3–7.*

WORTH NOTING

Iglesia Parroquial. Across from the Plaza de Armas is the squat little Iglesia Parroquial. The ornate altarpiece in this church depicts the town's founders, indigenous peoples, and the Virgin Mary all in front of the Torres del Paine. ✉ *Arturo Prat and Eberhard, Puerto Natales.*

Plaza de Armas. A few blocks east of the waterfront overlooking Seno Última Esperanza is the not-quite-central Plaza de Armas. An incongruous railway engine sits prominently in the middle of the square. ✉ *Arturo Prat at Eberhard, Puerto Natales.*

WHERE TO EAT

$$$ INTERNATIONAL 🍴 **Afrigonia.** Afrigonia's "taste of Africa in Patagonia" might sound cheesy but their unusual fusion menu is well rehearsed and flavor combinations are usually well-tuned and tasty. With bamboo shoots adorning the walls, you might forget you are in Puerto Natales, but then you'll see the local seafood, Patagonian lamb, and king crab on the menu, presented with enticing ingredients: masala curry, mango, and coconut cream. It is hard not to like Afrigonia, despite the long waiting times. [$] *Average main: 10000 pesos* ✉ *Eberhard 343, Puerto Natales* ☎ *61/241–2232* ⏲ *Closed Apr.–Sept.*

$$$ CHILEAN 🍴 **Asador Patagónico.** This bright spot in the Puerto Natales dining scene is zealous about meat. So zealous, in fact, that there's no seafood on the menu. Incredible care is taken with the excellent *lomo* and other grilled steaks, and the room is filled with the smell of roasting meat. The place used to be a pharmacy, and much of the furniture is still labeled with the remedies (*catgut crin* anyone?) they once contained. There's lively music, dim lighting, an open fire, and a friendly buzz; wear removable layers since it can get warm when the grill is cranking. [$] *Average main: 10000 pesos* ✉ *Prat 158, Puerto Natales* ☎ *61/241–3553* ⏲ *Closed June.*

$$ SEAFOOD 🍴 **Cangrejo Rojo.** Although it requires a taxi drive to the other side of town, this nautical-chic café is worth it for its maritime feel, good music and atmosphere, and the tasty, feel-good food prepared lovingly by the marine biologist owners, Francisco and Nuriys. As well as a plethora of sea dwellers, you'll find lamb and other meats on the contemporary menu. Add organic wine, homemade waffles, and nice loose leaf teas, and you are onto a winner. [$] *Average main: 7000 pesos* ✉ *Santiago Bueras Av. 782, Puerto Natales* ☎ *612/412–436* ⏲ *Closed Sun.*

10

$ CAFÉ Fodor's Choice ★ 🍴 **The Coffee Maker.** A coffee bar with steaming espressos and some of the best views in town, right on the water's edge and facing the mountains in the distance, the Coffee Maker serves the tastiest java in Chile. In the trendy lodge Kau, its breakfasts, cakes, and afternoon nibbles make it a good spot to enjoy the view and take advantage of the Wi-Fi. [$] *Average main: 4000 pesos* ✉ *Kau, Pedro Montt 161, Puerto Natales* ☎ *61/241–4611* 🌐 *www.kaupatagonia.com* 🕘 *No lunch in winter.*

$$ VEGETARIAN Fodor's Choice ★ 🍴 **El Living.** This bohemian, loft-style café offers comfy couches and tables covered in gossip magazines and tour info. The gluten-free and vegetarian options on the menu will tick the box in comfort and health. Fresh juices, warming hot drinks, and hearty breakfasts make this a good option during the summer, right in front of Plaza de Correo with a garden in the back. [$] *Average main: 6000 pesos* ✉ *Arturo Prat 156, Puerto Natales* 🌐 *www.el-living.com* 🕘 *Closed Apr.–Oct.*

$ CHILEAN 🍴 **Espacio Ñandu.** Right on the corner of the plaza, this modern artisan shop doubles as a restaurant, bar, café, post office, and the best Wi-Fi spot in town, where you can surf on your own computer or rent one of theirs. With empanadas, tacos, seafood, and salads, you've got all bases covered for lunch, dinner, or just coffee and a snack. In addition to hot beverages, the bar also stocks local beers and a decent wine selection. [$] *Average main: 5000 pesos* ✉ *Eberhard and Arturo Prat, Puerto Natales* ☎ *61/241–4382.*

$$ CHILEAN 🍴 **Kosten.** You'll watch the wind whip the Seno Ultima Esperanza from a comfortable lounge in front of the fireplace at this modern café and bar attached to Indigo Hotel. With a well-stocked bar upstairs, this is a nice spot for a Calafate Sour, and if you are feeling lazy, just amble downstairs to the small restaurant where they serve simple, modern Chilean cuisine. [$] *Average main: 7000 pesos* ✉ *Indigo Hotel, Ladrilleros 105, Puerto Natales* ☎ *612/613–450* 🌐 *www.indigopatagonia.cl* 🕘 *Closed in winter; months vary.*

$$ CHILEAN 🍴 **Restaurant Ultima Esperanza.** Named for the strait on which Puerto Natales is located, Restaurant Ultima Esperanza is perhaps your last chance to try Patagonian seafood classics in a town being overrun by hip eateries. This traditional restaurant is well known for attentive, if formal service, and top-quality, typical dishes. Poached conger eel in shellfish sauce, king crab stew, and cordero are specialties—dishes served with plenty of flavor and little fuss. The room is big and impersonal, and for this reason alone the restaurant may be losing ground to new arrivals more focused on atmosphere and comfort. [$] *Average main: 9000 pesos* ✉ *Av. Eberhard 354, Puerto Natales* ☎ *61/241–3626* 🌐 *Closed July.*

$$$$ CHILEAN Fodor's Choice ★ 🍴 **The Singular.** Don't let the five-minute taxi ride out of town or the entrance through a barn put you off. The Singular's luxurious restaurant offers possibly the best cuisine in Chilean Patagonia. Smartly dressed and attentive waiters welcome you with a long list of aperitifs and hand you fur-bound menus that list exquisitely original Patagonian dishes: ceviche of fresh king crab, scallops, salmon, and octopus; guanaco steak with native cracked wheat; and sweet and succulent king crab stew. The historic and handsome setting, along with roaring fireplaces and sultry jazz, make the Singular an unforgettable visit. [$] *Average*

main: 14000 pesos ✉ *Puerto Bories s/n, Puerto Natales* ☎ *61/2722–030* 🌐 *www.thesingular.com* 🕐 *Closed May–Sept.*

WHERE TO STAY

$$ B&B/INN 🏨 **Hostal Lady Florence Dixie.** Named after an aristocratic English immigrant and tireless traveler, this long-established hotel with an alpine-inspired facade is on the town's main street; its bright, spacious upstairs lounge is a good people-watching perch. **Pros:** convenient location; relaxed atmosphere. **Cons:** not quite the boutique hotel it purports to be; rooms have a dowdy feel in a town that's rapidly modernizing. 💲 *Rooms from: 70000 pesos* ✉ *Av. Bulnes 655, Puerto Natales* ☎ *612/411–158* 🛏 *19 rooms* 🍴 *Breakfast.*

$$$$ HOTEL 🏨 **Hotel CostAustralis.** Designed by a local architect, this venerable three-story hotel is one of the most distinctive buildings in Puerto Natales; its peaked, turreted roof dominates the waterfront. **Pros:** great views from bay-facing rooms; good restaurant; courteous and professional staff; startlingly low off-season rates. **Cons:** rooms are somewhat bland; endless corridors a little impersonal. 💲 *Rooms from: 155000 pesos* ✉ *Av. Pedro Montt 262, at Av. Bulnes, Puerto Natales* ☎ *612/412–000* 🌐 *www.hoteles-australis.com* 🛏 *105 rooms, 5 suites* 🍴 *Breakfast.*

$$$ HOTEL 🏨 **Hotel Martín Gusinde.** This modern hotel with a good downtown location has simple but well-equipped rooms. **Pros:** atmosphere is urbane. **Cons:** rooms are easily penetrated by hallway noise. 💲 *Rooms from: 110000 pesos* ✉ *Carlos Bories 278, Puerto Natales* ☎ *61/2712–180* 🌐 *www.hotelmartingusinde.com* 🛏 *28 rooms* 🍴 *Breakfast.*

$$ B&B/INN 🏨 **Kau Lodge.** This modern and attractive B&B offers great value with an intimate setting, some of the best sea views and certainly the best coffee in town, and excellent touring tips from the mountain-guide owner, Hernan, who also runs a tourism agency offering customized trips and activities. **Pros:** great views; excellent value; good Wi-Fi. **Cons:** rooms are all facing the coast and the windows can get a bit battered during strong winds; small breakfast. 💲 *Rooms from: 61000 pesos* ✉ *Pedro Montt 161, Puerto Natales* ☎ *612/414–611* 🌐 *www.kaulodge.com* 🛏 *9 rooms* 🍴 *Breakfast.*

$$$$ HOTEL Fodor's Choice ★ 🏨 **Índigo.** Chilean architect Sebastian Irarrazabel was given free rein to redesign this building along a nautical theme; inside, a maze of gangplanks, ramps, and staircases shoot out across cavernous open spaces, minimalist wood panels line walls and ceilings, and water burbles down a waterfall that borders the central walkway. **Pros:** steeped in hip luxury; rooftop spa; great views; excellent guiding on excursions. **Cons:** ultramodern aesthetic not for everyone; standard rooms do not have bathtubs. 💲 *Rooms from: 158200 pesos* ✉ *Ladrilleros 105, Puerto Natales* ☎ *612/413–609* 🌐 *www.indigopatagonia.cl* 🛏 *29 rooms* 🍴 *Breakfast.*

OUTSIDE PUERTO NATALES

Several lodges have been constructed on a bluff overlooking the Seno Ultima Esperanza, about a mile outside of town. The views at these hotels are spectacular, with broad panoramas and unforgettable sunsets. While some might complain about the 10- to 30-minute trek into town, it is an easy walk along the seafront. A taxi will set you back around 2,000–2,500 Chilean pesos.

$$$ **Altiplanico Sur.** This is the Patagonian representative of the Altiplánico

HOTEL line of thoughtfully designed eco-hotels, and nature takes center stage: the hotel blends so seamlessly with its surroundings, it's almost subterranean. **Pros:** couldn't be closer to nature; stellar views of the fjords and mountains, even from a low vantage point; outdoor Jacuzzi on request. **Cons:** staff speaks little English; few technological amenities. S *Rooms from: 110000 pesos* ⊠ *Ruta 9 Norte, Km 1.5, Huerto 282, Puerto Natales* ☎ *61/241-2525* ⊕ *www.altiplanico.cl* ⇨ *22 rooms* ⊘ *Closed mid-May–mid-Sept.* ⦿ *Breakfast.*

$$$$ **Remota.** For most guests the Remota experience begins with the

HOTEL safari-esque transfer from Punta Arenas Airport, during which the

ALL-INCLUSIVE driver stops to point out animals and other items of interest; on arrival,

Fodor's Choice you meet what seems like the entire staff, check into your ultramodern

★ room, have a drink from a top-shelf open bar, and run off to the open-air Jacuzzis and impossibly serene infinity pool. **Pros:** after a few days the staff feels like family; restaurant uses the freshest locally sourced ingredients; inspiring design. **Cons:** all-inclusiveness discourages sampling local restaurants; views not as good as those from hotels inside Torres Del Paine National Park. S *Rooms from: 195000 pesos* ⊠ *Ruta 9 Norte, Km 1.5, Huerto 279, Puerto Natales* ☎ *612/414-040* ⊕ *www. remota.cl* ⇨ *72 rooms* ⦿ *All-inclusive.*

$$$$ **The Singular Patagonia.** Taking the former Bories Cold-Storage Plant,

HOTEL once used for processing and exporting sheep, and turning it into a

ALL-INCLUSIVE sleek, modern hotel with all the comforts of the 21st century is no

Fodor's Choice easy task. **Pros:** one-of-a-kind historic setting; expeditions and tours

★ for all levels of fitness; multiple rate plans available. **Cons:** may feel too remote for some; families welcome but may find more child-friendly facilities elsewhere. S *Rooms from: 577543 pesos* ⊠ *Y-300 Rd., toward Torres del Paine National Park, Puerto Bories* ☎ *61/722-030* ⊕ *www. thesingular.com* ⇨ *54 rooms, 3 suites* ⦿ *All-inclusive.*

$$$$ **Weskar Patagonian Lodge.** Weskar stands for "hill" in the language

HOTEL of the indigenous Kaweskar, to whom owner Juan José Pantoja, a marine biologist, pays homage in creating and maintaining this cozy lodge, which is high on a ridge overlooking the Ultima Esperanza fjord. **Pros:** great views from your room; cozy log-cabin decor. **Cons:** less luxurious than neighbors for similar price; from the dining room you can really hear the traffic or wind when it's howling; bathrooms are so-so. S *Rooms from: 117000 pesos* ⊠ *Ruta 9 Norte, Km 1/Puerto Natales, Puerto Natales* ☎ *612/414-168* ⊕ *www.weskar.cl* ⇨ *30 rooms* ⊘ *Closed mid-May–Sept.* ⦿ *Breakfast.*

PARQUE NACIONAL TORRES DEL PAINE

80 km (50 miles) northwest of Puerto Natales.

A top global destination for hikers and nature spotters, Torres del Paine National Park is, quite simply, outstanding. With breathtaking mountains, glaciers, and lakes, along with wildlife like guanacos, rheas, and pumas, the Park offers plenty of picture-perfect moments. Frequently changeable Patagonian weather is the only blemish in this UNESCO World Heritage Site, which attracts more than 150,000 visitors a year.

ESSENTIALS

Visitor Information CONAF. The national forestry service, CONAF, has an office at the northern end of Lago del Toro with a scale model of the park and numerous exhibits (some in English) about the flora and fauna. ⊠ *CONAF station in southern section of park past Hotel Explora* ☎ *61/269–1931* ⊕ *www.conaf.cl* ✉ *Summer 15,000 pesos, winter 8,000 pesos* ⊙ *Ranger station: Nov.–Feb., daily 8–8; Mar.–Oct., daily 8–5:30* ⊠ *Baquedano 847, Puerto Natales* ☎ *61/241–1438* ⊠ *Av. Bulnes 0309, 4th fl., Punta Arenas* ☎ *61/223–8581.*

EXPLORING

Fodor'sChoice **Parque Nacional Torres del Paine.** About 12 million years ago, lava flows
★ pushed up through the thick sedimentary crust that covered the south-western coast of South America, cooling to form a granite mass. Glaciers then swept through the region, grinding away all but the twisted ash-gray spire, the "towers" of Paine (pronounced "pie-nay"; it's the old Tehuelche word for "blue"), which rise over the landscape to create one of the world's most beautiful natural phenomena, now the Parque Nacional Torres del Paine. The park was established in 1959. Snow and rock formations dazzle at every turn of road, and the sunset views are spectacular. The 2,420-square-km (934-square-mile) park's most astonishing attractions are its lakes of turquoise, aquamarine, and emerald waters; and the Cuernos del Paine ("Paine Horns"), the geological showpiece of the immense granite massif.

Another draw is the park's unusual wildlife; creatures like the guanaco and the ñandú abound. They are acclimated to visitors, and don't seem to be bothered by approaching cars and people with cameras. Predators like the gray fox make less frequent appearances. You may also spot the dramatic aerobatics of falcons and the graceful soaring of endangered condors. The beautiful puma, celebrated in a National Geographic video filmed here, is especially elusive, but sightings have grown more common. Pumas follow the guanaco herds and eat an estimated 40% of their young, so don't dress as one.

The vast majority of visitors come during the summer months of January and February, which means the trails can get congested. Early spring, when wildflowers add flashes of color to the meadows, is an ideal time to visit because the crowds have not yet arrived. In summer, the winds can be incredibly fierce. During the wintertime of June to September, the days are sunnier yet colder (averaging around freezing) and shorter, but the winds all but disappear. The park is open all year, but some trails are not accessible in winter. Storms can hit without warning, so be prepared for sudden rain or snow. The sight of the Paine peaks in clear weather is stunning; if you have any flexibility in your itinerary, visit the park on the first clear day.

EXPLORING THE PARK

There are three entrances to the park: Laguna Amarga (all bus arrivals), Lago Sarmiento, and Laguna Azul. You are required to sign in when you arrive, and pay your entrance fee (around US$35 in high season). *Guardaparques* (park rangers) staff six stations around the reserve, and can provide a map and up-to-the-day information about the state of various trails. A regular minivan service connects Laguna Amarga with

10

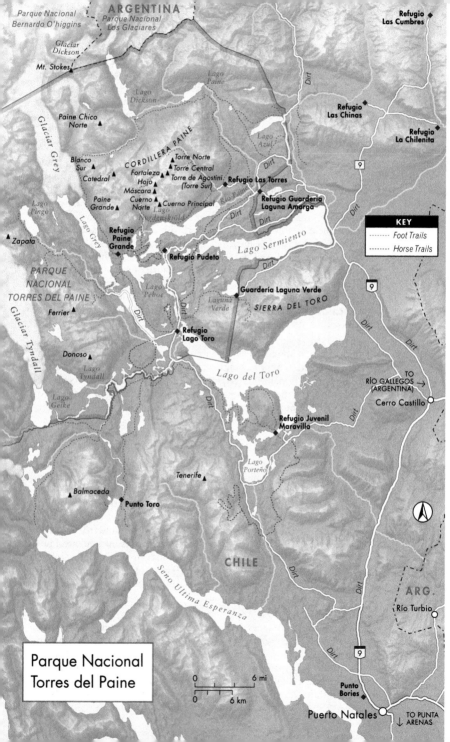

Parque Nacional
Torres del Paine

the Hostería Las Torres, 7 km (4 miles) to the west. Alternatively, you can walk approximately two hours before reaching the starting point of the hiking circuits.

Although considerable walking is necessary to take full advantage of Parque Nacional Torres del Paine, you need not be a hard-core trekker. Many people choose to hike the **"W" route,** which takes four days, but others prefer to stay in one of the comfortable lodges and hit the trails in the morning or afternoon. **Glaciar Grey,** with its fragmented icebergs, makes a rewarding and easy hike; equally rewarding is the spectacular boat or kayak ride across the lake, past icebergs, and up to the glacier, which leaves from Hostería Lago Grey *(⇨ below)*. Another great excursion is the 900-meter (3,000-foot) ascent to the sensational views from **Mirador Las Torres,** four hours one way from Las Torres Patagonia *(⇨ below)*. Even if you're not staying at the Hostería, you can arrange a morning drop-off there, and a late-afternoon pickup, so that you can see the Mirador while still keeping your base in Puerto Natales or elsewhere in the park; alternatively, you can drive to the Hostería and park there for the day.

If you do the "W," you'll begin (or end, if you reverse the route) at Laguna Amarga and continue to Mirador Las Torres and Los Cuernos, then continue along a breathtaking path up Valle Frances to its awe-inspiring and fiendishly windy lookout (hold on to your hat!) and finally Lago Grey. The W runs for 100 kilometers (62 miles), but always follows clearly marked paths, with gradual climbs and descents at relatively low altitude. The challenge comes from the weather. Winds whip up to 90 mph, and a clear sky can suddenly darken with storm clouds, producing rain, hail, or snow in a matter of minutes. An even more ambitious route is the "Circuito," which essentially leads around the entire park and takes from a week to 10 days. Along the way some people sleep at the dozen or so humble *refugios* (shelters) evenly spaced along the trail, and many others bring their own tents.

Driving is an easy way to enjoy the park: A new road cuts the distance to Puerto Natales from a meandering 140 km (87 miles) to a more direct 80 km (50 miles). Inside the national park more than 100 km (62 miles) of roads leading to the most popular sites are safe and well maintained, though unpaved. ■ TIP➜ **If you stick to the road, you won't need four-wheel drive.**

You can also hire horses from the Hostería Las Torres and trek to the Torres, the Cuernos, or along the shore of Lago Nordenskjold (which offers the finest views in the park, as the lake's waters reflect the chiseled massif). Alternatively, many Puerto Natales–based operators offer multiday horseback tours. Water transport is also available, with numerous tour operators offering sailboat, kayak, and inflatable Zodiac speedboat options along the Río Serrano toward the Paine massif and the southern ice field. Additionally, the Hostería Lago Grey operates the *Grey II,* a large catamaran making a three-hour return trip to Glaciar Grey four times daily as well as dinghy runs down the Pingo and Grey rivers. Another boat runs between Refugio Pudeto and Refugio Lago Pehoé.

10

Erratic Rock. For anyone seriously contemplating trekking the W or the full Circuit around Torres del Paine, the Erratic Rock hostel in Puerto Natales offers a free seminar on how best to make the journey. Rustyn Mesdag, the hostel's Oregonian co-owner, is a rambunctious, opinionated guide who gives the not-to-be-missed "Three O'Clock Talk" describing all the routes, tips, and tricks you need to complete one of South America's most challenging treks. His hour-long presentation to a room full of eager hikers starts promptly at 3 pm every day of the high season, and is full of advice on camping, equipment, food, and provisions, including the latest reports on weather and trail conditions inside the park. It's a great introduction to possible trekking partners, as CONAF doesn't allow you to complete the walk on your own. The irrepressible Mr. Mesdag also publishes the ubiquitous Black Sheep newspaper in English. ⊠ *Baquedano 719, Puerto Natales* ☎ *61/414–317* ⊕ *www.erraticrock.com.*

WHERE TO STAY

$$$$
HOTEL

Hostería Lago Grey. The panoramic view from the restaurant and bar, past the lake dappled with floating icebergs to the glacier beyond, is worth the journey here. **Pros:** great views in communal areas; location; heated bathroom floors. **Cons:** thin walls; staff speaks little English. Ⓢ *Rooms from: 154000 pesos* ⊠ *Lago Grey* ☎ *612/712–100* ⊕ *www.lagogrey.com* ⟿ *60 rooms* ⦿ *Breakfast.*

$$$
HOTEL

Hostería Tyndall. This wooden lodge, often surrounded by flocks of snow geese and other wild birds, has simple rooms with attractive wood paneling. **Pros:** cheaper lodging and dining options than other places in the park; great views of Los Cuernos (the Horns) on a clear day. **Cons:** hallways are poorly lit; the lodge itself can get noisy; frayed around the edges. Ⓢ *Rooms from: 92000 pesos* ⊠ *Lago Tyndall* ☎ *612/614–682* ⊕ *www.hosteriatyndall.com* ⟿ *36 rooms, 6 cottages* ⊗ *Closed Apr.–Sept.* ⦿ *Multiple meal plans.*

$$$
HOTEL
ALL-INCLUSIVE
Fodor'sChoice
★

Hotel Explora–Salto Chico. Hotel Explora is next to a gently babbling waterfall on the southeast corner of Lago Pehoé with a shimmering lake offset by tiny rocky islets and a perfect view of Torres del Paine. **Pros:** the grande dame of Patagonian hospitality and one of the best hotels in the country; heart-stopping views from the center of the national park. **Cons:** a bank breaker; terrible Wi-Fi. Ⓢ *Rooms from: 1110000 pesos* ⊠ *Lago Pehoé, Parque Nacional Torres Del Paine* ☎ *2/239–5280 in Santiago* 🖷 *2/395–2580 in Lake Pehoé* ⊕ *www.explora.com* ⟿ *49 rooms* ⦿ *All-inclusive.*

$$$$
HOTEL

Hotel Río Serrano. The main draw of this grand hotel are the views from certain rooms, which take in the entire Torres del Paine mountain range, with the Serrano River and a wind-stunted forest in the foreground. **Pros:** impressive public areas; a stunning location with all-encompassing views. **Cons:** standard rooms are tight on space. Ⓢ *Rooms from: 205750 pesos* ⊠ *Lago Toro, Torres del Paine* ☎ *61/222–4181 for reservations (Puerto Natales)* ⊕ *www.hotelrioserrano.cl* ⟿ *95 rooms* ⦿ *Multiple meal plans.*

$$$$
HOTEL

Las Torres Patagonia. Owned by one of the earliest families to settle in what became the park, Las Torres has a long history, and is the closest hotel to the main trails into the heart of the Torres del Paine itself.

Pros: friendly and efficient; homey atmosphere; couldn't be closer to the mountains. **Cons:** not cheap and prices keep rising. $ *Rooms from: 335000 pesos* ⊠ *Lago Amarga* ☎ *61/360–364* ⊕ *www.lastorres.com* ⇱ *84 rooms* ☉ *Closed mid-Apr.–mid-Sept.* ⦿ *Multiple meal plans.*

$$$$
RESORT
FAMILY

🖼 **Patagonia Camp.** Nestled in a dense forest just outside the Torres del Paine National Park, this is a nature-lover's haven, with luxurious yurts that look out onto a lake and the distant mountains. **Pros:** beautiful forest location; eco-friendly. **Cons:** finding the way back to your yurt can be tricky; wind and other guests are easy to hear from yurts; expensive. $ *Rooms from: 460000 pesos* ⊠ *Camino al Milodon, Km 74, Torres del Paine, Puerto Natales* ☎ *2/2882–1610* ⊕ *www.patagoniacamp.com* ⇱ *18 rooms* ☉ *Closed mid-May–mid-Sept.* ⦿ *Multiple meal plans.*

$$$$
RESORT
Fodor's Choice
★

🖼 **Tierra.** With stunning views of Lago Sarmiento and the Torres del Paine range from the huge interior windows, this luxurious hotel and spa keeps nature directly in the foreground at all time. **Pros:** gorgeous architecture and design; excellent spa; fabulous views. **Cons:** expensive; transfers in/out are limited. $ *Rooms from: 460000 pesos* ⊠ *Lago Sarmiento, Ruta Y, Torres del Paine* ☎ *2/3705–301* ⊕ *www. tierrapatagonia.com* ⇱ *40 rooms, 3 suites* ☉ *Closed May–Sept.* ⦿ *Multiple meal plans.*

OFF THE
BEATEN
PATH

Parque Nacional Bernardo O'Higgins. Bordering the Parque Nacional Torres del Paine on the southwest, Parque Nacional Bernardo O'Higgins marks the southern tip of the vast Campo de Hielo Sur (Southern Ice Field). As it is inaccessible by land, the only way to visit the park is to take a boat up the Seno Última Esperanza. The Navimag boat passes through on the way to Puerto Montt, but only the Puerto Natales-based, family-run outfit Turismo 21 de Mayo operates boats that actually stop here—the *21 de Mayo* and the *Alberto de Agostini.* (Several operators run trips to just the Balmaceda Glacier.) These well-equipped boating day trips are a good option if for some reason you don't have the time to make it to Torres del Paine. On your way to the park you approach a cormorant colony with nests clinging to sheer cliff walls, venture to a glacier at the foot of Mt. Balmaceda, and finally dock at Puerto Toro for a 1-km (½-mile) hike to the foot of the Serrano Glacier. Congratulations, you made it to the least-visited national park in the whole of Chile. In recognition of the feat, on the trip back to Puerto Natales the crew treats you to a *pisco sour* (brandy mixed with lemon, egg whites, and sugar) served over a chunk of glacier ice. As with many full-day tours, you must bring your own lunch. Warm clothing, including gloves, is recommended year-round, particularly if there's even the slightest breeze.

10

PUNTA ARENAS, CHILE

Founded a little more than 150 years ago, Punta Arenas was Chile's first permanent settlement in Patagonia. Great developments in cattle-keeping, mining, and wood production led to an economic and social boom at the end of the 19th century; today, though the port is no longer an important stop on trade routes, it exudes an aura of faded grandeur. Plaza Muñoz Gamero, the central square (also known as the Plaza de

Armas), is surrounded by evidence of its early prosperity: buildings whose then-opulent brick exteriors recall a time when this was one of Chile's wealthiest cities.

The newer houses here have colorful tin roofs, best appreciated when seen from a high vantage point such as the Mirador Cerro la Cruz. Although the city as a whole is not particularly attractive, look for details: the pink-and-white house on a corner, the bay window full of potted plants, and schoolchildren in identical naval pea coats reminding you how the city's identity is tied to the sea.

Although Punta Arenas is 3,141 km (1,960 miles) from Santiago, daily flights from the capital make it an easy journey. As the transportation hub of southern Patagonia, Punta Arenas is within reach of Chile's Parque Nacional Torres del Paine (a four-hour drive) and Argentina's Parque Nacional los Glaciares. It's also a major base for penguin-watchers and a key embarkation point for boat travel to Ushuaia and Antarctica.

The sights of Punta Arenas can be done in a day or two. The city is mainly a jumping-off point for cruises, and while tours to Torres del Paine do operate from here, a visit to Chilean Patagonia's main attraction is much more pleasantly done from Puerto Natales, a town that's gaining ground over Punta Arenas as a vacation destination and will likely affect the traffic into Punta Areas when the new airport opens there in 2016.

GETTING HERE AND AROUND

Most travelers will arrive at Aeropuerto Presidente Carlos Ibañez del Campo, a modern terminal approximately 12 miles from town. On a clear day you'll get a memorable fly-by view of Torres del Paine. Public bus service from the airport into the central square of Punta Arenas is 3,000 pesos although private transfers by small companies running minivans out of the airport (with no other pick-up points or call-in service) are most reliable and cost around 4,000 pesos per person, while a taxi for two or more is your best deal at 7,000 pesos.

Set on a windy bank of the Magellan Strait, eastward-facing Punta Arenas has four main thoroughfares that were originally planned wide enough to accommodate flocks of sheep. Bustling with pedestrians, Avenida Bories is the main drag for shopping, and O'Higgins for dining. Overall, the city is quite compact, and navigating its central grid of streets is fairly straightforward.

CRUISE TRAVEL TO PUNTA ARENAS

Arturo Prat Port is not far from the main drag of town. You can either walk five minutes from the pier or take a taxi for around US$5. Stroll along the portside a few minutes until you reach Calle O'Higgins, where you'll find many bars and restaurants, and then head up Calle Roca or Pedro Montt to the main plaza.

The small town center is easy to walk around, although you'll want to bring layers with you, as you never know when the wind might pick up. Also remember to bring a warm jacket for the evening, as nighttime temperatures are cold year-round.

ESSENTIALS

Bus Contacts **Buses Fernández** ⊠ *Armando Sanhueza 745* ☎ *61/2242–313* ⊕ *www.busesfernandez.com.*

Rental Car Contacts **Avis** ⊠ *Pedro Montt 969* ☎ *61/2241–182* ⊕ *www. avis.cl* ⊠ *Aeropuerto Presidente Ibañez.* **Hertz** ⊠ *Av. Bernardo O'Higgins 931* ☎ *61/261–3087* ⊕ *www.hertz.com.* **International Rent A Car** ⊠ *Aeropuerto Presidente Ibañez* ☎ *61/2212–401* ⊕ *www.recasur-rac.com.* **Payne** ⊠ *José Menéndez 631* ☎ *61/2240–852* ⊕ *www.payne.cl.*

Visitor and Tour Information **Punta Arenas City Tourism** ⊠ *Plaza Muñoz Gamero* ☎ *61/2200–610* ⊕ *www.puntaarenas.cl.* **Sernatur Punta Arenas** ⊠ *Lautaro Navarro 999* ☎ *61/2225–385* ⊕ *www.sernatur.cl* ☉ *Winter: weekdays 8:30–6, Sat. 10–4; summer: weekdays 8:30–8, weekends 9–1 and 2–6.*

EXPLORING

TOP ATTRACTIONS

Cementerio Municipal (*Municipal Cemetery*). The fascinating history of this region is chiseled into stone at the Municipal Cemetery. Set among long paths lined with eerily sculpted cypress trees, ornate mausoleums honor the original families who built Punta Arenas. In a strange effort to recognize the region's indigenous past, there's a shrine in the northern part of the cemetery where the last member of the Selk'nam tribe was buried (look for the copper dome). Local legend says that rubbing the statue's left knee brings good luck. ⊠ *Av. Bulnes 949* 🎫 *Free* ☉ *Daily dawn–dusk.*

Fodor'sChoice **Monumento Natural Los Pingüinos** (*Penguin Natural Monument*). Punta
★ Arenas is the launching point for a boat trip to see the more than 120,000 Magellanic penguins at the Monumento Natural Los Pingüinos on Isla Magdalena. Visitors walk a single trail, marked off by rope, and penguins are everywhere—wandering across your path, sitting in burrows, skipping along just off the shore, strutting around in packs. The trip to the island, in the middle of the Estrecho de Magallanes, takes about two hours. To get here, you must take a tour boat. If you haven't booked in advance, you can stop at any of the local travel agencies and try to get on a trip at the last minute, which is often possible. You can go only from December to the end of March; the penguin population peaks in January and February. The ferry that crosses the strait to Porvenir runs a daily morning service (except Monday) and occasional midweek afternoon service to the island (5,800 pesos per person). Almost all cruise ships that stop at Punta Arenas visit the colony. However you get here, bring warm clothing, even in summer; the island can be chilly, and it's definitely windy, which helps with the odor. If you like penguins, you'll have a blast. If you don't like penguins, what are you doing in Patagonia?

Museo Naval y Marítimo (*The Naval and Maritime Museum*). This museum extols Chile's high-seas prowess, particularly where Antarctica is concerned. In fact, a large chunk of ice from the great white continent is kept just below freezing in a glass case. The exhibits are worth a visit by anyone with an interest in merchant or military ships and sailing, but

Punta Arenas

Restaurants ▼

Café Tapiz	4
Dino's Pizza	1
Kiosko Roca	3
La Cuisine	9
La Marmita	2
Parrilla Los Ganaderos	8
Puerto Viejo	7
Sotito's Restaurant	6
Taberna Club de la Unión	5

Hotels ▼

Hotel Cabo de Hornos	4
Hotel Dreams	1
Hotel José Nogueira	3
Hotel Rey Don Felipe	2

the real highlight is in the screening room, where you can watch Irving Johnson's incredible film *Around Cape Horn*—his account of the hardship faced by crews in frigid southern waters in the early 20th century. His astounding black-and-white footage of daredevil crew members and mountainous seas is accompanied by a gruff and often hilarious voiceover. ⊠ *Av. Pedro Montt 981* ☎ *61/2205–558* ⊕ *www.museonaval. cl* 🖼 *1,000 pesos* ⊙ *Tues.–Sat. 9:30–5.*

Museo Regional de Magallanes (*Regional Museum of Magallanes*). Housed in what was once the mansion of the powerful Braun-Menéndez family, the Regional Museum of Magallanes is an intriguing glimpse into the daily life of a wealthy provincial family in the early 1900s. Lavish Carrara marble hearths, English bath fixtures, a billiard room that was a social hub in the city's glory days, and cordovan leather walls are all kept in immaculate condition, helped by the sockettes you wear over your shoes. The museum has an excellent group of displays depicting Punta Arenas's past, from prehistoric animals to European contact to its decline with the opening of the Panama Canal. The museum is half a block north of the main square. ⊠ *Av. Magallanes 949* ☎ *61/2244–216* ⊕ *www.museodemagallanes.cl* 🖼 *1,000 pesos* ⊙ *Winter, Wed.–Mon. 10:30–2; summer, Wed.–Mon. 10:30–5.*

Chocolatta. Tea and coffee house, chocolate shop, and bakery, Chocolatta is a perfect refueling stop during a day of wandering Punta Arenas. The interior is warm and cozy, the staff is fast and friendly, but there's no pressure. You can hang out, perhaps over a creamy hot chocolate, for as long as you like. ⊠ *Bories 852* ☎ *61/224–8150* ⊕ *www.chocolatta.cl.*

Museo Salesiano de Maggiorino Borgatello. Commonly referred to simply as "El Salesiano," this museum is operated by Italian missionaries whose order arrived in Punta Arenas in the 19th century. The Salesians, most of whom spoke no Spanish, proved to be daring explorers. Traveling throughout the region, they collected the artifacts made by indigenous tribes that are currently on display. They also relocated many of the indigenous people to nearby Dawson Island, where they died by the hundreds (from diseases like influenza and pneumonia). The museum contains an extraordinary collection of everything from skulls and native crafts to stuffed animals. ⊠ *Av. Bulnes 336* ☎ *61/222–1001* ⊕ *www.museomaggiorinoborgatello.cl* 🖼 *2,500 pesos* ⊙ *Tues.–Sun. 10–12:30 and 3–5:30.*

Palacio Sara Braun. This resplendent 1895 mansion, a national landmark and architectural showpiece of southern Patagonia, was designed by French architect Numa Meyer at the behest of Sara Braun (the wealthy widow of wool baron José Nogueira). Materials and craftsmen were imported from Europe during the home's four years of construction. The city's central plaza and surrounding buildings soon followed, ushering in the region's golden era. The Club de la Unión, a social organization that now owns the building, opens its doors to nonmembers for tours of some of the rooms and salons, which have magnificent parquet floors, marble fireplaces, and hand-painted ceilings. Unfortunately, the staff aren't all that friendly or enthusiastic. After touring the

10

rooms, head to the cellar tavern for a drink or snack. ✉ *Plaza Muñoz Gamero 716* ☎ *61/2241–489* 🎫 *1,000 pesos* 🕘 *Mon. 10–1, Tues.–Sat. 10–1 and 4–7:30.*

Plaza Muñoz Gamero. A canopy of pine trees shades this grandiose main square, which is surrounded by splendid baroque-style mansions from the 19th century. The heart of the city gives perhaps the strongest impression of Punta Arenas at its peak of wealth and power. A grandiose bronze sculpture commemorating the voyage of Hernando de Magallanes dominates the center of the plaza. Local lore has it that a kiss on the shiny toe of Calafate, one of the Fuegian statues at the base of the monument, will one day bring you back to Punta Arenas. ✉ *José Nogueira at 21 de Mayo.*

WORTH NOTING

Mirador Cerro la Cruz. The white cross that gives this hill its name marks a pretty good vantage point over the city, but it's not the best; to get to the best spot, climb down the stairs to the road just in front on the cross and turn right, until you reach a novelty road sign showing the distance to far-flung points of the globe. You'll have a panoramic view of the city's colorful corrugated rooftops and across the Strait of Magellan. Stand with the amorous local couples gazing out toward the flat expanse of Tierra del Fuego in the distance. ✉ *Fagnano at Señoret* 🎫 *Free* 🕘 *Daily.*

WHERE TO EAT

Over the last few years the restaurant scene has improved significantly in Punta Arenas. While there isn't much diversity, you'll find classic Chilean dishes that make the most of the abundant seafood and Patagonian lamb. Most restaurants close around midnight.

$ CAFÉ 🍴 **Café Tapiz.** This colorful and cozy café has a warm, inviting atmosphere, aided by the steaming hot chocolates and coffee on offer alongside sweet treats and Chilean sandwiches. Popular with locals and tourists, this place always has a buzz. You can buy local handicrafts here as well. [$] *Average main: 4000 pesos* ✉ *Roca 912* ☎ *9/8730–3481* 🌐 *www.cafetapiz.cl* 🕘 *Closed Sun.*

$ PIZZA FAMILY 🍴 **Dino's Pizza.** If you're wondering where everyone in Punta Arenas disappears to at lunchtime or on a cold and windy evening, they're here. This crowded pizzeria bursts with families, businesspeople, and teenage couples, all giving rapid-fire orders to an army of waiters in red polo shirts, who serve delicious thin-crust pizza and mountainous sandwiches with brisk efficiency. Take a seat at the counter and watch Dino and his chefs put together a string of takeaway orders smothered with seafood toppings (but not drowning in cheese). [$] *Average main: 6000 pesos* ✉ *Calle Carlos Bories 557* ☎ *61/224–7434* 🌐 *www.dinospizza.cl* 💳 *No credit cards* 🕘 *Closed Tues.*

$ CAFÉ 🍴 **Kiosko Roca.** This little bar is always packed with locals who come here for their specialty: a small sandwich with chorizo paste and béchamel sauce, and a banana milkshake. It might not seem like much, but Kiosko Roca is an institution in Punta Arenas. Pop in for a quick snack and see if you agree with what all the fuss is about. [$] *Average main:*

1000 pesos ✉ *Roca 875* 💳 *No credit cards* ⏲ *Closed Sun. No dinner Sat.*

$$ FRENCH Fodor's Choice ★ 🍴 **La Cuisine.** La Cuisine became one of the most popular restaurants in Punta Arenas by adding a French and European twist to typical Chilean seafood and meat dishes. Layered king crab lasagna and guanaco with calafate berry reduction are house favorites, as well as their signature pâté and three-flavor crème brûlée. La Cuisine is small, so it's best to make a reservation in the summer. [$] *Average main: 9000 pesos* ✉ *O'Higgins 1037* ☎ *61/2228–641* ⏲ *No dinner Sun.*

CORDERO AL ASADOR

In Argentine and Chilean Patagonia, lamb is deliciously prepared in the traditional manner: spit-roasted whole over an open fire. Restaurants offering *cordero al asador* often have grills positioned in their front windows to tempt you; you can smell, as well as see, the meat roasting to a delectable crispness.

$$ CHILEAN Fodor's Choice ★ 🍴 **La Marmita.** Fronting a small plaza lined with topiary, La Marmita is a family business just a short distance from downtown—but a long way from the usual Punta Arenas dining experience. The warm, rustic shack is charmingly decorated with an old kitchen stove, spatulas, whisks, shoe lasts, wooden children's toys from yesteryear, and an overflowing bread basket near the window. The short menu leans heavily on seafood, but with a twist; *ceviche de salmon* and crab dishes served with quinoa show a Peruvian influence, and the *pulmai* is a southern take on the famous seafood hotpot *curanto* from Chiloé. English-speaking staff will interpret the more obscure selections; the only thing missing is a decent wine list. With so few tables, make sure to book ahead. [$] *Average main: 8000 pesos* ✉ *Plaza Sampaio 678* ☎ *61/222–2056* 🌐 *www.marmitamaga.cl* 💳 *No credit cards* ⏲ *Closed Sun.*

$$ CHILEAN FAMILY 🍴 **Parrilla Los Ganaderos.** This bright restaurant resembles a rural *estancia* (ranch), with retro decor and waiters dressed in gaucho costumes serving up spectacular *cordero al ruedo* (spit-roasted lamb) cooked over a big fire in the dining room. A lamb serving comes with three different cuts of meat, or you can pick your way through other barbecue dishes. Complement your meal with a choice from the long list of Chilean wines. Black-and-white photographs of past and contemporary ranch life are displayed along the walls. [$] *Average main: 10000 pesos* ✉ *O'Higgins 1166* ☎ *61/222–5103* 🌐 *www.parrillalosganaderos.cl.*

$$ CHILEAN 🍴 **Puerto Viejo.** Owned by a local farmers' association, this restaurant down by the old port is a paragon of stylish modern design that offers traditional Patagonian lamb and seafood dishes. The maître d' station features the replica prow of a ship, and glass-and-untreated-wood partitions cordon off the smoking section. Start with *centolla* (king crab) or spicy scallops *al pilpil*, and then opt for the Magallenic lamb. Reservations are recommended. [$] *Average main: 8000 pesos* ✉ *Av. Bernardo O'Higgins 1166* ☎ *61/2225–103* ⏲ *Closed Sun.*

$$ SEAFOOD 🍴 **Sotito's Restaurant.** An institution in Punta Arenas, Sotito's has not rested on its reputation. Although it doesn't look like much from the outside, this restaurant is filled with attentive, bow-tied waiters who are chomping at the bit to take your order. Chileans make a pilgrimage

here from all over the country to this portside restaurant to enjoy some of the country's best *centolla* (king crab). [$] *Average main: 8000 pesos* ✉ *Av. Bernardo O'Higgins 1138* ☎ *61/2243–565* 🕒 *No dinner Sun.*

$$ CAFÉ 🍴 **Taberna Club de la Unión.** A jovial, publike atmosphere prevails in this wonderful, labyrinthine cellar redoubt down the side stairway of Sara Braun's old mansion on the main plaza. A series of nearly hidden rooms in cozy stone and brick have black-and-white photos of historical Punta Arenas adorning the walls. Some of the glamour has been lost with the decision to install large-screen TVs, but they tend to show tasteful concert films. Sip Patagonian beers like Austral served cold in frosted mugs while eating tapas-style meat, cheese, and seafood appetizers. The bar is affiliated with the Club de la Unión headquartered upstairs, and many members relax down here. [$] *Average main: 8000 pesos* ✉ *Plaza Muñoz Gamero 716* ☎ *61/2241–317* 🕒 *Closed Sun. No lunch.*

WHERE TO STAY

$$$$ HOTEL Fodor's Choice ★ 🏨 **Hotel Cabo de Hornos.** This hotel, part of the HotelesAustralis group, towers impressively over the main plaza. **Pros:** friendly, professional service; interesting design elements for such a large hotel. **Cons:** standard rooms don't match the brave design choices downstairs. [$] *Rooms from: 165000 pesos* ✉ *Plaza Muñoz Gamero 1025* ☎ *61/2715–000* 🌐 *www.hotelesaustralis.com* 🛏 *111 rooms* 🍽 *Breakfast.*

$$$$ HOTEL 🏨 **Hotel Dreams.** The most eye-catching of the new developments in Punta Arenas, Hotel Dreams is equipped with a big casino, convention center, and disco. **Pros:** great location and amenities; modern. **Cons:** can fill up with cruise passengers; noise from the casino crowds. [$] *Rooms from: 178000 pesos* ✉ *O'Higgins 1235* ☎ *600/626–0000* 🌐 *www.mundodreams.com/ciudad/punta-arenas* 🛏 *88 rooms, 16 suite* 🍽 *Breakfast.*

$$$ HOTEL Fodor's Choice ★ 🏨 **Hotel José Nogueira.** Originally the home of Sara Braun, this opulent 19th-century mansion has a superior location—just steps off the main plaza. **Pros:** central location; historic. **Cons:** some rooms are noisy and small. [$] *Rooms from: 115000 pesos* ✉ *Bories 959* ☎ *61/2711–000* 🌐 *www.hotelnogueira.com* 🛏 *17 rooms, 5 suites* 🍽 *Breakfast.*

$$$ HOTEL 🏨 **Hotel Rey Don Felipe.** This hotel is a great value stay in Punta Arenas, with comfortable rooms, a small gym and spa, and friendly staff. **Pros:** good value; quiet. **Cons:** a couple blocks from the main action; uninspiring views. [$] *Rooms from: 90000 pesos* ✉ *Armando Sanhueza 965* ☎ *61/229–5000* 🌐 *www.hotelreydonfelipe.com* 🛏 *45 rooms, 2 suites* 🍽 *Breakfast.*

NIGHTLIFE AND PERFORMING ARTS

During the Chilean summer, because Punta Arenas is so far south, the sun doesn't set until well into the evening. That means that locals don't think about hitting the bars until midnight. In the winter, on the other hand, it can be hard to persuade anyone to leave the warmth of the bar.

NIGHTLIFE
BARS
Jekus. This gastropub is a popular nightspot, where locals come for beer on the tap, live music, and karaoke at the weekends. They have a menu of local cuisine for when you get a bit peckish, too. ✉ *O'Higgins 1021* ☎ *61/2245–851* ⊕ *www.jekusrestaurant.com.*

Pub 1900. If you can't stay up late, try Pub 1900, which attracts an early crowd. It's a decent place for audible conversation. ✉ *Av. Colón 716* ☎ *61/2226–200.*

La Taberna Club de la Unión. The city's classic speakeasy, La Taberna Club de la Unión, hops into the wee hours with a healthy mix of younger and older patrons. It is also open for an early evening drink if you just want an aperitif before dinner. ✉ *Plaza de Armas.*

DANCE CLUBS
Club Madero. If you're in the mood for dancing and Latin beats, you can't beat Club Madero. This is the place where locals come to show off their salsa and bachata moves, which will undoubtedly keep you warm on a cold evening. There's karaoke once a week. ✉ *Bories 655* ☎ *61/2248–744.*

PERFORMING ARTS
FILM
Sala Estrella. In the early evening take in a movie at the only cinema in town. The charming Sala Estrella runs an eclectic mix of Hollywood and art-house films in an old-style, one-screen theater. ✉ *Mejicana 777* ☎ *61/2225–630* ⊕ *www.cinesalaestrella.cl.*

SHOPPING

You don't have to go far to find local handicrafts, pricey souvenirs, wool clothing, hiking gear, postcards, custom chocolates, or semiprecious stones like lapis lazuli. You will see penguins of every variety, from keychain size to larger than life. Warm wool clothing is for sale in almost every shop, but it isn't cheap. Unfortunately, few things are actually made in Chile—often a design is sent to England to be knitted and then returned with a handsome markup.

Plaza de Armas. The pretty Plaza de Armas in the center of town has a dozen small artisan kiosks that offer a wide range of tourist trinkets and souvenirs. ✉ *Plaza de Armas.*

Quilpué. Quilpué is a shoe-repair shop that also sells *huaso* (cowboy) supplies such as bridles, bits, and spurs. Pick up some boots for folk dancing. ✉ *José Nogueira 1256* ☎ *61/2220–960.*

Zona Franca. You can find real bargains on electronic goods, from digital cameras and laptops to thumb drives and USB devices, at the Zona Franca, a free-trade zone about 3 miles out of town along Bulnes. ⊕ *www.zonaustral.cl/en/zona-franca* ⊙ *Daily 10–9.*

10

PUERTO HAMBRE

50 km (31 miles) south of Punta Arenas.

In an attempt to gain a foothold in the region, Spain founded Ciudad Rey Don Felipe in 1584. Pedro Sarmiento de Gamboa constructed a church and homes for more than 100 settlers. But just three years later, British navigator Thomas Cavendish came ashore to find that all but one person had died of hunger, which some might say is a natural result of founding a town where there isn't any fresh water. He renamed the town Port Famine. Today a tranquil fishing village, Puerto Hambre still has traces of the original settlement, a sobering reminder of bad government planning.

EXPLORING

Fuerte Bulnes. In the middle of a Chilean winter in 1843, a frigate under the command of Captain Juan Williams Rebolledo sailed southward from the island of Chiloé carrying a ragtag contingent of 11 sailors and eight soldiers. In October, on a rocky promontory called Santa Ana overlooking the Estrecho de Magallanes, they built a wooden fort, which they named Fuerte Bulnes, thereby founding the first Chilean settlement in the southern reaches of Patagonia. Much of the fort has been restored. ⊠ *5 km (3 miles) south of Puerto Hambre* ☎ *61/2723–195* ⊕ *www.phipa.cl* 🖃 *12,000 park entrance* ⊗ *Daily 9-6:30.*

Monolith. About 2 km (1 mile) west of Puerto Hambre is a small white monolith that marks the geographical center of Chile, the midway point between northernmost Arica and the South Pole.

Reserva Nacional Laguna Parrillar. The 47,000-acre Reserva Nacional Laguna Parrillar, west of Puerto Hambre, stretches around a shimmering lake in a valley flanked by hills. It's a great place for a picnic, if the weather cooperates. A number of well-marked paths lead to sweeping vistas over the Estrecho de Magallanes. ⊠ *Off Ruta 9, 52 km (32 miles) south of Punta Arenas* 🖃 *1,500 pesos* ⊗ *Oct.–Apr., weekdays 8:30–5:30, weekends 8:30–8:30.*

PINGÜINERA DEL SENO OTWAY

65 km (40 miles) northwest of Punta Arenas.

This protected colony has more than 11,000 feathered residents in peak season. Just an hour from Punta Arenas, this is one of the best spots on mainland Chile to visit penguins.

GETTING HERE AND AROUND

The colony is 65 km (37 miles) northwest of Punta Arenas and just an hour's drive up the Ruta 9 and off a gravel road. If you don't have your own car, there are many tour operators and transfers from Punta Arenas, most of which offer half-day excursions in the morning or afternoon usually returning back to the city in less than four hours.

EXPLORING

Pingüinera de Seno Otway. Magellanic penguins, which live up to 20 years in the wild, return repeatedly to their birthplace to mate with the same partner. For about 2,000 penguin couples—no singles make the trip—home is this desolate and windswept land off the Otway Sound. In late September the penguins begin to arrive from the southern coast of Brazil and the Falkland Islands. They mate and lay their eggs in early October, and brood their eggs in November. Offspring are hatched mid-November through early December. If you're lucky, you'll see downy gray chicks stick their heads out of the burrows when their parents return to feed them. Otherwise you might see scores of the adult penguins waddling to the ocean from their nesting burrows. They swim for food every eight hours and dive up to 30 meters (100 feet) deep. The penguins depart from the sound in late March.

The road to the sanctuary begins 30 km (18 miles) north of Punta Arenas, where the main road, Ruta 9, diverges near a checkpoint booth. A gravel road then traverses another fierce and winding 30 km (18 miles), but the rough trip should reward you with the sight of hundreds of sheep, cows, and birds, including, if you're lucky, rheas and flamingos. The sanctuary is a 1-km (½-mile) walk from the parking lot. It gets chilly, so bring a windbreaker.

The best time to appreciate the penguins is in the morning before 10 am, or the evening after 5 pm, when they are not out fishing. If you don't have a car, many tour companies based in Punta Arenas, offers tours to the Pingüinera. The tours generally leave from Punta Arenas and return about 3½ hours later; most charge around 20,000 pesos. ✉ *Off Ruta 9* 🎫 *6,500 pesos (plus 2,500 road toll)* ⊗ *Oct.–Mar., daily 8–7.*

EL CALAFATE, EL CHALTÉN, AND PARQUE NACIONAL LOS GLACIARES, ARGENTINA

The Hielo Continental (Continental Ice Cap) spreads its icy mantle from the Pacific Ocean across Chile and the Andes into Argentina, covering an area of 21,700 square km (8,400 square miles). Approximately 1.5 million acres of it are contained within the Parque Nacional los Glaciares (Glaciers National Park), a UNESCO World Heritage Site. The park extends along the Chilean border for 350 km (217 miles), and 40% of it is covered by ice fields that branch off into 47 glaciers feeding two enormous lakes—the 15,000-year-old **Lago Argentino** (Argentine Lake, the largest body of water in Argentina and the third largest in South America) at the park's southern end, and **Lago Viedma** (Lake Viedma) at the northern end near **Cerro Fitzroy**, which rises 11,138 feet.

Plan on a minimum of two to three days to see the glaciers and enjoy El Calafate—more if you plan to visit El Chaltén or any of the other lakes. Entrance to the southern section of the park, which includes Perito Moreno Glacier, costs around US$20 for non-Argentineans.

Prices for restaurants and hotels in the Argentina sections are given in U.S. dollars. As of this writing, the exchange rate was US$1 to 618 Chilean pesos.

10

WHAT IT COSTS IN U.S. DOLLARS			
$	$$	$$$	$$$$
Restaurants	Under $9	$9–$12	$13–$18	over $18
Hotels	Under $116	$116–$200	$201–$300	over $300

Restaurant prices are the average cost of a main course at dinner or, if dinner is not served, at lunch. Hotel prices are the lowest cost of a standard double room in high season.

EL CALAFATE

320 km (225 miles) north of Río Gallegos via R5; 253 km (157 miles) east of Río Turbio on Chilean border via R40; 213 km (123 miles) south of El Chaltén via R40.

Founded in 1927 as a frontier town, El Calafate is the base for excursions to the Parque Nacional Los Glaciares, which was created in 1937 as a showcase for one of South America's most spectacular sights, the Glaciar Perito Moreno. Because it's on the southern shore of Lago Argentino, the town enjoys a microclimate much milder than the rest of southern Patagonia.

To call El Calafate a boomtown would be a gross understatement. In the first decade of this millennium the town's population exploded from 4,000 to more than 25,000, and it shows no signs of slowing down; at every turn you'll see new construction, with many luxury and boutique hotels cropping up. As a result, the downtown has a new sheen to it, although most buildings are constructed of wood, with a rustic aesthetic that respects the majestic natural environment. One exception is the casino in the heart of downtown, the facade of which seems to mock the face of the Glaciar Perito Moreno. Farther out of the city is another glacier lookalike, the brand new Glaciarium museum, architecturally modeled on Perito Moreno and with Argentina's only ice bar.

Now with a paved road between El Calafate and the glacier, the visitors continue to flock in to see the creaking ice sculptures. These visitors include luxury-package tourists bound for handsome estancias in the park surroundings, backpackers over from Chile's Parque Nacional Torres del Paine, and *porteños* (from Buenos Aires) in town for a long weekend.

GETTING HERE AND AROUND

Daily flights from Buenos Aires, Ushuaia, and Río Gallegos, and direct flights from Bariloche transport tourists to El Calafate's 21st-century glass-and-steel airport with the promise of adventure and discovery in distant mountains and glaciers. El Calafate is so popular that the flights sell out weeks in advance, so don't plan on booking at the last minute.

If you can't get on a flight or are looking for a cheaper option, there are daily buses between El Calafate, El Chaltén, Río Gallegos, Ushuaia, and Puerto Natales in Chile—all of which can be booked at the bus terminal. El Calafate is also the starting (or finishing) point for the legendary Ruta 40 journey to Bariloche. If you can bear the bus travel for

CASH WOES

For a town that lives and dies on tourism, one of the most infuriating elements of the boom is the cash shortage that strikes El Calafate every weekend during high season. The four ATMs in town frequently run out of money starting as early as Friday evening, and there's often no respite until midday Monday.

The shortage is compounded by tour companies who offer steep discounts for cash on combined glacier, ice-trekking, and estancia tours. Apart from stocking up during the week, the best plan to ensure that you won't run out is to bring all the cash you'll need for your stay here. If worse comes to worst, most hotels and many restaurants will accept credit cards, or exchange dollars.

a few days, you'll pass some exceptional scenery, and most operators allow you to hop on and hop off at canyons, lakes, and the famous handprint-covered caves en route.

Driving from Río Gallegos takes about four hours across desolate plains enlivened by occasional sightings of a gaucho, his dogs, and a herd of sheep, and *ñandu* (rheas), shy llama-like guanacos, silver-gray foxes, and fleet-footed hares the size of small deer. Esperanza is the only gas, food, and bathroom stop halfway between the two towns. Driving from Puerto Natales is similar, although snow-topped mountains line the distance; arriving by road from Ushuaia requires four border crossings and more than 18 hours.

Avenida del Libertador San Martín (known simply as Libertador) is El Calafate's main street, with tour offices, restaurants, and shops selling regional specialties, sportswear, camping and fishing equipment, and food.

A staircase ascends from the middle of Libertador to Avenida Julio Roca, where you'll find the bus terminal and a very busy Oficina de Turismo with a board listing available accommodations and campgrounds; you can also get brochures and maps, and there's a multilingual staff to help plan excursions. The tourism office has another location on the corner of Rosales and Libertador; both locations are open daily from 8 to 8 (during high season). The Oficina Parques Nacionales, open weekdays 8 to 4, has information on the Parque Nacional Los Glaciares, including the glaciers, area history, hiking trails, and flora and fauna.

TIMING

During the long summer days between December and February (when the sun sets around 10 pm), and during Easter vacation, tens of thousands of visitors come from all corners of the world and fill the hotels and restaurants. This is the area's high season, so make reservations well in advance. October, November, March, and April are less crowded and less expensive periods to visit, although some estancias might still be closed. March through May can be rainy and cool, but it's also less windy and often quite pleasant, and the autumn colors can be quite stunning. The only bad time to visit is winter, particularly May, June, July, and August, when many of the hotels and tour agencies are closed.

TOURS

In El Calafate, each tour has to be approved by the local government and is assigned to one tour operator only. On the upside you'll never fall foul of a shady operator, but on the downside there is no competition to keep prices low. Whether you book a tour directly with the operator who leads it, with another operator, or through your hotel or other tour agency, the price should remain the same. Take note that most tour prices do not include the park entrance fee, an extra US$30 for foreigners.

ESSENTIALS

Bus Contacts Cal Tur ⊠ *Terminal Ómnibus* ☎ *2902/493–801* ⊕ *www.caltur. com.ar* ⊠ *Av. Libertador 1080* ☎ *2902/491–842* ⊕ *www.caltur.com.ar.* **Freddy** ☎ *2902/492–127.* **TAQSA** ⊠ *Bus terminal* ☎ *2902/491–843* ⊕ *www.taqsa.com. ar.* **Turismo Zaahj** ⊠ *Bus terminal* ☎ *2902/491–631* ⊕ *www.turismozaahj.co.cl.*

Currency Exchange Casa de Cambio Thaler ⊠ *Av. del Libertador 963* ☎ *2902/493–245.*

Remis El Calafate ⊠ *Av. Roca 1004* ☎ *2902/492–005.*

Rental Cars Fiorasi ⊠ *Av. Libertador 1319* ☎ *2902/495–330.* **Hertz** ⊠ *Av. del Libertador 1822* ☎ *2902/493–033.* **ServiCar** ⊠ *Av. Libertador 695* ☎ *2902/492–541.*

Visitor and Tour Information Oficina de Turismo ⊠ *Rosales at Libertador* ☎ *2902/491–090* ⊕ *www.elcalafate.gov.ar* ⊠ *Bus terminal* ☎ *2902/491–476.* **Oficina Parques Nacionales** ⊠ *Av. Libertador 1302* ☎ *2902/491–005, 2902/491–545* ⊕ *www.parquesnacionales.gov.ar.*

EXPLORING

Glaciarium. This out-of-town glacier museum gives you an educational walk through the formation and life of glaciers (particularly in Patagonia) and the effects of climate change, as well as temporary art exhibitions. A 3-D film about the national park and plenty of brightly lit displays, along with the stark glacier-shaped architecture, give it a modern appeal. Don't miss the Glaciobar—the first ice bar in Argentina—where you can don thermal suits, boots, and gloves, and where a whisky on the rocks means 200-year-old glacier rocks from Perito Moreno. ⊠ *Ruta 7, Km 6* ✛ *Arrive by taxi (US$10 each way), 1 hr walking, or by shuttle service from the tourism office leaving every hr (US$5 return)* ☎ *2902/497–912* ⊕ *www.glaciarium.com* ▨ *Museum US$18; bar US$14 for 25 minutes with 1 drink* ☉ *Daily 9–8 (shorter opening hrs in winter); bar noon–6:30.*

Fodor's Choice ★ **Glaciar Perito Moreno.** Eighty km (50 miles) away on R11, the road to the Glaciar Perito Moreno has now been entirely paved. From the park entrance the road winds through hills and forests of lenga and ñire trees, until all at once the glacier comes into full view. Descending like a long white tongue through distant mountains, it ends abruptly in a translucent azure wall 5 km (3 miles) wide and 240 feet high at the edge of frosty green Lago Argentino.

Although it's possible to rent a car and go on your own (which can give you the advantage of avoiding large tourist groups), virtually everyone visits the park on a day trip booked through one of the many travel agents in El Calafate. The most basic tours start at US$50 for the round-trip and take you to see the glacier from a viewing area composed of a series of platforms wrapped around the point of the Península de Magallanes. The platforms, which offer perhaps the most impressive view of the glacier, allow you to wander back and forth, looking across the Canal de los Tempanos (Iceberg Channel). Here you listen and wait for nature's number-one ice show—first, a cracking sound, followed by tons of ice breaking away and falling with a thunderous crash into the lake. As the glacier creeps across this narrow channel and meets the land on the other side, an ice dam sometimes builds up between the inlet of Brazo Rico on the left and the rest of the lake on the right. As the pressure on the dam increases, everyone waits for the day it will rupture again. The last time was in July 2008, when the whole thing collapsed in a series of explosions, heard as far away as El Calafate, that sent huge waves across the lake.

In recent years the surge in the number of visitors to Glaciar Perito Moreno has created a crowded scene that is not always conducive to reflective encounters with nature's majesty. Although the glacier remains spectacular, savvy travelers would do well to minimize time at the mad-house that the viewing area becomes at midday in high season, and instead encounter the glacier by boat or on a mini-trekking excursion. Better yet, rent a car and get an early start to beat the tour buses, or visit Perito Moreno in the off-season when a spectacular rupture is just as likely as in midsummer and you won't have to crane over other people's heads to see it.

Glaciar Upsala. The largest glacier in South America, Glaciar Upsala is 55 km (35 miles) long and 10 km (6 miles) wide, and accessible only by boat. Daily cruises depart from Puerto Banderas (40 km [25 miles] west of El Calafate via R11) for the 2½-hour trip. Dodging floating icebergs (*tempanos*), some as large as a small island, the boats maneuver as close as they dare to the wall of ice that rises from the aqua-green water of Lago Argentino. The seven glaciers that feed the lake deposit their debris into the runoff, causing the water to cloud with minerals ground to fine powder by the glacier's moraine (the accumulation of earth and stones left by the glacier). Condors and black-chested buzzard eagles build their nests in the rocky cliffs above the lake. When the boat stops for lunch at Onelli Bay, don't miss the walk behind the restaurant into a wild landscape of small glaciers and milky rivers carrying chunks of ice from four glaciers into Lago Onelli. Glaciar Upsala has diminished in size in recent years. *Cruises start from $50USD.*

Nimez Lagoon Ecological Reserve. A marshy area on the shore of Lago Argentino just a short walk from downtown El Calafate, the Nimez Lagoon Ecological Reserve is home to many species of waterfowl, including black-necked swans, buff-necked ibises, southern lapwings,

Restaurants ▼

Casimiro Biguá .. **2**
Isabel **1**
La Lechuza **4**
La Tablita **3**
Pura Vida **5**

Hotels ▼

Eolo **5**
Estancia Cristina .**6**
Helsingfors **8**
Hotel Kau-Yatun ..**9**
Kosten Aike **2**
Los Ponchos Apart Boutique **7**
Madre Tierra **1**
Nibepo Aike **4**
Posada Los Alamos **3**

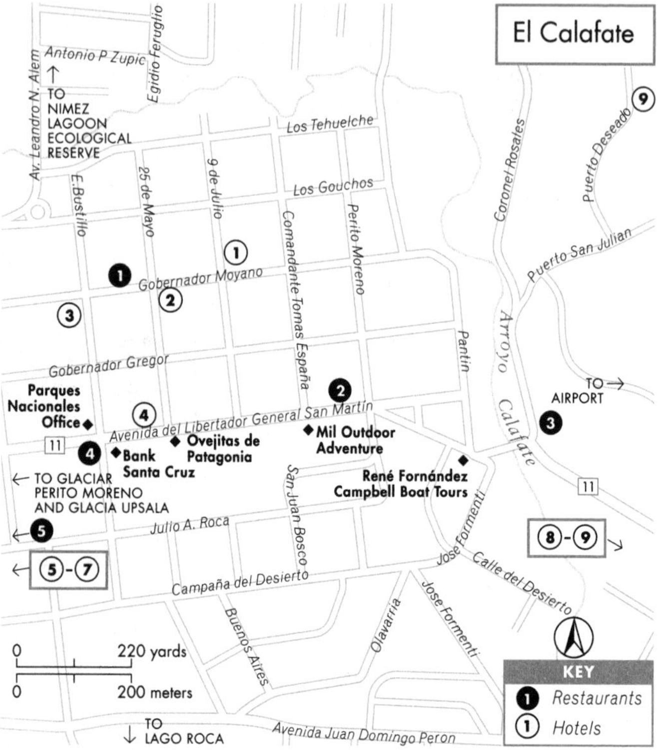

and flamingos. Road construction along its edge and the rapidly advancing town threaten to stifle this avian oasis, but it's still a haven for birdwatchers and a relaxing walk in the early morning or late afternoon. Strolling along footpaths among grazing horses and flocks of birds may not be as intense an experience as, say, trekking on a glacier, but a trip to the lagoon provides a good sense of the local landscape. During high season the nature reserve is open from 8 am until 9 pm. Don't forget your binoculars and a telephoto lens. ✉ *1 km (½ miles) north of downtown, just off Av. Alem* ☎ *2902/495–536* 🎟 *About $3USD.*

WHERE TO EAT

$$$$ ARGENTINE 🍴 **Casimiro Biguá.** This restaurant and wine bar boasts a hipper-than-thou interior and modern menu serving such delights as Patagonian lamb with *calafate* sauce (calafate is a local wild berry). The **Casimiro Biguá Parrilla,** down the street from the main restaurant, has a similar trendy feel but you can recognize the *parrilla* by the *cordero al asador* (spit-roasted lamb) displayed in the window. A third branch, also on Libertador, offers Italian dishes in a less formal setting. Each closes periodically during winter. [$] *Average main: US$25* ✉ *Av. Libertador 963* ☎ *2902/492–590* 🌐 *www.casimirobigua.com.*

VISITING LAGO ROCA

Lago Roca. This little-visited lake is inside the national park just south of Brazo Rico, 46 km (29 miles) from El Calafate. The area receives about five times as much annual precipitation as El Calafate, creating a relatively lush climate of green meadows by the lakeshore, where locals come to picnic and cast for trophy rainbow and lake trout. Don't miss a hike into the hills behind the lake—the view of dark-blue Lago Roca backed by a pale-green inlet of Lago Argentino with the Perito Moreno glacier and jagged snowcapped peaks beyond is truly outstanding.

Camping Lago Roca. There are gorgeous campsites, simple cabins, fishing-tackle rentals, hot showers, and a basic restaurant at Camping Lago Roca. Make reservations in advance if visiting over the Christmas holidays; at other times the campground is seldom crowded. In high season Cal Tur offer shuttles from Lago Roca to Perito Moreno. For more comfortable accommodations, you can arrange to stay at the Nibepo Aike Estancia at the western end of Lago Roca, about 5 km (3 miles) past the campground. The national park entrance fee is collected only on the road to Perito Moreno Glacier or at Puerto Banderas, where cruises depart, so admission to the Lago Roca corner of the park is free. ☎ 2902/499–500 ⊕ www.losglaciares.com/campinglagoroca ⊗ Closed May–Sept.

$$$
ARGENTINE
Fodor's Choice
★

✕ **Isabel.** It takes a lot of moxie to open a restaurant not serving *cordero*, barbecue, or pizza in Patagonia, and former "fancy" chefs José and Leandro show they have just that with their homely restaurant, Isabel. They use vintage plow wheels to cook a traditional and ultimately delicious stew-style dish known as *al disco*. The *al disco* menu offers all sorts of meats and veggies cooked in beer, red wine, or white wine; more creative and quasi-modern options like Bife al Napolitana; or you can create your own. And you've got to love a restaurant that tells you not to bother with starters but rather just dunk your bread in the disco sauce. Great atmosphere, laid-back charm, and effortlessly tasty food have made this one of the most popular new additions in town. $ *Average main: US$14* ⊠ *Gob. Moyano 1226, at 25 Mayo* ☎ *2902/489–000.*

$$
ARGENTINE

✕ **La Lechuza.** This bustling joint is known for having some of the best pizza in town. The brick oven and thin crust make for a more authentic, Italian-style taste and texture than at most spots. Their empanadas are just as good—pick up a few and you have the perfect pastry pick-me-up during a long day's exploring. With two other branches on the main strip (one with a kids' playground and the other for more Patagonian-style dishes), the secret is out, but stick with the original pizzeria, as the locals do. If it's not crowded, you're in the wrong one. $ *Average main: US$12* ⊠ *Av. Libertador at 1 de Mayo* ☎ *2902/491–610.*

$$$
ARGENTINE

✕ **La Tablita.** It's a couple of extra blocks from downtown and across a little white bridge, but this *parrilla* is where the locals go for a special night out. You can watch your food as it's cooking: Patagonian lamb and beef ribs roast gaucho style on frames hanging over a circular asador, and an enormous grill along the back wall is full of steaks, chorizos,

10

and *morcilla* (blood sausage). The whole place is filled with a warm glow despite the lackluster decor. It's slightly more expensive than other parillas in the center of town—and almost always fully booked—but has a classier atmosphere that will make you want to linger for dessert, if you have room. $ *Average main: US$14* ⊠ *Coronel Rosales 28* ☎ *2902/491–065* ⊕ *www.la-tablita.com.ar.*

$$
ARGENTINE

✕ **Pura Vida.** Bohemian music, homey cooking, and colorful patchwork cushions set the tone for this unpretentious, vegetarian-friendly restaurant several blocks from downtown. You'll be surrounded by funky artwork, couples whispering under low-hung lights, and laid-back but efficient staff as you try to decide which big-enough-to-share dish you'll order while working your way through a great dome of steaming bread. Choose between soups, pies, and bakes; the stew served inside a *calabaza* (pumpkin) is the signature dish. The cooking isn't quite up to the rest of the restaurant's charms, and the wine list is thin, but Pura Vida is more than the sum of its parts, attracting a curious blend of diners. $ *Average main: US$12* ⊠ *Av. Libertador 1876* ☎ *2902/493–356* ⊗ *No Lunch. Closed Wed.*

WHERE TO STAY

$$$$
HOTEL
ALL-INCLUSIVE

🏨 **Eolo.** A luxury lodge on the road to Perito Moreno, Eolo offers full-board stays in handsome accommodations where you can take in the beauty of Patagonia's vast, empty lands and see Lago Argentino in the distance. **Pros:** beautiful location; luxury service. **Cons:** expensive; no drinks included; far from town or any services. $ *Rooms from: US$950* ⊠ *Ruta Provincial N 11, Km 23,000* ☎ *2902/492–042* ⊕ *www.eolo.com.ar* 🛏 *12 rooms, 5 suites* ⊗ *Closed mid-Apr.–mid-Oct.* ⧫ *All-inclusive.*

$$$$
HOTEL
ALL-INCLUSIVE

🏨 **Estancia Cristina.** Boarding a catamaran for the four-hour journey across Lago Argentina, you pass a field of giant icebergs in front of the Upsala Glacier—as spectacular as Perito Moreno, minus the crowds—then disembark at Punta Bandera for a short drive up to the three guest lodges, their stark green roofs mirroring the mountain ridges beyond. **Pros:** combines a glacier visit with a stay in a genuine estancia; gourmet packed lunches; knowledgeable guides; incredible mountain views from comfortable, well-appointed rooms. **Cons:** long boat journey to get here; pricey for a one-night stay. $ *Rooms from: US$620* ⊠ *Punta Bandera* ☎ *2902/491–133* ⊕ *www.estanciacristina.com* 🛏 *20 rooms* ⊗ *Closed mid-Apr.–mid-Nov.* ⧫ *All-inclusive.*

$$$$
HOTEL
ALL-INCLUSIVE
Fodor's Choice
★

🏨 **Helsingfors.** This luxurious converted ranch house has an absolutely spectacular location in the middle of the national park on the shore of Lago Viedma. **Pros:** unique location; wonderful staff; comfy atmosphere; beautiful blue lake. **Cons:** three hours by dirt road from El Calafate; very remote; expensive. $ *Rooms from: US$725* ⊠ *Lago Viedma, 3 hrs by dirt road from El Calafate* ☎ *11/5277–0195 in Buenos Aires* ⊕ *www.helsingfors.com.ar* 🛏 *9 rooms, maximum 20 guests* ⊗ *Closed May–Sept.* ⧫ *All-inclusive.*

$$
HOTEL
FAMILY

🏨 **Hotel Kau-Yatun.** From the homemade chocolates and wildflower bouquets that appear in the rooms each evening to the sweeping backyard complete with swing sets for the kids, there are many thoughtful details in this converted ranch. **Pros:** good food; nice details; central location. **Cons:** water pressure is only adequate; lost a bit of personality from chain takeover. $ *Rooms from: US$180* ⊠ *25 de Mayo* ☎ *2902/491–059* ⊕ *www.kauyatun.com* ⏎ *44 rooms* ☽ *Closed Apr.– Sept.* ⧉ *Breakfast.*

$$$ ⊡ **Kosten Aike.** Lined with wooden balconies, high beamed ceilings, and
HOTEL   a slate floor, this hotel is a paragon of Andean Patagonian architecture.
Pros: large rooms; central location; great views from the spa; good value at this price point. **Cons:** dining room decor is uninspired. $ *Rooms from: US$208* ⊠ *G. Moyano 1243, at 25 de Mayo* ☎ *2902/492–424* ⊕ *www.kostenaike.com.ar* ⏎ *78 rooms, 2 suites* ☽ *Closed May–Sept.* ⧉ *Breakfast.*

$$$ ⊡ **Los Ponchos Apart Boutique.** Cozy and handsomely designed two-floor
B&B/INN   apartments in this boutique complex have beautiful views over Lago
Argentina and offer some independence and privacy with a self-catering kitchen and homey, gaucho-chic decoration. **Pros:** warm service; cozy; private. **Cons:** a bit of a walk from town. $ *Rooms from: US$220* ⊠ *Los Alamos 3321* ☎ *2902/496–330* ⊕ *www.losponchosapart.com. ar* ⏎ *8 rooms, 2 double apartments, 1 cabin* ☽ *Closed June–mid-Sept.* ⧉ *Breakfast.*

$$ ⊡ **Madre Tierra.** The friendly welcome from the owners makes staying at
B&B/INN   this B&B feel like visiting a friend's home (with great attention to detail
in design and well-chosen furnishings). **Pros:** personalized and friendly service, central location, authentic. **Cons:** accept cash payments only, walls are thin and noise travels. $ *Rooms from: US$165* ⊠ *9 de Julio 239* ☎ *2902/489–880* ⊕ *www.madretierrapatagonia.com* ⏎ *7 rooms* ⧉ *Breakfast.*

$$$$ ⊡ **Nibepo Aike.** This lovely estancia is 1½ hours from El Calafate in
RESORT   a bucolic valley overlooking Lago Roca and backed by snowcapped
mountain peaks; sheep, horses, and cows graze among purple lupine flowers, and friendly gauchos give horse-racing and sheep-shearing demonstrations. **Pros:** spectacular scenery; yummy food; welcoming staff. **Cons:** long drive by dirt road from downtown; two-night minimum stay; no Wi-Fi. $ *Rooms from: US$340* ⊠ *For reservations: Av. Libertador 1215* ☎ *11/5031–0755 reservations (Buenos Aires), 2902/492–797 day visits (El Calafate)* ⊕ *www.nibepoaike.com.ar* ⏎ *10 rooms* ☽ *Closed May–Sept.* ⧉ *Multiple meal plans.*

$$$ ⊡ **Posada los Alamos.** Surrounded by tall, leafy alamo trees and con-
HOTEL   structed of brick and dark *quebracho* (ironwood), this enormous com-
plex incorporates a country manor house, half a dozen convention rooms, a spa, indoor swimming pool, and mini-golf course to offer all the trappings of a top-notch hotel. **Pros:** modern and distinctive reception and public areas; beautiful gardens; long breakfast hours. **Cons:** it's easy to get lost in the maze of corridors; rooms are indifferently furnished; overly formal staff. $ *Rooms from: US$245* ⊠ *Moyano at Bustillo* ☎ *2902/491–144* ⊕ *www.posadalosalamos.com* ⏎ *144 rooms* ⧉ *Breakfast.*

10

SPORTS AND THE OUTDOORS
BOAT TOURS

Glaciares Gourmet. If fine dining and sipping wine while admiring the glaciers is more your style, this is the no-effort-required cruise for you. With a maximum of 28 passengers, the deluxe cruise liner is never overcrowded. You get a full day of cruising around the Spegazzini and Upsala glaciers, a short leg-stretching walk at beauty spot Puesto de las Vacas, and a six-course gourmet lunch with wine. If a full day isn't enough, you can opt for the two-night cruise option where you'll visit four glaciers (Spegazzini, Upsala, Perito Moreno, and Mayo) and access views that no one else can. ⊠ *Cruceros Marpatag, 9 de Julio (Local 4, Galleria de los Pajaros)* ☎ *2902/492–118* ⊕ *www.crucerosmarpatag. com* ⊠ *From US$288.*

Safari Náutico. Boats depart from a small port 7 km (4 miles) from Perito Moreno glacier and take tourists on an hour-long cruise around the glacier's south face for a closer inspection of the advancing glacier and floating icebergs. On a good day, you can stand on the deck for the best up-close photo opportunities. Tours happen all year and can be reserved at the port or in advance in the downtown office or other tour agencies. ⊠ *Hielo y Aventura, Av. Libertador 935* ☎ *2902/492–205* ⊕ *www.hieloyaventura.com* ⊠ *From US$50.*

Solo Patagonia. With two different full-day boat excursions, Solo Patagonia has been navigating the milky waters for years. Their fleet of large cruisers offers access to some of the best views of the Perito Moreno, Upsala, and Spegazzini glaciers from October to March. ⊠ *Av. Libertador 867* ☎ *2902/491–155* ⊕ *www.solopatagonia.com* ⊠ *From US$70.*

HIKING

Although it's possible to find trails along the shore of Lago Argentino and in the hills south and west of town, these hikes traverse a rather barren landscape and are not terribly interesting. The mountain peaks and forests are in the park, an hour by car from El Calafate. If you want to lace up your boots in your hotel, walk outside, and hit the trail, go to El Chaltén—it's a much better base than El Calafate for hikes in the national park. Good hiking trails are accessible from the camping areas and cabins by Lago Roca, 50 km (31 miles) from El Calafate.

HORSEBACK RIDING AND ESTANCIAS

Alta Vista. Convenient to El Calafate, Alta Vista is a solid choice for the standard estancia activites (horses, sheep, asados) and offers good guidance for local hikes. ⊠ *33 km (20 miles) from El Calafate on Ruta 15* ☎ *2902/499–902* ⊕ *www.hosteriaaltavista.com.ar.*

Estancia El Galpón del Glaciar. This estancia welcomes guests overnight or for the day—for a horseback ride, bird-watching, or an afternoon program that includes a demonstration of sheep dogs working, a walk to the lake with a naturalist, sheep-shearing, and dinner in the former sheep-shearing barn served right off the *asador* by knife-wielding gauchos. ⊠ *Ruta 11, Km 22* ☎ *2902/497–793–503, 11/5217–6719* ⊕ *www. elgalpondelglaciar.com.ar.*

Nibepo Aike. This pretty estancia 1½ hours from El Calafate offers a range of horseback experiences from hour-long excursions to full-day, nine-hour rides to view glaciers in the distance. It's possible to visit Nibepo Aike by booking a day trip at the office in downtown El Calafate, or you can stay overnight at the estancia. ⊠ *53 km (31 miles) from El Calafate near Lago Roca on Ruta 15* ☎ *2902/492–797, 2902/492–859* ⊕ *www.nibepoaike. com.ar.*

ICE TREKKING

Hielo y Aventura. For the most unusual and up-close-and-personal experience with Perito Moreno glacier, book yourself onto an ice trekking day where you'll don crampons and walk over the glacier studying crevasses and ice lakes before finishing with a whiskey on the rocks using ice from the glacier. The Mini Trekking excursion is a 10-hour trip and includes a 90-minute ice trek, a short trek in the forest, a 20-minute boat ride, and a transfer to the park from your hotel. You'll have to pay your own park entrance, bring a packed lunch, and wear the right clothing (crampons are provided), but you also get over an hour to enjoy the view of Perito Moreno Glacier from the park. For a more in-depth and challenging ice day, Hielo y Aventura also offers the Big Ice trek, which includes more time on the ice and ducking through bright-blue ice tunnels. This excursion has around seven hours' walking in total and is a longer day (ages 18–50 only). During high season, tours can get a bit crowded, but with a glacier the size of Buenos Aires, there is plenty of white space to feel true isolation. Ice trekking is available May to mid-September. ⊠ *Av. Libertador 935* ☎ *2902/492–205* ⊕ *www. hieloyaventura.com* ✉ *From US$100.*

KAYAKING

Viva Patagonia. Those brave enough to get in the milky ice waters can get dropped off by a boat on the glacier's edge and take a two-hour guided kayaking excursion with this outfitter. Available November through March, weather permitting. ⊠ *Calafate Mountain Park (Viva Patagonia), Av. Libertador 1037* ☎ *2902/491–446* ⊕ *www. calafatemountainpark.com* ✉ *From US$30.*

10

LAND ROVER EXCURSIONS

MIL Outdoor. If pedaling uphill sounds like too much work, check out the Land Rover expeditions offered by MIL Outdoor October to April. These trips use large tour trucks to follow dirt tracks into the hills above town for stunning views of Lago Argentino. On a clear day, you can even see the peaks of Cerro Torre and Cerro Fitzroy on the horizon. MIL's Land Rovers are converted to run on vegetable oil, so environmentalists can enjoy bouncing up the trail with a clean conscience. During the winter, the same company (also known as Calafate Mountain Park) runs a children's snow park with sledding, beginners' slopes, and more advanced off-piste skiing, snowshoeing and tearing around on snowmobiles. Open winter only, the snow park is 15 kms

(9 miles) from El Calafate city. ⊠ *Mil Aventura (Calafate Mountain Park/Viva Patagonia), Av. Libertador 1037* ☎ *2902/491–446* ⊕ *www. calafatemountainpark.com* ✆ *From US$50.*

MOUNTAIN BIKING

Alquiler de Bicicletas. Mountain biking is popular along the dirt roads and mountain paths that lead to the lakes, glaciers, and ranches. Rent bikes and get information at Alquiler de Bicicletas. ⊠ *HLS, Perito Moreno 65* ☎ *2902/493–806.*

EL CHALTÉN

222 km (138 miles) north of El Calafate (35 km [22 miles] east on R11 to R40, then north on R40 to R23 north).

Founded in 1985, El Chaltén is Argentina's newest town, and it's growing at an astounding rate. Originally just a few shacks and lodges built near the entrance to Parque Nacional Los Glaciares, the town is starting to fill a steep-walled valley in front of Cerro Torre and Cerro Fitzroy, two of the most impressive peaks in Argentina.

Famous for the exploits of rock climbers who started their pilgrimage to climb some of the most difficult rock walls in the world in the 1950s, the range is now drawing hikers whose more earthbound ambitions run to dazzling mountain scenery and unscripted encounters with wildlife including condors, Patagonian parrots, red-crested woodpeckers, and the *huemul,* an endangered deer species.

GETTING HERE AND AROUND

The three-hour car or bus trip to El Chaltén from El Calafate makes staying at least one night here a good idea. The only gas, food, and restroom facilities en route are at La Leona, a historically significant ranch 110 km (68 miles) from El Calafate where Butch Cassidy and the Sundance Kid once hid from the long arm of the law.

Before you cross the bridge into town over Río Fitzroy, stop at the Parque Nacional office. It's extremely well organized and staffed by bilingual rangers who can help you plan your mountain treks and point you to accommodations and restaurants in town. It's an essential stop; orientation talks are given in coordination with arriving buses, which automatically stop here before continuing on to the bus depot.

There's only one ATM in town (it's in the bus station), and it's in high demand; because of servicing schedules, on the weekend El Chaltén runs into the same cash availability problems that El Calafate does, though on a smaller scale. ⚠ **During the week, stockpile the cash you'll need for the weekend, or bring it with you if you're arriving between midday Friday and midday Monday.**

ESSENTIALS

Visitor Information **Parque Nacional Office** ⊠ *Av. M.M. de Güemes 21, El Chaltén* ☎ *2962/493–004* ⊕ *www.losglaciares.com/en.*

EXPLORING

Cerro Torre and Cerro Fitzroy. You don't need a guide to do the classic treks to Cerro Torre and Cerro Fitzroy, each about 6 to 8 hours round-trip out of El Chaltén. If your legs feel up to it the day you do the Fitzroy walk, tack on an hour of steep switchbacks to Mirador Tres Lagos, the lookout with the best views of Mt. Fitzroy and its glacial lakes. Both routes, plus the Mirador and various side trails, can be combined in a two- or three-day trip. ✉ *El Chaltén.*

Chorillo del Salta (*Trickling Falls*). Just 4 km (2.5 miles) north of town on the road to Lago del Desierto, the Chorillo del Salta waterfall is no Iguazú, but the area is extremely pleasant and sheltered from the wind. A short hike uphill leads to secluded river pools and sun-splashed rocks where locals enjoy picnics on their days off. If you don't feel up to a more ambitious hike, the short stroll to the falls is an excellent way to spend the better part of an afternoon. Pack a bottle of wine and a sandwich and enjoy the solitude. ✉ *El Chaltén.*

Laguna del Desierto (*Lake of the Desert*). A lovely lake surrounded by lush forest, complete with orchids and mossy trees, the Laguna del Desierto is 37 km (23 miles) north of El Chaltén on R23, a dirt road. Hotels in El Chaltén can arrange a trip for about US$40 for the day. Locals recommend visiting Lago del Desierto on a rainy day, when more ambitious hikes are not an option and the dripping green misty forest is extra mysterious. ✉ *El Chaltén.*

WHERE TO EAT AND STAY

$$$ ARGENTINE

🍴 **Aonikenk.** In a dark wooden dining hall you'll share hearty steaks, warming soups, and wine poured from penguin-shaped ceramic jugs, in a family restaurant that includes a hostel upstairs. It's rustic, and the food is not spectacular, but you can't beat the friendly atmosphere in what is easily El Chaltén's largest and most popular restaurant. It's also the only one that's consistently open for lunch and dinner in the off-season. [$] *Average main: US$13* ✉ *Av. M.M. de Güemes 23, El Chaltén* ☎ *2962/493–070* 💳 *No credit cards.*

$$ ARGENTINE Fodor's Choice ★

🍴 **La Cervecería.** While El Chaltén is still building all it needs to become a full-fledged town, it already has a successful microbrewery. The owners of this restaurant and bar pride themselves on handmade beers, with the stout or *negra* not to be missed. They call the place a "Hausbrauerei," but it's not just the hops bringing in the crowds: they also cook up delicious soups, snacks, empanadas, and a great *locro* (hearty traditional northern Argentine stew). [$] *Average main: US$10* ✉ *San Martin 320, El Chaltén* ☎ *2962/493–109* ⏲ *Closed May–Oct.*

$$$$ HOTEL

🏨 **Aguas Arriba Lodge.** Accessible only by boat or a three-hour trek, Aguas Arriba has a privileged location right on the Lago del Desierto, with a glimmer of Mount Fitzroy in the distance. **Pros:** fantastic location; attended by owners. **Cons:** noise travels between rooms; private shuttle to lake required in addition to walk/boat; no phone signal. [$] *Rooms from: US$375* ✉ *Lago del Desierto, El Chaltén* ☎ *11/4152–5697 Buenos Aires* 🌐 *www.aguasarribalodge.com* 🛏 *6 rooms* ⏲ *Closed mid-Apr.–Sept.* 🍽 *Breakfast.*

$ B&B/INN

🏨 **Nothofagus.** A simple B&B off the main road, Nothafagus is named after the southern beech tree, and the lodge has a rough-hewn, woodsy feel with exposed beams and leaves stamped into the lampshades. **Pros:** great views; bright and sunny breakfast room. **Cons:** staff energy too low for some; spartan rooms and bathrooms, some of which are shared. [$] *Rooms from: US$85* ✉ *Hensen, at Riquelme, El Chaltén* ☎ *2962/493–087* 🌐 *www.nothofagusbb.com.ar* 🛏 *9 rooms* 💳 *No credit cards* 🕒 *Closed June–Sept.* 🍴 *Breakfast.*

$$ HOTEL 🏨 **Posada Lunajuim.** A traditional A-frame roof keeps the lid on a funky, modern lodge filled with contemporary artwork, exposed brick masonry, and a spacious lounge and dining room complete with a roaring fireplace and a library stacked with an intriguing mix of travel books. **Pros:** you could spend all day in the common areas; staff and owners are pleasantly energetic and will make you a packed lunch for hikes. **Cons:** not all rooms have views; baths are quite small; a little pricey compared to the rest of town. [$] *Rooms from: US$165* ✉ *Trevisan 45, El Chaltén* ☎ *2962/493–047* 🌐 *www.lunajuim.com* 🛏 *26 rooms* 🍴 *Breakfast.*

SPORTS AND THE OUTDOORS

El Chaltén owes its existence to those who wanted a base for trekking into this corner of Los Glaciares National Park, specifically Cerro Torre and Cerro Fitzroy. It's no surprise that nearly everyone who comes here considers hiking up to those two mountains to be the main event—though the *locro* (hearty stew) and microbrews at the end of the day are a plus.

HIKING

Both long and short hikes on well-trodden trails lead to lakes, glaciers, and stunning viewpoints. There are two main hikes, one to the base of Cerro Fitzroy, the other to a windswept glacial lake at the base of Cerro Torre. Both hikes climb into the hills above town, and excellent views start after only about an hour on either trail. The six-hour round-trip hike to the base camp for Cerro Torre at Laguna Torre has (weather permitting) dramatic views of Torres Standhart, Adelas, Grande, and Solo.

Trails start in town and are very well marked, so if you stick to the main path there is little danger of getting lost. Just be careful of high winds and exposed rocks that can get slippery in bad weather. The eight-hour hike to the base camp for Cerro Fitzroy passes Laguna Capri and ends at Laguna de los Tres, where you can enjoy an utterly spectacular view of the granite tower. If you have time for only one ambitious hike, this is probably the best choice, though the last kilometer of trail is very steep. At campsites in the hills above town, hardy souls can pitch a tent for the night and enjoy sunset and dawn views of the mountain peaks. Ask about current camping regulations and advisories at the national park office before setting off with a tent in your rucksack. Finally, use latrines where provided, and under no circumstance should you ever think about starting a fire—a large section of forest near Cerro Torre was devastated several years ago when a foolish hiker tried to dispose of toilet paper with a match.

MOUNTAIN CLIMBING

Casa de Guias. A guide is required if you want to enter the ice field or trek on any of the glaciers in Los Glaciares National Park. Casa de Guias is a group of professional, multilingual guides who offer fully equipped multiday treks covering all the classic routes in the national park, and longer trips exploring the ice field. They even offer a taste of big-wall climbing on one of the spires in the Fitzroy range. ✉ *Av. San Martín 310, El Chaltén* ☎ *2962/493–118* ⊕ *www.casadeguias.com.ar.*

El Chaltén Mountain Guides. Five mountain guides offer expeditions in and around El Chaltén, as well as many other destinations in Argentina. One-day and multiday treks and ascents to rock and ice-climbing expeditions are available. In the winter they also offer backcountry skiing tours. ✉ *San Martín 187, El Chaltén* ☎ *2962/493–329* ⊕ *www. ecmg.com.ar.*

USHUAIA AND TIERRA DEL FUEGO, ARGENTINA

Tierra del Fuego, a more or less triangular island separated from the southernmost tip of the South American mainland by the twists and bends of the Estrecho de Magallanes, is indeed a world unto itself. The vast plains on its northern reaches are dotted with trees bent low by the savage winds that frequently lash the coast. The mountains that rise in the south are equally forbidding, traversed by huge glaciers slowly making their way to the sea.

The first European to set foot on this island was Spanish explorer Hernando de Magallanes, who sailed here in 1520. The smoke that he saw coming from the fires lighted by the native peoples prompted him to call it Tierra del Humo (Land of Smoke). King Charles V of Spain, disliking that name, rechristened it Tierra del Fuego, or Land of Fire.

Tierra del Fuego is split in half. The island's northernmost tip, well within Chilean territory, is its closest point to the continent. The only town of any size here is Porvenir. Its southern extremity, part of Argentina, points out into the Atlantic toward the Falkland Islands. Here you'll find Ushuaia, the main destination, on the shores of the Canal Beagle. Farther south is Cape Horn, the southernmost point of land before Antarctica (still a good 500 miles across the brutal Drake Passage).

10

USHUAIA

914 km (567 miles) south of El Calafate.

At 55 degrees latitude south, Ushuaia (pronounced oo-swy-ah) is closer to the South Pole than to Argentina's northern border with Bolivia. It is the capital and tourism base for Tierra del Fuego, the island at the southernmost tip of Argentina.

The city rightly (if perhaps too loudly) promotes itself as the southernmost city in the world (Puerto Williams, a few miles south on the Chilean side of the Beagle Channel, is a small town). You can make your way to the tourism office to get your clichéd, but oh-so-necessary, "Southernmost City in the World" passport stamp. Ushuaia feels like a frontier boomtown, at heart still a rugged, weather-beaten fishing village, but exhibiting the frayed edges of a city that quadrupled in size in the '70s and '80s and just keeps growing. Unpaved portions of Ruta 3, the last stretch of the Pan-American Highway, which connects Alaska to Tierra del Fuego, are finally being paved. The summer months (December through March) draw more than 120,000 visitors, and dozens of cruise ships. The city is trying to extend those visits with events like March's Marathon at the End of the World and by increasing the gamut of winter activities buoyed by the excellent snow conditions.

A terrific trail winds through the town up to the Martial Glacier, where a ski lift can help cut down a steep kilometer of your journey. The chaotic and contradictory urban landscape includes a handful of luxury hotels amid the concrete of public housing projects. Scores of "sled houses" (wooden shacks) sit precariously on upright piers, ready for speedy displacement to a different site. But there are also many small, picturesque homes with tiny, carefully tended gardens. Many of the newer homes are built in a Swiss-chalet style, reinforcing the idea that this is a town into which tourism has breathed new life. At the same time, the weather-worn pastel colors that dominate the town's landscape remind you that Ushuaia was once just a tiny fishing village, snuggled at the end of the Earth.

As you stand on the banks of the Canal Beagle (Beagle Channel) near Ushuaia, the spirit of the farthest corner of the world takes hold. What stands out is the light: at sundown the landscape is cast in a subdued, sensual tone; everything feels closer, softer, and more human in dimension despite the vastness of the setting. The snowcapped mountains reflect the setting sun back onto a stream rolling into the channel, as nearby peaks echo their image—on a windless day—in the still waters.

Above the city rise the last mountains of the Andean Cordillera, and just south and west of Ushuaia they finally vanish into the often-stormy sea. Snow whitens the peaks well into summer. Nature is the principal attraction here, with trekking, fishing, horseback riding, wildlife spotting, and sailing among the most rewarding activities, especially in the Parque Nacional Tierra del Fuego (Tierra del Fuego National Park).

GETTING HERE AND AROUND

Arriving by air is the preferred option. Ushuaia's Aeropuerto Internacional Malvinas Argentinas (⊠ *Peninsula de Ushuaia* ☎ *2901/431–232*) is 5 km (3 miles) from town and is served daily by flights to and from Buenos Aires, Río Gallegos, El Calafate, Trelew, and Comodoro Rivadavía. There are also flights to Santiago via Punta Arenas in Chile. A taxi into town costs about US$8.

Arriving by road on the Ruta Nacional 3 involves Argentine and Chilean immigrations/customs, a ferry crossing, and a lot of time. Buses to and from Punta Arenas make the trip five days a week in summer, four in winter. Daily buses to Río Gallegos leave in the predawn hours, and multiple border crossings mean an all-day journey. Check prices on the

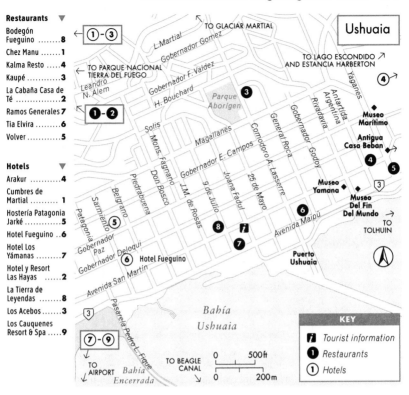

Restaurants ▼

Bodegón
Fueguino **8**
Chez Manu **1**
Kalma Resto **4**
Kaupé **3**
La Cabaña Casa de
Té **2**
Ramos Generales **7**
Tia Elvira **6**
Volver **5**

Hotels ▼

Arakur **4**
Cumbres de
Martial **1**
Hostería Patagonia
Jarké **5**
Hotel Fueguino ..**6**
Hotel Los
Yámanas **7**
Hotel y Resort
Las Hayas **2**
La Tierra de
Leyendas **8**
Los Acebos **3**
Los Cauquenes
Resort & Spa **9**

KEY

🛈 Tourist information
❶ Restaurants
① Hotels

55-minute flight, which can be a much better value. There is no central bus terminal, just individual company locations.

There is no regular passenger transport (besides cruises) by sea.

CRUISE TRAVEL TO USHUAIA

As you sail into Ushuaia, the captain almost always takes you around the picturesque lighthouse at the "end of the world": a beacon for the southernmost city perched on the edge of the Canal Beagle. The port is just two blocks from the main street, leaving you in a central location once you disembark.

Before undertaking the five-minute walk into town, stop at the Tourism Office (right in front of the port), where you can gather information and take advantage of the free Wi-Fi. Most city attractions can be reached on foot, although if you're spending the night here, you may need to take a taxi to your hotel. If you're in Ushuaia only for the day, lace on some good shoes, as the city is built on a hill and requires calves of steel.

ESSENTIALS

Bus Services Tecni-Austral ⊠ *Roca 157* ☏ *2901/431–408.*

Visitor Information Ushuaia Tourist Office ⊠ *Av. San Martín 674* ☏ *2901/432-001, 2901/424-550* ⊕ *www.turismoushuaia.com* ☉ *Weekdays 9*

10

am–10 pm, weekends 9–8 (reduced hrs in winter) ✉ *Av. Prefectura Naval Argentina 470* ☎ *2901/437–666.*

EXPLORING

TOP ATTRACTIONS

Canal Beagle. Several tour operators run trips along the Canal Beagle, on which you can get a startling close-up view of sea mammals and birds on **Isla de los Lobos, Isla de los Pájaros,** and near **Les Eclaireurs Lighthouse.** Catamarans, motorboats, and sailboats usually leave from the tourist pier at 9:30, 10, 3, and 3:30 (trips depend on weather; few trips go in winter). Trips start at US$50 and some include hikes on the islands. Check with the tourist office for the latest details; you can also book through any of the local travel agencies or scope out the offers yourself by walking around the kiosks on the tourist pier.

Estancia Harberton (*Harberton Ranch*). This property—50,000 acres of coastal marshland and wooded hillsides—was a late 19th-century gift from the Argentine government to Reverend Thomas Bridges, who authored a Yamana–English dictionary and is considered the patriarch of Tierra del Fuego. His son Lucas wrote *The Uttermost Part of the Earth,* a memoir about his frontier childhood. Today the ranch is managed by Bridges's great-grandson, Thomas Goodall, and his American wife, Natalie, a scientist and author who has cooperated with the National Geographic Society on conservation projects and operates the impressive marine mammal museum, **Museo Acatushun** (⊕ *www. acatushun.com*). Most people visit as part of organized tours, but you'll be welcome if you arrive alone. They serve up a tasty tea in their home, the oldest building on the island. For safety reasons, exploration of the ranch can only be done on guided tours (45–90 minutes). Lodging is available, either in the Old Shepherd's House or the Old Cook's House (US$400 for a double, with breakfast). Additionally, you can arrange a three-course lunch at the ranch by calling two days ahead for a reservation. Most tours reach the estancia by boat, offering a rare opportunity to explore the **Isla Martillo** penguin colony and a sea-lion refuge on **Isla de los Lobos** (Seal Island) along the way. ✉ *85 km (53 miles) east of Ushuaia* ☎ *2901/422–742* ⊕ *www.estanciaharberton.com* ✉ *Approx. $10USD* ☉ *Oct.–Apr. by tour only; daily 10–7, last tour 5:30.*

Fodor's Choice
★

Glaciar Martial. If you've never butted heads with a glacier, and especially if you won't be covering El Calafate on your trip, then you should check out Glaciar Martial, in the mountain range just above Ushuaia. Named after Frenchman Luís F. Martial, a 19th-century scientist who wandered this way aboard the warship *Romanche* to observe the passing of the planet Venus, the glacier is reached via a panoramic *aerosilla* (ski lift). Take the Camino al Glaciar (Glacier Road) 7 km (4 miles) out of town until it ends (this route is also served by the local tour companies). Even if you don't plan to hike to see the glacier, it's a great pleasure to ride the 15-minute lift, which is open daily 10–4:30, weather permitting (it's often closed in winter), and costs about $3USD. If you're afraid of heights, you can instead enjoy a small nature trail here, and the pretty teahouse. You can return on the lift, or continue on to the beginning of a 1-km (½-mile) trail that winds its way over lichen and shale straight up the mountain. After a steep, strenuous 90-minute hike, you can cool your heels in one of the many gurgling, icy rivulets that cascade down water-worn shale shoots or enjoy a picnic while you wait for sunset (you can walk all the way down if you want to linger until after the *aerosilla* closes). When the sun drops behind the glacier's jagged crown of peaks, brilliant rays beam over the mountain's crest, spilling a halo of gold-flecked light on the glacier, valley, and channel below. Moments like these are why this land is so magical. Note that temperatures drop dramatically after sunset, so come prepared with warm clothing. ⊠ *Glaciar Martial.*

Fodor's Choice **Museo Marítimo** (*Maritime Museum*). Part of the original penal colony, the Presidio building was built to hold political prisoners, murderous estancia owners, street orphans, and a variety of Buenos Aires' most violent criminals. Some even claim that singer Carlos Gardel landed in one of the cells for the petty crimes of his misspent youth. In its day it held 600 inmates in 380 cells. Today it's on the grounds of Ushuaia's naval base and holds the Museo Marítimo, which starts with exhibits on the canoe-making skills of the region's indigenous peoples, tracks the navigational history of Tierra del Fuego and Cape Horn and the Antarctic, and even has a display on other great jails of the world. You can enter cell blocks and read about the grisly crimes of the prisoners who lived in them and measure yourself against their eerie life-size plaster effigies. Of the five wings spreading out from the main guard house, one has been transformed into an art gallery and another has been kept untouched—and unheated. Bone chattering cold and bleak, bare walls powerfully evoke the desolation of a long sentence at the tip of the continent. Well-presented tours (in Spanish only) are conducted at 11:30 am, 4:30 pm, and 6:30 pm daily. ⊠ *Gobernador Paz at Yaganes* ☎ *2901/437–481, 2901/436–321* 🖃 *Approx. $13 USD (valid for 2 days)* ☉ *Daily 9–8 (summer), 10–8 (winter).*

Tren del Fin del Mundo (*End of the World Train*). Heavily promoted but a bit of a letdown, the Tren del Fin del Mundo purports to take you inside the Parque Nacional Tierra del Fuego, 12 km (7½ miles) away from town, so you have to drive to get there, and it leaves visitors a long way short of the most spectacular scenery in the national park. The touristy 40-minute train ride's gimmick is a simulation of the trip El Presidio prisoners were forced to take into the forest to chop wood; but unlike them, you'll also get a good presentation of Ushuaia's history (in Spanish and English). The train departs daily at 9:30, noon, and 3 (only 10 and noon in low season). One common way to do the trip is to hire a remis that will drop you at the station for a one-way train ride and pick you up at the other end, then drive you around the Parque Nacional for two or three hours of sightseeing (which is far more scenic than the train ride itself). ⊠ *Ruta 3, Km 3042* ☎ *2901/431–600* ⊕ *www.trendelfindelmundo.com.ar* 🖃 *$36USD.*

WORTH NOTING

Antigua Casa Beban (*Old Beban House*). One of Ushuaia's original houses, the Antigua Casa Beban long served as the city's social center. Built between 1911 and 1913 by Fortunato Beban, it's said he ordered the house through a Swiss catalog. In the 1980s the Beban

10

family donated the house to the city to avoid demolition. It was moved to its current location along the coast and restored, and is now a cultural center with art exhibits. ✉ *Maipú at Pluschow* ☎ *2901/431–386* 🖫 *Free* ⊗ *Weekdays 10–8.*

Canal Fun. This unconventional tour goes to **Monte Olivia**, the tallest mountain along the Canal Beagle, rising 4,455 feet above sea level. You also pass the **Five Brothers Mountains** and go through the **Garibaldi Pass**, which begins at the Rancho Hambre, climbs into the mountain range, and ends with a spectacular view of Lago Escondido. From here you continue on to Lago Fagnano through the countryside past sawmills and lumber yards. To do this tour in a four-wheel-drive truck with an excellent bilingual guide, contact Canal Fun; you'll drive *through* Lago Fagnano (about 3 feet of water at this point) to a secluded cabin on the shore and have a delicious *asado,* complete with wine and dessert. In winter they can also organize tailor-made dogsledding and cross-country skiing trips. ✉ *Roca 136* ☎ *2901/437–395, 2901/1551–1827* ⊕ *www.canalfun.com.*

Lago Escondido (*Hidden Lake*). One good excursion in the area is to Lago Escondido and **Lago Fagnano** (Fagnano Lake). The Pan-American Highway out of Ushuaia goes through deciduous beech forests and past beavers' dams, peat bogs, and glaciers. The lakes have campsites and fishing and are good spots for a picnic or a hike. This can be done on your own or as a seven-hour trip, including lunch, booked through the local travel agencies (around $60USD standard tour, $100USD with lunch and 4x4).

Museo del Fin del Mundo (*End of the World Museum*). See a large taxidermied condor and other native birds, indigenous artifacts, maritime instruments, a reconstruction of an old Patagonian general store, and such seafaring-related objects as an impressive mermaid figurehead taken from the bowsprit of a galleon at this museum. There are also photographs and histories of El Presidio's original inmates, such as Simon Radowitzky, a Russian immigrant anarchist who received a life sentence for killing an Argentine police colonel. The museum is split across two buildings—the first, and original, is in the 1905 residence of a Fuegonian governor at Maipu 173. The newest museum building, opened in 2008, is farther down the road at Maipu 465, where you can see extended exhibitions of the same style. ✉ *Maipú 173, at Rivadavía* ☎ *2901/421–863* 🖫 *Approx. $9USD (covers both museums)* ⊗ *Weekdays 10–7, weekends 2–8 (summer); Tues.–Fri. 10–5, weekends 2–7 (winter).*

Museo Yamana. Tierra del Fuego was the last land mass in the world to be inhabited—it was not until 9,000 BC that the ancestors of those native coastal inhabitants, the Yamana, arrived. The Museo Yamana chronicles their lifestyle and history. The group was decimated in the late 19th century, mostly by European diseases. The bicentenary of Charles Darwin's birth passed with great fanfare in 2009, but his attitudes towards the indigenous people, dismissing them as "miserable, degraded savages" in *The Voyage of the Beagle*, are belied here by descriptions of the Yamana's incredible resourcefulness in surviving a bitter climate. Photographs and good English placards depict the Yamana's powerful, stocky build and bold body-paint; their use of seal fat to stay warm; their methods of carrying fire wherever they went, even in small canoes; and their way of hunting cormorants, which were killed with a bite through the neck. ✉ *Rivadavía 56* ☎ *2901/422–874* 🌐 *www.tierradelfuego.org.ar/mundoyamana* 🎟 *Approx. $8USD* ⏲ *Daily 10–8 (summer), noon–7 (winter).*

OFF THE BEATEN PATH

Tres Marias Excursions. Although there are a number of boat tours through the Canal Beagle or around the bays to Tierra del Fuego National Park, one offers an experience that will put you in the shoes of the earliest explorers to visit the far south. The operators of Tres Marias Excursions offer a half-day sailing trip to Island H, an outcrop in the middle of the channel, with cormorant colonies, families of snow geese, seaweed stands, and a weather station that records the howling winds blowing in from the misnamed Pacific Ocean. The guides are skillful sailors and storytellers. On a gusty day you'll marvel at the hardiness of the Yamana people, who survived frigid winters wearing little or no clothing by setting fires behind natural and manmade windbreaks. You'll find the same plant and moss species that grow in the high Andes; they thrive here at sea level because the conditions kill off less hardy, temperate species. On the way back you visit a sea lion colony, but won't soon forget arriving in Ushuaia under full sail as the late sun hits the mountains. At $60USD it's only a little more expensive, and a lot more adventurous, than the motorized alternatives trawling for business at the dock. Tours only October to March. ✉ *Port* ☎ *2901/436–416* 🌐 *www.tresmariasweb.com.*

WHERE TO EAT

$$$$ ARGENTINE

🍴 **Bodegón Fueguino.** A mustard-yellow pioneer house that lights up the main street, this traditional eatery is driven by its ebullient owner Sergio Otero, a constant presence bustling around the bench seating, making suggestions, and revving up his staff. Sample the *picada* plate (king crab rolls, Roma-style calamari, marinated rabbit) over an artisanal Beagle Beer—the dark version is the perfect balm on a cold windy day. Lamb dominates the mains, and the emphasis is on hearty rather than fashionable. Tables filled with locals and visitors make for a boisterous atmosphere. Don't worry about the no-reservations policy as you won't have to wait long. [$] *Average main: US$18* ✉ *San Martin 859* ☎ *2901/431–972* 🌐 *www.tierradehumos.com* ✍ *Reservations not accepted* ⏲ *Closed Mon.*

$$$$ SEAFOOD Fodor's Choice ★

🍴 **Chez Manu.** *Herbes de provence* in the greeting room, a tank of lively king crabs in the dining room: French chef Manu Herbin gives local seafood a French touch and creates some of Ushuaia's most memorable meals with views to match. Perched a couple of miles above town across the street from the Hotel Glaciar, the restaurant has stunning views of the Beagle Channel. The first-rate wine list includes Patagonian selections, while all dishes are created entirely with ingredients from Tierra del Fuego. Don't miss the baby scallops or the *centolla* (king crab) au gratin. [$] *Average main: US$33* ✉ *Camino Luís Martial 2135* ☎ *2901/432–253* 🌐 *www.chezmanu.com* ⏲ *Closed Mon. No lunch Tues. Closed 2 wks in May/June.*

10

$$$$ ✕ **Kalma Resto.** Beautiful dishes and a contemporary twist on traditional
MODERN Patagonian flavors meet at this funky little restaurant at the end of
ARGENTINE the world. Owner and chef Jorge says that recipes are inspired by his
grandma's classics, but there is also a hint of Peruvian and Mediterranean with signature dishes like octopus ceviche, centolla and Beagle
Channel mussels, and paella. The wine list has plenty of Patagonian
wines to help you while away a couple hours at this slow-paced and
charming restaurant. $ *Average main: US$26* ✉ *Antártida Argentina
57* ☎ *2901/425–786* ⊕ *www.kalmaresto.com.ar* ☾ *No lunch July–Oct.
Closed May–June.*

$$$$ ✕ **Kaupé.** The white picket fence, manicured lawns, and planter boxes
ARGENTINE play up the fact that this out-of-the-way restaurant used to be a family
home. Inside, polished wooden floors, picture windows, and tables covered in wine glasses offer a sophisticated dining experience with an intimate touch. The star ingredient is centolla, best presented as chowder
with a hint of mustard. This restaurant is on a steep ridge above town
and offers good views, only a little bit spoiled by the radio antennae
sticking up from plots next door. Still, it's seafood served with panache
and warmth in a dining room that belies the status quo of the kitschy
restaurants near the waterfront. But it can be hard to find; even taxi
drivers get lost in the warren of streets above town. $ *Average main:
US$22* ✉ *Roca 470* ☎ *2901/422–704* ⊕ *www.kaupe.com.ar* ⌛ *Reserva-
tions essential* ☾ *Closed Sun.*

$$$$ ✕ **La Cabaña Casa de Té.** This impeccably maintained riverside cottage
ARGENTINE is nestled in a verdant stand of lenga trees, overlooks the Beagle Channel, and provides a warm, cozy spot for delicious loose leaf tea or
comforting snacks before or after a hike to the Martial Glacier (it's
conveniently located at the end of the Martial road that leads up from
Ushuaia, tucked in behind the ski lift). An afternoon tea with all the
trimmings will satiate any peckish trekker, fondues are served at lunch-
time, and at 8 pm in summer the menu shifts to pricier dinner fare with
dishes like salmon in wine sauce (mainly for the guests at the adjoining
cabin accommodation). $ *Average main: US$20* ✉ *Camino Luís Martial 3560* ☎ *2901/434–699* ⊕ *www.lacabania.com.ar* ☾ *Closed Apr.
and May.*

$$$$ ✕ **Ramos Generales.** Entering this café on the waterfront puts you in
ARGENTINE mind of a general store from the earliest frontier years of Ushuaia,
which is why locals call it the *viejo almacen* (old grocery store). As you
walk from room to room admiring the relics (like the hand-cranked
Victrola phonograph), the hubbub around the bar reminds you that
a warehouse like this was not just a store to pick up supplies; it was
also a place for isolated pioneers to socialize and gather all the latest
news from the port. Burgers and picada platters are uninspiring; choose
fresh-baked bread or scrumptious lemon croissants instead, and try
the *submarino*—a mug of hot milk in which you plunge a bar of dark
chocolate (goes well with a panini). $ *Average main: US$18* ✉ *Maípu
749* ☎ *2901/424–317* ⊕ *www.rgramosgenerales.com.ar* ☾ *Closed 3
wks in May.*

$$$$ ✕ **Tia Elvira.** On the street that runs right along the Beagle Channel,
ARGENTINE Tia Elvira is a good place to sample the local catch. Garlicky shellfish

appetizers and centolla are delicious; even more memorable is the tender *merluza negra* (black sea bass). The room is decked out with nautical knickknacks that may seem on the tacky side for such a pricey place. The service is friendly and familial. $ *Average main: US$28* ⊠ *Maipú 349* ☎ *2901/424–725* ⊘ *Closed Sun.*

$$$$
ARGENTINE

✕ **Volver.** A giant king crab sign beckons you into this red-tin-walled restaurant, where the maritime bric-a-brac hanging from the ceiling can be a little distracting. The name means "return" and it succeeds in getting repeat visits on the strength of its seafood. Newspapers from the 1930s line the walls in this century-old home; the service is friendly and relaxed. The culinary highlight is the centolla, which comes served with a choice of five different sauces. ■ TIP→ **This is among the best places to try Tierra del Fuego's signature dish.** $ *Average main: US$25* ⊠ *Maipú 37* ☎ *2901/423–977* ⊘ *No lunch Sun. Closed Mon.*

WHERE TO STAY

Choosing a place to stay depends in part on whether you want to spend the night in town, several miles west toward the national park, or uphill in the hotels above town. The hotels with the best views all require a taxi ride or the various complimentary shuttle services to reach Ushuaia.

$$$$
RESORT

🏨 **Arakur.** You can see this brand-new luxury hotel towering in the distance in front of Monte Olivia; it's one of the most extensive spa-and-resort complexes in Ushuaia and overlooks the entire bay and town from its own nature reserve out of town on the road to Cerro Castor. **Pros:** brand new; modern design with luxury fittings; sweeping views; nature reserve at doorstep. **Cons:** expensive; sterile atmosphere; far from town. $ *Rooms from: US$639* ⊠ *Cerro Alarken, access via Av. Héroes de Malvinas 2617* ☎ *2901/442–900* ⊕ *www.arakur.com* 🛏 *125 rooms, 6 suites* ⎜⎜ *Breakfast.*

$$$$
B&B/INN

🏨 **Cumbres de Martial.** This charming complex of cabins and bungalows, painted a deep berry purple, is high above Ushuaia in the woods at the base of the ski lift to the Martial glacier; each spacious room has an extremely comfortable bed and a small wooden deck with terrific views down to the Beagle Channel. **Pros:** easy access to the glacier and nature trails; stunning views of the Beagle Channel; romantic cabins; spa. **Cons:** you need to cab it to and from town; few restaurant options or services within walking distance. $ *Rooms from: US$332* ⊠ *Camino Luís Martial 3560* ☎ *2901/424–779, 2901/434–699* ⊕ *www. cumbresdelmartial.com.ar* 🛏 *6 rooms, 4 cabins* ⊘ *Closed Apr. and May* ⎜⎜ *Breakfast.*

$$
B&B/INN

🏨 **Hostería Patagonia Jarké.** Jarké means "spark" in a local native language, and this B&B is a bright, electric addition to Ushuaia; the three-story lodge cantilevers down a hillside on a dead-end street in the heart of town. **Pros:** warm, welcoming rooms with decent views; good price for Patagonia. **Cons:** steep walk home; can't compete with the views from the larger hotels farther uphill; noise travels through walls. $ *Rooms from: US$135* ⊠ *Sarmiento 310, at G. Paz* ☎ *2901/437–245* ⊕ *www.patagoniajarke.com.ar* 🛏 *15 rooms* ⎜⎜ *Breakfast.*

$$$
HOTEL

🏨 **Hotel Fueguino.** In downtown Ushuaia, the Fueguino boasts all the modern amenities: a conference center; a gym; a spa; shuttle service; outgoing, professional, multilingual staff; and one of the better Wi-Fi

10

signals in town. **Pros:** modern; central. **Cons:** barking dogs can keep you up all night in downtown location. *Rooms from: US$280 Gobernador Deloqui 1282 2901/424–894 www.fueguinohotel.com 53 rooms Breakfast.*

$$$ HOTEL **Hotel Los Yámanas.** This cozy hotel 4 km (2½ miles) from the center of town is named after the local tribe and offers a rustic mountain aesthetic. **Pros:** some stunning views from rooms; peaceful location; sauna is lovely. **Cons:** far from town; questionable taste in decoration. *Rooms from: US$230 Costa de los Yámanas 2850, Km 4 2901/446–809 www.hotelyamanas.com.ar 41 rooms Closed May Breakfast.*

$$$$ HOTEL **Hotel y Resort Las Hayas.** In the wooded foothills of the Andes, Las Hayas overlooks the town and channel below; ask for a canal view and, since the rooms are all decorated differently and idiosyncratically, sample a variety before settling in. **Pros:** good restaurant; charming staff and managers speak English; good spa. **Cons:** decor doesn't suit everyone; wall prints can be distracting; needs a refurb. *Rooms from: US$305 Camino Luís Martial 1650, Km 3 2901/430–710, 11/4393–4750 in Buenos Aires www.lashayashotel.com 88 rooms Breakfast.*

$$$ B&B/INN **La Tierra de Leyendas.** "The Land of Legends" is a honeymooners' delight; it sweeps up awards often, meaning the secret's out, but this adorable B&B run by Sebastian and Maria still bears their personal touch down to the family photos on the walls. **Pros:** an extraordinarily quaint find for western Ushuaia; enthusiastic, personal, and attentive service; all seven rooms have views. **Cons:** the street name is no joke—it's insanely windy; the immediate surroundings are a bit barren; need to book a month or more in advance; closed during winter. *Rooms from: US$208 Tierra de Vientos 2448 2901/446–565 www.tierradeleyendas.com.ar 7 rooms Closed mid-Apr.–mid-July Breakfast.*

$$$ HOTEL FAMILY **Los Acebos.** From the owners of Las Hayas (just around the corner on the winding mountain road), Los Acebos is a modern hotel on a forested ridge with a commanding view over the Beagle Channel; spacious and superclean rooms feature the same iconoclastic decor as Las Hayas, including the trademark fabric-padded walls, only this time with a '60s-style color scheme. **Pros:** good price for spacious and superclean rooms; expansive views of the channel from the restaurant. **Cons:** a tad out of the way for a spa-less facility. *Rooms from: US$269 Luis F. Martial 1911 2901/424–234, 11/4393–4750 (reservations from Buenos Aires office) www.losacebos.com.ar 60 rooms.*

$$$$ HOTEL Fodor's Choice ★ **Los Cauquenes Resort and Spa.** Right on the shore of the Beagle Channel about 8 km (5 miles) west of town, this resort is in a private community with privileged beach access and a nature hike that starts right outside your room. **Pros:** luxurious spa offers comprehensive range of treatments and massages; free transfer into city; private boat excursions offered. **Cons:** rooms can get uncomfortably hot; thin walls can make for noisy nights. *Rooms from: US$343 De la Ermita 3462, Barrio Bahía Cauquén 2901/441–300 www.loscauquenesushuaia.com.ar 54 rooms Breakfast.*

NIGHTLIFE

Ushuaia has lively nightlife in summer, with its casino, discos, and intimate cafés all close to each other.

Bar Ideal. This cozy and historic bar and café opens from 9 am onward. ✉ *San Martín 393, at Roca* ☎ *2901/437–860* ⊕ *www.elbarideal.com.*

El Náutico. The biggest and most popular pub in town, El Náutico attracts a young crowd with disco and techno music. ✉ *Maipú 1210* ⊕ *www.nauticodiscopub.com* ☉ *Closed Sun.–Thurs.*

Tante Sara. This popular café-bar in the heart of town has a casual, old-world feel. Locals kick back with a book or a beer; they pour the local artisanal brews, too. During the day it's one of the few eateries to defy the 3–6 pm siesta and stays open late. Their other branch, at San Martín 175, closes at 8:30 pm. ✉ *San Martín 701* ☎ *2901/423–912* ⊕ *www.tantesara.com.*

SHOPPING

Boutique del Libro–Antartida y Patagonia. Part of a bookstore chain, this branch specializes in Patagonian and polar exploration. Along with dozens of maps and picture books, postcards, and posters, it offers adventure classics detailing every Southern expedition from Darwin's Voyage of the Beagle to Ernest Shackleton's incredible journeys of Antarctic survival. While books in English are hard to come by in the rest of Argentina, here you're spoiled for choice, and the Antarctica trip logbooks on sale at the counter might inspire you to extend your travel farther south. ✉ *San Martín 1120* ☎ *2901/432–117* ☉ *Closed Sun.*

Laguna Negra. If you can't get to South America's chocolate capital Bariloche, you'll find some of the best sweets in Argentina at this boutique/café in the center of town. Planks of homemade chocolate include coconut crunches, fudges, and brittles, along with Tierra del Fuego's best selection of artisanal beers, chutneys, and spices. In the small coffee shop at the back, drop a glorious slab of dark chocolate into a mug of piping hot milk—one of the best *submarinos* in town. Locals pop in for a quick cup of hot chocolate at all hours, even as other cafés close for the lull between 3 and 8 in the evening. If you get hooked, there's another branch on the main street of El Calafate. ✉ *San Martin 513* ☎ *02901/431–144* ⊕ *www.lagunanegra.com.ar* ☉ *Closed 9–9.*

10

PARQUE NACIONAL TIERRA DEL FUEGO, ARGENTINA

21 km (13 miles) west of Ushuaia.

This park is one of the main reasons that travelers make a trip to the tip of Argentina. Its deep forests, glistening lakes, and wind-whipped trees will not disappoint. An easy day trip from Ushuaia, this 60,000-hectare park offers varied outdoor experiences and many wildlife-spotting opportunities.

EXPLORING

Fodor's Choice
★

Parque Nacional Tierra del Fuego. The pristine park offers a chance to wander through peat bogs, stumble upon hidden lakes, trek through native *canelo, lenga,* and wild cherry forests, and experience the wonders of wind-whipped Tierra del Fuego's rich flora and fauna. Everywhere, lichens line the trunks of the ubiquitous lenga trees, and "chinese lantern" parasites hang from the branches.

Everywhere, too, you'll see the results of government folly, *castoreros* (beaver dams) and lodges. Fifty beaver couples were first brought in from Canada in 1948 so that they would breed and create a fur industry. In the years since, without any predators, the beaver population has exploded to plague proportions (more than 100,000) and now represents a major threat to the forests, as the dams flood the roots of the trees; you can see their effects on parched dead trees on the lake's edge. Believe it or not, the government used to pay hunters a bounty for each beaver they killed (they had to show a tail and head as proof). To make matters worse, the government, after creating the beaver problem, introduced weasels to kill the beavers, but the weasels killed birds instead; they then introduced foxes to kill the beavers and weasels, but they also killed the birds. With eradication efforts failing, some tour operators have accepted them as a permanent presence and now offer beaver-viewing trips.

Visits to the park, which is tucked up against the Chilean border, are commonly arranged through tour companies. Trips range from bus tours to horseback riding to more adventurous excursions, such as canoe trips across Lapataia Bay. Entrance to the park is about $17USD.

Several private bus companies travel through the park making several stops; you can get off the bus, explore the park, and then wait for the next bus to come by or trek to the next stop (the service only operates in summer; check providers with the tourism office). Another option is to drive to the park on R3 (take it until it ends and you see the famous sign indicating the end of the Pan-American Highway, which starts 17,848 km [11,065 miles] away in Alaska, and ends here). If you don't have a car, you can also hire a private *remis* to spend a few hours driving through the park, including the Pan-American terminus, and perhaps combining the excursion with the Tren del Fin del Mundo. Trail and camping information is available at the park-entrance ranger station or at the Ushuaia tourist office. At the park entrance is a gleaming restaurant and teahouse set amid the hills, **Patagonia Mia** (*Ruta 3, Entrada Parque Nacional www.patagoniamia.com*); it's a great place to stop for tea or coffee, or a full meal of roast lamb or Fuegian seafood. A nice excursion in the park is by boat from lovely **Bahía Ensenada** to **Isla Redonda,** a wildlife refuge where you can follow a footpath to the western side and see a wonderful view of the Canal Beagle. This is included on some of the day tours; it's harder to arrange on your own, but you can contact the tourist office to try. While on Isla Redonda you can send a postcard and get your passport stamped at the world's southernmost post office. You can also see the Ensenada bay and island (from afar) from a point on the shore that is reachable by car.

Other highlights of the park include the spectacular mountain-ringed lake, **Lago Roca,** as well as **Laguna Verde,** a lagoon whose green color comes from algae at its bottom. Much of the park is closed from roughly June through September, when the descent to Bahía Ensenada is blocked by up to 6 feet of snow. Even in May and October, chains for your car are a good idea. No hotels are within the park—the only one burned down in the 1980s, and you can see its carcass as you drive by—but there are three simple camping areas around Lago Roca. Tours to the park are run by **All Patagonia** (*Juana Fadul 58* ☎ *2901/433–622* ⊕ *www.allpatagonia.com*). ⊕ *www.parquesnacionalesargentina.com* ✉ *About $17USD.*

WHERE TO STAY

EN
ROUTE

If you're in Ushuaia in the days leading up to New Year's Eve, drop in on **La Pista del Andino** campsite, on the edge of town. You'll be dwarfed by a mad mix of four-wheel-drive vehicles, enormous customized German trucks, and worn-out bicycles with beaten panniers. It's a tradition among overland explorers to spend Christmas and New Year's in the southernmost city in the world, and this turns out to be one of the most unusual "motorhog" celebrations around. Their routes zigzag across South America and are often painted on the sides of their vehicles—which have been known to be equipped with everything from rooftop tents to satellite dishes. Travelers share stories of crossing places like Siberia or northern Africa, and if you're lucky you'll encounter some who've ridden, driven, or pedaled the Pan-American Highway all the way from Alaska down to Ushuaia, a 17,000-mile journey that takes years to complete.

SPORTS AND THE OUTDOORS

FISHING

The rivers of Tierra del Fuego are home to trophy-size freshwater trout—including browns, rainbows, and brooks. Both fly- and spin-casting are available. The fishing season runs November through April; license fees range from US$50 per week to US$65 per season for nonresidents. Fishing expeditions are organized by the various local companies.

Asociación de Caza y Pesca. Founded in 1959, the Asociación de Caza y Pesca is the principal hunting and fishing organization in the city. ✉ *Av. Maipú 822* ☎ *2901/423–168* ⊕ *www.cazaypescaushuaia.org.*

Rumbo Sur. The city's oldest travel agency can assist in setting up fishing trips. ✉ *Av. San Martín 350* ☎ *2901/421–139* ⊕ *www.rumbosur.com.ar.*

Wind Fly. In summer this outfitter is dedicated exclusively to fishing, and offers classes and arranges trips. ✉ *Av. 25 de Mayo 155, Ushuaia* ☎ *2901/431–713, 2901/1551–6809* ⊕ *www.windflyushuaia.com.ar.*

MOUNTAIN BIKING

A mountain bike is an excellent mode of transport in Ushuaia, giving you the freedom to roam without the rental-car price tag. Good mountain bikes normally cost about US$10 for a half day or US$15 for a full day. Guided tours are about the same price.

All Patagonia. Guided bicycle tours (including rides through the national park) are organized by All Patagonia. ✉ *Juana Fadul 40, Ushuaia* ☎ *2901/433–622* ⊕ *www.allpatagonia.com.*

Rumbo Sur. One of the city's biggest travel agencies, Rumbo Sur can arrange cycling trips. ✉ *San Martín 350, Ushuaia* ☎ *2901/421–139* ⊕ *www.rumbosur.com.ar.*

Ushuaia Extreme. You can rent bikes or do a tour with Ushuaia Extreme. ⊠ *San Martin 1306, local A, Ushuaia* ☎ *2901/423–582* ⊕ *www. patagoniabiketour.com.*

SCENIC FLIGHTS

The gorgeous scenery and island topography of the area is readily appreciated on a Cessna tour.

Aeroclub Ushuaia. Half-hour- and hour-long trips are available through Aeroclub Ushuaia. The half-hour flight (US$105 per passenger; US$140 for one passenger alone) with a local pilot takes you over Ushuaia, Tierra del Fuego National Park, and the Beagle Channel with views of area glaciers, waterfalls, and snowcapped islands south to Cape Horn. A 60-minute flight (US$175 per passenger; US$235 for one passenger alone) crosses the Andes to Escondida and Fagnano lakes. ⊠ *Antiguo Aeropuerto, Luis Pedro Fique 151, Ushuaia* ☎ *2901/421–717* ⊕ *www. aeroclubushuaia.org.ar.*

Heli-Ushuaia. All sorts of helicopter trips are available from Heli-Ushuaia, beginning with a seven-minute spin at US$99 per person. There are plenty of longer trips and excursions if you have money to burn. ⊠ *Laserre 108, Ushuaia* ☎ *2901/444–444* ⊕ *www.heliushuaia.com.ar.*

SKIING

Canopy Ushuaia. Located at the Martial Glaciar, Canopy Ushuaia offers skiing in winter and canopy lines in summer. ⊠ *Cerro Martial, Luis Fernando Martial 3551, Ushuaia* ☎ *2901/1550–3767* ⊕ *www. canopyushuaia.com.ar.*

Cerro Castor. With off-piste and alpine skiing and almost guaranteed snow, this has become a popular ski haunt for European Olympic teams looking for summer snow. Pistes range from beginners to black-diamond runs with more than 31 trails and four high-speed lifts. You can rent skis and snowboards and take ski lessons at this resort 26 km (17 miles) northeast of Ushuaia on R3. Day passes are around US$70 in high season, and there are restaurants, bars, and a ski lodge on-site. The resort is open June to October. ⊠ *Ruta 3 Km 26, Ushuaia* ☎ *2901/422–244* ⊕ *www.cerrocastor.com.*

Club Andino. Ushuaia is the cross-country skiing (*esqui de fondo* in Spanish) center of South America, thanks to enthusiastic Club Andino members who took to the sport in the 1980s and made the forested hills of a high valley about 20 minutes from town a favorite destination for skiers. It's a magnet for international ski teams who come from Europe to train in the northern summer. ⊠ *Fadul 50, Ushuaia* ☎ *2901/422–335* ⊕ *www.clubandinoushuaia.com.ar.*

Haruwen. You can ride in dog-pulled sleds, rent skis, go cross-country skiing, get lessons, and eat at Haruwen, Hostería Los Cotorras, and Hostería Tierra Mayor; contact the Ushuaia tourist office for more information.

PUERTO WILLIAMS, CHILE

75-min flight southeast from Punta Arenas; 82 km (50 miles) southeast of Ushuaia, Argentina.

On an island southeast of Ushuaia, the town of Puerto Williams is the southernmost permanent settlement in the world (even though Ushuaia in Argentina often makes this claim, Ushuaia is in fact the southernmost city). Originally called Puerto Luisa, it was renamed in 1956 in honor of the military officer who took possession of the Estrecho de Magallanes for Chile in 1843, just after the country was founded. Most of the 2,500 residents are troops at the naval base, but there are several hundred civilians in the adjacent village. A tiny community of indigenous Yaghan peoples makes its home in the nearby Ukika village.

THE SOUTHERN DEBATE

The southernmost town on the globe, Puerto Williams, is just above the 55th parallel. It's closer to the South Pole than to the northern border of Chile. Bigger, and just to the northeast of Puerto Williams, is Ushuaia, Argentina, the world's southernmost *city*. At least, that's how the Argentineans describe it. The Chileans like to say that Puerto Williams is a city, too, resenting how Ushuaia has claimed that moniker in its tourist literature. Visit both, and decide for yourself.

GETTING HERE AND AROUND

Even though it's a short distance across the Canal Beagle from Ushuaia, there are no regular ferry services from Argentina to Puerto Williams. This is due in part to, according to whom you talk to, the desire among tour operators in Ushuaia to restrict the smaller Chilean town's claims to the lucrative tourist market. A workaround: Aeroclub Ushuaia now offers private flights (except Sunday) to Puerto Williams, Chile, for US$215 per person for two, or US$340 for a single passenger. There's a 15-kg baggage limit. You can book a passage with one of the private boats that regularly make the journey, for a fee.

Stop in at the Oficina de Turismo at Ibañez 130 (☉ *Dec.–Mar., weekdays 10–1 and 3–6* ☎ *61/2621–011*), but don't expect much beyond maps. Accommodation offerings are simple and huddled around the center of town.

EXPLORING

Aerovís DAP. Weather permitting, Aerovís DAP offers charter flights over Cabo de Hornos, the southernmost tip of South America. Although the water looks placid from the air, strong westerly winds make navigating around Cape Horn treacherous. Over the last few centuries, hundreds of ships have met their doom here trying to sail to the Pacific. ✉ *Av. Bernardo O'Higgins 891, Punta Arenas* ☎ *61/2616–100* ⊕ *www.aeroviasdap.cl.*

Museo Martín Gusinde. For a quick history lesson on how Puerto Williams evolved, and some insight into the indigenous peoples, visit the Museo Martín Gusinde, named for the renowned anthropologist who traveled and studied in the region between 1918 and 1924. ✉ *Aragay 1* 🔲 *500 pesos* 🕙 *Weekdays 10–1 and 3–6, weekends 3–6.*

WHERE TO STAY

When you arrive in Puerto Williams, your airline or ferry company will recommend a few of the hospedajes available, then take you around to see them. With the exception of Lakutaia Hotel, all are rustic inns that also serve meals.

$$$$ 🏨 **Lakutaia Hotel.** The most southern luxury hotel in the world, Hotel
B&B/INN Lakutaia takes advantage of Navarino's beautiful surroundings to offer
Fodor's Choice a range of unique outdoors activities including kayaking and trekking
★ in Lauta, mountain biking, golf, horseback riding, sailing, walks to
Castors Lagoon, and matches of Rayuela, a typical Chilean sport. **Pros:**
offers an impressive range of activities; sailboats offers stunning journey
into untouched parts of Tierra del Fuego. **Cons:** comes with a high price
tag. 💲 *Rooms from: 125000 pesos* ✉ *Seno Lauta s/n* ☎ *61/2621–721*
⊕ *www.lakutaia.cl* 🛏 *24 rooms* 🍽 *Breakfast.*

SPORTS AND THE OUTDOORS
HIKING

Cerro Bandera. A hike to the top of Cerro Bandera is well worth the effort if you have the stamina. The trail is well marked but very steep. The view from the top toward the south to the Cordón Dientes del Perro (Dog's Teeth Range) is impressive, but looking northward over the Beagle Channel to Argentina—with Puerto Williams nestled below and Ushuaia just visible to the west—is truly breathtaking. Near the start of the trail, 3 km (2 miles) west of Puerto Williams, is the Parque Etnobotánico Omora visitor center, which got its name from the Yahgan word for hummingbird. In the Yahgan cosmology, Omora was more than a bird; he was also a revered mythological hero. The Omora Foundation is a Chilean NGO dedicated to biocultural conservation in the extreme southern tip of South America. Their work led UNESCO to designate the Cape Horn Biosphere Reserve in 2005. Within the park's interpretive trails, explore the various habitats of the Isla Navarino region: coastal coigue forests, lenga parks, nirre forests, Sphagnum bogs, beaver wetlands, and alpine heath. Additionally, the Robalo River runs through the park and provides potable water to the town. ✉ *3 km (2 miles) west of Puerto Williams* ⊕ *www.cabodehornos.org* 🕙 *Open daylight hrs.*

EASTER ISLAND

WELCOME TO EASTER ISLAND

TOP REASONS TO GO

★ **Astounding archaeology:** Whether it's the ubiquitous moai statues, petroglyphs, or cave paintings, Easter Island is an open-air museum with a turbulent and mysterious past.

★ **Wonderful walking:** Easter Island's rolling hills, with the white-flecked ocean rarely out of sight, hold some glorious walking trails, especially along the north coast.

★ **Extraordinary diving:** Diving into the cobalt-blue waters is one of the most popular pastimes on Easter Island. Visibility is up to 120 feet, so you don't miss the bright tropical fish or the turtles. Coral formations like the Cavern of the Three Windows make for an unforgettable underwater experience.

★ **Souvenir shopping:** Locals have carved a living out of the stone and driftwood, making handicrafts like miniature moai, elaborate bowls, eerie masks, and shell jewelry.

1 Hanga Roa. Almost all hotels on Easter Island are in or near Hanga Roa, the only town, as are the offices of tour operators and car rental companies. Hanga Roa also has its own sights, including the Iglesia Hanga Roa, which has a magnificent expansive view of the Pacific Ocean. Next door is the better of the town's two craft markets. A short walk along the coast to the north leads to the unique town cemetery, the Tahai moai statue, and the island's small but attractively didactic anthropology museum.

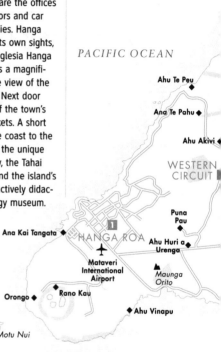

2 The Southeastern Circuit. Most of the archaeological sites on the island are along its southeastern coast. Lined with moai, including Ahu Tongariki with its 15 statues, re-erected after being toppled by a tidal wave, this road also leads to Ankena Beach and the so-called moai factory in the side of Rano Raraku volcano.

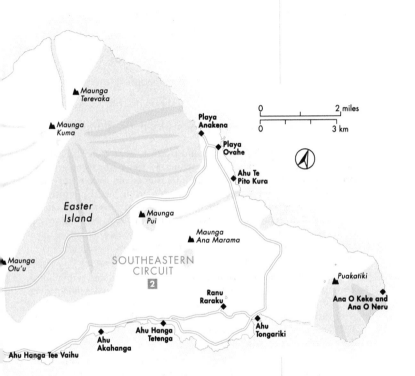

3 The Western Circuit.
A visit to the west of the
island has really only one
objective—to see the stone
houses and petroglyphs in
Orongo ceremonial village,
the center of the island's
birdman cult. On the way
is the water-filled crater of
the now-extinct Rano Kau
volcano.

GETTING ORIENTED

It's nearly impossible to
get lost on Easter Island.
It's just 22 km (14 miles)
from end to end and has
only three roads that fan
out from Hanga Roa: one
crosses the island north-
east to Anakena beach;
another curves along
the southeastern coast

before turning north and
then west to Anakena;
and the third, a dirt track,
snakes up the Rano Kau
volcano to the southwest.

Updated by
Eileen Smith

Easter Island, the most isolated inhabited island in the world—2,985 km (1850 miles) from its nearest populated neighbor and 3,700 km (2,295 miles) off the Chilean coast—is a tiny speck in the Pacific ocean. All over the island are hundreds of giant stone statues called moai, which overlook the ruins of the settlements that constructed them. The mystery of the moai, why the Rapa Nui (as the locals call themselves) constructed and later toppled them, and the natural beauty of the island continue to attract explorers, archaeologists, and tourists to this far-flung island.

The practice of carving, carrying, and erecting the large-headed, small-bodied stone moai, sometimes reaching 37 feet high, seems to have been central to the historical culture of Easter Island. Said to represent deceased leaders, the statues stand on an ahu, or burial platform, to watch over the communities they had once ruled. Several reconstructions and archaeological digs have confirmed the Rapa Nui had strong engineering skills, because the moai weigh many tons, and putting them in place using traditional materials and techniques must have been a tremendous strain on human and natural resources.

The reconstructions of various ahus with their moai, are quite photogenic, and invite visitors to marvel at the effort required, while posing for photos to share with friends and relatives. Many travelers come here with various questions in mind. First, how did the Rapa Nui get here? Then, why did they build and how did they move the moai? Why were the moai later toppled?

Theories abound, and a combination of local oral history and European observations and guesswork tell the following story. King Hotu Matu'a and his family sailed here, and landed on a beach at the north shore, which began the population of the land. Norwegian explorer Thor Heyerdahl believed that the original settlers came from South America, and sailed from Peru in a balsa-wood boat called the Kon-Tiki in 1947, to prove that it was possible. Despite this, it is now commonly believed that the Rapa Nui are of Polynesian descent, and if you look for it, this influence can be seen in traditional dance, food names and preparation, and the greeting used all over the island, "iorana."

Easter Island reached a peak historical population of 10,000–15,000 people. Between 1722, when the first European, Dutch Jacob Roggeveen set foot on the island, and the 1774 arrival of British Captain James Cook there was extreme population loss and the toppling of many moai. Less than a hundred years later, 1,000 islanders were captured and enslaved by Peruvian slave traders to work in guano mines. When they were eventually returned to the island, they brought smallpox with them, which further decimated the population, which dwindled down to just 110 people.

Chile claimed the island for its own in 1888, with little regard for the inhabitants, and leased it to a British sheep company, which corralled the Rapa Nui people into the town of Hanga Roa. The company departed in 1953, but it wasn't until 1967, when the airport was constructed, that the quality of life began to improve again for the people of Easter Island.

The geographical isolation and the archaeological history are two main draws for many visitors to Easter Island. A visit to the quarry at Rano Raraku, where most moai were sourced and sculpted, especially impresses, considering the engineering effort and knowhow required. The Rapa Nui also had the only written language in all of Polynesia called rongo rongo, which no one has yet deciphered, and petroglyphs can be seen at certain sites, such as the ceremonial village of Orongo where the "birdman" culture thrived.

The culture of the Rapa Nui is indeed another attraction to Easter Island, which despite the tumult in its history, continues to thrive, in language, cuisine, carving, dance, song, and the summer festival of Tapati, which takes place every February. These, together with the history, geology, and archaeology, clear water, white sand, and fiery sunsets bring tourists from all over the world. There is also a special energy or mana (as it is locally called) here at Te Pito o Te Henua (the navel of the world) that adds an intangible element, making a journey to Easter Island a once-in-a-lifetime trip that few get to share.

PLANNING

WHEN TO GO

Most people visit in summer, between December and March, often coinciding with Tapati Rapa Nui, a two-week celebration of music and dancing in the first two weeks of February. Temperatures can soar above 27°C (81°F) in summer. In winter, temperatures reach an average of 22°C (72°F), although brisk winds can often make it feel much cooler. Be sure to bring a light jacket. The wettest months are June and July.

FESTIVALS

The annual Tapati Rapa Nui festival, a two-week celebration of the island's heritage, takes place every year in February. The normally laid-back Hanga Roa bursts to life in a colorful festival of singing and dancing. The Día de la Lengua (Language Day), which usually takes place toward the end of November, celebrates the Rapa Nui language.

PLANNING YOUR TIME

In a few days, you can visit the island's major sights. Spend one day in Hanga Roa, stopping by the Iglesia Hanga Roa, the cemetery, and the Museo Antropológico Padre Sebastián Englert. Finish the day with sunset at Tahai. On your second day, tour the coastal road, visiting the hundreds of moai in the quarry at Rano Raraku and the lineup of 15 at Ahu Tongariki. On your last day, visit the volcano of Rano Kau, where the ceremonial village of Orongo is. In the afternoon head inland to the small quarry of Puna Pau to see the seven statues of Ahu Akivi and where the red topknots that crown some moai were crafted.

GETTING HERE AND AROUND
AIR TRAVEL

Easter Island's shoe-box-size Aeropuerto Internacional Mataveri is on the southern edge of Hanga Roa. LAN Airlines operates all flights from Santiago to the east and Tahiti to the west. Eight flights a week arrive from Santiago throughout the year (but none on Tuesdays), and one from Tahiti. Planes are often full in January and February, so it's best to book far ahead and reconfirm your flights.

Tickets to Easter Island are expensive—up to $1,000 for a round-trip flight from Santiago. There are better deals, however, if you buy your Santiago to Easter Island ticket as part of a multileg ticket that includes your flight from your city of departure to Santiago.

At the airport, the CONAF (national parks service) office outpost sells tickets for Rapa Nui National Park, which you need to get into Rano Rakaru and Orongo. As these tickets are sold in only one other place, a small office near Tahai, it's usually best to fork over your US$60 at the airport.

CAR TRAVEL

To see Easter Island's less traveled areas, a four-wheel-drive vehicle is sometimes a necessity. There are three well-maintained, paved roads. The first traverses the island from Hanga Roa to Playa Anakena, the second goes to Ahu Akivi and forks off of the Anakena road, and the third runs along the southern coast. Other roads are loose gravel or packed dirt (or mud if it has rained recently) particularly those that take visitors to some of the most isolated spots. Though in some cases, there are no roads at all.

None of the international car rental chains have offices on Easter Island, but there are two reputable local agencies, Insular and Oceanic, which have vehicles for rent, as do the main tour operators. The minimum charge is about 45,000 pesos per day for a basic Jeep. Helmet use is mandatory on an ATV or scooter, which rent for 40,000 pesos and 20,000 pesos, respectively. If you plan on visiting during January and February, call a few days ahead to reserve a car.

You can also rent cars at many restaurants, souvenir shops, and guest-houses. If you ask around, you may find a significantly cheaper rate than what the rental companies charge. It is important to note that there is no vehicle insurance on Easter Island and any damage is charged to the client.

TAXI TRAVEL

With no buses on Easter Island, taxis are a common form of transport, so it's never difficult to flag one down. Vehicles of the three main companies are identified by a yellow sign on the roof, but many local car owners also work as taxi drivers. They have a cardboard sign on the windscreen (and tend to be cheaper than radio taxis). Most trips to destinations in Hanga Roa should cost no more than 2,000 pesos (rates are lower for residents), but after 8 or 9 pm the price generally goes up to 3,000.

RESTAURANTS

Compared to mainland Chile, Easter Island is expensive. Almost everything has to be shipped or flown in, and you may sometimes feel you're not getting value for money. The upside is the wonderful fresh fish and, in summer, mangoes and small, sweet pineapples. The guavas on the bushes are ripe (and plentiful) when yellow, and there are some other interesting island-only fruits around, which you can try in the local ice creams. Don't leave Easter Island without trying the local banana bread known as *poe* (best bought at the Riro bakery opposite the church), at 1,000 pesos per hearty square.

At restaurants, local fish such as kana kana are nearly always on the menu. The only restaurants are in Hanga Roa or at the luxury hotels. There are some simple eateries at Playa Anakena, and a few other snack or fast food places around town, serving sandwiches or empanadas. Most other restaurants serve fish, salads, ceviche, and some more international items such as pasta, but there are plenty of imported ingredients as well, such as shrimp, which are generally imported from Ecuador.

Most restaurants are open for lunch and dinner, and a few scattered cafés are open for breakfast, but most people eat breakfast at their hotel. At restaurants, check your bill before leaving a tip; some restaurants add on a 10% service charge (which you are not legally obliged to pay).

HOTELS

A key factor in where to stay is whether you're prepared to rent a car or do quite a lot of walking. There are a few good hotels in the center of Hanga Roa, the only town, but most others are on the town's outskirts, a 15-minute walk or a 2,000-peso taxi ride away. Budget accommodation can be found at the many *residenciales*—often a few rooms attached to a private home—but standards vary enormously; rather than booking ahead, try to arrive on an early plane and talk to the representatives of the resedenciales, or take a taxi into town and scout out the best bargains. Except in January and February, rooms are always available. Three of the luxury hotels require a vehicle, though they, like most other hotels, provide transportation from the airport.

Most hotels now take credit cards but quite a few add a surcharge (as much as 10%). Ask ahead and, if there's a surcharge, consider getting money out of one of the two ATMs. *Hotel reviews have been shortened. For full information, visit Fodors.com.*

WHAT IT COSTS IN CHILEAN PESOS (IN THOUSANDS)				
	$	**$$**	**$$$**	**$$$$**
Restaurants	Under 6	6–9	10–13	over 13
Hotels	Under 51	51–85	86–115	over 115

Restaurant prices are the average cost of a main course price at dinner or, if dinner is not served, at lunch. Hotel prices are the lowest cost of a standard double room in high season, excluding tax.

ESSENTIALS

Air Travel Aeropuerto Internacional Mataveri ⊠ *Av. Hotu Matu'a s/n, Hanga Roa, Easter Island* ☎ *32/2210–0277, 32/2210–0278.* **LAN** ⊠ *Av. Atamu Tekena s/n, Hanga Roa, Hanga Roa, Easter Island* ☎ *600/526–2000* ⊕ *www.lan.com.*

Car Rental Contacts Aku Aku ⊠ *Av. Tu'u Koihu s/n, Hanga Roa, Hanga Roa, Easter Island* ☎ *3/2210–0770* ⊕ *www.akuakuturismo.cl.* **Insular** ⊠ *Av. Atamu Tekena s/n, Hanga Roa, Easter Island* ☎ *3/2210–0770* ⊕ *www.rentainsular.cl.* **Kia Koe** ⊠ *Av. Atamu Tekena s/n, Hanga Roa, Easter Island* ☎ *3/2210–0852* ⊕ *www.kiakoetour.cl.* **Oceanic Rapa Nui** ⊠ *Av. Atamu Tekena s/n, Hanga Roa, Hanga Roa, Easter Island* ☎ *3/2210–0985 Atamu Tekena, 3/2255–1392 Te Pito O Te Henua* ⊕ *www.rapanuioceanic.com.*

Visitor Information Sernatur ⊠ *Av. Policarpo Toro s/n, Hanga Roa, Hanga Roa, Easter Island* ☎ *3/2210–0255* ⊗ *Mon.–Thurs. 9–5:30, Fri. 9–4:30, Sat. 10–1.*

TOURS

There are several ways visitors arrange tours on Easter Island. Book it all ahead of time before setting foot on the island, which is recommended even for the plan-averse, especially for more strenuous, time consuming hikes or horseback rides to the north coast and Poike. Fans of the all-inclusive experience opt for hotel-based tours, while more spontaneous travelers can arrange tours on-site with hotels and, agencies, which can get you on tours the following, or even same day, depending on the activity.

Otherwise, simply wander the streets of Hanga Roa, looking for storefronts that offer tours, which can also yield good results, but may not be the most time-efficient and keeps you away from some of the smaller, more innovative agencies that don't have them. Sernatur, the local tourist office has fairly extensive knowledge of options and opportunities and can point you in the right direction.

Easter Island Traveling. An unlikely transplant to Easter Island, Marcus Edensky, a Swedish man married to a Rapa Nui woman, runs some of the best-reviewed tours on the island. He's always been an outdoorsman, and leads multiday hiking tours, horseback riding, and spiritual tours, among others, often on the north coast. He speaks Swedish, Spanish, English, and Rapa Nui. Easter Island Traveling specializes in small group tours, and the north coast tour ends (optionally) with *tunu ahi*, or food cooked directly on hot rocks. Private day-long hiking tours cost 105,000 pesos, three-day adventure tours start at 210,000 pesos, both with a two-person minimum. ⊠ *Policarpo Toro, Hanga Roa, Easter Island* ⊕ *www.easterislandtraveling.com* ▭ *From 69,000 pesos.*

Kava Kava Tours. This local company runs small full- and half-day tours taking in major sites, including moai and caves. One of its half-day tours goes to Puna Pau, the quarry from which the red stone topknots that sat atop the moai were carved. Another day-long tour goes around the Poike Peninsula, the oldest part of the island, and one of two areas open to hikers or people on horseback with guides only and not accessible by vehicle. ⊠ *Av. Ana Tehe Tama, Hanga Roa, Easter Island* ☎ *9/9352–4972* ⊕ *kavakavatour.cl* ▭ *From 25,000 pesos.*

Kia Koe. One of the largest and oldest tour companies on the island, this company runs full- and half-day excursions with pick-up and drop-off from some of the major hotels. ⊠ *Av. Atamu Tekena s/n, Hanga Roa, Easter Island* ☎ *3/2210–0852* ⊕ *www.kiakoetour.cl* ⚑ *From 25,000 pesos.*

Makemake Tours & Rental. A metal sculpture of a bike signals the entrance to this shop, slightly hidden from the street. It rents mountain bikes and surfboards, both to use alone or with a guide and instructor. Guided walks, private tours, snorkeling, and boat and fishing tours are also available. A mountain bike rental runs 11,000 pesos for eight hours, 13,000 pesos for a day, and 21,000 pesos for two days. A guided day-tour on mountain bike is 26,000, and a horseback-riding tour over the north coast is 80,000 pesos per person, with a two-person minimum. ⊠ *Atanu Tekena s/n, Hanga Roa, Easter Island* ☎ *3/2255–2030* ⚑ *From 26,000 pesos.*

Rapa Nui Travel. This large tour company, which runs the usual half- and full-day tours, has been awarded a seal of tourism quality by the local tourism board. The office is just beside the Hotel Gomero, with whom it works. ⊠ *Av. Tu'u Koihu s/n, Hanga Roa, Hanga Roa, Easter Island* ☎ *3/2210–0548* ⊕ *www.rapanuitravel.com* ⚑ *From 25,000 pesos.*

Toki Tour Aventura. In addition to group and private tours by car, van, or foot, this company rus a tour that follows the route the moai traversed (with help from humans) from Rano Rakaru quarry to some of their final resting places. Another day-long or half-day tour visits Orongo ceremonial village. Travelers need to pay for national parks entry separately, which is easiest to do upon arrival to Easter Island. Toki Tour Aventura also rents cars. ⊠ *Av. Pont s/n, Hanga Roa, Hanga Roa, Easter Island* ☎ *9/8205–9721, 9/9810–0604.*

EXPLORING EASTER ISLAND

An adventurous spirit is a prerequisite for visiting Easter Island. Certainly, package tours are available and common, but you only visit a handful of the sights. Tour buses often fly past fascinating, off-the-beaten-path destinations or simply don't go to places that are harder to access with groups, like the west coast caves of Ana Kai Tangata (bring a flashlight or headlamp). To fully experience the island, hire a private guide. Better yet, rent a four-wheel-drive vehicle, ATV, scooter, or mountain bike and head out on your own. Even in the height of the peak season you can find secluded spots if you time it well. A comprehensive guide to archaeological sites, including when to best find them empty is James Grant-Peterkin's "A Companion to Easter Island," available on the island and in Santiago bookstores catering to tourists.

Almost all businesses close for a few hours in the afternoon. Most are open 9 to 1 and 4 to 8, but a few stay open late into the evening. Many are closed Sunday. Smaller restaurants and shops don't usually accept credit cards. Be aware that outside of Hanga Roa, the only place to buy anything to eat or drink is at Anakena, or at one of the more remote luxury hotels, which are quite off the beaten path.

HANGA ROA

Hugging the coast on the northwest side is the island's capital of Hanga Roa. Of the 6,000 residents, about half are indigenous Rapa Nui and the rest from continental Chile or abroad. Few people live outside Hanga Roa because the bulk of the island forms the Rapa Nui National Park or is state owned. The town's two main roads intersect a block from the ocean at a small plaza. Avenida Atamu Tekena, the road which runs the length of the village, is where to find most of the tourist-oriented businesses. Avenida Te Pito o Te Henua begins near the fishing pier and extends two blocks uphill to the church.

> ### CURRENCY EXCHANGES
>
> The official currency is Chilean pesos, but U.S. dollars and euros are accepted just about everywhere. There are two banks on the island: BancoEstado, the Chilean state bank, and Santander, both in Hanga Roa. They are open weekdays 9 to 2 and can exchange U.S. dollars or give a cash advance on your Visa card. Both banks have an ATM, and the machine at Santander (unlike that at BancoEstado) accepts all usual international credit and debit cards.

Buildings are not numbered and signs nonexistent (street names are sometimes painted on curbstones), so finding a particular building can be frustrating at first. Locals give directions in terms of landmarks, so it's not a bad idea to take a walk around town as soon as you arrive so you can get your bearings. Important landmarks in town are the fishing cove and pier, the Catholic church, the Cruz Verde pharmacy, and the LAN (airline) office. A little farther away to the south and southeast, respectively are the Hanga Pika pier and the airport.

TOP ATTRACTIONS

Iglesia Hanga Roa. Missionaries brought Christianity to Easter Island, but the Rapa Nui people brought their own beliefs to Christianity. Find the two intertwined in this white church on the hill overlooking Hanga Roa. The paintings of the Via Crucis on the walls are what you would find in any Catholic church, but the wood figures have a clear Rapa Nui flavor and one of the altars rests on a block of local volcanic stone. At the first mass on Sunday morning at 9, hymns are sung in Rapa Nui. ✉ *Av. Te Pito o Te Henua s/n, Hanga Roa, Easter Island.*

FAMILY
Fodor's Choice
★

Museo Antropológico Sebastián Englert. This small museum, named for a German priest who dedicated his life to improving conditions on Rapa Nui and is buried beside the church, provides an excellent summary of the history of Easter Island and its way of life, as well as its native flora and fauna. Here, too, is one of the few female moai on the island and a coral eye found during the reconstruction of an ahu at Playa Anakena. The museum underwent extensive renovations in 2013 and now has text in English. ✉ *Tahai s/n, Hanga Roa, Easter Island* ☎ *3/2255–1021* ⊕ *www.museorapanui.cl* 🎟 *1,000 pesos* ⊙ *Weekdays 9:30–5:30, weekends and holidays 9:30–12:30.*

Tahai. The ancient ceremonial center of Tahai, where much of the annual Tapati Rapa Nui festival takes place, was restored in 1968 by

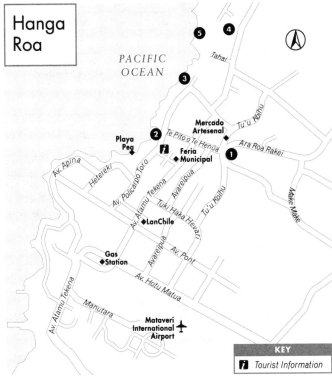

Hanga Roa

PACIFIC
OCEAN

Tahai

Mercado
Artesenal

Playa
Peg

Te Pito o Te Henua

Ara Roa Rakei

Feria
Municipal

Av. Apina

Hetereki

Av. Policarpo Toro

Av. Atamu Tekena

Avareipua

Tuki Haka Hevari

Tu'u Koihu

Make Make

Tu'u Koihu

LanChile

Gas
Station

Avareipua

Av. Pont

Av. Hotu Matua

Av. Atamu Tekena

Manutara

Mataveri
International
Airport

KEY

🛈 *Tourist Information*

archaeologist William Mulloy, who is buried nearby. Tahai consists of three separate ahus facing a wide plaza that once served as a community meeting place. You can still find the foundations of the boat-shape dwellings where religious and social leaders once lived. In the center is Ahu Tahai, which holds a single weathered moai. To the left is Ahu Vai Uri, where five moai, one little more than a stump, cast their stony gaze over the island. Also here is Ahu Kote Riku, with a splendid moai and red topknot intact; this is the only moai on the island to have its gleaming white eyes restored. ■ TIP→ **This is an especially good place to come to see the island's blazing yellow sunsets.** ✉ *On coast near Museo Antropológico Sebastián Englert, Hanga Roa, Easter Island.*

WORTH NOTING

Caleta Hanga Roa. Colorful fishing boats bob up and down in the water at Hanga Roa's tiny pier. Here you may see fisherfolk hauling in the day's catch of tuna, or a boatload of divers returning from a trip to the neighboring islets. Nearby is Ahu Tautira, a ceremonial platform with a restored moai. ✉ *Av. Policarpo Toro at Av. Te Pito o Te Henua, Hanga Roa, Easter Island.*

Cementerio. Hanga Roa's colorful walled cemetery occupies a prime position overlooking the Pacific and is visually unlike most. With artificial flower arrangements, white tombstones, and orange nasturtiums spread over the stone walls, the cemetery has a cheerful feeling. The central cross is erected on a *pukao,* the reddish topknot (routinely called a "hat") that might have topped a moai at some point. The cemetery is currently expanding towards the ocean, but by 2020, the newly deceased will have to be buried elsewhere, as it will likely be full. ⊠ *Av. Policarpo Toro at Petero Atamu, Hanga Roa, Easter Island.*

THE SOUTHEASTERN CIRCUIT

Most of the archaeological sites on the island line the southeastern coast. Driving along it, you pass many ahus, where moai once stood, most of which have not been reconstructed. Busloads of tourists hurry past these on their way to Rano Raraku, the quarry where around 400 moai wait in stony silence, and Ahu Tongariki, where 15 moai stand in line.

TOP ATTRACTIONS

Ahu Nau Nau. Beside the swaying palm trees on Playa Anakena stand the island's best-preserved moai on Ahu Nau Nau. Buried for centuries in the sand, these five statues were protected from the elements. The minute details of the carving—delicate lips, flared nostrils, gracefully curved ears—are still visible. On their backs, fine lines represent belts. It was here during the 1978 restoration that a white coral eye was found, leading researchers to speculate that all moai once had them; the eye is now on display at the Museo Antropológico Sebastián Englert. Staring at Ahu Nau Nau is a solitary moai on nearby Ahu Ature Huki. This statue was the first moai to be re-erected on its ahu. Thor Heyerdahl conducted this experiment in 1955 to test whether the techniques islanders claimed were used to erect the moai could work. It took 12 islanders nearly three weeks to lift the moai into position using rocks and wooden poles. ⊠ *1 km (½ mile) west of Playa Ovahe, at Playa Anakena, Easter Island.*

Fodor's Choice ★ **Ahu Tongariki.** One of the island's most breathtaking sights is Ahu Tongariki, where 15 moai stand side by side on a 200-foot-long ahu, the longest ever made. Tongariki was painstakingly restored after being destroyed for the second time by a massive tidal wave in 1960. The moai here, some whitened with a layer of sea salt, have holes in their extended earlobes that might have once been filled with chunks of obsidian. They face an expansive ceremonial area where you can find petroglyphs of turtles and fish, and the entrance is guarded by a single moai, which has traveled to Japan and back for exhibition. ■ **TIP→ The perfect morning sunrise behind the moai at Tongariki lasts only from December 21 to March 21.** ⊠ *2 km (1 mile) east of Rano Raraku on coastal road, Easter Island.*

MAIL AND POSTAGE

Correos de Chile, the island's tiny post office, is on Avenida Te Pito o Te Henua across from Hotel O'Tai. Postage is the same as in the rest of Chile. Bear in mind that mail is sent via LAN flights, so you're likely to travel back to the mainland on the same plane as the letter you posted. If you want an Easter Island postmark, you might want to bring your own stamps. The post office sometimes runs out.

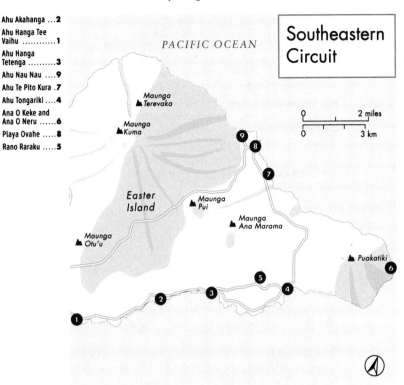

Southeastern Circuit

PACIFIC OCEAN

Maunga Terevaka

Maunga Kuma

Easter Island

Maunga Pui

Maunga Ana Marama

Maunga Otu'u

Puakatiki

0 — 2 miles
0 — 3 km

Fodor's Choice ★ **Rano Raraku.** When it comes to moai, this is the motherlode. Some 400 have been counted at the quarry of this long-extinct volcano, both on the outer rim and clustered inside the crater. More than 150 are unfinished, some little more than faces in the rock. Among these is El Gigante, a monster measuring 22 meters (72 feet). Also here is Moai Tukuturi, the only moai in a kneeling position; it's thought to predate most others. Look out also for the moai with a three-masted boat carved on its belly; the anchor is a turtle. CONAF checks but does not sell tickets here. They are sold at the airport upon arrival or at the CONAF office near the Anthropological Museum, paid in dollars. The same ticket gives access to the Orongo ceremonial village as well. ■TIP→ **It's best to buy your national parks ticket upon arrival at the airport.** ⊠ *5 km (3 miles) east of Ahu Hanga Tetenga on coastal road, Easter Island* ⌑ *US$60 for non-Chileans.*

WORTH NOTING

Ahu Akahanga. Tradition holds that this is the burial site of Hotu Matu'a, the first of the island's rulers. The 13 moai lying face down on the ground once stood on the four long stone platforms. There are also several "boat houses," oblong, boat-shape outlines that were once the foundations of homes. ⊠ *5 km (5 miles) east of Ahu Vaihu on coastal road, Easter Island.*

Ahu Hanga Tee (Vaihu). Eight fallen moai lie face down in front of this ahu, the first you encounter on the southern coastal road. Three reddish topknots are strewn around them. Even after the ahu was destroyed, this continued to be a burial chamber, evidenced by the rocks piled on the toppled moai. ⊠ *10 km (6 miles) southeast of Hanga Roa on coastal road, Easter Island.*

Ahu Hanga Tetenga. Lying here in pieces is the largest moai ever transported to a platform, measuring nearly 10 meters (33 feet). The finishing touches were never made to its eye sockets, so researchers believe it fell while being erected. ⊠ *3 km (2 miles) east of Ahu Akahanga on coastal road, Easter Island.*

Ahu Te Pito Kura. The largest moai ever successfully erected stands at Ahu Te Pito Kura. Also here is the perfectly round stone (believed to represent the navel of the world) that Hotu Matu'a is said to have brought with him when he arrived on the island. ⊠ *9 km (5½ miles) north of Ahu Tongariki on coastal road, Easter Island.*

Ana O Keke and Ana O Neru. Legend has it that young women awaiting marriage were kept here in the Caves of the Virgins so that their skin would remain as pale as possible. You need an experienced guide to find the caverns, which are accessible only on foot and hidden in the cliffs along the coast. Take a flashlight to see the haunting petroglyphs of flowers and fish thought to have been carved by these girls. ⊠ *Reached via dirt road through ranch on Poike, Poike Peninsula, Poike, Easter Island.*

Playa Ovahe. The beautiful cove of pinkish sand at often-overlooked Playa Ovahe is delightful, and the pile of volcanic rocks jutting out into the water is actually a ruined ahu. There are no facilities here, and both the national parks service and the local tourism office advise against setting up here, as there is some landslide potential and dangerous undercurrents, though it is lovely for a quick photo stop. Access is on the approach road to Anakena beach and requires a taxi or private vehicle, since tours do not stop here. As on most of the island, there is no cell coverage at Ovahe. ■TIP→ **Come in the morning; by afternoon due to the angle of the sun you'll be sitting in the shade. Amenities:** none. **Best for:** solitude; sunrise. ⊠ *10 km (6 miles) north of Ahu Tongariki on coastal road, Easter Island.*

THE WESTERN CIRCUIT

On the western tip of the island are the cave paintings of Ana Kai Tangata and the petroglyphs near the ceremonial village of Orongo. You'll also be treated to a spectacular view of the crater lake inside the long-dormant volcano of Rano Kau as well as the three islets or motu in the ocean below.

TOP ATTRACTIONS

Ahu Vinapu. The appeal of this crumbled ahu isn't apparent until you notice the fine masonry on the rear wall. Anyone who has seen the ancient Inca city of Machu Picchu in Peru can note the similar stonework. This led Norwegian archaeologist Thor Heyerdahl to theorize

FOLLOW THE TRAILS

Sights outside Hanga Roa are conveniently located on two main routes: the Southeastern and Western circuits. The first showcases the large moai carved at the height of the island's civilization, while the second gives insight into its decline, especially at Orongo ceremonial village. The following itineraries take you to each circuit's attractions (allow one day for each) or, if you're short on time, check out our Top Attractions for the can't-miss spots.

The Southeastern Circuit. Heading out of Hanga Roa along the island's southern coast, the road leads to Ahu Vaihu, with its eight fallen moai; Ahu Akahanga, the burial site of the island's first ruler; and Ahu Hanga Tetenga's large, unfinished moai. Farther along, at Ahu Tongariki, encounter your first standing moai, but that's just a warm up for the jackpot at Rano Raraku quarry where the moai were improbably carved

out of the hillside. Grab a guide to take you to the caverns of Ana O Keke and Ana O Neru; then, visit the "navel of the world" stone at Ahu Te Pito Kura and the beautiful, pink-sand Playa Ovahe before ending the day at Playa Anakena.

The Western Circuit. Divide this circuit into two, with a break for lunch in Hanga Roa. In the morning, start by visiting Ahu Vinapu, with its unusual masonry, before heading up the Rano Kau volcano, with its water-filled crater and wonderful views, to Orongo. On the way down, consider stopping by the cave paintings at Ana Kai Tangata. After lunch, visit the Puna Pau quarry, origin of the moai's red topknots, and the inland moai at Ahu Huri a Urenga, before carrying on north to Ahu Akivi's seven moai, the underground caverns at Ana Te Pahu, and the remains of the so-called boat houses at Ahu Te Peu.

that Rapa Nui's original inhabitants may have sailed here from South America. By now it has been established that the first settlers were Polynesian, though evidence points to contact with South America early on. The moai here still lie where they were toppled, including one face up, which is unusual, as most were knocked face down. ✉ *Southeast of Hanga Roa along Av. Hotu Matu'a, Easter Island.*

Fodor's Choice ★ **Orongo.** The 48 oval stone houses of this ceremonial village, likely constructed in the late 1600s and used by locals until 1866, were occupied only during the ceremony honoring the god Make-Make. The high point of the annual event was a competition in which prominent villagers designated servants to paddle small rafts to Motu Nui, the largest of three islets just off the coast. The first servant to find an egg of the sooty tern, a bird nesting on the islets, would swim back with the prize tucked in a special headdress. His master would become the *tangata manu*, or birdman, for the next year. The tangata manu was honored by being confined to a cave until the following year's ceremony. Dozens of petroglyphs depicting birdlike creatures cover nearby boulders along the rim of Rano Kau. CONAF checks but does not sell tickets here. They are sold at the airport or at the CONAF office near the Padre Sebastian Sebastian Englert Anthropological Museum, and are good for Orongo and Rano Raraku, which are currently the only sites to which there is

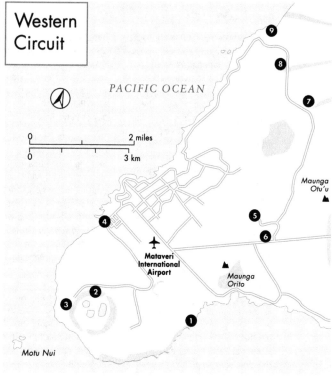

Western Circuit

PACIFIC OCEAN

0 ——— 2 miles
0 ——— 3 km

Mataveri
International
Airport

Maunga
Otu'u

Maunga
Orito

Motu Nui

controlled entry. ⊠ *South of Hanga Roa on Rano Kau, Easter Island* ▣ *US$60 for non-Chileans.*

Puna Pau. Scoria, the reddish stone used to make the topknots for the moai, was once excavated at this quarry. About two dozen finished topknots are still here. ■ TIP→ **The views of the island from the top of the hill are well worth the short climb.** ⊠ *Off road branching north from road to Playa Anakena, signposted "Puna Pau" and "Ahu Akivi," Easter Island.*

Fodor's Choice
★

Rano Kau. This huge volcano on the southern tip of the island affords wonderful views of Hanga Roa. The crater, which measures a mile across, holds a lake nearly covered over by reeds. The opposite side of the crater has crumbled a bit, revealing a crescent of the deep blue ocean beyond. Entering the crater is forbidden, except in signposted areas. It is protected, and the ground is unstable. ⊠ *South of Hanga Roa, Easter Island.*

WORTH NOTING

Ahu Akivi. These seven stoic moai—believed by some to represent explorers sent on a reconnaissance mission by King Hotu Matu'a—are among the few that gaze out to sea, though researchers say they face a ceremonial site. Others say that the oral history of the explorers has been folded into stories about the moai, and that there is no connection between

CLOSE UP

Mysteries of the Moais

Most people are drawn to Easter Island by the moai, the stone statues that have puzzled and intrigued outsiders since the first Europeans arrived there almost three centuries ago. These squat, minimalist figures with oversize heads are believed to have been the crowning glory of a family shrine, standing on an ahu—or stone platform—beneath which ancestors were buried and transmitted mana, or power, to the living family chief. They most likely overlooked the settlements that erected them.

Most of the moai were carved at the Rano Raraku quarry in the east of the island, where many can still be seen at different stages of completion. That, in itself, was a mammoth task, with only stone tools to chisel the statues laboriously out of the volcanic hillside. It was, however, nothing compared to transporting the finished statues to their ahu. Locals claim the moai "walked" to their destination, but most archaeologists believe they were either dragged on wooden platforms or rolled along on top of tree trunks. It's not clear how they could have been moved miles without damaging the statues en route, though their eye sockets were not carved until they arrived at the ahus.

Once the moai arrived at their ahu, how were they lifted into place? In 1955, Norwegian explorer Thor Heyerdahl and a team of a dozen men were able to raise the single moai on Ahu Ature Huki in 18 days. In 1960 archaeologists William Mulloy and Gonzalo Figueroa and their men raised the seven moai at Ahu Akivi. They struggled for a month to lift the first, but the last took only a week.

Both teams used the same method—lifting them with a stone ramp and wooden poles. This technique would be unwieldy for lifting the larger moai, however. It also fails to explain how the pukao, or topknots, were placed on many of the heads.

Why were the moai subsequently toppled? The reason posited by some is that creating them required a tremendous amount of natural resources, particularly wood, and as these were depleted, family groups that had once worked in harmony began to squabble, attacking the source of their opponent's mana—their moai.

That, at least, is the theory put forward by Jared Diamond in his book *Collapse: How Societies Choose to Fail or Succeed*. If that is the case, the moai are not only Easter Island's glory but, as the island was deforested, the cause of the decline of the civilization that created them. But, in a way, the moai are still serving their original purpose. Mana meant prosperity, and the moai continue to bring this today in the form of tourism.

It is unclear whether any additional moai will ever be stood back up. Archaeologists, such as Sergio Rapu, are looking at the possibility of leaving them where they are and using digital platforms to show both past (moais upright) and present (moais toppled) without damaging the statues.

statues and explorers. Archaeologists William Mulloy and Gonzalo Figueroa restored the moai in 1960. ⊠ *Past Puna Pau on road branching north from paved road to Playa Anakena, Easter Island.*

Ahu Huri a Urenga. One of the few ahus to be erected inland, Ahu Huri a Urenga appears to be oriented toward the winter solstice. Its lonely moai is exceptional because it has two sets of hands, the second carved above the first. Researchers believe this is because the lower set was damaged during transport to the ahu. ⊠ *3 km (2 miles) from Av. Hotu Matu'a on paved road to Playa Anakena, Easter Island.*

Ahu Te Peu. As at Ahu Vinapu, the tightly fitting stones at the unrestored Ahu Te Peu recall the best work of the Incas. The foundations for several boat-shape houses, including one that measures 40 meters (131 feet) from end to end, are clearly visible. From here you can begin the six-hour trail-less hike around the island's northern coast to Playa Anakena. CONAF (national parks service) recommends a guide, and you may walk past many of the archaeological sites if you do not have one. ⊠ *Past Ana Te Pahu on gravel road branching north from paved road to Playa Anakena, Easter Island.*

Ana Kai Tangata. A small sign just past the entrance of Hotel Iorana points toward Ana Kai Tangata, a seldom-visited cavern on the coast that holds the island's only cave paintings. Directly over your head are images of red and white birds in flight. Dramatic cliffs shelter the cave from the crashing surf. ⊠ *South of Hanga Roa, Easter Island.*

Ana Te Pahu. A grove of banana trees marks the entrance to these underground caverns that once served as dwellings. Partly shielded from the blazing sun, a secret garden of tropical plants thrives in the fissure where the caves begin. Below ground is a passage leading to a second cave where the sunlight streams through a huge hole. ■ TIP→ **Bring a flashlight, and be careful of the dripping water within a week or so of rain.** ⊠ *Past Ahu Akivi on gravel road branching north from paved road to Playa Anakena, Easter Island.*

BEACHES

HANGA ROA

FAMILY **Playa Pea.** Hanga Roa has only two tiny beaches: Playa Pea, a stretch of sand near the bay, and another small beach on the northern edge of the town, with a sea pool for swimming. Both are popular among local families with small children. This is more of a jump-in-because-I'm-hot kind of beach than one you want to spend time at, though you could sit and read a book while watching the waves. **Amenities:** food and drink. **Best for:** swimming; snorkeling. ⊠ *Policarpo Toro, Hanga Roa, Easter Island.*

THE SOUTHEASTERN CIRCUIT

FAMILY
Fodor's Choice
★

Playa Anakena. Easter Island's earliest settlers are believed to have landed on idyllic Playa Anakena. Legend has it that the caves in the cliffs overlooking the beach are where Hotu Matu'a, the island's first ruler, dwelled while constructing his home. It's easy to see why Hotu Matu'a might have selected this spot: on an island ringed by rough volcanic rock, Playa Anakena is the widest swath of sand. Ignoring the sun-worshipping tourists are the five beautifully carved moai standing on nearby Ahu Nau Nau. On the northern coast, Playa Anakena is reachable by a paved road that runs across the island or by the more circuitous coastal road. For 15,000 pesos (or ask your hotel to negotiate a better price), a taxi takes you from Hanga Roa and picks up at the agreed-upon time later. ■ TIP→ **Bring snacks and water from Hanga Roa.** **Amenities:** toilets; parking; food and drink. **Best for:** snorkeling; swimming. ✉ *Easter Island.*

Playa Ovahe. A lovely strip of pink sand, Playa Ovahe isn't as crowded as neighboring Playa Anakena. The fact that most tourists pass it by is what makes this secluded beach so appealing. Families head here on weekends for afternoon cookouts, but swimming is dangerous because of strong undercurrents. The cliffs that tower above the beach were once home to many of the island's residents. Locals proudly point out caves that belonged to their relatives. **Amenities:** none. **Best for:** sunrise; solitude. ✉ *Easter Island.*

WHERE TO EAT

$$$ BELGIAN 🍴 **Au Bout du Monde.** This Belgian-Polynesian restaurant serves some of Easter Island's best food from a small menu of mostly fish and meat. Try the seared tuna with Tahitian vanilla sauce, and one of the many chocolate-based desserts. There are no longer performances at the restaurant, but the owner sends patrons to her brothers-in-law's show with Grupo Maori Tupuna at the Vai Te Mihi events center next door. [$] *Average main: 13000 pesos* ✉ *Av. Policarpo Toro s/n, Hanga Roa, Easter Island* ☎ *3/2255–2060* 🌐 *www.restaurantauboutdumonde.com* 🕒 *Closed Tues.*

$$ CAFÉ 🍴 **Café Caramelo.** The cheesecake at this airy, colorful café is fantastic, and not just by island standards. The coffee is also better than most on the island, with beans from major international roasters. Choose café favorites like salads with olives, a sandwich with cream cheese and serrano ham, or a vegetarian sandwich with hard boiled eggs. ■ TIP→ **Carmelo serves a filling brunch, enough for two or three people, for 14,000 pesos.** [$] *Average main: 6000 pesos* ✉ *Av. Atanu Tekena, Hanga Roa, Easter Island.*

$$$ SEAFOOD 🍴 **Haka Honu.** This festive restaurant on the street that runs along the beach serves hearty portions of local foods like kana kana (fish) and seafood. It is rumored to get some of the best picks of fish on the island. In the evening, a slightly younger set comes here for drinks, but it never gets too rowdy. Business is especially good at lunch and dinner. Desserts are enormous. ■ TIP→ **In winter, this is often the most lively place on the island at night.** [$] *Average main: 12000 pesos* ✉ *Policarpo Toro s/n, Hanga Roa, Easter Island* ☎ *3/2255–2260.*

$ CHILEAN 🍴 **Kona Tunu Kai Hua Maria Pika.** This spot looks like a small, no-frills, rustic shack, but at lunchtime it is always full, which speaks to the food's quality. It's just on the far side of the Hanga Roa Hotel, and in fact, was built to feed the laborers who worked there. The menu is written on a flowerly whiteboard on the wall of the raw-wood interior and includes owner Maria Luisa Ikanakoi's big, filling Chilean sandwiches as well as ceviche and a daily menu for 5,000 pesos—a great antidote to big, expensive meals on the island. Expect to be well-accompanied by a crowd of young locals, many of whom come here on their lunch break. $ *Average main: 5000 pesos* ⊠ *Av. Apiña s/n, Hanga Roa, Easter Island* ☎ 9/9140–6767 ⊟ *No credit cards* ⊗ *No dinner.*

$$$
SEAFOOD
✕ **La Kaleta.** This restaurant draws in patrons with its fairly unbeatable views from the point of Caleta Hanga Roa, seen from the terrace by the breaking waves. The food, while good, is pricey, so you might prefer to linger over a drink at sunset rather than having a full meal here if you're trying to keep costs down, though there are a range of options, with locally caught fish being cheaper than imported seafood, for example. $ *Average main: 12000 pesos* ⊠ *Caleta Hanga Roa, Hanga Roa, Easter Island* ☎ 3/2255–2244.

$
CAFÉ
✕ **Mikafe.** This coffee shop with outdoor seating down on the pier does swift business with divers coming off the boats, locals needing coffee, and school kids in search of their after-school ice cream. Flavors include ordinary strawberry and cream, the slightly unusual *pepino* (a fruit that tastes like melon), and occasionally, island-specific flavors like *tipanie* (a flower). Guava, which grows wild everywhere in the summer, shows up in ice cream as well. $ *Average main: 4500 pesos* ⊠ *Caleta Hanga Roa, Hanga Roa, Easter Island.*

$$
SEAFOOD
✕ **Tataku Vave.** On the next bay south from Hanga Roa, this delicious, all-fish restaurant is worth the 15-minute walk. At 5,000 pesos, the set main course at lunchtime is especially good value, but the giant portions of ceviche are even more popular. The bay, which is where most of Easter Island's supplies are brought ashore, is not exactly pristine—it's as near to industrial as there is on Easter Island—but it is still a prime place for spotting turtles on your way in or out of the restaurant. ■ TIP➔ **The view from the restaurant is spectacular over the ocean, but can be very breezy.** $ *Average main: 6000 pesos* ⊠ *Hanga Piko Pier, Hanga Roa, Easter Island* ☎ 3/2255–1544 ⊟ *No credit cards.*

$$$$
SEAFOOD
Fodor's Choice
★
✕ **Te Moana.** If you stay any length of time on Easter Island, you may find yourself returning to this inviting blue and wood restaurant on the waterfront with an expansive ocean view. Generous portions of fish, meat, pasta, and pizza are attractively presented, and the service is excellent. Try any of the ceviches or on a cool evening the Thai fish soup, which is a meal in itself. The restaurant specializes more in mixed drinks and beer than wine, which is sold only by the bottle. $ *Average main: 14000 pesos* ⊠ *Policarpo Toro s/n, Hanga Roa, Easter Island* ☎ 3/2255–1578 ⊗ *Closed Sun.*

WHERE TO STAY

$$$$
HOTEL
🏨 **Altiplánico Rapa Nui.** This hotel, part of a relatively new chain of boutique hotels in popular Chilean vacation spots, has minimalist design—beds are mattresses on a cement platform and some rooms have indoor-outdoor showers. **Pros:** expansive coastal view, particularly from the lower of the three rows of rooms; total peace and quiet, Aka Pu moai visible from the hotel. **Cons:** 40-minute walk from Hanga Roa, so guests

Restaurant ▼
Au Bout du Monde **1**
Café Caramelo ...**5**
Haka Honu **4**
Kona Tunu Kai
Hua Maria Pika ...**7**
La Kaleta **3**
Mikafe **2**
Tataku Vave **8**
Te Moana **6**

Hotels ▼
Altiplanico R. N. ..**2**
Aukara Lodge ...**16**
Chez María Goretti **3**
Explora
Rapa Nui **6**
Hangaroa Eco **9**
Hare Noi **15**
Hotel Gomero ..**13**
Hotel Iorana **17**
Hotel Monovai ...**9**
Hotel O'Tai **5**
Hotel Taha Tai ..**10**
Hotel Taura'a ...**11**
Hotel Tupa **12**
Mana Nui Inn **1**
Puku Vai **14**
R. Taniera **8**
Vai Moana **4**

Where to Eat and Stay in Hanga Roa

PACIFIC OCEAN

KEY
Restaurants
Hotels
Tourist information

either rent a car or rely on taxis and tours to get around. $ *Rooms from: 228000 pesos* ⊠ *Sector Hinere s/n, Easter Island* ☎ *3/2255–2190* ⊕ *www.altiplanico.com* ⇗ *17 cabins* ⦾ *Breakfast.*

$$
B&B/INN
Fodor's Choice
★

Aukara Lodge. Located just behind the LAN airline office, this *residencial* is owned by a professor of history and a local sculptor, whose work is displayed in the adjacent art gallery. **Pros:** tours available; contact with local artists in the workshop; airport transport included. **Cons:** few rooms and high popularity make it difficult to get a space here; early booking is essential. $ *Rooms from: 70000 pesos* ⊠ *Av. Pont s/n, Hanga Roa, Easter Island* ☎ *3/2210–0539* ⊕ *www.aukara.com* ⇗ *5 rooms* ▭ *No credit cards* ⦾ *Breakfast.*

$$
B&B/INN

Chez María Goretti. The beautiful garden and lovely, airy, plant-filled dining room are the main attractions of this guesthouse on the northern edge of town between Hanga Roa and Museo Antropológico Sebastián Englert. **Pros:** the new rooms are good value; friendly atmosphere. **Cons:** some rooms could use a paint job; about a 10-minute uphill walk from town. $ *Rooms from: 56000 pesos* ⊠ *Av. Atamu Tekena s/n, Hanga Roa, Easter Island* ☎ *3/2210–0459* ⊕ *www.chezmariagoretti. com* ⇗ *20 rooms* ⦾ *Breakfast.*

$$$$
ALL-INCLUSIVE

Explora Rapa Nui. This luxury property is built in local volcanic stone and imported wood, and curves discretely along a hillside overlooking the island's south coast in an emulation of the ceremonial village at

Orongo. **Pros:** well-guided hikes; excellent food; superb service. **Cons:** a 15-minute drive from Hanga Roa; somewhat isolated; costs considerably more than others. $ *Rooms from: 997000 pesos* ✉ *Sector Vaihu s/n, Hanga Roa* ☎ *2/2395–2800* ⊕ *www.explora.com* ⤴ *26 rooms, 4 suites* ⦿ *All-inclusive.*

$$$$
ALL-INCLUSIVE
Fodor's Choice
★

🏠 **Hangaroa Eco Village & Spa.** The latest green initiatives meet traditional architecture and hospitality at this peaceful retreat on the coast of remote Easter Island. **Pros:** romantic, great spa; one free nightly cocktail for guests. **Cons:** may be too remote for some travelers. $ *Rooms from: 274415 pesos* ✉ *Av. Pont s/n, Hanga Roa, Easter Island* ☎ *2/2957–0300* ⊕ *www.hangaroa.cl* ⤴ *69 rooms, 6 suites* ⦿ *All-inclusive.*

$$$$
HOTEL
ALL-INCLUSIVE

🏠 **Hare Noi.** A series of modern-yet-rustic constructions set on a gentle sloping hill on the drive out to Anakena Beach from the town of Hanga Roa is the home of five-star hotel Hare Noi, a name that means "our home," with words taken from Italian (Noi, our) and Rapa Nui (Hare, home). **Pros:** design oriented, yet comfortable; excellent restaurant **Cons:** a bit far from town; not private enough for some. $ *Rooms from: 472000 pesos* ✉ *Av. Hotu Matua s/n, Hanga Roa, Easter Island* ☎ *3/2255–0134* ⊕ *www.noihotels.com/hotel/hare-noi* ⤴ *9 rooms* ⦿ *All-inclusive.*

$$$
HOTEL

🏠 **Hotel Gomero.** A drive lined by palm and papaya trees leads to this charming small hotel. **Pros:** an inviting swimming pool sits in a beautifully attended garden; transport to and from airport available; owners run a tour service; impeccably tidy. **Cons:** on the outskirts of town and up a hill. $ *Rooms from: 99000 pesos* ✉ *Av. Tu'u Koihu s/n, Hanga Roa, Easter Island* ☎ *3/2210–0313* ⊕ *www.hotelgomero.com* ⤴ *17 rooms* ⦿ *Breakfast.*

$$$$
HOTEL

🏠 **Hotel Iorana.** Perched high on a cliff that juts out into the ocean, this hotel entices its visitors with unmatched views. **Pros:** a lovely setting; rooms are attractively, if simply, decorated; airport transportation available. **Cons:** more expensive than other similar midrange hotels; 15–20-minute walk from town. $ *Rooms from: 150000 pesos* ✉ *Ana Magaro s/n, Hanga Roa, Easter Island* ☎ *3/2210–0608* ⊕ *www.ioranahotel.cl* ⤴ *50 rooms, 2 suites* ⦿ *Some meals.*

$$
HOTEL
FAMILY

🏠 **Hotel Manavai.** This hotel has 30 simple wood-paneled rooms around a long garden that's perfect for kids to play in. **Pros:** perfect for families; peaceful garden; knowledgeable hosts. **Cons:** no ocean view from rooms. $ *Rooms from: 82000 pesos* ✉ *Av. Te Pito O Te Henua, Hanga Roa, Easter Island* ☎ *3/2210–0670* ⊕ *www.hotelmanavai.cl* ⤴ *30 rooms* ⦿ *No meals.*

$$$
HOTEL

🏠 **Hotel O'Tai.** Although the hotel is right in the center of town, its beautiful gardens make you feel like you're miles from anywhere. **Pros:** great location; good value for money. **Cons:** some of the standard rooms could do with redecoration; extra charge for hotel transfer. $ *Rooms from: 94000 pesos* ✉ *Av. Te Pito o Te Henua s/n, Hanga Roa, Easter Island* ☎ *3/2210–0250* ⊕ *www.hotelotai.com* ⤴ *40 rooms* ⦿ *Breakfast.*

$$$$
HOTEL

🏠 **Hotel Taha Tai.** Open and airy, this hotel seems to have sunlight streaming in from everywhere. **Pros:** rooms are spacious, clean, and comfortable; staff are friendly and helpful. **Cons:** a 10-minute walk along the sometimes windy or very sunny coast from the center of town. $ *Rooms* *from: 129000 pesos* ✉ *Av. Apina Nui s/n, Hanga Roa, Easter Island* ☎ *3/2255–1192* 🌐 *www.hoteltahatai.cl* 🛏 *30 rooms, 10 bungalows* 🍴 *Breakfast.*

$$$ HOTEL Fodor's Choice ★ **Hotel Taura'a.** This lovely hotel on Hanga Roa's main street is owned by Bill Howe, an Australian, and his Rapa Nui wife, Edith Pakarati. **Pros:** good breakfasts—they're different every day of the week—and coffee (a rarity on Easter Island); airport transport available; owners run a tour service. **Cons:** no pool. [$] *Rooms from: 106000 pesos* ✉ *Av. Atamu Tekena s/n, Hanga Roa, Easter Island* ☎ *3/2210–0463* 🌐 *www.tauraahotel.cl* 🛏 *17 rooms* 🍴 *Breakfast.*

$$ HOTEL **Hotel Tupa.** Owned and managed by local archaeologist and former governor of the island, Sergio Rapu, this hotel has three kinds of rooms: budget, garden, and beach. **Pros:** lovely location overlooking the Hanga Roa bay; transport to and from airport available; owner-run tour service; very connected and knowledgeable owners. **Cons:** long, twisty hallways; some areas not in perfect repair. [$] *Rooms from: 76000 pesos* ✉ *Sebastian Englert s/n, Hanga Roa, Easter Island* ☎ *3/2210–0225* 🌐 *www.tupahotel.com* 🛏 *43 rooms* 🍴 *Breakfast.*

$$ B&B/INN **Mana Nui Inn.** This collection of seven freestanding rooms and three simply furnished cabins are laid out in a grassy yard with paved paths, banana trees, and blooming bougainvillea and hibiscus flowers, some of which you might recognize from your welcome flower necklace (just one of many homey touches). **Pros:** friendly owner; ocean-view breakfast room; a shared kitchen. **Cons:** the 10-minute walk from town on a dirt road gets muddy in the rain. [$] *Rooms from: 55000 pesos* ✉ *Sector Tahai, Hanga Roa, Easter Island* ☎ *3/2210–0811* 🌐 *www.mananui.cl/rapanui* 🛏 *10 rooms* 🍴 *Breakfast.*

$$$$ HOTEL **Puku Vai.** Within walking distance of the airport, Puka Vai is clean, airy, bright, and spacious. **Pros:** clean, efficient construction; owners have a good relationship with taxi companies, car rental, and tour agencies. **Cons:** 15-minute walk from town; few elements of Easter Island culture present. [$] *Rooms from: 120000 pesos* ✉ *Hotu Matua s/n, near airport, Hanga Roa, Easter Island* ☎ *3/2255–1838* 🌐 *www.pukuvaihotel.com* 🛏 *13 rooms* 🍴 *Breakfast.*

$$ B&B/INN **Residencial Taniera.** The guestbook of this little *residencial,* located by the side of the church, testifies to a decade of satisfied customers. **Pros:** a riotous garden of coffee, cotton, and different varieties of banana trees; attractively decorated; spotlessly clean rooms. **Cons:** very basic rooms. [$] *Rooms from: 55000 pesos* ✉ *Simón Paoa s/n, Hanga Roa, Easter Island* ☎ *3/2210–0491* 🌐 *www.taniera.cl* 🛏 *4 rooms* 💳 *No credit cards* 🍴 *Breakfast.*

$$$$ RESORT **Vai Moana.** The name of this lodging means "blue sea," and it's easy to see why. **Pros:** owner is interested in the living culture (not just historical culture) of Easter Island. **Cons:** a 15-minute walk from the center of Hanga Roa. [$] *Rooms from: 116000 pesos* ✉ *Av. Atamu Tekena s/n, Hanga Roa, Easter Island* ☎ *3/2210–0626* 🌐 *www.vai-moana.cl* 🛏 *26 rooms* 🍴 *Breakfast.*

NIGHTLIFE AND PERFORMING ARTS

NIGHTLIFE

You're in for a late night if you want to sample the scene in Hanga Roa. There seem to be two sets of nightlife, the one that goes on at restaurants until around midnight, and the second one that starts around that time, or much later, at the local clubs, where it's mainly locals, as tourists are off to bed to make the most of daylight hours on the island.

DANCE CLUBS

Piriti. You might think Piriti, a dance club close to the airport, is locals-only, but really, anyone is welcome. The soundtrack is a mix of recorded Latin and pop early on; later in the night (as late as 2 or 3 am), live bands play. There are two parts of the club: the outer, rustic part, and the inside, which resembles a disco that could be found anywhere in the world. In August 2014, the outer part of the club was damaged by fire, so check with locals to see if it's back up and running during your visit. ⊠ *Av. Hotu Matu'a s/n, Easter Island.*

Toroko. On weekends, the younger set heads to Toroko, a dance club a stone's throw from the beach. You won't need directions—just follow the thumping disco beat. Toroko has historically had more of a locals-only vibe, but with the closing of a few other venues, this may change. ⊠ *Av. Policarpo Toro s/n, Hanga Roa, Easter Island.*

PERFORMING ARTS

DANCE SHOWS

Grupo Maori Tupuna. One of three traditional dance groups on the island, this one performs at the Vai Te Mihi cultural center next to Au Bout du Monde Restaurant. Part of every show involves willing visitors pulled up onto the stage to dance with the traditional Rapa Nui dancers. The dances here are supposed to be among the least influenced by other Polynesian styles, and feature traditionally (read: barely) clad, body-painted men and women telling stories through dance. They perform Monday, Thursday, and Saturday. ■TIP→ **If you'd like to be pulled up on stage, increase your chances by sitting in the front row for 17,000 pesos extra (you need a reservation).** ⊠ *Policarpo Toro s/n, Hanga Roa, Easter Island* ☎ *3/2255–0556* 🎫 *12,000 pesos standing, 15,000 regular seat, 17,000 pesos front row.*

Kari Kari. This dance group spends most of the show getting members of the audience on the stage to dance with the performers. It's done with little technology (no flashing lights or microphones), and is in a fairly small space on the main street. Members also perform a very good *sau sau,* the island's famous courtship dance. They perform on Monday, Tuesday, Thursday, and Saturday. ⊠ *Av. Atamu Tekena, Hanga Roa, Easter Island* ☎ *32/210–0767* 🎫 *15,000 pesos.*

Peu Tepuna Tongariki (Tongariki Cultural Center). This cultural center is aimed at the school-aged children of the island, to keep Rapa Nui traditions, including songs, poetry, and dance alive. Performances are frequent (often by the children) and free to the public. You can usually find the kids rehearsing in the garden outside. ⊠ *Policarpo Toro s/n, Hanga Roa, Easter Island* ☎ *3/2210–0226.*

Te Ra'ai. This dance group brings participants off the tourist track to the host's home, where there is traditional face painting, an explanation of the ceremonial type of cooking called *umu*, and finally a dance performance (or you can attend just the dance performance) put on by the collective Haha Varua. The dance is traditional Polynesian and Rapa Nui and interactive with the audience. Performances take place Monday, Wednesday, and Friday. ⊠ *Av. Kaituoe s/n, Hanga Roa, Easter Island* ☎ *3/2255–1460* ⊕ *www.teraai.com.*

SPORTS AND THE OUTDOORS

Haka pei, or sliding down hillsides on banana trunks, is one of the more popular activities during the Tapati Rapa Nui festival. Another is racing across the reed-choked lake that's hidden inside the crater of Rano Raraku.

Visitors who take to the water usually prefer swimming at one of the sandy beaches or snorkeling near one of the offshore islets. The now astroturf soccer pitch is usually filled with teams practicing, but if it's an informal game, you might be able to join in.

DIVING

The crystal-clear waters of the South Pacific afford great visibility for snorkelers and divers. Dozens of types of colorful fish as well as turtles flourish in the warm waters surrounding the island's craggy volcanic rocks. Some of the most spectacular underwater scenery is at Motu Nui and Motu Iti, two adjoining islets just off the coast.

Mike Rapu Diving Center. Mike Rapu Diving Center arranges first dives (no certification necessary) for 40,000 pesos, and for those with NAUI or PADI certification (they are a PADI partner), it's 30,000 pesos. A photographer can be provided for an additional 10,000 pesos. Snorkeling trips are available as well. ⊠ *Caleta de Hanga Roa, Hanga Roa, Easter Island* ☎ *3/2255–1055* ⊕ *www.mikerapu.cl.*

Orca Diving Center. Orca Diving Center provides a boat, guide, and gear for 36,000 pesos per person or 47,000 for a night dive. The outfitter also rents snorkeling masks and fins if you'd like to go out independently, but the guided boat trips let you see much more. ⊠ *Caleta de Hanga Roa, Hanga Roa, Easter Island* ☎ *3/2255–0877, 3/2255–0375* ⊕ *www.orcadivingcenter.cl.*

HIKING

The breezes that cool the island even in the middle of summer make this a perfect place for hikers, and because such a large part of the island is a national park, you can walk more or less wherever you want without worrying if you might be on private property. Be careful, though, as the sun is much stronger than it feels. Slather yourself with sunblock and bring along plenty of water.

Numerous hikes leave from Hanga Roa. You can take a short walk roughly north along the coast and onto the grassy field before it takes you to Ahu Tahai. More strenuous is the hike on the unpaved road from Ahu Te Peu to the seven moai of Ahu Akivi, about 10 km (6 miles) north of town. One of the most rewarding treks is along a rough dirt path on the northern coast that leads from Ahu Te Peu to Playa Anakena. The six-hour journey around Terevaka takes you past many undisturbed archaeological sites that few tourists ever see. CONAF (parks service) recommends a guide for this route. If you insist on going without one, pick up an *Easter Island Trekking Map* at any local shop.

HORSEBACK RIDING

One popular way to see the island is on horseback, which typically costs around 35,000 pesos for a half-day or 70,000 pesos for a group tour with a guide, but you may get a discount if you pay cash. Trips past Ahu Akivi and up to Terevaka (the highest point on the island) are popular, and full-day tours of the north coast are also possible. Some outfitters may offer multiday tours, with a minimum of two passengers.

MOUNTAIN BIKING

Mountain biking is a great way to get around Easter Island's sights. Most car rental agencies also rent mountain bikes for 11,000 for 8 hours or 13,000 pesos for 24 hours. Remember to pack water, as you won't find much (if any) outside of town.

SURFING

When the weather is right, you can find surfboard rentals near Playa Pea, or at Makemake, the bike rental shop in Hanga Roa, for about 20,000 pesos for the board or 25,000 pesos with a lesson. Alicia Ika, at Easter Island Traveling teaches surfing as well. Vendors at beachfront stands near the SERNATUR (local tourism office) can also take you out.

SHOPPING

Souvenir shops line Hanga Roa's two main streets, Avenida Atamu Tekena and Avenida Te Pito o Te Henua. The most popular souvenirs and gifts are reproduction stone moai in a variety of formats (keychain size to the length of your forearm), and shell necklaces. Go farther afield to the sculptor Bene Tuki's workshop at Aukara Lodge or visit Amaya Vai's painting studio two streets back from Atamu Tekena on Tu'u Koihu.

Amaya Art Gallery. Originally from mainland Chile, Amaya Vai has lived on Easter Island for more than 25 years and makes colorful paintings, some on paper made from local products, such as the spiky part of the pineapple fruit and banana pulp. Her work tends toward natural designs, flowers, and some from petrolyphs found on the island, in acrylic, watercolor, and mixed media. ⊠ *Tu'u Koihu, Hanga Roa, Easter Island* ☎ *9/136–6102*.

Feria Municipal. The Feria Municipal, the town's fruit, vegetable, and fish market, also has a crafts section. ⊠ *Av. Atamu Tekena s/n, Hanga Roa, Easter Island* ☎ *3/2255–2049*.

Mercado Artesanal. Next to the church is the Mercado Artesanal, a large building filled with crafts stands. Here, local artisans whittle wooden moai and string together seashell necklaces. It's open Monday–Saturday 9–8 (until 7 pm May–October) and Sunday 10–1:30. When specific vendors leave temporarily, they cover their wares with a blanket. ⊠ *Ara Roa Rakei s/n, Hanga Roa, Easter Island* ☎ *3/2255–1346*.

Rapa Nui Natural Products. This quirky natural products store is filled with everything from local soaps, scented oils, jams (such as guava) and honey, to candy. English, Spanish, and Dutch are spoken. ■ TIP➜ **Pick up some white and dark chocolate moai here.** ⊠ *Hanga Roa, Easter Island* ☎ *3/2255–2204* ⊕ *www.rapanui-shop.com*.

Vai a Heva. This small store stocks professional and souvenir-quality carvings of moai and other important symbols of the Rapa Nui culture, as well as jewelry made of shells and bone, pearls from the South Pacific, and imitation *rongo rongo* tablets on wood. ⊠ *Te Pito O Te Henua s/n, Hanga Roa, Easter Island* ☎ *3/2255–1385*.

SPANISH VOCABULARY

ENGLISH	SPANISH	PRONUNCIATION

BASICS

Yes/no	Sí/no	see/no
Please	Por favor	pore fah-**vore**
May I?	¿Me permite?	may pair-**mee**-tay
Thank you (very much)	(Muchas) gracias	(**moo**-chas) **grah**-see-as
You're welcome	De nada	day **nah**-dah
Excuse me	Con permiso	con pair-**mee**-so
Pardon me	¿Perdón?	pair-**dohn**
Could you tell me?	¿Podría decirme?	po-dree-ah deh-**seer**-meh
I'm sorry	Lo siento	lo see-**en**-toh
Good morning!	¡Buenos días!	**bway**-nohs **dee**-ahs
Good afternoon!	¡Buenas tardes!	**bway**-nahs **tar**-dess
Good evening!	¡Buenas noches!	**bway**-nahs **no**-chess
Good-bye!	¡Adiós!/¡Hasta luego!	ah-dee-**ohss**/**ah**-stah **lwe**-go
Mr./Mrs.	Señor/Señora	sen-**yor**/sen-**yohr**-ah
Miss	Señorita	sen-yo-**ree**-tah
Pleased to meet you	Mucho gusto	**moo**-cho **goose**-toh
How are you?	¿Cómo está usted?	**ko**-mo es-**tah** oo-**sted**
Very well, thank you.	Muy bien, gracias.	**moo**-ee bee-**en**, **grah**-see-as
And you?	¿Y usted?	ee oos-**ted**
Hello (on the telephone)	Diga	**dee**-gah

NUMBERS

1	un, uno	oon, **oo**-no
2	dos	dos
3	tres	tress
4	cuatro	**kwah**-tro
5	cinco	**sink**-oh

6	seis	saice
7	siete	see-**et**-eh
8	ocho	**o**-cho
9	nueve	new-**eh**-vey
10	diez	dee-**es**
11	once	**ohn**-seh
12	doce	**doh**-seh
13	trece	**treh**-seh
14	catorce	ka-**tohr**-seh
15	quince	**keen**-seh
16	dieciséis	dee-**es**-ee-**saice**
17	diecisiete	dee-**es**-ee-see-**et**-eh
18	dieciocho	dee-**es**-ee-**o**-cho
19	diecinueve	**dee**-**es**-ee-new-**ev**-eh
20	veinte	**vain**-teh
21	veintiuno	**vain**-te-**oo**-noh
30	treinta	**train**-tah
32	treinta y dos	train-tay-**dohs**
40	cuarenta	kwah-**ren**-tah
43	cuarenta y tres	kwah-**ren**-tay-**tress**
50	cincuenta	seen-**kwen**-tah
54	cincuenta y cuatro	seen-**kwen**-tay **kwah**-tro
60	sesenta	sess-**en**-tah
65	sesenta y cinco	sess-**en**-tay **seen**-ko
70	setenta	se-**ten**-tah
76	setenta y seis	se- t **en**-tay **saice**
80	ochenta	oh-**chen**-tah
87	ochenta y siete	oh-**chen**-tay see-**yet**-eh
90	noventa	no-**ven**-tah
98	noventa y ocho	no-**ven**-tah-**o**-choh
100	cien	see-**en**

101	ciento uno	see-**en**-toh **oo**-noh
200	doscientos	doh-see-**en**-tohss
500	quinientos	keen-**yen**-tohss
700	setecientos	set-eh-see-**en**-tohss
900	novecientos	no-veh-see-**en**-tohss
1,000	mil	meel
2,000	dos mil	dohs meel
1,000,000	un millón	oon meel-**yohn**

COLORS

black	negro	**neh**-groh
blue	azul	ah-**sool**
brown	café	kah-**feh**
green	verde	**ver**-deh
pink	rosa	**ro**-sah
purple	morado	mo-**rah**-doh
orange	naranja	na-**rahn**-hah
red	rojo	**roh**-hoh
white	blanco	**blahn**-koh
yellow	amarillo	ah-mah-**ree**-yoh

DAYS OF THE WEEK

Sunday	domingo	doe-**meen**-goh
Monday	lunes	**loo**-ness
Tuesday	martes	**mahr**-tess
Wednesday	miércoles	me-**air**-koh-less
Thursday	jueves	hoo-**ev**-ess
Friday	viernes	vee-**air**-ness
Saturday	sábado	**sah**-bah-doh

MONTHS

January	enero	eh-**neh**-roh
February	febrero	feh-**breh**-roh
March	marzo	**mahr**-soh

April	abril	ah-**breel**
May	mayo	**my**-oh
June	junio	**hoo**-nee-oh
July	julio	**hoo**-lee-yoh
August	agosto	ah-**ghost**-toh
September	septiembre	sep-tee-**em**-breh
October	octubre	oak-**too**-breh
November	noviembre	no-vee-**em**-breh
December	diciembre	dee-see-**em**-breh

USEFUL PHRASES

Do you speak English?	¿Habla usted inglés?	**ah**-blah oos-**ted** in-**glehs**
I don't speak Spanish	No hablo español	no **ah**-bloh es-pahn-**yol**
I don't understand (you)	No entiendo	no en-tee-**en**-doh
I understand (you)	Entiendo	en-tee-**en**-doh
I don't know	No sé	no seh
I am American/ British	Soy americano (americana)/ inglés(a)	soy ah-meh-ree-**kah**-no (ah-meh-ree-**kah**-nah)/in-**glehs(ah)**
What's your name?	¿Cómo se llama usted?	koh-mo seh **yah**-mah oos-**ted**
My name is . . .	Me llamo . . .	may **yah**-moh
What time is it?	¿Qué hora es?	keh **o**-rah es
It is one, two, three . . . o'clock.	Es la una./Son las dos, tres . . .	es la **oo**-nah/sohn lahs dohs, tress
Yes, please/No, thank you	Sí, por favor/No, gracias	**see** pohr fah-**vor**/no **grah**-see-us
How?	¿Cómo?	**koh**-mo
When?	¿Cuándo?	**kwahn**-doh
This/Next week	Esta semana/ la semana que entra	**es**-teh seh-**mah**-nah/lah seh-**mah**-nah keh **en**-trah
This/Next month	Este mes/el próximo mes	**es**-teh mehs/el **proke**-see-mo mehs

This/Next year	Este año/el año que viene	**es**-teh **ahn**-yo/el **ahn**-yo keh vee-**yen**-ay
Yesterday/today/tomorrow	Ayer/hoy/mañana	ah-**yehr**/oy/mahn-**yah**-nah
This morning/afternoon	Esta mañana/tarde	**es**-tah mahn-**yah**-nah/**tar**-deh
Tonight	Esta noche	**es**-tah **no**-cheh
What?	¿Qué?	keh
What is it?	¿Qué es esto?	keh es **es**-toh
Why?	¿Por qué?	pore **keh**
Who?	¿Quién?	kee-**yen**
Where is . . . ?	¿Dónde está . . . ?	**dohn**-deh es-**tah**
the train station?	la estación del tren?	la es-tah-see-on del trehn
the subway station?	la estación del tren subterráneo?	la es-ta-see-**on** del trehn la es-ta-see-**on** soob-teh-**rrahn**-eh-oh
the bus stop?	la parada del autobus?	la pah-**rah**-dah del ow-toh-**boos**
the post office?	la oficina de correos?	la oh-fee-**see**-nah deh koh-**rreh**-os
the bank?	el banco?	el **bahn**-koh
the hotel?	el hotel?	el oh-**tel**
the store?	la tienda?	la tee-**en**-dah
the cashier?	la caja?	la **kah**-hah
the museum?	el museo?	el moo-**seh**-oh
the hospital?	el hospital?	el ohss-pee-**tal**
the elevator?	el ascensor?	el ah-**sen**-sohr
the bathroom?	el baño?	el **bahn**-yoh
Here/there	Aquí/allá	ah-**key**/ah-**yah**
Open/closed	Abierto/cerrado	ah-bee-**er**-toh/ser-**ah**-doh
Left/right	Izquierda/derecha	iss-key-**er**-dah/dare-**eh**-chah
Straight ahead	Derecho	dare-**eh**-choh
Is it near/far?	¿Está cerca/lejos?	es-**tah sehr**-kah/**leh**-hoss
I'd like . . .	Quisiera . . .	kee-see-ehr-ah
a room	un cuarto/una habitación	oon **kwahr**-toh/**oo**-nah ah-bee-tah-see-**on**
the key	la llave	lah **yah**-veh
a newspaper	un periódico	oon pehr-ee-**oh**-

		dee-koh
a stamp	un sello de	oon **seh**-yo deh
	correo	koh-**reh**-oh
I'd like to buy . . .	Quisiera	kee-see-**ehr**-ah
	comprar . . .	kohm-**prahr**
cigarettes	cigarrillos	ce-ga-**ree**-yohs
matches	cerillos	ser-**ee**-ohs
a dictionary	un diccionario	oon deek-see-oh-**nah**-ree-oh
soap	jabón	hah-**bohn**
sunglasses	gafas de sol	**ga**-fahs deh sohl
suntan lotion	loción	loh-see-**ohn** brohn-seh-ah-**do**-rah
	bronceadora	
a map	un mapa	oon **mah**-pah
a magazine	una revista	**oon**-ah reh-**veess**-tah
paper	papel	pah-**pel**
envelopes	sobres	**so**-brehs
a postcard	una tarjeta postal	**oon**-ah tar-**het**-ah post-**ahl**
How much is it?	¿Cuánto cuesta?	**kwahn**-toh **kwes**-tah
It's expensive/ cheap	Está caro/barato	es-**tah kah**-roh/ bah-**rah**-toh
A little/a lot	Un poquito/ mucho	oon poh-**kee**-toh/ **moo**-choh
More/less	Más/menos	mahss/**men**-ohss
Enough/too much/too little	Suficiente/ demasiado/ muy poco	soo-fee-see-**en**-teh/ deh-mah-see-**ah**-doh/**moo**-ee **poh**-koh
Telephone	Teléfono	tel-**ef**-oh-no
Telegram	Telegrama	teh-leh-**grah**-mah
I am ill	Estoy enfermo(a)	es-**toy** en-**fehr**-moh(mah)
Please call a doctor	Por favor llame a un médico	pohr fah-**vor ya**-meh ah oon **med**-ee-koh
Help!	¡Auxilio! ¡Socorro!	owk-see-lee-oh/ soh-kohr-roh
Fire!	¡Incendio!	en-sen-dee-oo
Caution!/Look out!	¡Cuidado!	kwee-dah-doh

ON THE ROAD

Avenue	Avenida	ah-ven-**ee**-dah
Broad, tree-lined boulevard	Bulevar	boo-leh-**var**
Fertile plain	Vega	**veh**-gah
Highway	Carretera	car-reh-**ter**-ah
Mountain pass	Puerto	poo-**ehr**-toh
Street	Calle	**cah**-yeh
Waterfront promenade	Rambla	**rahm**-blah
Wharf	Embarcadero	em-bar-cah-**deh**-ro

IN TOWN

Cathedral	Catedral	cah-teh-**dral**
Church	Templo/iglesia	**tem**-plo/ee-**glehs**-see-ah
City hall	Casa de gobierno	kah-sah deh go-bee-**ehr**-no
Door, gate	Puerta portón	poo-**ehr**-tah por-**ton**
Entrance/exit	Entrada/salida	en-**trah**-dah/sah-lee-dah
Inn, rustic bar, or restaurant	Taverna	tah-**vehr**-nah
Main square	Plaza principal	plah-thah prin-see-**pahl**
Market	Mercado	mer-**kah**-doh
Neighborhood	Barrio	**bahr**-ree-o
Traffic circle	Glorieta	glor-ee-**eh**-tah
Wine cellar, wine bar, or wine shop	Bodega	boh-**deh**-gah

DINING OUT

A bottle of . . .	Una botella de . . .	**oo**-nah bo-**teh**-yah deh
A cup of . . .	Una taza de . . .	**oo**-nah **tah**-thah deh
A glass of . . .	Un vaso de . . .	oon **vah**-so deh
Ashtray	Un cenicero	oon sen-ee-**seh**-roh

Bill/check	La cuenta	lah **kwen**-tah
Bread	El pan	el pahn
Breakfast	El desayuno	el deh-sah-**yoon**-oh
Butter	La mantequilla	lah man-teh-**key**-yah
Cheers!	¡Salud!	sah-**lood**
Cocktail	Un aperitivo	oon ah-pehr-ee-**tee**-voh
Dinner	La cena	lah **seh**-nah
Dish	Un plato	oon **plah**-toh
Menu of the day	Menú del día	meh-**noo** del **dee**-ah
Enjoy!	¡Buen provecho!	bwehn pro-**veh**-cho
Fixed-price menu	Menú fijo o turístico	meh-**noo fee**-hoh oh too-**ree**-stee-coh
Fork	El tenedor	el ten-eh-**dor**
Is the tip included?	¿Está incluida la propina?	es-**tah** in-cloo-**ee**-dah lah pro-**pee**-nah
Knife	El cuchillo	el koo-**chee**-yo
Large portion of savory snacks	Ración	rah-see-**ohn**
Lunch	La comida	lah koh-**mee**-dah
Menu	La carta, el menú	lah **cart**-ah, el meh-**noo**
Napkin	La servilleta	lah sehr-vee-**yet**-ah
Pepper	La pimienta	lah pee-me-**en**-tah
Please give me	Por favor déme	pore fah-**vor deh**-meh
Salt	La sal	lah sahl
Savory snacks	Tapas	**tah**-pahs
Spoon	Una cuchara	**oo**-nah koo-**chah**-rah
Sugar	El azúcar	el ah-**thu**-kar
Waiter!/Waitress!	¡Por favor, señor/señorita!	pohr fah-**vor** sen-**yor**/sen-yor-**ee**-tah

TRAVEL SMART CHILE

GETTING HERE AND AROUND

■ AIR TRAVEL

Traveling between the Americas is usually less tiring than traveling to Europe or Asia because you cross fewer time zones. Miami (8½ hour flight), New York (11 hours), Dallas (9½ hours), and Atlanta (9½ hours) are the primary departure points for flights to Chile from the United States, though there are also frequent flights from Los Angeles, Boston, Washington, D.C., and other cities. Other international flights often connect through other major South American cities like Buenos Aires and Lima.

Arriving from abroad, Canadian travelers have to pay US$132 and Australian citizens US$117 on entry as a "reciprocity fee." Credit cards and cash are accepted for payment. Since 2014, U.S. citizens are exempt from paying the fee of US$160.

Always confirm international flights at least 72 hours ahead of the scheduled departure time. This is particularly true for travel within South America, where flights tend to operate at full capacity and passengers often have a great deal of baggage to process.

LAN offers the LANPASS program, where customers can earn miles (actually, kilometers) by flying with LAN or other members of the One World Alliance (American Airlines, British Airways, Qantas, and others) or through car rentals or hotel stays with affiliated companies.

AIRPORTS

Most international flights head to Santiago's Arturo Merino Benítez International Airport (SCL) about 30 minutes west of the city. Domestic flights leave from the same terminal.

Airport Information Comodoro Arturo Merino Benítez International Airport ✉ Pudahuel, Pudahuel, Santiago, Chile ☎ 2/2690-1752 ⊕ www.aeropuertosantiago.cl.

FLIGHTS

The largest North American carrier is American Airlines, which has direct service from Dallas and Miami; Delta flies from Atlanta. LAN flies nonstop to Santiago from both Miami and New York and with a layover in Lima from Los Angeles. Air Canada flies nonstop from Toronto. Most of the major Central and South American airlines also fly to Santiago, including Aerolíneas Argentinas, Avianca (Taca), Copa, and Tam.

LAN and Sky have daily flights from Santiago to most cities throughout Chile.

Airline Contacts Aerolíneas Argentinas ☎ 800/333-0276 in North America, 2/2210-9300 in Chile ⊕ www.aerolineas.com. ar. **American Airlines** ☎ 800/433-7300 in North America, 2/2601-9272 in Chile ⊕ www. aa.com. **Avianca (Taca)** ☎ 800/284-2622 in North America, 2/2270-6613 in Chile ⊕ www. avianca.com. **Copa** ☎ 800/359-2672 in North America, 2/2200-2100 in Chile ⊕ www.copaair. com. **Delta Airlines** ☎ 800/221-1212 for U.S. reservations, 800/241-4141 for international reservations, 800/202-020 in Chile ⊕ www. delta.com. **LAN** ☎ 866/435-9526 in U.S., 600/526-2000 in Chile ⊕ www.lan.com. **Sky** ☎ 600/600-2828 in Chile ⊕ www.skyairline. cl. **Tam** ☎ 888/235-9826 in North America, 600/526-2000 in Chile ⊕ www.tam.com.br.

■ BOAT TRAVEL

Boats and ferries are the best way to reach many places in Chile, such as Chiloé and the Southern Coast. They are also a great alternative to flying when your destination is a southern port like Puerto Natales or Punta Arenas. Navimag and Transmarchilay are the two main companies operating routes in the south. They both maintain excellent websites (Spanish-only in the case of Transmarchilay) with complete schedule and pricing information. You can buy tickets online, or book through a travel agent.

Boat Information Navimag ☎ 2/2442–3120 in Santiago, 65/2432–360 in Puerto Montt ⊕ www.navimag.com. **Transmarchilay** ☎ 65/270–700 in Puerto Montt ⊕ www.transmarchilay.cl.

CRUISES

Several international cruise lines, including Celebrity Cruises, Holland America, Norwegian Cruise Lines, Princess Cruises, and Silversea Cruises, call at ports in Chile or offer cruises that start in Chile. Itineraries typically start in Valparaíso, following the coastline to the southern archipelago and its fjords. Some companies, such as Holland America, have itineraries that include Antarctica. Victory Adventure Expeditions and Adventure Associates are tour companies that offer cruises to Antarctica.

You can spend a week aboard the luxury *Skorpios,* which leaves from Puerto Montt and sails through the archipelago to the San Rafael glacier. In Punta Arenas, you can board *Cruceros Australis* and motor through the straights and fjords to Ushuaia and Cape Horn.

International Cruise Lines Celebrity Cruises ☎ 800/647–2251 ⊕ www.celebrity.com. **Holland America Line** ☎ 206/286–3900, 877/932–4259 ⊕ www.hollandamerica.com. **Norwegian Cruise Line** ☎ 866/234–7350 ⊕ www.ncl.com. **Princess Cruises** ☎ 800/774–6237 ⊕ www.princess.com.

Silversea Cruises ☎ 800/722–9955 ⊕ www.silversea.com.

Chilean Cruise Lines Cruceros Australis ☎ 877/678–3772 in North America, 2/2442–3115 in Chile ⊕ www.australis.com. **Skorpios** ☎ 718/831–7149 in U.S., 2/2477–1900 in Chile ⊕ www.skorpios.cl.

Cruise Tour Companies Adventure Associates ☎ 61/2–8916–3000 Australia ⊕ www.adventureassociates.com. **Victory Adventure Expeditions** ☎ 61/2227–098 in Chile ⊕ www.victory-cruises.com.

▌ BUS TRAVEL

Long-distance buses are safe and affordable. Luxury bus travel between cities costs about one-third that of plane travel and is more comfortable, with wide reclining seats, movies, drinks, and snacks. The most expensive service offered by most bus companies is called *cama premium* or simply *premium,* which indicates that the seats fold down into an almost horizontal bed. Service billed as *semi-cama, ejectivo,* and *cama* are other comfortable alternatives.

Without a doubt, the low cost of bus travel is its greatest advantage; its greatest drawback is the time you need to cover the distances involved. A trip from Santiago to San Pedro de Atacama, for example, takes about 23 hours. Be sure to get a receipt for any luggage you check beneath the bus and keep a close watch on belongings you take on the bus.

Tickets are sold online, at bus company offices, and at city bus terminals. Note that in larger cities there may be several bus terminals (Santiago has three major terminals, for example), and some small towns may not have a terminal at all: pick-ups and drop-offs are at the bus line's office, invariably in a central location. Expect to pay with cash, as only the large bus companies such as Pullman Bus and Tur-Bus accept credit cards.

Reservations are recommended all year round, but are essential for holidays and travel during high season. You should arrive at terminals extra early for travel during peak seasons when the terminals can be packed with travelers.

Pullman Bus and Tur-Bus are two of the best-known companies in Chile. Their websites are Spanish-only.

Bus Information Pullman Bus ☎ 600/320–3200 ⊕ www.ventapasajes.cl. **Tur-Bus** ☎ 600/660–6600 ⊕ www.turbus.cl.

■ CAR TRAVEL

Certain areas of Chile are most enjoyable when explored on your own in a car, such as the beaches of the Central Coast, the wineries of the Central Valley, the ski areas east of Santiago, and the Lake District in the south. Some regions, such as parts of the Atacama Desert, are impossible to explore without your own wheels.

Drivers in Chile are not particularly aggressive, but neither are they particularly polite. Some common sense rules of the road: Before you set out, establish an itinerary. Be sure to plan your daily driving distance conservatively, as distances are always longer than they appear on maps. Pick up a CHILETUR guide to the part of Chile to which you are traveling (North, Center, or South) before departing. The guides have excellent maps indicating gas stations along the major highways, as well as recommendations for different routes and car trips for each region of Chile. You can buy CHILETUR guides (Spanish only) at gas stations affiliated with COPEC and at bookstores in Chile. More information about the CHILETUR guides, including prices and content, is available at ⊕ *www.chileturcopec. cl*. Bring enough change to pay tolls on highways.

Obey posted speed limits and traffic regulations, and keep your lights on during the day as well as the night. And above all, if you get a traffic ticket, don't argue—and plan to spend longer than you want settling it.

GASOLINE

Most service stations are operated by an attendant and accept credit cards. They are open 24 hours a day along the Pan-American Highway and in most major cities, but not in small towns and villages. Attendants will often ask you to glance at the zero reading on the gas pump to show that you are not being cheated. A small tip is expected if attendants clean your windows or check your oil level.

PARKING

You can park on the street, in parking lots, or in parking garages in Santiago and large cities in Chile. Expect to pay anywhere from 500 to 3,000 pesos approximately, depending on the length of time. For street parking, a parking attendant (either official or unofficial) will be there to direct and charge you. You should tip the unofficial parking attendants, called *cuidadores de autos*; 1,000 pesos is a reasonable tip for two to three hours.

ROAD CONDITIONS

Between May and September, roads and underpasses can flood when it rains. It can be dangerous, especially for drivers who don't know their way around. Avoid driving if it has been raining for several hours.

The Pan-American Highway runs from Arica in the far north down to Puerto Montt and Chiloé, in the Lake District. Much of it is now two-lane and bypasses most large cities. The Carretera Austral, a mostly unpaved road that runs for 1,240 km (770 miles) as far as Villa O'Higgins in Patagonia, starts just south of Puerto Montt. A few stretches of the road are broken by water and are linked only by car ferries (check ferry schedules before departing, as schedules may change depending on the time of year). Some parts of the Carretera can be washed away in heavy rain; it is wise to consult local police for details.

Many cyclists ride without lights in rural areas, so be careful when driving at night, particularly on roads without street lighting. This also applies to horse- and bull-drawn carts.

ROADSIDE EMERGENCIES

El Automóvil Club de Chile offers low-cost road service and towing in and around the main cities to members of the Automobile Association of America (AAA). But if you don't speak Spanish, you're probably better off contacting your rental agency, or having your hotel concierge communicate with the automobile club or your rental agency.

Auto Club Information El Automóvil Club de Chile ☎ 600/464-4040 ⊕ www. automovilclub.cl.

RULES OF THE ROAD

Keep in mind that the speed limit is 60 kph (37 mph) in cities and 120 kph (75 mph) on highways unless otherwise posted. The police regularly enforce the speed limit, handing out *partes* (tickets) to speeders.

Right-hand turns are prohibited at red lights unless otherwise posted. Seat belts are mandatory in the front and back of the car, and police give on-the-spot fines for not wearing them. There is a zero tolerance alcohol policy for drivers in Chile. If the police find you with more than 0.3 milligrams of alcohol in your blood, you will be considered to be driving under the influence and arrested.

Plan to rent snow chains for driving on the road up to the ski resorts outside Santiago. Police will stop you and ask if you have them—if you don't, you will be forced to turn back.

It is obligatory to keep your headlights lit during the day and night.

CAR RENTAL

On average it costs 25,000 pesos (about US$50) a day to rent the cheapest type of car with unlimited mileage. Vehicles with automatic transmissions tend to be more luxurious and can cost twice as much as the basic rental with manual transmission. Many companies list higher rates (about 20%) for the high season (December–February). Hertz, Avis, and Budget have locations at Santiago's airport and elsewhere around the country.

To access some of Chile's more remote regions, it may be necessary to rent a four-wheel-drive vehicle, which can cost 80,000 pesos (about US$165) a day. You can often get a discounted weekly rate. The rate you are quoted usually includes insurance, but make sure to find out exactly what the insurance covers and to ask whether there is a deductible you will have to pay in case of an accident. You can usually pay slightly more and have no deductible. An obligatory extra that all companies charge for rentals out of or returning to Santiago is TAG, an electronic toll-collection system used in that city. This charge is currently about 5,000 pesos (about US$10) per day. If you don't want to drive yourself, consider hiring a car and driver through your hotel concierge, or make a deal with a taxi driver for some extended sightseeing at a longer-term rate.

Major international rental companies (Alamo, Avis, Budget, Hertz, National) operate in Chile, but local companies are sometimes a cheaper option. Rosselot, Bengolea, and Chilean are reputable local companies with offices in Santiago and other cities.

To drive legally in Chile you need an international driver's license as well as your valid national license, although car rental companies and police do not often enforce this regulation. The minimum age for driving is 18, but to rent a car you have to be 22 (or 23 depending on the company).

Major Rental Agencies Alamo ☎ 786/231-5053 in U.S., 2/2655-5255 in Chile ⊕ www. alamo.com. **Avis** ☎ 800/633-3469 in U.S., 2/2795-3932 in Chile ⊕ www.avis.com. **Budget** ☎ 800/218-7992 in U.S., 2/2795-3952 in Chile ⊕ www.budget.com. **Hertz** ☎ 800/654-3131 in U.S., 2/2360-8600 in Chile ⊕ www.hertz.com. **National Car Rental** ☎ 877/222-9058 in U.S., 2/2228-7637 in Chile ⊕ www.nationalcar.com.

Local Agencies Bengolea ✉ Av. Francisco Bilbao 1047, Providencia, Santiago, Chile ☎ 2/2204-9021. **Chilean** ✉ Bellavista 0183, Bellavista, Santiago, Chile ☎ 2/2963-8760 ⊕ www.chileanrentacar. cl. **Rosselot** ✉ Comodoro Arturo Merino Benítez International Airport, Santiago, Chile ☎ 2/2690-1374 ⊕ www.rosselot.cl ✉ Av. Francisco Bilbao 2032, Providencia, Santiago, Chile ☎ 2/2381-3692.

ESSENTIALS

■ ACCOMMODATIONS

The lodgings that we list are the cream of the crop in each price category. All hotels listed have private bath unless otherwise noted. In Chile, a national rating system is used, classifying hotels on a scale of one to five stars. The rating is determined by SERNATUR, the national tourism agency, and is based on the services offered and the physical attributes of the hotel and its property. The system is somewhat perfunctory, however, and doesn't allow for true qualitative analysis.

It's always good to look at any room before accepting it. Expense is no guarantee of charm or cleanliness, and accommodations can vary dramatically within one hotel. If you ask for a double room, you'll get a room for two people, but you're not guaranteed a double mattress. If you'd like to avoid twin beds, ask for a *cama matrimonial.*

Hotels in Chile do not charge taxes (known as IVA) to foreign tourists. When checking the price, ask for the *precio extranjero, sin impuestos* (foreign rate, without taxes). If you are traveling to Chile from neighboring Peru or Bolivia, expect a significant jump in prices. Also, note that you can always ask for a *descuento* (discount) out of season or sometimes midweek during high season.

HOTELS

Chile's urban areas and resort areas have hotels that come with all of the amenities that are taken for granted in North America and Europe, such as room service, a restaurant, and a swimming pool. Elsewhere you may not have television or a phone in your room, although you will usually find them somewhere in the hotel. Rooms that have a private bath may have only a shower, and in some cases, there will be a shared bath in the hall. In all but the most upscale hotels you may be

asked to leave your key at the reception desk whenever you leave.

RESIDENCIALES

Private homes with rooms for rent, *residenciales* (also called *hospedajes*) are a unique way to get to know Chile, especially if you're on a budget. (Many rooms cost less than US$30 per night.) Sometimes residenciales and hospedajes are small, with basic accommodations and not necessarily in private homes. Some will be shabby, but others can be substantially better than hotel rooms. Staying in these types of accommodations allows you to interact with locals (though they are unlikely to speak English). Contact the local tourist office for details on residenciales and hospedajes.

MOTELS

If you spot motels while road tripping in Chile—often recognizable by their palm trees and love hearts signage—you should think twice before heading in for a night cap. Motels in Chile are usually pay-per-hour love hotels and range from seedy or shabby to colorful themed rooms.

■ COMMUNICATIONS

INTERNET

Chileans are generally savvy about the Internet, and in most cities you'll find Wi-Fi spots and Internet cafés. Connection fees at cybercafés are about 1,000 to 2,000 pesos for an hour, and Wi-Fi is always free for paying customers. In Santiago there are also many free Wi-Fi hubs, particularly in metro stations.

If you're planning to bring a laptop or tablet into the country, check the manual first to see if it requires a converter. Newer laptops and tablets will require only an adapter plug. If you are planning on using your cell phone, check your service providers' roaming charges before leaving. Buying local pay-as-you-go phone cards are available at phone shops and kiosks in most towns, although they are unlikely to offer Internet service unless you sign on for a long-term contract.

While most people in Chile walk around the streets with smart phones in hand, carrying anything valuable could make you a target for thieves. Act with caution by concealing your devices in a generic bag and keeping it close to you at all times, especially on public transportation.

PHONES

The good news is that you can now make a direct-dial telephone call from virtually any point on earth. The bad news? You can't always do so cheaply. Calling from a hotel is almost always the most expensive option; hotels usually add surcharges to calls, particularly international ones. Chile has many call centers, and you can also purchase calling cards at street kiosks or phone shops. Mobile phones are usually cheaper than calling from your hotel.

The country code for Chile is 56. When dialing a Chilean number from abroad, drop the initial 0 from the local area code. The area code is 2 for Santiago, 58 for Arica, 55 for Antofagasta and San Pedro de Atacama, 42 for Chillán, 57 for Iquique, 51 for La Serena, 65 for Puerto Montt, 61 for Puerto Natales and Punta Arenas, 45 for Temuco, 63 for Valdivia, and 32 for Valparaíso and Viña del Mar. Mobile phone numbers are preceded by the number 9 (sometimes you'll see it written as 09). Dial the "0" first if you're calling from a landline within Chile; otherwise, drop it if you're calling from abroad or from another cell phone in Chile.

CALLING WITHIN CHILE

A 100-peso coin is required to make a local call in a public phone booth, or 200 pesos to dial a cell phone. It is increasingly difficult to find pay phones in Chile, since most people now use cell phones. *Centros de llamadas* (call centers), small phone shops with individual booths, are common and are priced fairly. Simply step into any available booth and dial the number.

The charge will be displayed on a monitor near the phone.

You can reach directory assistance in Chile by calling 103. English-speaking operators are not available.

To call a landline from a cell phone, dial "0" and then the city code and number.

For national long-distance calls, you may need to dial a long-distance carrier code (try 123 or 133—two commonly used codes) then the area code and number.

CALLING OUTSIDE CHILE

The country code is 1 for the United States and Canada, 61 for Australia, 64 for New Zealand, and 44 for the United Kingdom. You must add a zero before these country codes when dialing from Chile, and may also be required to add an international service provider (or "carrier") code before the 0 (try commonly used codes 123 or 133). Using a Telefónica/Movistar phone (the top service provider in Chile), dial 800/207-300 to reach MCI international operator assistance.

CALLING CARDS

If you plan to call abroad while in Chile, it's in your best interest to buy a local phone card (sold in kiosks and call centers). EntelTicket phone cards, for example, are widely available in different denominations.

MOBILE PHONES

If you have a multiband phone (some countries use frequencies other than those used in the United States), and your service provider uses the world-standard GSM network (as do T-Mobile, AT&T, and Verizon), you can probably use your phone abroad. Roaming fees can be steep, however, and overseas you normally pay the toll charges for incoming calls. It's almost always cheaper to send a text message than to make a call.

If you just want to make local calls, consider buying a new SIM card (note that your provider may have to unlock your phone for you to use a different SIM card) and a prepaid service plan in the destination. You'll then have a local number and

A NOTE ABOUT THE LANGUAGE

Chile's official language is Spanish. Even just mastering a few basic words and terms is bound to make chatting with the locals more rewarding.

Although staff at large hotels generally speak adequate English and in Santiago you are also likely to find one person with basic English in most tourist-oriented restaurants and shops, be prepared elsewhere for people to be helpful but to speak little or no English. Taxi drivers, except for the (very expensive) services provided by hotels, won't in general know English, and menus are mostly in Spanish only.

Chilean Spanish is fast, clipped, and chock-full of colloquialisms. For example, the word for police officer isn't *policía*, but *carabinero*. Even foreigners with a good deal of experience in Spanish-speaking countries may feel like they are encountering a completely new language—particularly for food-related words.

The most common way of asking for directions in Chile is "*¿Dónde queda...?*" (Where is...?). If you need to get someone's attention first, you can add "*Disculpe*" (Excuse me). When giving directions, Chileans seldom use left and right, indicating the way instead with a mixture of sign language and *para acá, para allá* (toward here, toward there) instructions. At their rapid-fire rate, these often come off as two-syllable exchanges ("*pa'ca*," "*pa'ya*").

can make and receive local calls at local rates. If your trip is extensive, you could also simply buy a new cell phone in your destination, as the initial cost will be offset over time. SIM cards and prepaid service plans can be purchased at offices of the major cell phone companies in Chile, like Entel and Movistar.

Contacts Cellular Abroad. Cellular Abroad rents and sells GSM phones and sells SIM cards that work in many countries. ☎ 800/287–5072 ⊕ www.cellularabroad.com. **Mobal.** Mobal rents mobiles and sells GSM phones (starting at US$29) that will operate in 140 countries. Per-call rates vary throughout the world. ☎ 888/888–9162 ⊕ www.mobal.com. **Planet Fone.** Planet Fone rents international cell phones, but the per-minute rates are expensive. ☎ 888/988–4777 ⊕ www.planetfone.com.

■ CUSTOMS AND DUTIES

You may bring into Chile up to 400 cigarettes, 500 grams of tobacco, 50 cigars, 2.5 liters of alcoholic beverages, and gifts to the value of US$300. Prohibited items include plants, fruits and vegetables, seeds, meat, and honey. Spot checks take place at airports and border crossings, and fines are common. It's always better to declare all animal and vegetable products you are carrying, rather than risk being fined.

Visitors, although seldom questioned, are prohibited from leaving with handicrafts and souvenirs worth more than US$500. You are generally prohibited from taking antiques out of the country without special permission.

Information Chilean Embassy ✉ 1732 Massachusetts Ave. NW, Washington, District of Columbia, United States ☎ 202/785–1746 ⊕ chileabroad.gov.cl/estados-unidos. **U.S. Customs and Border Protection** ⊕ www.cbp.gov.

▌ EATING OUT

The restaurants that we list are the cream of the crop in each price category. It is customary to tip 10% in Chile; tipping above this amount is uncommon among locals. Credit cards are generally accepted in big cities (although the tip should preferably be left in cash), but when visiting smaller towns and rural areas, always bring enough cash.

Chileans like to eat three staple meals a day, if not more. You can expect a typically light breakfast to be served between 7 am and 10 am; lunch is usually eaten between 1 pm and 3 pm; and dinner won't usually be served before 8 pm, often running till midnight. Reservations are advisable but generally not necessary unless you are visiting a popular restaurant or are taking a large group.

The dress code for lunch is fairly casual, but eating out in the evening is often a special occasion for locals. You should dress like you care. Chileans can be conservative with dress; if you bare too much flesh you might attract scornful looks or meandering gazes.

▌ ELECTRICITY

Unlike the United States and Canada—which have a 110- to 120-volt standard—the current in Chile is 220 volts, 50 cycles alternating current (AC). The wall sockets accept plugs with two round prongs.

Consider making a small investment in a universal adapter, which has several types of plugs in one lightweight, compact unit. Most laptops and mobile phone chargers are dual voltage (i.e., they operate equally well on 110 and 220 volts) and so require only a plug adapter. These days the same is true of small appliances such as hair dryers. Always check labels and manufacturer instructions to be sure. Don't use 110-volt outlets marked "for shavers only" for high-wattage appliances such as hair dryers.

WORD OF MOUTH

Was the service stellar or not up to snuff? Did the food give you shivers of delight or leave you cold? Did the prices and portions make you happy or sad? After your trip, rate the places you visited and describe your experiences and travel tips with us and other Fodor's travelers on Fodor's Travel Talk Forums at www.fodors.com. Yes, you, too, can be a correspondent!

▌ EMERGENCIES

The numbers to call in case of emergency are the same all over Chile and work from both cell phones and landlines. Operators will generally not speak English, however; your embassy is your best bet for most emergencies.

Foreign Embassies United States ✉ Av. Andrés Bello 2800, Las Condes, Santiago, Chile ☎ 2/2330–3000 ⊕ chile.usembassy.gov.

General Emergency Contacts Ambulance ☎ 131. **Fire** ☎ 132. **Police** ☎ 133.

▌ HEALTH

From a health standpoint, Chile is one of the safer countries in which to travel. To be on the safe side, take the normal precautions you would traveling anywhere in South America.

In Santiago there are several large private *clínicas,* and many doctors speak at least a bit of English. In most other large cities there are one or two private clinics where you can be seen quickly. Generally, *hospitales* (hospitals) or *postas* (centers for emergency first aid) are for those receiving free or heavily subsidized treatment, and they are often crowded with long lines of patients waiting to be seen.

Altitude sickness—which causes shortness of breath, nausea, and splitting headaches—may be a problem in some areas of the North or hiking in the Andes. The best way to prevent *puna* is to ascend slowly and acclimate, spending at least one night at a lower altitude if possible. If symptoms persist, return to lower elevations. Over-the-counter medications to help prevent altitude sickness are available. If you have high blood pressure and/or a history of heart trouble, you should check with your doctor before traveling to high altitudes.

When it comes to air quality, Santiago ranks as one of the most polluted cities in the world. The reason is that the city is surrounded by two mountain ranges that keep the pollutants from cars and other sources from dissipating. The pollution is worst in winter.

What to do? First, avoid strenuous outdoor exercise and the traffic-clogged streets when air-pollution levels are high. Santiago has a wonderful subway that will whisk you to almost anywhere you want to go. Spend your days in museums and other indoor attractions. And take advantage of the city's many parks.

Visitors seldom encounter problems with drinking the water in Chile. Almost all drinking water receives proper treatment and is unlikely to produce health problems. But its high mineral content—it's born in the Andes—can disagree with some people. In any case, a wide selection of still (*sin gas*) and sparkling (*con gas*) bottled waters is available.

Food preparation is strictly regulated by the government, so outbreaks of food-borne diseases are rare. But use common sense. Don't risk restaurants where the hygiene is suspect or street vendors where the food is allowed to sit around at room temperature.

SHOTS AND MEDICATIONS

Although no vaccinations are required for entry into Chile, all travelers to Chile should get up-to-date tetanus, diphtheria, and measles boosters, and a hepatitis A inoculation is recommended. Children traveling to Chile should have current inoculations against mumps, rubella, and polio. Always check with your doctor before leaving.

If you have traveled to an area at risk for yellow fever transmission within five days before entering Chile, you may be asked to show proof that you have been vaccinated against the disease.

According to the Centers for Disease Control and Prevention, there's some risk of food-borne diseases such as hepatitis A and typhoid. There's no risk of contracting malaria, but a very limited risk of dengue fever, another insect-borne disease, on Easter Island. The best way to avoid insect-borne diseases is to prevent insect bites by wearing long pants and long-sleeve shirts and by using insect repellents with DEET. If you plan to visit remote regions or stay for more than six weeks, check with the CDC's International Travelers Hot Line.

The Hanta virus, a serious respiratory disease, exists in Chile, particularly in rural areas where rats are found (long-tailed rats are the most common carriers). Pay particular attention to warnings in campgrounds, and make sure to keep camping areas as clean as possible.

Health Information Centers for Disease Control and Prevention (*CDC*). ☎ 800/232-4636 ⊕ www.cdc.gov/travel. **World Health Organization** (*WHO*). ⊕ www.who.int.

OVER-THE-COUNTER REMEDIES

Mild cases of diarrhea may respond to Imodium (known generically as loperamide). Pepto Bismol is not available in Chile (though Maalox is), so pack some chewable tablets. Drink plenty of purified water or tea—chamomile (*manzanilla* in Spanish) is a soothing option. You will need to visit a *farmacia* (pharmacy) to purchase medications such as *aspirina* (aspirin), which are readily available.

▌ HOURS OF OPERATION

Most retail businesses are open weekdays 10–7 and Saturday until 2; most are closed Sunday. Some businesses and shops in regional cities and towns close for lunch between 1 and 3 or 4, though this is becoming less common. Supermarkets often stay open until 10 or 11 pm, as do large malls.

Most banks are open weekdays 9–2. *Casas de cambio* are open weekdays 9–7 and weekends 9–3 for currency exchange.

Gas stations in major cities and along the Pan-American Highway tend to stay open 24 hours. Others follow regular business hours.

Most tourist attractions are open during normal business hours during the week and for at least the morning on Saturday and Sunday. Most museums are closed Monday.

HOLIDAYS

New Year's Day (January 1), Good Friday (April), Labor Day (May 1), Day of Naval Glories, or the Battle of Iquique (May 21), Corpus Christi (June), Feast of St. Peter and St. Paul (June), Feast of the Vírgen de Carmen (July 16), Assumption of the Virgin Mary (August 15), Independence Day (September 18), Army Day (September 19), Discovery of the Americas or Columbus Day (October 12), Day of the Evangelic and Protestant Churches (October 31), All Saints Day (November 1), Immaculate Conception (December 8), and Christmas (December 25).

Many shops and services are open on most of these days, but transportation is always heavily booked up on and around the holidays. The two most important dates in the Chilean calendar are September 18 and New Year's Day. On these days shops close and public transportation is reduced to the bare minimum or is nonexistent. Trying to book a ticket around these dates will be difficult unless you do it well in advance.

▌MAIL

The postal system (CorreosChile) is efficient and reliable; on average, letters take about 10 days to reach the United States, Europe, Australia, and New Zealand. They will arrive sooner if you send them *prioritario* (priority) post. You can send them *certificado* (registered), in which case the recipient will need to sign for them. Vendors often sell stamps at the entrances to larger post offices, which can save you a potentially long wait in line— the stamps are valid, and selling them this way is legal. There are no mailboxes in Chile. You must mail letters from a post office or through your hotel. Post offices are open from 9 to 6 or 7 on weekdays and from 10 to 2 on Saturday.

Postage on regular letters and postcards to the United States and Europe cost around 700 pesos, but depend on the destination and origin.

▌MONEY

Unlike in some other South American countries, U.S. dollars are rarely accepted in Chile. (The exception is larger hotels, where prices are often quoted only in dollars.) Credit cards and traveler's checks are accepted in most resorts and in many shops and restaurants in major cities, though you should always carry some local currency for minor expenses like taxis and tipping. Once you stray from the beaten path, you can often pay only with pesos.

Typically you will pay 1,000 pesos for a cup of coffee, 1,500 pesos for a glass of beer in a bar, 1,500 pesos for a ham sandwich, and 1,000 pesos for an average museum admission.

Prices throughout this guide are given for adults. Substantially reduced fees are almost always available for children, students, and senior citizens.

▌TIP➔ Banks never have every foreign currency on hand, and it may take as long as a week to order. If you're planning to exchange funds before leaving home, don't wait until the last minute.

ATMS AND BANKS

Automatic teller machines, or *cajeros automáticos,* dispense only Chilean pesos. They are ubiquitous but, although most have instructions in English, not all are linked to the Plus and Cirrus systems. Look at the stickers on the machine to find the one you need. Most ATMs in Chile have a special screen—accessed after entering your PIN—for foreign-account withdrawals. In this case, you need to select the "extranjeros/foreign clients" option from the menu. ATMs offer excellent exchange rates because they are based on wholesale rates offered only by major banks.

Your own bank will probably charge a fee for using ATMs abroad; the foreign bank you use may also charge a fee. Nevertheless, you'll usually get a better rate of exchange at an ATM than you will at a currency-exchange office or even when changing money in a bank. And extracting funds as you need them is a safer option than carrying around a large amount of cash.

■ TIP ➜ PINs with more than four digits are not recognized at ATMs in Chile. If yours has five or more, remember to change it before you leave.

Banco de Chile is probably the largest national bank; its website ⊕ *www.bancochile.cl* lists branches and ATMs by location if you click on the "surcursales" (locations) link, then the "cajeros automáticos" link. Banco Santander (⊕ *www.santander.cl*) is another fairly common option.

CREDIT CARDS

It's a good idea to inform your credit-card company before you travel, especially if you're going abroad and don't travel internationally often. Otherwise, the credit-card company might put a hold on your card owing to unusual activity—not a good thing halfway through your trip. Record all your credit-card numbers—as well as the phone numbers to call if your cards are lost or stolen—in a safe place, so you're prepared should something go wrong. Both MasterCard and Visa have general numbers you can call (collect if you're abroad) if your card is lost, but

you're better off calling the number of your issuing bank, since MasterCard and Visa usually just transfer you there.

If you plan to use your credit card for cash advances, you'll need to apply for a PIN at least two weeks before your trip. Although it's usually cheaper (and safer) to use a credit card abroad for large purchases (so you can cancel payments or be reimbursed if there's a problem), note that some credit-card companies *and* the banks that issue them add substantial percentages to all foreign transactions, whether they're in a foreign currency or not. Check on these fees before leaving home, so there won't be any surprises when you get the bill.

Dynamic currency conversion programs are becoming increasingly widespread. Merchants who participate in them are supposed to ask whether you want to be charged in dollars or the local currency, but they don't always do so. And even if they do offer you a choice, they may well avoid mentioning the additional surcharges. The good news is that you *do* have a choice. And if this practice really gets your goat, you can avoid it entirely thanks to American Express; with its cards, DCC simply isn't an option.

Credit cards are widely accepted in hotels, restaurants, and shops in most cities and tourist destinations. Fewer establishments accept credit cards in rural areas. You may get a slightly better deal if you pay with cash (ask about discounts), and some businesses charge an extra fee for paying with a non-Chilean credit card.

Chile has implemented a security system for credit-card transactions called PinPass, which requires you to enter a previously established PIN in a hand-held machine. As a foreigner, you should explain that you haven't activated your PinPass, and the merchants should be able to process the transaction with your signature.

Credit card receipts in Chile have a line for signatures as well as for national ID numbers, or RUTs. You may be asked to put your passport number on this second line; otherwise, you can leave it blank.

CURRENCY AND EXCHANGE

The peso is the unit of currency in Chile. Note that Chilean currency may be written as $1,000 or CLP$1,000. Chilean bills are issued in 1,000, 2,000, 5,000, 10,000, and 20,000 pesos, and coins come in units of 1, 5, 10, 50, 100, and 500 pesos. Note that getting change for larger bills, especially from small shopkeepers and taxi drivers, can be difficult. Make sure to get smaller bills when you exchange currency. Always check exchange rates in newspapers or online for the most current information; at this writing, the exchange rate was approximately 618 pesos to the U.S. dollar. As long as the U.S. dollar hovers around 500 pesos it's easy to figure out how much you're paying for something in Chile: simply multiply what you're being charged by two and remove three zeros (e.g., a 10,000-peso dinner is about US$20).

Common to Santiago and other mid- to large-size cities are *casas de cambio*, or money-changing stores. Naturally, those at the airport will charge premium rates for convenience's sake. It may be more economical to change a small amount for your transfer to the city, where options are wider and rates more reasonable. Note that exchange houses will not accept damaged dollar notes.

The U.S. State Department warns travelers that Chilean banks, casas de cambio, and businesses may refuse US$100 bills due to past problems with counterfeiting. Chilean banks and police officers have been trained by the U.S. Secret Service to identify counterfeit bills, but some places still won't accept them. If you plan to exchange U.S. currency, bring bills smaller than US$50.

▌ PACKING

You'll need to pack for all seasons when visiting Chile, no matter what time of year you're traveling. Outside the cities,

especially in the Lake District and Southern Chile, long-sleeve shirts, long pants, socks, sneakers, a hat, a light waterproof jacket, a bathing suit, and insect repellent are all essential. Light colors are best, since mosquitoes avoid them. If you're visiting Patagonia or the Andes, bring a jacket and sweater or a fleece pullover. A high-factor sunscreen is essential at all times, especially in the far south where the ozone layer is much depleted.

Other useful items include a screw-top water bottle that you can fill with purified water, a money pouch, a travel flashlight and extra batteries, a medical kit, binoculars, and a pocket calculator to help with currency conversions. A sarong or light cotton blanket can have many uses: beach towel, picnic blanket, and cushion for hard seats, among other things. You can never have too many large resealable plastic bags, which are ideal for storing film, protecting things from rain and damp, and quarantining stinky socks.

▌ PASSPORTS AND VISAS

While traveling in Chile you might want to carry a copy of your passport and leave the original in your hotel safe. If you plan on paying by credit card you will often be asked to show identification (the copy of your passport or a driver's license, for example). Citizens of the United States, Canada, Australia, New Zealand, and the United Kingdom need only a passport to enter Chile for up to three months. Keep hold of the customs slip you receive on arrival; you'll need to hand it over when you leave.

▌ SAFETY

The vast majority of visitors to Chile never experience a problem with crime. Violent crime is a rarity; far more common is pickpocketing or thefts from purses, backpacks, or rental cars. Be on your guard in crowded places, especially markets and festivals. It's best to avoid wearing flashy jewelry, and handling money in public. Always remain alert for pickpockets, and take particular caution when walking alone at night, especially in the larger cities.

Volcano climbing is a popular pastime in Chile, with Volcán Villarrica, near Pucón, and Volcán Osorno the most popular. But some of these mountains are also among South America's most active volcanoes. CONAF, the agency in charge of national parks, cuts off access to any volcano at the slightest hint of abnormal activity. Check with CONAF before heading out on any hike in this region.

Many women travel alone or in groups in Chile with no problems. Chilean men are less aggressive in their machismo than men in other South American countries (they will seldom, for example, approach a woman they don't know), but it's still an aspect of the culture (they will make comments when a woman walks by). Single women should take caution when walking alone at night, especially in larger cities.

In the event of an earthquake in Chile, exercise common sense (don't take elevators and move away from heavy objects that may fall, for example) and follow instructions if you are in a public place (metro, museum, etc.). If you are in a coastal location, listen for tsunami sirens, or simply follow the tsunami evacuation route (indicated by signs in the streets) or head to high ground.

Contacts CONAF ☎ *45/229–8148 in Temuco, 2/2328–0300 in Santiago* ⊕ *www.conaf.cl.*

▌TAXES

A 19% value-added tax (called IVA in Chile) is added to the cost of most goods and services in Chile; often you won't notice because it's included in the price. When it's not, the seller gives you the price plus IVA. At many hotels you may receive an exemption from the IVA if you pay in American dollars or with a credit card in U.S. dollars.

▌TIME

All of Chile is in the same time zone: UTC/GMT minus 4 hours (or 3 hours during daylight saving time). Daylight saving time in Chile begins in October and ends in March.

Depending on the time of year, New York is the same time as Santiago or 1 to 2 hours behind, and Los Angeles is 3 to 5 hours behind. London is 3 to 5 hours ahead of Santiago, and New Zealand and Australia are 16 to 17 and 14 to 15 hours ahead respectively.

▌TIPPING

In restaurants and for tour guides, a 10% tip is usual, unless service has been deficient. Taxi drivers don't expect to be tipped. Visitors need to be wary of parking attendants. During the day, they should only charge what's on their portable meters when you collect the car but, at night, they will ask for money—usually 1,000 pesos—in advance. This is a racket but, for your car's safety, it's better to comply.

▌VISITOR INFORMATION

The national tourist office, Servicio Nacional de Turismo, or Sernatur, with branches in Santiago and major tourist destinations around the country, is often the best source for general information about a region. The Sernatur office in Santiago is open 9–6 weekdays, and 9–2 on Saturday. The hours of Sernatur's regional offices vary, but can be found on its website.

Municipal tourist offices, often located near a central square, usually have better information about their town's sights, restaurants, and lodging. Many have shorter hours or close altogether during low season, however.

Contact Sernatur ☎ *2/2731–8310* ⊕ *www. sernatur.cl.*

INDEX

PHOTO CREDITS

NOTES

NOTES

NOTES

NOTES

NOTES

NOTES

NOTES

NOTES

Fodor's CHILE

Publisher: Amanda D'Acierno, *Senior Vice President*

Editorial: Arabella Bowen, *Editor in Chief*; Linda Cabasin, *Editorial Director*

Design: Tina Malaney, *Associate Art Director*; Chie Ushio, *Senior Designer*; Ann McBride, *Production Designer*

Photography: Jennifer Arnow, *Senior Photo Editor*; Mary Robnett, *Photo Researcher*

Production: Linda Schmidt, *Managing Editor*; Evangelos Vasilakis, *Associate Managing Editor*; Angela L. McLean, *Senior Production Manager*

Maps: Rebecca Baer, *Senior Map Editor*; David Lindroth and Mark Stroud, *Cartographers*

Sales: Jacqueline Lebow, *Sales Director*

Marketing & Publicity: Heather Dalton, *Marketing Director*; Katherine Punia, *Publicity Director*

Business & Operations: Susan Livingston, *Vice President, Strategic Business Planning*; Sue Daulton, *Vice President, Operations*

Fodors.com: Megan Bell, *Executive Director, Revenue & Business Development*; Yasmin Marinaro, *Senior Director, Marketing & Partnerships*

Writers: Barbara Balfour, Amanda Barnes, Sam Edwards, Anthony Esposito, Jimmy Langman, Eileen Smith

Editor: Luke Epplin

Editorial Contributor: Mike Dunphy

Production Editor: Jennifer DePrima

6th Edition

ISBN 978-1-101-87817-0

ISSN 1535-5055

SPECIAL SALES

This book is available at special discounts for bulk purchases for sales promotions or premiums. For more information, e-mail specialmarkets@penguinrandomhouse.com

PRINTED IN UNITED STATES OF AMERICA

10 9 8 7 6 5 4 3 2 1

ABOUT OUR WRITERS

Barbara Balfour is an award-winning public speaker, writer, and editor who has traveled to more than 35 countries. Her work has appeared in media outlets such as the BBC, *ELLE Canada,* the *Economist Group,* and most major newspapers in Canada. One of her favorite pastimes is spending an afternoon at Isla Negra and seeing the country through Pablo Neruda's eyes. For this edition, Barbara updated the Experience chapter.

After working as a journalist at British newspapers, **Amanda Barnes** headed to South America six years ago in search of sunshine, a real-life Borges fantasy, and mastering the art of a good *asado.* When she isn't trotting around on travel assignments Amanda is based in Mendoza, Argentina. She is editor of the *Squeeze* magazine and wine guide, and writes for numerous international travel and wine publications. For this edition, she updated the El Norte Grande, The Central Valley, Southern Chilean Patagonia and Tierra del Fuego, and Travel Smart chapters.

British-born **Sam Edwards's** infatuation with Latin America began at the tender age of four when his seasoned traveler parents took him to Ecuador for 18 months. After graduating from university, he promptly abandoned the gray skies of his home country to explore jungles, dive bars, deserts, and soccer stadiums from Guatemala to Patagonia. Five years later he still dances like a gringo. When he's not on the road, Sam has worked as an editor at the *Santiago Times* and reported on Chilean current affairs for *Vice* and *Al Jazeera* among others. For this edition, he updated the El Norte Chico chapter.

Born and bred in New Jersey, **Anthony Esposito** was attracted to Chile by the lure of the Andes and Pablo Neruda's poetry. He's been living and working as a writer there for the last decade. He is currently a correspondent for Reuters, but has written for the *Wall Street Journal, Time, USA Today,* and *Monocle.* Apart from writing, he is an avid cyclist and loves trekking. For this edition, Anthony updated the Central Coast chapter.

Jimmy Langman lives in southern Chile, where he is executive editor of *Patagon Journal,* a magazine about travel, nature, culture, and outdoor sports in the Patagonia region of Chile and Argentina. Since 1998, he has also worked as a freelance journalist, writing regularly for *Newsweek, National Geographic News, Globe and Mail,* the *Independent* (London), and other publications in the United States, Canada, and Britain. Jimmy updated the Lake District, Chiloé, and Southern Coast chapters.

Eileen Smith is a long-term expat in Chile, where she lives in Santiago. She is a freelance writer and photographer and an urban cyclist. She loves interesting fonts on signs and exploring small, old-school stores selling buttons, batteries, and other assorted treasures. She writes about Chilean culture, Spanish, travel, and food for online and traditional media. For this edition, she updated the Santiago and Easter Island chapters.

Santiago
Metro Network

VESPUCIO NORTE
Zapadores
Dorsal
Einstein
Cementerios
Cerro Blanco
Patronato
Puente Cal y Canto

SAN PABLO
Lo Prado
Blanqueado
Santa Ana
L2
Plaza de Armas
Bellas Artes

PUDAHUEL
L1
Neptuno
Gruta de Lourdes
QUINTA NORMAL
Cumming

Barrancas
Laguna Sur
Las Parcelas
Monte Tabor
Del Sol
Santiago Bueras
Plaza de Maipú

Pajaritos
Las Rejas
Ecuador
San Alberto Hurtado
U. de Santiago
Estación Central
U.L.A.
República

Los Heroes
La Moneda
U. de Chile
Santa Lucía
U. Católica

Baquedano

Salvador
Manuel Montt
Pedro de Valdivia
Los Leones
Tobalaba

El Golf
Alcántara
Escuela Militar
Manquehue
Hernando de Magallanes
LOS DOMINICOS

Cristóbal Colón
Francisco Bilbao
Príncipe de Gales
Simón Bolívar
Plaza Egaña
Los Orientales
Grecia
Los Presidentes
Quilín
Las Torres
Macul

Vicuña Mackenna

Vicente Valdes

Toesca
Parque O'Higgins
Rondizzoni

Parque Bustamante
Santa Isabel
Irarrázaval
Ñuble
L5
Rodrigo de Araya
Carlos Valdovinos
Camino Agrícola
San Joaquín
Pedrero
Mirador
Bella Vista de La Florida
Santa Julia

Franklin
El Llano
San Miguel
Lo Vial
Departamental
Ciudad del Niño
Lo Ovalle
El Parrón
L4A
La Cisterna
San Ramón
Santa Rosa
La Granja

Rojas Magallanes
Trinidad
San José de la Estrella
Los Quillayes
Elisa Correa
Hopital Sótero del Río
L4
Protectora de la Infancia
Las Mercedes

PLAZA DE
PUENTE ALTO

KEY

Metro lines

O Stations

◎ Transfer service